THE KNOTTED SUBJECT

THE KN⬡TTED SUBJECT

▶ HYSTERIA AND

ITS DISCONTENTS

ELISABETH BRONFEN

PRINCETON UNIVERSITY PRESS · PRINCETON, NEW JERSEY

Library of Congress Cataloging-in-Publication Data

Bronfen, Elisabeth.
The knotted subject : hysteria and its discontents / Elisabeth Bronfen.
p. cm.
Includes bibliographical reference and index.
ISBN 0-691-01231-8 (cloth : alk. paper). — ISBN 0-691-01230-X (pbk. : alk. paper)
1. Hysteria. 2. Hysteria in literature. 3. Hysteria in motion pictures.
4. Navel—Symbolic aspects. I. Title.
RC532.B76 1998 616.85′24—dc21   97-45157 CIP

This book has been composed in Sabon

Princeton University Press books are printed on acid-free paper and meet the guidelines for
permanence and durability of the Committee on Production Guidelines for Book
Longevity of the Council on Library Resources

Printed in the United States of America

1 2 3 4 5 6 7 8 9 10

1 2 3 4 5 6 7 8 9 10

(pbk)

FOR GEORGE B. BRONFEN

10 JUNE 1922–14 APRIL 1995

The hysteric is a divine spirit that is always at the edge, the turning point, of making. She is one who does not make herself . . . she does not make herself but she does make the other. It is said that the hysteric "makes-believe" the father, plays the father, "makes-believe" the master. Plays, makes up, makes-believe: she makes-believe she is a woman, unmakes-believe too . . . plays at desire, plays the father . . . turns herself into him, unmakes him at the same time. Anyway, without the hysteric, there's no father . . . without the hysteric, no master, no analyst, no analysis! She's the *unorganizable* feminine construct, whose power of producing the other is a power that never returns to her. She is really a wellspring nourishing the other for eternity, yet not drawing back from the other . . . not recognizing herself in the images the other may or may not give her. She is given images that don't belong to her, and she forces herself, as we've all done, to resemble them.

—*Hélène Cixous*

CONTENTS

IN THE COURSE of its long medical history, hysteria—that infamously resilient somatic illness without organic lesions—has stubbornly remained elusive to any precise definition and has thus proved itself a useful screen on which to project the diagnostic fantasies of doctors faced with their own impotence and helplessness. Precisely because the hysteric seems to be imitating other illnesses while her psychosomatic symptoms are clearly aimed at an addressee—be this a physician, other family members, or a public audience—she readily appears to be an arch simulator, deceiver, and seductress. Nevertheless, by keenly responding to the hermeneutic task exemplified by the hysteric's bodily enactment of psychic discontent and anguish, analysts seeking to offer an interpretive cure inevitably find themselves drawn into scenes of mutual implication. For even though the hysteric appears to be a particularly fruitful object for scientific speculation because of her protean symptoms, she also develops one symptom after another whenever the cure for any given ailment is offered. In so doing, she insists that no solution is ever complete. Faced with this nosological enigma, physicians in past centuries have found themselves trapped in a mixture of fascination and resignation—so much so that Lasègne called hysteria the wastebasket of medicine, where one throws everything one has no use for, and Charcot repeatedly maintained that his hysteric patients were making much ado about nothing.

It is commonly thought that hysteria as a psychosomatic ailment died out at the beginning of the twentieth century, and the fourth edition of the *Diagnostic and Statistical Manual* used by American psychiatrists and social workers accordingly no longer lists hysteria as a syndrome. Nevertheless, in recent years hysteria once again, has become the topic of a lively critical debate. Beginning in the late 1970s feminist scholars such as Hélène Cixous, Catherine Clément, and Christina von Braun (and, more recently, Janet Beizer, Evelyn Ender, and Claire Kahane) have invoked a return to the question of hysteria as a means to discuss the exclusion of feminine subjectivity inherent in patriarchal culture. At the same time, cultural historians like Mark S. Micale have strongly argued for an inclusion of the discussion of male hysteria, and art historians and literary scholars such as Georges Didi-Huberman and Sander Gilman have emphasized the issue of visualization in medical representations of this ailment. Elaine Showalter has even suggested that an array of psychosomatic illnesses, such as chronic fatigue syndrome or war shock, could easily be viewed as postmodern forms of hysteria. Concurrent with this critical reappraisal of hysteria—and perhaps taking a cue from such authors as Gustave Flaubert, who insisted on calling himself a hysteric, and from the surrealist poets Aragon and Breton, who praised hysteria for being the greatest poetic discovery of the nineteenth century—contemporary popular culture celebrities have embraced this seductive and deceptive manner of self-performance. Psycho-rock singers Sinead O'Connor and P. J. Harvey, laying bare their torment and anguish on stage, recall the public performance of private traumas conducted by Charcot during his Tuesday lectures at the Salpêtrière. Madonna exhibits her astonishing ability to find ever new guises and roles (including the writing on her back she flaunts in nude photographs), strangely matching the versatile histrionics, deceptive seduction, and dermography displayed by the hysteric patients housed in the nineteenth- and early twentieth-century clinics of Europe and North America. Similarly, a photopage headlined "Hysteric Glamour" (published in 1996 in a Berlin-based newspaper) displays two models posing in seductive attitudes next to a text that reads, "We were girlies, sweet and nasty, tired of having no idea. We wanted to be glamourous . . . burned down the house. Now we are women, hysteric + cool."

Moreover, in response to Jacques Lacan's inclusion of hysteric discourse as one of four discourses at work in psychoanalysis, critics Slavoj Žižek, Gérard Wajeman, and Bruce Fink have discussed hysteria as a paradigmatic example of a radically ambiguous relationship between the subject and the so-called Master in response to whom the subject's identity is constituted. Within this reformulation, the hysteric subject emerges as one who both supports the desire for a figure of paternal authority and recognizes that it requires the Other as an addressee—even while the hysteric subject also radically protests against this interpellation. Indeed, following Lacan's schema, Lucien Israël suggests that the language of hysteria be considered a mode of communication, an attempt to establish a relation with the Other, to broadcast the message of a recognition of lack—"I am not complete"—yet accomplishing this, in contrast to all other forms of neurosis, by transforming anxieties and desires into somatic manifestations.

In concert with this renewed interest in hysteria, this book sets out to reinvestigate medical discourses and cultural performances relating to this elusive, protean, and enigmatic psychosomatic disorder as they were developed in diverse psychiatric and psychoanalytic writings; in fictional texts; and in operatic, cinematic, and visual representations from 1800 to the present. If traditional conceptions of hysteria persist in the notion of much ado about nothing, I suggest taking this "nothing" and its relation to the resilience of self-fashionings, as well as the crisis in interpellation engendered by the hysteric performance, quite seriously and quite literally and reading it as a language that allows the subject to voice both personal and cultural discontent. My wager is that by shifting away from a gendered notion of hysteria, which considers all its symptoms to be the expression of dissatisfied feminine sexual desire, and instead by returning to Sigmund Freud's initial interest in finding a traumatic rather than a sexual etiology of hysteria, this conversion of psychic anguish into a somatic symptom can be interpreted as the enactment of a message in code. Yet what the hysteric broadcasts is a message about vulnerability—the vulnerability of the symbolic (the fallibility of paternal law and social bonds); the vulnerability of identity (the insecurity of gender, ethnic, and class designations); or, and perhaps above all, the vulnerability of the body, given its mutability and mortality.

To bring a psychoanalytically informed discussion of the language of hysteria into dialogue with readings of specific narrative and visual representations, my introductory chapter develops most of the theoretical issues I will return to in the course of the book. At stake in this preliminary discussion is not only the exploration of a traumatic etiology of hysteria but also the manner in which this trauma can be conceptualized as a snarled knot of memory traces, which as a wandering foreign body haunts the psyche. At the same time, given my interest in exploring a discussion of hysteria that is not solely defined by a relation to phallic symbolism, I revisit Sophocles' tragedy of *Oedipus*. Finding matricide to be as much at the core of this text as are the two desires that Freud postulates as the lynchpins of his Oedipal theory— namely, the desire for the maternal body, as well as patricide—I suggest including another anatomic sign in our discussion of psychic developement: the navel. For this cut, this knotted scar marks a moment of castration not only in the sense that it commemorates the loss of the mother but also in the sense that it marks our mortality, the vulnerability of our bodies, and thus radically protests against any phantasies of omnipotence and immortality. Looking at a modern day Oedipal story, Hitchcock's *Psycho*, I investigate those "navel moments" in the film where the traumatic knowledge of vulnerability is either hidden behind protective fictions of plenitude or horrifically erupts from behind such screens. The navel, I suggest, could serve as a particularly fruitful sign for a discussion of the traumatic nothing about which the hysteric makes so much ado, because the hysteric's complaint revolves precisely around a knowledge of fallibility and fragility, and it goes hand in hand with a need for protective phantasies and a desire for imagining what the condition of happiness and plenitude might be. As a counter-text, thus, I offer Woody Allen's *Zelig*, the story of a happy hysteric who, rather than repressing the traumatic knowledge of privation, learns to convert it into a stabilizing protective fiction of transference love.

Building on the navel as an anatomic sign that is at once highly suggestive and fundamentally unreadable, my first chapter offers a discussion of the plethora of critical readings of Freud's specimen dream of Irma's injection, and in so doing returns to the notion that hysteria defies closure. For in response to his recalcitrant hysteric who will not be cured, Freud finds at the navel of his dream an unplumbable spot, a knot tying together all the strands of his nocturnal phantasy scenario but one that cannot be unraveled. And all the while he desperately seeks to arrive at a symbolic formula for dream work to counter the traumatic knowledge of mortality and fallibility of this dream, both analyzing and identifying with the resistant hysteric. My discussion explores the ways in which each critic of Freud's interpretation, seeking to fill the original text's gaps, repeats the inability to find closure that haunts Freud's own rendition. These attempts, given that they themselves are never complete, suggest that the figure that best describes the rhetoric of Freud's specimen dream and its interpretations is a counter-directional gesture, one that knots together the sublimation afforded by a coherent narrative solution and the desublimation that serves to articulate the traumatic knowledge of fallibility inherent in the analytic effort, with the result that the analysis can do nothing but repeat the hysteric's broadcast. I end with a reading of Barthes's *Camera Lucida*. Though writing more than half a century later, like Freud, Barthes investigates the power of our collective image repertoire—using photography, however, rather than dreams. His discussion also revolves around a navel point—though not explicitly designated as such—namely, the empty page standing for the one true image that ties him to the maternal body, to an acceptance of her loss and an embrace of his own death.

Having installed my theoretical framework, I move in the second part of the book to the historical moment when, with the birth of the bourgeois family, hysteria bloomed as the language within which the daughter could articulate her discontent. Tracing the development of both medical and cultural formations of hysteria forward to the year in which Freud and Breuer published their *Studies in Hysteria* (1896), I interlace a critical reevaluation of the archival texts on hysteria, using such diverse aesthetic texts as Mozart's *Magic Flute*, Radcliffe's gothic *The Romance of the Forest*, Stoker's *Dracula*, and Wagner's *Parsifal*.

In the third part I look more closely at versions of the case history beginning with three distinct yet interrelated sets of psychiatric discussions: Freud's and Breuer's work on hysteric patients, Jasper's work on criminal nostalgics, and Pierre Janet's work with hysteria. I also explore the cultural exchange between medical and artistic discourses. Anne Sexton was diagnosed as a manic-depressive hysteric, yet after her first failed suicide attempt, she turned into one of the most successful American poets of her day. Using her biography and writings I suggest that her case history illustrates not only how she used her writing to keep psychic disturbances at bay, but also how in her hysteric protest against paternity she used her poetry to rewrite Freud's Oedipal story to articulate her poetic version of the daughter's discontent. I end this third section of case studies with a text in which an aesthetic representation feeds upon a medical discussion of hysteria, though in a more distanced and ironic mode. Arguing that Hitchcock's *Marnie* can be read as a cinematic version of the psychoanalytic case history of hysteria, I particularly contend that, far from simply paraphrasing Freud, Hitchcock—in imitation of the hysteric's discourse—radically challenges some of the tacit presuppositions of Freud's insistence on a sexual cure. For the outcome of the hero's dramatic enactment of the heroine's scene of trauma is not a cure but the horrific rebirth of a monstrous girl-woman.

The last section returns to the historical beginnings of this book—the cultural moment when enlightenment begins to reveal the obscene desires inherent in the symbolic system of law—only to transpose this gothic note into the language of postmodernity. I offer the films of David Cronenberg as a cinematic rendition of hysteric hallucinations. By focusing once again on navel scenes, I explore how Cronenberg's cinematic enactment of womb anxiety–womb envy offers a visual performance of how trauma is present in the psyche as a wandering foreign body of nonabreacted memories and desires. My final example for a postmodern performance of the language of hysteria is a discussion of Cindy Sherman's photography. Although she never speaks about herself in terms of hysteria, and indeed works with no explicit references to medical and psychoanalytical discourses, I place her work within the context of contemporary women artists who directly address the issue of hysteria. She uses a constant masking and refashioning of her body to broadcast a message about how we are haunted by the elusive and protean sense of vulnerability, implenitude, and fallibility, even while the mise-en-scène of desire created by phantasy work seeks to hide this traumatic knowledge.

ACKNOWLEDGMENTS

DIALOGUE was very much part of writing this book, and I thank first and foremost Birgit Erdle for her untiring comments, criticism, and support. For assistance in many aspects of both writing and putting together the manuscript my thanks go also to Benjamin Marius and Therese Steffen. Furthermore, I acknowledge the members of the English Department of Sheffield Hallam to whom I presented many portions of this book: especially Judy Simons, Robert Miles, Jill LeBihan, Allison Chapman, and Fred Botting. I also wish to thank Jörg Huber at the Schule für Gestaltung in Zurich for organizing a conference on hysteria to celebrate the centennial of Breuer's and Freud's *Studies in Hysteria*, a forum that included presentation of parts of this project. I thank Alaida Assmann, Peter Hughes, Margaret Bridges, Evelyne Ender, Greg Poletta, Rick Waswo, Wlad Godzich, Eric Santner, Maria Tatar, Sander Gilman, Griselda Pollock, Slavoj Žižek, Diane Middlebrook, Petra Eggers, Mathias Landwehr, Yvonne Studer, Marianne Dada-Buechel, Nikolaus Schneider, and Christina von Braun for their collegial support throughout the writing process. Additional thanks go to Susanne Hermanski, Sophie Manham, Maurice Biriotti, and Astrid Heinrich for the references to hysteric moments in popular culture, My thanks go as well as to Anne M. Heiles for her work as copyeditor. And finally appreciation goes to Anita Roy, who first asked me to write the book; Mary Murrell, my editor at Princeton University Press; and Dieter Simon, my publisher in Berlin at Volk und Welt.

A preliminary version of the introduction was published as "From Omphalos to Phallus: Cultural Representations of Femininity and Death," in *Women. A Cultural Review* 3:2 (1992). Parts of the first chapter appeared as "Death: The Navel of the Image," in *The Point of Theory*, edited by Mieke Bal and Inge Boers, Amsterdam University Press. Parts of chapter 3 appeared as "Hysteria, Phantasy, and the Family Romance—Ann Radcliffe's *Romance of the Forest*" in *Women's Writing: The Early Period* I, no. 2 (1994) and as "The Perforated Text of Origins—Radcliffe Camera" in *Imprints & Revisions: The Making of the Literary Text, 1759–1818, Spell* 8. Parts of chapter 4 appeared as "Kundry's Laughter," in *Richard Wagner. New German Critique* 69 (Fall 1996). Parts of chapter 5 appeared as "Freud's Hysterics, Jasper's Nostalgics," in *Parallax* 3 (September 1996). Preliminary versions of chapter 9 appeared as an entry to the exhibition catalogue *Cindy Sherman: Photographic Work 1975–1995*, Schirmer and Mosel, and as "The Knotted Subject: Hysteria, Irma, and Cindy Sherman" in *Generations and Geographies in the Visual Arts: Feminist Readings*, edited by Griselda Pollock.

Throughout this book, all translations from French and German are my own, unless otherwise attributed, and reference is given to the original text. Further, references to a cited text will appear with page reference after quotations and, unless otherwise stated, refer to the same text throughout; passages without page references are from the last-cited page. Unless otherwise stated, all italics are the author's and all ellipses, mine.

PART ONE

► THE HYSTERICAL SUBJECT OF THEORY

INTRODUCTION

Navel Inversions

> Home is where they buried my umbilical cord.
>
> —*Derek Walcott*

I

IN THE REPERTORY of western imagery, the navel is the firmly privileged representative for the origin of human existence. Literally a skin mark and an index of the primal cut made at the belly of a newborn, and figuratively a culturally codified symbol for the making of an independent human being, the navel refers in retrospect both to the child's bond with the maternal body and its bond with divinity. Though this bond is physically severed at birth, it remains psychically sustained and ritually renewed throughout the life of each individual. The navel marks centrality. Anatomically placed at the body's center, it becomes a symbol of the world's spiritual center as well. At the same time, however, it also functions as a sign of bondage, namely to the law of genealogy and mortality. Whereas angels and artificially created simulacrums of the human body have no navels, Adam and Eve (created in the image of their divine father, rather than born of woman), are often depicted with a belly button. Precisely this theologically debated detail of the body comes to highlight their fallen, human status, their difference.

Visualized as a common point of connection but also as an incision and severing, the navel emerges as a cultural image fraught with reticence. Although it is often prominently displayed in sculptures of the human body and frequently a significant detail in paintings of the nude, it yet remains an oversight. Most dictionaries of subjects and symbols in art, or motives and themes in literature and folklore, will ignore the navel or merely include a cursory entry mentioning its multifarious usage as trope for conceptualizations of the center. Nor has the navel been privileged theoretically in psychoanalytically informed semiotic and cultural studies of the body, as have other body parts such as the breast, penis, vagina, eye, nose, or foot. Indeed, however suggestive the navel appears, it is yet a willfully unexplored part of the human body, an obscene detail that fascinates even as it repels, owing perhaps precisely to its intangibility.

Marking an earlier opening to the body, it seems to echo the vagina as well as the anus, transforming the stomach into an erotically exciting but also a cultural taboo zone. At the turn of the century, for example, a performance of Richard Strauss's *Salome* in New York City provoked a scandal because the soprano displayed her navel while performing the "Dance of the

Seven Veils." As the dancer moved, the navel kept changing its shape, dangerously opening and closing—and offending the censors—with each new gesture. Under the Hays production code it was considered improper to offer an unmitigated view of the navel, so that Hollywood actresses could exhibit their belly only if its central point was filled with a jewel or covered with an ornament. Given the navel's deceptive appearance, then, and its simulation of an erotogenic orifice as well as an undecipherable cavity whose function and destiny remain obscure, anecdotes about this body part abound. Naive lovers look to the navel as the most natural site for sexual intercourse, while children often believe babies emerge from this indeterminate hole. Youngsters ponder the seeming fragility of its structure. When told that the navel was created by being tied off from the umbilical cord, they readily phantasize that it can come undone: the little boy who equates his navel with a screw, frustrated that no one can tell him what it is for, takes a screw driver and opens it. In this child's phantasy the bottom finally falls off.[1]

Above all, the navel is a flashback or an analeptic index of a bodily wound. In its anatomic sense, after all, it is a slight, round depression in the center of the abdomen, containing a bulging scar where the umbilical cord, connecting the fetus with the placenta in the womb, had been attached. That this individually unique somatic sign can also become transformed semiotically within our image repertoire so as to signify the vulnerability of human existence in general was illustrated poignantly for me in a story told by a friend. Going through an art gallery, she tried to help her daughter distinguish between images of the baby Jesus and those of the crucified Christ. "Christ," her mother explained, "is different from the baby Jesus because he has four wounds: two on his hands, one on his feet and one on his side." Her daughter cannily replied, "But I see a fifth wound," pointing to the navel.[2]

What ultimately renders the navel such a suggestive and irresistible aperture is in part its protean quality, for, depending on the shape of the stomach, its appearance will change as well—an opulent belly will produce a round navel, a flat one a vertical slit. Equally crucial, however, although the naval perfectly simulates an opening with a designated aim, it actually serves no purpose and leads nowhere. Functioning neither as an entrance nor an exit, it displays a hole that is nothing. As it represents the interface between an opening and a closed-off cavity, between what is internal and what is external to the body, it also delineates what is off-limits to visualization. For although the navel is open to the exploration of the touch, its most intimate point remains impenetrable to the eye, already inside the folds of the body— though it is separated as well from the actual body interior by a piece of knotted skin. Functioning as a demarcation between the intimate and the external, it remains inaccessible to the gaze both from the outside and the inside. The navel, one could say, is obscene precisely because it is so indeterminate, suggestively visible yet ultimately hidden, a useless, surplus skin pointing belatedly to a prior urgency, namely the site of originary nourishment for the child in the uterus and the wound that produced its birth. Signifying a human commonality, it is also a mark par excellence of singularity. Each navel is a radically unique shape, the sign of individuality, for though we all have a navel, yet no navel completely resembles another.

It is precisely this challenge to specularity posed by the navel that Marie-Ange Guilleminot exploits in *Point commun. Vues de l'intérieur.*" Since 1991 this Paris-based visual artist has made more than ninety plaster casts of navels. As she explains, in her work she is motivated by the desire to approach a person in a virginal situation, to create a new kind of relationship between artist and model.[3] The intimate practice played through in her performance is defined by a language and by tools usually attributed to other activities. Guilleminot sets up a rendezvous during which she initially treats the models as clients, speaking with them about their attitudes toward their navels, about why they are willing to have an imprint taken, and how they imagine this imprint will look. Evoking both a medical and a sexual setting (these two domains so poignantly coming together in the psychoanalytic session), she then asks each respective model to lie down and expose his or her navel. This can occur either in a private space (as was the case in the finissage to her show at the Galerie Chantal Crousel on 3 March 1995), or as a public demonstration.

Placing a five-by-five inch wooden frame around the navel of the model, she first cleans the aperture and lubricates it with Vaseline to eliminate any particles that might alter the imprint and to prevent hair from sticking to the mold. She then fills the frame with warm plaster and asks the model to remain lying down until the plaster is firm enough to be removed, soliciting from each model associations that come to mind in the course of the molding procedure. In that the plaster requires a certain amount of time to set, Guilleminot's navel casting, resembles moments of waiting in photographic practice, both the time of exposure (which in the early days of photography could stretch to several minutes), and the time of developing the negative and the print in a dark room. Once the plaster cast has hardened, she helps the model slowly lift the inverted imprint of the navel from the belly and displays it to his or her expectant gaze. The first exhibition of Guilleminot's navel casts took place on 20 June 1992, when a series of about seventy frames was presented lying flat on tables in the apartments of five people who had been *moulée*—molded, matrixed, and cast. Her project continues, depending on the new people she encounters since all her models must be accquaintances to some degree. Unlike the medical and the psychoanalytic meeting, the process of taking someone's navel imprint involves familiarizing herself with the other person; at the same time, the scene of molding is suggestive, like the navel around which it revolves, never becoming entirely intimate.

Seminal to Marie-Ange Guilleminot's performance is that the innermost folds of the navel, which remain inaccessible to the eye, can be rendered

Marie-Ange Guilleminot, *Point commun. Vues de l'intérieur.* (By permission of the artist.)

visible by virtue of representation—but only as an inversion of this intimate body part. Hers is a self-conscious staging of misrepresentation, capturing what is otherwise intangible and indeterminate in a decipherable form but at the cost of conversion and displacement. The mold we see perfectly fills out the space that the navel touches, thus *ex negativo* exposing the shape of this suggestive, irresistible detail. Drawing out what is normally withheld, rendering publicly what is intimate, Guilleminot extracts an improper portrait of the model. Though not a copy of the face, the body part that is usually privileged in portraiture, her molded navels nevertheless can be read as fairly precise renditions of the individuality of the models. Indeed, the fantasies and anxieties about what this intimate body part will look like, which are called forth in the course of the navel molding, find their acme as each model contemplates the sculpted inversion of her or his navel. As though echoing the old practice where midwives would read the knots on umbilical cords as prophetic signs that allowed them to predict how many more pregnancies a woman would undergo,[4] model and audience scan the imprint to produce an explanatory narrative of its donor: "What does my navel really look like?" "What will it say about me?" "How will others read this intimate self-image?"

Furthermore, the act of representation, as it is ritually performed by Marie-Ange Guilleminot's navel moldings, also implies a scene, one self-consciously staged for an audience (be this only the artist and the model) or, as at the gallery with its group of spectators, a scene calling forth a story to boot. Imitating the gesture of giving birth, it repeats the severing and doubling undertaken in parturition, and though the object brought forth through the molding is a plaster cast rather than a living body, it is formed indexically in the image of the donor, duplicating precisely the cutting point between maternal body and newborn. Indeed, one of the women working at the Gallerie Crousel read these molds as entirely accurate portraits, quite confident that she knew the personality of each owner, knew whom she would be able to get along with and whom she would never want to meet. Even without going so far as to draw inferences about the hidden personality traits of a model from its navel cast, the singularity each mold displays is striking. The folds, knobs, fissures, and peaks that distinguish one cast from all the others calls for an interpretive story, this hermeneutic gesture supported by the fact that each mold not only exhibits clearly a unique shape but is also the product of an impression whose referentiality is binding. It is the imprint of an authentic skin mark.

There are, then, two bodies involved in Marie-Ange Guilleminot's navel moldings: one is a somatic representation, a protean scar on the skin, intangible and indeterminate because only partially visible; the other is a plaster cast that converts this skin mark into a tangible and legible semiotic sign, open to multifarious interpretive narratives attempting to explore and name this obscenely irresistible body detail. Explicitly demonstrating the process of dislocation, fragmentation, and isolation by which an obscure body part can become the privileged object in the staging of fantasies of intimate encounters with otherness and visualizations of the impenetrable, Guilleminot self-consciously reflects the process of aesthetic parturition itself. Indeed, her navel moldings function self-reflexively like a mise-en-abyme of the strategy of conversion and replacement that lies at the core of all strategies of representation.

The trajectory that Marie-Ange Guilleminot's performance traces parallels, in a nutshell, what is at stake in my inquiry into the configurations of hysteria seen in western culture. Her point of departure is a perturbing and irresistible body detail, the somatic sign of naught. Quite literally no thing, a cut knotted together to form a scar, the tracing of the figure O, of no anatomical value, the navel is at once a worthless body part and a cipher for obscene fantasies of erotic or horrific nature involving penetration into the body interior or extracting something from this intimate, unknown site. The parturition of the plaster casts then renders this intimate and impenetrable part of the human anatomy external. By converting what is an indeterminate body boundary written on the skin into a decipherable representation, Guilleminot's navel molds produce an inverted sculpture of this body scar, this knotted point of incision that touches upon without ever disclosing the naught from which it shields but which it also preserves. Yet one must not forget that the navel itself is an improper representation, marking after the fact an inaccessible and yet unencompassable nothing—a nonevent, a nonsite, a nonbody—at the origin and core of all subjectivity. To return to the anecdote about Christ's wounds, this knotted scar demarcates by giving (an improper) shape to the nothing subtending psychic processes and by moving the viewer with its traumatic impact, a piercing injury that is naught because it is only recognized belatedly. As Cathy Caruth argues, "The impact of the traumatic event lies precisely in its belatedness, in its refusal to be simply located, in its insistent appearance outside the boundaries of any single place or time" (1995, 9). Yet this indeterminate traumatic impact not only of parturition itself but also of the fragility and mutability it encompasses, staunchly inhabits our imaginary phantasies and symbolic codes, even without taking on any definitive form. It impacts as a resilient trace of bondage, vulnerability, and incision—as the persistence of a remainder. Guilleminot's navel molds thus emerge as "metarepresentations," inversions of a somatic sign that is itself a transformation of sorts and that has been produced to mark an ineluctable impression that radically resists representation. I maintain that it is precisely this ubiquitous and impenetrable traumatic impact—this injurous blow to the tissues of the body and the mind—that representations of hysteria obliquely address by converting naught into exuberant and resilient protean symptoms.[5]

However, before developing more precisely the enmeshment between the language of hysteria and those traces of traumatic impact, deprivation, and loss at the core of all self-representations, I should explain what is to be gained by privileging the navel as a critical category in a discussion of subjectivity. In the 1980s critics explored the potential of poststructuralist terminology in their effort to describe how the subject—grafted onto a complex network of significatory difference, deferral, and displacement—came to embody and perform gender constructions. To describe the shift in literary and cultural studies in the past decade, concepts such as emplacement, ensoulment, coherence, closure, ethics, and moral commitment seem to be emerging as the compelling concern of the 1990s.[6] In an essay called "Identity and the Writer," A. S. Byatt notes this change, explaining

> Lately—and I think this is a cultural observation—I've replaced the post-romantic metaphor with one of a knot. I see individuals now as knots, in say, the piece of lace that one of Vermeer's lacemakers is making. Things go through us—the genetic code, the history of the nation, the language or languages we speak . . . the constraints that are put upon us, the people who are around us. And if we are an individual, it's because these threads are knotted together in this particular time and this particular place, and they hold. I also have no metaphysical sense of the self, and I see this knot as vulnerable: you could cut one or two threads of it . . . or you can, of course, get an unwieldy knot where somebody has had so much put in that the knot becomes a large and curious, and ugly object. We are connected, and we also are a connection which is a separate and unrepeated object. (1987, 26)

At stake for Byatt in the metaphor of the individual as knot is the transformation *from* emphasizing how a subject is inscribed by multiple codes and understands the self as a result of this inscription, with each individual subject to the symbolic discourses and representations of a given cultural context *to* an emphasis on the subject's particularity, to the very specific individually differentiated form of knotting the subject. The pun contains the seminal ambivalence I am concerned with in regarding the navel as a critical category for cultural analysis, namely, the enmeshment between connection, incision, bondage, and negation, that is, the bond constructed over naught. To speak of the knotted subject emphasizes not that the subject is split and multiple but *how* this multiplicity offers a new means of integration. The metaphor of the knotted subject yields an image for the condition of being culturally determined, with identity resulting from the inscription of cultural representations. At the same time this metaphor calls into question the specificity, particularity, or uniqueness of each cultural determination, ultimately favoring a notion of an individual who integrates fantasies of coherence with an acknowledgment of fallibility.

What makes the metaphor of the knotted subject so compelling to me is precisely that it allows one to move beyond a notion of the subject as exclusively constructed by representations, indeed beyond the conventional postmodern dictum "all is representation," even as it doesn't deny the supremacy of symbolic inscription. To speak of a knotted subject also allows me to underscore the way notions of want or implenitude, flaw, and vulnerability are inscribed into human existance.[7] If one moves toward a concept of subjectivity that argues for individual integration of incoherences, one can account for another element omitted from the exclusive privileging of the simulacrum—namely, the way that our body makes us each fallible, our mutatability imposes constraints on us. At the same time, this critical shift also addresses the impact of a traumatic knowledge specific to each person and how it returns to haunt not only any sense of plenitude and integrity offered by narcissistically informed self-fashionings and phantasies but also vexes the sense or security that what fundamentally splits the subject is its alienation within language.

Shifting our critical interest to the navel as signifier for a knotted scar that covers and touches upon a nonrepresentable wound ultimately allows us to address another moment of the uniquely unrepeatable cut that binds each human together, a wound which is parallel to but not subsumed by symbolic castration.[8] In one of the crucial marks of poststructuralist criticism, namely Derrida's claim for dissemination against Lacanian determination, as this emerged in the debate over Edgar Allan Poe's tale "The Purloined Letter," Derrida countered the notion of fate addressed by Lacan by suggesting that "a letter can always not arrive at its destination. . . . It belongs to the structure of the letter to be capable, always, of not arriving" (Muller 1988, 187). Slavoj Žižek, in turn, shrewdly inserts into the picture precisely the category so fundamentally neglected by poststructuralism, namely the notion of the *real*. He suggests, "We can say that we live only insofar as a certain letter (the letter containing our death warrant) still wanders around, looking for us. . . . Such is the fate of all and each of us, the bullet with our name on it is already shot . . . at the end of the imaginary as well as the symbolic itinerary, we encounter the Real" (1992, 21). It is precisely this wandering body, the traumatic knowledge of our mutability that hysteria communicate so spectacularly by virtue of its many protean symptoms.

If I suggest speaking of a knotted subject, then, with the navel as a signifier for the way the individual is constructed out of and over an originary traumatic wounding, I do so to emphasize that the acculturated subject only in part fades before the diacritics of the symbolic field that dictates its subjugation to language and cultural codes, that is, subjects itself to symbolic castration. Still another fading is at stake, however, referring to actual castration, given that the acculturated subject also fades before the real law of mortality: at birth, mutability, fragility, and fallibility all inscribe human existence. As the narrative of the Oedipal trajectory teaches us, sexual and symbolic castration stand in for a real lack. By being subject to symbolic laws *and* sexual anatomy, to representations *and* to the body, each human, precisely because subject to individual death, is individual and connected. The inscription of mortality at birth—ironically called the big leveler—also marks the singularity of each mortal existence. Therein lies the crux of the ambiguity between connection and negation implied by the notion of the knotted subject, for which the navel is both a somatic and a semiotic figure. This signifier points to the vulnerability inhabiting the individual, namely, that the knotting occurs over a wound, both shielding and constructing a site within which are the remains of the traumatic impact.

However, as Judith Butler (1990) has shown, sexuality cannot be discussed independently of the symbolic discourses on gender that produce it. In addition to distinguishing symbolic and sexual castration, now, however, I would suggest exploring the distinction between processes of language and Lacan's *real*. Bruce Fink defines the psychic realm of the real as an unrent, undifferentiated fabric, a seamless surface or space that doesn't exist, since it precedes language, yet which serves as the matrix onto which symbolic and imaginary processes are grafted. In other words, he views the real as the material that cultural codes and phantasies transform into narratives meant to sustain them. Obviously these articulations of the real are registered belatedly, or after the fact; Fink notes, "Insofar as we name and talk about the real and weave it into a theoretical discourse on language and the "time before the word," we draw it into language and thereby give a kind of existence to that which, in its very concept, has only ex-sistence" (1995, 25). So to distinguish between "symbolic castration" and the real incision (symbolically rendered only belatedly and in the gesture of a dislocated figure), which harks back to the traumatic wound at the onset of mortality yet defies any direct representation by not referring to any clearly marked single experience or event, I propose the concept of "denaveling." Its force comes directly from the delay and dislocation of its articulation though, in contradistinction to symbolic castration, it refers to an actual cut.[9]

By introducing this set of categories into our consideration of the subject's position and representation within the symbolic field of culture, my interest lies in writing such concepts as transcience and mutability back into the psychoanalytic account of psychic processes. The entire paradigm of mortality is as crucial to our discussion of visual and narrative representations as such already well-established and related categories as body, gender, desire, or ethics. For this hermeneutic enterprise, which places traumatic impact at its center—namely, the fragility of the body, the precariousness of the image repertoire, and the fallibility of the symbolic—I will use the term *navel*. Signifying the paradigm of concepts that are both literally and figuratively connected with this anatomical body sign as well as its symbolic counterpart, *omphalos* (the Greek term for navel, referring to ancient sculptures), the navel is devoid (like the phallus) of any direct reference to bodily reality; that is, referring to the representational quality of an articulation. In so doing, I suggest both a theoretical divergence from and a debt to Freud's discussion of castration, for which the Oedipus complex is the linchpin. For in this theoretical model, the issue of having or not having the phallus is the pivotal indication for the position one can take within a culture, whether one follows the classical patriarchy's privileging of the phallus or a more modern feminist critique of phallocentricity. As Griselda Pollock (1991, 32f) accurately notes,

> If everything is allowed to hinge only on castration, with its overly anatomical associations, men, who have penises to lose, appear not to be afflicted by lack. . . . The focus on castration gives undue and absolute significance to the sexing of the subject which then is read back as the end towards which all preceding processes drive. . . . But we are all subject to many psychic moments of lack in the process that begins with birth. . . . The Oedipal story as Freud and company invented it, and western bourgeois families institutionalised it, can be read as a defensive, masculinist representation, distancing men from the lack which forms all human subjects by making feminine bodies the exclusive and visual bearers of deficiency.

One of the premises underlying my argument about cultural configurations of hysteria is that the hysteric strategy of self-representation and self-performance negotiates between the phallus and the omphalos, staging as it does the child's questioning whether having or not having the phallus is all that determines a subject. For what the hysteric is so painfully aware of is precisely another law that dictates an individual's phantasies and symptoms; namely, the inevitable yet also inaccessible traumatic impact that she or he can neither fully repress nor directly articulate. In choosing the navel as an anatomical sign to designate this other force field constituting the subject, I follow Mieke Bal. She argues that whereas the phallus refers to gender in terms of "to have it" versus "to be it," the omphalos, in contrast, "is fundamentally gender specific—the navel is the scar of dependence on the mother—but it is also democratic in that both men and women have it. And unlike the phallus and its iconic representations disseminated throughout post-Freudian culture, the navel is starkly indexical" (Bal 1991, 23).

By rewriting symbolic castration under the aegis of the navel, speaking of denavelment and of the omphalos, I seek a way out of the impasse in psychoanalytic theory, all division and separation inevitably turning into a discussion of sexual differences, so that feminine castration is necessarily viewed as different from masculine castration as are the phantasies concomitant with sexual castration revolving around the phallus. Instead I suggest shifting our critical attention to nongendered psychic moments of loss, severance, deprivation, and the persistent production of narratives commemorating the impact of traumatic vulnerability at the core of our psychic and aesthetic representations. These phantasies and symptoms hark back to an indeterminable yet ineluctable originary wound and look forward to the equally indeterminable, inevitable human demise that threatens the human subject above and beyond the symbolic significance of a culturally privileged organ.

II

Before discussing how the language of hysteria can interrogate and sustain the Oedipal trajectory as described by Freud, it is worthwhile to review the origin of his psychoanalytic project, namely his formulation of the castration complex. With and against this primal theoretical phantasy, I will offer a rereading of Sophocles' *Oedipus the King* to shed light on a moment in this play that Freud chose *not* to read. In *The Interpretation of Dreams*, Freud isolates this tragedy as the illustration par excellence of the distressing disturbance brought about in the child's relation to his parents by the first stirrings of sexuality. The Oedipus legend, according to Freud, springs from some primeval dream material that corresponds to two universally persistent dreams: that men dream of having sexual relations with their mother is not only the key to the tragedy of Oedipus but also "the complement" to a second dream, namely the dream of the father being dead (Freud 1900–1901, 261–264). He calls *Oedipus the King* a "tragedy of destiny," whose lesson for the spectator is the "submission to the divine will and realization of his own impotence." One could say that it serves as a core scenario for symbolic castration, admonishing the subject to curtail his desire in accordance with the law dictated by culture. However, the compelling force moves us even today, Freud adds, precisely because Oedipus's destiny "might have been ours—because the oracle laid the same curse upon us before our birth as upon him. It is the fate of all of us, perhaps, to direct our first sexual impulse toward our mother and our first hatred and our first murderous wish against our father. *Our* dreams convince us that that is so." Thus they add a sexual encoding to the scenario of cultural forbiddance. The acculturated subject, according to Freud, is one who accepts this sexually encoded, symbolic castration. Abandoning the childhood wishes articulated by Sophocles this acculturated subject can detach his sexual impulses from his mother and forget his jealousy of his father.

Incest and patricide are the essence Freud draws from the play, and it is interesting to look carefully at his summary of it. The action of the play, he suggests, "consists in nothing other than the process of revealing with cunning delays and ever-mounting excitement—a process that can be likened to the work of a psycho-analysis—that Oedipus himself is the murderer of Laïus, but further that he is the son of the murdered man and of Jocasta. Appalled by the abomination he has unwittingly perpetrated, Oedipus blinds himself and forsakes his home. The oracle has been fulfilled." Yet if we turn to Sophocles' play we can see that the mother-wife is eliminated in a far more radical sense than is implied by the standard psychoanalytic formulation of a renunciation of the maternal body. Freud suggests that this story is about man's destiny, to recognize his fundamental impotence. He further reads it as an allegory about the subject's move from a drive-oriented "natural" existence to a renunciation of his "drives." This renunciation, this acceptance of symbolic castration, is concomitant with his becoming an acculturated being. However, in so doing Freud elides a significant moment— the death of Jocasta.

In Sophocles' rendition, Jocasta initially pleads with Oedipus not to pose any more questions to the messenger, as the latter is about to confront him with the devastating story of his origins. She hopes that the terrible family secret may remain unrevealed and that the illusory integrity of her marriage be upheld, however precariously. Even before the messenger can convey the truth about Oedipus's family debt, she turns from her husband, warning him, "God keep you from the knowledge of who you are." Returning home, she goes straight to her marriage chamber, the fatal site of double procreation. Tearing her hair, she calls upon her dead first husband, Laïus, groaning and cursing her bed in which, in the words of the messenger, "she brought forth husband by her husband, children by her own child, an infamous double bond" (Sophocles 1954; lines 1250–51). In choosing the act of suicide, Jocasta acknowledges her guilt at precisely that moment when the disclosure of the dangerous knowledge she has sought to keep from Oedipus appears to be inevitable. Taking her life means resigning herself to the inheritance she had tried to avert. In suicide she faces her legacy directly, without any fantasies of an intact family as shields from the traumatic impact. Significantly, her actual death is elided in the play; the rest of the messenger's report renders it only obliquely, concentrating instead on Oedipus's rage and distress. The messenger explains, "How after that she died I do not know— for Oedipus distracted us from seeing. He burst upon us shouting and we looked to him as he paced frantically around, begging us always: Give me a sword, I say, to find this wife no wife, this mother's womb, this field of double sowing whence I sprang and where I sowed my children! . . . Bellowing terribly and led by some invisible guide he rushed on the two doors— wrenching the hollow bolts out of their sockets, he charged inside" (lines 1252–1263).[10]

Sophocles' play thus articulates a dream other than the one about our incestual desires for the mother and our patricidal hatred and murderous wishes directed against the father, namely a dream of matricide. Just before

Oedipus becomes appalled at the crimes he has unwittingly committed, indeed immediately after he discovers that he is the murderer of his father, his response is not atonement but rather the desire to commit another murder. With sword in hand he rushes into the bedroom of his mother-wife, hoping to strike with his sword at this field of double sowing. The phantasy he embarks on is that in destroying the body that was the origin both for himself and his progeny he might discharge the guilt he is suddenly burdened with. He might thus assert his potency against the curse of knowledge that Jocasta brought on him in the double gesture of giving birth to him and bearing his children. However, Jocasta has thwarted his efforts. As he and his servants enter the room, they find her hanging, the rope twisted around her neck. "When he saw her, he cried out fearfully and cut the dangling noose. Then, as she lay, poor woman, on the ground, what happened after was terrible to see. He tore the brooches—the gold chased brooches fastening her robe—away from her and lifting them up high dashed them on his own eyeballs, shrieking out such things as: they will never see the crime I have committed or had done upon me!" (lines 1263–1272).

What would Oedipus have done if Jocasta hadn't committed suicide? I venture a speculation: he would have deflected his aggressive instincts from himself onto her, as his initial response indicates he wanted to, and killed her. And if he had been successful in this initial matricidal urge, would he have had to blind himself? I would further speculate that the answer would be 'no'. By destroying "this mother's womb, this field of double sowing whence I sprang," he would have also destroyed the site of his origin and, by extension, the so-called curse laid on him before birth. He thus could have given birth anew to himself, and in this self-engendered refashioning could have cleansed himself from the family debt, the legacy of his birth. Destroying the maternal body would have reinstated his imaginary fiction of omnipotence and would have sustained a phantasy scenario of a second denaveling, symbolically undoing the first umbilical incision. So one might then read his matricidal impulse as a universal desire distinct from the one isolated by Freud, namely the desire to obliterate the incoherences and flaws inflicted on us by genealogy. That birth position forces the individual to oscillate between phantasies of wholeness (whether an integrity of the body or family bond) and a recognition that this notion itself is perhaps a necessary, but an illusory, phantasy. The dream of matricide, in other words, establishes the illusion that we can become or remain innocent, not fallible or responsible for our implenitude.[11] It is precisely because Oedipus cannot sever himself from the history of his genealogy, just as he cannot move beyond the mortality that the maternal body (the "field of double sowing") so tragically inscribed in his life, that he must resort to blinding himself. He thus conflates symbolic and actual castration in a gesture repeating the traumatic incision of denaveling that is at the root of his story.

One might speculate that Oedipus becomes appalled at his own abomination (to return to Freud's formulations) precisely because he cannot kill

Jocasta. At the sight of her dead body he recognizes his own impotence before fate. Not only has it become a sign for the mutability and fallibility that
any notion of potency would require he repress, but also, and maybe above
all, it signals his impotence precisely in the fact that he himself could not kill
this site of his origin. I would add that he wishes to escape more than the
crimes of patricide and incest. Freud read the gesture of self-blinding as a
symbol for sexual castration and as a disavowal in response to the guilt felt
about incestual and patricidal instincts. Yet Oedipus's response can also be
read as a disavowal of a different guilt: his reaction of matricidal desire
when the oracle told him he was not omnipotent but rather vulnerable and
fallible. Over and above incest and patricide we share another fate, perhaps
common to men and women alike in a way the gendered Oedipus complex
is not, another curse that the oracle laid upon us with the cutting of the
umbilical cord, whose nonarbitrary, indexical sign is the navel, not the phallus. This curse, or prophecy, is about the mutability of our bodies and our
need to accept the parental debt; much as Oedipus cannot escape the fatal
enmeshment of his mortality and responsibility for the fallibility he inherited
from his parents, we can negotiate but never elide our common fate.

Any fundamental realization of what Freud calls impotence, I would
argue, involves a recognition of the traumatic knowledge of vulnerability
that grounds our existence. The reversal of this recognition, the dream of
omnipotence, is thus directed toward two moments that Freud's discussion
of sexual castration elides: the desire for immortality in the face of the mutability of the human body and the desire to be innocent of the matrix of
psychic incoherences we each inherit from a given family structure. Both
desires elicit the wish for a sacrificial cleansing, posited against the recognition that we must accept responsibility both for the mortality of our body
and the flaws of our family history, a double legacy inherited with the cutting of the umbilical cord and bespoken by the navel. The desire to refashion
ourselves mythically, outside and beyond anatomical and historical facticity, is related to—and is as illusory as any—myths about immortality.[12]
These, myths, I would argue, are two equally fundamental dreams that we
carry from childhood on and that Sophocles articulates in his play through
the dead body of Jocasta.

By shifting the emphasis in my reading of the Oedipal story from incest
and patricide to failed matricide, and by interpreting the ensuing self-castra-
tion as the metonymic substitute for a desire to eradicate the site of one's
origin—the mother's womb and the child's remnant of this connection via
the navel—I am moving away from the sexual encoding of castration. I want
to suggest instead that at the epicenter of all traumatic knowledge, including
what Freud calls the recognition of human impotence, lies a recognition of
mortality. Freud's psychoanalytic theory purports, that the Oedipal subject
handles this awareness of death as an *Unheimlichkeit*—as the state of not
being fully at home in the world because one's somatic and psychic state is
fragile and mutable. By having recourse to a sexually encoded act of dis-

placement, aggression is directed either outside of or displaced among other body organs, only to be converted into phantasies or realizations of partial dismemberment. Oedipus, unable to kill Jocasta, blinds himself, thus shifting the fear of death to an issue of seeing. Freud's psychoanalytic narrative readily transforms these pierced eyes into a metaphor for the male sexual organ, in a hermeneutic gesture that the existential therapist Irvin Yalom (1980, 59–74) calls a press for translation engendered by an unwillingness to directly theorize the traumatic impact of our mortality. Indeed, as Yalom argues, Freud ultimately came to view the nature of trauma as explicitly and exclusively sexual, emphasizing abandonment and castration as primary and privileged sources of anxiety in his effort to avoid or exclude a discussion of death.

Freud's inattention to death is particularly striking in the case studies on which he initially based his early theories about anxiety, trauma, castration, and femininity (see the *Studies in Hysteria*) where death pervades the clinical histories of his patients. The traumas precipitating the hysterical symptoms of the three main patients—Anna O., Emmy von N., and Elisabeth von R.— quite markedly involve death, either because the patient was involved in nursing a dying parent or because the deaths of various family members forced these women to confront not only the truth of their own mortality but also the fallibility of symbolic codes when faced with the total disintegration of the family bond. Yet Freud, in his interpretation of each case, either overlooks the connection between hysterical trauma and mortality or translates it into issues of sexually encoded loss: castration (e.g., the loss of the penis) or abandonment (e.g., the loss of love). Freud's phallic reading, Yalom argues, overlooks that the common denominator of abandonment, separation, and castration is the loss and annihilation connected with death. In his very late writings on the death drive Freud returned to the issue of mortality, which he had minimized at the turn of the century in writing his *Interpretation of Dreams* and his *Studies on Hysteria*. However, he never abandoned the primacy of sexual castration as an explanatory model for psychic organization and disturbance.[13] Freud's work on hysteria, in which he reads hysteric symptoms not as representations of death anxiety and traumatic impact but as articulations of a sexual scenario (an actual event of sexual abuse or a phantasy of seduction) resulted in the so-called "riddle of femininity." The narrative of phallic monism posits woman as an enigma, eliding the other story Freud's hysteric patients were telling him: a story about real death anxiety. Similarly, the insistence on incest and patricide, ignoring the desire for matricide, in *Oedipus the King* translated issues of mortality and facticity into sexuality, thus repressing the knowledge that death is the metaphorical navel of all feelings of impotence.

Under the aegis of the phallus, as Christa Rhode-Dachser (1991) argues, the Oedipal story translates femininity into an enigma for the masculine subject by devising a twofold symptom-representation: the sexually cas-

trated and demonic woman. This construction of femininity is how the masculine subject projects the recognition of mortality and fallibility. In the double strategy characteristic of symptom formation, the phallic narrative
represses this traumatic knowledge by deflecting all the values connected
with the paradigm of mortality onto the sexually different feminine body,
finding its oblique articulation there. Psychoanalytic theory can be said to
screen a recognition of mortality by sexually encoding narratives about the
traumatic knowledge of human vulnerability in terms of the castrated or the
demonic woman. As the feminine equivalent of the phallic masculine subject, she comes to harbor the denied recognition of death.

If making the feminine body the exclusive and visual bearer of fragility
and want sustains the masculinist Oedipal story, as Griselda Pollock puts it,
then for feminist hermeneutics to interrogate its linchpin, the so-called riddle
of femininity, requires undoing the boundary that distances men "from the
lack which forms all human subjects" (1991, 33). Such a dismantling of
phallic strategies above all involves abandoning the distinction between a
masculine and a feminine subject of castration. By returning to the masculine subject those aspects of human existence that culture has projected onto
femininity—lack, drives, deprivation, fallibility, implenitude—we no longer
focus our critical attention on gender distinction. Rather, shifting critical
attention from phallus to omphalos implies confronting the way the subject
emerges as a knot shielding itself from its originary wound by avoiding this
traumatic knowledge of mortality. In other words, the initial incision produces a split in the subject from which sexual desire, cultural images of potency and immortality (as well as neurotic symptoms) may emerge as secondary screen phantasies. At the same time, this traumatic incision is also
what knots the subject *together* at the navel of its being.

III

The field of mythopoetics has seen the navel as a symbol for the site not only
of origin but also of termination. In speaking of the navel of the world,
concomitant with the idea of a centered existence is the notion that all life
departs from and also returns to a sacred center. Thus, Christian mythology
sees the altar as an *umbilicus terrae*, and stories of antiquity have always
drawn on the connection between the navel and the grave, vault, or tomb,[14]
this anatomical mark signifying the mortal wound that taints all human life
from birth. For example, in Plato's *Symposium* (1961, 543), Aristophanes,
describing the birth of sexuality, claims that because the initially androgy-
nous humans tried to reach up and set upon the gods, they were punished by
being cut in half. The sight of the gash was meant to frighten them into
keeping quiet, and although Apollo tied the skin together over the one opening, "smoothing most of the creases away," Aristophanes suggests "he left

a few puckers round the navel, to remind us of what we suffered long ago." As a mythopoetic symbol, then, the navel signifies that the centeredness of human existence is constructed over a gap, a fissure, a void.

This image of human existence emerging from a center that is split recalls the priestess at Delphi in a cave-like shrine, chanting the oracle's truth over a cleft in the earth, inspired by mephitic vapors that rose from the earth, a scenario that allows me to specify the symbolic resonance with the omphalos. In Greek mythology the omphalos referred to a mound-shaped, stone, cult object, a supremely sacred fetish to which the suppliant used to cling, the most famous example of which was found in Apollo's temple in Delphi. Jane Ellen Harrison (1927, 386–429) suggests that this religious fetish was a crucial stake in the conflict between the old matrilinear order of the daimones of Earth and the Olympian Apollo, representative of the new patriarchal order. The omphalos was initially the sanctuary of Gaia—herself transparent, representing Earth as a maternal divinity. In her power to nourish and protect, Gaia represented a cyclical divinity, giving forth mortal existence and reclaiming it. The cult of Gaia acknowledged human mortality and its debt to Earth, and in this religious order the omphalos as maternal emblem was meant to relate both nourishment and mortality to the realm of a feminine originary divinity. In Harrison's reading, the sequence of cults from Gaia to Apollo, during which the progenitress of all generations of gods was transformed into an antagonistic demonic nature force, was seen as the conflict between the dream-oracle of Earth and Night and the truth of heaven's light and sun. This conflict crystallized in the myth of Apollo's slaying of the snake Python, who was both Gaia's child and guardian of the omphalos. Indeed, one Pompeian fresco shows the Python, still coiled around the omphalos, with the high pillar behind it giving it a grave-like look.[15]

However, after the displacement of Gaia by Apollo through this sacrificial murder, the general apparatus of her cult, the mephitic cleft in the earth and the omphalos as site of oracle, were maintained. The fetish-stone and maternal emblem, however, received a new encoding and were transformed into the sign of the earth's center on which Apollo's monistic faith in a paternal God could be based. The story of Gaia's prophetic powers was exchanged for those of Zeus who, seeking to find the center of the earth, released two eagles from the eastern and western edges of the world, only to have them meet over Delphi. In the cult of Apollo, the omphalos also served as the site of prophecy, only now it was in the form of the Delphic navel stone transformed into a grave-mound commemorating the sacred snake Python. One could say that this new religious realm was constructed at the grave of the sacred snake, and indeed navel stones are often seen in conjunction with gravestones.

Yet the Apollonian omphalos functions like a symptom that negates even as it articulates the impact of disavowed knowledge. Re-encoded, it displaces Gaia and with her an acknowledgment of the vulnerability of life, of the mortal's debt to Earth; it does so precisely by commemorating the killing of the snake, which, functioning as manifest connection to this maternal divinity, can be read as the mythopoetic rendition of the umbilical cord. In other words, even as the Apollonian omphalos displaces the snake, now no longer encircling the navel-stone but buried beneath it, it reminds us of the visible connection to the source of life, which is also the source of death. The trajectory from Gaia's to Apollo's omphalos might then be read in the following way. Initially, the omphalos signified the maternal emblem, marking the site of a manifest worship of the chasm at the center of existence—Earth's cleft—with a visible connection to the transparent maternal force given shape in the figure of Python. In the second, Apollonian phase, the omphalos was transformed into an apotropaic emblem, a shield from any direct acknowledgment of our mortal debt to the maternal Earth. After this shift in belief, brought about by virtue of a form of matricide, the omphalos came to serve as site of purification and prophecy, at the same time, however, commemorating the now invisible umbilical cord. So that Apollo's omphalos, whose manifest function lay in marking the center of the world and the site of truth, had a supplementary function as a gravestone, rendering a displaced acknowledgment of death as well. The navel was symbol of a ritually marked central source of life and fertility and of sacrifice and commemoration (as a gravestone monument).

The omphalos that interests me is not Gaia's altar but rather Python's grave-mound: there it functions as a symbol of loss and commemoration, articulating how values connected with the maternal divinity—the Earth, the night, the bond between birth and death—ground any paternal symbolic system. In this function the omphalos describes an aspect of the destiny of our anatomy distinct from Freud's story of the phallus. It invites us to think of the navel as a gravestone commemorating the death of our Python, the umbilical cord we have lost. In the interpretive narrative I am advocating, the navel marks a double matricide: the bodily severing at childbirth and the psychic renunciation of the maternal body required by symbolic castration. Although the omphalos thus functions as the edifice on which phantasies of potency and immortality can be erected, as the apotropaic gesture that can mitigate the anxiety induced by human vulnerability, this navel-grave also is the trace of the incision we carry with us as we move into the paternal cultural order. It is, after all, the signature of the lost maternal body, admonishing us of our debt to death.

My redefinition of the omphalos follows Jacques Lacan's discussion of the psychic history of the subject as structured by a fundamental loss of the maternal body—a loss we never own or represent but one that we repeat. For Lacan the lack of this or that object is not at stake but rather the very lack of being. Far from assuaging this traumatic impact, the sublimation of drives and desires that results from a symbolic castration works against fictions of potency and immortality. It recreates the void left by this loss of the mother, pointing to what is fundamentally *unheimlich* in our way of inhabiting the world and the cleft that underlies phantasies of plenitude. Indeed, in his article, "The Function and Field of Speech and Language," Lacan (1966, 105) suggests, "When we wish to attain in the subject . . . what is primordial to the birth of symbols, we find it is in death, from which his existence takes on all the meaning it has." For Lacan castration involves coming to terms with what one is not, with what one does not have, with what one cannot be; with a recognition of finitude and that something crucial is always already lost—and irretrievably so. As Richard Boothby suggests, Lacan's notion of castration "is only incidentally related to a paternal threat of violence," or to the threat of sexual dismemberment, and he adds, "Acceptance of castration means [instead] abandoning the narcissistic dream of absolute self-adequacy and submitting to an original being at-a-loss" (1991, 149).

It is precisely because the paternal threat and its privileged signifier, the phallus, are only incidental to a castration that addresses the fallibility and vulnerability of the subject, whereas the maternal loss is endemic to it, that I speak of denaveling along with symbolic castration. I locate the site of this other incision at the navel, a remainder or residue written into the body, "which harkens back to the primordial object of satisfaction, that original object in relation to which every subsequent attempt at satisfaction must be deemed a refinding of the object: the mother" (Boothby 1991, 165–167). While the force of phallic castration resides in producing ongoing signification and deferral of desire, the omphalos points to the real, traumatic knowledge of human existence grounded by mortality. In other words, I am exploring an omphalic form of signification based not on the repression of traumatic enjoyment, in the way sublimation is. This omphalic form of signification neither forgets nor substitutes for the originary traumatic relation to the maternal body (its excessive presence and then its loss) but rather constructs a site within the symbolic for this knowledge.

In other words, an omphalic signification neither directly satisfies desire by moving from representation to action (in what Lacan has called the *passage à l'acte*) nor directly sublimates desire by keeping it unrealized, allowing the object at stake to remain lost. Rather, it addresses the mortal vulnerability of the subject; it enjoys the trace of this traumatic kernel. Sublimation would require that something be successfully repressed in order to be symbolized. The omphalos, in contrast, commemorating a lost body and the traumatic impact of vulnerability that could only be articulated in its wake, addresses a different knowledge. Since the traumatic kernel was never fully present to the psychic process, it can also never be fully lost. Representation here implies a strategy of conversion that preserves bits of the lost body, which is why the navel scar, index of parturition's incision, appears as such an adequate somatic metaphor for the process.

Yet this lost body, as Michèle Montrelay astutely notes, appears as an object of desire and anxiety not only belatedly, but also refers to "a time when nothing was thinkable: then, the body and the world were confounded in one chaotic intimacy which was too present, too immediate—one continuous expanse of proximity or unbearable plenitude. What was lacking was lack" (1977, 233). Omphalic, then, I want to call a strategy of representation that is firmly in place within the symbolic and not to be relegated to a realm beyond cultural laws. At the same time this strategy oscillates between sublimation and the celebration of a traumatic remnant harking back to the site of unbearable plenitude. Evoking anxiety, the traumatic impact calls for sublimation; never really repressed, however, it persistently wanders, as a foreign body, through the psychic and somatic systems.

IV

Alfred Hitchcock's *Psycho* (1960), is a postmodern rewriting of *Oedipus the King*. In the movie Normal Bates succeeds at the matricide that eluded his mythic forefather, only to displace his unappeased aggressive impulses by making a fetish of the lost maternal body, subsequently killing young women who threaten to be not only rivals to but moreover repetitions of Mother. Rather than offering an interpretation of the entire film, however, I will concentrate on three scenes revolving around navel inversions, which illustrate what is at stake in omphalic representation.[16] Hitchcock begins his narrative with a panorama of a city, whose name, Phoenix, Arizona, is then set into the center of the shot; the bird-like camera seeks out a building, swoops down, slips through the bottom slit left open from the pulled-down blinds of a window, and enters a dark space, only to arrest its flight by revealing the body of the protagonist, Marion Crane, lying half-dressed on a bed.

As we discover in the following scenes, she (like the camera introducing her), is a wanderer, lacking a clear position in her social order and in search of a place of habitation. Meeting her lover clandestinely during a lunch break, she seeks to legitimate their relationship through marriage and to gain respectability before the law; she is thwarted in her desire because Sam insists that he must first pay off his dead father's debts and his ex-wife's alimony. The next scene confirms the instability of her position within the symbolic, staging it, however, as an ambivalence toward paternal authority. Like an hysteric, Marion, who has no father of her own, plays to the father's gaze, responding to her customer's, Mr. Cassidy's, flirtation by taking on the coyly submissive pose of the daughter as he boasts about how he intends to pay $4o,ooo in cash to buy a house to give to his "sweet little girl" for her wedding. Significantly he looks suggestively at Marion only to correct himself, "Oh, oh no, not you," as he sits on her desk and continues his seductive speech, describing how his gift is meant not to buy happiness but rather to "buy off unhappiness," constantly addressing the similarity between Marion and his "baby" with such questions as "Are *you* unhappy?"

Though it remains unclear whose unhappiness is to be bought off—the daughter's—as she moves into the unknown territory of marriage, or the father's, bereft of his daughter, the fact that Cassidy prides himself in being

potent enough to ward off any sense of vulnerability evokes the exact opposite message to Marion. What his seduction provokes is her recognition not
only of her implenitude (she is unhappy precisely because she does not have
a home) but also of the fallibility of paternal authority. Cassidy jokingly
explains that this is "private money," that he has not declared before the
law. By thus offering his unhappy surrogate daughter a piece of the knowledge he keeps from his real daughter, that is, a glimpse of the hole in symbolic consistency, he shows her how to profit from his flaw by herself questioning the authority of the law. Demurely obeying the command of her boss
to take the money to a safe-deposit box, she no longer sustains but rather
dismantles paternal authority. She steals the money. With this act of parturition—Marion cuts the money, the symbolic baby Cassidy has nourished in
private as the father—she also cuts herself from the community of law-abid-
ing citizens. She renders visible the obscene, unspoken detail on which the
entire transaction of buying off unhappiness is based: She acts out the fact
that the father's potency feeds off illegal, private funds.

Marion's theft is the first omphalic moment in the film. The navel, as
signifier of a founding incision, shielding from but also addressing vulnerability, is here rendered in the image of the envelope that contains the illegal
money. The camera repeatedly seeks out this bundle, folded in half, un-
sealed, held shut by a rubber band, now referring both to the father's and the
daughter's fallibility before the law. The envelope now figures as the mark
of both Marion's and Cassidy's transgressive cut that jettisons them from
social codes, with the daughter imitating the father's effort at another gesture of parturition: buying off unhappiness. As Marion changes in her room,
the camera views this knotted scar five times, from all sides, the last shot
showing Marion plunging it into the dark caverns of her purse. From here
she extracts it when a policeman on the highway stops her to see her licence,
then again in the garage restroom, where she exchanges her car. Later she
opens the envelope to fold the money into a newspaper, and she leaves it,
like Poe's purloined letter, excessively exposed on her bedside table in Bates
Motel, somewhat shielded from the view of Norman. Significantly, it is the
last object that he clears from her room when he seeks to make Marion's
corpse, along with her effects, disappear from sight.

Throughout Marion's scenes, she remains ambivalent toward the law,
acknowledging its authority even as she transgresses it. On the manifest level
she reaches the Bates Motel only on the second night of her trip to bring the
stolen money to Sam in Fairville and sell him on the idea of marriage: The
policeman had stopped her that morning while she was sleeping in her car at
the side of the road. On the latent level, however, in turning off the highway
Marion follows a fateful call to discover the truth of her desire for marriage,
this bond that could sustain a fantasy of integrity and belonging that might
shield her from a sense of abandonment and implenitude. We will discover
that this lack, based on subjectivity because it ensures individuality, or the
distinction from other objects and bodies, though traumatic, nevertheless

preserves her from the equally disturbing and unbearable excess of plenitude that would extinguish all life-sustaining differentiation. As Montrelay, commenting on Oedipus's discovery of the truth, writes, "The realization of unconscious desire is always so catastrophic that the subject can never bring it about on its own" (1977, 234). Indeed it needs a symptom of sorts which, as Žižek puts it, "is a compromise formation. . . . In the symptom, the subject gets back, in the form of a ciphered, unrecognized message, the truth about his desire, the truth that he was not able to confront, that he betrayed" (1993, 187).

In Norman Bates, Marion finds herself confronting precisely such a signifying double, one who also lost a father early on and thus only imperfectly subjected to "symbolic castration," hovers between supporting and transgressing the authority of paternal law.[17] To analyze both the ciphered message Norman broadcasts to Marion and the self-representation he has designed, which culminates in the shower scene, we must see how the film's second omphalic moment is embedded in a narrative sequence. Marion's realization of her desire begins, after all, with a discussion about Norman's mother: "My mother—what is the phrase?—she isn't quite herself today." After he invites Marion to have dinner with him in his homey kitchen, indeed just as she is about to cautiously place the stolen money wrapped inside the newspaper on the bedside table, she hears a disembodied female voice coming from the house in which Bates lives, calling out, "No, no." Although Norman describes Marion as "just a stranger" who is hungry on a wet night, the mother forbids him (on a manifest level) to feed her "ugly appetite with my food or my son." Yet screened out by the sexual narrative (the maternal voice's castrative interdiction that the son enjoy a potential bride) lies a different message about another appetite satisfied by cutting open any idealized fictions of sexual or marital pleasure. Because it is disembodied the maternal voice is itself a foreign body, wandering bereft of any corporality through the Bates Motel. It harks back in a ciphered way to an earlier traumatic parturition, namely the matricide committed by Norman, and prophesies a repetition of this fatal incision. This voice of the murdered mother is the trace of a lost object haunting Norman's psychic system, for which the house, itself an omphalos of sorts, is a visual externalization. A lost body, this maternal voice was not successfully repressed, forgotten, or sublimated, and thus came to be embodied in this vault of Norman's mind as the repeated recollection of trauma.

The jettisoned, freely floating voice that now belongs neither to Norman nor to his mother, as indeterminate a body as the navel, points out to Marion the fallibility of her phantasy that she could build a happy marriage with Sam based on the money stolen from Cassidy. In the ensuing conversation with Norman, Marion's decision to accept symbolic castration is confirmed. Thanking him for the exchange, she decides to go back to Phoenix the next morning and return the money, both acknowledging her guilt and relinquishing her romantic idealization. But by rendering an intimate, traumatic trace external, a second desire is awakened in both Marion and her symptom, Norman, directed not at sublimating lack but rather at enjoying unbearable plenitude, filling the hole in paternal authority with an excessive presence of the maternal body. As though to pave the way for the total obliteration of the differences underlying the origin and sustainment of individual subjectivity, body boundaries seem to blur in the course of their conversation. It is no longer clear who is stuffing and who is being stuffed; who is alive and who, inanimate; what is outside and what, inside.

On the one hand, Norman speaks of his hobby, "stuffing things . . . taxidermy," shown by the many stuffed birds on the parlor wall and whose crowning achievement, at the end of the film, is the transformation of his mother's corpse into a fetish. On the other hand, Hitchcock lays the trace for the discovery of a second, far more disturbing fetish, namely, that it is Norman's body which has in fact been stuffed, transformed into the living host of the lost maternal body. Norman's preservation of a bond twice severed, by parturition and then by matricide when he stabbed his mother in repetition of the umbilical cut, keeps alive the traumatic impact. Overtly he justifies his unwillingness to leave the "trap" he was "born into," having recourse to a screen fiction, namely his filial responsibility toward keeping Mother. If he were to leave, he explains, "the fire would go out. It would be cold and damp like a grave." Furthermore, while Marion had read Cassidy's confession of the illegality of his funds as an invitation to imitate him in his transgression of the law, Norman interprets Marion's revelation of her fraud as an invitation to embark on his transgressive desire.

Showing us Norman smiling at the discrepancy between the name Marion gives in parting and the signature in the register, Hitchcock begins the sequence that will end with the car containing her corpse sinking into the swamp behind the motel. One could say the shower scene that follows enacts the content of the conversation preceding it: namely, that escape is impossible; one is born into an irrevocable knot and caught within constraints from which complete liberation would be a fiction. It visualizes, as a hallucination in the real,[18] what has been insufficiently repressed. The hallucination evokes first as a disembodied voice and then as the object of the conversation, namely, the maternal body in her traumatizing intimacy "too present, too immediate—one continuous expanse of proximity or unbearable plenitude," (Montrelay 1977, 233) which appears before Marion as her nemesis. As Barbara Creed notes, interpretations of this scene tend to see it either as representing the mother's desire to get rid of a rival or as a symbolic form of rape. She suggests that it be seen, instead, as a rendition of the son's response to a castrating parent: "Norman 'becomes' mother largely to turn the tables on mother, to ensure his own survival—to castrate rather than be castrated" (1993, 148). I would call this scene omphalic, however, because it ties together the two castrative constraints that are of concern here. Like Oedipus, Norman enters into the privacy of a feminine realm, knife in hand, ready to stab Marion Crane. On the manifest level of the story he thus interrupts her during her shower, a gesture of cleansing, meant to ritually mark her acceptance of symbolic castration. By going back to Phoenix and returning the money, she not only acknowledges her guilt but also relinquishes the phantasy of an intact home brought about through marriage. If, however, one stays with the less literal reading within which Norman and his alter-representation, Mother, are symptoms of Marion's unconscious desire, a second aspect of castration, what I am calling *denavelment*, comes into play. Whereas the shower marks Marion's ability to sublimate the inadequacy of her social existence, the lack of a marital bond, it also enacts her wish to enjoy what lies beyond (and precedes) this lack—precisely by enmeshing a representation of vulnerability with its actual performance.

If we accept the hybrid Norman-Mother as personifying the engulfing plenitude first felt in the maternal body, so overwhelming because the undifferentiated proximity allows for no autonomy and thus engenders a traumatic vulnerability from which lack shields, then its entrance into Marion's privacy has, as William Rothman notes, an uncanny, dual function: "First she is compelled to acknowledge this apparition as her own projection. Second, she is compelled to acknowledge this nightmare figure also as real, beyond her control" (1982, 301). At the navel of the film, Marion and Norman are actually conjoined. Their union is not erotic, but because of their desire to enjoy the traumatic kernel at the navel of their existence, they come together as one and the same phantasic body: Mother, engulfing the child, undoing the umbilical cut, and claiming back the body she gave forth. In Norman's case, as the narrative at the end of the film explains, this is a moment of psychosis when the son relinquishes all individuality and becomes the mother he killed. In Marion's case, the disembodied maternal voice had already given her a ciphered message about the frailty of her family romance and phantasies of marital plenitude with Sam. The appearance of its embodiment as Norman-Mother transmits two further messages about vulnerability. Just as marriage will not buy off unhappiness, so the symbolic is inconsistent: there is no restitution for her crime and she cannot undo the wound her theft has inflicted. As she is confronted with the irrevocable truth of her mortality, the vanity underlying her fantasies of romantic plenitude and social refashioning is utterly disclosed. At all three levels—phantasy, public position, and reality of the body—the message the phantastic figure of Norman-Mother brings is that to close the gap and undo the navel is a form of traumatic enjoyment commensurate with death. As Norman-Mother repeats the gesture of stabbing, which had itself given birth to this phantastic figure, repeating the matricide at the root of his psychosis, both Norman and Marion enjoy the traumatic kernel subtending any act of sublimating representation. They relinquish themselves to the archaic body of destructive impulses, which are curbed in the course of castrative representations leading to sublimation. Indeed, they enact a breakdown, in which symptoms become exclusively flesh.

That this scene cannot be interpreted merely as a phantasy of sexual penetration but must also be seen as a return to the traumatic impact of an earlier cut is shown by our viewing the knife actually stabbing the body only

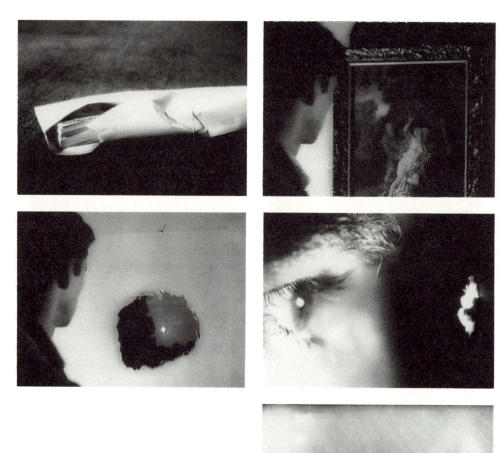

Alfred Hitchcock, scenes from *Psycho*: the
envelope of money; removing the painting;
the hole in the wall; the gaze; the shower murder; the drain; the dead eye; the mother fetish;
the grinning Mother-Norman; the merged
Mother-Norman; recovering the car.

when its blade is pointed not at the genitals or the breasts but rather at the
abdominal area, just above her navel—at the site of Marion's womb.[19] Norman-Mother, one could say, wants not only to kill Marion but to pierce her
at exactly the site from which she could become a mother herself. In attacking the site of motherhood he seems to take from her, in a preventive gesture,
the ability to give birth to men like himself. With this doubly coded gesture
he cuts into the feminine womb; as with "the field of double sowing," he
attacks both the maternal body and himself, sustaining his phantasy work.

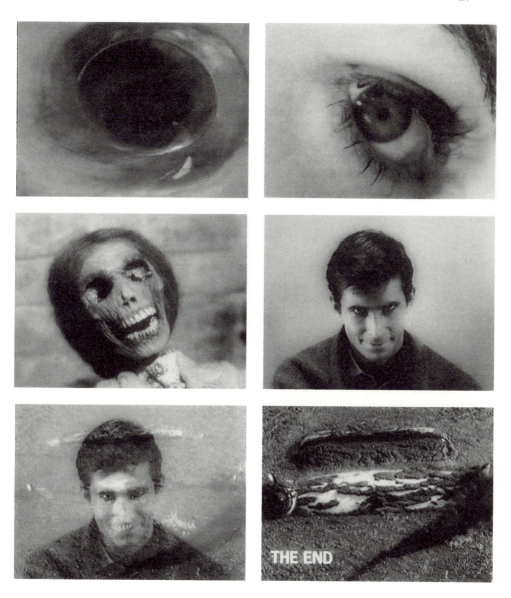

For Marion, however, returned in denaveling to the site at which her subjectivity began, it is as if, sliding down along the bathroom wall, she wakes up from a moment of phantastic trauma beyond language only to realize it was not a hallucination but actuality. The truth she has acquired, the most intimate tip of the navel, cannot be rendered in representation. Hitchcock thus gives us only an inversion: the dead eye.

On the narrative level, which self-reflexively comments on the act of representation, Hitchcock insists that the navel remains an indeterminate boundary, a site marking the entrance, exit, and return of mutable bodies, along with debris one wants to reject. It is a shield from direct access to the inevitable, inaccessible matrix of vulnerability. This dual message, I suggest, comes across visually through the sequence of holes introducing and concluding the murder scene. Hitchcock shows us Norman removing a painting of "Susanna and the Elders" so as to gaze at Marion undressing through a hole in the wall. Significantly, this clandestine hole appears to be precisely behind the navel Susanna so tauntingly flaunts in the painting that screens it, and it resembles a belly with a navel. Hitchcock, in a close-up, then explicitly focuses on the eye and the hole, the latter a navel behind a navel, that Norman seeks to penetrate with his gaze. Covering the hole again, Norman returns to the house. Meanwhile Marion, having calculated whether she can pay back from her own savings the stolen money she has already spent, throws the torn bits of figures and paper into the toilet bowl and flushes these down, a navel image Hitchcock frames but does not penetrate.

In the shower itself he then rapidly aligns the showerhead—spouting water—with Marion's opened mouth—screaming in terror—and the bathtub drain, only partially visible as we see Norman-Mother pressing Marion against the wall. Her navel is struck by the knife; after Norman's exit, we once again see the showerhead emitting water and the drain absorbing its bloody transformation. The scene closes with the camera moving toward the bathtub drain until it has completely filled the frame, and superimposing on this Marion's dead eye, from which the camera then recedes, this navel image signifying the interface between traumatic knowledge and the limits of visualization. The camera then travels from Marion's head, passing by the showerhead and the toilet bowl (without showing its interior) through the room to alight on the newspaper containing the money. Through the open window we see the Bates house and now hear not the maternal voice but Norman's, calling out his horror. This signals another reason why I would call the cinematic language in this scene omphalic: by virtue of the technique of rapid sequence of shots (more than forty in as many seconds), it constructs a cinematic space that preserves traumatic knowledge without representing it directly. It avoids sublimating the impact into a single, fixed, and semantically encoded image.

In the final scene of revelation Norman-Mother, with the same gesture he entered his seductive guest's bathroom, breaks into the cellar room with knife in hand, ready to stab Marion's sister. Lila had gone there hoping to find Norman's mother, but had turned around in horror when she discovered that the person she had hoped to learn from now exists only as the remains of a corpse. As she turns, however, she finds herself confronted with a resurrection of this dead mother. Yet Lila, in contrast to her sister firmly emplaced within the symbolic, indeed seeks merely to cover the cleft her sister's theft created. The message she receives, between these two foreign bodies of the fetish and the phantastic figure of Norman-

Mother, enacts for her the truth of her sister's death, not her own. At the same time, however, this scene initiates the last sequence I am calling omphalic, one that again blurs the boundary, before a final fusing of bodies into traumatic plenitude.

Lila is facing the fetish just before she turns around, so that both she and the mother fetish are virtually in the same position; it is unclear who is to be the object of Norman's thrust. As she turns from the fetish, Lila's out-flung arm causes the bulb to swing back and forth. Casting shadows and then returning with its light, this swinging bulb transforms the cellar into a mutable phantasmagoric space. While Sam overpowers Norman-Mother, Lila first notes the wig fallen to the ground and then, once more, the maternal fetish. If the stable light had initially emphasized the deadness of the preserved head, the movement of the light now reanimates the maternal face. Roger Dadoun calls this "the most horrific moment of the film, the scene that is the fantasmatic and emotional pivot of the whole story [because] the mother is everywhere, occupying the whole screen from one edge of the frame to the other" (1989, 50–51). Hitchcock dissolves this traumatic image of excessive maternal plenitude, obliterating all distinctions—between the dead and the animate, the self and the other—into that of the county courthouse, and in doing so this image continues to haunt the viewer, just as, in Creed's words, "The all-pervasive presence of the mother . . . continues to haunt the subject even after the mother's death" (1993, 150).

If the omphalos as gravestone buries and recalls the absent Python and, with it, our connection to the maternal body, we also find several articulations in *Psycho* that correlate to Oedipus's castrative self-blinding. On the one hand, the serial murder of women, recalling and potentially replacing the psychically preserved, dead, mother with the significant cut, at least in Marion's case, is shown to be directed at the navel. On the other hand, the omphalos gravestone also finds articulation in Norman's effort to create a two-sided maternal fetish: the perfectly harmless stuffed fetish and his own murderous impersonation of her. Rather than sublimating her death by acknowledging his crime, he preserves and repeatedly performs this traumatic knowledge at his own body, by transforming himself into the host that harbors the parasitical dead mother's voice and language as well as by dressing in her clothes whenever he is once more overwhelmed by the impulse to kill potential mothers. While the failed murder of Lila structurally repeats the successful killing of Marion, it does so with a significant difference, marking the peripeteia of Hitchcock's narrative. Both scenes hinge on a breakdown of the symbolic, the first one opening up the hole through which the unbearable excessive proximity of the Mother can reemerge as a hallucination in the real, and the second case, when the desire is satisfied, a scene in which Norman is the object against which the force of too much maternal presence is directed. Although it costs him life as a differentiated subject, the result is not murder, but transformation. Before our eyes he enacts the phoenix, with which the film began, as we notice the wandering voice of Mother arising from the ashes of Norman's body.

With the explanation "Bates no longer exists," the psychoanalyst embarks on an interpretive narrative of Norman's transformation. After the early death of the father, matricide was Norman's response to too much maternal presence, an incestuous desire gone awry, provoked when Norman found himself unable to contain his murderous jealousy once it was aroused by the presence of a rival. Oedipus, faced with Jocasta's corpse, blinds himself and thus embraces a psychic trajectory in which sublimation occurs because desire is repressed and symbolization performed, repeating the cutting of the mortal thread Jocasta undertook when she hanged herself. Norman, able to commit matricide, actually binds himself ever more closely to Mother. In order to erase any memory of this traumatic event, which he cannot sublimate because he cannot fully repress it (it actually gains force from the impact of an earlier cut, the loss of the father), he has recourse to another register of representation, namely, the body. As the analyst explains, "He was simply doing everything possible to keep alive the illusion of his mother being alive." He cannot psychically symbolize her death to himself, given that this realization is shielded by the psychic blank with which he registered the traumatic impact of matricide.

Preserving the dead mother who cannot be buried, he encrypts her in his own psychic register, so that he harbors not only the signature of parturition—the navel—but also the traces of the dead mother: her voice, her sentences, her clothes. Possessed by this foreign body, he either splits his personality, carrying on conversations with her, or dissociates himself completely, falling into a trance as Mother takes over completely; "He was never all Norman but he was often only Mother." Owing to successful matricide, he, unlike Oedipus, does not need to blind himself; rather he can continue to perform the act of severance from other potential maternal bodies, the potential brides that attract him. Yet, while the analyst's narrative is meant to assuage the horror evoked by the revelation of Norman's deeds, the closure of *Psycho* is extraordinarily perturbing because it ends not with a victim but with a haunting image.

Sitting in the cell of the courthouse, Mother-Norman now takes his symptom no longer as a ciphered message but as the truth, and no longer keeps the maternal fetish alive but rather feels assured that he is this dead body. Supporting the law and utterly displaying its limitations s/he sits in the police cell, pondering, "It's sad when a mother has to condemn her own son, but I couldn't allow them to believe that I would commit murder. They will put him away now, as I should have, years ago." To prove her subjection before the law she explains that she will simply sit and stare, without even harming the fly that moves across her hand. As the camera moves toward the sitting figure, it once more fills the frame with a face uncannily hovering between being alive and dead. Grinning, Mother-Norman oscillates: this figure both is and is not mother, both is and is not dead; is neither masculine nor feminine, mother nor son; fetish, corpse, nor living body. Rather it is all of these states amalgamated into one phantastic body, into whose presence Hitchcock has drawn us. Like Lila, we enraptured spectators are dangerously close to this all-engulfing, uncanny body of traumatic enjoyment, and although we can assure ourselves that Norman will no longer thrust his knife at us, we also know that there also is no Sam to come and save us.[20]

The shower scene, structured on a sequence of hole images that signify the point of disposal but also the limit to visual penetration, culminates in the disappearance of the car in the swamp behind the house. The only release Hitchcock offers us from the horrific image of overwhelming plenitude is an equally terrifying image of birth, the final omphalic representation of traumatic knowledge, unsuccessfully repressed and returning. Rather than cutting to the scene of the police dragging the swamp, Hitchcock instead superimposes over Bates's grinning face the earlier image of the grinning mother-fetish, merging the two in a cinematic hallucination for the spectator. The next and final shot shows an iron chain pulling Marion's car out of the swamp. Fundamentally disquieting, for a split second the iron chain as umbilical cord is superimposed over the throat of Mother-Norman, as if it were this phantastic body—not the car and with it Marion's corpse—that is reborn (a superimposition like the one at the end of the shower scene, where Marion's dead eye emerges out of the drain). Only after the traumatic imprint of this superimposed image on us does Hitchcock switch to showing only the car borne out of the muddy water, the eyes and grinning smile of Mother-Norman seeming to fade into the swamp's cleft of departure and return. These three superimposed images are all tropes for traumatic parturition: Norman, giving birth to himself as his dead mother; then the maternal fetish, the artificial body he produced; and finally the police, bringing all that was imperfectly repressed back to daylight, namely Marion's corpse and the stolen money. Returning to life, as a body already dead, Marion both displaces and recalls the superimposed images of Norman and the maternal fetish that are the visual progenitors of this stillborn. It is as though the phallic register of sublimation, meant to assuage the shock of Norman's murder and his fatal transformation, is actually imploded by the omphalos, for the car the police are about to bring forth is quite literally a vault containing Marion's preserved corpse. The chain, Python, retrieves into light the lost bodies that remained as traces of traumatic knowledge.

This horrific repetition of parturition, making external something intimate, is precisely what Lacan sought to describe when he coins the term *extimacy* to indicate that "The most intimate is at the same time the most hidden. . . . The most intimate is not a point of transparency but rather a point of opacity. . . . Extimacy says that the intimate is Other—like a foreign body, a parasite" (Jacques-Alain Miller 1988, 123). As such, these final superimposed images also recall Marie-Ange Guilleminot's plaster cast inversions of the navel, documenting the need to make visible the impenetrable, inevitable traumatic kernel but rendering a visualization that neither deflates the boundary between representation and traumatic enjoyment (which would entail a psychotic entering of the navel crevice) nor represses the lost body in the act of symbolization. Rather, these superimposed images articulate within cinematic language, like a scenario or an amalgamated image, what has no single site, no single body, and no event. Harking back to the shower scene, Hitchcock imposes closure on the visual sequence of holes with an image of return that is also a disappearance. If the maternal fetish, along with the car, rises out of the swamp, it does so only for a moment, as part of the sequence and not as a frozen image. As an articulation of extimacy, this uncanny foreign body now begins to wander in the image repertoire that *Psycho* has implanted in its audience's memory. Like the dead eye of Marion, which on the diegetic level of the narrative is about to reemerge from the swamp, but which is related on the level of cinematic language, the superimposed eyes of the maternal fetish and the psychically dead Norman will now haunt us as a splice of visualization with prohibition. What we get is an inversion, a symbolic imprint of the traumatic impact: not a referential image of death's body returned to light, but rather a phantastic image liberated from all bodily attachments.

V

Working with hysteric patients at the end of the nineteenth century, Sigmund Freud not only discovered the unconscious but also developed a theory about the traumatic etiology of symptom formation.[21] In an early text he presents the syndrome he will maintain throughout his work with hysterics: "The symptoms of hysteria . . . are determined by certain experiences of the patient's which have operated in a traumatic fashion and which are being reproduced in his psychical life in the form of mnemic symbols" (1896, 193). The cure of psychoanalysis consists, he suggests, in locating the scene in and through which the symptoms arose and, during the reproduction of this primal traumatic scene, undertaking a belated correction of the psychical events that occurred earlier. Two forms of repetition thus compete in hysteric representation and its cure: on the one hand, the hysteric continually converts a traumatic scene into ever new symptoms: on the other hand, the analyst enacts a reproduction of the past scene. Whereas the hysteric conversion seeks interminability, the analyst seeks closure by encoding the scene as a primal location of "premature sexual experience" (203).

Freud's early theory raises the question, of course, of whether such an encoding is valid. More crucial, however, is whether analysis can ever gain access to such an originary traumatic scene or whether the scene the patient finally retrieves isn't performative, generated within (and limited by) the discursive parameters set up by analysis. In other words, when an analyst at last seems to have discovered the primary scene of trauma, is he perhaps not simply falling prey to the convincing performance of the hysteric? From the beginning Freud, seeking to find the solution to any case of hysteria, was painfully aware that this originary scene of trauma kept receding from his interpretive grasp. However, the impenetrability of trauma, far from devaluing Freud's early theory, is in fact compelling in speaking about a knotted subject because it rests on the notion that hysteric symptoms are constructed like knots: "No hysterical symptom can arise from a real experience alone, but that in every case the memory of earlier experiences awakened in association to it plays a part in causing the symptom" (197).

Hysteric symptoms are overdetermined, excessive, exaggerated precisely because they weld together several syntagmatically unconnected, psychic moments. They are the derivatives (*Abkömmlinge*) of a chain of memory traces (*Erinnerungsketten*) that have to have remained present in the unconscious in order for them ultimately to be engendered (*erzeugen*). Using the language of parturition that resonates in Freud's own formulations, one could say the hysteric symptom functions like a navel, given that it is a mark for the process by which psychic material of traumatic impact, which has been harbored in the womb of the unconscious, has been brought forth at a particular site of the body: the lump in the throat, the anaesthetized limb, the disturbance of vision. Yet these surface marks, resulting from the production of symptoms, only articulate the fact that these belated stagings are not the effective ones, while the actually effective ones at the origin of traumatic impact initially beget no product. Each symptom as navel merely marks the tip of a complex knot of psychic woundings that consciously and unconsciously resonate with many, more intense, prior injuries, "behind all of which there lies in addition the memory of a serious slight in childhood (*eine schwere, nie verwundene Kränkung*) which has never been overcome" (217).

In *Studies on Hysteria*, which I will explore in greater detail in chapter 5, the formula Freud and Joseph Breuer settle on is that "Hysterics suffer mainly from reminiscences" (1893–95, 7); their symptoms enact memories that are residues of symbolic-mnemonic representations of "traumatic experiences that never can be sufficiently abreacted" (1893–95, 10). Yet the hysteric interlacing several scenes—these memory traces obliquely but belatedly articulating scenes of trauma in a dislocated and transformed manner—not only suffers from not having abreacted memories but more still from being unable to unravel this knot of memory traces. She cannot decide what impressions are relevant and worth preserving (or, conversely, irrelevant and worth relinquishing) so that all impressions remain present to her, the past indeed at times replacing the present.

Hysteria is thus the lynchpin of my own theorizing, given my interest in exploring the individual as being knotted together over a wandering body, the traumatic knowledge of its mutability, and driven by a libido of vulnerability.[22] Although postponing a detailed presentation of the rich history of medical discourses on hysteria until chapter 2, I would note that hysteria was considered so vexing a disturbance because its protean, creative, and resilient symptoms evolved from a complete absence of organic lesions. This led physicians from Hippocrates onward to view it as a malady of the matrix, occurring whenever the womb came unhooked; in the course of its peregrinations, it would upset normal bodily functions by settling in improper sites. If one focuses on the structural implication Howard Colvin notes (1994; 15), namely, that *hysteresis* in physics "refers to the erratic wandering behaviour of inorganic systems about some ideal central tendency," one could read the "wandering uterus" of classical medicine figuratively, namely, as a metaphor for the body of traumatic knowledge wandering through the psychic apparatus. Furthermore, at least one old custom confirms that the lack of a clearly determinable organic dysfunction, the nothing about which hysteric symptom formation revolves, was indeed aligned with the navel in the image repertoire of some medical discourse. As Ilza Veith notes, certain physicians recommended putting tight bandages or plasters onto the navel, not because this was thought to restrain the uterus, but because these navel bandages would repress and compel into order the spirits ready to leap forth, thus preventing the hysteric fit from occurring (1965, 136).

In my inquiry into the cultural performance of hysteria I return to the birth of psychoanalysis, however, because of my discontent with the direction Freud ultimately took in his explanation of hysteria. As did Jacqueline Lubtchansky (1973) I ask myself if sexual impressions and desires of love are at the origin of hysteria, whether they are enough to create neurosis. Reading Freud's early case histories, one is most impressed with how these narratives keep returning to painful scenes of lack, deprivation, fallibility, and vulnerability, to impressions connected with the death of loved ones, misfortunes, and losses.[23] I want to stay with one of the basic definitions of hysteria, therefore, namely, that this psychosomatic disorder renders visible ideational contents (*Vorstellungen*) gone awry, the somatic conversion standing in for a psychic distress.[24] But I want to focus on the way that the hysteric enacts a ciphered message. Hysteric symptoms are consequences of and witnesses to occurrences emanating from the intimate site; Freud designates this as the *andere Schauplatz*, acting as displaced representations of this otherness. But they do not broadcast a message harking back to a discrete primal scene, which a narrative encoding would resolve and thus extinguish. Rather, the message at stake addresses the lack of plenitude and completion as a structural phenomenon, be this the vulnerability of the symbolic (the fallibility of paternal law and social bonds), of identity (the insecurity of gender, ethnic, and class designations), or of the body (its mutability). Hysteric symptoms reproduce, as Lubtchansky demonstrates, traumatic impressions.

Returning to Freud's initial theory of the *traumatic* rather than the *sexual* etiology of hysteria, I am interested in hysteria as a clinical syndrome only insofar as the nosology points to cultural constructions that set up the category hysteria—and negotiate theories of representation. My interest lies in hysteria as a structuring of the subject, as a strategy using multiple self-fashionings, even as these are constructed over—but also shield from—radical negativity. That is, the structure comes from (yet also screens out) the traumatic kernel at the core of all systems of identity, the *Urverdrängung*, on which all later repressions, phantasy work, and symptom formation feeds without ever directly touching it. If traditional notions of hysteria, in the absence of organic lesion, kept returning to the image of much ado about nothing, I want to take quite seriously and literally this *nothing* and its resilience of self-representations engendered by the hysteric performance. I argue that the traumatic impact, itself a figuration of nothing, can be located as the indeterminable lesion at the core of hysteria. I want to privilege the traumatic etiology of hysteria, therefore, because it addresses the problem of horrific impact that speaks to us of our woundedness. It tells the unbearable plenitude subtending all division and the interface of this traumatic kernel to symbolic codes, and it explains as well fantasy and symptom formation.

Cathy Caruth defines trauma as an overwhelming event that has not been assimilated or experienced fully at the time but only belatedly as a repeated possession of the one who experiences it: "To be traumatized is precisely to be possessed by an image or an event," (1995, 5) but by an event "that is itself constituted in part by its lack of integration into consciousness" (152).[25] Trauma articulates how one is moved against one's conscious control by the impression of an overwhelming occurrence, by a remainder, that returns insistently and against the will of the person inhabited by this knowledge. Thus, while the temporal delay initially carries the individual beyond the hold of the first impact, "Trauma is a repeated suffering of the event, but it is also a continual leaving of its site" (10). To speak of a traumatic etiology to hysteria's symptoms thus means emphasizing the act of screening something out rather than recovering what is screened. Owing to its belated articulation, trauma cannot be reduced to an incident.

Instead trauma gives figure to an experience not directly available to consciousness that has attached itself as a latent presence, like a foreign body. The force of this distressing presence comes from its articulating a vulnerability, as Kai Erikson puts it, a blow to the tissues of the body or the mind that smashes whatever defenses the psychic system has set up (Erikson 1995, 183). However, given that the experience was not integrated into consciousness when it occurred and has never been transformed into a memorable symbol, the traumatic event can be neither repressed, forgotten, nor translated into a narrative memory. On the contrary, while trauma calls out to be integrated into a story, to convert trauma also means "to lose both the precision and the force that characterizes traumatic recall" (Caruth 1995, 153). The solution, as Alaida Assmann (1995) argues, resides in a dislocated articulation, for trauma uses the body as the material for its impression, encrypts the disturbing experience psychosomatically rather than encoding it into a story, and as such marks the limit of narrative. Furthermore, given that trauma wanders through the body as a latent presence, moving the individual whose direct linguistic access to this impact is barred, it is also trauma that acts when language fails.[26]

Caruth is primarily associated with the renewed interest in trauma as part of psychiatry's acknowledgment of "Posttraumatic Stress Disorder" (PTSD), particularly in relation to victims of sexual abuse and of the Holocaust. Yet her discussion also sheds light on parts of Freud's correspondence to Fliess in which Freud develops the notion that hysteria emerges from an overwhelming of the ego by a passive experience of an unpleasure so great that it can neither be resisted nor translated into a psychic symptom; rather it produces an "excessive expression of excitation," a manifestation of *Angst* followed by a gap in the psyche (*Psychische Lücke*). Repression and the formation of defensive symptoms occur only subsequently, not in response to the actual trauma but in connection with a memory trace of this traumatic impact, such that "Thenceforward defence and overwhelming . . . may be combined to any extent in hysteria" (1892–1899, 228). Repression takes place, to quote Freud, "by the intensification of a boundary idea, which thereafter represents the repressed memory in the passage of thought," oscillating, so to speak, between the ego and the undistorted portion of the traumatic memory. The compromise each hysteric symptom affords is displacing the attention "along a series of ideas linked by temporal simultaneity," representing the traumatic impact after the event. Freud concludes, therefore, that it isn't some idea that is being suppressed at each hysteric repetition of the primary attack; rather, "It is a question in the first instance of a gap in the psyche" (229).

Urtrauma remains unrepresentable and inaccessible. It designates an untranslatable surplus, whereas any symbolization of memory scenes occurs belatedly, knotting these memory traces together in strands and layers at another site so that they converge on a few symptoms. Freud thus maintains that memory is "present not once but several times over" (1892–1899, 233). The implication is that the psychic gap, the nothing (of which the hysteric makes so much ado), is a representational impossibility even as it is precisely what makes representation possible. The hysteric must convert this gap, but she can do so only by leaving unsymbolized that traumatic residue demarcated by the psychic gap, itself. But the gap, though not accessible to representation, is precisely not repressed but, as a radical reading of Freud suggests, still present—in a register other than that of verbal articulation. Indeed, conversion occurs precisely because the traumatic kernel cannot be directed into symbolic representations. Freud will later similarly divide repression into two moments: first, a primal repression (*Urverdrängung*), when the psychical representative of the instinct is denied entrance into the consciousness and instead forms a fixation that preserves both the representative in question and the instinct attached to it; second, the repression proper, which affects mental derivatives (*Abkömmlinge*) of the repressed representative. These other bodies then "experience the same fate as what was primally repressed." Freud concludes, "Repression proper, therefore, is actually an after-pressure (*Nachdrängen*)" (1915, 148).

The discovery that a psychic gap lies at the origin of traumatic attacks and their conversion into symptoms of aggression or mutilation is crucial: it allows Freud to speak of hysteric symptoms as memory traces. These break into conscious life in a form distorted by compromise, namely, refracted by phantasies, protective fictions, or protective structures (*Schutzdichtung, Schutzbauten*). Embellishing and mitigating traces of traumatic impact, these phantasies are psychical facades constructed to bar memories—even as they help refine memories (1892–1899; 248). In other words, although the aim of memory traces seems to be to arrive back at the primal scene of trauma, any symptom formation stops before the psychic gap that irrevocably demarcates the initial traumatic knowledge. Along with the unsuccessfully repressed material, therefore, what returns in symptom formation is inevitably this impenetrable dead zone between Urtrauma, Urverdrängung, and any modalities of "after-pressure."

The schema Freud presents in his "Architecture of Hysteria" (1892–1899, 148–251) draws a trajectory with the inaccessible traumatic moment farthest away, demarcated by a psychic gap, a moment of psychic parturition, or psychic "denavelment." This original trauma, which is to be conceived structurally, is then semantically encoded in a series of representations of traumatic impact; it occurs belatedly in the language of the symptom, both in the unconscious and the conscious register. Like the navel, the symptom articulates an incision without allowing penetration of the wound lying beneath the knotted scar they construct. Negotiating between an Urtrauma and its vicissitudes, the symptom takes on the form of memory traces, phantasies, screen memories, somatic conversions, and, I would add, the interpretive narratives seeking to encode what evades symbolic representation. Freud himself insists on a clear linearity, with phantasies rewriting and falsifying the memory traces only to result in symptoms. "Making inaccessible the memory from which the symptoms have emerged" (252), phantasies distort by fragmentation, then join up one fragment with another left over from another phantasy, and, rearranging the sequence and content of the scenes, produce a new amalgam.

Yet I suggest not highlighting linearity, whose aim is ultimately a rewriting of memory to disclose, rather than falsify, the truth, to solve the knot (so that, as in the little boy's childhood fantasy, the entire button will come undone). Rather, I would use the trope Freud did to describe this act of shielding and preserving, *Schutzdichtung*, which brilliantly exemplifies that these hysteric constructions both protect and seal off. They prevent something from directly penetrating into or emanating out of the hole they cover (like the image of Marion's eye, which Hitchcock superimposes on the drain at the end of the shower scene). Given that these mnemonic protective fictions preserve and encrypt, whereas psychic symbolization relinquishes and represses, I suggest calling this omphalic rather than symbolic representation of the impact of a remembered event. The knotted subject, articulated by the language of hysteria, comprises the memory traces, phantasies, and somatic symptoms emerging as the psychic process demarcates all work of representation from an originary psychic gap.

In *Studies on Hysteria*, Freud and Breuer argue "Psychical trauma or more precisely the memory of the trauma—acts like a foreign body which long after its entry must continue to be regarded as an agent that is still at work" (1893–95, 290). Their clinical evidence suggests that the ideational materials formed during hypnoid states, when the *condition seconde* is powerful, gain control of the body and the psyche, not only dictating the behavior in this second state, but also infiltrating into the first, so-called normal, state. If one of the side effects of hysteric symptoms, like navels marking the workings of the foreign body, is that these arise from amnesia, from a gap in memory, the cure they posit is returning to the scene shielded by this gap to remove the conditions that led to producing of the symptom.[27]

One is now compelled to critique Freud for believing he could retrieve a primal scene—rather than staying with the more radical aspect of his theory that maintained precisely the *inaccessibility* of any scene preceding the psychic gap underlying the representation. Equally one would argue against his cathartic model: that the narrative or scenario used to fill this gap in memory is simply yet another protective fiction, one that perhaps better shields the analysand from traumatic impact, but that does not necessarily undercut the resilience of trauma. Indeed, as we rethink Freud's, theories, the crux may be whether the line can really be drawn between these two acts of psychic filling—the hysterical and the analytical. In other words, if the hysteric finds herself responding to the fact that she exists as an interpellation of representatives of alterity—the father, the analyst, or culture in general—is it not equally the case that she draws any interlocutor into her performances of psychic distress? The analytic narrative can merely repeat, and in so doing it substitutes for the hysteric performance even as it remains on the level of representations, retouching the after-pressures, not the *Urtrauma* itself. And if the key factor in the hysteric's proclivity toward an overabundance of phantasy is to neglect "the distinction between phantasy and reality" (1917, 374), might it not also be the case, as my concluding discussion of Woody Allen's *Zelig* will seek to demonstrate, that hysteric neurosis is so fascinating—but also so irritating—to medical discourses precisely because it infects the analyst in the process?

What makes Freud's *early* theory of the traumatic etiology of hysteria so compelling today is that it rests on a fundamental contradiction. Though related to an origin, the crucial point about psychic representations of trauma is that no one primary event can be located. All symbolization occurs *after* the significant event, demarcated by a psychic gap. Though we need phantasies and symptoms to lend consistency to our psychic and social reality, the fact that they run parallel to another knowledge, namely, the impact of trauma, leads us to recognize them as protective fictions. This is precisely what Lacan addresses in his work on the structure of hysteria, which he came (in Bruce Fink's words) to consider as embodying "a unique configuration with respect to knowledge."[28] The hysteric sustains the system of knowledge proclaimed by the figure representing paternity. Supporting the father's desire, at the same time, the hysteric also calls into question the consistency of his law, endlessly demanding that he prove the authority of his power. As Bruce Fink notes, "The hysteric pushes the master—incarnated in a partner, teacher, or whomever—to the point where he or she can find the master's knowledge lacking. . . . In addressing the master, the hysteric demands that he or she produce knowledge, and then goes on to disprove his or her theories" (1995, 134). Indeed, this dialectic subtends Freud's entire project of psychoanalysis, given that his discovery of the unconscious emerged from listening to hysterics even as they insisted on refusing his solution, thus proving to him the inadequacy of his knowledge.

However, as the hysteric produces a versatile and seemingly infinite array of self-representations, alternating between sustaining and interrogating paternal desire, she can traumatize those toward whom her discourse is directed—her family members, teachers, analysts, or audience—precisely because the inconsistent number of masks she dons actually displays the inconsistency of the symbolic system ruled by the paternal metaphor. Moving seamlessly from seductive obedience to calculated derision and insolence, manipulating the masks, the hysteric awakes the sense of how impossible it is to determine whether there is a consistent subject behind them. As Slavoj Žižek puts it, the spectator of a hysterical self-display is made anxious because it seems that "behind the multiple layers of masks there is nothing; or, at the most, nothing but the shapeless, mucous stuff of the life-substance" (1994, 150). Yet while this traumatic experience of symbolic inconsistency remains at the level of paternal phantasy, it points to the other definition Lacan offers of the hysterical discourse. Within Lacan's algebraic formulas for the hysterical discourse, as Bruce Fink demonstrates, the *object (a)* appears in the position of truth, meaning that "the truth of the hysteric's discourse, its hidden motor force, is the real" (1995, 134), the kernel of traumatic knowledge that is both inevitable and inaccessible. Recognizing this screened site of knowledge as the source of her truth, the hysteric also perceives the hole within the symbolic, its point of inconsistency. In other words, because she knows that hers is an irretrievable truth (demarcated by the psychic gap of trauma) she simulates the truth that paternity seeks. She stages its truth but always also insists through her excessively protean and inconsistent symptoms that this is a protective fiction.[29] The hysteric dissimulates, as Regula Schindler argues, by placing a representation where there is nothing, the psychic gap. Yet she also articulates the truth insofar as this "nothing" is indeed the grounds of her psychic distress (1994, 54). Thus, when I propose calling the hysterical discourse omphalic, I wish to highlight this bifurcation, which insists that hysteric self-representations cannot wholly be subsumed by the phallic function but must exist alongside it.

VI

In the following chapters, rethinking the implications of a traumatic etiology of hysteria, I will offer readings of diverse psychoanalytic and cultural texts so as to explore the language of hysteria as a strategy of self-representation and as a structuring of the subject in relation to knowledge. Because I am interested in the phenomenon of hysteria as a cultural construction, rather than as a strictly clinical syndrome, when I address medical discourses, I will treat them as interpretive narratives embedded within an existent repertoire of cultural images. By considering hysteria a malady of representation, I follow Lucien Israël (1976), who suggests that any attempt at defining this strange psychosomatic disturbance should be shifted from a semantic to a structural level of discussion. Hysteria is a mode of communication, an attempt to set up a relation with the Other, be this a system of laws and codes or that unknown site, which our conscious activity can only feebly reflect. It broadcasts the fallibility of the symbolic and the subject, a recognition that neither are complete. In some sense hysteria always involves a theatrical manifestation—be this an attack, a fainting spell, or the staging of some bodily dysfunction—with the displayed symptom an external manifestation of the internal psychic conflict, played out in the private or intimate theater of the unconscious.

Stavros Mentzos hightlights precisely this notion of hysteric performance, acting out or simulation, though like Freud he accepts the "much ado about nothing" rather than morally denigrating it. He claims, therefore, that individuals affected by hysteria move internally (in accordance with their experience) and externally (in accordance with public appearance) into a state in which they experience themselves as quasi-other; in the eyes of those nearby they appear as other than who they are. They move into a psychic state in which their own body functions, psychological functions, character traits are experienced and appear as an (apparently) *other*, a quasi-altered, self-representation (1980, 75). Symptoms of the hysterical tendency to experience and present oneself as other than one is constitute histrionic behavior, emotional instability, overexcitability, and seductive gestures, although Mentzos is careful to qualify his definition. Expressive behavior and heightened excitability can be called hysterical only when the self-presentation is not the spontaneous expression of a momentary experience but rather the inverse. Excitability and histrionic behavior are chosen, and a particular scene is staged and played through, as though such an experience and such a dramatic situation had in fact occurred (1980, 92).

Given that the seminal characteristic of hysteria, once one sees it first and foremost as a form of communication, is its making visible an inconsistency between self-representation and the real self, these acts of simulation ultimately are the staging or performative quality of gender, indeed of subjectivity, in the manner described by Judith Butler (1990). Using linguistic speech-act theory, which designates the performative as an utterance that constitutes some act, especially the act described by the verb of a sentence, she argues that when a female subject assumes a particular gender position within a given cultural space, this self-representation is a performance, constituted by the discursive position this particular self chooses to define herself. One might say that, the hysteric's gesture of presenting herself other than she is enacts that the act of self-representation is the verb of her public performance. Her much ado about nothing seems to say, "I am a performance, indeed, I am only as a performance, as the knotting together of languages that have determined me."

According to psychoanalysis, of course, all neuroses are the product of the work of the unconscious; they articulate the rejection of an unmitigated desire. Israël, therefore, isolates one aspect specific to this particular neurosis that remains constant in the midst of all the protean shapes within which hysteria may choose to present itself. While obsessions and phobias translate repressed desire into verbal language, or into symptoms expressed by verbal language, hysteria transforms words and anxieties (themselves already secondary representations of a repressed desire) into somatic manifestations. In other words, hysteria emerges as the one neurosis that articulates an inundation of the psychic apparatus by *Vorstellungen*, the pathological abundance of imaginations, of phantasies gone awry: it hooks to the body its message of the return of repressed desire.[30]

The hysteric conversion, its representational force grounded on a psychic gap and the lack of any organic lesion, clearly marks that it is signifying other, namely as a *version*, etymologically a sort of turning. Here the body speaks in place of symbolic language, belatedly and at another site, rendering, as do Marie-Ange Guilleminot's plaster casts, an intimate detail external: the hysterical symptom emerges as a form of representation, which, must be distinguished as Birgit Erdle argues (1996), from a historiographic manner of dealing with memory and commemoration. In its resiliently protean quality, the language of hysteria radically defies closure. The traumatic knowledge it seeks to articulate obliquely is infinitely convertible. Unlike other psychosomatic illnesses, hysteria produces mutable body disorders. Thus, while a historiographic symbolization aims to exchange indeterminate traumatic impact for a linear narrative, an encoded story, a monumental image, hysteria resists all cures. It offers instead ever new versions of reworked memory traces, addressing—without ever touching—the initial traumatic event.

Indeed, rather than accepting the solution, the undoing of the knot, hysteria preserves the knot in all its ambivalence and inconsistency. In encountering the real, the hysteric is neither submerged by the traumatic gap—this nothing around which its representations revolve—nor brought to repress and symbolize it: hysteria preserves the traumatic kernel by converting it into a space constructed around nothing. Its language engenders symptoms and performs phantasy scenarios, and it produces psychic configurations that one could call omphalic crypts.[31] Dismantling the very protective fictions it seeks to establish, the exaggeration and clear dissimulation written into the language of hysteria, it shields from the naught it also preserves. In other words, even as the hysteric's much ado converts traumatic knowledge, it keeps intact what it displaces.

Significantly these conversions work by blurring boundaries. As the foreign body of trauma wanders through the psychic structure, articulating traumatic desires by producing somatic disorders, the language of hysteria—known as a malady of the matrix or womb—also articulates the flaw written into symbolic structure. Duplicitous in both preserving and shielding from traumatic knowledge, the language of hysteria supports the very paternal law it also seeks to dismantle. In other words, hysteria traces an oscillation. It commemorates the traumatic enjoyment of the abundant presence of the maternal body: one could read the "wandering womb of hysteria" as referring to the subject's desire being doomed to endlessly seek an impossible satisfaction. The hysteric also, however, pursues a paternal figure who might represent symbolic consistency, who could fulfill her phantasy of a love that would abolish all flaws; her constant undermining of paternal authority can in turn be read as an expression that a satisfaction of this desire, too, is an impossibility.[32] Embellishing Freud's dictum that hysterics suffer mainly from reminiscences, the formula I propose is that the exaggerated, overabundant, disconcertingly mutable language of hysteria aims to disclose the fallibility of the cultural system within which it performs, as well as the vulnerability at the navel of all its resilient self-fashionings. In the manner proposed by Luce Irigaray, it is well worth exploring the dark continent of the hysteric subject without "converting her to a discourse that denies the specificity of her pleasure by inscribing it as the hollow, the intaglio, the negative, even as the censured other of its phallic assertions" (1974, 141). Yet listening to this specificity, I would add, ultimately means exploring how the language of hysteria—the body symptoms and phantasy scenarios—allows the subject to organize an enjoyment of the inevitable and inaccessible kernel of traumatic knowledge subtending self-representation. By obliquely addressing the desire for a destructive, all-encompassing plenitude, fatal attraction and protective fiction balance each other.

VII

I close these prefatory remarks by discussing another postmodern film, Woody Allen's *Zelig* (1983). Its narrative discloses not only how the multiple self-fashionings of the hysteric revolve around an indeterminate traumatic impact but also how fallibility is written into any interpretive project that interrogates hysteria. I mean to set up Zelig, the "human chameleon," as the mirror inversion of Norman-Mother, the phantastic figure of traumatic plenitude. This opposition establishes the counterdirectional movement that will subtend my own presentation of the language of hysteria in the course of this book; namely, alternating between representations such as *Psycho* that move toward desublimation, having a traumatic naught as their vanishing point, and representations such as *Zelig* that are pure simulacrums having nothing as their point of reference.

In an interview with Stig Björkman, Woody Allen explains the conception of this film: "I was thinking that I wanted to do a story about a person whose personality changed all the time to fit in everywhere. He wants so badly to be liked that he changes his personality to fit in with every group that he's with. Then I thought it would be very interesting to see the physical changes. He becomes who he is with. Then I thought, it would be very interesting to present him as an international phenomenon and that his story should be told in a very documentary way, as though this was a famous international figure. . . . I wanted to make a comment with the film on the specific danger of abandoning one's own true self, in an effort to be liked, not to make trouble, to fit in, and where that leads one in life in every aspect and where that leads on a political level (Björkman 1994, 136; 141). Creating a film about a man who appears *as though* he were like those interpellating him, within a medium that appears *as though* it had historical verisimilitude, while in fact the hero is at times interpolated into preexistent documentary footage having nothing to do with him, and the scenes are staged *as though* they were authentic documentary material, Allen raises all the central issues at stake in discussing hysteria as a malady of representation.

First, by constantly changing his personality because he wants to be liked and to be "safe . . . like the others," as Leonard explains to his analyst, Eudora Fletcher, Zelig confirms Lucien Israël's structural definition of hysteria. He communicates with the Other, broadcasting a message of vulnerability: "I am lacking that something which would allow me to believe in the protective fiction of fitting in—so I might cover up the lack at the navel of my being, the traumatic knowledge of paucity subtending mortal existence." Yet by merging to excess, Zelig dismantles the very fiction he seeks to sustain, fundamentally risking the economy of satisfaction he so desperately seeks. Second, characteristic of a language of hysteria, Woody Allen admits that his interest is broader than a psychic disturbance, in which the self represents itself other than it is (in the manner described by Mentzos 1980), taking on multiple personality roles to support the desire of the Other interpellating him. This conversion into a quasi-altered, self-representation must be somatic: staging phantasies, gone awry, at the body. Third, by locating the story in a historical moment, Allen points to another aspect of hysteria. Mentzos notes that the hysteric is like a chameleon, taking on diverse forms and fitting into the style or modes of expression and concerns of different cultures and epochs. In other words, if the hysteric self-representation aims to mimic other roles, donning gestures and behaviorisms to mask a lack, it also imitates the cultural discourses that produced the hysterical symptom. The hysteric, in other words, performing an illness of mimesis, mirrors not only the desire of an individual interpellator but that of culture at large: the ciphered message conveyed by the hysterical symptom is not only directed at the hysteric himself but also at his audience.

In discussing Woody Allen's film, therefore, I focus on two contradictions. On the one hand I argue that the perfect simulations of the hysteric articulate the naught he seeks to cover up in such a resistent manner that any "cure" is already caught up in this representatorial chain. Even though the soothing message of *Zelig* is that one should not abandon "one's own true self," that "the love of one woman can cure," the disturbing question that the film leaves unanswered is whether this self can indeed be neatly severed from all quasi-altered representations that are aimed at supporting the desire of the Other or whether it can exist only as a performance. Locating his "true self" in the role of Eudora Fletcher's husband, does Zelig not simply don his most successful and resilient masquerade? On the other hand, although at the diegetic level the film offers a so-called solution to this case history—the cure through transference love—its own cinematic language emerges as a hysterical undercutting of the very closure it purports.

The film significantly begins with three experts belatedly attempting to locate Zelig historically. In it Susan Sontag describes how astonishing it was that "he was *the* phenomenon of the twenties," while Irving Howe emphasizes that it was a very strange case, even though "his story reflected the nature of our civilization, the character of our times. . . . Yet it was also one man's story . . . and all the themes of our culture were there." Finally, Saul Bellow concludes it "certainly is a very bizarre story," highlighting the irony that Zelig should have faded from memory so quickly and so completely, given that he perhaps touched a nerve in people in a way "they would prefer not to be touched." As is so typical for narratives about hysteria, this psychic disturbance emerges as an enigma that calls for an interpretive solution, so that the story about to unfold is set against what is ultimately an irresolvable bafflement. Imitating the style of documentary film, Woody Allen constructs an amalgamation. He knots together actual historical film material, fictitious comments from actual historical personages, interviews with fictitious people involved in the story of Zelig, and comments from the experts about this extraordinary case, the latter two sets of witnesses treating the story *as though* it were part of history; a narratorial voice holds together all the individual strands. The extraordinary cinematic trick that gained Allen praise at the film's release is the creating of what looks like historical footage—in three places Woody Allen, playing Zelig, was artificially engrained into original documentary material.[33]

From the onset of the film, then, an interplay is established between hysterical performance and the manner in which the audience is made hysteric. Each one of the experts uses certain turns of phrase to emphasize the strangeness of the entire affair. They merely reiterate rhetorically the fact that in the incidents that initially made the public aware of Zelig, he literally appears as a foreign body. The "first small notice taken of Leonard Zelig," as the narrator explains, occurs during a party at the Long Island estate of Mr. and Mrs. Henry Porter Sutton, where Scott Fitzgerald, "casting perspective on the twenties for all future generations" observes the strange transformation of a curious little man whose name he has not quite caught. Leon Selwyn or Zelman, he notes, "seemed clearly to be an aristocrat and extolled the very rich as he chatted with socialites. He spoke adoringly of Coolidge and the Republican party, all in an upper-class Boston accent." Yet an hour later Fitzgerald adds, "I was stunned to see the same man speaking with the kitchen help. Now he claimed to be a Democrat, and his accent seemed coarse, as if he were one of the crowd." Zelig is noted as a foreign body not because he changes to fit in with the company he keeps, but because this ability to adapt to the desire of the Other is excessively protean and versatile. By performing more than one quasi-altered self, he actually dismantles the previous self-representation, and with it puts in question those he was imitating as well.

Similarly, two other events noted before his delivery into Manhattan Hospital are "odd incidents" in which Zelig is disturbing precisely because his imitation, far from allowing him to blend in, shows him to be a foreign body. At the training camp for the New York Yankees, Lou Zelig appears behind Babe Ruth as the latter is about to bat. He is removed by security guards and called an impostor in the local newspaper. During a private party at a speakeasy on the South Side of Chicago, the waiter Calvin Turner first notes him among the guests; afraid that Zelig is a police infiltrator, Turner is reassured by a fellow waiter who admits not knowing him but adds, "I know one thing, he's a tough-looking hombre!" Yet precisely the assuredness of identity through visual self-presentation is disturbed in the next incident, for this stranger suddenly disappears only to reappear in the jazz band playing trumpet, looking "just like that gangster," as Turner notes, only "The gangster was white, and this guy is black."[34]

Ironically, however, it is not these disturbing appearances but rather Zelig's disappearance that brings about his arrest. Acting on the fact that his landlady and employer have both reported him missing, the authorities ultimately find a "strange-looking Oriental who fits the description" in an establishment in Chinatown. Realizing that what they think is a disguise cannot be peeled off, the police deliver Zelig to Mannhattan Hospital instead, where, under the guidance of Eudora Fletcher, his malady is diagnosed and ultimately cured. One sequence that is significant for the narrative development of Allen's film is (before the mutable body of Leonard Zelig is found and the process of explaining this foreign body begins) that we see the two images that our hysteric selects as favorite self-representations. The "only two clues" the police find in his Greenwich Village home are two photographs. One shows Zelig standing next to Eugene O'Neill, both men lean in stature and casually dressed, flanked by a young child standing just in front of them, all three staring somewhat wistfully at the camera. The other shows Zelig as Pagliacci, obese, wearing a clown costume, and sitting at the edge of a big brass drum; about to strike it, he is smiling at the camera expectantly.

These two photographs, I propose, form the navel of the film, addressing a traumatic knowledge of vulnerability as well as the psychic gap that demarcates all representations from this knowledge. The two adjacent images enact the naught, marking the primal scene of trauma by belated representation about which all Zelig's other hysterical chameleon acts revolve and on which they feed. As Graham McCann notes, what is poignant and haunting in the way Allen has *engrained* himself into old documentary images is the deathly stillness of these photographs. "Zelig stares out at us, his face registering a hunted look, as though he senses that now, at this moment, we have pinned down a part of his fugitive self. In contrast to the newsreel images of Zelig, clowning for the camera and constantly moving and gesturing, the still images come as a shock, a mortifying glimpse of a figure flattened out by history" (1990, 182). Yet, I would add, only these two photographs in conjunction with each other unsettle the viewer in such an uncanny manner, bringing forth in the grain of the image an impression that a phantom has returned from the past to deanimate its model in the present. Unlike earlier scenes that disturb viewers because Zelig can play any role he is confronted with so convincingly, and unlike later scenes where Zelig, spliced into documentary footage, appears to be moving with actual historical personages, these two versions of Zelig do more than simply pin down a fugitive part of his self. They actually enact the subject escaping, by blurring all boundaries between actor, character, and historical past; the present moment of the spectator viewing the images; and the scene of fictitious rendition.

Given that these are the only two self-portraits Zelig has decided to keep, we can read them as the two quasi-altered, self-representations he identifies with. These are significantly two phantasy scenarios that enact an identification with the artistic process—one, the condition of the writer (O'Neill) and the other, the clown (Pagliacci) self-consciously donning the mask of a mask. Dressed up to perform the scene in Leoncavallo's opera, where the jealous actor Canio appears on the stage to sing the tragic aria "No, Pagliacci non son" only to kill on stage the wife who in reality is betraying him with another man, Zelig here imitates the actor's distress when reality and fiction converge. In his refusal to continue to be Pagliacci, declaring his nonidentity with this comic role, Canio tries to pull off not only his own disquise but also his faithless wife's, only to find that he is irrevocably caught within the staging of a scenario. Though he shifts from comedy to tragedy, the fatality he performs is merely an imitation of another scripted operatic plot.

Zelig finds himself caught between the writer producing fictions and the clown self-consciously performing them. We as spectators cannot be sure whether this double portrait is not also a self-representation of Woody Allen, the author of *Zelig*, himself wavering between the role of director pulling together the various composite parts and of clown, whose disguise cannot be torn off, even though his sole wish is to be loved. Though the self-conscious mirroring of author and character is a dramatic convention, what makes this particular conjunction of the two photographic images so haunting is that at their vanishing point both the protagonist Zelig and the author Allen, playing the chameleon protagonist, disappear into a vortex of representations whose referentiality has become entirely indeterminate. Though the Pagliacci photograph can be located as a purely fictional scene, Woody Allen engrained into the frame with Eugene O'Neill points to a historical moment made uncanny by the presence of a foreign body. Depending on what semantic level one chooses as focus, the image either negates the real of history (the authenticity of documentary photographs is radically called into question by the hysteric engrainment) or allows the reality of history to traumatically flood the quasi-safe representations with its truth (not only does the protagonist Zelig fade before the role of author he imitates, but so, too, does Woody Allen, the author of the film, once he is in the same frame with another dead author). As Roland Barthes (whose *Camera Lucida* will be analyzed in greater detail in the next chapter) notes, the essence of the photographic image resides in the stubbornness of the referent's always being there. Something in the image remains that is *actually* gone, an irretrievable nothing that can only be pinned down as a representational trace. Thus each photograph has, as its ultimate signifier, the nothing of mortality.

As maker and creature converge in this truly strange, double image, and with them the facticity of a historical past and the protective fiction of a present that changes with each viewing, the nothing of representation and representations of nothing keep changing places. If the symptom rendered in the image with Eugene O'Neill seems to convey the message, "I will not have existed because I represent myself as someone who is already dead," the image of Pagliacci reads, "I never existed except as a mask." Yet knotted together, these two images also declare, "I do exist, but not as the self I represent in each one image. I exist as the vulnerable point of connection between historic facticity and protective fiction."[35] Standing in for the navel of Eudora Fletcher's act of parturition, which is about to take place in a

Manhattan hospital and whose product is a cured Leonard Zelig, we thus find the indeterminacy of identity reflected in the indeterminacy of two photographic images. While in *Psycho* the omphalic representation emerged in the superimposition of images knotting together a drain and a dead eye with the dead eyes and grinning mouth of a maternal fetish as these rise out of the face of the deanimated son, in *Zelig* this moment is located in the double portrait of Zelig imitating Eugene O'Neill and performing Pagliacci. Engrained into a fifty-year-old frame, the composite Zelig-Allen fits precisely as a foreign body, pitting this filmic moment outside the trajectory of its story line but also outside historic referentiality.

Once Zelig has been delivered to the hospital and his diagnosis begins, he resolutely enacts a seemingly endless array of hysterical, quasi-altered, self-representations over naught. The doctors soon discover his ability to take on many roles, to transform into a professional type (the perfect psychiatrist), an ethnic type (French, Black, or Asian) or simply change his physiognomy. Yet, even as none of these performances are simply a surface disguise that can be peeled off, so, too, no organic lesion can be found in the depth of the body to explain the symptom. As such a "nonperson," in whom the self fades beneath all its diverse roles, Zelig becomes famous precisely as a nonentity, drawing his audience into a hysterical exchange. As the narrator explains, his "own existence is a nonexistence," devoid of personality; he is "a cipher, a nonperson, a performing freak." Leaving "such diverse impressions everywhere," the audience imitates his mutability by itself producing a protean array of reactions as diverse as his roles. Some see in his ability to transform, the lucky person whose wishes might come true; others, the personification of the capitalist exploiting workers or, as with the Klu Klux Klan, a multiple threat to white supremacy.

While Zilig's true self eludes the grasp of both the doctors and the public-at-large, their reactions to the stimulus he represents becomes entirely tangible. In fact, Allen seems to use his chameleon man as a symptom for the malaise written into both the medical discourse as well as the popular discourse of the time. Any medical discourse attempting to diagnose hysteria is constantly confronted with its own fallibility (see chapter 2), for in the absence of clearly distinguishable organic lesions and stable symptom formations, physicians ultimately speak about their own nosological desires. Thus, the narrator explains, "Although the doctors claim to have the situation in hand, no two can agree on a diagnosis," their explanations as mutable as the patient's symptoms. Whether they diagnose a glandular dysfunction, an eating disorder, or a neurological etiology, the analysis (even as it misses the mark), touches on their own situation. That Zelig in fact broadcasts a message about the identity of his *interpellator* is shown most poignantly in the case of Dr. Birsky, who diagnoses the brain tumor in his patient that he himself will die of two weeks later.

But Zelig also imitates the cultural discourse at large, the jazz age: as the narrator explains, "America, enjoying a decade of unequaled prosperity, has gone wild." The commercialism elicited by Eudora Fletcher's explanation that Zelig is a human chameleon who "protects himself by becoming whoever he is around"—the songs, objects, games, dances, costumes, jokes, advertisements, and Hollywood film—are as hysterical in their seemingly endless mutability and fickleness as the medical curiosity they have as their object. Allen, furthermore, explicitly enacts the fallibility of interpretation by self-consciously inserting statements by the three leading cultural critics whom he chooses for their "patina of intellectual weight and seriousness" (Björkman 1994, 139). They do not simply demonstrate that Zelig is a cipher for their own intellectual project. Blum argues, "It was all symbolism—but there were no two intellectuals who agreed about what it meant," only to be proved true when Sontag's claim that Zelig should be read as a "triumph of aesthetic instincts" is pitted against Irving Howe's insistence that Zelig's story reflects "the Jewish experience in America." The film also plays with the endless circulation of much ado about nothing: these comments not only say nothing about Zelig, the famous nonentity, but they also produce an interpretive narrative about a historical nonentity, a nonperson who never existed.

Zelig performs an infinite mirroring of quasi-altered, self-representations, itself emerging as a hysterical cinematic rendition of Leonard Zelig's hysteric performances of the self and of the hysterical responses this elicits from the public at large as well as from physicians and cultural critics. And if it is the excess of Zelig's symptoms that disturbs the very security he seeks through assimilation (because this overabundance undercuts the security of those he mimics when they find themselves reflected in a foreign body), it is also the excess of Allen's quasi-authentic documentary images that disturbs. In the same gesture that Allen uses in undercutting his authorial potency, setting up an ambivalent identity between himself and his protagonist, he also dismantles the authority of intellectual opinion precisely as he elicits it, by asking Sontag, Blum, and Howe to stand in for interpretive consistency that is self-consciously staged as insubstantial.

In other words, on the extradiegetic level, the film is much ado about nothing. Not only does Zelig fade behind the roles he assumes and dissolves into the photographs that frame him within specific historical moments, but the film's technique, by pretending to be a documentary, also imitates the hysteric performance of the quasi-altered, self-representation of its protagonist. There is no verifiable historical reference for the overabundant cinematic phantasies displayed. Pretending to be a documentary about a historic figure who pretends to be like those interpellating him, the nonentity of a protagonist is mirrored in the technique, which explicitly states its nondocumentary character. Like Leonard Zelig, the entire film does not belong to the genre it seeks to fit: it is a generic foreign body. As a conglomeration of mock-documentary images, the footage pretends to be what it is not: actual archival material. At the same time the film is a *hysterical* documentary about nothing because the protagonist of the film never existed. If the message Zelig proves is that every true self is a knot of masks, so too the hysteric message of the technique is that it shows all documentary style to be infected by moments of pretense. A documentary about nothing, it is as close as cinema can come to straddling perfect simulation with an articulation of the nothing subtending the representational gesture.

However, although the extradiegetic level of the film outside the story level insists that the enigma that hysteria poses inevitably eludes both a narrative and visual rendition, Allen embeds a counternarrative. The fact that Eudora Fletcher succeeds in transforming Zelig into a subject with a stable self-representation illustrates a solution to hysteria through transference love. The cure is thwarted initially because Leonard identifies with her and thinks he is a doctor. Significantly, the peripeteia of the cure occurs when she decides to consciously enact her own fallibility, the nothing subtending any self-assured appearance. Telling Leonard she is not a doctor, but rather has come to him as a patient asking for help, she elicits from him the first articulation of his actual helplessness. As Zelig declares, "I'm not a doctor!" she seeks to fix his identity onto a representation: "Who are you?" Zelig's response, however, acts out the core of his self-representation, where no name standing in for a stable identity kernel lies but rather the engulfing traumatic knowledge of vulnerability. Asking, "What do you mean, who am I, I, I don't know. These are tough questions. . . ." He refuses to acknowledge her interruption. When she offers the suggestion, "Leonard Zelig?" he replies, "Yes. Definitely. Who is he?" As she continues trying to give a name to his identity, "You," he responds, "Pshaw . . . no, I'm nobody, I'm nothing . . . I . . . Catch me, I'm falling." Zelig is responding to her desire that he accept symbolic castration. But rather than offering a figure of an intact self, he insists that at the navel of his being he is nothing; his given name is an empty designation, he acknowledges, even as it does not contain his identity. In so doing, Zelig articulates the Lacanian dictum: far from assuaging traumatic impact, an acceptance of symbolic castration recreates the gap inherent in human existence, the fissure, the denavelment that constitutes the speaking and desiring subject and underwrites all phantasies of plenitude and security.

Although the cure Eudora Fletcher undertakes is built on this psychic gap—she induces a trance and posthypnotic suggestion to return her patient to this sense of being nothing in all future sessions—the explanatory scenes that Zelig ultimately draws from his unconscious continue to circle around this nothing. Indeed, as Birgit Erdle (1995, 16) notes, the memory traces Zelig offers stage a circulation of repetitions that defy any origin and any solution: "My brother beat me. . . . My sister beat my brother. . . . My father beat my sister and my brother and me. . . . My mother beat my father and my sister and me and my brother. . . . The neighbors beat our family. . . . People down the block beat the neighbors and our family." The subjectivity subtending all his hysteric self-representation can only be designated an inscription within this circling of traumatic impact. His urge to assimilate not only enacts the protective fiction of belonging, meant to assuage an earlier psychic wound of not fitting in. More importantly, the excess within this gesture refers to the fact that traumatic impact cannot be assimilated. It can only be reiterated in memory traces staging the nonassimilation of traumatic impact in a scenario where the subject casts himself as a foreign body. Even though Zelig never names what is at the core of his disorder, precisely because the trauma has no name, he articulates that something disturbs him and that this elusive knowledge remains as a disturbance.

Yet traumatic impact can also be articulated through an inversion, with the hysteric seeking to support the desire of his interpellating Other precisely because he hopes to exchange memory traces of vulnerability for a protective fiction of plenitude. Fletcher, for example, fails to discover the primal scene of trauma during the sessions' trances, when Zelig brings forth unconscious material, but she does elicit a proposal of love. Significantly, his declaration once more encircles a recognition of vulnerability: as Zelig explains, "You're sweet. . . . 'Cause you're . . . you're not as clever as you think you are. You're all mixed up. . . . oh . . . I love you. . . . I want to take care of you. . . . uh . . . No . . . no more pancakes." Projecting his own vulnerability onto her, he constructs a countercirculation of desire aimed at recuperation, rather than at the preservation of psychic wounds. One might say that he finally succeeds in supporting the desire of the interpellating Other, in a way his previous chameleon acts did not, because he has constructed a phantasy in which he supports the very person who also supports him.

Of course, the narrative of the film deconstructs the cure through transference love, illustrating that Fletcher has produced a successful, but, in its stability, vulnerable, knotted subject. Zelig, in fact, simply continues to exhibit his hysteric symptoms. Now, however, he has learned to imitate the dominant cultural ideology that privileges the role of the individualist who speaks up and says what is on his mind, whereas earlier he had acted the chameleon who blends in. Fletcher herself points to the contradiction at stake when she admits to having "molded him too far." During the first meeting with the other physicians, Zelig appears overly opinionated, staunchly disagreeing with any opinion that is not his own. The fine-tuning from which Leonard Zelig ultimately emerges as "at last his own man" is a precarious protective fiction. It is in constant need of renegotiation, poignantly evident when the others allege he has misused or betrayed them, provoking a return of Zelig's old chameleon nature.

This contradiction, both dismantling and sustaining the fantasy that a subject can be his own man, plays through to the end of the film. Zelig, once again the chameleon, finds in the mass hysteria of Nazi party members a celebration of individual nonentity much like his own desire to blend in (even amidst another fantasy set up to screen traumatic impact). The presence of Eudora Fletcher at the Nazi rally, however, causes him to wake from his trance, but it is once again his hysteric ability to transform as a particular situation requires that allows him to believe he is a pilot and able to save both of them from Nazi punishment. Indeed, Allen emphasizes the contradiction once more with his recourse to an expert: Saul Bellow explains, "his sickness was also at the root of his salvation [. . . .] It was his very disorder that made a hero of him."

As we watch the home movies documenting the simple marriage ceremony between Leonard Zelig and Eudora Fletcher, we hear the narrator quote Scott Fitzgerald: "One wonders what would have happened if, right at the outset, he had had the courage to speak his mind and not pretend. In the end, it was, after all, not the approbation of many but the love of one woman that changed his life." And we cannot help wondering about another family story told in the film in the interview with Mrs. Catherine Fletcher. Tucked between the scenes showing her daughter Eudora receiving awards and christening ships and those of the celebrities at the Hearst estate, posing with Leonard and Eudora, the interview remains a foreign body within the narrative. Behaving the way Zelig has just been taught to do, Catherine Fletcher disagrees with the reporter and insists on presenting a story about her family that does not fit into the happy fiction he is soliciting from her. Yet while the reporter simply tunes out the story she insists on telling—about family wealth coupled with depression, difficulties, and alcohol problems—her silenced maternal voice haunts the happy family romance of the final home movie. Something disturbing remains.

As Slavoj Žižek notes, the problem with the destructive, clandestine enjoyment that Lacan calls *jouissance* is not that we never find it but that we cannot get rid of it. If we displace it, it returns somewhere else. All we can do is heroically *accept* this loss by converting its traumatic impact into protective fictions that alternate between the horrific return of the phantastic body of discarded plenitude (as in *Psycho,*) or the protective fiction of a family romance (as in *Zelig*). This is the message that hysteria broadcasts, this much ado about nothing, the language in which nothing sustains the protean fictions located not beyond the fissures; much ado obliquely articulates the naught hysterics seek to shield.[36]

CHAPTER 1

The Navel of Sigmund Freud's Inaugural Dream

> I know of a young chronophobiac who experienced something like panic
> when looking for the first time at homemade movies that had been taken a
> few weeks before his birth. He saw a world that was practically unchanged—
> the same house, the same people—and then realized that he did not exist
> there at all and that nobody mourned his absence. He caught a glimpse of his
> mother waving from an upstairs window, and that unfamiliar gesture dis-
> turbed him, as if it were some mysterious farewell. But what particularly
> frightened him was the sight of a brand-new baby carriage standing there on
> the porch, with the smug, encroaching air of a coffin; even that was empty, as
> if, in the reverse course of events, his very bones had disintegrated.
>
> —*Vladimir Nabokov*

I

LITERARY CRITICS who use psychoanalysis justify the enmeshment of these
two disciplines by pointing out that both explore the way we tell, write, and
interpret the stories we are born into, stories that allow us to remember the
past and stories we create so as to make sense of our world (L. R. Williams
1995, E. Wright 1984). Along these lines, Peter Brooks argues that psychoanalysis is necessarily a narratology, a study of how narratives work, given
that the analyst seeks to help the patient redress the gaps in memory, the
contradictions and inconsistencies in narrative chronology, and the lack of
explanatory force with which a patient tells his or her story. "The work of
the analyst," he claims "must in large measure be a recomposition of the
narrative discourse to give a more coherent—and thus more therapeutic—
representation of the patient's story, to reorder its events, to foreground its
dominant themes, to understand the force of desire that speaks in and
through it" (1993, 232).
    A basic premise behind Freud's talking cure, after all, is that the hysteric,
like all other neurotics, becomes a patient precisely because the story she tells
is fragmentary and discontinuous. With an hysteric unable to tell the complete story of the origin and development of her symptoms—leaving out,
distorting, and rearranging information—the analyst faces an elusive and
enigmatic version and his responsibility becomes the reconstructing of a
complete and logical narrative. However, as critics suspicious of Freud's

self-assurance have counterintuitively noted (Showalter 1985, Mentzos 1980), the hysteric's inability to give a coherently ordered narrative of her life may not be a characteristic simply of this psychosomatic disorder, but rather of the very meaning of hysteria. Thus, Freud's belief that the analyst can reconstruct what remains intangible in the self-presentation of the hysteric is itself part of an analytic narrative, justifying and reassuring the very enterprise of psychoanalysis.

In this chapter I will address the incompatibility subtending the exchange between the hysteric and her interpellator. The analyst seeks a solution, in the sense of a conclusive narrative that will either disband the symptoms altogether or stabilize them into one livable symptom, whereas the hysteric resiliently resists closure, producing ever new conversions and ever changing narratives. Furthermore, far from allowing the analyst to use his interpellation to clearly delineate the abnormal from the normal and draw a clear boundary between himself and his so-called deviant object of analysis, the hysteric draws the analyst into the hysteric exchange, infecting him with her knowledge that any interpretive closure—therapeutic as it may be—is necessarily inadequate, inconsistent, and fallible.

I will explore the problem that the hysteric poses to the analyst in performing, as she does, the interface between narrative representation and its limitations, precisely because her stories revolve around the impact of traumatic woundings to the psychic apparatus. The navel is a critical metaphor, therefore, because both the hysteric and the analyst of hysteria keep harking to the question of origins. If the conversion of hysterical memory traces feeds endlessly on an originary traumatic impact without ever fully returning to the scene of origin for its psychic disturbance, so too does Freud's architecture of hysteria seek an infinitely receding point of origin, which constitutes precisely the vanishing point of his own structural schema. Freud's early work on hysteria marks the scene of his own analytic parturition. Identifying with the voice and the symptoms of the hysteric, indeed at times placing himself in her position, he discovers the meaning of dreams and gives birth to psychoanalysis in the same gesture in which he brings forth an autobiographical narrative, a self-representation that disturbingly conflates analyst and object of analysis.

I begin, therefore, by exploring Freud's dream of Irma's injection in his *Interpretations of Dreams* (1900–1901), and, more specifically, the moment he designates as the "navel of the dream." This first specimen dream, of which Didier Anzieu says, "Few dreams have been the subject of so much comment," (1975, 137) perfectly illustrates the way an interrogation of hysteria results in a hysterization of the interpretive process, not only by undercutting any desire for closure, but also, equally importantly, by eliciting explanations as protean as the hysteric symptom itself. Indeed, what Professor Blum claims for Zelig's chameleon act can just as easily be claimed for the vicissitudes of this "metadream" within the canon of psychoanalytic criticism: everyone acknowledges that its dream symbolism is significant, but no two intellectuals seem to agree about what it means. In the following discussion, I will begin, therefore, by tracing Freud's own interpretation and then turn to several critical interpretations of his reading, a selection not meant to be exclusive but rather illustrative. At stake, of course, in my own reading of these interventions is precisely what elisions are brought to the fore, what semantic encodings are privileged, and what is left unexplored in this ongoing narrative exchange in which no two critics seem to agree. To conclude I will turn to Roland Barthes's *Camera Lucida*, in which I suggest Freud's investigation into the universalities underlying his personal dream work is transposed into the collective image repertoire created by photography. While Freud directly invokes the navel as a seminal interpretive metaphor, Barthes does not explicitly use this term. His discussion, in contradistinction, directly addresses the issue of *mutability*, at the navel of the photographic representation. Through the photographic image Barthes delineates how the quest for a contact with death and mortality connects and disconnects with the loss and commemoration of the maternal body—in precisely the rhetorical gesture I am calling omphalic representation.

Freud, in seeking to establish his theory that dreams are always a form of wish fulfillment (not *what* a dream means but *that* it signifies is at stake), arrests his discussion by invoking the metaphorical "navel of the dream," where the intimacy of Irma's throat is conflated rhetorically with the extimacy marked by the navel. In this inaugural dream interpretation Freud has recourse to this pivotal metaphor to illuminate the moment of psychic self-representation that marks the absolute specificity of the dreamer—and with it what resists interpretation as well. Invoking a knot that is cut and severed, this impenetrable moment of connection would lead the analyst "far afield." Yet it is precisely this detail, unfathomable and fatefully inevitable, that suggests a story about individuation, enmeshing connectedness with vulnerability. That is to say, both Freud's self-representation and his critical technique are intimately linked with resistance to normative containment—thematically, his identification with hysteria and rhetorically, his invocation of the navel of a dream. In so doing Freud, at the outset of psychoanalysis at least, unfolds a different story of the individiual's acquisition of a self-representation marked by specificity, a narrative not limited to positioning the subject in relation to the phallus as the privileged signifier of the symbolic. Rather Freud's narrative conceives the subject in relation to the mutability of the body and encourages a responsibility toward its own fallibility. Analogously, Barthes, in seeking to prove that photographs are moments of facticity, arrests his discussion once he has found the seminal maternal photograph, for this, too, brings him to the point of his own mortal implenitude. In both cases, turning to images—to dream representations and photographs—is meant to illustrate and support the construction of a theory. Conversely, only the theoretical concern can illuminate the significance of the two images, of the intimate part of Irma's throat and of the five-year-old French girl. My own theoretical point is to explore how each text rhetorically invokes the concept of the navel to conceptualize how the subject is knotted. The individual's self-representation involves a counter movement that balances integration and dissolution, connection and negation, and coherence and difference, that points to the vulnerability inhabiting the particular and the traumatic impact inscribing any effort at sublimation and symbolization.

To flesh out this notion of a knotted subject I will borrow the critical categories developed by Roland Barthes in a much earlier text, his "Introduction to the Structural Analysis of Narratives" (1966). Starting with the premise that any discourse is a long "sentence," Barthes argues that structural analysis involves distinguishing several levels or instances of description and placing them within a hierarchical (integrationary) perspective. To understand a narrative, he claims, "is not merely to follow the unfolding of the story, it is also to recognize its construction in 'storeys,' to project the horizontal concatenations of the narrative 'thread' onto an implicitly vertical axis" (1966, 87). The three levels he proposes—functions (irreducible units), actions, and narration—are bound together according to a mode of progressive integration, in a process of knotting. Similarly, one might say that the individual is constructed of storeys—genetic and cultural codes bound together through the language of the body—but has a knot over psychic wound.

Crossing a psychoanalytic with a structuralist discursive model, Barthes explains that the "essence of a function is, so to speak, the seed that it sows in the narrative, planting an element that will come to fruition later," a polyvalent detail whose final meaning is fixed only once the narrative is considered as a whole. But even at the most basic level, Barthes distinguishes two narrative forces. Units either have correlate units on the same level that belong to what he calls the distributional function, involving metonymic *relata*, or (their saturation requiring a change of level) belong to the class of integrational functions, forming metaphoric *relata*. In the act of interpreting, we treat each narrative element as a polysemous detail that spreads its meaning in seemingly unrestrained fashion on the selective level of each individual sequence—even as we try to integrate each individual narrative moment into a coherent meaning on the combinatory level of narration. That is to say, by virtue of an interpretive gesture, details on the distributional axis are knotted together on the higher level of narration so that the structural trajectory of each narrative analysis moves from an interpretation of the distributional form to the production of an integrated meaning. Integration joins what has been disjoined; it guides the understanding of discontinuous elements, simultaneously contiguous and heterogeneous. Narrative—and analogously any construction of identity employing narrative—works through the concourse of two movements. In a gesture of sublimation, it "recovers itself, pulls itself together"; in a counter gesture of desublimation "the structure ramifies, proliferates, uncovers itself" (1966, 122). What Barthes's enmeshment of the integrational and distributional axes affords my discussion of the language of hysteria is a recognition that a distributional free play of signification always calls also for both narrative integration and the vulnerability in such a knotting of the subject and its story into a coherent whole. His is an awareness that any narrative integration, any desire for coherence and wholeness, even as it is fundamentally necessary constructs itself over and out of a matrix informed by a traumatic *jouissance* whose traces can neither be fully excluded nor effaced.

II

Before turning to the dream representation Freud used as a specimen to exemplify his method of interpretation, it seems useful to recall how, from the start, he set an analogy up between dreams and symptoms. Freud credited his hysteric patients, with teaching him "that a dream can be inserted into the psychical chain that has to be traced backwards in the memory from a pathological idea. It was then only a short step to treating the dream itself as a symptom and to applying to dreams the method of interpretation that had been worked out for symptoms" (1900–1901, 101). In either case, To interpret means substituting one representation for another, assigning a meaning that recodes, restructures, and thus replaces the prior psychic formation "by something which fits into the chain of our mental acts as a link having a validity and importance equal to the rest" (96). The dream of Irma's injection proves to be so ingenious a specimen, therefore, because its content performs what is at stake in interpretation itself, namely the act of *substitution*. As a composite figure, Irma stands in for several women who were significant to Freud at this point in his life. The narrative plot of the dream, moreover, ultimately replaces Irma with a formula written on a wall and with a male friend.

This specimen dream comments self-reflexively as an interpretive representation. Like Freud's interpretation, which as a secondary rendition stands in for his nocturnal phantasy scenario and turns what is riddled with gaps and discontinuity into a coherent narrative, the dream itself is a representational structure, embodying in images (*Vorstellungen*) the desires, anxieties, and drives that would otherwise remain unarticulated. However, the dream representation introduces a protean, polysemantic, and heterogeneous matrix of images and sequences; like the hysteric symptom that disobeys the laws of anatomy, it jars precisely because it doesn't seem to follow the logic that the conscious subject has learned to live by. In contrast, the interpretive representation arrests endless semantic proliferation. It fashions a coherent narrative by excluding those stories/storeys that do not fit. In other words, Freud adds an interpretation to his own dream representation, not only demonstrating how drives, by being fixed onto an image, find entrance into the unconscious but in so doing also emerge as the stuff of symptom formations, be this hysterical conversions or dreams. His interpretation becomes a second kind of fixative, replacing the semantic heterogeneity of the dream representation with a critical representation that aims at an enclosure of meaning. At the same time, however, Freud exposes the cost of any interpretive substitution by obliquely articulating not only what falls from the unconscious representation but also what is purposefully excluded from his interpretation so that the solution can appear coherent. This fissure, this gap, this elision is what adjoins at the navel of the dream—as well as at the navel of each critical interpretation after Freud. Dark and impenetrable, the navel of each dream functions as the vulnerable point as the critic tries to integrate into his or her critical narrative what remains nonintegrated in Freud's own interpretation. But this dark spot is also the sign of parturition, as its impenetrability brings forth a plethora of critical rereadings.

Freud explains in a preamble to his transcription of the dream he had during the night of 23–24 July 1885 (1900–1901, 106) that in the summer of that year he had been seeing a young woman. Using the pseudonym Irma, he describes her as being on very friendly terms with him and his family, although her relatives did not look favorably at the psychoanalytic treatment he was giving her. Analysis had provided relief from her hysterical anxiety without, however, ending her other somatic symptoms. Freud admits that at this stage in his inquiry into hysteria he "was not yet quite clear in my mind as to the criteria indicating that a hysterical case history was finally closed." Irma had been unwilling to accept the solution he had proposed and instead had broken off the treatment. Freud's dream is in direct response to the return of a junior colleague, Otto, from the summer resort where Irma and her family were; the colleague stated that she was better but not quite well—a report Freud reads as an implicit criticism of his psychoanalytic work by his friend Otto, an echo of Irma's relatives' displeasure (who also have long been his friends).

In one sense he directly names what is at stake in his dream representation, a form of unconscious self-representation that attempts through a sequence of images to knot together: desires and anxieties namely, his reputation as a friend and as a theorist. This reputation is endangered by his failure both to relieve his patient of her physical pains and to determine the right moment of closure for this case history of hysteria. After all, it is not only an illness signifying a "suffering of the womb" but one, more importantly, that Freud and his contemporary Pierre Janet considered an illness *by representation (maladie par representation)*. He confesses his uncertainty as to whether he can impose a solution onto his analysand, replacing the language of her body with his analytic narrative, or whether the interpretive narrative (meant to stand in for the hysteric symptom and thus relieve her of her pain) is one which she must bring forth herself. Freud's preamble also articulates, more obliquely, how his patient's resistance—psychically in that she breaks off the treatment and physicall in that her pain persists—cuts off his power to terminate the case, to integrate her pain and hysteric self-representation into his narrative solution. Irma's resistance castrates him in the sense that it points to his vulnerability as an analyst. Her resistance is the moment of failure in his interpretive system. She thwarts his desire to find a conclusion to her case history, to designate a stabilizing solution in the form of a coherent narrative: against his wish for closure she pits the insistence of her hysterical symptoms, an insistence so disturbing that it activates something in Freud's own unconscious, calling forth the return of repressed material.

By writing out Irma's case history as an integrated narrative that he can show to Dr. M. (Josef Breuer) and thereby build a new alliance confirming his authority as a scientist, the conscious Freud hopes to gain power over what he experienced as a wounding of his analytic potency. Yet the unconscious Freud responds to the challenge posed by Irma's insistence with a dream that gives figure to this moment of failure, staging an intricate scenario of apertures and closures. Then, even as the recuperative interpretation is meant to patch up the wound, Freud turns to the metaphorical "navel of the dream," undertaking a rhetorical gesture I call omphalic, a simultaneous movement in two opposite directions: integration and dissolution.

The dream itself is structured over two scenes. The first involves only Freud and Irma. It begins with a dialogue, Freud faulting her for not accepting his solution, and Irma countering by pointing out the persistence of her somatic pain, and it ends as Freud, after an initial resistance on the part of his patient, looks into the intimacy of her throat and discovers there a big, white patch and extensive whitish-grey scabs. The second scene repeats the first, but now Freud and the woman resisting both his solution and analytic gaze are joined by three men (Dr. M., Otto, and Leopold), and all four probe the body of a completely passive Irma. Uncertainty translates into certainty, the disturbance Irma stands for is expelled, and an origin for the mysterious persistence of her pain is found. Although the analytic solution Irma rejects remains unspecified, the dream ends with the mysterious emergence of another solution, the formula for trimethylamine, which Freud sees before him printed in heavy type (though he does not write it out in his dream transcription).

In other words, this dream representation involves four solutions: Freud's unnamed psychoanalytic solution, which Irma rejects as an explanation of her hysteric symptoms; Otto's solution injected into her with a dirty syringe, which calls forth her somatic pains; Dr. M.'s solution of diagnosing an infection—putting an end to hysterical resistance and pain when he shifts a psychic disturbance for which no organic lesions can be found to a clearly designated organic disorder; and the formula's (Otto's) solution specifying trimethylamine (NC_3H_9). Irma's speech in the first part of the dream, disagreeing with Freud's analytic explanation, is elided and replaced by Dr. M.'s speech, by contrast distinctly offering greater clarity. Freud's accusing Irma of resisting his treatment, and her questioning Freud's skill as a physician because of the persistence of her pains, are replaced in Dr. M's speech by an accusation of Otto. As the agent of a thoughtlessly made injection delivered with an unclean syringe to boot, Otto now stands in for the physician's guilt, which was initially directed at Freud. The result is a chiasmus between preamble and dream representation: if Otto in the preamble uses Irma's hysterical symptoms to accuse Freud, Freud later replaces Irma's hysteria with an organic disturbance so as to accuse Otto, hoping that through this substitution his guilt will disappear.

The constellation of actors in this scenario initially is a twosome, with the dreamer and his wife receiving the guests in a hall. As Freud explains, this detail anticipates the birthday party Martha and he were about to give. The German "*Wir empfangen*," referring both to biological conception (*Empfängnis*) and to a reception (*Empfang*), explicitly links the medical with the sexual and family themes of the dream. Yet what starts as a birthday reception for Freud's pregnant wife readily translates into another birthday celebration, commemorating his discovery of the functioning of dreams, relying on the analogy between procreation and the germination of intellectual creation; that is, between the maternal parturition of offsprings and the paternal discovery of and coming forth with ideas. Along these lines, the final footnote to this specimen interpretation, added by the editors, significantly refers to a letter written to Fliess, on 12 June 1900: "Do you suppose that some day a marble tablet will be placed on the house, inscribed with these words?—'In This House, on July 24th, 1895, the Secret of Dreams was Revealed to Dr. Sigm. Freud. At the moment there seems little prospect of it" (121).

Once Irma arrives, the dreamer's wife disappears only to reappear in a footnote, which Freud adds, as a model for Irma. Concomitant with the more figural reduction to Freud and his patient, the visual field shrinks from a hall to a space by a window and then further to the aperture of Irma's opened mouth. After she has fallen passive, the couple is replaced by Dr. M. and Freud, the new couple, expanded, however, to include the group of colleagues. After Freud acknowledges his identification with the object of analysis (the hysterical feminine body) (a point I will return to), analytic consent is reached. The "We were receiving" ("*Wir empfangen*") of the first scene transforms into the "We were directly aware, too, of the origin of the infection" ("*Wir wissen auch unmittelbar*"), replacing the earlier parental couple with a bond of male physicians. As Erik Erikson (1954) suggests, the dream abides by the conventional plot development of religious narratives about conversion or confirmation. A dreamer is cast in the role of a guilty figure and isolated from his peer group as a lonely investigator; he becomes a patient, having appealed to the help from a higher authority, and finally a joiner, his self-doubt translated into empowerment.

Freud's own analysis of the Irma dream is quite explicitly undertaken under the aegis of his theoretical interests. He seeks to prove that once the act of interpreting a dream has been completed, each unconscious sleeping representation will emerge as the fulfillment of a wish. He maintains an untroubled analogue between dream and events of the previous day, such that the preamble and dream representation are meant to be mirror inversions.

Yet he ultimately demonstrates that while the preamble is a conscious, written narrative, the dream representation remains an unconscious narrative available, like all traumatic imprints (and like the navel imprints cast by Marie-Ange Guilleminot), as a belated transcription—as a representation that converts as much as it reveals. Furthermore, the interpretation itself, trying to uncover the intra- and interpersonal connections between the dream scenario and the dreamer's life, continues the process of conversion even as it seeks to shed light on obscurities.

As Freud embarks on his interpretation, the reproaches he makes Irma are readily understood as an attempt to rid himself of his responsibility toward his disobedient patient. This part of the dream, he claims, could as easily have been spoken by the conscious Freud, for in offering a solution the physician dismisses all further responsibility as well as his own guilt. Thus, on a manifest level the dream performs the sentence, "If [the pains] were [Irma's] fault, they could not be mine." However, seeking to penetrate the dream's latent strata, Freud moves toward those points that cannot be attributed to a conscious speaker. The first layer—the choking that Irma feels in her throat, abdomen, and stomach—Freud cannot explain, since it played no significant part in Irma's illness, just as the pale and puffy appearance cannot be attributed to her. The distressing thought that he might have missed an organic illness, however, can, easily be applied to the material of the preamble. It marks a moment of denial for, far from being horrified, Freud the analyst is pleased. Since he is accountable for the removal only of hysteric and not organic pains, this thought actually allieviates his responsibility toward this resisting patient: "I was actually wishing that there had been a wrong diagnosis; for, if so, the blame for my lack of success would also have been got rid of" (1900–1901, 109).

The peripeteia of the first scene occurs in the passage at whose end Freud inserts the footnote about the navel of the dream: "I took her to the window and looked down her throat, and she showed signs of recalcitrance, like women with artificial dentures. I thought to myself that there was really no need for her to do that. She then opened her mouth properly [*Der Mund geht dann auch gut auf*] and on the right I found a big [white] patch; at another place I saw extensive whitish-grey scabs upon some remarkable curly structures which were evidently modelled on the turbinal bones of the nose" (107). Quite explicitly, one (crucially, not the only) point of identification for Freud in this unconscious self-representation is the image of a hysteric patient resisting an investigation of her oral cavity and, upon submitting to Freud's gaze, presenting the spectacle of a void marked by a white patch and whitish-grey scabs, which, after all, are crustlike exudate or cracked dead tissue over a healing skin wound. Now, if we bear in mind that Irma complains of pains in her throat, stomach, and abdomen choking her, what the dream plot reveals is that it is precisely in order to discover the organic origin of this sense of a knotted throat, indeed a knotted body, that Freud tries to visually penetrate the interior of Irma's body.

Starting then with the somatization of a knot, Freud interprets the figure of Irma as a representational knot—as his own psychic condensation of various women. Because the attributes given so far do not fit the patient for whom Irma is a screen name, Freud begins to untangle the different women who coalesce in this figure. An oral examination revealing bad teeth allows him first of all to associate to a governess he had treated in the past. She "seemed a picture of youthful beauty," he claims, but her open mouth revealed "false teeth" (109). Freud presents this governess as an example of the way medical examinations may reveal "little secrets" that satisfy neither party. In so doing he addresses a theme as seminal to the dream sequence as the one he seeks to prove about alleviation of guilt, namely, the desire to keep certain fallibilities clandestine. These secrets are articulated only obliquely, either because one does not want or is unable to name them directly. At the same time, the governess might also refer to the *vanitas* tradition, feminine beauty shown as the illusory tissue that covers and diffuses the fragility of the human body, namely its mutability and decay. Following this strand, Freud's "little secret" can be read as a metonymic displacement for corporeal vulnerability.

The image of a woman standing by a window allows Freud to disentangle a second referent for Irma: one of Dr. M.'s patients and a friend of Irma's. She had in fact suffered from hysterical choking, and Freud finds confirmed in the "recalcitrance" of Irma her shy nature. His impression that "there was no need for her" to behave in the manner of a resisting patient further fits the description of Irma's friend, who had so far been able to master her hysterical condition without having had to consult Freud. Having thus replaced the hysteric (so distressing to Freud because she questions the fallibility of his analytic powers) for whom Irma was initally the screen name with two other women, namely the governess and the friend who require no psychoanalytic treatment, he proceeds to decode the image of a woman with bad teeth, usually pale, puffy looking, and recalcitrant, as yet another displaced representation: Martha Freud.

That his wife is named only in the explanatory footnote and that Freud omits explaining that the "pains in the abdomen" refer to the fact that at the time she was pregnant with a child neither of them wanted (a child he was going to call Wilhelm to commemorate his friendship with Fliess), illustrates Freud's interpretive desire to keep certain fallibilities hidden. Freud concludes, "I have been comparing my patient Irma with two other people who would also have been recalcitrant to treatment," thereby making two significant elisions. Although his wife is named, the reference to her maternity is not mentioned; further, the governess, representing bodily mutability, is completely effaced from the interpretive narrative. In other words, even as Freud decodes the composite parts of Irma, producing coherence where his dream offered contradictions, he obscures what is at stake more obliquely: the way the feminine body evokes anxieties about mortality, in that beauty hides decay and pregnancy proleptically invokes the death of the maternal body and of the child. Instead, he privileges the third woman replacing the real-life Irma, namely Dr. M's patient and Irma's friend, as he deciphers why he should have undertaken this exchange in his dream. This third woman is a reassuring figure. Standing in not only for Irma but also for the duplicitously beautiful governess and the pregnant wife, she leads the interpretation away from the disturbing theme of the vulnerability of the body, which the unconscious Freud produces as a ciphered message once he finds himself confronted with a hysteric's resistance to his theory. Furthermore, seeking to prove that this dream enacts a wish fulfillment, Freud can read her as a reassuring figure who represents his desire for complicity—for a confession from the hysteric that would support his analytic solution.

He explains the exchange: "Either I felt more sympathetic towards her friend or had a higher opinion of her intelligence. For Irma seemed to me foolish because she had not accepted my solution. Her friend would have been wiser, that is to say she would have yielded sooner. She would then have opened her mouth properly, and have told me more than Irma" (110–111). In other words, Freud implicitly shows himself, as a dreamer, performing the very dissimulation he finds in his hysteric patients, his dream functioning like a hysteric symptom. He knows that the image of the pliable woman opening her mouth to broadcast the consistency of his theory is a protective fiction, screening the far more traumatic knowledge of his fallibility. Yet he insists that to privilege this strand of the feminine knot that Irma configures, to arrest his interpretation at the utterance of the conditional "She would have told," is fully in line with a coherent narrative interpretation. It is analogus to the hysteric who claims she believes in the consistency of the narratives offered her by a representative of paternal law even as she radically dismantles their authority.

Significantly, then, Freud situates his footnote after his comment that the disturbing Irma is exchanged for an acquiescing friend whose mouth opens properly, in a figurative sense, so as to give him the solution he seeks. On the other side of the footnote, which one could call a distributional detail in the text that forces our gaze to plunge to the bottom of the page, Freud gives an image of what he sees inside this compliant mouth. This second dream representation is a specular inversion of the protective fiction that would have come out of the mouth of Irma's friend, pitting against the reassuring confession Freud imagines in the conditional "she would have . . ." a horrific revelation of whitish-gray spots and scabs, which Freud reads as a condensed index for potentially fatal body wounds. In the footnote itself he explains, "I had a feeling that the interpretation of this part of the dream was not carried far enough to make it possible to follow the whole of its concealed meaning. If I had pursued my comparison between the three women, it would have taken me far afield.—There is at least one spot [*Stelle*] in every dream at which it is unplumbable [*unergründlich*]—a navel, as it were, that is its point of contact with the unknown [*mit dem Unerkannten zusammenhängt*]" (111).

Although I will later discuss the metaphoric navel of the dream more fully, it is worth noting here how the suggested analogy links maternity and parturition with mortality. But it specifies also a site in the processes of the psychic apparatus that is not only impenetrable but also not open to explorations. A dream relates to the *unknown* in the act of interpretation, just as the child relates to the prenatal maternal body at the moment of birth.[1] In other words, with any interpretive, integrative narrative whose aim is to find a solution, Freud designates a distributional detail that, like the hysteric's resistance and protean dissimulations, resiliently undermines the entire project of analysis, pointing to its vulnerable spot. He allows his comment about this wounding moment of interpretive failure to follow, from the protective fiction of a confessing woman. Furthermore, this footnote whose point of origin is Irma's resistance—like Freud's resistance to addressing his wife's pregnancy—even as it refers to the resistance inherent in any interpretation—also straddles two dream images. The footnote is about a "navel of the dream" and functions *structurally* like a navel as well. It points to a theoretical thought, cut off from the main text, while actually knotting together on one side of the navel the condensation, or complex, of three women (occurring over the body of the hysteric Irma), with the white spots and the gray scabs inside the hysteric's throat on the other side. And it is precisely this narrative contiguity between a knotted, hysterical subject and a disturbing image of an organic malfunction, a knot of scars, that has been left unread by other critics. This placement strikes me as seminal: it not only aligns the hysteric's complaint with the fallibility inherent in any act of interpretation but also with the inevitable mutability of the body. Freud glosses over the whitish-gray scabs as a composite index of his anxiety about his eldest daughter's serious illness and his own precarious health; he was suffering from a heart condition and also using cocaine to relieve himself of troublesome nasal swellings. The misuse of cocaine was particularly worrisome for him because it had led to serious disorders in one of his female patients who had followed his example and hastened the death also of a dear friend of his. With the traumatic reference to the threat of death to himself and his daughter, the analysis of the first scene of the dream ends.

In the second scene, where Freud calls Dr. M. to repeat the examination of Irma, the phrase *at once* reintroduces the theme of mortality. Here, Freud recalls a "tragic event" (111) in his practice, when he had been forced to call on the assistance and support of an experienced senior colleague because the drug, sulfonal, that he had repeatedly prescribed to one of his patients had produced a severe toxic state. Once more a fatal threat to his daughter's life surfaces as a latent thread of the dream: like her, the patient who had ultimately "succumbed to the poison" was named Mathilde. Although he entertains the thought that the replacement brought forth by the dream representation serves to articulate an unconscious anxiety, namely, that he would have to give his daughter in exchange for having caused the death of his patient—"this Mathilde for that Mathilde"—he nevertheless shifts the issue of fallibility back into the less threatening realm of medical competence. Thus, he favors the interpretation that substitutes various women, over Irma's body, to come up with a narrative about how he collects evidence that proves both his "lack of medical conscientiousness" at the same time that it confirms the opposite: his competence as an analyst. The interpretation he repeatedly resists, in turn, is that the condensation and displacement occurring over Irma's body (the composite figure of hysteric patients, wife, and daughter)—merges with a self-representation, one that ultimately solicits associations about his own physical vulnerability.

As Freud interprets the second scene of the dream, he notes how characters addressed in the first half have transformed into new characters in the second. Dr. M. appears as the mirror inversion of Irma: both serve as the Other to whom Freud addresses his complaint, only to vindicate himself. Furthermore, like the women condensed into the figure of Irma, the two models for Dr. M.—his colleague Josef Breuer, with whom he developed his first case histories on hysteria, and his elder brother—both rejected a "certain suggestion," poignantly remaining unnamed. Yet while the former relation involves a dialogue, suddenly interrupted by the traumatic impression Freud has of the somatic irregularity inside Irma's mouth, the latter centers on a monologue, only to end with a symbolic formula's appearing uncannily before Freud's eye. Otto and Leopold, Freud's assistants when he worked in the children's hospital, mirror the disobedient Irma and her compliant friend, with Otto corresponding to the former and the "prudent Leopold" to the latter.

As Freud and his colleagues investigate Irma's body, the second moment of identity between analyst and patient is represented by the discovery that "a portion of the skin on the left shoulder was infiltrated." Commenting that this is the rheumatism in his own shoulder, Freud connects this detail to the tuberculosis that Irma's friend had imitated as one of her hysteric symptoms. Above all, he claims that the comment, "I noticed this, just as he did," was to be understood as "I noticed it in my own body, that is." Shoshana Felman reads this discovery as Freud's finding the hysteric's complaint inscribed in his own body, which leads to an identification between the two. "The subject of the dream is saying: I am myself a patient, a hysteric; I am myself creative only insofar as I can find a locus of fecundity in my own suffering" (1993, 111). In a sense one could call this the epicenter of the dream interpretation, for it is at this point that Freud and his resisting object of analysis conflate, completing the recognition of identity that began when he saw his own complaint inside Irma's throat. This is not, however, the strand Freud favors, for as he offers a reading of Dr. M.'s monologue, the interest once more lies in drawing a boundary between himself and the hysterical body he unwittingly identifies with.

Dr. M.'s diagnosis, "infection, but no matter" is read, then, as a complex solace. On the one hand, it supports the dreaming Freud's wish to have Irma suffer from an acute somatic illness for which he, as a psychoanalyst, would not be responsible. On the other hand, the fact that the paternal figure of authority, to whom the dreaming Freud has appealed for an absolution of his guilt, assures him that the patient will be relieved of her pain offers another consolation as well. Freud is embarrassed, in the course of the dream, at the fact that he had invented such a serious illness for Irma "simply in order to clear myself," and his interpellator's assurance seems to counteract Freud's own sense of cruelty. However, even as Dr. M's diagnosis apparently mitigates the revenge the dreamer Freud has taken against his hysteric patient, the fact that his consolation is so nonsensical indicates to Freud that he is also ridiculing his colleague for being ignorant of the hysteric basis to the somatic disorder. Thus, two rhetoric moves introduce the solution to the origin of Irma's distress. First, Freud discerns that he cannot untangle the contradiction inherent in his own relation to Irma's hysteria, for while the dream alleviates his guilt by endowing the composite figure of Irma and her friend with an organic disturbance lying outside his field of competence, it still insists that hysteria is the cause for the symptoms of tuberculosis Irma's friend displays. In what can be seen as a perfect hysteric strategy of its own, the dreamer Freud cannot decide whether he wants the diagnosis of hysteria to be the answer to his patient's complaint. Second, Freud now successfully severs any identification between himself and Irma by instead positing a relation of identity between her and Dr. M. Both function as his adversaries, given that the doctor agrees as little with his solution as did Irma. They also are the objects for his retribution: "I had already revenged myself in this dream on two people: on Irma with the words, 'If you still get pains, it's your own fault,' and on Dr. M. by the wording of the nonsensical consolation that I put into his mouth"(115). Here, too, however, the appeasing rhetoric is duplicitous, pointing to Freud's continued hysterization. Once again the words uttered by the interpellating Other function as a protective fiction to the specular signs of vulnerability he finds inside or emerging from the mouth of the Other.

This counterdirectional gesture of absolution with implication continues, as Freud interprets the fact that suddenly the origin of Irma's pain becomes known. As he finds the factual source of the injection given to Irma, Freud comes up not only with the story Otto had related the previous day about giving an injection to someone in a nearby hotel while he was staying with Irma and her family, but also recalls the cocaine injections that had caused the death of his friend Fleischl. Thus, although he reassures himself of his innocence in never having given an injection with an unclean syringe, he must acknowledge his own involvement in the fatal cocaine injections. Freud traces the ingredients of the injection, "propyl, propyls . . . propionic acid" back to a pineapple liqueur Otto had once given him and his wife, and which, he had suggested in jest, might poison those who drank it. The formula for trimethylamine, which in turn is read as the other source of Irma's disturbances, allows Freud to evoke, his friend Wilhelm Fliess, without directly naming him, the person, along with Breuer, with whom he developed his early theories on hysteria. The fact that the formula for trimethylamine was not only spelled out in his memory but actually appeared in heavy type suggests to Freud "the desire to lay emphasis on some part of the context as being of quite special importance" (116). This leads him to the fact that Fliess had determined trimethylamine to be one of the products of sexual metabolism—and thus to his desire to determine a sexual etiology for every case of hysteria. With this string of associations in place, Freud is now able not only to fully redraw the boundary between himself and his hysteric patient which had become fluid in the course of the interpretation) but also to jettison off all those strands of the dream representation and his interpretation that invoke bodily mutability and analytic fallibility as the ciphered message broadcast by the hysteric symptom.

Instead, formulating an integrative sentence under which all aspects of the dream can be subsumed, he now convinces himself that the origin of Irma's as well as her friend's disturbance can be located in an unappeased sexual desire, the wandering feminine uterus. Both women, after all, are widows. Furthermore, even as the appearance of the formula for trimethylamine allows Freud to assure himself that he knows the solution to any case of hysteria—namely, that he must construct a narrative about sexuality and its dissatisfactions—it also finally introduces an Other who does not resist this solution the way Irma and Dr. M. have. The formula, after all, is not only an allusion to sexuality but also to Fliess as "a person whose agreement I recalled with satisfaction whenever I felt isolated in my opinions" (117). To support the suggestion that Fliess is an invisible presence in the dream, the fourth investigator of Irma's body, Freud also recalls that his friend had postulated a connection between the turbinate bones and the female sexual organs. While this association allows Freud to decipher the "three curly structures in Irma's throat" as displaced images for her sexuality, it once again renders the boundary between a representation of feminine sexual disorder and the vulnerability of his own body fluid by reintroducing his own nasal discomforts from using cocaine.

The reference to a thoughtlessly made injection demonstrates how the theme of mortal vulnerability persists against Freud's conscious wish till the end of both the dream and any interpretation. Freud readily interprets the reference as an accusation aimed at Otto, that he was so ready to side against him. Yet it also knots this accusation against his friend together with one launched at himself, invoking one last time the cocaine injection his friend Fleischl had so hastily resorted to and the fatal sulfonal injections he had so thoughtlessly given his patient Mathilde. Similarly, the unclean syringe, though a reference to his own conscientiousness as a doctor, also knots together a string of women whose physical suffering in some manner relates to injections: an old woman patient, now residing in the country; his wife, Irma; and the dead Mathilde. Trying "to keep at bay all the ideas which were bound to be provoked by a comparison between the content of the dream and the concealed thoughts lying behind it," Freud finally offers a coherent, integrative narrative for the wishes the dream sought to fulfill, an interpretive story about how the motive for the dream representation is his wish not to be responsible for the persistence of Irma's pains; its fulfillment can be located in the twofold manner in which the dream scenario places guilt elsewhere.

The dreaming Freud first relegates the guilt to Otto, thus avenging the implicit critique he felt his friend had expressed. He also acquits himself secondly by offering a string of reasons other than his own failure as underlying Irma's persisting illness. Accordingly, Freud concludes that the dream affords satisfaction by enacting substitutions. Each of the characters that displeases him by rejecting his solution is replaced by more congenial addressees: Irma, by her friend; Otto, by Leopold; and Dr. M., by Fliess, as though the dream were saying, "Take these people away! Give me three others of my choice instead! Then I shall be free of these undeserved reproaches!'" (119) Freud admits that the interpretive solution he finally reaches, reducing the dream to a narrative about his exculpation of Irma's illness, does not adequately explain the other theme that involves his daughter's illness; his patient Mathilde's and his friend Fleischl's deaths; and his concern about his wife's, his brother's, Dr. M.'s, and his own health. Yet he ultimately transposes the entire paradigm connected with bodily vulnerability and mortality into a different register, labeling it "concern about my own and other people's health—professional conscientiousness" (120).

As Freud ultimately moves from the semantic encoding to the structure of the dream, the rhetoric of substitution undertakes a final turn: duplicitously articulating an identity between Freud and his hysteric patient, sharing not only Irma's traumatic knowledge of vulnerability but also Freud's equally traumatic knowledge of the fallibility of his analytic work, and exchanging this identification for a coherent interpretive solution that redraws the boundaries. Psychoanalysis is not so much born of Freud's ability to decode the latent meaning of the manifest dream representations. Rather, its birth is marked by his having replaced a hysteric body in pain and the challenge it poses to his authority with a narrative about his guilt and conscientiousness as a physician, ultimately ending up with the representation of a symbolic formula. For his project of psychoanalysis to be consistent, what is crucial is not that the formula of trimethylamine can be interpreted to mean something but rather that he now can postulate a formula that is universally true: every dream, far from being the expression of fragmentary mental activity, really has a meaning. While Freud's own adventure into self-discovery is nourished by the particular semantic encoding his interpretation brings forth, ultimately at stake for the birth of psychoanalysis is not what a particular dream means, but rather that it *signifies* and in so doing that it exhibits a universal structure.

III

In the first biographical reading of Freud's interpretation that I want to discuss, John Forrester (1980) takes the formula for trimethylamine as his starting point for an inquiry into Freud's favoring the symbolic structure over the semantic content of the dream.[2] For here—with nitrogen broken into three sets of carbon, and each in turn broken into three sets of hydrogen—the triad emerges as the dominant structuring principle. Forrester then grafts onto this formula Freud's claim that the dream is structured by the relation that a man has to three women. As Forrester points out, Karl Abraham had written Freud in January, 1908, "I should like to know whether the incomplete interpretation of 'Irma's injection' dream . . . is intentional. I find that trimethylamine leads to the most important part, to sexual allusions which become more distinct in the last lines. After all, everything points to the suspicion of syphilitic infection in the patient." To this Freud had responded, "Syphilis is not the subject-matter. . . . Sexual megalomania is hidden behind it, the three women, Mathilde, Sophie and Anna, are my daughters' three godmothers, and I have them all! There would be one simple therapy for widowhood, of course. All sorts of intimate things, naturally!" (Freud and Abraham 1965, 18 and 20). Forrester then expands the triadic structure to encompass Freud's entire narrative about a wish to denigrate others so as to justify and acquit oneself of guilt. The pattern he discerns works with four terms: the self, a rival, a representative of paternal authority, and an object of exchange. With Freud in the position of N, each of the three C's is once more tripled: (1) the condensation of the rivals, colleagues, and friends breaking down into Otto, Leopold, and the unnamed friend Fliess; (2) the condensation of the paternal figures of authority breaking down into Dr. M./Breuer, his brother Emmanuel, and his dead friend Fleischl; and (3) the object of exchange—the daughters, widows, and patients—breaking down into Irma (Anna Hammerschlag), her friend (Sophie Schwab-Paneth), and his wife-Mathilde (Mathilde Breuer). In so doing, Forrester leaves unaccounted a second, more fateful feminine triad: namely, the daughter Mathilde whose health is threatened, the patient Mathilde who died of the sulfonal injection, and the governess who represented bodily decay.

Having offered this biographical decoding of the formula, Forrester follows Freud in concluding that what is significant about the dream is not its meaning per se, but rather its symbolic structure, which organizes Freud's associations about the relation that the male subject has with females. In a later article "The Theme of the Three Caskets," Freud isolates the mythopoetic motive found in Shakespeare's *Merchant of Venice* and *King Lear*, citing the primal scene of desire illustrating the three inevitable relations a man has with a woman: "the woman who bears him, the woman who is his mate and the woman who destroys him . . . the mother herself, the beloved one who is chosen after her pattern, and lastly the Mother Earth who receives him once more" (1913, 301). The choice of the third woman, he suggests, is a trope for accepting one's mortality: "Choice stands in the place of necessity, of destiny. In this way man overcomes death, which he has recognized intellectually. No greater triumph of wish-fulfilment is conceivable" (299). Freud's inaugural specimen dream and his interpretation of it repeatedly invoke precisely this superlative triumph of wish-fulfilment—only to replace them with a narrative about sexuality as the origin of hysteria and about the sexual megalomania behind the composite figure of Irma. Thus he assuages the dreamer's narcissism as physician and lover, reassuring himself against the wound inflicted by the hysteric. For like King Lear, Freud does not choose the third woman, the fairest one who is silent, who represents death, but he nevertheless designs a phantasy scenario for himself, which Shakespeare had denied his king. Freud gets all three women at once, only to abandon the scene of femininity so dangerously connected with mutability and fallibility, turning to a different love story, the one about his invisible friend and the symbolic formula they bring forth.

In his book *Freud's Self-Analysis* Didier Anzieu focuses on masculine rivalry with and appropriation of feminine parturition: Freud's own hysteria, which he repeatedly confessed to Fliess in his correspondence, emerges as the desire to have a wandering womb of his own. Anzieu, who views the dream of Irma's injection as a fragmented Freud "searching for his true unity" (1975, 132), was the first to decode the biographical context for the dream—Freud's family and friends, his health, and his work—shedding light on those historical facts that Freud, in line with a Victorian proclivity toward reticence and secrecy, had kept concealed. His aim is to prove that for Freud sexuality is the pregnant metaphor for the hermeneutic quest of the analyst. Anzieu argues that the first of the two scenes dividing the dream in half, the tête-à-tête between Freud and Irma, exhibits an intense heterosexual attraction "where the desire to observe—to observe the mystery of conception—is satisfied." The second, staging a discussion among men, in turn, illustrates how "the desire for knowledge is realized in the form of a search for causes." Anzieu locates the unifying principle of the dream in its description and explanation of sexuality. In a gesture Freud resists, Anzieu reduces most of the heterogeneous dream imagery to homogeneous sexual metaphors. In his interpretation, the hall with its guests and Irma's throat are recoded as representations of the female genital organs; to open properly is read as an image of coitus; Irma's choking, her palor, and the pains in her abdomen are seen as indices for pregnancy; and the scabs are transformed into traces of sperm and read as representations of impregnation. Somewhat more speculatively Anzieu suggests that the toxin, which Dr. M. claims will be eliminated, can be read as an allusion to the miscarriage Freud hoped for, while the injection made with a dirty syringe refers to the need for developing trustworthy and safe contraception, one of Fliess's preoccupations at the time of his friendship with Freud. At the same time Anzieu acknowledges that Freud is refracted among the various characters, not only the observing and penetrating Irma but also identifying with her pain, which evokes his own heart trouble. He is doubly present "as a theoretician of the sexual aetiology of neuroses and as a patient suffering from a possibly fatal cardiac complaint," with the investigation of sex and the ascultation of the heart representing "rather accurately the self-analysis that Freud had been intending to carry out for some time using one of his dreams" (Anzieu 1975, 137). Thus the second unifying principle, perhaps superior to sexuality, is self-representation. Anzieu constructs yet another interpretive triad implicitly: sexuality, configured over the body of the hysteric, combines with mortality, configured over the body of the dreaming investigator, and is knotted together with a dream confirming the unity of the self as it emerges out of its disparate, fragmentary parts.

Anzieu further argues that the formula for trimethylamine actually matches the formal construction of the dream "where figures mostly appear in sets of three": by virtue of this triadic structure "the dream contains a symbolic representation of its own structure" (Anzieu, 150), a symbolic structure from which, in fact, its meaning derives. Giving the historical models for the various characters in the dream scenario, grafting these onto the formula of trimethylamine, Anzieu comments on the way the entire sequence is structured around an exchange between human figures and other elements, "diseases, substances that cure or kill and Death" itself. Thus, personal responsibility and the origin of pain is conclusively explained by the emergence of the formula: "The merry-go-round of cocaine, sulphonal, amyl and propyl has jolted to a halt: Freud has found the formula he was looking for" (139). Not only can he now convince himself that sexuality, or rather sexual dissatisfaction, lies at the origin of hysterical symptoms: trimethylamine can also be read, Anzieu speculates, as a "formula" of life. With an antidote to the expelled toxin, or the dream representation of miscarriage, Freud is here warding off his "furies who desire the death of the child" (139). The formula, Anzieu speculates, also stands for the product of his wife's satisfied sexuality—the unborn child they will call either Wilhelm or Anna.[3]

In Freud's endowing the formula with being a symbolic representation of sexuality, he elides the other possible interpretations he has hinted at, dealing with his fear of death and his countertransference. Anzieu continues to decode the historical material that emerges for these other thematic strands, placing the dream in the context of Freud's friends and patients, his infantile wishes, and body imagery. He embellishes points I have already raised: Freud's ambivalence toward his wife's pregnancy and his dependence on Fliess, seeking not only to aggrandize his friend but also wishing to compete with Martha's pregacy by not only conceiving a new science but also refashioning himself as the discoverer of the secret of dreams, with Fliess acting as midwife (1975, 146). He finally offers an interpretation of Freud's

claim that behind the figure of Irma one could discern his sexual megloma-
nia. Although entirely speculative, his interpretation fits the discussion I am
presenting because it touches on the subject of matricide. Desiring the three
widows might mean, on a latent level, Freud's wishing that Martha might
die in the course of her difficult pregnancy, giving him access to one of the
attractive widows Irma stands in for. Anzieu connects this matricide fantasy
with a desire for the forbidden maternal body, while the reference to a navel
of the dream opens to question the belief in a successful and conclusive interpretation afforded by the formula that his friend Fliess gave him. Over this
image, a phantasy enters the scenario about intellectual parturition and self-
creation—reintroducing the traumatic knowledge of one's physical and intellectual fallibility. Behind Freud's desire for Irma, Anzieu detects the phantasy that "the woman we dream of is the woman to whom we were once
connected by the umbilical cord, and who remains 'unknowable' by us in
the biblical sense." Anzieu, thus, does not understand the impossibility of
fully interpreting a dream or a hysterical symptom as a structural matter—
the consequence of an inadequacy written from the start into Freud's theory.
Rather, he binds it semantically with the Oedipal conflict, recoding it as "an
internal resistance caused by the barrier against incest" (154). In line with
the very structural claim Freud insists on, Anzieu ultimately locates the wish
that the dream of Irma's injection fulfils in "the paradisiacal wish to possess
the mother's body and to merge the child's body into it."

Anzieu disregards the Lacanian emphasis that this impossible maternal
body belatedly evoked by the navel refers to a state of unbearable plenitude
(and traumatic enjoyment beyond difference and distance). He fashions his
own interpretive narrative along the lines of the Oedipal story that Freud
postulates in *The Interpretation of Dreams*. He places or locates the desired
body of the unpossessed mother at the core of Freud's unconscious phantasy
work, triggered by hysteric resistance, so that the guilt Freud articulates in
the dream is a version of his knowing that he must renounce this desirable
body, on the carnal level, while the exculpation he performs allows him to
regain possession on a symbolic level. By virtue of the symbolic replacement
that interpretation affords, according to Anzieu, Freud can distance himself
from the unconscious (at whose navel he finds the forbidden, desirable
mother), even as he can establish its existence and enjoy its meaning. Two
processes fall by the wayside, however, as Anzieu semantically fixes what
Freud so astutely and so self-critically leaves indeterminate: the persistence
of the hysteric's pain—her insistence that her complaint be heard—and the
associations of vulnerability and fallibility this so poignantly evoked in
Freud. Because these disturbances to any integrative story remain, they call
forth in him a desire to cover this wound with a protective screen, namely
the symbolic formula that makes it impossible to reduce the dream to a
semantic encoding or to directly articulate real pain of traumatic impact
from which symbols and images shield the dreamer.

IV

Jacques Lacan, as part of his 1954–1955 seminar on the developmental stages in ego formation, traces the theme of disempowerment unfolding in the dream of Irma's injection and comes up with a reversal of her formulaic narrative sentence. The concept of wish fulfillment as the goal of all dream work does not mean the recuperation of the narcissistically wounded ego for him, but rather the decentering of the subject in relation to the ego. Lacan does not simply focus on the dream's biographical configurations of triads but rather works these into the context of the two-part structure of the dream plot. While the first scene stages the dreamer's attempt to imagine the symbol, and put symbolic discourse into a figurative form (the dream representation), the second scene stages the dreamer's attempt to symbolize the image, or to *interpret* the dream (Lucan 1978, 184). Interested in this double transformation, Lacan concentrates on the two moments when each plot sequence seems to be completed and can be broken off.[4]

The first of these culminations occurs at the end of Freud's dialogue with Irma, when the horrific vision of the scabs inside her throat forces him to confront a visualization of trauma. Lacan calls this moment the horrible discovery of the flesh one never sees, the ground of all things, the underside of the face, its reverse, the flesh that in its shapeless, vulnerable state provokes anxiety. This moment of extimacy (rendering what is profoundly intimate in an external representation), produces an identification with anxiety, a revelation of human mutability and decay: "You are this, which is the farthest away from you, which is the most formless" (Lacan 1978, 186). In other words, the grayish-white scabs reveal the traumatic impact of the real in what is least penetrable without mediation, the essential object, no longer something concrete but rather a structural moment before which all language comes to a halt and all categories fail, "the object of anxiety par excellence" (196). For Lacan, the fact that the dialogue between Irma and Freud ends with this horrific vision does not simply silence Irma. Far from confirming the ego of the analyst-dreamer, it signals a blow to his ambition as an analyst, to the sense of his ego's plenitude and intactness, a narcissistic injury that harks back to the sense of vulnerability evoked by Irma's resistance and described in the preamble.

Asking himself (as Erikson had) why Freud, faced with such a traumatic vision, doesn't wake up, Lacan argues that the continuation of the dream indicates a shift in register. The second scene of the dream no longer revolves around the ego Freud, but rather around a paternal figure of authority. Thus, whereas the first scene culminates in the revelation by a female triad— the composite figure of Irma—in a final reference quite simply of death (188), the second stages the rivalry of three brothers (Freud, Otto, Leopold) in relation to an imaginary father, Dr. M., who functions intact as represen-

tative of paternal law. For Lacan, this second triad is not an index for death
(i.e., for the traumatic knowledge that emerges from the real and whose
signifier is the mutable flesh inside the hysteric's mouth). Instead, it stands in
for judicial speech uttered under the aegis of symbolic law (i.e., for the question of justice and injustice: "Am I conscientious or guilty of a misde-
meanor?"), for truth and its dissimulations, for the solution to an enigma
and a complaint. Pitting two oracular messages against each other—the
traumatic revelation of mutability and the symbolic formula for trimethylamine—Lacan translates Freud's inaugural dream into a narrative sentence.
The dream's first point of culmination occurs once the ego is faced with a
horrific image, and the second occurs with the appearance of the written
formula, which like the Babylonian Menetekel is a performative figure of
warning that lacks any specific semantic content, offering the significant answer to what makes a dream meaningful. Highlighting a different dimension
of the dream's self-reflexivity, Lacan locates the significance of the dream in
its symbolic enunciation: "There is no other word, no other solution to your
problem but the word itself" (190).

Like Rohde-Dachser, Lacan sees this dream as the inauguration of psychoanalysis because it performs the sentence to which Freud will reduce analytic practice, "Where id was, there ego shall be." He emphasizes, however,
that to recognize oneself as being a subject of the unconscious, one's ego
must do more than traverse the experience of a traumatic impact of vulnerability in the face of death. Arriving at an appropriation of the unconscious,
which after all is the aim of analysis, the subject fades before symbolic law.
By not waking up, and instead moving seamlessly from a dialogue with a
representative of death to making an appeal to a representative of paternal
authority, Freud performs this subjection to the symbolic order. There is no
longer a Freud who can say "I," Lacan claims: only the symbolic father who
speaks for him and an unidentified other speaker who brings forth the uncanny formula from some unknown realm, more impenetrable than Irma's
open mouth because it remains utterly unrepresented by the dream. For
Lacan, then, the significant function of this inaugural dream work is that it
produces a narrative representation of the unconscious, revealing its location in the subject, of the subject, and yet also beyond it. The seminal value
of the dream resides not in the biographical material it converts, but rather
in its performing a search for *meaning*. Though for Lacan the dream also
revolves around parturition, he argues that the scenario at stake illustrates
how the subject of the unconscious comes into existence only when it recognizes itself in relation to a symbolic formula.

Concerned with the way the two scenes mirror each other, Lacan suggests
that the dream's first scene illustrates the division of the object of hermeneutic desire into a triadic feminine figure, whereas the second scene illustrates
the spectral decomposition of the ego into a series of self-representations.
In other words, the first scene stages the ego in relation to its desired object.
Trauma ensues once the other—the hysteric from whom the analyst desires

a confirmation for his solution—reveals itself not only to be irrevocably separate and noncompliant, but also inevitably fallible. In so doing the other disappoints precisely the sense of plenitude the imaginary relation is meant to afford. Without directly discussing how the navel that Freud invokes in the footnote relates to the image of Irma's open mouth, Lacan decodes this dream image of a female aperture as a trope for the abyss from which all life emerges, which promises or threatens to engulf the ego with its unbearable proximity and to which all life returns. He thereby presents Irma's open mouth precisely in the terms that mythopoetic texts have used to discuss the cleft at the center of the temple of Gaia, adorned and shielded by the omphalos.

The implication, of course, is that the imaginary relation leads ultimately to anxiety. Once the ego penetrates the surface of its desired object, it finds a reflection of its own vulnerability before the enjoyment of a destructively excessive presence, which Lacan designates as *jouissance*, as well as before death. From this profoundly wounding vision of what is at the navel of the imaginary, the ego is released by entering into a symbolic relation with the otherness. The narcissistic ego is replaced by a headless subject of the unconscious, refracted and multiplied, no longer in possession of an ego. Yet this very disempowerment is also a moment of empowerment, for the entrance into a symbolic relation to the world also alleviates the subject from its imaginary relations to the world, which are tragic not only because they frustrate the sense of wholeness but also because their final referent is death. Lacan agrees with Freud that the wish fulfillment performed by the dream revolves around the question of exculpation and self-vindication, but for him guilt is not effaced by being transferred to other figures in the dream (to Otto and to Irma). Rather, with a traumatic kernel at the navel of Freud's dream representation, a discourse devoid of meaning enters the game, reassuringly conclusive and consistent. The message the dream broadcasts to the dreamer and any interpretors of this symptom thus reads "the creator is someone greater than myself. It is my unconscious, it is that word which speaks for me, beyond myself." Though Lacan insists on the authority of this message, I maintain that the meaning of the dream he posits, despite its being a structural one devoid of biographically encoded semantic content, is a reassuring solution because it offers yet another protective fiction to shield from its counterpart, the emergence of the real within Irma's throat. Still, the resistance of the hysteric and the somatization of her persisting pain, though inaugurating the discovery of the meaning of dreams, because their traumatic revelation engender the replacement of imaginary psychic processes by symbolic ones, are once again excluded not only from the final moment of the dream plot but also from the interpretive narrative.

Copjec's defense of Lacan's reading focuses precisely on what he elides, namely, that what is excluded from the symbolic may persist, nevertheless, as an enjoyment (*jouissance*) where knowledge fails. While the interpretive narrative Lacan develops tells the story of how the proper response to the

anxiety elicited by an encounter with the object (a) (the remainder or trace
of the real configured in the grayish-white scabs) is to take flight into the
symbolic "which shields us from the terrifying real" (Copjec 1994, 120),
this symbolic salvation of the subject, he astutely notes, "must include the
negation of what it is not," must include this surplus element (121). To
exclude the real, declaring this act of sublimation to be the inaugural gesture
of symbolic processes, one must also *declare* the real as absented and forbidden, existing as an impossibility. The law, for example, positioned as the
apotropaic shield against the real, can support the avoidance of this traumatic point only by acknowledging that its authority is coterminous with its
impotence. Supporting a desire not to know anything about the real always
also implies the failure to say the real. Copjec thus points to a terminological
condundrum within Lacan's interpretation. The object (a), the scabs inside
Irma's mouth, mark both the emergence of the real and the symbolic's
avoidance of this traumatic point, the absence of the real. In her critique
Copjec insists that the culmination of the dream's first scene cannot be effaced from the end of the second scene. Psychoanalysis can claim to found
itself on the unconscious and on the desire of woman, Copjec concludes,
because instead of fleeing the real Freud duplicitously holds on to it. Because
he so rigorously registers the inaccessibility of the real at the navel of his
unconscious dream representation and of the hysteric's desire—refusing to
interpret this traumatic impact—he also maintains its impact. Fleeing the
real through recourse to symbolic sublimation means acknowledging that
this protective fiction is secured only by negating what it shields from, or
through its failure to be completely consistent within itself. Affirming this
traumatic impression, Copjec concludes, "What Freud confronts in his moment of anxiety is a gap in symbolic reality, a point that interpretation . . .
cannot bridge. In response, he does not bridge it; he records its unbridgeabil-
ity and in this way circumscribes it" (126). Though she does not directly
address how an unbridgeable gap is connected with the navel as a signifier
for the circumscribed trace of a cut, her insistence on the trace of the real
within the symbolic allows me to return to Freud's pregnant footnote.

V

I have chosen two final rereadings of the inaugural dream of psychoanalysis
because they focus so explicitly on the "navel of the dream," this strange
distributional detail. Shoshana Felman (1985) investigates the connection
between Freud's construction of femininity, the question of female desire,
and analytic interpretation. She starts with the fact that at the end of his life
Freud admitted his failure at answering the question, "What does woman
want?" Following Paul de Man, she explores the way Irma's composite
body and the footnote it elicits mark the representational failure from which
a text, narrating the impossibility of its own reading, still demands to be

read. Felman sees at stake the double birth performed by the dream of Irma's injection, not only producing a formula to answer the question of what a dream means, but also introducing the fact that something remains *answerless*. Though using different terminology, she traces a figure not unlike the one Copjec presents, offering another narrative about how any symbolic negation of the real contains traces of what it seeks to avoid.

Regarding the feminist intervention, Felman concentrates on a seminal moment when an argument is broken off, namely the footnote in which Freud explains, "If I had pursued my comparison between the three women, it would have taken me far afield. There is at least one spot (*Stelle*) in every dream at which it is unplumbable—a navel, as it were, that is its point of contact with the unknown" (Freud 1900–1901, 111). Given that in her reading the dream "is about female *resistance*, and about *female complaint*," this navel comes to function as the rhetorical figure for failure at the base not only of all dream work but also of Freud's interpretive system. Her reading revolves about the following conundrum. Freud is concerned with Irma's resistance to his solution, made manifest in the persistence of her pain, because it points to a moment of failure within his analytic system. At the same time, the entire dream interpretation revolves around this moment of failure. In other words, the dreaming and interpreting Freud, who seeks closure to the hysteric's much ado about nothing willingly refuses to pursue a question; this missed chance subverts all answers he subsequently brings forth, he himself hysterically producing a representational site (*Stelle*) that demarcates nothing but about which his overdetermined interpretations make much ado. As Felman suggests, once his dream narrative has been turned into an interpretive sentence that seeks to offer a solution to the complaint of the hysteric, in the same gesture it also constructs her as "unknown, unreadable, misunderstood, miscured, dissatisfied," so that the dream not only performs the dreamer's wish fulfillment but also places it in relation to his hysteric claimant. Putting closure on one question (that of the dreamer's desire) invariably opens another, for to a feminist reader such as Felman the dream seems to ask, "Is there a difference between female wish fulfillment and male wish fulfilling fantasies of female wish fulfillment?" (62)

Felman locates precisely this difference between masculine and feminine desire at the navel of Freud's dream, finding a connecting point between Freud's effort at giving birth to a universally true formula for the meaning of dreams and Martha Freud's unacknowledged pregnancy. In choosing the navel as the best trope to designate the dream's resistance to understanding, Freud obliquely articulates the real somatic sign on the belly of his pregnant wife, indeed proleptically refers to the same mark on the body of their unborn child. His choice of trope indicates a counterdirectional rhetorical gesture, signifying by analogy "the disconnection and the connection between a maternal body giving birth and a newborn child," transposed onto the register of knowledge to embody how the dream is "*tied up* with the unknown and disconnected from its knowledge, *disconnected* from the knowledge of its own begetting" (63). Within the terminology I am seeking to establish, the dream is the umbilical cord to an impenetrable point in the unconscious, at whose visible end we find an omphalic knot of hysteric differentiality with respect to any given definition of this complaint. For the hysteric invokes in her interpellator the desire to discover her identity, even as she frustrates such a project by her protean symptoms that point instead to the inexhaustibility and unaccountability of her difference from and within the symbolic.

As Felman persuasively argues, the hysteric's resistance enacts not only the analogy between the dream and feminine identity but also Freud's own identification with hysteria. The analogy between the hysteric's resistance to an analytic solution (embodied by Irma's complaint and the knot of women configured within her body) and the dream's resistance to coherent and complete interpretation (the navel of the dream) thus emerges as a signifying structure of difference as seminal to this inaugural dream as the triadic formulas presented by Anzieu and Forrester. In other words, the same gesture that allows Freud to discover the principle of wish fulfillment, meant to efface the threat of feminine difference and, to negate the hysteric's complaint within the symbolic formula that ends the dream, allows him also to discover the navel of the dream, subverting all conclusive interpretive formulas and inscribing precisely the "pregnancy of the difference which its wish fulfillment narcissistically erases" (1985, 64). At issue for Felman is whether there is a way to articulate this point of resistance, of narrative fallibility, without explaining it away. Can the resistance be spotlighted without subsuming it by what is known—preserved, I would add, omphalically, as an impenetrable site within the symbolic, as the aporia of representing negation?

This radical, unknown is given voice, according to Felman, in the three moments of resistance knotted at the navel of Freud's dream: the silenced navel of Freud's pregnant wife, the painful knot in Irma's throat, and the metaphorical navel. Speaking for the "unaccountability of female difference," condensing the hysteric's nonacceptance of the analyst's solution and her pain at the issue of maternity and female sexuality, this narrative knot comes to stand for analytic parturition. It signifies Freud's discovery "that resistance is a textual knot, a nodal point of unknown significance . . . that the psychoanalytic dialogue is a new way of reading and working with, the pregnancy of this unknown and the fecundity of this resistance" (Felman 1985, 66). The navel of the dream thus traces the countermovement of connection and disconnection, for in rhetorically addressing a site and meaning he does not command, Freud can construct a narrative of integration over a distributional detail that "separates as much as it unites," subverting the very desire for solution his dream also fulfills. Were he to follow what would lead "far afield," the navel of the dream would lead him both to the differentiality of pain spoken by the body and to the unspeakability of sexual difference—to the physical gap in speech. And it is precisely this gap in language, thus my own argument, that the hysteric endlessly performs, knotting together in the message her symptom broadcasts to the interpellating analyst the two resistances at stake in this inaugural specimen dream: a point of fallibility in any representation and its interpretation, on the one hand, with the persistence of physical pain on the other. Both are exterior and irreducible to the very interpretive narrative they engender and sustain, namely, to the analyst's desire to patch the wound inflicted on him by this resistance, revealing somatic and representational vulnerability. The seminal aporia arising from the dream is the insight brought into the limits of Freud's interpretive system, even as this system, by converting her complaint into a symbolic formula, tries to silence the resistance and subversion the hysteric performs. Rewriting Freud's concluding interpretive sentence—that the significance of every dream resides in its offering a meaningful, albeit encoded, message of psychic wish fulfillment—the structural sentence Felman gleans from the dream of Irma's injection is that "in every theory, interpretation or conscious meaning there is a disconnection" (67).

We have seen that Forrester connects the subversive moment Freud introduces into his discourse by using a figure of the resistant female who insists on remaining silent or elusive to avoid a recognition of mortality. His reading suggests that once this revelation has been displaced onto a female Other, the traumatic knowledge of vulnerability can be circumvented. Felman, emphasizing that "the navel is a knot that is cut" and suggesting that its metaphorical value for Freud lies in its sanction of a theoretic blindness ("to sever what cannot be disentangled"), seeks to align Freud's navel of the dream with de Man's conviction that to read, and to know is to forget, erase, deface, or repeat. Irma's silence, far from confirming the male analyst, instead affirms the process of failure written into any interpretation reading the hysteric's persistent pain that belatedly bespeaks the impact of trauma. Felman thus understands the uncanny emergence of the formula at the end of the dream in the sense of de Man's redefinition of prosopopeia, "by which the dead are made to have a face and a voice which tells the allegory of their demise and allows us to apostrophize them in our turn" (de Man 1984, 122).

Perhaps what makes this dream so fascinating is that ultimately it remains indeterminable who is defaced and who reanimated in this merry-go-round of effacing replacements and silenced voices: Who disappears? Irma? Freud? Both? Or neither? And what remains? The empowered masculine ego or the silenced feminine difference? The negated real or the unanswered unconscious? Is the uncanny shadow to the strange formula, arising out of nowhere at the dream's end, perhaps also the hybrid hystericized body of Irma-in-Freud? These questions must remain unanswered. Yet they clearly relate to the navel as the knotted scar of a cut that also commemorates something lost at birth: the prenatal mother, her body dead, forgotten, unfathomable, yet persisting as a memory trace. In resorting to the metaphorical navel of a dream, Freud apostrophizes this lost maternal body and the unbearable plenitude it so seductively and so threateningly recalls; he turns the vulnerable spot in his representation into a figure of the unfathomable. He constructs a narrative, explicitly acknowledging that his interpretation was not carried far enough because, he insists, the concealed meaning would take one far afield. However, if the trope navel of the dream thus articulates mortality by elision, calling it out as that which resists interpretation, it does so in the gesture of a countermovement. It knots together and cuts off the very dream material that could articulate an anxiety about death, much as Freud ultimately disconnects all the strands that deal with fatal illnesses from his narrative interpretation.

Using as his interpretive point of departure, Freud's proposition that every dream reveals itself as a meaningful structure, Samuel Weber presents the dream of Irma's injection as his speciman example of the way analysis "leads away from the known toward the unknown, away from elucidation (*Aufklärung*) to the murky realm of hypothesis and supposition (*Annahmen*)" (1982, 71). For Weber some speculation is always afoot within any interpretation of a dream and functioning as its uncanny internal difference, given that each dream is a "dissimulating distortion" that by definition never offers a transparent presentation of its meaning. The problem with any interpretation of dreams being not that there is too little, but rather too much meaning, a dream representation is always overdetermined in meaning, so the analyst always faces the problem of determining what connection of distributional details is right to pursue. Speculation is thus written into any decision about whether pursuing a question would lead far afield or whether material brought up by a dream should be truncated.

Weber also focuses on the navel of a dream to explore the mutual implication of interpretation and speculation, analyzing, however, Freud's second mention of this disturbing detail:

> There is often a passage (*Stelle*) in even the most thoroughly interpreted dream which has to be left obscure (*im Dunkel*); this is because we become aware during the work of interpretation that at this point there is (*anhebt*) a tangle of dream-thoughts which cannot be unravelled and which moreover adds nothing to our knowledge of the content of the dream. This is the dream's navel, the spot where it reaches down into the unknown (*dem Unerkannten aufsitzt*). The dream-thoughts to which we are led by interpretation cannot, from the nature of things, have any definite endings; they are bound to branch out in every direction into the intricate network (*netzartige Verstrickung*) of our world of thought. It is at some point where this meshwork is particularly close that the dream-wish grows up (*erhebt sich*), like a mushroom out of its mycelium. (1900–01, 525)

That Freud designs the topographical structure of the dream in such a manner that it becomes impossible to designate a transcendental point of origin from which an interpretation can emerge is crucial for Weber. Dream work instead contains a shadowy place at its navel, that defies (even as it provokes) interpretation, rendering any analytic narrative uncertain. Even more

seminal for Weber, however, is that the term *navel* contains its own deconstructive moment. On the one hand, the term sounds reassuring because it
refers to the most primordial mark on the body, one that carries a sense of
continuity, generation, and origin and recalls the site of connection to one's
maternal origins. On the other hand, this metaphor signifies "the site of a
trace and of a separation, but also of a knot" (1982, 76). Freud's metaphorical language of the "intricate network," and "tangle" and his insistence that dream thoughts can have "no endings," suggests that the dream-
navel, far from spreading into the reassuring solidity of a tree, seems to
mushroom into a disquieting snare or a trap: "The consoling inexhaustibility of infinite ramification is overshadowed by the unsettling entanglement
in a familiarity that is no longer quite as familiar as it seemed" (77). In other
words, as I have argued in relation to a primal scene of trauma, the point of
any dream's origin, known or unknown, is not a fixed place but rather a site
marked by the movement of difference. This navel of the dream, as it straddles the unknown or rises above the rest of the dream material, is a turning
point in the analytic narrative precisely because interpretation here "reaches
its enabling limit" and "threatens to get out of hand" (77).

Yet Weber goes on to deconstruct the very notion of a fixed, determinable
site of origin. The navel of the dream—where the dream wish grows up
like a mushroom out of its mycelium—is far from marking the spot where
an interpretation must stop. Instead it marks the absence of any determinable point of engendering. Given that the dream wish antedates the dream
itself and (like any narrative of trauma) can be formulated only belatedly,
the essence of the dream with its navel as metaphor "is the movement
of dislocation to which that thought, that wish, is submitted in and through
the dream-work" (77). It is neither central, empty, nor simply an abyss;
rather it vexes the notion of a point of origin because it *straddles* the unknown. The navel of the dream "seems curiously full, oversaturated, and if
it presents difficulties to our understanding, it is because it contains too
much rather than too little" (80). In Weber's discussion the navel emerges
not only to mark a gap but also a site of disturbingly abundant presence,
recalling for me the double function of the navel as a knotted scar. Signifying
a wound to the newborn, it refers also to the separation from the overwhelming plenitude of the prenatal maternal body, the scar knotting together the vulnerability induced by loss and the empowerment induced by
the introduction of differentiation and separation from this site of abundant
traumatic jouissance.

Weber ends his discussion by unpacking semantic layers from within the
second metaphor, which Freud embedded in the navel of the dream, comparing the dream work to a mushroom rising out of its mycelium. Whereas the
mycelium is defined as "the vegetative part of the thallus of fungi," this
thallus in turn is defined as "a vegetable structure without vascular tissue, in
which there is no differentiation into stem and leaves, and from which true
roots are absent" (Weber, 81).[5] Contrasting the thallus with Freud's use of

phallus, Weber concludes "If the dream-wish erects itself, phallic-like, out of the mycelium," then its navel "cannot be reduced to a question of the phallus," which is to say, to "the split or absent center of a subject, for one simple reason: the thallus." For, as Weber insists, "The essence of this curious figure can be articulated only in negations—no differentiation, without vascular tissue, absent roots" (81). Felman had built her argument on the omission of Martha's pregnancy from Freud's footnote, and Weber also rests his interpretation on an oversight, namely the fact that Freud finishes his description of the mycelium without mentioning the thallus. To do so would have led Freud's aim of a conclusive definition of dream work in a different direction, much as discussing Jocaste's dead body within the story of Oedipus or unraveling the connection between the three figures within Irma would have led him far astray from the formula he sought to prove. The metaphor of the thallus would have led to a narrative about the foundation of any dream wish being defined by an absence of true roots. Such a story would distort and distend, dislocate and disfigure in a far more radical way than the notion of an abyss, an unplumbable center Freud designates as the limit of any interpretation. With a last look at Freud's imagery, Weber comments that the German verb *aufsitzen* means both to sit atop or to straddle something and to be taken in or duped by something or someone. Within Freud's second description of the navel of the dream, then, we find a curious image of parturition. The navel of the dream marking the end of the umbilical cord that reaches down into the unknown and impenetrable area of the unconscious, is where any attempt at representation, be this through dream work or interpretation, is always somewhat deluded by the unconsious it seeks to convert. At the other end of this umbilical cord we find the thallus, so that the duping that occurs therefore emerges from an un-differentiated structure, a matrix without roots.[6] From this imagery Weber concludes that Freud's conception of interpretation "originates and ends in a kind of calculated deception: in a posture necessarily, and structurally, an imposture, and perhaps also an imposition" (82).

Embellishing Weber's discussion, we can once more locate in the navel of the dream the resilient and distressing point of identification between Freud and his hysteric patient. His dream, a symptomatic conversion of his unconscious thoughts, imitates the dual strategy of the hysteric's complaint, given that this system provokes his fantasy of reaching the enabling limit of his analytic ability, only to frustrate his authority. The analogy is this: If Freud is taken in by his hysteric's dissimulation, so too his dream representation is taken in (*aufsitzen*) by the unconscious. And if the hysteric's symptoms dissimulate by performing much ado about nothing, so too the navel of Freud's dream presents an overdetermined tangle of material knotted together over a hidden structure without roots. Like the hysteric, who calls forth the desire for an analytic solution, Freud's interpretation finds itself face-to-face with its own hysterical strategy, the calculated deception it cannot avoid.

I return one last time to the footnote in Freud's text involving the navel of the dream, this time to focus on the way it negotiates between Freud's effort to construct an integrated self-representation and his experience of the vulnerability of such a construction. His experiencing of vulnerability is induced by the revelation of his fallibility as an analyst (the complaint coming out of Irma's mouth) and his impotence in the face of mortality (the traces of the real inside Irma's mouth). As an interjection between two sentences, this interpretive footnote knots and dissevers what is syntactically combined in the dream narrative, namely the two images of the scar that remains after a wound: the navel and the scabs. The first of these markings, the trope navel of the dream, refers to Freud's recognition of the psychic material that eludes and resists any interpretive closure. The second marking, the scabs, refers to Freud's vulnerability before the possibility of fatal disturbances (Irma's pain is an index of his own heart condition). Furthermore, both the navel and the scabs refer to an entering of and being resisted by the dark interior realms of the female body. The footnote itself, therefore, seems to heal by its displacement: it puts closure on one moment of analytic failure by converting it into metaphor, which in turn signifies the necessary curtailment of the interpretive abilities of the analyst.

Freud's rhetorical displacement is particularly salient, I want to argue, because the insertion of the footnote forecloses what it also foreshadows. It cuts off the very message it presages, namely, the alliance between an *unplumbable spot* leading *far afield* and *reaching down into the unknown*, and the grayish-white spots that offer themselves with horrific abundance to Freud's gaze as he penetrates Irma's oral cavity, leading him down into the unknown of the body, far afield from hysteria as the female complaint about sexual dissatisfaction and into a discussion of hysteria as a complaint that broadcasts the message of body mutability and vulnerability. In other words, in his interpretive story Freud jettisons off the thematic storey that is specularly at least the correlative of the metaphorical navel of the dream, or the whitish-gray scabs. This narrative is about resistance, a woman not readily accepting a solution to her complaint, a moment in a dream that eludes interpretation; these scabs mark a resistance on Freud's part that allows him to evade the question of mortality as the final point of reference of any dream interpretation. By insisting that to decode the connection between the three women would lead far afield, Freud foreshadows the other act of cutting off significant strands of the dream. The footnote's omission anticipates his silencing those parts he admits "are not so obviously connected with my exculpation from Irma's illness"; that is, all indices to body ailments and the inevitable mortality of human existence; signposts of those vulnerable points in the knot of identity that thwart without entirely undoing connectedness.

By focusing on the metaphorical navel of the dream, and on the white scabs as the visual realization of a somatic navel, we confront not only the theoretical notion of a limit to any interpretation (what must be left obscure

because it can't be unraveled) but also what pierces a coherent and integrated narrative about how rhetoric replacement can produce exculpation—
and the integrated self-representation of Freud resulting from it. This dream
articulates the discursive sentence that what pierces any recuperative gesture
of narration is mortality as the final and urgent referent not only of all body
disorders but also of all systems of representation. For the scabs indicate the
wounding to any sense of plenitude or infallibility that the disorder of the
body might recall. By jettisoning these scabs from his narrative Freud
rhetorically stages their actual function in his dream. As I have discussed,
one could interpret Irma's open mouth as a dream representation of the
limbo that leads to what Lacan calls the real, with the whitish-gray scabs
representing the *object (a)*, a trace that Žižek (in a more visual and less formulaic sense) calls the blot or stain of traumatic jouissance.

I would argue that the navel of the dream—the unique point of connectedness, the knotted site of feminine difference and hysteric complaint, a descriptive, impenetrable site—provokes a countermovement. Irma, a representational knot (condensation) of three other women signifying the enigma
of Woman, draws the text in one direction; the scabs, symptom for a body
knot and signifying mutability, draw the text in the opposite direction. The
footnote self-reflexively marks the spot of the representation of representation. The double navel (the metaphorical navel of the dream and the representation of the white scabs) mediates between symbolic sublimation and
the return of the nonsymbolized real, the jouissance Montrelay relates to the
traumatic, excessive presence of the maternal body of plenitude. The symbolic sublimation occurs as a narrative interpretation transforms the lack of
a signifier into a signifier of lack (hence, the designation navel of the dream
marking the site that must remain obscure, lacking not only transparency
but also any fixed point of origin). The nonsymbolized real appears in the
guise of a traumatic object stain, the sight of the white scabs in Irma's throat;
it is omphalic because despite these blots' appear in Freud's dream representation, he can find no interpretation for them other than encrypting them in
a paradigm he calls "professional conscientiousness."[7]

In my reading, the counter movement of the navel and scabs negotiates
the articulation of real mutability within symbolic representation. While the
figural knot (the navel) points to how a subject connects various representations, the somatic knot (the scabs), points to how the body makes all representation vulnerable. In other words, the navel and scabs not only give voice
to death, which, as de Man's prosopopeia suggests, underlies the commemorative gesture, but also point to the traumatic knowledge of vulnerability,
which interpretation fails to penetrate but still draws upon for its urgency.
To read this counterdirectional moment—navel and scabs—as a metarepresentation illustrates precisely the double gesture through which mortality
and representation are mutually implicated. The subject, knotting together
various cultural codes, not only has to subject itself to symbolic laws and the
shift from an imaginary to a symbolic relation to the world (under the aus-

pices of a privileged, though empty, master signifier), the formula at the end of the dream arising out of nowhere. Rather, the dream of Irma's injection also commemorates another form of fading. It is that the knotted subject is also subject to the real law of mutability; the navel points not only to the inevitability of mortality but also to the fact that any narrative that gives a coherent explanation of this constitutive vulnerability of the human subject is a necessarily protective fiction. At the navel of Freud's interpretation, emerging from its rootless thallus and coming together in its omphalos, one can, then, locate a knot of counterdirectional tendencies. They are the revelation of impotence, evoking the desire to reassert an integrated notion of connectedness; the resistance of an enigma, encroaching on the subject and on the translation of an unanswerable question into a trope for representational narrative; analytic failure and exculpation; and symbolic sublimation as it diffuses the threat of the traumatic real and the persistence of a trace of this negated knowledge.

At this point we should recall that Freud (1915) uses the concept *Vorstellungs-Repräsentanz* (ideational representation, as distinct from affect) to designate the drive's representative within the psychic apparatus. The relation of the somatic to the psychic is that of the drive to its representation. The somatic drive can be repressed and thus inscribed in the unconscious only insofar as it is fixed onto a representation. This is a moment of severing a knot resembling the structure of the production of the navel. As Freud writes, "We have reason to assume that there is a primal repression, a first phase of repression, which consists in the psychical representative of the drive being denied entrance into the conscious. With this a fixation is established; the representative in question persists unaltered from then onwards and the instinct remains attached to it"(Freud 1915, 148). Žižek argues that the ideational representation does not so much stand in for drives as it signifies what the representational field necessarily excludes; it functions as a metarepresentation because it represents the primordially repressed or real by virtue of belated conversion, displacement and dislocation. He sketches two modalities for the way the primordially repressed real returns into the representational field in the guise of an outstanding surplus element. On the one hand, the object (a) is a "stain of the Real, a detail which sticks out from the frame of symbolic reality"; on the other hand, the *phallus* is "master" or "surplus signifier." To distinguish these two modalities he describes the first as a surplus of the real over the symbolic and the second as a surplus of the symbolic over reality. Applying this view to the dream of Irma's injection, one might say that the scabs inside Irma's mouth function as the surplus of the real over the symbolic, whereas her composite figure, who condenses several female figures into one representation only to be jettisoned from the interpretive narrative and replaced by the trope navel in the footnote, functions as the surplus of the symbolic over reality. The surplus symbolic—in Freud's text the navel of the dream—can be read as a symptom signifying the return of the repressed. Žižek writes of it, "What is excluded from reality reappears as a signifying trace on the very screen through which we observe reality" (1992, 238). The surplus real—in Freud's text the scabs—signifies the return, in the guise of a traumatic object stain, of what remains unsublimated within the symbolic.

Žižek writes of these two modalities, "*Vorstellungs-Repräsentanz* designates a signifier which fills out the void of the excluded representation, whereas a psychotic stain is a representation which fills out a hole in the Symbolic, giving body to the 'unspeakable'" (239). In the counterdirectional movement around Freud's dream navel, sublimation tames the real, integrates distributional elements, and turns the lack of a signifier (site where words fail in the dream) into a signifier for lack (the trope navel of the dream). Žižek likens sublimation, to a "primordial metaphor": functioning as a constitutive exclusion it translates a stain that cannot be symbolized into an empty signifier, the formula at the end of the dream representation. It likewise translates the interpretive sentence Freud (and any critic after him) ultimately brings forth at the end of each reading. At the same time, a remainder of this excluded real eludes the significatory process; it persists as a nonsymbolized stain to induce moments of desublimation, omphalic because as a trace they enjoy the trace of the traumatic kernal of the real. While the act of sublimation allows the subject to knot itself into an integrated self-representation, the stain of this traumatic knowledge insistently points to the vulnerability of this construction. It is precisely this double gesture—a severing that leaves a commemorative scar—that the navel's anatomy so brilliantly materializes. For the navel commemorates the primordial maternal body, reminding us of the loss of overabundant presence and presaging our demise.

My own analytic point is this: Freud's dream of Irma's injection circles around or encompasses that a navel is both indeterminate and overdetermined, connecting these two modalities of lack. In Freud's dream transcription and its interpretation we have sublimation on the one hand, namely, his metaphorical navel of the dream and his interpretive narrative, which stand in as representatives for an excluded, unnameable representation. And we have indexes of mortality, on the other hand, signifying the finitude where words fail, the facticity grounding life. These moments of desublimation are obliquely represented in Freud's dream by the white scabs visible in the void inside Irma's throat. The moment I want to call omphalic is precisely the counterdirectional gesture that knots symbolic death, incurred by any troping to or narration of real mutability, even as the knotting is also a form of severing, leaving the thallus—the traumatic kernel—without any roots, point of origin, direct representation, accounted for but nevertheless submerged. Begetting and preserving psychic and cultural representations, the gesture negotiates between the *surplus signifier* (the phallic master signifier for the symbolic function), and the object (a) (the signifier for the traumatic stain). In contrast to Freud's trope navel of the dream, the omphalos not only marks the point where interpretation fails, but also knots this fallibility with an encroachment of traumatic impact into the field of representation and with the desire. It constructs a coherent self-representation (Freud's autobiographical impetus) and produces a consistent, interpretive narrative (Freud's theory on the significance of dream work). The omphalos thus works as the troubled and troubling interface between Freud's recuperative trope and the horrific revelation inside Irma's throat; it broadcasts to the subject, knotted together over these two forces, that the only ethical choice resides in alternating between protective fictions of symbolic salvation and the recognition of human vulnerability. Neither fully relies on the fallacy of symbolic coherence but neither fully gives in to an enjoyment of traumatic plenitude.

VI

To illustrate a narrative knotting of the traumatic knowledge of death with the protective fiction of a consistent self-image I turn to one last rereading of Freud's dream of Irma's injection. Although *Camera Lucida* is dedicated to Jean-Paul Sartre's work *L'Imaginaire*, I would speculate that structurally and thematically Roland Barthes's investigation into the essential feature distinguishing the photograph from the community of images is haunted by Freud's specimen dream. Like Freud in his dream interpretation, Barthes, who is concerned with the photograph's seeming to evade classification, skillfully performs the point of representational failure at the center of his analysis, so much so that he, too, has provoked many critical readings. As Martin Jay notes, "Few texts have been subjected to as thorough an exegesis. . . . Everything from its title . . . to its dedication . . . has been probed for meaning. No less energy has been spent analyzing the absence of a photo of Barthes himself . . . and even more significantly, the absence of an image of his mother, whose haunting presence in a photograph is described, but not shown" (1993, 451). Furthermore, like Freud, Barthes is concerned with the meaning of a visual representation, and although the image repertoire he explores is a public collection of photographs made by others rather than self-engendered dream images, his focus is on the personal meaning that emerges from a dialogue between spectator and image. For his inquiry he chooses only those few photographs that he feels certain "existed for me" (Barthes 1980, 8). He uses as his guide the knowledge his body has of these photographs, "the attraction certain photographs exerted upon me" in the sense of adventure: "This picture *advenes*, that one doesn't" (19). Thus, although his objects of analysis may be other people, reading photographs leads Barthes as much to the question of self-representation as Freud's reading of dreams ultimately brings him to his inaugural, autobiographical narrative.

Moreover, in discussing portrait photography Barthes raises the theme that most intimately links his inquiry to Freud's specimen dream: the way a photographic image records the traumatic knowledge of death within symbolic codes of connotation. In an early article, "The Photographic Image," Barthes was concerned with the way a photograph links two messages, one without a code (the photographic analogue to a given reality) and the other with a code (the aesthetic or rhetoric conversion of this reality). He had already discussed how the photograph's structural paradox coincides with an ethical one: "When one wants to be 'neutral,' 'objective' one strives to copy reality meticulously, as though the analogical were a factor of resistance against the investment of values. . . . How then can the photography be at once 'objective' and 'invested'" (1961, 19). Demonstrating that the signification of a photograph emerges only thanks to the code of connotation, so that all attempts to read the denotated reality necessarily emerge from and remain within a historical and cultural frame, Barthes claims that if pure denotation exists, it cannot be on the level of neutral, objective language (since this is already coded) but rather on the level of absolutely traumatic images: "Trauma is a suspension of language, a blocking of meaning" (1980, 30). While any traumatic situation can be recoded rhetorically so as to distance, sublimate, and pacify its impact, the truly traumatic photograph does not depend on the certainty that its denoted scene really occurred. Rather, "The traumatic photograph . . . is the photography about which there is nothing to say; the shock-photo is by structure insignificant: no value, no knowledge, at the limit no verbal categorization can have a hold on the process of instituting the signification" (31). The ability to produce a coherent interpretive narration is inversely proportional to the traumatic effect; within the language of hysteria I am proposing, the code of connotation revolves around a significatory nothing.

It is precisely this kernel of traumatic knowledge emanating from the photographic image that Barthes returns to in *Camera Lucida*. Attributing the discontent aroused by the attempt to classify photography to the fact that what the image can mechanically reproduce ad infinitum can occur only once existentially, Barthes argues that the photograph itself bespeaks the contingency of an event or a person, it being but "the weightless, transparent envelope" (1980, 5). The photograph denotes something absolutely particular and singular, "what Lacan calls the Tuché, the Occasion, the Encounter, the Real, in its indefatigable expression" (4). From the start Barthes encounters the "stubbornness of the referent in always being there," in persistently adhering; the referent resists any neat translation into a symbolic encoding, thus drawing his attention away from the level of symbolic connotation. From the start this disturbing referent, somewhat like the hysteric pain Irma so resiliently uses to confront Freud's desire for a symbolic solution, also brings mortality into play. Barthes proceeds to call the referent, the *eidolon* emitted by the photographed object, the *spectrum* because the word not only relates to spectacle but also refers to "that rather terrible thing which is there in every photograph: the return of the dead" (9).

Even as the dead return in any photographic reproduction of what is past and lost, the dialectic of animation and deanimation is, such, however, that the photograph always also mortifies the subject it reproduces by transforming it into an object imitating the subject. When he is photographed Barthes experiences hysteric quasi-altered self-representation, the self shown other than it really is. He writes, moreover, "I invariably suffer from a sensation of inauthenticity, sometimes of imposture" (13). He understands the hysteric's self-effacement before his multifarious roles as a microversion of death: "I am neither subject nor object but a subject who feels he is becoming an object . . . a specter." The hysteric quality of the photograph thus resides in its dual insistence on a referent to the image, whose final denominator is mortality: preserving the dead, commemorating or holding onto a past that will not be abreacted, this photographic referent also presages the demise of the spectator.[8] Barthes recognizes that "what I am seeking in the photography taken of me is Death: Death is the *eidos* of that Photograph" (15).

To return to the analogy of Freud's interpretation of dreams, I want to suggest that even while photographs give pleasure because they seem to satisfy a desire and pose as the figuration of wish fulfillment, they also contain a disturbing detail recalling for the spectator that this image connects to what is excluded from historical and cultural encoding. They evoke the navel of an imaginary umbilical cord harking back to the referent outside representation, the uncoded death where past and future conflate. Like Freud, who faced Irma's hysterical complaint, Barthes finds himself infected by the hysterical duplicity of the photography. He seeks a consistent interpretive narrative that will give a name to photography's essence, a universally applicable formula, yet he recognizes the fallibility of this enterprise since each photograph is essentially "only contingency, singularity, risk" (20). Like the hysteric's complaint, the photograph's image displays the inevitable truth of death against the very symbolic codification it also demands.

Like the dream of Irma's injection, Barthes's text is structured by two scenes separated by a navel, a knotted scar commemorating the wound of parturition, and thus is also about the loss of the maternal body. As I will later show in more detail, the blank page separating the twenty-four sections of part one from the twenty-four sections of part two marks the death of Roland Barthes's mother. While this traumatic event remains unrepresented, the latter part of *Camera Lucida* conjoins Barthes's initial desire to define the fascination certain photographs hold for him, (as a potential source of a universal formula for the meaning of photography) with his work of mourning. His unexpectedly finding a photograph of his now-dead mother taken when she was five years old, leads Barthes to realize that the essence of photography can be expressed in the formulation "this-has-been." At the same time, like Freud's, experiencing Irma's pain at his own body, this photograph allows Barthes to identify with his own vulnerability before death.

Yet it is precisely at (and around) the navel of the photograph and his analytic narrative that Barthes significantly diverges from Freud's interpretive gesture. Indeed, speculating about an analogy between these two texts allows me to surmise that Barthes explores the path Freud believed would lead far afield. Whereas Freud would investigate neither the significance behind the knotting together of at least three women into the figure Irma nor the connetion between this figure and the horrific revelation inside her mouth, Barthes travels far afield from his initial interest in the enjoyment afforded by photographs, instead coming face-to-face with death as the referent of the photographic image. In other words, the traumatic revelation Freud evades, although its theme keeps catching up with him, is what Barthes explicitly confronts as the universal structure of the photographic image. The analogy, however, goes further, for like Freud, Barthes also insists that a certain reticence be retained within this demystificational process. He will not reproduce the image of his mother from which he gleans the essence of the photograph; this suppressed image therefore comes to function in exactly the manner Freud discusses for the navel of the dream. Within Barthes's text the absent image marks the spot where a figurative umbilical cord leads the interpreter of photographs to an impenetrable site linked to the lost maternal body (Anzieu), the feminine begetter (Felman), death (Forrester), that final image without representation in his narrative whose absence produces a gap, the blank page that is abundantly full (Weber), and a narrative about the noncodified matrix, the traumatic kernel, from which the subject of representation emerges (Lacan). This marked absence or reticence, this representational nothing, which the second half of Barthes study resiliently and resolutely revolves about, performs an omphalic representation, with a textual presence drawing power from its being an encrypted, nonsublimated and nonsymbolized embodiment of the stubborn referent. Constructed as a knot between a maternal body twice lost, enacting the fluid identity between mother and son in the act of begetting and parturition, this strange detail infiltrates the text in both directions.

The analogy I am proposing is the following. Freud identifies with the hysterical complaint, questioning the infallibility of his solution, broadcasting the message of vulnerability by producing a hysterical symptom of his own, the dream. Interpreting this dream is meant to put closure on both Irma's and his own hysterical complaint, replacing all the ambiguities and inconsistencies it touches upon with a formula. Barthes, for his part, also addresses a symptom that broadcasts the language of hysteria. For in recording events and persons of the past, photography registers history, but the history itself "is hysterical: it is constituted only if we consider it—only if we look at it—and in order to look at it, we must be excluded from it" (1980, 65). The photograph, in other words, speaks a language of hysteria in that it converts an otherwise unavailable event into the rhetoric of images that can become meaningful to the spectator. However, like any hysterical symptom, the image is duplicitous, supporting the desire of the interpellator to appropriate a knowledge that is inaccessible to him—the past—even as it dismantles any authority this knowledge may have. The photograph can render this other event only in a quasi-altered representation, as an image that is by definition *other* than the event it stands in for, a dislocated and belated impression drawing its significance from the associations the spectator brings to it and also changing with every viewing. In other words, borrowing from the pure denotation it also transforms, the photograph envelops the real, traumatic impact of the past within a cultural, historical encoding. Far more self-consciously than Freud, Barthes identifies with the hysterical rhetoric of the photographic image as it wavers between pure denotation, which escapes all signification, and conveying of a protective historical fiction, replacing the lack of language with a cultural encoding.

Barthes introduces two terms for discussing the coexistence of a paradoxical force coming from photographs—that they pull the spectator in the direction of pleasure only to wound this sense of plenitude. Firsthand, he distinguishes a *studium* for each photograph, "a field of cultural interest" (1980, 26) that regulates the viewer's ability to decode the image, calling upon him to take an interest in it and to participate in its signification. The studium makes the photographer's intentions apparent and appeals to the inconsequential taste—the unconcerned desire of the spectator to accept or disapprove with these—and the sympathetic interest of the viewer as a cultural subject. At the same time, because "every photograph is contingent" (34) and thus outside meaning, it is by assuming the mask of the studium that photography can signify: along the lines used to describe hysterical language, "the mask is the meaning." The studium (always coded) engenders a coherent interpretive narration and shields from the contingency inevitably invoked by the denotative referent of the photographic image. Second, Barthes notes a *punctum*, a detail that, like the object (a), shoots out from the frame of symbolic reality to wound the viewer. The punctum performs an unexpected prick, a cut or sting that disturbs the legibility of any culturally connotated meaning, defies reduction to a code, and insists on the pictorial referent (an "analogon" contained in the photograph that points to something prior to codification). In this sense the punctum functions precisely like a somatic navel, harking back to the body the photographic image was cut from, that is, the denoted reality it can recall though never fully recapture. Indeed, Barthes quite explicitly sees the photographic image as an imaginary reference to the maternal body. The studium, untraversed by a disturbing detail, produces a pleasurable photograph, which Barthes relates to the sense of familiarity, of having already been there.[9] Such images awake in him the Mother, he claims, "but never the disturbing Mother" (40). Though Barthes does not explain the relation between the punctum and the maternal body, I would conjecture that it invokes not the phantasy of the maternal body one can return to, but the disturbing revelation that this body is impenetrable, irretrievably lost, and unbearably abundant.

Along with this somatic image, marking a bodily wound, the more rhetoric version of this anatomic scar (as a textual knot that severs as much as it ties together) also comes into play in Barthes's definition of the punctum.

For like the navel of Freud's dream it points to what evades representation—"what the chemical action develops is undevelopable, an essence (or a wound), what cannot be transformed but only repeated under . . . the insistent gaze" (Barthes 1980, 49). It disturbs because it cannot be named; it is a "blind field" (57), an addition to the image, because it is what the spectator adds once he has been pierced. Yet it is also "nonetheless already there" (55) because it emanates from the contingency of the photograph's referent; in short, it is a "subtle beyond" that promises to satisfy desire at the same time that it launches "desire beyond what it permits us to see" (59). For the referentiality that Barthes locates as the essence of the photo—the object we see was there and the subject who saw it was there—is one of mortality. The uncoded past of the depicted object indicates the future of the *spectator's* own demise. In other words, the significatory knot emerging from the end of part one—connecting the studium with the punctum to form the two structuring forces of the photograph—declares meaning to be the product of a hysterical mask. In the guise of a familiar cultural code this hysterical symptom shields from the traumatic impact of contingency, about which one can say nothing, yet which enters the image through its punctum, or its wounding detail.

Barthes ends the first part of his text after having established his critical terms. Returning to my speculation that his narrative structure duplicates Freud's dream of Irma's injection, the first textual scene traces a hedonistic investigation into the pleasure a photograph affords, constructing the spectating subject in relation to imaginary objects (the photos and the pleasure they invoke). Indeed, Barthes self-critically notes the failure of an interpretive project conducted under the aegis of desire: "I had not discovered the nature . . . of Photography. I had to grant that my pleasure was an imperfect mediator, and that a subjectivity reduced to its hedonist project could not recognize the universal" (60). The revelation of the real inside Irma's mouth, which according to Lacan brings about a shift in register in Barthes's text, occurs in the empty page between the two parts of *Camera Lucida*. For in the blank page that separates and connects the two parts of the narrative, we find knotted together all the strands that Irma and Freud's resistance to her came to represent: the maternal body as source of life and threatened by death, which engender an autobiographical narrative along with the author's recognition of his own vulnerability. Only when going through some photographs, after his mother's death does Barthes discover the Winter Garden image, and here he finds not only the "truth of the face" he had loved but also an accurate, "just image" that achieves for him "the impossible science of the unique being" (71).

In other words, he is able to discover the essence of what photography means in this representation of his mother taken before his own conception and birth. Barthes locates the "truth of the image, the reality of its origin" in the way the superimposition of reality and of the past provokes in the willing spectator the emotion that the image is true, just, and accurate precisely by its convincing him that the referent has really existed: "What I see has been there, in this place which extends between infinity and the subject. . . . It has been here, and yet immediately separated; it has been absolutely, irrefutably present, and yet already deferred" (77). The represented object has been real, and for the viewer it is alive; but the reality is of the past, so that in the image what is alive is also already dead, "the corpse is alive, *as corpse*" (79). Although the image certifies that what it represents "has been," the viewer can respond to this referent to human facticity with indifference or with sympathy. At this point in the argument Barthes explicitly equates the punctum with a navel of the photograph by suggesting "a sort of umbilical cord links the body of the photographed thing to my gaze" (81). In performing how the referent stubbornly persists in its claim, the photo links the spectator concretely to the realm of death, not as the protective fiction of a memory narrative, an imaginative reconstitution, but rather as "reality in a past state: at once the past and the real" (82). Barthes's punctum, however, emerges with a Janus face. The detail that pierces a coherent narrative, functioning as the rhetorical navel of Freud's dream and pointing to a blind spot, has a temporal correlative in that the object in the image will die, has already died, and has returned as a dead person. This punctum is also a textual navel; by marking a connection to the past, it articulates the impact of trauma on the biography and on the body of the spectator, the denotative reality of his parturition from the maternal body and his inevitable return to the site of origin. As the spectator empathizes with the punctum, he becomes the reference of every photograph. What wounds him, as the photograph broadcasts its message that something has been, is that this spectral identification unsettles the interpellating spectator in the narcissistic self-assurance of his survival: "Why is it that I am alive *here and now*?"

Thus, in the second textual scene, Barthes responds to the traumatic impact of this event, and, in contrast to Freud, he is unconcerned with fleeing from the imperious sign of his future death; rather, he embraces this wounding revelation. As in the dream of Irma's injection we find a shift from the imaginary to the symbolic register, but relinquishing the narcissistic state of pleasure becomes coterminous with positioning the subject relative to what the symbols and cultural codes seek to negate and exclude—the traumatic stain of real death. Freud, using his dream work to fashion a narrative about himself as subject of the unconscious, unwittingly encircles the navel he wishes to leave unexplored only to replace it with a formula for trimethylamine. This empty master signifier on the one hand represents sexuality, offering Freud a solution to the cause of hysteria. On the other hand, because it is exclusively symbolic, it offers Freud the answer to his inquiry into dream work, namely that significance in dreams does not depend on reference but is instead located in the structure being meaningful. This is a protective analytic narrative because it leaves the theme of mortality and vulnerability, the stubbornness of the referent, behind and instead favors the uncanny appearance of a formula lacking point of origin and a clear point of reference.

Barthes instead consciously delves into the navel of his narrative and encircles the maternal picture he will not repoduce because anyone else would respond only indifferently to it, simply as a culturally knowledgeable spectator. He, too, comes up with an interpretive narrative about the origin of the subject; his story, however, is about how the subject of the unconscious, beyond any sexual encodings, is always subject to the traumatic knowledge of its mortality. He thus also reaches a formula, the *noematic* "that has been." Yet this sentence is authenticated by an irrevocable referent, the knowledge of his own demise, certified by the presence of his lost mother in an image: that is, the fact that her absence, though a loss or gap, emerges as being abundantly full.[10] What I wish to emphasize is the countermovement in Barthes's reading of the Winter Garden photograph; this image knots and also cuts the connection between a commemorative narrative of mourning that seeks to sublimate the loss of the mother and a traumatic recognition of the spectator's own mortality. The phantasy this representation presents enmeshes two modalities of desire, an omphalic oscillation between sublimation and the preservation of a traumatic impact and between a memory narrative's recuperative gesture and its piercing.

In the first phantasy scenario Barthes describes how the death of the mother repeats the cutting of the umbilical cord: it is the second, final separation from her, and an analeptic reference to the parturition of birth. "I was then losing her twice over, in her final fatigue and in her first photography," he explains (71). As part of the mourning process he recalls how in nursing her he had imagined her as his "little girl," his "feminine child," becoming the maternal parent of his dying mother: "I, who had not procreated, I had, in her very illness, engendered my mother. As in Freud's narrative, failure translates into success by virtue of a trope. The dead mother becomes a *Vorstellungs-Repräsentanz* for his creative triumph over her death. In this scene, the image serves as a surplus signifier to fill the gaping void amid representational reality; loss is compensated by an image of male progeny, even as the dead mother leads him to discover the essence of photography. Seeing the image of his mother before his birth, before his own history, he images his own death; the mother who gave birth to him also becomes a harbinger of his "total, undialectic death." This trajectory—losing the maternal body, recovering it in an image, reading not only his mother's but also his own mortality in that image—traces a series of narcissistically recuperative gestures.

Rediscovering the mother in the image not only reconstitutes an umbilical cord to this lost body but also stirs the awareness of a death beyond any pleasurable image, indeed beyond any cultural encoding, and so Barthes, in a second phantasy scenario, rewrites the revelation the Winter Garden photograph affords him. In this scenario he traces a trajectory running in the opposite direction, sublimation (where mourning turns the lack of a signifier into a signifier of lack) now reversing into a "mad realization of one's own death" (turning the signifier of lack back into a lack of signifier). Even as the Winter Garden photo, as the navel of his inquiry, incites an empowering narrative about his creativity in the face of death, the wound it produces signifies that his grief cannot be transformed into mourning (90). The photo's punctum invokes the recognition that even as death calls for narratives, it evades representation. His mother's photograph, so meaningful to him, lacks a cultural context—it cannot convert the negation of death and cannot use the power of representation to purify, contemplate, or reflect death. It instead underlines the "unendurable plenitude" of the absent/present, dead maternal body. Barthes thus returns to his discussion of how trauma is the inverse of the hysterical mask supplied by a historical encoding of photography. Discovering his mother, even as words fail him, Barthes argues there is "nothing to say about the death of one whom I love most, nothing to say about her photograph, which I contemplate without ever being able to get to the heart of it, to transform it. The only 'thought' I can have is that at the end of this first death, my own death is inscribed; between the two, nothing more than waiting." (93) This image of his mother signifying the future anteriority of his own death functions like a traumatic stain that draws him and counterbalances the tropic surplus signifier, the first phantasy of resolving death. Barthes's certainty that it is a just and accurate photograph, a true representation, is proportional to the fact that it arrests his interpretive narrative. Unlike Freud, who marks the navel of his dream as the moment that must be left obscure, Barthes recognizes that this is the spot which precisely does not lead astray: "I exhaust myself realizing that 'this-has-been.' . . . I passed beyond the unreality of the thing represented, I entered crazily into the spectacle, into the image, taking into my arms what is dead, what is going to die" (117).

If Barthes calls history hysterical, he does so to emphasize the paradox between the irrevocability and inevitability of his unique biography, the story of his demise originating before his birth and of history as a protective cultural code, supporting the imaginary activity of the subject. What is unique about the photographic image is its stubborn insistence on its *reference* to the past: "Every photograph is a certificate of presence" (87). Yet I have also been arguing that the photograph is hysterical because (even as it poses as a pleasurable image of the past) its punctum also pierces the hedonism of the studium. Converting the traumatic certainty of the past into a bearable historistic narrative, into a "memory fabricated according to positive formulas" (93), it nevertheless also allows the unique emotion of a completely personal "fugitive testimony" to remain. Though Barthes maintains through the end of his narrative that any reader of photographs alternates between the studium and the punctum, it also becomes clear that the punctum itself is split. Referring to a detail that pierces codification, the navel of the photograph reveals *another* punctum, namely time, as the horrific revelation of "an anterior future of which death is the stake" (96). While the studium has a visualization, a disturbing detail like the scabs inside Irma's mouth, the punctum can only be perceived as an intensity. Here what pricks the spectator is the discovery of the equivalence between the absolute past (this has been) and death in the future. The punctum, marking a "tenuous umbilical cord" (110) resurrects the specter of the lost maternal body (like de Man's prosopopeia) only to speak of both the maternal and the filial demise. This navel of the photograph also connects the "unheard-of identification of reality (*'that-has-been'*) with truth (*'there-she-is!'*)." (113) While Monique Schneider (1980) sees in Freud's dream of Irma's injection the traces of a matricidal and infanticidal fury, Barthes exhibits a fury of his own—the madness of plunging into the navel of the photographic spectacle to embrace both the other's and his own death.

The essence of photography's power is that it can be either tame or mad. Under the aegis of the studium the disturbing message about mortal vulnerability at the navel of the image, the "this-has-been" threatening to wound the viewer, can be tempered. This manner of reading, relying on the protection of a cultural encoding, resists the photo's traumatic effect, deflects its wound, forgets its denotative reality. The second response gives in to the force of the punctum, eliciting a madness Barthes calls ecstasy, because it allows the conscious subject to embrace its own temporality. By insisting that the spectator choose between the tame and the mad image, between perceiving a relative or an absolute realism, Barthes himself remains in the position of the hysteric, dismantling his own authority and turning the responsibility for truth back onto the reader of the *Camera Lucida*. The choice, he maintains, is his but also ours: to subject the spectacle of the photograph "to the civilized code of perfect illusions, or to confront in it the wakening of intractable reality" (Barthes 1980, 119).[11]

I have been treating Freud's dream of Irma's injection as a symptom whose studium offers a formula to explain the origin and meaning of both dreams and hysterical complaints and whose punctum proclaims maternity and death to be at the navel of the dream, I have also been arguing that it mirrors the hysteria it is meant to solve. Not only does Freud at two crucial moments identify with Irma's pain as an index for his own physical vulnerability; rather, he imbues the structuring principles of both the dream and his interpretation with two aspects of the hysterical symptom: the gesture of the complaint that defies a coherent solution by bringing forth ever new conversions and the gesture of simulation that poses to please its interpellator and mask the traumatic knowledge it also purports. In Barthes's *Camera Lucida* the photograph also emerges as a hysteric message; it vacillates between madness and tameness and in so doing induces an indecision in the spectator as it circles with much ado about the traumatic impact of death, of which there is nothing to say and which, insofar as it has a representation (the Winter Garden photograph), has an exclusively private meaning. Barthes conceives of the photograph as a hysterical textual knot, binding together a detail (*punctum*), which wounds any historistic narrative the spectator seeks to construct by insisting that the essence of the image resides in its reference to death, with the hysterical play of culturally codified signs (*studium*), which pose as a protective fiction to mask the traumatic knowledge they also address. Returning to the critical vocabulary introduced at the beginning of the chapter, one could conclude that to read a photograph means connecting its visualized "storeys" into an integrational narrative over a detail that pierces this narration, a detail pointing to the intractable real. Two notions of history thus come into play, one, the time before we were born—a knowledge available to us only belatedly—as a cultural text, and, the second, the time of the past as a future anterior message about the truth of our own demise. In rereading Freud with Barthes, I have explored the impossibility of avoiding either one of these two aspects, because the photograph, the dream, and indeed the language of hysteria all seem to draw their power precisely from the way they call upon the spectator to constantly reconsider the act of reading. Even if we were to endow the studium—the cultural code—as the symbolic formula (as Freud seemingly does), still the detail that pierces any coherent sentence—the trace of the negated real— would remain. We can choose not to include it in the protective fiction our interpretation constructs, but we cannot efface it. In the midst of the hysteric's protean conversions and the surplus of analytic responses to these, the *nothing*, where language fails, will insist, persist, and resist with its traumatic impact. Forbidding any easy identity with the laws of authority and the codes of culture, the indeterminacy and overdetermination the language of hysteria performs *shields* from the psychosis that an unmitigated experience of traumatic enjoyment would entail. Indeed, the ultimate paradox of *Camera Lucida* is that although Barthes lauds what Freud shies away from—namely an unconditional entrance into self-destructive ecstasy—his own text partakes with such virtuosity and expertise the very taming through cultural codes he also seeks to pierce.

Having come to the end of the first part of my own inquiry, which aimed to set up the theoretical framework for discussing a variety of analytic discourses about and aesthetic renditions of hysteria, I can now isolate three modalities for how the subject knots together a self-representation in relation to the traumatic knowledge of vulnerability. All three, I would argue, should be seen as offshoots of Freud's own hysteric rhetoric, articulated in his identification with Irma as well as in the inclusion of a surplus element, a blind spot within an interpretive narrative that poses as coherent. The first is an unconditional embracing of destructive jouissance, conceived as an undifferentiated identity with the dead maternal body or the maternal body before birth; a psychosis represented by Norman-Mother in *Psycho*. The second is a hysteric embracing of protective fictions of infalliblity, invincibility, and plenitude, in which the excess of these protean performances, these simulations and dissimulations, obliquely articulates the jouissance of traumatic knowledge they also successfully evade, a figuration represented by

_____ **PART TWO**

▶ HISTORY'S HYSTERIAS

CHAPTER 2

Medicine's Hysteria Romance: Is It History or Legend?

> There doesn't seem to be anything medicine has not said about hysteria: it is multiple, it is one, it is nothing; it is an entity, a malfunction, an illusion; it is true and deceptive; organic or perhaps mental; it exists, it does not exist.
>
> —*Gérard Wajeman*

I

THE DIAGNOSIS and treatment of hysteria have perplexed physicians throughout its medical history. Self-consciously exposing hysteria as the neurotic symptom par excellence that broadcasts the fallibility of any medical discourse seeking a cure for the vicissitudes and transformations of the body, the seventeenth-century physician Thomas Willis claimed, "If a disease of unknown nature and hidden origins appears in a woman in such a manner that its cause escapes us, and that the therapeutic course is uncertain, we immediately blame the bad influence of the uterus, which, for the most part, is not responsible at all. . . . what has so often been the subterfuge of so much ignorance we take as the object of our treatment and our remedies" (Foucault 1961, 138). The polymorphism and variability of hysteria's symptoms caused the nineteenth-century physician Charles Lasègue to declare that hysteria had never been adequately defined, and furthermore, that no precise definition would ever be found by a physician (Israël 1976, 3). In a somewhat more nostalgic mode, but also addressing the mutability of this neurosis, Lasègue's contemporary Pierre Janet felt that the word hysteria "should be preserved, although its primitive meaning has much changed. It would be very difficult to modify it nowadays, and truly, it has so grand and so beautiful a history that it would be painful to give it up" (Veith 1965, ix). Next, recognizing that the lack of a precise nosology could be a strength rather than weakness, the surrealist poets André Breton and Louis Aragon proclaimed hysteria the greatest poetic discovery of the nineteenth century (Aragon and Breton 1928).

This abundant and versatile nosological propositions led the historian Mark S. Micale (1995) to conclude, in his comprehensive overview of the medical literature on hysteria, that the extraordinary accumulation of meanings of hysteria over more than a millennium actually produced an interpretive overload: "Hysteria during the European fin de siècle came to mean so

many different things that by around 1900 it ceased to mean anything at all"
(1995, 220). In other words, not simply the symptoms brought forth over
the centuries by hysteria as a syndrome, but rather its discursive function
within medical and aesthetic texts can be characterized and classified. Two
striking features remain consistent within the protean history of this concept. First, the language of hysteria forces its investigator to realize he cannot
define or identify his subject, and thus it demarcates the limitations of the
system of representation that seeks to classify—and also produces hysterical
symptomology. In response to the unanswerable questions "Is hysteria an
illness like any other? Is hysteria an illness or not?" Etienne Trillat notes,
"Hysteria, in so far as it is an illness, is a reduction, but also an original
creation, the fruit of a process, of a type of thinking which, by drawing the
thing it dreads into the interior of certain parameters, certain medical can-
ons, transforms it into a perceptible object. Which is why it is quite in vain
to ask oneself what hysteria might have been before the advent of medicine"
(1986, 10).

In a sense the language of hysteria stages the performative quality of any
syndrome; it presents a parody of psychosomatic illnesses, in the way Judith
Butler has described for the construction of gender. Making the claim for
hysteria that she makes for femininity, one might argue that symptoms assume a particular position within the parameters set up by any given medical
nosology only as a performance. In other words, like gender, hysteria comprises what the physician chooses, dislocates, or excludes in order to support
the position he seeks to ascribe to this disorder. The persistent inability of
medical professionals to find a universal, systematic definition for hysteria
ultimately illustrates that hysteria can have no autonomous and original
identity outside its discursive formations. Instead, hysteria and its medical
discourse are mutually constitutive. Hysteria exists only insofar as it results
from a given network of medical, supernatural, religious, and aesthetic discourses, and it does so by marking the blind spot or impossibility of the
physician's representational gesture.

Of course, nosology, like any other system of classification, must necessarily construct a class to encompass what does not fit anywhere else, that
cannot be accounted for in any other of the classes. As Slavoj Žižek notes,[1]
every structure needs a class for what eludes the general and universal—the
purely negative defined as being not x, not x^1, not x^2—an element that re-
serves a place for what is excluded from classification and that marks the
lack in and of the structure, its inconsistency. In fact, only when this paradoxical element is added can the structure be completed. The existence of a
class whose definition resides in being purely negative is also the condition
that makes all other elements in a given structure possible. Now, if the hysteric, as I have already suggested, defines her desire by trusting in her phantasies of happiness and plenitude, even while she insists that neither this
desired object nor that desired situation is really *it*, so too the syndrome of
hysteria is treated by its analysts and interpellators as that element which

explodes all other classes in the effort at classifying disease. It is precisely not this syndrome, not that disorder, and perhaps not even a sickness in the strict sense. The one question about hysteria that remains constant throughout the plethora of semantic encodings is whether to include it in a given nosological classification (whether it is called an observable somatic disturbance, an illness of the soul, or a sacred or supernatural phenomenon)—or whether it acts as the exclusion that grounds all other inclusions.

What also remains strikingly consistent in the medical history of hysteria, as Micale notes, is, the "extreme, almost obscene interpretability" of what defies definition. Hysteria has elicited commentary in the most diverse historical settings and styles of disease reasoning: "The disorder has been viewed as a manifestation of everything from divine poetic inspiration and satanic possession to female unreason, racial degeneration and unconscious psychosexual conflict. It has inspired gynecological, humoral, neurological, psychological, and sociological formulations, and it has been situated in the womb, the abdomen, the nerves, the ovaries, the mind, the brain, the psyche, and the soul. It has been construed as a physical disease, a mental disorder, a spiritual malady, a behavioral maladjustment, a sociological communication, and as no illness at all" (1995, 285). In other words, while the individual hysteric daunts her physician because she exhibits an extraordinary ability to transform her symptoms according to any alterations in her psychosocial conditions, so too the syndrome of hysteria in general appears to adapt its symptoms to the prevailing ideas and mores in a given historical, social, and cultural context. To add one more area of discrepancy, while Micale concludes that hysteria, having exhausted its metaphorical potential by the end of the early twentieth century, receded rapidly from the medical, aesthetic, political, and social arena,[2] the psychoanalyst André Green (1976) notes at the end of his overview, of then-recent psychoanalytic work in hysteric disorders that far from having disappeared, hysteria has merely adjusted yet again to the times; even at the end of the twentieth century it continues to live among us in travesty.

Defying any definitive nosology, hysteria is a neurosis that elicits two opposing responses. On the one hand, physicians argue that since it cannot be defined within the parameters of existing medical discourse, this psychosomatic disturbance is actually nothing. Lucien Israël calls this an attitude of rejection, one which claims that the illnesses brought forth by the hysteric are not real and that these patients, who make so much ado about nothing, in fact have no valid complaint. On the other hand, other physicians affirm hysteria by subsuming it among psychosomatic disturbances, claiming it is like any of these other neurotic disorders (Israël 1976, 3). Clearly these two attitudes, far from being mutually exclusive, are mirror images of each other. For even if hysteria is nothing in and of itself but rather mimics the symptoms of other diseases, the anguish, pain, and disorder that hysteria causes is real to its patients and their peers. At the same time, if hysteria should be taken seriously as a psychosomatic disorder as real as any other neurosis, it also cannot be denied that its history within medical literature (as well as the cultural transformations of this discourse) is specific, if only because hysteria has repeatedly been the illness par excellence for drawing nosological lines of demarcation. Thus, as Israël notes, hysteria as a subject of medical history mirrors back to its interpellators and analysts—to us— precisely the same gesture of indecision that the hysteric's unsatisfied desire also performs. It forces us to incessantly ask whether it is history or legend. Is it real or simulated? And what is the difference?

Micale highlights the simultaneous construction of demarcations and blurring of boundaries at the core of hysteria's vicissitudes within medical discourse, suggesting the reason it is so difficult to classify hysteria is that it has two histories: a medical-scientific and a popular-cultural one. And while hysteria sometimes seems to be a metaphor or icon in visual and narrative arts, quite distinct from the nonmetaphorical concept of it in medical theory and clinical practice, these two realms usually prove to be intimately and inextricably entwined. As the protean and resilient mimetic force of hysteria infects the very discourses meant to contain and explain it, "the standard distinction between scientific and fictional texts dissolves and the traditional division within the history of science and medicine between professional theory, enlightened lay opinion, and popular belief is utterly untenable" (1995, 180).

I would add two other aspects that are crucial in hysteria's murky interface between medical theory and cultural legend. For one, if hysteria is to be understood as the performance of a given historical moment, then the hysteric's voicing discontent allows the critic to analyze what has gone awry in this particular cultural formation. For another, as Barbara Johnson notes about the interplay between allegorization and identity politics, "Just because identities are fictions does not mean that they have not had, and could not have, real historical effects. . . . It is just that the 'cause' of the cultural messages cannot easily be tied to intentions" (1994, 73). I will therefore briefly sketch some of the metaphors medical discourse has brought forth in its valiant effort to explain hysteria. I will follow Foucault's argument in the *Archaeology of Knowledge* (1969) that statements distinct in form and dispersed in time form a group if they refer to one and the same object, yet it is also the case that the hysteric of ancient Greece is a differently constructed category than the hysteric on the eve of modernism.

At the same time it is worth remembering, as Martha Noel Evans has noted, that although the word *hysteria* derives from the Greek word for the womb, *ustera*, its neuter form *usteron* signifies what comes late or behind, what falls short or is inferior: "At the intersection of uterus and that which comes after, the neuter plural, *usteria* (meaning literally 'things of the uterus') signifies the placenta, or more precisely, the afterbirth" (1991, 4). From this etymology she deduces that hysteria is not only a knot that combines a scientifically observable manner of pathological behavior with a mythopoetic creation of language, an actual disorder with its verbal con-

struction, but furthermore, that, any discussion of hysteria is belated, coming after the spectacle its host performs: "The hysteria that generates theory
is in a sense invisible, like the uterus, and can become known only as an
afterbirth, as what comes after the mysteries of love—the product of the
gendered encounter between theory and its object" (5). In other words, the
discursive exchange I am interested in[3] is one where the metaphors chosen
by physicians are in part taken from cultural texts that were popular at the
time, only to engender new cultural representations in turn. Hysteria, precariously negotiating the interface between mimesis, imagination, representation, and deception, involves not only a sympathetic correspondence between mental and somatic disturbances but also an identification between
analyst and patient, whether this transference is based on supporting a mutual desire or sustaining a mutual dislike. Not the truth of any one definition
of hysteria but rather that a wish for such a classification generated such a
grand historical narrative is what interests me about the vicissitudes of this
concept within medical discourse. What intrigues me is the richly resilient
conversions and inversions that wish continues to find in cultural texts.

II

The story of hysteria's excessively abundant and diverse history within western medical discourses, which comes to mirror the mutable and intangible
quality of this psychosomatic phenomenon, invariably begins with Hippocrates' treatise *On the Diseases of Women*. In it he introduces the association of hysteria with the female reproductive organs and defines it as a disturbance caused by the pathological peregrinations of a restless, dissatisfied
womb.[4] Considered to be a small, voracious animal, a foreign body that had
dried up, lost weight, and come unhooked, this wandering uterus was
thought to seek for nourishment throughout the body of sexually dissatisfied
women, such as widows and spinsters.[5] As a result, the uterus would upset
the normal body functions by settling in improper sites, causing overall per-
spiration and palpitations. If it came to rest in the hypochondrium, an im-
pediment of the flow of breath would result in epileptic convulsions, spas-
modic seizures and suffocation. If it attached itself to the heart, the patient
would feel anxious and oppressed and would begin to vomit; if to the liver,
the patient would lose her voice and grit her teeth, and her complexion
would turn ashen. If its motion was arrested in the loins, the patient would
feel a lump on her side; if it settled in the legs or arms she would become
paralyzed; if in the throat, she would experience strangulation.[6] Finally, if
the uterus mounted to the head, the patient would feel pains around the eyes
and nose and feel drowsy or lethargic. The cure Hippocrates recommended—apart from a uterine fumigation meant to lure the uterus back to
its proper place—was marriage. Yet this, Veith notes, "translates the sexual
element, initially implied in the earliest concepts of hysteria, into tangible

terms" (1965, 13), a conversion on the part of the physicians that continued as the standard prescription for more than two thousand years (and that I will discuss, in another chapter, as the protective fiction favored by Freud in his case histories).

Just as crucial for Veith, the physicians of ancient Greece not only maintained the uterine origin of the hysteria syndrome, excluding it from the category of mental disease, but they also insisted on a natural origin over any divine or demonic causation. The belief that evil spirits were at fault, foreshadowed in the medical discourses of antiquity by the linking of hysteria to bestial instincts, did not take hold until monotheism supplanted the pantheism of ancient Greece, finding its first ardent proponent in Augustine. The earlier emphasis on dissatisfied sexuality as the primary cause of hysteria readily transferred to Christian notions of human suffering the manifestation of innate evil, a result of original sin. In the course of the Middle Ages, mental illness became coterminous with spirit possession—the devil tricking humans by taking over the imagination rather than the body—and hysteria came to be understood as the illness par excellence of the soul. Now the hysteric was no longer the sexually dissatisfied woman but rather a figure that appeared different than she really was, in the guise of a normal person when in fact she was the dangerous host of evil spirits. In her alliance with the unholy powers of the devil, the hysteric (who could be either male or female) was considered to be demonically possessed. In this configuration, as Trillat notes, medieval practice anticipates the writings of such Enlightenment physicians as Thomas Sydenham, in part because hysteria becomes linked with melancholia as a state of possession occurring whenever a vulnerable woman becomes the victim of her dark humors. At the same time, it is at this juncture, when hysteria came to be connected with demon possession, that the trace is set to knot hysteria with deceit. For Sydenham and many theorists after him, as I will show, the essential trait of hysteria is found in the patient's ability to fool the physician, to simulate illnesses, to present herself other than she really is.

The crucial difference, of course, is that while the physicians of the early Enlightenment felt sympathy with hysterics, indeed to a certain degree identified with them, medieval culture transformed a medical question into a moral one and shifted all interest in understanding and curing into an issue of punishment. Nevertheless, these physicians and witch hunters also articulated the murky interface between body and mind, between true representation and the trickeries of simulation that would both fascinate and distress future analysts of hysteria. The medieval cultural assumption was that whereas the so-called healthy imagination *represented* material objects in shapes and figures that were clearly distinct from their point of reference, the devil *presented* these objects, insofar as he produced a hallucinatory scene, so that what was represented appeared to actually be present. Imagination perverted by the devil, for which hysteria came to be considered a perfect example, allowed one to believe that the deceptive image was identical with the object (Trillat 1986, 44).

The devil's deception goes in two directions. On the one hand, he tricks the hysteric into believing that the products of her imagination are real, while on the other, he deceives the world into believing those under his influence continue to belong to normal society. That the imagination thus led astray emerges as multifarious and chameleon-like is an equation that subtends the gothic literature of England (and also points to a much later phenomenon, which I will return to in discussing Cronenberg's postmodern, hysterical performances of the imagination gone awry). At the same time the deception raises the disturbing question of intent. For if the hysteric, with her imagination so disordered that phantasy and body language jarringly conflate, seeks to deceive, why express such excess in her performance? As with Woody Allen's *Zelig*, the chameleon hysteric, seeking to trick the interpellator into believing, presents a strategy noticeable as deceit precisely because it misses the mark, offering up a surplus in the mimicking and disclosing the simulation.

The central text of the inquisition, the *Malleus Maleficarum* (1494), argued that hysterics, exhibiting strange paroxysms, sudden and transient attacks of paralysis and body pains, partial numbness, mutism and blindness—falling into a trance and behaving in shocking, lascivious ways—were witches, whose bodies had been paralyzed and whose senses were bewildered by a spell cast upon them. As though in response to a salient symptom of medieval hysteria—strange confessions made by hysterics that included phantasies of intercourse with the devil—the proposed cure was interrogation, whose aim was to exact a confession from the possessed soul, and subjecting the hysteric to often cruel bodily investigations. Although physicians in the late-nineteenth century were no longer interested in punishing the hosts of evil spirits, art historian Georges Didi-Huberman has meticulously documented the influence that iconographic representations of demon possession did in fact have on the work of Jean-Martin Charcot, who sought to make tangible the hysterics' symptoms—their convulsions, stigmata, anesthesia—with recourse to the age-old metaphors transmitted from medieval culture.[7] Indeed, one could view psychoanalysis as the hybridization of ancient and medieval medicine: namely, between an organic disorder that occurs when a foreign body takes possession of the human soma, on the one hand and a mental disorder that results when a person is possessed spiritually by a mental construct, a fancied voice emanating from outside of, or other to, the conscious, rational self. This slow merging of two initially distinct attitudes began when early Renaissance theorists such as Paracelsus rejected the demonic model of explanation, returning to Hippocrates' discussion of the altered womb as the cause of a loss of reason and sensibility (only to argue that one of the manifestations of the hysteric disorder was its inducing a state of unconscious phantasies where reason is taken and perverted into an imagined idea) (Veith 1965, 106). As Trillat suggests, "If one was able to maintain that hysteria in the age of the Renaissance could pass as the daughter of the devil, this slightly diabolic daughter gave birth to a child at the beginning of the 19th century, which would turn into psychoanalysis; all psychoanalytic theory was of hysteria born. Only the mother died after delivery" (1986, 212).

The turning point in medical discourses about hysteria occurred in the seventeenth century. Physicians such as Edward Jordan argued that although hysteria originated in the womb, it emerged only when vapors emanating from a disturbed uterus would ascend to produce symptoms in other body parts or when a sympathetic interaction between another organ and the uterus made the latter a partaker of grief. The faculty afflicted most often by emanations from the uterus or in sympathy with it was the brain; for Jordan, the perturbations of the mind were actually responsible for the disease, that is, not the uterus but the *usteria*, the afterbirth, resulting from a sympathetic consent between organs. As the organ governing the imagination, reason, and memory, the brain's sympathetic involvement with the disturbed womb would result in hallucinations, impairment of intelligence, or mental alienation. With the brain as controlling point for the five senses, the affliction resulted in loss of sight, hearing and anesthesia: as the organ monitoring body motion, an afflicted mind could understandably cause the spasms, paroxysms, palsies, fainting spells, convulsive dancing, and other motoric attacks for which hysterics had come to be known. Knotting together the dissatisfied womb with a brain that, in sympathy, comes to be equally dissatisfied, Jordan was the first to point out the interface between wandering desire and wandering phantasy, which was to become such a rich topos in romantic literature.

As Jordan's contemporary Robert Burton argued in *The Anatomy of Melancholy*, calling hysteria the melancholy of maids, nuns, and widows, we are torn to pieces by our passions. The brain is troubled "not in essence, but by consent" with the vapours originating in the womb, "that inflammation, putridity, black smoky vapours, etc; from thence comes care, sorrow and anxiety, obfuscation of spirits, agony, desperation, and the like, which are intended or remitted should the amatory passion be aroused, or any other violent object or perturbation of the mind" (1621, 415). The symptoms he lists (uncannily presaging the ailments of Radcliffe's gothic heroine, Adeline, in *The Romance of the Forest*) include diverse body pains, troublesome sleep, world weariness, discontent, a longing for solitude, despondency and despair, a proclivity for visions, and the sense of conferring with spirits while in a state of dissociation. Yet this distress exists only while the influence of the vapors lasts. Significantly, the afflicted, under normal circumstances, are pleasant and merry by disposition and cannot explain the origin of the symptoms that come on them so mysteriously, only to disappear as suddenly as they came. Burton's argument is particularly interesting in that hysteria be seen as an illness by consent. Furthermore, he reflects on his own implication in his object of inquiry: for, arguing against enforced sexual abstinence only to conclude that the best and surest remedy for hysteria is marriage, he first recognizes the futility of prescribing a cure for women "that out of strong temperament, innate constitution are violently carried away with this torrent of inward humours and though very modest of themselves, sober, religious, virtuous, and well given . . . yet cannot make resistance." But he stops his narrative. Astonished, he notes, "But where am I? Into what subject have I rushed? What have I to do with nuns, maids, virgins, widows? I am a bachelor myself, and lead a monastic life in a college, it is certainly very foolish of me to speak thus, I confess 'tis an indecorum. . . . Though my subject necessarily require it, I will say no more" (417–18). We are strangely reminded of Freud, of course, some three hundred years later checking himself similarly once he finds himself on a path that might lead far afield of his proposed theoretical trajectory.

Perhaps the most significant turning point in medical discussions of hysteria can be read in the writings of Thomas Sydenham, for whom hysteria was (next to fever) the most common disease of his time.[8] Like Thomas Willis, he did not limit hysteria to women, maintaining instead that they were simply more susceptible to hysteria than men. He was not only the first—in his *Epistolary Dissertation*—to compare the multifarious and inconstant appearances of hysteric disease with the shapes of proteus and the colors of the chameleon, but moreover he also included-hysteria among the afflictions of the *mind*: "The frequency of hysteria is no less remarkable than the multiformity of the shapes which it puts on. Few of the maladies of miserable mortality are not imitated by it. Whatever part of the body it attacks, it will create the proper symptom of that part. Hence, without skill and sagacity the physician will be deceived; so as to refer the symptoms to some essential disease of the part in question, and not to the effects of hysteria" (1679, 85). In other words, for Sydenham hysteria is baroquely representative; like an actor it can assume countless different figurations. Its symptoms not only appear in great and varied forms, but in so doing also follow no rules, instead making up a confused and irregular assemblage. Never ultimately adhering to any one illness, exchanging one symptom formation for another, this array of imitations of illness arises not from one organ but from the sympathetic alliance between the vapors and the brain as locus of the animal spirits. As Trillat notes, hysteria is not an illness like others for Sydenham, and it won't readily fit into any nosographic system: it emerges superimposed on a parallel level; it imitates all other illnesses, it renders these in a deceptive guise. "Hysteria is the *grand fallace* (fallacy)." Its particular power resides in the ability to deceive, and a physician facing the deception nevertheless seeks to contain this strange phenomenon within the parameters of his respective medical discourse by reading it under the aegis of the phallus, that symbolic function that assures the difference between true and false, authenticity and simulation. For Trillat, then, the ambiguity of hysteria so poignantly articulated by Sydenham is that it is "a malady, which isn't one, while being one. . . ." (1986, 54).

Sydenham describes physical disfunctions, pains, fits, and motoric disturbances noted by other physicians, but above all he distinguishes the mental anguish that seems far greater than somatic pain. By explaining that the nature of the disease is first and foremost an incurable despair, which induces in the patient the sense of having to suffer "all the evils that can befall humanity," Sydenham not only moves the seat of hysteria from the womb to the brain, but he also tacitly leaves behind the traditional explanation that sexual dissatisfaction is at the root of the hysteric attack. With the brain's distressing insight into human vulnerability, Sydenham notes melancholic symptoms of "forebodings, brooding over trifles, cherishing them in their anxious and unquiet bosoms. Fear, anger, jealousy, suspicion, and the worst passions of the mind arise without cause." When these patients feel joy, hope, or cheerfulness, they do so only at intervals "few and far between," whereas both the joyful and the painful passions are indulged without moderation: "All is caprice. They love without measure those whom they will soon hate without reason. Now they will do this, now that; ever receding from their purpose" (1679, 89). Anticipating Freud's discovery that our dreams broadcast to us a truth we cannot directly confront, Sydenham also traces the melancholic etiology of hysteria to the hysteric's dream work: "All that they see in their dreams are funerals and the shadows of departed friends. Thus they are racked both in mind and body, even as if life were a purgatory wherein they expiated and paid the penalty of crimes committed in a previous state." And like Freud some two hundred years later, Sydenham explains that those afflicted by hysteria are neither maniacs nor madmen but rather "persons of prudent judgement, persons who in the profundity of their meditations and the wisdom of their speech, far surpass those whose minds have never been excited by such stimula" (89).

Agreeing with Hippocrates' claim that the womb is the cause of innumerable sorrows and troubles, "in calculation (though not in the view of the nature of the disease)," Sydenham is saying that the symptoms are numerous and multiform, a "farrago of disorderly and irregular phenomena." But for him the remote or external causes are overordinate actions of the body coupled with overordinate commotions of the mind "arising from sudden bursts of anger, pain, fear." Thus, when a patient complains of an ailment he as physician cannot determine by the usual rules of diagnosis, Sydenham inquires about mental suffering: "I never fail to carefully inquire whether they are not worse sufferers when trouble, low-spirits, or any mental perturbation takes hold of them. If so, I put down the symptoms for hysterical." Like Jordan and Willis, he explains the hysteric's imbalance of the mind-body relationship as arising from a disorder of the animal spirits—yet not in the manner of an explosion. Rather, he postulates an economic model that Freud would ultimately return to. Attuned to where the body has already been weakened, the animal spirits leave their proper station and violently take over the vulnerable site. Sydenham's discussion of an irregularity of the spirits, held at bay while both mind and body are firm and strong but brought into full force once mental or somatic constancy is lacking, anticipates Freud's discussion of the foreign body wandering through the psychic apparatus and calling forth (in sympathy), somatic responses. These spirits, after all, are messengers broadcasting a knowledge of vulnerability and mutability that is audible once the body and mind can no longer hold onto their protective shield of firmness and strength.

Rejecting both the sexual encoding of hysteria and its organic site in the womb, Sydenham concludes, "It is clear then, to me, that it is not any corruption of either the semen or the menstrual bood, to which, according to the statements of many writers, this disease is to be referred. It is rather the faulty disposition of the animal spirits," of vapors led astray from their proper site in the body, activating the animal spirits in the brain to produce imaginations equally strange to the normal state of mind. The origin of hysteria is not lodged in the humors but because the organs are weakened, a disorder of the animal spirits can reign. As a cure he proposed purifying and fortifying the body and the mind by restoring the blood, so that the patients could withstand attack from foreign bodies working in sympathy with each other and prevent these spirits, vapors, and imaginations from even setting out on their faulty paths. In that sense Sydenham must be seen as a product of the baroque age, even if his dictum—that hysteria is chameleon-like and multiform—transformed the privileged definition of hysteria in the eighteenth century. Unlike his successors Whyatt and Cheyne, Sydenham incorporates a knowledge of death into his definition of hysteria, indeed recognizes that hysteria broadcasts a message about human frailty and vulnerability. Yet at the same time he, too, ultimately seeks to make the patient's body and mind strong enough to resist this knowledge.

By the eighteenth century, the shift undertaken by Sydenham had become firmly entrenched. Transforming the discussion from vapors into hypersensitivity and excitation, hysteria gained recognition as a disorder of the nervous system. The symptoms that described hysteria now included some familiar ones but also new ones reflecting the rise of bourgeois culture: paroxysms, sudden sensations of cold, trembling, shivering, feelings of oppression and suffocation, physical pains that migrated from one place to another, fainting spells, lethargy, despondency, catalepsy, nervous asthma, nervous cough, giddiness, dimness of sight, ringing in the ears, delirium, hallucinations, amnesia, and a histrionic vacillation between laughter and crying. In contrast to Sydenham's appraisal, however, which considered hysteria as common as fever and thus neither class nor gender specific, the new view of hysteric disorder limited it to a certain part of the population, those well-born and idle, of delicate nervous constitution, and sexually or socially dissatisfied (the latter no longer called spinsters or widows but mythomaniacs or nymphomaniacs). The hysteric of the late-eighteenth and early-nineteenth centuries was a sensitive creature, prone to dreaming, melancholic somnambulance, or febrile insomnia but also capricious, fantastic, unforseeable, deceitful, and lustful. As the French psychiatrist Pinel claimed, she was the product of the conditions of the bourgeois family; a young woman was encouraged in her genital neuroses by an imagination obsessed with lascivious reading and resided within a domestic situation that imposed severe restraint and a secluded life. She first found an outlet for her frantic desires in the habit of masturbation, then in lewd behavior, and finally in the hysteric fit.

In his study *Madness and Civilization*, Michel Foucault analyzes the transformation within medical discourses of the "classic age of hysteria," through which this psychosomatic illness came once more to be considered the feminine illness par excellence.[9] The significant nosographic shift, according to Foucault, is that by the mid-eighteenth century, physicians were forced to admit their failure to define the organic reality of hysteria. Instead they conceptualized both hysteria and its masculine counterpart, hypochondria, as diseases of the nerves and as pathologies of the mind. Physicians of the Enlightenment felt completely safe in assuming that hysterics were young girls looking for husbands or young widows who had lost theirs, while they viewed hypochondriacs as individuals too much given to study and meditation. Thus, Joseph Raulin notes "this disease in which women invent, exaggerate, and repeat all the various absurdities of which a disordered imagination is capable, has sometimes become epidemic and contagious" (Foucault 1961, 139). Yet when it came to determining the actual disturbances in the qualities of the nervous fluids, the dynamic properties of other body fluids such as blood or lymph, or the secret nature of the chemical makeup of the body, only contradictory qualities annulling each other seem to have prevailed. "Hysteria," Foucault concludes, "is indiscriminately mobile or immobile, fluid or dense, given to unstable vibrations or clogged by stagnant humors" (142).

Faced with this impasse, during a century in which neither theoretical nor experimental innovation occurred in the area of pathology, physicians suddenly decided to replace the theme "of a dynamic upheaval of corporeal space," one that accepted the brain's controlling and distributing a disease whose origin was visceral by using a morality of sensibility. This change developed because physicians had decided to view hysteria as a *disorder* in which the body had become indiscriminately penetrable to the influence of animal spirits, that is, to the imaginations located in the brain: "the hysterical body was thus given over to that disorder of the spirits which, outside of all organic laws and any functional necessity, could successively seize upon all the available spaces of the body" (Foucault 1961, 147). This hysterical body emerged as a curious hybrid of real illness and deception. While the organic symptoms were imitations of all possible organic disorders, the actual defect lay in a derangement of internal mobility—in the disorder and excessive movement of the animal spirits.

The significant shift not only to a moral but also a gendered paradigm, however, ultimately took place as physicians claimed that "the more easily penetrable the internal space becomes, the more frequent is hysteria and the more various its aspects; but if the body is firm and resistant, if internal space is dense, organized and solidly heterogeneous in its different regions, the symptoms of hysteria are rare and its effects will remain simple" (Foucault

1961, 149). Once the resistance of the organs to the disordered penetration of the spirits is aligned with notions about the strength of the soul, which keeps thoughts and desires in order, the spatial density of the body readily converts into moral density. Concomitant with this construction, the female body, by the mid-eighteenth century conceived as more delicate and less firmly constituted, (especially when a woman leads a soft, idle, and luxurious existence) readily exhibits a laxity of the heart. This, in turn, once more is somatically confirmed when an internal space becomes so permeable and porous that hysteria breaks forth. For Foucault, this conversion of Hippocrates' metaphor of the perpetually mobile womb within the body into that of the body's interior ruled by a lawless whirlwind in a chaotic space creates a situation "where a certain manner of imagining the body and of deciphering its internal movements combined with a certain manner of investing it with moral values" (150).

One other element supported the shift from a discussion of the dynamics of corporeal space to the morality of sensibility: sympathy. While earlier physicians such as Sydenham had argued that sympathy was at the root of communication between such distant organs as the womb and the brain, the physicians of the mid-eighteenth century, such as Cheyne, Whytt, and Cullen expanded the notion of sympathy to mean the faculty of feeling and moving. Accordingly, separate organs, communicating with each other, suffered together or reacted jointly to an external stimulus. For Foucault, however, Whytt's claim that "all sympathy, all consensus presupposes sentiment and consequently can exist only by the mediation of the nerves, which are the only instruments by which sensation operates" illustrates that the nerves, far from being invoked to explain how movement or sensation is transmitted, actually serve to justify the body's sensibility "with regard to its own phenomena, and its own echo across the volumes of its organic space." Hysteria emerges not only as a disorder with sympathy gone awry, insofar as organs responding to each other and standing in for each other as Sydenham had argued, but, more crucially (and for the emergence of gothic literature even more significantly), it thus presupposes "a state of general vigilance in the nervous system which makes each organ susceptible of entering into sympathy with any other" (153). This exquisite internal sensibility—correlate to the image of the chaotic, porous interior body—once more functions as the organic metaphor for a moral value attached to the construction of femininity prevailing in the mid-eighteenth century. But the delicate and highly sensitive woman who suffers convulsions at the vivid description of a tragic event or faints at the slightest onset of pain is not the same person as Sydenham's melancholic who holds onto the past, allows memory traces to flood her body and her mind, and becomes incapacitated as she confronts the truth of death's presence in the world.

Instead, by the mid-eighteenth century the sensitive woman was imagined as being riddled by "obscure but strangely direct paths of sympathy . . . always in an immediate complicity with itself, to the point of forming a kind of absolutely privileged site for the sympathies . . . radiating through the entire body" (Foucault 1961, 154). Her sympathy was not an empathy with vulnerability and loss, but rather the result of an almost hermetic rarification of the body. She was seen as frail precisely because her body listened only to itself, drawing all external stimulus into a dialogue with the self and indeed excluding all moments of difference. And once organic frailty, rarity, or excessive refinement had become the accepted definition, the feminine body could as readily be invested with moral values that veered toward the more mobile; thus, as Whytt claimed, the feminine body was more subject to the nervous disease of hysteria. If earlier theories of hysteria saw the body as the site of a womb gone awry or as the host for supernatural spirits seeking to take possession of it, this new formulation of hysteria presented "a body too close to itself, too intimate in each of its parts, an organic space which is, in a sense, strangely constricted," that is a pathological proximity of the body with itself (Foucault, 154). In other words, while earlier medical discourses presented the hysteric as the victim of her crude body, with her psychosomatic disorder the violent response to a womb seeking satisfaction, the hysteric of the mid-eighteenth century fell ill owing to an abundance of feeling, an excessive sympathy with her environment, an uncurbed empathy for all that would move her body and soul—but a flow of organic and psychic energy that formed a closed circuit.

The correlate image to that of the feminine body's tenuous fiber and delicate constitution once again spliced a psychological with a moral value. Women, made of frail fibers, were seen to have easily impressionable souls and unquiet hearts readily carried away by lively imagination; this twofold sensation and mobility—of the organism and the imagination—came to account for their disposition to hysteria. At best, then, a notion of ideal femininity had been fashioned by the mid-eighteenth century, that rendered women as the more exquisite embodiments of the sensations of the soul. Yet, as Foucault concludes, the reverse of this feminine sensibility is the hysteric's unconsciousness, fainting spells, dissociations, and hallucinations, altogether an *overcharging* of the soul's capacity to feel that could lead to a complete extinction of all feeling. This construction of the hysteric as a victim of irritated nerves always had an implied moral judgment, as is clear in the equation found in the medical literature between the woman who cultivates affections, passions, and imaginations, for example by reading novels and the woman who loses all control over her sensuality and sensibility.

In the course of the nineteenth century hysteria came to be seen more and more as the inextricable knot between an expression of passion and a simulation of passion, where the body reproduced the texts it read or converted itself into a text of sorts. The psychosomatic expressions could be deciphered as sentences and scenes about psychic distress and social discontent that the afflicted women could find no other language to express. Hysteria produced both excessively excitable and histrionic patients, as well as languid and cataleptic ones. Exhibiting a helpless form of paralysis of the limbs, anesthesia of various body parts, uncontrollable coughing fits, trancelike states, and amnesia on the one hand, as well as a proclivity toward manipulation, caprice, seduction, and deception, on the other hand, the hysteric of the Victorian period further supported the notion that woman has a greater delicacy of the nervous system. Her emotional liability and suggestibility aimed at an incessant erotization of all social exchange, and she exhibited a more volatile and impressionable character, such that a want of proper work and physical exercise could make her prone to abundant sensibility and phantasizing, capricious role-playing, and errant sexuality.

Veith (1965) points out that the manifestations of hysteria changed from era to era according to the cultural mores and the state of medical knowledge, but that certain symptoms—convulsions, the *globus hystericus*, loss of consciousness, the acting out of possession and with it a variety of physical and mental delusions—kept returning. Edward Shorter contends that the unconscious, "not wishing to make itself ridiculous, brings itself medically up to date" (1992, 54). As medical theories themselves call the hysterical symptom into existence, these symptons concomitantly change proportionately to scientific trends and shifts in medical paradigms, exhibiting a wonderful symbiosis between doctor and patient, with the patients' perfecting the diagnosis of their physicians. Shorter's claim about hysteria's fickleness, aimed at supporting the physician's good feelings—so as to keep alive his interest in the patient—illustrates another constant in the otherwise so protean chronicle of hysteria's history, however: namely, this psychosomatic illness is represented by the phantasm of its interpellators. Rather than the physician's admitting that he, the propagator of medical progress, does not understand, hysteria is consistently shown as cheating the rules of the medical game (Israël 1976, 6).

Veith also notes that hysterical symptoms "were modified by the prevailing concept of the feminine ideal"; in the nineteenth century women were expected to be delicate and vulnerable both physically and emotionally, and this construction of femininity was reflected in the disposition to hysteria (1965, 209). Indeed, when Otto Weininger asserted that "hysteria is the organic crisis of the organic mendacity of Woman" (1903, 359), he was merely repeating a cliché that had firmly engrained itself in the cultural image repertoire of late-nineteenth-century Europe. At that historical moment hysteria and femininity could be called coterminous precisely because both were construed to represent emotional volatility, exquisite sensitivity, emotional exhaustion, and a proclivity to contradiction, controversy, duplicity, and falsehood. Describing the aporetic exchange between constructions of femininity and of hysteria, Christina von Braun (1985) argues that in the act of diagnosing the hysterical syndrome, the physicians (who were, after all, representatives of the discursive prejudices or preferences of their times) came to project their historically specific imaginations of what the feminine body should be onto their patients. At the same time, one also finds these imaginations reproduced by the hysterics themselves: in doing so, they used their bodies to exhibit symptoms of psychosomatic disorder that only served to exclude them again from being considered normal and possessed of the ideal feminine body—which, ironically, they were supposed to have embodied in the first place.

It is precisely this aporia at the navel of the history of hysteria—this murky enmeshment of mutual consent, deceit, and mutual desire on the part of the analyst, patient, and artists reproducing their exchange—that transformed the Salpêtrière, Jean-Martin Charcot's museum of living pathology. This most spectacular arena of hysteria became the site where Sigmund Freud, observing the work of his colleague, first encountered the language of hysteria that would lead him to that other scene, the unconscious, and with it to the birth of psychoanalysis. Because I will discuss both Charcot's nosology and Freud's case histories in later chapters, I will cut short my overview of the medical literature on hysteria at this point. However, before returning to the historical moment that is the subject of both this and the next chapter, the shift from the late Enlightenment to Romanticism, I want to highlight two currents that have thread their way through the otherwise protean discourses on hysteria.

First, any discussion of hysteria lives off a hermeneutic project that itself knots together two disparate strands. One thread of the discussion bases its theories on *observable* phenomena that can be compared to other phenomena; the other presents the most radical transformations in the writings on hysteria occurring whenever the analyst was willing to embark into the area of the *imaginary*, the world of the dream, into speculations about his patient's body interior and her subjective casting of the world—only to configure this elusive illness as a communication with a representative of radical otherness (be this a divine entity, a malign spirit, or the unconscious). This discourse, furthermore, is located beyond the boundaries of consciousness and the boundaries of the body—even as it so dramatically speaks in the register of the body; it is a discourse that requires an interpellating Other because it addresses itself to an audience, even as the message it bespeaks is precisely not part of the world of normalcy, a discourse of the uncontainable and intangible that by negation demarcates what is contained in such categories as the body or consciousness.

As Christina von Braun suggests, European culture traces a development within the notion of subjective consciousness and identity that initially posits an I (*ich*), seeking to define itself by virtue of distinguishing itself from the Other but also seeking to find itself confirmed in the existence of this radically different Other. This notion of the human subject came to be replaced by a second construction von Braun calls the omnipotent I (*Ich*), having at its disposal parthenogenetic powers because it can at will extinguish and recreate the Other—and with this itself. This second subject formation (*Ich*) conceives of itself as immortal, while the first subject formation (*ich*) is sustained by a knowledge of its own incompleteness, its own mortality (1995,

107). Von Braun is interested in the hysteric's jarring imitation of identities projected onto and elicited from her pathological body because of the contradictions this performance of difference so resiliently highlights in the many theories about this psychosomatic disorder, allowing one to hear another voice behind the self-identical, omnipotent, phallic subject of European culture. The fallacy of the hysteric voice offers no direct access to the other, more originary form of identity (*ich*), which, as I have argued earlier, corresponds to the destructive enjoyment of the traumatic knowledge of difference that only psychosis could sustain. Yet it brings about an oblique articulation of difference, its simulation pointing to the inconsistency that grounds any definition of a universal subject—as it grounds any definition of universal normalcy. Reformulating von Braun's argument slightly, I find it compelling that the chronicle of hysteria's history is not really a linear progression from a time when the subject was able to live its difference and its mortality (*ich*) to the era when this traumatic knowledge had successfully been exchanged for the protective fiction of parthenogenesis (*Ich*). Rather, the transformation within medical configurations of hysteria illustrates that this other voice has always been audible, even while the attempts to convert it into a stable and definite object of nosology varied. The difference is simply that some physicians were more willing than others to listen to this message about the subject's fallibility and vulnerability.

Second, it is seminal to bear in mind that hysteria is not just an illness of imitation and of sympathy but more a *maladie par representation*, as Freud's contemporary Pierre Janet (1894) termed it. It is the somatic voicing of traces of a psychically traumatic impact—be this sexual or melancholic—whose origin is unknown or repressed. As Roy Porter (1993) notes, the hysteria mystery is, so daunting, after all, because it hovers elusively between the organic and the psychological, muddling the medical and the moral and discrediting its own credentials as the hysteric articulation converts a traumatic impact into a simulation, into an unjust image that speaks obliquely and treacherously. Thus, to speak of hysteria as a malady of or by representation suggests two things. On the one hand, this disorder is constructed by the cultural images and medical discourses it imitates; on the other hand, it engenders condensed and displaced reproductions of an originary psychic disorder. With no organic lesions to be found and no initial trauma to be clearly determined, the body symptoms *stand in for* a disorder that cannot be located in the body, even as its message can be articulated only by proxy in the register of the body. In other words, to produce hysterical symptoms—be this the loss of consciousness, control over body functions, or control over the vagaries of the mind—is for those afflicted the only possible way to articulate a psychic disturbance, but the improper recourse to language of the body signals that the patient cannot effectively use symbolic language. As I will show in greater detail in discussing Freud's case histories, these symptoms form sentences, such as resorting to a paralysis of the legs to express "I am caught in an emotional impasse," or resorting to a loss of the self entirely or a split of the self into many roles for "I cannot live with the constraints imposed on my desire for self-development."

To speak of hysteria as an illness by representation means even more than focusing on the hysteric's being haunted by memories and stories she has incorporated and cannot shed, texts occupying her body as though it were their host and using her body to speak their alterity. Rather, as I argued in the introduction, one of the seminal definitions of the hysteric is that there is a noncoincidence between her self-representations and the being she really is, but in such a way that she not only plays roles, but that her existence resides in the performance of these roles. This is why (even as hysteria is connected with mimesis as mimicry, deceit, and simulation) one can isolate a distinct, indeed an authentic, voice emerging from the hysterical performance. To do so, however, means shifting one's critical point of view away from asking whether there is a true kernel of the self, which the hysteric is oblivious to or which she keeps hidden in the course of her public display. It means turning instead to the fact that the public display is the only way she can articulate her true self, even as she knows that this is a performance. As I will show with the spectacular self-display that young hysterics exhibited in Jean Martin Charcot's amphitheater during his infamous *leçon de mardi*, the extraordinary tales the hysterics produced for Freud as they lay on his couch in Bergstrasse 19, and the seductively fascinating self-fashionings poet Anne Sexton used to turn herself into a glamouros star in the wake of the Second World War, hysteric performance has always meant the public confession of an intimate trauma and of intimate phantasies. But this act of self-presentation has also always colluded with a given public's notions of what constituted a healthy body, a stable psyche, a safely contained imagination, or indeed a just representation of the self, on the one hand, and with what display of excess, abundance, difference, and disjuncture was necessary, on the other, to make these constructions hold.

III

Although by the end of the nineteenth century the concept of hysteria was as fatigued perhaps as the culture that had produced its symptoms (see the discussion of Wagner's *Parsifal*), the end of the eighteenth century marked a different, equally poignant, historical moment, given that the wish to discuss hysteria within the parameters of moral sensibility parallels the birth of the bourgeois family. In discussing the production of discourses on sexuality, Michel Foucault distinguishes four great strategic unities that emerged just before the end of the eighteenth century, claiming that these formed the specific mechanisms of knowledge and power centering on sex. The first, significantly, is the hysterization of women's bodies, which he describes as "a threefold process whereby the feminine body was analyzed—qualified and disqualified—as being thoroughly saturated with sexuality; whereby it was integrated into the sphere of medical practices, by reason of a pathology intrinsic to it; whereby, finally, it was placed in organic communication with the social body (whose regulated fecundity it was supposed to ensure), the family space (of which it had to be a substantial and functional element), and the life of children (which it produced and had to guarantee, by virtue of a biologico-moral responsibility lasting through the entire period of the children's education): the Mother, with her negative image of 'nervous woman,' constituted the most visible form of this hysterization" (1976, 104). As these strategic unities (along with the hysterical woman, Foucault includes the masturbating child, the Malthusian couple, and the perverse adult) turned into favored objects of medical, moral, and aesthetic discourses, thus simultaneously becoming "targets and anchorage points for the ventures of knowledge" (105), what was at stake was neither a struggle against sexuality nor an effort to mitigate and control it but rather the production of sexuality as a historical construct: "not a furtive reality . . . but a great surface network in which the stimulation of bodies, the intensification of pleasures, the incitement to discourse, the formation of special knowledges, the strengthening of controls and resistances, are linked to one another, in accordance with a few major strategies of knowledge and power" (106).

Foucault's central argument is that once the deployment of sexual strategies came to challenge the hitherto dominant deployment of alliances (ie., kinship codes), the bourgeois family, with its husband-wife and parents-children axes, emerged as the point of interpenetration between these two modes. Indeed, after the eighteenth century, the family became "an obligatory locus of affects, feelings, love . . . the most active site of sexuality." With this shift the issue of incest emerged as the central expression of the ambivalences in the interchange of alliance and sexuality. Incest—constantly solicited and refused—became "an object of obsession and attraction, a dreadful secret and an indispensable pivot. It is manifested as a thing that is strictly forbidden in the family insofar as the latter functions as a deployment of alliance; but it is also a thing that is continuously demanded in order for the family to be a hotbed of constant sexual incitement" (Foucault 1976, 109). As the deployments of alliance and sexuality became enmeshed, the family came to absorb and reorganize the threat that any intensification of the body initially posed to the system of kinship. But this shift also gave birth to the familiar figure of the family neurotic, the embodiment both "of an alliance gone bad and an abnormal sexuality." This figure might be a nervous woman, frigid wife, indifferent or murderous mother, hysterical or neurasthenic girl, or a precocious and already exhausted child.

Foucault's argument is particularly compelling in his emphasizing the gesture of duplicitous articulation. From the mid-eighteenth century on, even as the family proved to be the "keystone of alliance," it also emerged as the "germ of all misfortunes of sex" and vice versa. The alliance system, threatened by an intensification of the body, learned to assert its interests in precisely the endangering order of sexuality. What emerged from this unhappy but perhaps necessary marriage was a plea on the part of the family for assistance in its efforts to reconcile the conflicts between sexuality and alliance. Foucault calls this an elaborate "family broadcast" of its complaint, launched at experts (doctors, psychiatrists, priests) but also at the audiences of cultural texts, factoring and reproducing this complaint. His point is that these confessions assert that the family was the "source of a sexuality which it actually only reflected and diffracted" (1976, 111). However, applying Foucault's explanatory model to that of the hysteric daughter or son, one could also argue that having recourse to this psychosomatic disturbance allows the children to target the way the bourgeois family couples sexuality with the law of alliance, the way it sexualizes workings of kinship and incest.

I want to return to the notion of the performative, because the relation between the bourgeois family and the hysteric, confessing her complaint, is one of mutual implication and reflection. If the late-Enlightenment family couples the deployment of sexuality with the system of alliance, to avoid the risk "that sexuality would appear to be, by nature, alien to the law but rather constituted only through the law" (Foucault 1976, 113), the hysteric, I would argue, *questions the legitimacy* of the prohibitions and dictates of family law and its codes of sexuality, even while she articulates this complaint within this very discursive space. Like the family whose discontent she performs, the hysteric uses sexuality, an intensification of the body as site and language of self-representation, to prop up and regenerate the old deployment of alliance. And if her self-display aims to publicly confess her intimate trauma, to broadcast the family as site of the unhappy marriage of sexuality and alliance, it is intriguing that it becomes an endless and indeterminate vacillation. For as the hysteric uses her symptoms to keep reposing the question as to whether hers is a case for therapy or morality, she also keeps fluid precisely the boundary Foucault highlights between sexuality and alliance, that is, between personal and social illness. In that she always acts out her discontent in relation to the question of her position within family bonds, she insists on broadcasting the fact that to designate a disturbance as an illness of unsatisfied sexuality is always also an issue of social or family alliances.

In this and the next chapter the speculation I will pursue by exploring several texts from the end of the Enlightenment is the following: The hysteric uses her body, knotting together strife and gender, to articulate the difference at the heart of the family. She vacillates between accepting and questioning the paternal metaphor as the law dictating her being. As Jacques Lacan says, the hysteric places herself in relation to a figure of paternity, but her position before this paternal law is contradictory, both accepting that the question of her existence can be articulated only in relation to this paternal figure and perpetually renegotiating her relation to the other. This exchange takes the shape of performing the question, What am I? concerning her sexual designation and contingency in being. It means asking, on the one hand, "Am I a man or a woman?" and, on the other, "Am I or might I not be?" The enmeshment of these two paradigms weds the mystery of the hysterical subject's existence, "binding it in the symbols of procreation and death" (Lacan 1966, 194). Thus the question of her existence, repeatedly performed in relation to the paternal figure, will bathe, support, invade, and tear apart the hysteric thus forming the core of her protean, irritating resilience. She performs a disorder by refusing to undertake the so-called normal Oedipal journey, engaging with the paternal metaphor even as she makes manifest what is latent—the violence, sacrifice, and incest underlying the bourgeois family.

Catherine Clément (1979) was the first psychoanalytically informed cultural critic to analyze the libretti of classical European opera for family structures, incest, and the violence with which one generation follows another, as well as in relation to the punishment and eradication inflicted on those deemed abnormal or strange by a given community, those foreign bodies who transgress social laws. Opera enmeshes myth with history and stages love stories or family sagas to construct political narratives. It has recourse to old, mythopoetic tales, for example, about how a pagan, maternal principle of nocturnal superstition must be replaced by the paternal principle of diurnal reason or how polytheism must be exchanged for monotheism. Many of the operatic texts of the eighteenth and nineteenth centuries encode the violent struggle for power and the interchange between alliance and sexuality, beneath the surface of both the bourgeois family and its public counterpart, the European nation as a whole.

One of the key texts Clément isolates to support her thesis that opera stages such a politicized family affair is Emanuel Schikaneder's libretto to Mozart's *The Magic Flute*, which she reads as the *rite de passage* of two children who must learn to renounce the maternal principle and accept paternal law. Alongside this psychoanalytic narrative, however, *The Magic Flute* for her also celebrates the historical moment when the bourgeois ideology of a truly stable family unit is added to two existent family structures: the poor, peasant families, who lose their many children to the fatalities of life, and the rich, noble families, who care for their own by virtue of a complex system of alliances. This new sexualized alliance is one endowed with fewer children and dedicated instead to a contained and monogamous form of procreation. What Clément finds crucial is that this new construction of the family is so committed to eradicating those women who challenge their newly ascribed role as docile wives and daughters. The Queen of the Night, whose coloraturas signal a language of pure affect both terrible and brilliant, is barred from the portals of wisdom. Her daughter Pamina, taught to curb her loquacity and torn between her mother's hysteric madness and her surrogate father's Sarastro's, mysterious process of examination, altogether gives up her desire to know what role her parents have designed for her. Instead she submits herself to the silent suffering that is the linchpin of the bourgeois conception of the submissive wife. Concluding her reading,

Clément claims, "If there is an opera which, with all its verbal and musical power, commemorates the symbolical suppression of women by men, that opera is called *The Magic Flute*" (1979, 147).

Though Clément's reading is perhaps too reductive in its polemical gesture and too imprecise in its neglect of the Mozart score, I want, nevertheless, to follow her cue and examine more closely the part played by Pamina. For initially she is a resistant daughter, boldly questioning the mysterious priestly authority. Only at the very end does she relinquish expressing her discontent, transforming into the obedient daughter whose distinctive voice is silenced as it merges into the general harmonic configuration at the conclusion of libretto and score. Admittedly, Pamina is not yet a hysteric, though one could perhaps imagine her becoming one. Rather, her story sets up the narrative pattern that will structure all subsequent versions of what Foucault calls the family broadcast of its complaint. And at the navel of this story we find the hysteric's strange performance of discontent, so resiliently proclaiming that even as the bourgeois family conceives itself as the happy and healthy result of a sagacious father and supportive, protective mother, in reality the paternal command of obedience is as inconsistent and violent as is the maternal demand for unconditional love.

In other words, *The Magic Flute* indeed performs a narrative manifestly meant to commemorate the image of the bourgeois family, namely, the story of how paternal authority, with sublimation serving as its chief weapon, requires a scene of matricide as the symbolic act of violence marking a triumph over those drives and affects that hark back to a destructive (because undifferentiated and uncontained) enjoyment before the world of symbolic laws, only to reencode this entire family affair as a political narrative about the replacement of pagan superstition by reason.[10] However, if one reads the narrative of *The Magic Flute* against the grain (as Clément does not,) through the gothic rewritings of the bourgeois family story that were in a sense coterminous with its inauguration and whose interest lay in highlighting the horror that lurked from the start in the shadows of its enlightened claim for reasonable family bonds, a different interpretive narrative emerges. Clément merely mentions two moments that she believes "escape the misogynist imagination of their creator" (1979, 147): the duet in the first act when Pamina and Papageno sing about the luck of love and how man and woman should be complementary; and the duet when Pamina and Tamino declare their unconditional love for each other before Sarastro's initiation trial again separates them. Against this I would argue (both perfidious to the Mozart/Schikaneder text and compelling) the fact is that nothing escapes the ideology of the bourgeois marriage it seeks to proport. Rather, the entire plot is skillfully structured on two radical breaks in the narrative that self-consciously perform the very fissures that were from the start written into the protective fiction of a reasonable exchange between alliance and sexuality. Even though familial harmony is established in the end, my argument is that this text not only consciously articulates the violence necessary for the bourgeois family to be born, but that it also makes equally obvious the scars that remain once parturition has occurred.

A friend, describing his impressions as a twelve-year-old seeing *The Magic Flute* for the first time, assures me that the mysterious break in the opera when the Queen of the Night suddenly turns evil, not only stunned him but also left him totally confused. Occurring unexpectedly and left unexplained, this sudden shift of sympathy against the Queen of the Night is never really recuperated by the rest of the story; it remains an ever subtle trace of disjunction even after her voice has been silenced. Schikaneder and Mozart initially present her as the good, valiant, protective mother who convinces Tamino to save the daughter who has been stolen from her by Sarastro. They passionately recall the scene of maternal disempowerment, where she could only watch as Pamina, trembling, terrified, and struggling, called to her mother to save her ("Mit bangem Erschüttern / Ihr ängstliches Beben / Ihr schüchternes Streben / Ich musste sie mir rauben sehen: / 'Ach helft!' war alles, was sie sprach") ["With terrified tremor / her anxious shudder / her timid attempts / I had to watch as she was stolen from me: / 'Help' was all that she could say"]. As her three attending ladies present Tamino with the magic flute, the fetish object meant to protect and empower him, they sing of a world where deceit is overcome, where love and brotherhood replace hatred, defamation, and melancholy. Indeed, Tamino becomes omnipotent with the flute in hand; it is endowed with the power to change human passions, transforming despondency into joy (and converting bachelors into lovers). Though the flute will ultimately be used to support Sarastro's paternal law, which declares fortitude, patience, and reticence ("Sei standhaft, duldsam und verschwiegen!") ["Be steadfast, enduring and reticent"] the cardinal virtues, it actually represents precisely the fluidity and malleability the father's dictate lacks.

Furthermore, once Pamina appears on stage, having again failed to flee her imprisonment in Sarastro's palace, she does not so much lament the possibility of her own death as that her mother might die of grief over the loss of her daughter. Indeed, she calls to her warden Monostatos to kill her because he represents a world incapable of love ("O lass mich lieber sterben / Weil nichts, Barbar, dich rühren kann") ["oh, let me die / since nothing can move you, you barbarian"], and in the language of hysteria that her gothic brothers and sisters will imitate to perfection, Pamina faints. She stages not only her impotence before the rigidity of paternal authority but also, more disturbingly, her desire for self-sacrifice, for the archaic destructive enjoyment the maternal realm represents. As she wakes from her dream, she quite explicitly addresses the junction between her desire to return to her mother and her desire for death ("Mutter-Mutter-Mutter. Wie? / Noch schlägt dieses Herz? / Noch nicht vernichtet? / Zu neuen Qualen erwacht? / O das ist hart, sehr hart! / Mir bitterer als der Tod") ["Mother-mother. What? My heart is still beating / Not yet destroyed? / Awakened to new anguish? / Oh this is harsh, very harsh / more bitter than death"]. That Pamina should voice this traumatic knowledge before her encounter with Papageno, who tells her about Tamino's love for her, only further supports the alternative narrative that I suggest is told in the *The Magic Flute* alongside the official one seeking to justify the harshness of paternal authority. For this sequence of events allows me to speculate that the love story Papageno and Pamina bespeak ("Wir wollen uns der Liebe freun / Wir leben durch die Lieb' allein") ["We want to joyfully partake of love / We live only through love"] functions like a protective fiction, not only standing in for lack, given that at this point both feel utterly abandoned, but more importantly shielding from and containing her desire for the other, destructive enjoyment.

As we discover during the conversation the Queen of the Night has with her daughter in the second act, Sarastro had been a close friend of the family; when the King had died, he had left all his material possessions to his wife and daughter, but bequeathed to his friend power over the day, the all-consuming sevenfold orb of the sun, which Sarastro now wears on his breast. To his astonished wife he had explained it was her duty to submit herself and her daughter to the guidance of this wise man and his all-male club of initiates. Yet what mars the superficially reasonable last will of the dying father, as we discover in the course of the narrative, is that Sarastro is anything but a benign ruler. Indeed, recalling the gothic world of Matthew Lewis's *The Monk* and Charles Maturin's *Melmoth, the Wanderer*, Sarastro's domain includes slaves and prisoners who are tortured, impaled, or hanged (though these scenes of horror occur behind the stage), and his chief warden, Monostatos, is ready to commit both sexual abuse and murder.[11] Even the rite of initiation is tainted, for, as Tamino discovers, the ordeals, or tests, of these Masonic-like rites are so severe that some aspirants have died in the process.

Uncannily anticipating the lustful uncles and paternal friends who will reappear in the stories Freud's hysteric patients tell him, Sarastro abuses his power of surrogate father, bestowed on him at the deathbed of his friend, when he steals Pamina from her mother. Claiming at first that he feels morally obliged to remove her from the dangerous sphere of maternal influence, he recodes this act in explaining to Tamino that the theft was the necessary precondition for bringing the two lovers together under the aegis of the bourgeois marriage he seeks to inaugurate. For, in actuality, he wanted to enjoy her in a scene of incest that sexualizes the deployment of alliances along the lines Foucault describes. His representative, the Speaker, tries to convince Tamino that the Queen's version of the story is merely the concoction of an idle woman ("Ein Weib tut wenig, plaudert viel / Du Jüngling, glaubst dem Zungenspiel") ["A woman is idle, chatters much / you, youth, believed the play of her tongue"], using the language of simulation and deceit that has, as I have already sketched, a long tradition in the medical literature of hysteria. Indeed, the Queen of the Night is rendered in exactly the terms of the hysteric, making much ado about nothing, tricking the prince into believing she has been abused though her complaint is without substance. Yet only shortly after this speech by the King's Speaker, Schikaneder/Mozart include the scene where Pamina challenges Sarastro and points out the underlying inconsistency of his authority. For while the ideology he espouses insists on the reasonable curtailment of instinct, desire, and violence, on the exchange of nocturnal irrationality and mystery for the clarity of day, he himself is not free of these nocturnal drives. Pamina, who trusts in friendship's harmony as the only guarantee of worldly happiness, also insists on truthful action. Confronted by Sarastro after her flight has been intercepted, she courageously admits to having committed a crime, in seeking to flee his power, but also insists on her innocence, by implicating the warden whom Sarastro had assigned to her ("Der böse Moor verlangte Liebe / Darum, o Herr, entfloh ich dir") ["The wicked moor desired love / because of this, oh Master, I fled from you"]. It is at this point that Sarastro, in turn, obliquely acknowledges his own incestuous desire for Pamina, for while she accuses his representative Monostatos of untenable sexual advances, he applies the complaint to himself. By negation, thus, he admits what had been his real intention, yet he also insists on his authority ("Zur Liebe will ich dich nicht zwingen, / Doch geb' ich dir die Freiheit nicht") ["I will not force you to love me / but I also will not give you freedom"]. Indeed, he ultimately renounces Pamina only by releasing her into a second alliance, the marriage, which occurs not only within his exclusive and unconditional realm of power but also only after the completion of a ritual he has designed for the couple. It is seminal for my alternative reading, however, that to the end Pamina holds onto two desires. Even as she recognizes in Tamino the embodiment of her love ("Er ist's!") ["It is he!"], she does so only after her defiant attempt to defend her duty as a daughter and her insistent declaration of her longing for her mother ("Mir klingt der Muttername süsse") ["I still hear sweetly my mother's name"] has been twice interrupted by Sarastro's rebuke proclaiming the impropriety of maternal authority, (i.e., the necessity for paternal mastery over women's passions).

At the beginning of the second act, Tamino, having clearly changed camps, is now willing to support Sarastro in his battle to pit the light of reason against the maternal forces of the night.[12] Sarastro in turn explains to his initiates the design he claims to have had in mind all along and denies his earlier confession to Pamina. His theft of her, he explains, was from the start intended to forge the Tamino-Pamina couple as a last bulwark against the proud mother, whom he describes as vaingloriously seeking to bewitch the populace with her deception, tricks, and superstition. Throughout his exchanges with Tamino, Sarastro (repeatedly prescribing reticence over loquacity) defines manhood as fortitude against the wiles of women ("Weibertücken"). The language Sarastro uses to describe the Queen of the Night in all these instances resonates with phrases used to describe hysterics—possessed by evil, demonic spirits, seeking to trick and beguile the world. Indeed, once the distraught mother appears, her coloratura-studded aria, calling for unconditional revenge, now refutes the image of the protective mother conveyed in the first act. As she gives her daughter a gift—significantly not an enchanted flute that can bring out the protean quality in the world but rather a dagger meant to kill Sarastro once and for all—she embodies pure destructive jouissance unleashed on the world ("Tod und Verzweiflung flammet um mich her!") ["Death and despair enflame me"]. Hers is now a sternly relentless command to steal the orb of the sun and to relinquish Tamino, whom as a member of the initiates her daughter may no longer love; she threatens that if Pamina does not kill the priest Sarastro (commit patricide), she will relinquish all natural maternal bonds to her ("Verstossen sei auf ewig, verlassen sei auf ewig") ["Be forever rejected, forever abandoned"].

Yet to me, Clément's reading of the Schikaneder/ Mozart libretto overlooks a fact that is far more disturbing than any purely misogynist statement would be: namely, that Sarastro's paternal law is as tainted as the queen's maternal demand. His enlightened project of the marriage between Tamino and Pamina is explicitly shown to be based on a lie; the theft of Pamina was first and foremost intended to satisfy his own incestuous desires. Furthermore, his law is harsh, inflexible, and indeed merely the mirror inversion of the queen's relentless demand for revenge. After all, the initiation trial requires complete obedience unto death ("Dich allen unseren Gesetzen zu unterwerfen / und selbst den Tod nicht zu scheuen") ["To subject yourself to all of our laws / and even not to fear death"]. In other words, only those who subject themselves unconditionally to his dictates and codes can enter the temple of wisdom, while those who do not accept his teaching are vengefully excluded from the category Sarastro designates as human ("Wen solche Lehren nicht erfreun, / Verdienet nicht, ein Mensch zu sein") ["He who has not pleasure with such teachings / does not deserve to be considered human"]. Based on this totalitarian law of universality, the Queen of the Night, her three attendant women, and Monostatos are finally cast into hell, no longer like the hysteric who has no clear classification but can alternate between being protective and destructive, they now are clearly stereotyped as the embodiments of evil that must be sacrificed for the order of the initiates to stand phallically erect against all fallacious powers of the night.

As Nikolaus Harnoncourt explained in liner notes to his recording of *The Magic Flute* in Zürich in 1987, in this manifestly misogynist opera in which neither of the parents is morally blameless, the queen harbors a mortal hatred against the man who has betrayed her, and Sarastro is neither as virtuous, devoted to truth, or sagaciously protecting all forms of life as he repeatedly claims, the only person who remains flawless and pure is, oddly enough Pamina. Indeed, while she cannot convince herself to kill Sarastro, she also cannot give in to Monostatos's demand for love, even after he has threatened to kill her. Furthermore, she continues to plead in favor of her mother once Sarastro finds out about the murder plot, although she knows her mother's desire is criminal. What perhaps makes Pamina the only truly compelling figure in *The Magic Flute*, I would suggest, is the following tragic

irony. Although her actions ultimately support Sarastro's symbolic universe
with its exclusivist law, she does not act in reference to his word, which she
has already disclosed as inconsistent. Rather, in contrast to Tamino who
will only speak to her once Sarastro's representatives allow him to do so, she
acts ethically, in reference to the judgment her own heart dictates and, to use
Lacan's definition of the ethical act, not compromising her desire, even if this
act suspends the symbolic network of paternal laws. This ethical desire is not
the narcissistic desire for plenitude, represented by the birdman Papageno
seeking relentlessly to satisfy his pleasure and procreate himself once he has
found his Papagena, nor the traumatic desire for revenge seeking to utterly
destroy the symbolic network, represented by the Queen of the Night.
Rather it is a desire for law that vexes and challenges the confines of the
existing law, that acts against its inconsistencies but from within, not beyond, the symbolic realm.

Slavoj Žižek argues in relation to Kantian ethics that the moral subject,
under the laws dictated by the interpellating Other, remains forever plagued
by uncertainty. Even as the subject abides by the prescribed dictate, she has
no guarantee of having truly understood the desire of the Other. Žižek therefore locates guilt in an acceptance "that the big Other exists in the guise of
a transcendent agency which plays a perverse game of cat and mouse with
us, knowing very well what our duty is yet concealing it from us, letting us
grope around and make blind guesses" (1996, 171). In Schikaneder's libretto Sarastro purports to be precisely such a transcendent agent, inserting
the lovers Pamina and Tamino into a intentionally obfuscated Masonic rite
of passage that insists that ignorance and blind trust is a requirement for the
entry into the temple of wisdom. An ethical act that does not compromise
desire, however, occurs because "we leave the domain of superego guilt behind the moment we become aware that the Other itself does not know what
my duty is" (1996, 171). Pamina's attitude is ethical in that she recognizes
the inconsistency of the paternal figure of authority, although she is willing
to acknowledge the duty he prescribes even as she also insists on following
an obverse duty toward her mother. She acts as she does, not from any
pressure exerted by the voice of consciousness, the paternal voice of Sarastro, but simply because she cannot act otherwise.[13]

Thus, just after the finale to the second act has begun, and once Tamino
has abandoned her to undergo the final stages of Sarastro's ritual tests, she
embraces the death she imagines will also be his fate. With the dagger meant
for Sarastro in her hand, she sings her only aria, passionately addressing this
instrument of death as the only bridegroom available to her ("Du also bist
mein Bräutigam?") ["You then are to be my bridegroom?"], painting in desperate but longing language her marriage with death. At this moment the
two desires that have driven her conflate, for her suicide addresses not only
Tamino but also her mother. In other words, she seeks death because her
lover has appeared treacherous ("Falscher Jüngling, lebe wohl! / Sieh, Pamina stirbt durch dich") ["False youth, farewell / Look, Pamina dies for

you"], seemingly able to leave her without confessing his love to her, and she cannot deflect this narcissistic wound or convert love's grief ("Liebesgram") into hatred. Yet seeking death is also the gesture of reconnecting with the maternal figure and represents the lure of the total self-expenditure. The dagger, given to her by the Queen of the Night, proves to be a symbolic umbilical cord that fatefully draws her back into the traumatic knowledge of destruction the mother embodies. Overdetermined, the despair she feels is both the result of Tamino's unconditional surrender to Sarastro's laws and the result of her mother's relentless curse ("Mutter, durch dich leide ich, / Und dein Fluch verfolget mich") ["Mother, through you I suffer, / and your curse haunts me"]. Indeed, one could even conflate the two bridegrooms into one, given that the Queen of the Night first sent Tamino to Pamina and only replaced the first gift with the dagger once her first emissary proved unreliable.

With this configuration Schikaneder's libretto sets up the paradigm of the bourgeois family narrative, which historically is to be followed almost immediately by a gothic broadcast of its complaint. On the one hand we have the son, compelled to follow a paternal authority that runs counter to his sentiment, who abandons his beloved in favor of the call of duty, even if this means death (a trajectory so brutally brought to its logical conclusion by Mary Shelley in *Frankenstein*, where the solitary hero will destroy his entire domestic world as he relentlessly pursues his scientific project). On the other hand we have the daughter, willing to sacrifice herself for love and to follow the path of her mother who found recourse in madness and self-destructive passion as answers to the treachery committed by her husband and then his representative (a narrative abundantly filling the pages and stages of the nineteenth century, from Sir Walter Scott's *Lucia di Lammermoor* to Edith Wharton's Lily Bart in *House of Mirth*: Bronfen 1992).

It is at this point in the opera that I would locate the second seminal break, for although Schikaneder/Mozart prevent tragedy, they do so by showing that the alternative is a totalitarian harmony barring all differences. Pamina is distracted from her suicidal desire by the three boys who assure her that if she were to see Tamino, she would realize that he, also, loves only her ("Denn er liebet dich allein") ["For he loves only you"]. She follows them to the final scene of Tamino's trial, the walk between fire and water that leads into the temple of the initiates. As he is about to embark alone on this path, she calls to her lover to stop. Significantly, Tamino will speak to her and indeed confess their love is mutual only after the two accompanying, armed men allow him to do so and only because Pamina's willingness to sacrifice herself now makes her worthy of the paternal cause he has dedicated himself to ("Ein Weib, das Nacht und Tod nicht scheut, / Ist würdig und wird eingeweiht") ["A woman, who fears neither night nor death, / is worthy to be initiated"]. Pamina, in turn, willingly interpolates herself into his ritual ("Ich werde aller Orten / An deiner Seite sein, / Ich selbsten führe dich / Die Liebe leitet mich)" ["At all places / I will stand by your side, /

while I myself led you, / love leads me"]. She stands by his side, indeed leads the way, as they walk the dangerous path, and she suggests he play the magic flute to protect them. Both are now united under the aegis of Sarastro's paternal authority, and having curbed their drives and affects, having learned sublimation, they can leave the nocturnal and maternal realm of destructive jouissance ("des Todes düstre Nacht") ["the dismal night of death"].[14] This symbolic matricide is then literally fulfilled when two scenes later the Queen of the Night, along with her attendant ladies and newly won ally Monostatos, is plunged into the endless night, successfully banned from the sun-filled stage.

But an unbreachable difference has developed in the bourgeois couple, about whom Jacques Lacan has so apodictically said that the imaginary love between man and woman does not work. For their bond of love has not resulted from a dialogue. Rather, it has grown from the subjection of both lovers to a third position, the paternal law. This peripeteia, through which Pamina's desire for death converts into the protective fiction of the bourgeois marriage but which bars any future, unmediated communication between the two lovers, is poignantly supported by the transformation occurring in Mozart's score, as the Andante (B major) anticipating their journey through fire and water turns into the March (C major) celebrating their triumph over all perils. At the beginning of the scene, Tamino and Pamina express their fortune in seeing each other again. Their duet is structured as a dialogue, and they almost never sing together. Vocally they either echo one another or interlace their mutual declaration of love, while Pamina further embellishes her joy with grace notes and coloraturas. As they bespeak the journey they are about to undertake ("Wir wandeln durch des Tones Macht, / Froh durch des Todes düstre Nacht") ["Supported by the power of the musical sound we wander / happily through the dismal night of death"], the harmony of their mutual undertaking is still articulated in two separate voices, supporting each other yet also distinct. Furthermore the voices of the two lovers, singing contrapuntally, are pitted against the two voices of the armed men who resolutely sing together (homophonically).

After the march has begun, and once Pamina and Tamino have successfully entered the domain of Sarastro's temple, their voices again replace the sound of the enchanted flute. Yet as they describe their triumph over fire and water, using the same words with which they embarked on the final stage of their *rite de passage*, they sing everything in parallel sixths and tenths, now fully supporting the harmonic unity without counterpoint or embellishment. Furthermore, while in the Andante both lovers had been supported *colla parte* by the first and second violins, their voices are now supported *colla parte* by wind instruments, Pamina by the oboe and Tamino by the bassoon, in a harmonic unity encompassing a greater tonal range than at the beginning of the ritual. In other words, they no longer alternate in singing their duet, but rather blend their voices perfectly, together and with the orchestration. However, in so doing they have given up their individual voices, so that

on the level of the libretto their unity is performed under the aegis of paternal dictation, and on the level of the score their independence is resolved into
a dominant (harmonic) chord.[15]

This harmonic solution of the score and the libretto nevertheless leaves us,
as spectators, with a certain sense of unease. For, after all, how wholesome
can a family bond, representing the sexualization of alliances under the strict
law of a paternal authority, be if it requires not only the unmitigated expulsion of those elements that disturb Sarastro's order but also a willful blindness toward the tyrannical aspects of his rule? Seeking to refute the reproach
of misogyny that has so often been launched against this opera, the Lacanian
critic Michel Poizat describes the narrative trajectory of *The Magic Flute* as
"the peaceful journey—with all that this implies in relation to loss, suffering,
and even a certain violence—which leads from the place of mortifying enjoyment (*jouissance mortifère*), of neurosis, indeed psychosis and imaginary
passion, to the place where a desire has been recognized and accepted, which
allows both man and woman to fulfill themselves beyond destructive phantasms" (1991, 225). The fact that the Queen of the Night, who had initiated
the relationship by giving Tamino a portrait of Pamina, disappears is final
proof for Poizat that at the end of their trials the two lovers have more than
a phantasmatic relationship.

My own reading is concerned less with arbitrating this dispute than showing that, whichever way one decides the case, something disturbing remains.
While it is true that the destructive enjoyment sustained by the maternal
realm with its phantasmic structuring of desire must be contained with the
help of symbolic laws, so as to prevent psychosis, it is equally true that the
symbolic realm also remains precariously fallible, not because it contains a
figure like Monostatos, as Poizat notes, but because it seeks to subject difference into harmony. As in my reading of the conflict between Gaia and
Apollo, which actually traces a similar mythopoetic pattern, I suggest shifting our critical interest to what remains after parturition, for one final point
must be made about the maternal gifts that circulate within the opera. If I
have spoken of the knife as a symbolic umbilical cord, drawing Pamina back
into the destructive maternal realm, then the flute is its inversion. Significantly, it is Pamina who insists Tamino should play the magic flute to protect them as they cut through the crevice between the two mountains—and
in doing so symbolically cut the umbilical cord that connects them to the
Queen of the Night. On the other side of matricide, the magic flute functions
like the omphalos, a fetish object that moves from one domain of power to
the other, representing and annihilating, the maternal authority, as Poizat
notes, a "fatal attraction and the bearer of the breath of life" (1991, 226).
But I would add that like the omphalos, the flute is an insignia within the
realm of paternal authority, and it also bears the message that the traumatic
knowledge of destructive enjoyment this order seeks to repress will inevitably return. It is the knotted scar on the symbolic body of the Pamina-Tamino
couple that emerges after the Queen of the Night has been jettisoned off, the

navel that in one and the same gesture buries and commemorates the maternal loss. Its voice, so uncannily resembling the highest notes of the queen's coloraturas in her aria of revenge, encrypts what has no designated space within Sarastro's realm.

Indeed, if any one voice in the opera can be designated as hysteric it would be the sound of the flute, for even as Tamino plays it to tame the perilous elements (and thus confirms Sarastro's designs), it remains a duplicitous instrument. Ultimately it will enchant, regardless of who its master is, and just because it has been so successfully appropriated by Tamino to work against the Queen of the Night is no guarantee its power might not at a later point work in the other direction. As pure music in serving more than one master eludes any one exclusive and unconditional symbolic encoding, so too the flute bespeaks the maternal power that can never be fully eradicated, but it does so like the *hysterus*—as an afterbirth.

IV

Having presented *The Magic Flute* as a paradigmatic for illustration of the birth of a family narrative, whose discontent the hysteric begins to proclaim at the end of the eighteenth century, I want to turn to a historical case, the story of the hysteric Maria Theresa von Paradis, a contemporary of Mozart. In the next chapter, I will move on to the gothic rewriting of this family broadcast. Admittedly my presentation of this case history is framed by my interest in hysteria as a disturbance of the voice, of body movements, and of mental states expressed without directly naming the difference what has been left so violently unarticulated within the bourgeois family. Broadcasting the message of a family gone awry from the moment of its inception, the hysteric's scenario yet remains within the familial, discursive parameters. One could say, the hysteric performs an illness in and of the family, dismantling the notion of harmony between the familial sexuality and alliance, even though her complaint involves incessantly rewriting the family narrative. She uses the dysfunction of her body to return to phantasy scenes of the family that point simultaneously to the uncanny difference at its center and to her conviction that this familial difference can be arbitrated. In other words, if the hysteric is the one in the family who performs the internal fissure, if she unremittingly insists that something is amiss, she is also haunted by the phantasy that she could embody what is lacking in the figure of paternal authority and make the family whole.

Maria Theresa von Paradis, named after the Austrian Empress in whose court of justice her father, Joseph Anton von Paradis, served as a civil servant, was born in 1759. During the first three years of her life she appeared to be healthy though prone to infections, only to wake up one morning in her fourth year unable to see. While her parents initially thought this disorder would pass as quickly as it had come, they proved to be wrong. She remained blind, forced to adjust herself to her affliction. At the same time her father soon recognized her great artistic talent and drew upon the most prominent Viennese musicians to train her. Under the tutelage of the virtuoso Leopold Koželuch, who composed several concertos for her, she learned to master the piano and organ. Vincenzo Righini trained her voice, while Antonio Salieri and Carl Friberth taught her dramatic composition. At the age of eleven, accomplished enough as a musician to entertain the royal family, she was awarded a pension by the Empress, to compensate her for her disability. By the time she was eighteen and able to perform more than sixty piano concertos by heart, she came to be esteemed by the Viennese public as the blind pianist.

Still, her parents continually sought the help of physicians, who had speculated that the disorder was either the result of an apoplectic fit resulting from gout or that it had been caused by nocturnal anxiety. With no improvement in sight, they finally recognized that because the optic nerve had clearly remained undamaged, hysteria was the real cause for Maria Theresa's blindness, though they could neither determine the origin of the symptom nor designate a cure. An amazing alteration did occur, however, when the parents turned to Dr. Franz Anton Mesmer, known for his work with animal magnetism. Believing that diseases were the result of an imbalance in the universal fluid of the human body, which regulated the relation of the soma to its cosmic influences, he had developed a cure that most of his peers considered to be the machinations of a charlatan. In order to bring his patients, who were predominantly women, in contact again with the cosmic source of these fluids, he would place them into a somnolent trance or "mesmeric" sleep, hoping that once in this state, the body would, like a magnet, attract the cosmic fluids and set the imbalance right. From these trances, his patients would awake refreshed and healed (Veith 1965, 221–223), a practice Jean-Martin Charcot, Joseph Breuer, Sigmund Freud, and Pierre Janet were to have recourse to when they began to use hypnosis to treat hysteria, roughly one century later (Tatar 1978).[16]

In his *Memoirs* Mesmer recalls having diagnosed the eighteen-year-old Maria Theresa Paradis at his first encounter with her in 1777; "It was a complete amaurosis attended by spasms in the eyes. As a consequence, she suffered from deep depression and from obstructions of the spleen and liver, which caused her to go into transports of delirium bad enough to make her fear she was losing her mind" (1779, 40). Up to this point in her life, Maria Theresa had been subjected to a variety of somatic treatments, ranging from bleedings, purgings, and blisterings to wearing a plaster helmet and undergoing electrotherapy. Mesmer, by contrast, was fully intent on curing her blindness by addressing it as a hysterical, not a somatic, disorder; he therefore dispensed with all these operations and instead concentrated on building up trust between himself and his patient. Having acheived this, he began stroking and touching her with his hand and his wand, and sought (as many psychoanalysts would do after him) to reproduce the moment of traumatic impact, so that in a state of utter vulnerability Maria Theresa could receive the healing flow of animal magnetism. Of course, we have only Mesmer's account of the curative process, making it impossible to discover what really happened during these sessions and whether there was scientific validity to Mesmer's treatment. The facts of the case, however, do corroborate that Maria Theresa demonstrated an almost miraculous improvement. Owing to previous therapies, her eyes had become horribly swollen and distorted, forced out of their alignment. Within a very short period Mesmer had restored her eyes to their normal position, and as Maria Theresa came more and more readily to respond to Mesmer's suggestion, indeed learning to induce an autosuggestion of her own, the symptoms of hysteria also began to clear away.

Yet healing, as Jacques Derrida has so astutely noted for the notion of the *pharmakon*, is a sword that cuts both ways. Depending on its dosage and on the condition of the body receiving the treatment, one and the same substance can either harm or cure. In the case of Maria Theresa von Paradis, as her optic nerve was resuscitated, the prickling she felt made her head jerk and caused her to suffer recurrent attacks of vertigo. She had the sensation her head was spinning because she could not adjust to the information her eyes were sending her brain after so many years of seeing only darkness. Though throughout her illness Maria Theresa had apparently wanted to be cured, now that something like a cure was about to take place, she began to be disturbed by the thought of a life different from the protective darkness she was familiar with. To be able to see was unfamiliar, perhaps the uncanny return of a psychic state her blindness had allowed her to contain, and it was threatening. As my discussion of *Zelig* sought to demonstrate, any alliance between analyst and hysteric is sustained by a mutual desire for improvement, which is why the analyst is so prone to be duped by the transference of his patient, who, if she is both intelligent and submissive, will produce the symptoms and narratives the physician wishes to receive from her to confirm his treatment. While it was probably only Maria Theresa's faith in Mesmer that allowed her to overcome any doubts she may have had that the cure was what she really wanted, one might speculate that regaining her vision was in part the result of her shift in interpellator. For as Mesmer took the place of Joseph Anton von Paradis, whose paternal desire the daughter had come to sustain so spectacularly well by virtue of her blindness, being able to see again was the way she could not only assure herself of Mesmer's attention, but also give to him what he lacked—proof that his cure of animal magnetism was effective.

Thus, what is intriguing about this incident is not the question of whether Mesmer was a charlatan. Rather, as the next stage in Maria Theresa's story illustrates, her hysteric disorder was a way to articulate the lack that she felt at the heart of the family, but could express only by negotiating paternal authority. To assure the continuation in his patient's improvement, Mesmer asked Maria Theresa to stay in his clinic, partly because he wanted to keep her under close observation, but more crucially because by relocating her he could remove her from the family situation to which she had apparently only been able to respond with blindness. As the hysteric daughter began more and more to regain her sight, what also progressively came to light was that for both paternal figures she was merely a stake in their own symbolic projects. Joseph Anton Paradis sought to enhance his authority as impressario, while Anton Mesmer sought to cement his authority as psychic healer. For both "fathers," Maria Theresa's hysterical body was the site at which each sought to broadcast his paternal power and knowledge. It actually makes perfect sense that the first part of the treatment was documented by Joseph Anton von Paradis in a statement of more than twenty-three pages testifying to the efficacy of the Mesmerian method, which Mesmer appended to his *Memoirs* as a footnote. Thus, throughout this curious autobiography we have on the upper part of the pages Mesmer's testimony wherein he defends himself and his cure against his critics, including the vituperative father Paradis. And on the lower part of the pages, in turn, we have the father's voice praising Mesmer and the way he cured his daughter. In the blind spot between these two paternal voices, the bar demarcating the difference between the two, we obliquely sense Maria Theresa's position, articulated in the oscillation between blindness and sight, between performing music and falling silent. Torn between these two paternal desires that ultimately had nothing to do with the traumatic knowledge she was converting in her hysteric symptoms, Maria Theresa found herself in a psychic impasse.

Like *The Magic Flute*, this incident revolves around an inexplicable lacuna. Mesmer never adequately explains why Joseph Anton von Paradis suddenly turned against him in the second act. The interpretation he offers, that his enemies in the medical profession convinced Paradis to call off the treatment by assuring him that Mesmer was having a pernicious influence on his daughter, dovetails with his own conspiracy theory. However, given that (at least superficially) Mesmer's treatment was entirely wholesome, only a mind obsessed with its own persecution phantasies could have located his advocate's change in attitude in some outside source. One might speculate that although Mesmer never recorded any personal antagonism between himself and von Paradis, a paternal rivalry must have developed, whereby the father resented his daughter's dependence on the healer. To a degree monetary interest could also have informed von Paradis' antagonism toward Mesmer, for the impressario could well have begun to anticipate a substantial loss of income from his daughter's cure. Maria Theresa's playing begin to deteriorate once her sight was partially restored because the presence of an audience she had before never actually seen began to make her nervous as a musician. Von Paradis had not factored into his desire to have his daughter returned to perfect health that, should her sight be fully restored, she would no longer be the performing curiosity she had been and perhaps lose not only her income but also the pension granted by the empress. Whether von Paradis actually convinced himself that his daughter would never be happy with her eyesight restored, that Mesmer would never be able to really cure her, or that a successful treatment would deprive her of favor with her public and the empress one thing was certain: the father, much like Sarastro, wanted to remove Maria Theresa from what he considered a pernicious sphere of influence.

What ultimately made the case so controversial for those commenting on it later is that Maria Theresa initially objected to returning to her parents. One can only conjecture that, on the one hand, this had to do with the fact that she had learned to trust her physician, perhaps even felt a certain erotic attraction to him. On the other hand, however, her fear of returning home also began to suggest what the cause for her hysteric blindness might have been. For once the parents discovered that Maria Theresa refused to come home, they enacted a violence against their daughter within the public space of the clinic, which one is tempted to see as a reproduction of the violence within the confines of the home that had probably first precipitated her flight into blindness. And if Joseph Anton later supported Viennese society's gossip about sexual abuse, as a psychoanalytically concerned critic I feel compelled to wonder whether the rigor with which he did so might not also indicate paternal denial. Indeed, Mesmer explicitly accuses the father that in "seeking to cover his excesses, he spread the most atrocious imputations about me amongst the public" (1779, 56).

Recounting the family affair in his *Memoirs*, Mesmer first describes how Rosalia Maria von Parades suddenly arrived on 29 April, at his clinic, demanded that Maria Theresa be released, and, when this request was denied, fell into a violent frenzy, stamping and shouting until her daughter, who was present, fell into one of her old convulsive attacks. Mesmer writes that the mother, "hearing her cries, left me briskly, pulled her daughter furiously away from the attendant holding her, and, saying 'unhappy creature, you are part of the intrigue of this house,' flung her with rage headlong against the wall" (1779, 50). Trying to help the traumatized daughter, Mesmer found the mother attacking him. He then continues his narrative with the entrance of the father, who, having been ordered away by one of the servants, "came storming into my house waving a sword. Another servant barred the door to the room where we were and struggled to push him away. They finally succeeded in disarming this madman, and he rushed from the house calling down maledictions on me" (52). Whether Maria Theresa was simply shocked by this Oedipal violence or whether it recalled the traumatic impact of the violence she had come to associate with her filial position, in either case its onset caused her to relapse back into her hysteric symptoms. As Mesmer notes, after the mother had finally left, the daughter "had vomit attacks, convulsions, and anxiety attacks brought about by the least sounds, above all the ringing of the church bells. She had fallen back into her prior blindness, by virtue of the blow her mother had given her" (53).

As pecuniary concerns, parental desires, and scientific interests came to be so inextricably knotted together that no reasonable compromise could be found between the two parties, the Paradis parents decided to launch their complaint against Mesmer at the Viennese public, which, of course, was only too eager to believe the accusation that the physician was holding the blind daughter against her will. For the parents chose to broadcast the scenario of Mesmer confined alone with an eighteen-year-old blind girl behind closed doors in his clinic, corroborating the rumors that had already cast the physician in the role of a wizard doing strange things in his laboratory and seducing his female patients. Meanwhile the notion of the nominally healthy bourgeois family that began to circulate forbade any speculations about what the Paradis parents might have themselves been doing with their daughter behind the closed doors of their home. This exchange was so fraught with phantasies that only a figure whose symbolic mandate remained unquestioned could finally arbitrate. The Empress Maria Theresa, scandalized at the stories that involved her protégée, asked her chief physician Stoerck on 2 May 1777 to order Mesmer to cease his hoax ("finir cette supercherie" was her expression) and return the girl to her parents.

Apparently Maria Theresa tried one last time to make her voice heard. Told that she was to leave the clinic, she fell back into her old hysteric symptoms, exhibited convulsions, delirium, and blindess. Now able to forbid her removal on medical grounds, Mesmer once more used his hypnotic powers to restore her sight. Finally, however, Joseph Anton von Paradis got his way. Learning of her improvement, he persuaded Mesmer to send Maria Theresa home, promising that she could return for further treatment whenever she should need it. Of course the parents kept her, and Maria Theresa lapsed back into her accustomed blindness from which she was never to emerge again. However, while one would think that under such circumstances the outcome would have been sheer tragedy for the blind Maria Theresa, her story takes a different turn, for she got over her dependence on Mesmer, no longer wished to have her sight restored, and instead readjusted herself with alacrity to the familiar world of eternal darkness.

What I find most compelling in Maria Theresa's story, however, is that it brings to the fore precisely the ambivalence Mozart evades when he so unequivocally celebrates the extinction of the night: namely, the disquieting possibility that both the blindness, which set in so suddenly, and then the equally miraculous regaining of her sight were hysterical symptoms. For I would speculate that both were nourished by a darkness far more archaic than either the violence brought about by her neurotic parents or the suggestion imposed by the physician—that is, by a traumatic knowledge that makes itself heard only in belated traces, in the protective fiction by which the hysteric believes she can support the desire of the paternal figure and make the father whole, traces that, consequently, are always only as lasting as the Other to whom they are addressed. Put another way, the volatility of Maria Theresa's ability to see is not necessarily indicative of the proficiency of Mesmer's cure. Rather, it indicates that the traumatic knowledge on which hysteric symptoms feed, regardless of what concrete scenes of violence or vulnerability finally give shape to this intangible impact, can be converted but cannot be extinguished. Whether blindness or sight prevails, what ultimately persists is the insight that both are belated articulations of an originary conflation of power, knowledge, and sexuality, which has no scene, no narrative, and no characters.

The second, equally disturbing, message one may glean from the story of Maria Theresa's encounter with Mesmer is that the hysterical symptom might be more empowering than its cure. For hers is the story of a happy hysteric. She returned to her career as a pianist, playing not only in Vienna but also successfully touring in Paris and London. Her virtuosity on the keyboard was so great that Mozart composed the Concerto in B-Flat Major (K. 456) for her, which she premiered in Paris in 1784 at the Tuileries before Louis XVI and Marie Antoinette. She also became a successful composer in her own right, producing songs, piano literature, and operas. Toward the end of her life she even founded a school for educating women pianists. She died at the age of sixty-five, having lived forty-seven years in the dark, sustained by the music her fingers and her voice brought forth. One final point of almost tragic irony is that while Mesmer's failure to cure Maria Theresa's hysteria was at the core of her success as a famous professional musician at a time when few women were able to carve a place for themselves within this public domain, it drove the infamous physician away from Vienna, estranging him from his wife, home, and comfortable life, and even came to haunt him years later when he was seeking to promote his work on animal magnetism in Paris. In 1784 Maria Theresa von Paradis arrived to perform a concert in Paris, and the journalist Friedrich Melchior Grimm notes with spite the strange discrepancy in their respective situations: "Her ability on the harpsichord, in spite of her total blindness, is the most astonishing thing in the world; but one may well believe that her appearance in Paris at the time surprised Mesmer in a most disagreeable manner" (quoted in Simons 1987, 86). Maria Theresa knew the cost of taking up her father's magic flute but, unlike Pamina, did not give up this powerful tool to enter into the protective fiction of a bourgeois marriage. Rather, she continued to play, not only bringing the sound of the night into the most renowned salons and concert halls of late-eighteenth-century Europe, but exhibiting her own proximity to the world of darkness. Therein lies the force of her hysterical oscillation.

The point that feminist scholars Martha Noel Evans (1991) and Elaine Showalter (1985) have convincingly made is that hysteria can be interpreted as a pathological response to prescribed gender roles and social helplessness. Symptoms like inertia, overexcitation, excessive role-playing, or motoric function disorders signal a recourse to body language that stands in for the stifling domestic situation women found themselves in as the nineteenth century progressed. Along these lines, Carroll Smith-Rosenberg (1985), basing her research primarily on the bourgeois women of Victorian New England, argues that this flight into illness came to serve as an appealing form of indirect dissent that preserved notions of ideal femininity (frailty, docility, and subordination to men) even as it allowed women to enter covertly into a power struggle with the dictates of patriarchal law. The astonishing difference between the life stories of these mid-nineteenth-century hysterics and that of Maria-Theresa von Paradis, whose hysteric blindness was used to launch a complaint at the earllier bourgeois family when it had just begun to take hold, is that Maria Theresa's act of transforming her body into a ciphered message about the terrifying situation of a daughter should have so inextricably been tied up with her success as a professional musician. In contrast, for the women, who consulted psychoanalysts such as Freud or Janet, hysteria was the language chosen to bespeak precisely their failure to enter the public domain. Having recourse to this psychosomatic illness defeated their husbands' and families' demands to support the domestic order, given that they concomitantly left the household unattended, as it also defeated the male physicians, whose remedies proved to be so ineffectual. This late-nineteenth-century hysteria, Smith-Rosenberg concludes, must be understood as an oblique way of voicing discontent with a paternal value system. The distraught daughters chose a dislocated articulation because, fully ingrained in the fiction of the bourgeois family, they couldn't directly admit their dissatisfaction to themselves in private, let alone in public. At the same time, they could also no longer fully disavow this discontent. In my exploration of some cases of hysteria presented by Freud and Jaspers, I will return to stories about what happens when the ideal woman, culturally constructed to guarantee the stability of the hearth, is dislocated, leaves her home, and thereby offers yet another rendition of the wandering womb come unhooked. At this point, however, as I move to my discussion of an exemplary gothic rewriting of the hysteric's broadcast of familial complaint, another issue is at stake: how to write like a proper lady and, nevertheless, find a way to articulate dissenting wishes.

CHAPTER 3

Gothic Hysterics: Ann Radcliffe's
The Romance of the Forest

> What does it mean to be hysterical? Perhaps I've also been so, perhaps I am
> now, but I know nothing about it, having never examined the matter thor-
> oughly and having only heard about it secondhand without studying it. Isn't
> it a malaise, a great distress, caused by the desire for an impossible *some-*
> *thing*? In that case, all of us who have imagination are afflicted with it, with
> that strange sickness. And why would such a malady have a sex?
>
> —*George Sand*

I

IN HER DISCUSSION of eighteenth-century English literature and culture,
Terry Castle uses the psychoanalytic category of the *uncanny* to explore an
articulation like the one Foucault isolates in describing the bourgeois family
as both the keystone of alliance and the germ of all misfortunes connected
with sexuality. For, in claiming that the eighteenth century gave rise to the
uncanny, which Freud referred to a century later in his elaborations on psychic ambivalence, Castle seeks to suggest how "the very psychic and cultural
transformations that led to the subsequent glorification of the period as an
age of reason or enlightenment—the aggressively rationalist imperatives of
the epoch—also produced, like a kind of toxic side effect, a new human
experience of strangeness, anxiety, bafflement, and intellectual impasse"
(1995, 8). In other words, in this historic period of Mozart/Schikaneder's
The Magic Flute, the spirit of rationality was meant to render all belief in
magic and superstition obsolete, thereby casting reason as the basis of all
social behavior, the historic internalization of rationalist protocols proved,
however, to also be the germ of psychic unease. The equation that Castle
postulates for this era is "The more we seek enlightenment, the more alienat-
ing our world becomes": the more forcibly superstition is banned to the
realm of eternal night, the more persistently this repressed material returns
in configurations of the uncanny. Equally important, she adds, is the fact
that "the more we seek to free ourselves, Houdini-like, from the coils of
superstition, mystery and magic, the more tightly, paradoxically, the uncanny holds us in its grip" (Castle 1995, 15).[1]
  Of the many examples Castle offers to substantiate her claim, the most
relevant one to my discussion is Ann Radcliffe's gothic romances as a liter-

ary response to this new sensibility of the late-eighteenth century, played upon a sense of the uncanny in human consciousness. Speaking of a spectral-ization or ghostifying of mental space, Castle uncovers the following dialec-tic for the psychological and literary discourse of the time. While ghosts and apparitions were recoded as hallucinations, or projections of the mind, the mind itself came to be viewed as a phantom zone, the home of spectral pres-ences and haunting obsessions. This was in part the result of the rationalist project's "supernaturalization" of the mind, which sought to explain away the traditional supernatural realm, only to find it return in an inverted form, contaminating the very language of mental experience that had been in-vented to exorcise it. At the same time, as romantic self-absorption grew, however, the Other—be this people or the external world—came to be re-duced more and more to a mental effect, devoid of corporeality, valued as an internalized image, a mental phantom, until these phantasmatic objects had come to seem increasingly real. Such a "spectralization of the other" resulted in an inflated belief in the omnipotence of thought as well as in a valuing of absence over presence, of the dead over the living, of phantasied objects or mental simulacrums over concrete people. Indeed, Castle notes the contra-diction that while "the 'ghost' of the dead or absent person, conceived as a kind of visionary image or presence in the mind, takes on a new and compel-ling subjective reality," on the other hand, "real human beings become ghostly too . . . in the sense that they suddenly seem insubstantial and un-real" (Castle 1995, 136).

Castle's point is that the spectralization of the Other can be seen as an ambivalent way of negating one's own death, not by explicitly banning it to the margins of social and psychic reality, as members of the enlightened rationality sought to do, but rather by valorizing a life beyond death, an eternal presence of the deceased as phantasmatic object. In this preference for the specter, furthermore, Castle sees an important link between late-eigh-teenth-century and postmodern sensibility. Her interrogation of Radcliffe's texts leads her to ask whether, in our late twentieth century, we do not also deny our own corporeality or the corporeality of others, whether we do not also cherish the life of the mind over life itself. She thus draws from gothic literature a plea to recognize "the denatured state of our own awareness: our antipathy toward the body and its contingencies, our rejection of the pres-ent, our fixation on the past (or yearnings for an idealized future), our long-ing for simulacra and nostalgic fantasy" (137).[2]

Although Castle does not discuss this new sensibility, which encouraged a fluid boundary between life and death or between somatic bodies and men-tal phantoms, in relation to hysteria as a malady of the imagination, this is precisely the analogy I will explore now. For as I have been arguing, the language of hysteria articulates a similar conviction that the distinction be-tween life and death, between body and phantasied Other, is irrelevant pre-cisely because the dead live on in the mind of the hysteric as memory traces, although still alive, because the inhabitants of the hysteric's world exist first and *foremost* as characters in phantasy scenarios that make up her psychic reality. However, I propose the hybrid gothic hysterics in order to indicate that the ambivalence written into any spectralization of the other, as it emerged as the uncanny underbelly of the rationalist imperative of the Enlightenment, may have sought not only to reject the present and deny death or corporeality by translating bodies into phantoms. Rather, at least with hysteric performances, spectralization may well also have embraced mortal contingency by restaging the phantasmatic objects—precisely at the site of the body. The valuing of absence over presence, similarly, is less at stake than is the existence of several presences, or, rather, acknowledging the presence of a phantom, which as an actual presence would be unbearable and impossible.

In still another sense, the paradox underlying psychoanalytic explanation of the Enlightenment's spectralization can be fruitfully aligned with the exchange the hysteric sets up with her peers. Castle rightly notes that within the Freudian cure to escape being possessed by the past involves an absorption in the phantasmatic: "One denies ghosts by raising them, frees oneself of one's memories by remembering, escapes the feeling of neurotic derealization by plunging into an unreal reverie. . . . Seen in historical terms, as an offshoot of the radically introspective habit of mind initiated in the late eighteenth century, psychoanalysis seems both the most poignant critique of romantic consciousness to date, and its richest and most perverse elaboration" (139). In light of the link that Castle sets up between the double-sided sensibility prevalent at the end of the eighteenth century and Freud's discussion of the uncanny, it is perhaps no coincidence that what gave birth to psychoanalysis was the late-nineteenth-century hysteric's richly suggestive performance of romantic consciousness gone awry. A spectralization of the other is that psychic articulation that assumes taking on a different guise with each new historical period and yet remains constant. One may speculate whether the reason why the language of hysteria continues to irritate and fascinate analysts and spectators is partly that this psychosomatic disorder begs the questions whether an escape from one's family neurosis is ever really possible, whether the finality of death can ever be unequivocably denied, and whether the traces of traumatic impact can ever be fully effaced.

My reading of Ann Radcliffe's early gothic *Romance of the Forest* will be framed by a psychoanalytic discussion of phantasy as a pointer to what is inconsistent in the rationalist project—what is repressed or yet unaddressed. I want to highlight not only the way gothic phantasmagoria can be seen as a symptom, admonishing us to recognize the contingency of our mortal existence, but also the contradictory doubleness in articulation that links the hysteric's complaint launched at the family, with her obsession with phantasmatic objects. Castle's self-absorbed romantic subject has recourse to a spectralization of the other so as to nourish a fixation on the past and a yearning for an idealized future that renders the present phantasmatic. The hysteric imitates this late-eighteenth-century sensibility when she insists on articulating what is wrong with the present family, insisting with a belief in the ideal family in mind. For her complaint is not aimed against the family per se, but simply that *her* family does not satisfy her desire for perfection. She points to what is wrong in the present coterminously with indulging in phantasmatic objects so as to explore the possibility of other filial bonds for the future. Apodictically put, hysteric spectralization involves not so much discovering as inventing the ideal family—in a gesture that conflates nostalgia with utopia.

II

As Laplanche and Pontalis note in *The Language of Psychoanalysis*, the word phantasy or fantasy refers to an "imaginary scene in which the subject is a protagonist, representing the fulfilment of a wish . . . in a manner that is distorted to a greater or lesser extent by defensive processes" (1973, 314). The two spellings of the word, however, already indicate how ambiguous the concept is. *Phantasie* in German exploits associations connected with the world of the imagination; it invokes the creative activity that both invents and invigorates phantasy scenarios and the products of this activity, the contents of this imaginary world. *Fantasie* is closer to the French notion of *fantasme*, "referring to a specific imaginary production, not to the world of phantasy and imaginative activity in general" (314). It implies a dynamic, structuring activity that in the act of articulation constantly draws in new material. As Elizabeth Cowie also notes, the word fantasy derives from the Greek term "to make visible": "However, rather than a notion of revelation, making visible what we would not otherwise be able to see—as with a microscope allowing us to see bacteria, etc., invisible to the 'naked' eye—fantasy as a term has come to mean the making visible, present, of what isn't there, of what can never directly be seen" (1990, 154).

Thus the word phantasy invariably evokes the impression that one is speaking about something existing only as an expression of unrestrained fancy, something unreal, extravagant, bizarre, eccentric, foreign in origin, and alluring in effect—something that is strongly influenced by caprice or whimsy rather than by fact, reality, reason, or experience. Yet it is also precisely because the term phantasy inevitably makes it impossible to distinguish between imagination and reality that it plays such a crucial role in Freud's discussion of the etiology of neuroses and, in particular, hysteria. As he notes, "If hysterical subjects trace back their symptoms to traumas that are fictitious, then the new fact which emerges is precisely that they create such scenes in phantasy, and this psychical reality requires to be taken into account along side practical reality" (1914, 17). In other words, if psychical reality is not to be confused with material reality, it is because Freud's aim was to explain the coherence and efficiency of the subject's *phantasy* life, always insisting that the subjective, the imaginary, is not only the object of psychoanalysis, but that it possesses a reality of its own. As Laplanche and Pontalis explain, Freud refused to restrict himself to a choice between treating "phantasy as a distorted derivative of the memory of actual fortuitous events" and seeing it as deprived of any specific reality, treating it "merely as an imaginary expression designed to conceal the reality of the instinctual dynamic" (1973, 315). Rather, phantasy murkily interfaces between the traumatic impressions, memory traces, repressed desires, and culturally transmitted narratives that are the matrix within which it can express in a converted form what can find no direct psychic articulation.

For Freud, the most important manifestations of phantasy work are daydreams: the scenes, episodes, and romances an individual creates for him- or herself in either a waking or hypnoid state. Conceiving phantasies to be among the "most intimate possessions" of the patient, cherished but also concealed with great sensitivity, Freud argues that they function along the same lines as nocturnal dreams. Given that both represent unconscious desires obliquely by staging an imagined scene of wish fulfillment and correcting an inadequate reality, Freud adds, "A happy person never phantasises, only an unsatisfied one" (1908, 146). While every dream represents through coded language a knowledge the dreamer wishes to deny, so too every phantasy articulates something lacking by virtue of a compromise formation. Most phantasies, Freud explains, are either ambitious wishes revolving around self-aggrandizement or the fulfillments of erotic desires. In temporal structure they knot together three events: a current impression that provokes dissatisfaction in the present, a memory of an earlier experience when the wish was fulfilled, and the phantasized future event that promises satisfaction once again. "Past, present and future are strung together, as it were, on the thread of the wish that runs through them" (Freud 1908, 148).

Though each daydream is distinctly configured, Freud believed he had discovered a common denominator in many of the phantasies patients related to him. Projected into the future, the daydreamer often designs a scenario where she regains the plenitude she believed to have possessed in her happy childhood—the protective house, the loving parents, and the first, usually autoerotic, objects of the dreamer's affectionate feelings (1908, 148). Significantly, Freud calls this typical phantasy "the neurotic's family romance" (1909a), arguing that it is a response to the fact that the psychic development of each individual calls for a liberation from the authority of one's parents. Because it is easier to abandon something one disparages, the family romance allows the daydreamer to use this scenario to voice her sense of being dissatisfied with the current family bond. In this staging of desire, discontent with the present family relations is converted into a phantasy of being a stepchild or an orphan, while the parents one needs to get free of—converted not only into foster parents but endowed with a low opinion to boot—are readily replaced by others of higher social standing. As in the phantasy scenario involving the theme of the three caskets (see chapter 1), necessity is thus translated into choice. Separation from the familiar family and a loss of the protection it affords becomes desirable because the threat has been converted into a more idealized version. At the same time, however, the faithlessness, illegitimacy, and ingratitude which the daydreamer ascribes to his real family are benign forms of vengeance and hostility. The humble parents are merely recast as aristocratic ones, along the lines of the child's memory of his childhood. Far from getting rid of parents, Freud concludes, the family romance, actually exhalts them: "The whole effort at replacing the real father by a superior one is only an expression of the child's longing for the happy, vanished days when his father seemed to him the noblest and strongest of men and his mother the dearest and loveliest of women" (241).

Yet the ambivalence of articulation played through when a correction of reality leads back to phantasies that are all too familiar to us, I would argue, is more complex. Even as phantasy work knots together a memory trace of satisfaction with a contemporary event of discontent so as to project a redressing of dissatisfaction into the future, the reminiscence on which the phantasy of triple plenitude is based is coded as a protective fiction. The past that the daydreamer imagines is inevitably reshaped to fit the story she needs to tell herself so as to make sense of her world. When Freud notes that the family romance gives voice to two distinct expressions of unease—to a dissatisfaction with the present and a regret that the "happy days" of childhood "have gone"—he admits that here "the over-valuation that characterizes a child's earliest years comes into its own again" (1909a, 241). Yet acknowledging that the parents seemed exhalted, in this nostalgically reinvoked past, Freud also implicitly contends that the vanished days were happy. His own theory, however, actually suggests the inverse conclusion: any sense of early childhood satisfaction is already a phantasy, albeit a necessary one. For in his architecture of hysteria Freud quite explicitly argues that phantasies are both psychical façades constructed to bar the memories they bespeak and that they serve to refine these memories, to sublimate them (1892–1899, 248).

Along these lines, Freud finds another trait common to many daydreams, namely that the protagonist appears to be enjoying the protection of a special providence. Such phantasy scenarios, articulate a desire for invulnerability in that they revolve around the sentence "nothing can happen to *me*"(1909a; 150). Indeed they offer a complementary version of the desire for protection and plenitude, recast in the family romance. For the blind spot in both scenarios, their point of inconsistency, is that in both the script of a happy childhood and that of an invulnerable protagonist, protective fictions are recast as familiar reminiscences so as to shield from a knowledge of the traumatic kernel at the heart of the family, the difference at its hearth. Indeed, it is this underbelly of the idealized family invoked so nostalgically that returns uncannily when the hysteric offers her exaggerated adaptation of the family romance, the happy daydream gone too far and become fanciful. As Freud posits in his discussion of daydreams, while phantasies of restoring a lack may satisfy the daydreamer, once phantasies become overluxuriant and overpowerful, the conditions are laid for an onset of neurosis. This is so, I would add, because having traversed satisfaction, the daydreamer is still confronted with whatever lack set the entire process of phantasizing in motion—with the inevitable psychic unhappiness of deprivation and fallibility for which the navel is the somatic sign. For the conversion that neurosis offers merely transforms fate into choice (as the family romance illustrates), once the chosen symptom has made bearable, even enjoyable, the truth that satisfaction is impossible.

By the mid-nineteenth century, hysteria had become the paradigmatic neurosis of psychic exchange between a lack of satisfaction and phantasy work: this psychosomatic disturbance had come to be seen as a malady by representation. Freud notes that even without having knowledge of this ideational complex "the mind of the hysterical patient is full of active yet unconscious ideas; all her symptoms proceed from such ideas. It is in fact the most striking character of the hysterical mind to be ruled by them" (1912, 262). Every hysterical attack ultimately proved to be "an involuntary irruption of daydreams" (1908a, 160), of phantasies initially banished by repression to the unconscious, translated into the register of the body there only to be portrayed in pantomime (1909, 229). Unconscious phantasies thus emerged as the immediate psychical precursors of hysteric symptoms, the latter nothing other than pathogenic "unconscious phantasies brought into view through conversion" (1908a, 162). Analysis, of course, aimed to turn from the conspicuous symptom to the latent content of the unconscious phantasy from which it originated, hoping to eliminate both the origin of the pathogenic phantasy and the symptom itself through the course of interpretation. However, the presupposition subtending the analytic cure casts symptoms as articulations of phantasies and not of actual events; insofar as these symptoms refer back to memory traces, reminiscences must be conceived as protective fictions or an expression of psychic reality, which is inevitably demarcated from the real traumatic impact whose traces it also records.

The hysteric symptom proves to be a complex and highly equivocal knot, seminal to the architecture of hysteria that Freud proposes at the beginning of his psychoanalytic project. A particular symptom or hysterical attack does not simply relate to one unconscious phantasy: rather, it represents several phantasies simultaneously, through condensation. This representation however, occurs "not in an arbitrary manner but in accordance with a regular pattern" (1908, 163). Seeking universal formulas to characterize the relation between phantasy and symptom formation, Freud argues that the hysteric symptom emerges as a mnemic representation of traumatic impressions and experiences and serves as the substitute for the uncanny return of these traumatic experiences. Yet hysteric symptoms also are seen as staging the fulfillment of a wish, or the realization of an unconscious phantasy that serves the fulfilment of a wish, becoming the substitute mode of sexual satisfaction that refers back to real satisfaction during infantile life (which also has been repressed). In other words, the hysteric symptom blurs the boundary between traumatic impression and originary autoerotic satisfaction. In light of this, the loss of consciousness, the *absence* so common in hysterical attacks, indeed performs the acme of satisfaction. Freud suggests that the mechanism of these *absences* begins with the subject's attention concentrated on satisfying a particular desire articulated through the phantasy scenario. Once satsifaction occurs, once the phantasy seems fulfilled, however, this investment of attention is suddenly removed. Significantly, what ensues is a momentary void in consciousness, and this "gap in consciousness . . . is widened in the service of repression, till it can swallow up everything that the repressing agency rejects" (1909, 234). Although Freud aligns the lapse of consciousness to the one observable at the climax of every intense sexual satisfaction, one could just as easily compare it to the climax of every traumatic experience: to that excessive expression or excitation that the ego experiences in moments of overwhelming anxiety, which is followed by a gap in the psyche. For what is so poignantly performed by the hysteric's absence, I would argue, is that once phantasy has been traversed we find ourselves confronting not the face of satisfaction but rather the psychic gap setting traumatic impact apart from all gestures of representation.[3]

The compromise the hysteric symptom affords knots together two opposite affective and instinctual impulses: on the one hand, the desire to articulate repressed knowledge and on the other hand, the desire to suppress it. The content of the knowledge negotiated so duplicitously not only combines sexual impulses with traumatic impressions involving the idea of mortal danger or a threat to life (1893, 28). Further, Freud notes, the bisexuality of hysteric symptoms represent both a "compromise between a libidinal and a repressing impulse" and a union of a masculine and a feminine unconscious, sexual phantasy (1908a, 165). As a result, during a hysterical attack the patient can attempt to carry out the activities of various figures appearing in the phantasy, performing a multiple identification: for example, simultaneously staging a contradictory action that splices being agent of an action *and* its object.

As such, phantasies emerge as a knot connecting symptom formations, conscious daydreams, and unconscious desires. Under the censorship of repression, they screen traumatic impact by modulating this forbidden knowledge into a belated and distorted articulation. Phantasies mediate between a primal enjoyment of traumatic knowledge that lies before the psychic gap on which all representations are grounded and the symbolic laws of social reality that demand *forgoing* this clandestine enjoyment. As a result of this renunciatory conversion, the subject can preserve a fallible albeit efficient self-identity—but only at the cost of symptom formation. Like nocturnal dreams, phantasies perform a psychic compromise, refract traumatic knowledge, and deflect its power in the name of repression and sublimation. As an interface between two poles, phantasies cast scenes of wish fulfillment in the language of psychic reality around a refused and denied traumatic enjoyment. In other words, a phantasy is linked on one side to the deepest unconscious wish—and marks the navel of any representation—which feeds on this unknown and unknowable material of desire grounding the psychic apparatus. On the other side, a phantasy functions as the navel from which any secondary revisions are brought forth, masterminding all representations of this inevitable and inaccessible knowledge.

As Freud notes in his discussion of the unconscious, phantasies "are highly organized, free from self-contradiction, have made use of every acquisition of the system *Cs*. [conscious] and would hardly be distinguished in our judgement from the formations of that system. On the other hand they are unconscious and are incapable of becoming conscious. Thus qualitatively they belong to the system *Pcs*. [preconscious], but factually to the *Ucs*. [unconscious] Their origin is what decides their fate. We may compare them with individuals of mixed race (*Mischlinge*) who, taken all round, resemble white men (*die Weissen*), but who betray their coloured descent by some striking feature or other, and on that account are excluded from society and enjoy none of the privileges of white people" (1915, 190f.). As such, phantasies cannot be seen only as foreign bodies, which do not belong to the realm in which they act. Rather, as Freud describes, they point to the strategy of hysteric language. Both, after all, are deceptive and chameleon-like, hard to distinguish from the formations of the system, yet ultimately betraying through some detail their deviation from the norm—be it consciousness, in the case of phantasy in general, or normalcy, in the case of hysteric phantasies in particular. The crux, therefore, lies not in the distinction between conscious, subliminal, and unconscious phantasy work but rather in what analogies they share and what transitions occur between the three levels, as repressed desire uses phantasy as the threshold that allows it uncannily to return in the guise of symptoms.

Though phantasy is intimately linked with desire, Laplanche and Pontalis insist that it cannot be reduced to an intentional aim on the part of the subject, who seeks to recover phantasy-objects that are bound to early experiences of satisfaction. The two writers therefore, offer several additions to Freud's theory of particular relevance to my discussion of the language of hysteria (given their insistence on the notion of phantasy as performance). Phantasy, they argue, is not the object of desire, but its setting. Phantasies are scripts of organized scenes that can be dramatized, usually in a visual form. The subject is inevitably present in these scenarios, both as an observer and as a participant. The subject does not imagine a desired object nor aim the scene at it. Rather the individual crafts a scenario in which she plays her own part and in which permutations of roles and attributions are possible. By virtue of enactment, phantasy knots a denied, refused enjoyment of unbearable plenitude, of destructive, traumatic knowledge, with the very law of sublimation that forbids it. Because it thus serves as the double-sided site where the articulation of desire is joined with defensive operations, Laplanche and Pontalis designate it as "the mise-en-scène of desire—a mise-en-scène in which what is prohibited is always present in the actual formation of the wish" (1973, 318).

Freud, as part of his argument that psychic, not material, reality is the decisive constituent of neurosis precisely as it welds the latent content (the unconscious desire) with manifest data (the phantasy representation), believed he could ultimately uncover "real" phantasy scenes (*Urszenen*), unconscious schemata that not only lie behind but also structure all belated articulations of traumatic impact. In other words, these typical phantasies, which he claimed to have uncovered beneath the diversity of individual stories, also transcend the individuals' lived experiences. Freud came to call these originary scenes—the navel point of all symptom formation and of the entire neurotic organization of any personality—"primal phantasies of phylogenetic endowment." He felt that here an individual reaches beyond his or her own experience into primeval experience and reencodes traumatic traces, with recourse to inherited memory traces. "The seduction of children, the inflaming of sexual excitement by observing parental intercourse, the threat of castration (or rather castration itself)," Freud suggests, "were once real occurrences in the primaeval times of the human family, and . . . children in their phantasies are simply filling in the gaps in individual truth with prehistoric truth (1917, 371).

As they elaborate Freud's discussion of primary phantasies, Laplanche and Pontalis underline two implications subtending the proposed topology. For one, the original phantasy is "first and foremost fantasy—it lies beyond the history of the subject but nevertheless in history—a kind of language and a symbolic sequence, but loaded with elements of imagination" (1964, 18). The notion of a primal phantasy, one might say, works with the same duplicity in articulation that leads Barthes to call history hysterical, arguing that narratives convert the certainty of the past, which excludes the subject, into a story fabricated according to conventional formulas. Laplanche and Pontalis find equally significant the fact that "the origin of fantasy is integrated in the very structure of the original fantasy," given that all three primal phantasy scenes—of heritage, castration, and seduction—revolve around the individual's desire to explore and solve the riddle of his origins: Who am I in relation to my family heritage? What is the origin of my body's vulnerable and mutable anatomy? What is the cause of my drives, my desires, my phantasies? "The original fantasies" they argue, "also indicate a postulate of retroactivity: they relate to origins. Like myths, they claim to provide a representation of, and a solution to, the major enigmas which confront the child. Whatever appears to the subject as something needing an explanation or theory, is dramatized as a moment of emergence, the beginning of a history." With phantasies of origins, according to Laplanche and Pontalis, "The primal scene pictures the origin of the individual; fantasies of seduction, the origin and upsurge of sexuality; fantasies of castration, the origin of the difference between the sexes." Owing to these constructed scenarios, these quests for origins, "we are offered in the field of fantasy, the origin of the subject himself"(1964, 19).

The primal scene, then, functions like a foreign body introduced into the subject not so much as the result of perceiving or experiencing a given scene, but rather by being told a given phantasy scene that supports parental desire. If I earlier suggested that phantasy work knots together conscious, subliminal, and unconscious stories of the psychic register, what Freud's notion of primal phantasy introduces into the proposed topology of the mind is why the significant border does not run between unconscious and conscious phantasies. For the division at stake instead distinguishes between the original, or primal, phantasies (i.e., between any inherited memory traces—the archaic knowledge with which each subject fills the gaps in individual truth) and the other, secondary phantasies, whether repressed or conscious, in which the daydreams symptomize unconscious desires, and hallucination revives traumatic impact. One could say that the gap in knowledge and the gap in consciousness conflate in the hysteric's abundant and excessive symptoms.

Within psychoanalytic discourse, then, phantasy and hysteria come to represent each other. Yet when Freud postulates that these two forms of psychic expression are mutually exchangeable because they stand in for each other, he actually draws on precisely the psychological debate that had occurred some hundred years earlier. By the mid-eighteenth century hysteria had emerged as an illness of or by representation, a disorder of the imagination; nourished by memory traces that stubbornly resist effacement, it led not only to abundant phantasy work but more crucially to phantasy scenes converted into a somatic language. In other words, as the gothic hysteric performed an imagination gone awry, she did so within the context of cultural formations housing a newly discovered sensibility of the body and a spectralization of the mind as the side effects of a rationalist imperative.

Laplanche (1974, 468) argues that if the understanding of hysteria in the late-twentieth century has changed, it has been in part because the body now appears to be the "locus for a communication which is potential, implicit, veiled and fixed." Yet, insisting that the conversion the hysterical symptom performs must be understood as a manner of communication which privileges the body as its scene of articulation, rendering this body as subject and object, as me and not-me, he confirms Terry Castle's claim that the late-eighteenth century invented a spectralization of mental space, where the mind was not only conceived as the home for phantasmatic objects but also as the stage from which these foreign bodies of denied or refused knowledge could broadcast their inverted message. As Laplanche notes, to speak of hysterical attacks and crises as phantasy scenarios is useful, given that a scene is triangular in essence. Thus, equating hysteria with the performance of phantasy scenes allows one to describe how the language of a hysteric's performances knots together the various levels involved in the psychic articulation of inevitable dissatisfaction.

Given that a scene implies an action, which unfolds according to a certain scenario that is implicitly perceived in the other or is unconsciously transmitted, phantasy uses the rhetoric of *Nachträglichkeit* (belatedness) to reinterpret more archaic scenarios, offering modulations of what Freud calls the primal scene and primal phantasies. In his architecture of hysteria Freud notes that hysteric phantasies are made up of things heard and only *subsequently* made use of: "They combine things that have been experienced and things that have been heard, past events (from the history of parents and ancestors) and things that have been seen by oneself" (1892–1899, 248). A scene, however, also implies the stage where a given action is carried out. Once one conceives of hysterical phantasy work as a mise-en-scène of desire, a communication in which something is both revealed and hidden, *scene* comes to designate an element readily available to conversion, a sequence which is detachable and able to be isolated as it is staged in the phantom zone of the mind. Finally, *to make a scene* also refers to a public display of passion and temper, aimed at violently moving the interpellating spectator. It is in this triple sense that hysteria performs a scene.

My assumption in discussing gothic literature is that the hysteric can be seen as a phantasizer par excellence. To support my argument that hysterical phantasies articulate the desire of the bourgeois family gone awry at precisely the moment that the family is installed, I use a terminology fully developed only by psychoanalysis a century later; I do so keeping in mind Castle's claim for discovery of the uncanny at the end of the eighteenth century. Within a cultural moment, when two explanations of the world vied with one another—the rationalist project and the repressed supernatural returned as phantasmatic object—the hysteric's gothic text closely imitates this duplicitous self-conception by phantasizing two contending family romances. As I will show, the first scenario that the power of gothic fiction feeds on embellishes the dark underside of enlightened rationality and of the bourgeois family, which had come to serve as its linchpin. The second, abiding by an aesthetic dictate that paternal authority ultimately be recuperated, invents the ideal family and the ideal marriage. Within this discursive space, the hysteric's broadcast of her discontent comes to function as the bourgeois family's specter, speaking the unease on which its rationalist protocol was grounded. Yet in another sense its language spectralizes the other, for hysteria splices the malady of imagination with the pathology of reminiscences so that this particular phantasy work also entails a dialogue with the dead, a negotiation of origins, of inheritance, of the transmitted knowledge one cannot disclaim, and of the burden of one's lineage that one cannot deny.

One final aspect of the duplicitous articulation hysteric phantasy performs should be be raised. The family romance, lying at the heart of gothic fiction, is an inversion of what Foucault calls the family broadcast of complaint, dismantling its very foundation, exploring the inconsistency in the symbolic. However, this phantasy work also lends consistency to psychic and social realities because it is the belief that an infallible family exists and sustains the mise-en-scène of the family romance. As I have argued, the moment in phantasy when a desire seems to find its satisfaction is also dangerously close to encountering the traumatic knowledge that negates all imaginations or constructions of plenitude and infallibility. Focusing on this double gesture, Slavoj Žižek discusses the symptom as a coded message; it prolongs communication when words fail, by converting the failed, repressed words into a different mode of articulation. As he notes, by implication the symptom is not merely interpreted but also always addressed to a figure of alterity who is expected, retroactively, to confer on it its true meaning. In other words, it is formed not only with an eye to its interpretation but also with an eye to its addressee: "In its very constitution, the symptom implies the field of the big Other as consistent, complete, because its very formation is an appeal to the Other which contains its meaning." However, especially in light of the resilience of hysteric symptoms, this begs the question why symptoms persist, even after a complete interpretation has occurred. Žižek thus adds that a symptom "is not only a ciphered message, but also a way for the subject to organize his/her enjoyment" (1992b, 424).

Initially, Lacanian theory tried to position symptom and phantasy diametrically opposite each other. Aligning the dimension of an enjoyment that requires perpetual negotiation and organization exclusively with phantasy, the symptom came to be seen as a signifying formation that can be analyzed, whereas phantasy appeared to resist interpetation. While the symptom implies and addresses an accessible, consistent interpellator, a figure of infallible authority, phantasy in turn implies a blocked, barred inconsistent Other, a figure of "implenitude." The trajectory of the psychoanalytic cure thus begins by interpreting symptoms—so as to penetrate to the fundamental phantasy, "the kernel of enjoyment which is blocking the further movement of interpetation." In a second step analysis requires "going through the fantasy, obtaining distance from it, of experiencing how the fantasy formation masks and fills out a certain void, an empty place in the Other" (Žižek 1992b, 425), the nothing of the hysteric's abundant phantasy work. Yet once Lacan realized that certain symptoms will persist even after the subject has gone through her fantasy, he coined the notion of a *sinthome*, knotting together symptom and phantasy (as "phantomatic" sign), to indicate a signifying formation that also bears *jouissance* (jouir-sens), "enjoyment-in-sense (enjoy-meant)." Splicing the recognition that the authority of the interpellator is inconsistent with that of the subject's need for a support of its being, the symptom/phantasy emerges as "the only point that gives consistency to the subject." Merging these two definitions, Žižek concludes that phantasy work is the way the patient can avoid madness "by choosing something (neurotic symptom-formation) instead of nothing (psychotic autism, the destruction of the Symbolic universe, psychic suicide) through the binding of enjoyment to a certain Symbolic formation which assures a minimum of consistency to being-in-the-world" (425).

The counter-directional gesture of phantasy is such that even as the inadequacy of the hysteric's addressee (and the symbolic universe this interpellator represents) is uncovered, this Other is also recognized as the only support available to the hysteric. Noting that the difference between fantasy and phantasy "is sometimes more than orthographic," Robert Miles (1994) suggests that whereas the former traces the incursion of traumatic impact, the latter involves a shaping imagination that discloses by dramatizing this incursion: fantasy refers to the production of symptom formations, and phantasy refers to the text that emerges once one has gone through fantasy.

I will be applying this distinction between fantasy and phantasy to the romantic texts of self-absorption. I will discuss, without, however, distinguishing them by two separate orthographies. My point is that if the gothic family romance ultimately constructs a coherent, phantasy narrative, it does so through two simultaneous and contradictory phantasy scenarios. In the first the individual traces the search for the happy family of plenitude and infallibility, but in the process self-consciously exposes that discovering the ideal family bond is concomitant with writing it. The family that fully satisfies psychic reality is inevitably a textual family. In the second of these scenes, far from masking or filling out the empty place within paternal authority, the author explores a plethora of phantasmatic representatives of symbolic inconsistency—the perverse, transgressive, and suicidal configurations of family ties gone awry. If, then, I argue that gothic hysterics perform to abundance the duplicity of articulation that Freud finds at the heart of all hysteric phantasy work, I do so to emphasize that within the aesthetic constraints of narrative coherence these phantomatic texts bear the enjoyment of vulnerability and traumatic knowledge, indeed they perform an "enjoyment-in-sense (enjoy-meant)" par excellence. In other words, they constructively transform the kernel of destructive enjoyment into a story that preserves the subject from annihilation. Although they enjoy the hole in symbolic consistency, the narrative matrix within which they are cast is the enlightened family romance, meant to bar any knowledge of this traumatic kernel by resolving the phantasy scene of vulnerability and fallibility into the phantasy scene of marriage; in the process these romances exchange the cruel, impotent, or absent father and negligent or absent mother with an infallible spouse. Following Laplanche and Pontalis, who claim that the origin of phantasy is integrated into the very structure of phantasies of origin, I would add that phantasies of traumatic knowledge inevitably revolve around the trauma of phantasy. The gothic hysteric imitates a key malaise of her culture—the spectralization of the enlightened project—by using phantasy to convert the traumatic impact of this specter into two distinct but interrelated protective fictions. The first explores the lure of total self-expenditure, with the obscene father serving as the addressee of the hysteric symptom. The second resolves the complaint that the hysteric launches at an inadequate family by inventing an ideal lineage and, in so doing, abandoning what is on the other side of the equation: destructive archaic enjoyment.

III

By reading Ann Radcliffe's *The Romance of the Forest* (1791) as a hysterical mise-en-scène of desire, I want to suggest that in the course of her quest, the gothic heroine Adeline gains that triple site of plenitude Freud designated as the aim of a neurotic's family romance: a house, a family, and a reliable object of desire. If we follow Freud in recognizing Her Majesty the Ego as the heroine of every daydream (1908), then (in very general terms) Radcliffe's romance can be seen as a trope for the vicissitudes of feminine subjectivity and for the feminine Oedipal journey (Massé 1992, Langbauer 1990, Modleski 1982), with the daughter abandoning the forbidden maternal body and exchanging the equally forbidden paternal figure for a husband cast in his image. In a rather more specific manner, however, Radcliffe fashions her heroine as a hysterical phantasizer; even as Adeline searches for the perfect family bond—guided by her desire for maternal protection but also fleeing the mortal threat she believes her father to be posing—she challenges the very figure of paternal authority from whose symbolic system the narratives of infallibility and invulnerability she wishes to satisfy are derived. As Robert Miles notes, "Radcliffe's unsavoury father-figures may be construed as an assault on patriarchy, but this did not arise because 'patriarchy' was then strong; it arose because it was 'weak' and under attack." If in her phantasy scenario, then, the hysteric heroine articulates a duplicitous desire, dismantling the very paternal prestige she seeks, she also imitates the cultural malaise that was of particular concern to Ann Radcliffe and her audience. Miles adds that the power of these gothic plots must stem in part from their having been "in phase with one of the period's deep historical shifts" (1995, 110).

Because I am interested in reading this gothic text as a paradigmatic example of the hysteric's family romance, it will be necessary to begin with a brief summary of the intricate plot. In a forest outside Paris, the nineteen year-old beautiful and melancholic Adeline has just left the convent where she was raised. She is given to Pierre La Motte by ruffians as he flees creditors and persecution by the law. Together with his wife, his servant Peter, and this orphaned girl, La Motte seeks shelter in an abbey, the rumored local of a man forcibly confined and murdered. During one of her nocturnal explorations of this abbey, Adeline indeed discovers a secret chamber and in it a manuscript describing a man's agonies of confinement as he awaits execution. Soon after, La Motte's son Louis appears, falls in love with Adeline, proposes, and is rejected because she in turn has fallen in love with Theodore. Theodore is a soldier in the regiment of the Marquis de Montalt, the proprietor of the abbey, to whom La Motte is under obligation because he tried to rob and kill him. The Marquis also falls in love with Adeline, but his proposal is turned down as well. In response, the Marquis involves La Motte in a scheme to capture Adeline as she flees the abbey, so as to imprison her in his villa until she gives in to his seduction. Theodore, who had wanted to warn Adeline but was sent away by his jealous commanding officer before he could do so, unexpectedly reappears in the garden of the Marquis's villa and helps his beloved escape from her violator. At an inn the Marquis's men catch up with them, Theodore is wounded but manages to wound the Marquis. Now under arrest for desertion as well as for attacking a superior officer, he is brought to an army prison to await trial. Adeline, separated once more from her lover, is forcibly returned to the abbey, once again the prisoner of the Marquis. Now, however, because he has discovered her real family lineage, he no longer wishes to seduce her but rather to murder her.

At this point Adeline finds herself as the nexus from a surrogate father who has betrayed her (La Motte) to a lover who has been mutilated and awaits his death on her account (Theodore) and a jealous rival bent on vengeance and destruction (Phillipe, Marquis de Montalt). But like all heroines of daydreams, Adeline is invulnerable in the midst of her staged vulnerability. Aided by La Motte, she flees with Peter to his native village in Switzerland, where she is taken in by the La Luc family. While La Motte, arrested and emprisoned, awaits trial in Paris, La Luc embarks on a journey with Adeline and his daughter Clara to the south of France because his health requires a change in climate. There, accidentally meeting Louis La Motte again, they discover not only that Theodore is the son of La Luc, but that he also has been sentenced to death. They immediately go to the military prison in Vaceau and, on the morning of his execution, learn that the King has issued a reprieve, owing to information that has emerged during the trial. At this point we discover that Adeline is the daughter of Henry, Marquis de Montalt, who was taken prisoner and killed by his brother Phillipe. After the murder, the infant girl had been given to a foster father, Jean d'Aunoy, and later sent to a convent. After deciding not to stay there, she was taken away by the Marquis's men to be killed in the forest outside Paris—but instead given to La Motte. Due to the seal Adeline used on a letter to Theodore, which was intercepted by the Marquis, the latter discovered her real identity and sought again to have her killed. This seal belonged to Adeline's real mother who passed it on to the Marquis; it was stolen by d'Aunoy and given to his wife, who in turn gave it to her foster daughter, Adeline. She kept it as a memento of the woman she thought was her mother. Thus, Adeline, in the course of her family romance, exchanged lowly parents for superior parents—an obscene father for an ideal father and a seemingly perfect husband—what remained constant was the maternal insignia. On his deathbed Phillipe legitimizes Adeline, and as the reinstated Marquise de Montalt, she achieves a pardon for Theodore and the sentence of exile for La Motte. Having buried the skeleton of her father in the family vault, she is seemingly delivered of her hysteric symptoms, especially her melancholy, and with Theodore by her side she returns to Lelancourt in Savoy to live there as Madame La Luc.

Radcliffe's heroine, I want to argue, emerges as a hysterical phantasizer par excellence; she not only behaves like a foreign body once she has left the familiar confines of the convent but the sense of strangeness she experiences and imparts to her peers acts as a materialization of the phantasy scenarios that inhabit her inner mental theater. In other words, Adeline's hysteria entails converting into physical symptoms the dissatisfied desire wandering within her psychic apparatus, with this psychosomatic articulation, as I will show later, taking the shape of hallucinations or absences in consciousness, melancholic languor or body paralysis, and fits of excitation or anxiety. She embodies or performs precisely the sympathetic communication between animal spirits in the brain and body organs discussed earlier in relation to medical theories of the Enlightenment. On the other hand, this internal situation of a foreign body wandering uncontrolled within the confines of the body—a disorder metaphorically described by medical literature as the detached womb—is mirrored by Adeline's seemingly aimless peregrinations through the strange and threatening French and Swiss countryside, causing disturbances wherever she chooses to arrest her journey. To return to Terry Castle's formulation, Radcliffe's hysterical heroine displays a double spectralization of the Other. The mind becomes the stage for phantasmatic presences at the same time that the somatic conversion of a psychic disturbance allows this mental phantom zone to be projected onto an external stage, so that the social space within which the hysterical heroine wanders emerges as the scene where unconscious phantasies can be materialized.

In yet another sense one can call Adeline's gothic quest a hysterical mise-en-scène because, even as she uses her phantasy work to ultimately achieve the family romance of protection and plenitude, this conversion of unconscious phantasies into an adequate and resilient symptom, allowing her to organize her enjoyment in a less pathogenic manner than before, is nevertheless a tainted compromise formation. For example, in the final scene of happiness in Savoy, the assurance seemingly afforded by the phantasy of marriage and familial belonging is recognized in all its fallibility as the only positive support giving consistency to the hysteric. Furthermore, the resolution of the hysteric's dissatisfaction into a marriage plot with Theodore is inextricably intertwined with an enjoyment of mortal threat whose kernel persists, if only as a trace, even after the heroine has traversed her gothic fantasy. Adeline desires to pursue her origins, in the course of which she invents noble parents (Henry, Marquis de Montalt) whom she can exchange for her humble (Jean d'Aunoy) and malevolent (Philippe, Marquis de Montalt) foster ones; her wish responds to incompletely abreacted traumatic impressions, which articulate themselves in memory traces that have remained vivid in her psychic apparatus only to be converted into symptoms of hysteria. In other words, as Adeline wanders aimlessly from one hostile site to another, she is unwittingly moved by a foreign body of traumatic knowledge inside her (the rumors about the confined and murdered man, the unidentified maternal seal) even though, as Freud argues for hysterics in general, she is oblivious to the origin and meaning of this complex of pathological representations that haunt her. As these nonabreactable traumatic impressions (themselves inevitably demarcated from any representations through a psychic gap) are transformed into phantasmatic objects, which can be seen as the embodiments of nonabreacted reminiscences (the paternal manuscript found in the abbey), we find the hysterical heroine imitating what Castle calls the unease of the enlightened project in general. Her body and the world it moves in become the scene for a spectralization, where ghosts take on a compelling subjective reality and real human beings become ghostly. Recalling Syndenhams's conflation of hysteria and nostalgia, the Freudian dictum I have recourse to in this chapter is that the hysteric "can not get free of the past, and for its sake neglect[s] what is real and immediate" (1908a; 160).

Particularly with Radcliffe's heroine, however, the nonabreacted reminiscences from which Adeline suffers are more than representations of an unverbalized trauma or her own repressed traumatic memories. They are an unconscious legacy inherited from her parents. Her ambivalent negotiation of paternal authority is thus complex, for even as she challenges the threatening father figure, Philippe de Montalt, whose obscene desire literally haunts her and indeed provokes her continual flight, she is also haunted subliminally by his rival, Henry de Montalt, and unconsciously led to find his prison manuscript. In this phantasmatic text, as Robert Miles notes, Adeline is able to romanticize her origins, "supplanting her brutal father with an ideal one" (1995, 114). Moreover, she embeds this critique of patriarchy in a phantasy that prohibits the daughter from undermining the fictitious though necesssary infallibility and integrity of that paternal figure who, as addressee, forms the linchpin of the entire mise-en-scène of desire. The crux, then, is that both scenarios—the hysterical overexcitation that results in phantasies of mortal danger and the hysterical hallucinations that result in a phantasy of retrieved familial protection—revolve about the paternal figure of authority (which Žižek designates as the big Other), presumed to confer retroactively onto the symptom its true meaning.

If at the conclusion of the narrative, however, the consistency of benign paternal authority is recovered, the phantasy scenario itself works with the uncanny perforations of the big Other, not only because, as Miles notes, the "benevolent father is merely a form of compensation for the irremediable reality of his malign opposite" (1995, 114) but also because the paternal knowledge is itself riddled with gaps. In his discussion of primal phantasies as phylogenetic endowments, Nicolas Abraham argues that the foreign body of inherited knowledge, once seen as a buried secret, can fruitfully be compared to a phantom, by which he means a formation of the unconscious that has never been conscious, but rather has passed from the parent's unconsciousness to the child's, and thus exists like a stranger in the subject's mental topography. In other words, the concealment of knowledge by the parents' repression creates a gap, which the phantom then objectifies. As

Abraham notes, "What haunts are not the dead, but the gaps left within us by the secrets of others" (Abraham and Torok 1987, 171), pointing to the psyche's having become the crypt for someone else's unconscious phantasies. Thus, the return of the phantom does not entail a family truth that will disclose the secret and fill the gap, but rather it disturbingly broadcasts the message that a gap has been transmitted to the subject. The phantom objectifies a gap in knowledge as this conflates with the psychic gap that demarcates traumatic impressions from any belated representation. For Abraham, therefore, the difference between "*the stranger incorporated* through suggestion and the *dead returning to haunt*" is not crucial, since both "act as foreign bodies lodged within the subject." Rather, the heterogeneity of the phantom is at stake because faced with the phantom, the subject must recognize that at no times does the nature of the big Other bear any direct reference itself. Encoded as the bearer of a family secret, it marks history as what shapes the subject even as it is forever inaccessible to it. On the other hand, the phantom also indicates that the traumatic impressions it reintroduces into the subject cannot be abreacted, but merely designated (175).

Applying this to *The Romance of the Forest* one could say, in search of a home that would quell her dissatisfied desire, the hysteric Adeline transforms her hystericized body into the scene that not only stages the encroachment of traumatic impressions as the originating force behind phantasy, but also links this with phantasies of origin, shown in turn to function as the hysteric conversion symptom of a phantasmic presence. The encrypted foreign body of knowledge is converted into a search for origins that fixates on the past—on dead ancestors and family secrets—so as to fashion a scenario of satisfaction that can be projected into the future. Radcliffe's gothic phantasy, however, traces a crucial scenario where the hysteric symptom formation is shown to feed on this inherited legacy even as it shields from its unbearable impact; it turns the knowledge gap into a protective fiction of the family romance in which finding a home, loving parents, and an adequate object of desire makes bearable the unsurpassable dislocation of the subject, its psychic wound and physical vulnerability. Like the patients of Charcot and Freud who were called on to articulate the primal scene of trauma in order for their symptoms to disappear, the self-absorbed hysteric must also discover the origin of her trauma by reconstructing a narrative about her family origins based on an inherited knowledge whose archaic traces she finds inscribed in her unconscious. But if the narrative reconstruction ultimately puts an end to her hysterical symptoms, it does so by staging neither the heroine's nor the parents' trauma but a phantom text that stands in for the inherited gap.

In the course of her encounter with this traumatic return of repressed archaic knowledge, Adeline's dreams, hallucinations, and somatic symptoms perform hysteria as a malady by and of representation. The hysterical mise-en-scène of desire unfolds a text of origins, already representation, so that the primal scene, which the entire narrative encircles, is not sexual but textual. Adeline is uncannily attracted to her father's manuscript, as she is uncannily attached to her mother's seal, even though in both cases she cannot supply any concrete points of historical reference. She phantasizes a paternal death and a maternal indestructibility, although the knowledge she has access to is riddled with gaps. While the seal is attributed to the wrong woman (a maternal phantom), the manuscript that satisfies Adeline's phantasy of origins can be seen as a phantom text because far from lending a coherent meaning to her symptoms, it objectifies the gap transmitted to the hysterical subject: it exists only as a disfigured text, replete with blank spaces and faded passages. As Laplanche and Pontalis note, "The day-dream is a shadow play, utilising its kaleidoscopic material drawn from all quarters of human experience, but also involving the original fantasy, whose dramatis personae, the court cards, receive their notation from a family legend which is mutilated, disordered and misunderstood (1964, 22). For Adeline, any conscious memory of her parents is irrevocably lost, even though it is precisely this lack that forces her to fill in the gaps of her own romantic trajectory with the phylogenetic text of an archaic trauma inscribed in her unconscious. Within her daydream, then, the family legend appears as the barely legible fragments of a paternal manuscript and the falsely attributed maternal seal; it vexes the security these insignia are meant to afford even though, to recall Žižek's definition, they are the only consistent symbols that can give support to the hysterical subject's being, in the face of traumatic knowledge.

Rather than offering an in-depth discussion of Radcliffe's gothic romance, I will limit myself to two ways hysterical phantasy work veils—as it articulates—an originary, traumatic impact. Even though this pool of archaic knowledge, this phylogenetic endowment, is irrevocably demarcated by a gap in consciousness, it also engenders the three primal phantasies of heritage, seduction, and castration that allow the heroine to use phantasies of origin to fill in the gaps within her psychic topology created by others' secrets. I will first analyze Adeline's two dream-representations, to illustrate this transformation of traumatic knowledge into phantasy symptoms. Then I will offer a typology for the way the hysteric uses her phantasy-symptoms (*sinthome*) to organize her enjoyment into three questions that inevitably touch on the kernel of traumatic, archaic knowledge: What is the origin and solution of my family legacy? What is the origin and fate of my mutable body? What is the origin and aim of my dissatisfied desire?

The first dream occurs just after Adeline has left the convent and is waiting in the house she believes to be her father's, unaware that Philippe de Montalt has had her brought there to be executed. As she later explains to Mme. La Motte, "The anxiety of my mind prevented repose; gloomy unpleasing images flitted before my fancy, and I fell into a sort of waking dream: I thought that I was in a lonely forest with my father; his looks were severe, and his gestures menacing: he upbraided me for leaving the convent, and while he spoke, drew from his pocket a mirror, which he held before my face; I looked in it and saw, (my blood now thrills as I repeat it) I saw myself wounded, and bleeding profusely. Then I thought myself in the house again; and suddenly heard these words, in accents so distinct, that for some time after I awoke, I could scarcely believe them ideal, 'Depart this house, destruction hovers there' " (41). This dream representation will induce a fever attack, once La Motte has taken her away from the house of potential destruction, and in that sense it is the first of several sequences in which Adeline's hysteria literally acts out an illness through representation. Ideational material gone awry engenders physical dysfunction. The masochistic phantasy scene represents the threat of mutilation coming from her father who "castrates" her by showing her own wounded body to her—significantly, through a mirrored image. This phantasy could be read as a sign for her menstruation, for sexual violation having occurred, or even for the forbiddance of autoerotism, the classic encoding of the castration phantasy. However, rather than selecting a semantic encoding as the interpretation of this daydream, I suggest reading this scene structurally, as the staging of the questions Why am I cut? What is the origin of this wound? How do I explain the threatening incursion of sexuality or mutability into my body? Furthermore, given that hysteria enacts a malady of representation, the second structural point to note is that in this particular phantasy scenario Adeline is the passive object of a threat that is above all visual. Her father forces her to look at herself as she is alienated or cast into an image, an image of a wounded body, to boot.

The second dream, which also merges seduction and castration in a visualized staging of desire, is significant because it shifts from Adeline as threatened object to Adeline as active spectator. This product of her perturbed fancy occurs in the abbey, after she has discovered her love for Theodore and her ambivalent fascination with and abhorrence of the Marquis, and while her suggestible nature has incorporated La Motte's unexplained melancholy as well as the rumor about the mysteriously murdered man. This dream also will engender a malady of representation—hysterical langor, tears, and a fainting fit. However, because it stages a shift from a masochistic to a sadistic phantasy scene, the dream calls forth another hysterical symptom, the act of detection, during which Adeline finds the prison chamber and the gap-riddled manuscript of her actual father. This second dream phantasy is divided into three parts. In the first part Adeline finds herself in the prison chamber (which she will later discover) at the bed of a man "convulsed in the agonies of death." Shocked by the spectacle, she pulls back, but he stretches forth his hand and seizes hers violently. The sexualization of this scene of mortality transforms the dying person into a man of "about thirty, with the same features, but in full health, and of a most benign countenance," who smiles at her. As he is about to speak, "the floor of the chamber suddenly opened and he sunk from her view. The effort she made to save herself from following awoke her" (Radcliffe, 108). That is to say, in this phantasy Adeline not only collapses the dying father with the future husband but, more importantly, she merges anxiety about the inherited traumatic knowledge of physical vulnerability (represented by the spectacle of his dying) with the satisfaction of sexual desire promised by the younger man. Yet the satisfaction threatens to call forth a gap, to recall Freud's formulation early on that once the subject has traversed its phantasy, a gap will engulf the subject completely, subsuming her in the pool of archaic knowledge that so uncannily draws her into an identification with her father through death. This unbearable proximity to her traumatic kernel awakens Adeline from her dream.

The second part of the dream stages her pursuit of a man in a black cloak through a long passage. As she turns back, she finds that it is in fact she who is being pursued, and the terror this reversal occasions awakens her a second time. That the beautiful male body is not even a dissimulating shield of mortal threat is played out in the last part of the dream, for here Adeline gives in to the seduction of her pursuer and follows him into a funeral chamber where she once again finds the Chevalier lying in the coffin, his features serenely sunk in death: "While she looked at him, a stream of blood gushed from his side, and descending to the floor, the whole chamber was overflowed" (108–109). Once again the sound of a masculine voice brings the horror of the scene to an unbearable climax that merges satisfaction with trauma, and she finally wakes up completely.

The threat of mutilation that caused satisfaction in the first dream representation has been transferred to another body: satisfaction now resides in seeing a masculine body bleeding. Even though her own vulnerability is at stake in the representation, these scenes stage her proximity to her traumatic kernel of knowledge by casting her in the role of a sadistic spectator. Reading the scene structurally, we see the question it seems to pose: "In what sense is a paternal death the origin of my existence and the origin of my desire?" Seduction is welded with the primal scene in that the dying man tries to seduce her; castration merges with seduction in that Adeline is drawn by a cloaked man to the spectacle of a mutilated body, a sight of horror that promises to flood her with obscene satisfaction. That these two dreams show her wounded and as viewer of someone else's wound, as pursued and pursuer, illustrates the simultaneity of contradictory actions that Freud (1908a) calls the bisexual nature of hysterical phantasies when he notes that in staging her attack, the hysteric often plays both the masculine and the feminine parts, the subject *and* the object of mutilation or seduction. Above all, however, Adeline's dreams represent by displacement that the archaic trauma, whose mnemic traces haunt her only to draw her into a chamber of death, revolves around a recognition of mortal danger, vulnerability, and fallibility.

Phantasy scenarios, I have been arguing, modulate a kernel of traumatic knowledge so that they make this foreign body bearable within the psychic topography—by simultaneously shielding and articulating this repressed, impossible, obscene knowledge that calls for an enjoyment of self-expendi-

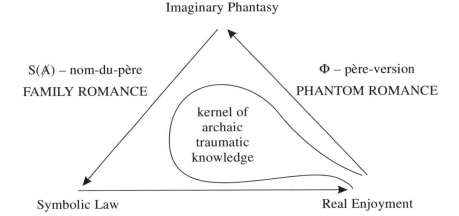

a – phantomatic object of desire

PHANTOM/SYMPTON

Žižek's Three Modalities of Desire

ture. To show how Radcliffe's gothic romance plays through the three primal phantasies that Freud isolates (the scenes of heritage, castration, and
seduction) I want to elaborate Slavoj Žižek's (1991) interpretation of the
Lacanian schema that positions three modalities of desire—represented by
the signifiers (Φ), S(Å) and *a*—in a triangular relationship that is in turn
structured by the three psychic registers, the Real, the Imaginary and the
Symbolic, as these are grafted upon this traumatic pool of enjoyment.

For Žižek each modality of desire functions as a screen, meant to help
distance the subject from unconscious traumatic jouissance and prevent her
from being engulfed by this gap and drawn into this nonsymbolized kernel.
Yet, as I will suggest, one could also relate each of the three positions to the
protective fictions that Freud designates as primal phantasies. After all, they
are belated representations that feed on this traumatic kernel even as they
are demarcated from it by the psychic gap. At the same time, functioning as
inherited phantasies, they also serve to fill gaps in individual knowledge. In
the Lacanian schema this fluidity of boundary between the protective fictions and jouissance is visually rendered by the opening at the bottom of the
triangle where jouissance leaks out.

In Žižek's rereading, the first position (if one follows the arrows along the
triangle) is represented by the signifier Phi (Φ) and designated as representing the *père-version* (or Father-of-Enjoyment) who signifies an embodiment
of an impossible jouissance, a fascinating image of lethal, nauseous enjoyment, the terrifying and fascinating materialization of trauma and forbiddance, an obscene and revengeful leftover after the father has been sacrificed
to become law. The second position is represented by the signifier of the

barred Other [S($\not{A}$)] and designated as representing the *nom-du-père* (or Name-of-the-Father), signifying the Other's inconsistency, exhibiting the failure of ordinary paternity and patriarchal law. It refers to a figure who guarantees that we will be able to endure the inconsistency of the symbolically structured culture as well as any sudden reappearance of the traumatic. At the same time it represents the father's impotence, that is, as the barred Other he is not able to live up to his name, to his symbolic mandate; he is lacking, surrogate, inconsistent himself. One could speak of the father as sacrificed to become law, because this figure sustains stability in the midst of inconsistency. Finally, the third position, represented by the signifier for the *object of desire* (*a*), refers to the object-cause that propels our desire to construct coherent narratives, to unravel the secret of desire. This indifferent object incessantly disappears and reappears; indeed, it consists exclusively of the fact that it has some significance for the heroine and is vitally important to her. One could say it marks the pure semblance sustaining the heroine in her Oedipal journey, which keeps the romanctic quest afloat. Comparing the three positions, Žižek suggests that while the signifier of the barred Other marks the point of impossibility around which a symbolic structure is articulated, and while the (Φ) is a manifestion of this impossibility, the *object a* is an imaginary concealment of the impossibility. At the same time, the (Φ) is neither exchangeable, like the father's name and his representatives, nor indifferent, like the *object a*.

Turning to the relation of the three psychic registers at each corner of the triangle, we find a visual formulation for the way phantasy negotiates enjoyment in relation to law. The Real, marking the place where primal enjoyment uncannily floods into the psychic topology on the level of unconscious desires and affects, is diametrically opposite the Symbolic, the guarantor of law (and with it, of ego stability). Positioned between these two, the Imaginary represents the function of phantasy. Marking the murky interface between the Real and the Symbolic, we find it at the tip of two phantasy scenarios: the first, the right side of the triangle, connects imagination with the Real by traversing the obscene object (Φ) to form a mise-en-scène of hallucinatory enjoyment; the second, on the left side, connects imagination with the Symbolic by traversing the flawed object [S($\not{A}$)] to form a mise-en-scène of sublimated desire. Applying this to the dialectic proposed by Terry Castle, one might say the former stages the horrific phantom romance, revolving around a clandestine traumatic knowledge about origins. This functions as the uncanny, toxic side effect of the latter, the family romance, revolving around a publicly proclaimed idealized story about family legacy meant to sustain the enlightened rationalist project. Furthermore, while the former can be attributed to the hysteric's broadcast of her complaint, the latter stages her belief in the perfect family and in the existence of an infallible law. As the schema indicates, what is crucial about these two phantasy scenarios is not only that they are inversions of each other, but also that the hysterical subject wavers between them.

Applying this triadic schema of protective fictions to *The Romance of the Forest*, I would place the castration phantasy in the position of the *father of enjoyment*, the heritage phantasy as the *name of the father*, and the seduction phantasy as the *object of desire* so that each phantasy scenario can itself be read as a triadic structure that negotiates enjoyment in relation to law. In the first triadic scenario, under the aegis of the fascinating object of lethal desire (Φ), which threatens to draw the subject into an obscene, self-expending enjoyment, hysteric conversions perform the question "Am I masculine or feminine, and how does my gender relate to my body's vulnerability?" Given that the issue of origin in this phantasy scene is the emergence of sexual difference and mutability, the privileged scene here is one of mutilation, where in a gesture of sexualizing mortality the subject imagines scenes of mutilation inflicted by the Other. In the second triadic scenario, under the aegis of the signifier of the Other's inconsistency [S(Å)], the failure of paternity, the hysteric's family romance stages the question "Who are my father and mother? What was the scene of my conception?" Given that the origin at issue here is the subject's family legend, this scene involves a rediscovery or rather invention of adequate parents, the solution to a family secret. Finally, in the third scenario, under the aegis of the constantly appearing and disappearing phantasic object of desire (*a*), a hysterical romance narrative is sustained, revolving around the question "What object would abate my dissatisfaction?" Here the question of origin revolves around the emergence of sexuality, and in the privileged phantasy a sense of plentitude is constructed over deferral.

Like the modalities of desire discussed by Žižek, these phantasy scenes stand in for and screen the repressed traumatic material, the pool of archaic knowledge from which they also stem. In a sense, they represent traumatic effects, riddled with gaps because the original phantasy scene they refer to, in Laplanche's and Pontalis's sense, is always retroactive. They stage the fulfillment of an unconscious wish, set in a sequence of scenes where Adeline is cast as an object of persecutions and desires, excluded from a secure position within the symbolic universe, and threatened by its representatives to violation, barter and murder. The implication, of course, is that just as all three primal phantasies concern the issue of origins, they also make a scene of the hysteric's attraction to an obscene enjoyment of her trauma. As the hysteric subject of *The Romance of the Forest* traverses the three phantasy scenarios—with the family romance ultimately offering the satisfaction of parental stability within an inconsistent symbolic system, and the desire romance presenting marital love as the concealment of vulnerability—the hysteric conversions insist on broadcasting a counter story. Adeline suffers not only from a malady of representation, which can be recuperated by reconstructing an inherited text, but also from nonabreacted reminiscences drawing her into an encounter with traumatic enjoyment. Because I wish to emphasize the way the obscene phantom romance is never completely contained by symbolic recuperation, I will begin with phantasies constructed in

Heritage Phantasy

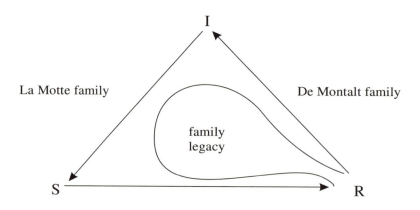

La Luc family

The Hysteric Family Romance

the name of the father, S($\hat{A}$), move on to those revolving around objects of desire, and end with those that address the obscene inversion of the family romance, the paternal figure who avoids forbiddances and is able really to enjoy.

Filling in the individual positions with details from Radcliffe's gothic romance produces three triadic schemas. Under the sign of the signifier of the barred Other, S($\hat{A}$), the hysteric family romance stages Adeline's alternation between three families, until the chain of surrogate fathers is replaced by a husband. These substitutions had begun after the murder of her real father, when Adeline was given to the lowly Jean d'Aunoy, sent to a convent, given to La Motte, handed over to the Marquis, stolen by Theodore, and returned to La Motte until, on discovering her real heritage as the Marquise de Montalt, she is finally in a position to marry Theodore Peyrou. Within this phantasy scenario, the position of the signifier of the barred Other is occupied by the La Motte family. Accepting her from the ruffians, the family offers her stability and a sense of belonging in the midst of an inconsistent world from which her supposedly natural father has abandoned her and still threatens to destroy her. Owing to their debts, however, the La Mottes themselves lack a fixed position within this symbolic universe. Thus, this surrogate family is itself inconsistent given that even as they protect and help her, they are also willing to sacrifice the surrogate daughter to protect their social status. The La Luc family functions as the object *a*, also a surrogate family but unconditional and secure in its willingness to accept Adeline as a member. She will ultimately find a coherent closure for her family romance by settling here in a plenitude one could describe as the imaginary concealing of the impossibility of the family. Yet this community of affection and reason works by virtue

Seduction Phantasy

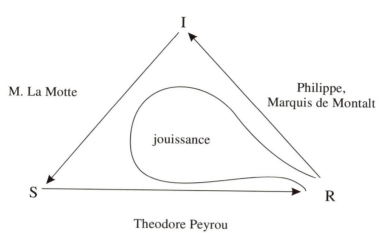

of deferral—the father's illness and the son's imprisonment mar the consistency and completion this family promises. If the family of the barred Other works on the basis of a dialectic between acceptance and nonacceptance and perpetuates a chain of false family origins, while the family of the object *a*, offering an ultimate and complete acceptance, leads to the adequate replacement for true origins, the family of the (Φ), the Montalt family functions on the basis of an impossible acceptance, the belated knowledge of origins that are true but irrevocably lost. As I have already shown, Adeline plays out her phantasy of origin in such a manner that initially her hysterical hallucinations help fill in the gaps in a fragmented and unsigned paternal manuscript, while the court testimonies during the La Motte trial fill in the knowledge gap that leads to the proper attribution of her mother's seal. Yet the family legend that emerges is a terrifying manifestation of trauma, and significantly Adeline faints on hearing about her mother's premature death and the uncle's murder of her father. This gap in consciousness becomes a symptom even as it shields her from the lethal, archaic knowledge about to engulf her. Furthermore, the incest taboo, so crucial to Freud's discussion of the primal scene, can also be discerned in this hysteric family romance. Adeline's dreams signify an incestual and necrophilic desire for the dead father, which finds its symptomatic manifestion in the figure of the obscene uncle who, as seducer turned murderous, functions as the phantomatic objectification of forbidden incestual and lethal desire.

If the first phantasy scenario, the family romance, stages a scenario of unsatisfied desire, where the hysteric is subject to a family secret barred from her consciousness, compelled to reconstruct the mutilated family legend, but always only retrieving representations of a traumatic truth that remains inaccessible, the seduction phantasy, under the sign of the object (*a*), stages how the hysteric is determined by her object choices. Again, the figure that allows the hysteric to endure an otherwise inconsistent, symbolic network is M. La Motte, representative of a chain of surrogate fathers who all point to a lack in the symbolic law (the sanctioned murder of Henry de Montalt) even as he is insufficent, or "not master of himself" (234). In the position of the father's name, he is nevertheless an impotent paternal figure, embodying the impossibility of the hysteric's appeal to paternal authority. Adeline's phantasmic desire for him resides in an identification with his melancholy (as this relates to some unexplained loss or crime) as well as in an identification with his exile, with his lack of a fixed social position. She desires him because he reflects her own inconsistency. Theodore, the imaginary lover of plenitude, represents the object (*a*), allowing for a deferral of a consummation of desire, even as he responds to the hysteric's desire for happiness by promising a concealment of the impossibility of satisfaction. As such he is the imaginary object that sustains the narrative of Adeline's romance, and her phantasmic desire for him is first as her savior, then as the lost lover, and finally as the wounded lover she must save from the death penalty. Significantly, their first meeting occurs in the forest as Adeline, in the mood of "pleasing melancholy," sings a sonnet to herself. Unexpectedly he echos back to her the last stanza, and in surprise she sees "a young man in a hunter's dress, leaning against a tree, and gazing on her with that deep attention, which marks an enraptured mind." Adeline desires Theodore because he mirrors her own state as the phantasizer. In the course of the novel he repeatedly disappears only to reappear suddenly; thus he embodies not lack but the imaginary recuperation always also implied in the loss of an object of desire. Throughout, his importance to her is as a stabilizing, nostalgic image of remembrance—even if the content of this nostalgia is that he "is lost to her for ever" (208) or suffering terrible tortures in her stead. As such, he is the imaginary support against the return of pieces of traumatic repressed material, represented by Philippe de Montalt, emboding the position of the (Φ) in the seduction phantasy. The Marquis is the politically powerful, dangerous, but fascinating object, the perverse father who manifests the impossibility of satisfaction. Given that within the phantasmic scenario projected onto Philippe he threatens to engulf Adeline in an obscene enjoyment of lethal desire, Adeline significantly enacts the symptom in her response to his seduction by fainting when the Marquis enters, succumbing to fits of anxiety when he remains near her, and finally fleeing from his presence.

The crucial point, however, is that all three figures of desired masculinity are interlinked: Theodore, as a soldier in the Marquis's troop, is in fact his representative, carrying out his commands. La Motte, under obligation to the Marquis owing to his crime, is willing to engage in a pact with him, and he too carries out his commands. The pattern for this enmeshment is set up in the scene where the Marquis first appears before Adeline. The moment he enters the abbey, Adeline faints, and her beauty "touched with the lan-

guid delicacy of illness . . . the negligence of her dress, loosened for the purpose of freer respiration" becomes the object upon which "he gazed with an
eager admiration, which seemed to absorb all the faculties of his mind"
while she experiences an absence, the hysterical performance of a gap in
consciousness. Only when Theodore also approaches Adeline and gazes at
her compassionately does she revive ("and saw him, the first object that met
her eyes, bending over her in silent anxiety"; (87–88). And only then does La
Motte enter, discover in the Marquis the man he had assailed, and consent
to support him in a plot to seduce Adeline. A similar configuration is repeated when Adeline, fleeing from a terrifying vision of the inebriated Marquis but really enjoying what the law forbids, finds herself in the garden
beyond the villa. She is being pursued by an unknown man and falls sense-
less to the ground, only to wake up and find herself in the arms of Theodore.
With these narrative sequences, Radcliffe poignantly deconstructs the phantasy scenes of her hysteric heroine to reveal how the inconsistent surrogate
father carries out the mandate of the perverse father—and how the satisfactory lover is merely the imaginary concealment of his impossible, traumatic
enjoyment.

Though the breakthrough of traumatic enjoyment will ultimately be
screened out, a trace of this agent of wounding remains. When Adeline recovers the history of her father, she does so by discovering that he was the
murder victim of Phillipe de Montalt. By accepting Theodore as a husband,
she chooses the victim of the Marquis's revenge. Thus, as these three figures
of masculinity modulate the traumatic effects of desire, they do so in connection with a threat of mutilation. In a way, these phantasies of seduction
rework the sadomasochistic scene Freud (1919) labeled "a child is being
beaten," for in relation to the impotent father, La Motte, Adeline phantazies
an identification with his lack in social position to perform the sentence, "I
am like my surrogate father, who is being punished by an obscene paternal
figure of authority," a phantasy that in a sense merely repeats her hallucinations about the torture of her real father. In relation to the object of imaginary plenitude, Theodore, her phantasy is that she will wound him; here the
sentence performed could be labeled "An object of desire satisfies me because I am the spectator of its mutilation." Finally, in relation to the obscene
father, Phillipe de Montalt, Adeline's fantasy is the masochistic scene, "My
surrogate father will mutilate me."

The phantasy of mutilation connects desire to the final phantasy scenario,
which, under the sign of (Φ) stages a plethora of hysterical conversions. The
issue of origins that is at stake here is the emergence of sexual differences,
which produce an indecision on the part of the hysteric as to how she wishes
to position herself in relation to castration: "Do I accept my castration as a
woman, do I remain masculine, do I oscillate between these options?" In
scenes that belong to this phantasy scenario, which is significantly placed on
the right closest to the opening or navel point that connects the traumatic
kernel to its phantasy representations (indeed initiating the oscillation

Castration Phantasy

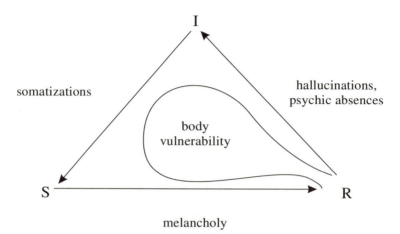

Hysteric Conversion

among the triangle of phantasy scenarios), the hysteric subject is constituted most directly through her engagement with the traumatic knowledge of her body mutability. Distributing Adeline's hysterical conversions of this knowledge among the three positions, one could say her phantasy-symptoms serve to stabilize her being in the midst of a symbolic universe that is unsatisfactory to the abandoned and bartered orphan Adeline. Whether the body speaks in fits of nervous excitability or fits of enfeeblement, the hysteric in either case uses conversion to address the fact that the Other, supposed to have the knowledge she requires, is barred. This fallibility in the father's name induces Adeline to wander along the corridors of the abbey seeking explanations for the anxiety that overcomes her or to flee repeatedly from her various persecutors. Anxiety attacks, however, also result in fits of tears, langor, palor, listlessness, and fever to the point of paralysis—conversions that repeatedly present the hysteric as some one suffering from a malady of representations not only because the symptoms stand in for a gap in knowledge but also because they are induced by mental images gone awry. For example, just after Adeline has been taken in by Peter's relatives in Savoy, the mutual support and protection she finds there force her to reflect on her own state of forlornness so intensively that she produces feverish symptoms, becomes delirious, and sinks into stupefaction. This somatic helplessness is a hysterical conversion of her psychic vulnerability, turning the representation impressed in her unconscious into a body image. This hysterical staging of vulnerability closes with Adeline awaking from her coma to find herself in the La Luc household, thus exchanging the protective fiction of fallibility for that of family plenitude.

At the same time, her hysterical suggestibility allows her to respond both to the sublimity of nature and the horror invoked by the abbey. The former evokes singing, composition, and recitation of poetry as well as melancholic daydreams. These symptoms in turn are formed under the aegis of the object (*a*), given that they are mitigating imaginary concealments of traumatic impact. Nostalgic in essence, these symptoms allow her to enjoy loss and the deferral of her desire. If in the psychosomatic disorders the repressed returns in a distorted manner, and if in melancholy the traumatic material is directed toward new nontraumatic objects, so that both hysterical conversions offer a mitigating compromise of sorts, the last set of symptoms, Adeline's absences, nightmares, and hallucinations stage how a foreclosure of trauma engenders its reappearance in the real. Formed under the sign of (Φ), these symptoms, staging the encroachment of trauma on the subject, occur when her impressionable imagination is drawn to horror. While the hysteric's psychosomatic conversions and nostalgia signify lack, these psychic absences show that what is at stake is actually the lack of a signifier, where the subject threatens to be engulfed by the traumatic gap of jouissance.

Belatedly materializing the two dreams I have already discussed, these hallucinations involve a masochistic phantasy scenario about finding and reading the gap-ridden manuscript, where the phantasizer is herself drawn toward mortality through the image of the dying father. Here the following recurring pattern emerges. Adeline is like a sleepwalker, for during these scenes her conscious reason is absent and these peregrinations often terminate in senselessness. In this state of a *condition second*, as Charcot and Freud would later call the hysteric's psychic absence, Adeline explores the abbey at night, finds and later reads the manuscript, and fills in the gaps she discovers there with the voices and images of her own hallucinations. One could say that the dark chamber corresponds to the psychic apparatus, and that through of her hysterical malady by representation she develops the mnemic traces she finds into images of her father's agony. During these scenes she experiences complete alterity and fears looking into a mirror, "lest some other face than her own should meet her eyes" (134). On the other hand, her hallucinations also involve sadistic scenarios, where she thrills herself by drawing mortality in the image of the tortured body of Theodore, loaded with chains, pale with sickness and grief, bleeding, calling her name in vain, and finally (at the place of execution) "pale and convulsed in death." Locked again in a dark chamber, "the image of Theodore, dying by the hands of the Marquis, now rose to her imagination, and the terrors of suspense became almost insupportable ... amidst the tumult. ... She clearly distinguished deep groans. This confirmation of her fears deprived her of all her remaining spirits, and growing faint, she sunk almost lifeless into a chair" (196). The hysteric performance of the phantasy of obscene lethal enjoyment was objectified at her body.

Žižek admonishes us to learn to love our symptoms because they bind enjoyment to a symbolic formation that assures consistency and shields from the pool of traumatic knowledge subtending psychic representations. The mise-en-scène of desire performed in *The Romance of the Forest*, which allows the heroine to organize her enjoyment to utmost satisfaction without the threat of being engulfed by it, positions as the origin of the hysteric phantasy the inherited knowledge of paternal fallibility whose traumatic impact, however, is retrievable only as a knot of phantasies of origin. These perform an exchange with surrogate figures of paternity, the transformation of masochistic into sadistic fantasy scenes, the staging of an obscene desire for mutilation progressing from a dream of her own wounded body, of dislocation and paternal threat, to that of her father's mortality as it becomes enmeshed with her lover's mutilation. However, if the hysteric Adeline finally brings closure to her family romance by accepting marriage as the most resilient and viable of all protective fictions at her disposal, she can do so because the abandonment that stood at the beginning of her peregrinations is ultimately exchanged for an act of parturition and self-progenation. At the end of the trial, Adeline gives symbolic birth to her real father, disclosing his manuscript and burying his skeleton in the family vault. She has not only found but also rewritten the mutilated family legend and filled its gaps with protective fictions that ultimately allow her to sublimate the traumatic knowledge it broadcasted. At the same time she also gives birth to herself as the Montalt heir and to Theodore who is saved first from execution by the disclosure of her parentage and then from legal persecution.

This narrative solution perhaps is yet another indication of the duplicity in articulating hysterical phantasy work, given that it not only splices passivity with agency, but also reinstalls the symbolic authority of paternity precisely by sublating paternity. Having been inseminated by the family secret his phantom text broadcasts, Adeline buries not only the dead father but with him his textual legacy. Yet the jarring oscillation, the refusal of closure I am claiming is the trademark of the language of hysteria, can be located at another textual detail. For in this phantasy narrative, where anxiety and desire are articulated in response to masculinity, an undercurrent of maternal longing calmly sustains the hysteric's histrionic turbulences. In a sense Adeline always had the knowledge of her heritage in the form of her mother's insignia, the seal. Thus the one stable signifier is attached to the signature of her real mother and the gift of her surrogate mother d'Aunoy. This insignia is neither an object of fascination, like the abbey or the manuscript, nor something to be repressed and returned to as an object of hallucination. The cherished object was simply always there. Functioning as the counterpoint to the economy of repression and conversion revolving about her paternal legacy, because it poses no hermeneutic task the maternal signature points to an origin for which the hysteric needs to produce no phantasy representations: her gap in knowledge induces neither anxiety nor desire. Adeline hesitates, taking the miniature of her mother when it is finally shown to her—perhaps because the archaic knowledge pertaining to her maternal legacy is so intimate a possession that—requiring neither repression, substitution, nor conversion—that it requires no material objectification.

If we compare the symbolic birth with which Radcliffe's gothic romance ends to that of Mozart's/Shikaneder's *Magic Flute*, a telling analogy emerges. In both narratives marriage is linked to a parturition from the maternal body but also to the preservation of a maternal gift. In Radcliffe's narrative the mother must not brutally be expelled because she is from the very beginning already lost, like Pamina's flute; Adeline's seal functions as the omphalos of the phantasy scenario. Commemorating the maternal bond precisely within the symbolic universe of paternal authority, this silent, nonconverted signature bears a message about the power that the dead have over the living, which moves beyond protective fictions about obscene lethal enjoyment or about concealing the impossibility of satisfaction. As omphalos, I want to argue, the seal is the textual detail knotting together the hysteric heroine's oscillations among the various phantasy scenarios. Recalling one last time the Lacanian schema for the triadic structure of desire, at the far-right corner, in the position of the Real, we find a psychic embrace of total self-expenditure outside any phantasy formations. Moving along the triangle, however, the phantasy of the lure of lethal enjoyment, whose addressee is the obscene father, performs a hysterical narrative about the fallacy of paternal authority. Its inversion, on the other side of the triangle, is the protective fiction sustains a narrative about phallic paternal authority, addressing its representative as one who guarantees that we will endure the inconsistency of the symbolic universe. The omphalos, marking the interface between fallacy and phallus, in Radcliffe's texts is represented by the maternal seal, outside, yet also masterminding the economy of phantasy scenarios, preserving the traumatic knowledge of an inherited gap which requires no symbolization and actually forbids it. The message this maternal gift broadcasts, over and against paternal phantoms, is that it is an impossible desire the hysteric seeks so resiliently and creatively to satisfy even as she can sustain her life only as long as she pits against this inevitable knowledge her belief that happiness can be found. Far from contradicting the power and necessity of protective fictions, the omphalos is what guarantees their survival.

As Miles notes, though the manuscript Adeline finds is incidental to the outcome of the plot, its importance lies in the fact that it "stands for 'romance,' for writing by women, for the secretive process whereby women romancers produce their ambiguous, multivalent texts." Thus his argument, on the one hand, is that the manuscript allows Adeline to romanticize her origins and exchange an obscene paternal figure for a benevolent one. On the surface or read literally, this sentimental closure to Adeline's abundant phantasy scenario supports the "gentlewoman's sense of propriety and modesty." On the other hand, the origins of the romance indict rather than idealize the father, given that his secrets engender the "subterfuge of coded writing" and offer a portrait of the woman writer as one who is forced "to secrecy, to figurative writing, to 'romance.' . . . The episode of the secret manuscript duplicates in miniature the wider conditions of the woman writer, where the disciplines of propriety enforce concealment" (1995, 115). This tension between two disparate readings—a conservative, sentimental one and its uncanny, radical underside—I would add, not only give structure to the hysteric heroine's oscillation between addressing her complaint to an idealized dead and an obscene, murderous paternal interpellator. Rather, they also allow one to speculate about the author's, Ann Radcliffe's, own language of hysteria, given that in choosing the gothic romance as her genre she, too, oscillates between two modes of authorial self-fashioning, the proper lady and the transgressive female author.

IV

In his presentation of the case history of Emmy v. N., at one point Freud records that "The night before she had had horrible dreams. She had had to lay out a number of dead people and put them in coffins, but would not put the lids on" (1893–95, 74). Now, this nocturnal self-representation is a particularly fitting image for ending a discussion of gothic hysterics, because here the hysteric fashions herself as one dressing, adorning, indeed even embellishing the dead, at the same time that she stages a phantasy scenario that involves commemorating the presence of the dead among the living by leaving their coffins open. Emmy v. N. offers not only a perfect example for what Freud claimed to be typical of hysteric phantasy work, namely, that the afflicted person so suffers from reminiscences that, haunted by a past, they neglect the present. Rather she also demonstrates how the hysteric performs the spectralization of the Other, which Terry Castle isolates as one of the toxic side effects of the enlightened rationalist project. In this nocturnal scene the hysteric Emmy v. N. uses her body to represent by proxy a phantasy scenario about a traumatic encounter with death. More importantly, in doing so, she oscillates between a restoration of the past and an obliteration of the present, between revitalizing what is dead and mortifying what is living—keeping the dead from being buried. Performing this double consciousness in the course of her phantasy scenario, she negotiates between a phallic law that requires the abandonment of the dead in favor of the living: that is, the sublimation of any traumatic knowledge of death [S(Ⱥ)] on the one hand, and the fallacious enjoyment of the lure of death Φ on the other (a desire that insists on a fluid exchange with the past) with the difference it inscribes in the world of the living, with a commemoration of mortality.

Freud's own interpretation of Emmy v. N.'s dream is that it obviously represents a recollection of the death of her husband. If one looks more closely at the case history he presents, however, given also that Emmy v. N. speaks about the dead in plural, it would be more accurate to see this dream as representing the many encounters with mortality that have informed her identity: when (aged five) her brothers and sisters often threw dead animals at her; when (aged seven) she unexpectedly saw her sister in her coffin;

when (aged eight) her brother used to terrify her by dressing up in sheets like a ghost; when (aged nine) she saw her aunt in her coffin and her jaw suddenly dropped; and the hallucinations she had (aged 19) at the deathbed of her brother and her coming home and suddenly finding her mother dead, with a distorted face. The sudden death of her husband while she was lying in bed after her second confinement is but the climax of these earlier events. I emphasize this crucial point because the language of hysteria stages the body in relation to past traumatic impressions, recasting these events belatedly into protective fictions that involve a sexualization, as they also involve phantasies about abandonment and plenitude. Indeed, Freud obliquely notes in respect to Emmy v. N.'s confessions, "It has also struck me that amongst all the intimate information given me by the patient there was a complete absence of the sexual element" (1893–95, 103). Worrisome though this admission may have been for him, given that he sought to establish sexual malaise as the etiology of all neurosis, what is more significant about this particular dream passage is that in it Emmy v. N. has actually given him another image for the seminal experience, which he claims is more liable than any other to provide occasion for traumas. Indeed, with precisely this image in mind I would suggest that one could perhaps more profitably read the hysteric adorning her dead, preserving the taint of death and the grief it calls forth among the living, as the paradigmatic representation par excellence of hysteria.

Jean-Martin Charcot's Vampires

> Hysteria is a more or less irreducible mental state, characterized by a subversion of the relations established between the subject and the moral world, of which the hysteric subject believes itself to be practically relieved, outside all delirious systems. This mental state is founded on the need for a reciprocal seduction, which explains the hurriedly accepted miracles of medical suggestion (or countersuggestion). Hysteria is not a pathological phenomenon and can, in all respects, be considered to be a supreme mode of expression.
>
> —*Aragon and Breton*

I

DISEASE FORMULATIONS in the medical construction of hysteria, as Roy Porter notes, "go with circumstances: doctors, patients, physical milieux, intellectual and cultural landscapes." He explains that "hysteria could be fashioned as a disorder, precisely because the culture-at-large sustained tense and ambiguous relations between representations of mind and body, which were, in turn, reproduced in the hierarchical yet interactive ontologies of morality and medicine, and, yet again, reflected by the sociological interplay of clinical encounters (1993, 265). In this chapter I continue my brief overview of the medical literature on hysteria with the argument that Jean-Martin Charcot's transformation of the Salpêtrière into a "museum of living pathology," as he called it, can be seen as a paradigmatic historic site for the murky enmeshment of mutual consent, mutual deceit, and mutual desire among the physician or analyst, his patient, and the artists representing this exchange. I return to this strand in the history of medical discourses on hysteria, however, neither to offer a critical survey of Charcot's teaching nor to evaluate its nosological merits and shortcomings. Rather, I am interested in the implications within Charcot's exploration of the somatic language of hysteria for how body disorders and intimate phantasies, reworking the traumatic impact of psychic anguish, can become a public spectacle and thus represent the vexed relation between mind and body.

I will be speaking of Charcot's vampires in part, at least, because his classification of hysteria—supported by a plethora of graphs, gravures, photographs, and public stagings—feeds off a well-established, visual iconography developed in conjunction with notions of demonic possession and exorcism.[1] By engendering visual reproductions of the movements, gestures, and poses of hysteria he also resurrects this mythopoetic estate, indeed feeds it with the blood of quasi-empirical evidence. His work at the Salpêtrière perfectly enacts the claim I made earlier that anyone making a radical transformation of the writings on hysteria, while basing a nosology on observable phenomena, must also be prepared to visit the intangible realm of vision, phantasy, and supernatural speculation. Given that the novelty of Charcot's scientific method stems from his insisting on the theatricality and visuality of hysteria and in his insisting on rendering the hysterical body as a public spectacle (which could be presented, recorded, and reproduced), his work also returns us to the notion of hysteria as a malady of or by representation. Charcot, though never theorizing a traumatic etiology of hysteria, nevertheless came to exploit the fact that the symptoms exhibited by his hysteric patients could be read as the somatic performance of traces of a psychically traumatic shock. More than any physician before him, he saw the symptoms as the belated and dislocated conversion of a knowledge of vulnerability, whose origin is not only repressed but inaccessible because it is demarcated by a gap in the psyche. As I have argued in chapter 2, precisely because the knowledge at stake is inevitable but also unknowable, hysteria always involves mimesis as simulation. It articulates through of an unjust image, speaking deceptively, obliquely, and even treacherously, even as it requires an interpellator and an audience. Though Charcot in one of his Tuesday lectures claimed, "You see how the hysterics cry. One could say this is much noise about nothing" (Trillat 1986, 119); it is precisely out of this nothing, whose margins are so histrionically demarcated, that a rich public display of resilient roles emerges, in which the afflicted hysteric offers a public confession not only of intimate phantasies but also of her inevitably evasive traumatic knowledge.

As J.-B. Pontalis notes, one best imagines Charcot as a man whose power resided in the hybridity of his personality. For the students whom he fascinated and who dedicated themselves to helping him construct his theoretical edifice he was both a professor and a magician. For the patients who made up his clinical *tableaux vivants*, serving as the objects of investigation and models for the iconography of hysteria he sought to fabricate in his pathological museum, he was both a miracle worker and a zoologist. Above all, however, his use of hypnotic suggestion to reconstruct the paralysis, anesthesia, or hallucinations that brought patients to the clinic in the first place is where Pontalis locates what he calls Charcot's phantasm of omnipotence. For even as Charcot was fully aware that his hysterics necessarily gave in to the perspicacity and charm of his gaze and knew that his audience was willingly mesmerized by his weekly performances as mastermind staging the infamous Tuesday lectures in the amphitheater of the Salpêtrière, he ultimately underestimated the extent to which he himself fell prey to the mise-en-scène of his patients' subservient desire: "And it is not nothing, the desire of the hysteric, especially if it is the desire of or for nothing" (1977, 16).

For Pontalis, then, the manner in which this perfectly circular setting, with physician, patient, and audience mutually entertaining and enjoying a performance of psychosomatic disturbance, is significant so that the distinction between empowered agent and disempowered object of investigation becomes imperceptible, working ultimately by virtue of a scene of almost unbearable visual presence. In Charcot's theater of living pathology the two sides of the hystericized body could be read and reproduced endlessly: the corporeal surface, skin, and gestures, poses, and attitudes that drew the interpellating Other into the field of vision. What was significantly absent in Charcot's spectacle of the hysteric body, however, was the inversion of specularity, namely, the psychic topology hidden beneath the body surface, impenetrable to any visual investigation of body organs. And it is this inverted site that Freud came to explore after he had studied with Charcot between October 1885 and February 1886 and translated some of his Tuesday lectures into German. In this fissure between a scene of total visuality—too full—and the invisible "other scene" of the unconscious—too empty—Pontalis locates the birth of Freud's spectral science of the mind. In the following discussion I will embark on a slightly different trajectory and explore this chasm as the point of origin for other, somewhat less wholesome, phantoms. Mapping Charcot's alphabet of hysteria onto two contemporary texts, Bram Stoker's *Dracula* and Richard Wagner's *Parsifal*, I will explore these discourses on healing and salvation as narratives that come dangerously close to designing total phantasies in which overabundant, hysterical delusions seek to endow what must remain unjust images with the aporetic status of truthful representation.

II

Jean-Martin Charcot became physician to the Salpêtrière Hospital in 1862, and within the next eight years he managed to establish his fame both as a scientist in neurology and neuropathology and as a charismatic teacher. Though his work with the five thousand inmates of the clinic—neurotics, epileptics, syphilitics, alcoholics, aging prostitutes, and insane patients deemed incurable—was not limited to hysteria, he openly declared this to be his favorite neurosis. It is with hysteria that he produced his most influential, but also highly contested, findings. Like many of the physicians of his time, Charcot acknowledged both a hereditary and sexual dimension to hysteria, though he is most credited for recognizing the role emotions played in the origin and persistence of this disorder. He would, for example, urge the removal of his patients from their psychopathogenic family environment: "It would not be possible for me to insist too much on the capital importance which attaches to isolation in the treatment of hysteria. Without doubt, the psychic element plays a very important part in most of the cases of this malady, even when it is not the predominating feature" (Charcot 1889,

210). Faced with being unable to locate organic lesions in his patients that might help him explain the somatic malfunctions they exhibited and finding that the autopsies conducted on the hysteric's corpse usually showed no pathology (Drinka 1984, 81), Charcot came to attribute psychic trauma one significant agent in the production of hysteria. He based this claim primarily on the observation that suggestion could be used to induce hysterical symptoms such as paralysis. Using hypnosis, he was able to get his patients to reproduce their physical symptoms, at the same time that in hallucinations equally induced by hypnosis they would offer information about prior traumatic experiences. Because these experimental simulations of paralysis occurring under hypnosis exhibited exactly the same symptoms as spontaneous and posttraumatic paralysis, they served to demonstrate that although hysterical symptoms took the form of genuine somatic contortions, paralyses, and anesthesias, they belonged neither to the conscious control of the patients nor to any organic malfunction. Charcot was always aware, of course, of the troubled implication between hysteric repetition induced by suggestion on his part and malingering on the part of his patients. In one of his lectures he explains, "This brings me to say a few words about simulation. It is found in every phase of hysteria and one is surprised at times to admire the craft, the sagacity, and the unyielding tenacity that especially the women, who are under the influence of this great neurosis, will put in play in order to deceive—particularly when the victim of the deception happens to be the physician. . . . It is incontestable that, in a multitude of cases, they have taken pleasure in distorting, by exaggerations, the principal circumstances of their disorder, in order to make them appear extraordinary and wonderful" (Charcot 1889, 368).

Indeed, the case of Geneviève, recorded by Bourneville and Régnard in their *Iconographie photographique de la Salpêtrière I* (1876–1877), enmeshes the plot of a conventional nineteenth-century novel of unrequited love and received ideas about martyrdom and demon possession with the narrative of real traumatic experience. Moreover, it reveals that in exchange between physician and patient the hysteric symptoms not only simulated a prior traumatic experience but also Charcot's own phantasies about the somatic grammar of hysteria, making it impossible to determine who was the arch duper—the master nosologist, the gifted hysteric, both, or neither. Geneviève was born as an orphan in Loudon, where the famous case of demon possession had occurred during the time of Richelieu. She spent her childhood in various foster homes; however, not unlike Charlotte Brontë's heroine Jane Eyre, she developed fits of anger early on and she was repeatedly hospitalized for these outbreaks of violence. At the age of fifteen she fell in love with a young man named Camille, who died of cerebral fever within a few months of their engagement. Because her foster father would not allow her to go to his funeral, fearing that she might have another attack of violence, Geneviève went to the cemetary one night to dig up the remains of her lover. She experienced a traumatic crisis and was found lying unconsious by his grave the next morning, a state she remained in for twenty-four hours. For the rest of her life Geneviève would repeatedly find herself hospitalized after a hysterical fit, escape from her asylum, work as a chambermaid in Poitiers or Paris, respond to the tragic romantic events of her life (most notably those involving seduction by a master, illicit pregnancies, or abandonment by a lover) by attempting suicide, only to be returned to the Salpêtrière, where in 1874 she first came to be treated by Charcot.

Geneviève won a prominent place in the annals of medical literature, however, because in the state of delirious hallucinations she oscillated between erotic gestures, pleading for sexual intimacy with the doctors (in part because she believed she recognized her lost lover Camille in one of the interns), and postures of saints, transfigured by ecstasy (the latter in imitation of Louise Lateau, a stigmatized nun living in Belgium about whom the Parisian newspapers were reporting at the time). Indeed, at one point in her life Geneviève, who considered Louise Lateau to be her sister, tried to undertake a pilgrimage to her but experienced a hysterical seizure before she reached Lille and was returned to the Salpêtrière. As Jacqueline Carroy-Thirard notes, Geneviève's case allowed the physicians at the Salpêtrière to secularize the theme of possession, given that she so adroitly merged divine ecstasy with amorous ecstasy (1980, 506). For all these symptoms—attacks of anger, hysterical seizures ending in a loss of consciousness, as well as the histrionic vacillation between poses of the prostitute and the saint—Charcot ultimately identified psychic trauma as the etiology. At the same time he used Geneviève as one of his favorite models for performances of the hysteric attack at his Tuesday lectures and for the photographic reproductions used to illustrate his written transcripts of case histories of hysteria. In a sense, Charcot's antidote to the traces of traumatic shock Geneviève came to articulate through her hysterical symptoms was itself the infliction of traumatic shock, be it hypnosis, pressure on sensitive points of the body, or abrupt sensual stimulation, so that symptom and treatment came to correspond with each other.

As George Drinka argues, without discarding the notion of a physical cause for hysteria, Charcot insisted that hysteria could not be perceived as a purely organic illness—given that he conceived of traumatic shock as a strain on the central nervous system. At the same time he held onto the belief that a major causative agent was hereditary, so that the predisposition to hysteria on some level did remain organic: "He started with the Zeus myth, which located the aetiological moment of neurosis in a shock in the environment . . . and then connected this shock with an idea of fright in the patient. This is what Charcot called autosuggestion: a terrifying idea of injury, or death, that grew in the mind and played a role in the development of the hysterical symptom" (1984, 277). At the same time the Salpêtrière could, as Carroy-Thirard suggests, be seen as the last theater of possession in France (1980, 501), given that Charcot always drew on the connection between demon possession, mystic visions, and hysteria, using his clinical observations to secularize religion by depicting celebrated religious figures such as Theresa of Avila, Saint Catherine of Siena, or their contemporary Bernadette of Lourdes as victims of hysterical neurosis, and the outbreak of witchcraft in Loudon and Salem as an epidemic of hysteria.[2] Indeed Charcot enjoyed comparing his cure of the hysteric to medieval representations of Christ casting out a demon from a possessed man or woman (Drinka 1984, 264). The case of Geneviève can thus be seen as a paradigm for the way Charcot's notion of hysteria knots together the vicissitudes of traumatic experience with the legacy of received cultural images of the feminine body contorted into fits of ecstasy, stigmatizing the presence of a foreign body within her.

Of course, Charcot's treatment of hysteria was limited largely to symptomatic therapy. As Veith explains, the psychological aspect of his treatment was directed toward neutralizing the originary psychic trauma by separating his patients from their psychopathogenic environments and assuring them that a cure was possible, while the physical aspect consisted in reinvigorating organs and extremities and stimulating muscles to alleviate somatic impairment (1965, 236). However, as the weekly lectures he gave for nearly twenty years demonstrated, Charcot was far less concerned with healing hysteria than with classifying its symptoms to come up with an all-encompassing nosological system that divided this psychosomatic dysfunction into two categories: the hysterical fit itself and the stigmata, that is, the symptoms occurring between the fits. Such stigmata, he argued, involved general sensory disturbance, disturbances of special senses, and motor disturbances, such as anesthesias and hyperesthesias, tremors, contractions and paralysis, difficulty in walking or standing, deafness, and tunnel vision. Apart from hypnosis, according to Charcot the hysterical symptoms could be controlled by manipulating another set of stigmatic symptoms, namely the hysterogenic points or zones on the body of the afflicted subject. He believed to have discovered that if he pressed a hysteric's body at certain points, this would either elicit or interrupt a hysterical attack. In his women patients, arresting the hysterical attack might require the application of pressure on the uterus or points located in its vicinity. Charcot never fully relinquished the notion that an unsatisfied sexual desire was one of the causes of hysteria; according to an anecdote Freud recounts, he overheard the master during a Tuesday reception asserting clandestinely to a colleague, "C'est toujours la chose génitale . . . toujours . . . toujours . . . toujours" (1914, 14). Nevertheless Charcot shifted his attention from the womb as privileged site of hysterical dissatisfaction to the ovaries, no longer recommending, as physicians before him had, a forceful penetration into the womb of a patient so as to reanchor in its proper place the supposedly peregrinating foreign body. Rather, he recommended the application of violent pressure to the abdominal area: "The doctor should plunge his closed fist in the area of the ovarian pain. He must, above all, call on all his strength in order to overcome the rigidity of the abdominal muscles" (Evans 1991, 29). At the same time he reinstituted the use of a belt-like ovarian compressor, meant to substitute for the fist of the physician, which would remain strapped on the patient's abdominal area for up to three days.

The originality of Charcot's work as a nosologist, however, ultimately lies in his insisting that the hysterical attack was uniform in all his patients, even if it was this belief that also made him such a contested medical figure. For his scientific analysis of this disease consisted not only in showing that the hysterical symptoms were mentally induced responses to experiences of traumatic shock, but, equally crucial, that the hysterical attack also followed a completely regular and uniform pattern. Charcot thus came to devise a complex graph, dividing hysterical attack, into four clearly distinguished phases, which each contained subphases. As part of his phantasm of nosological omnipotence, he insisted that these different periods could be precisely labeled and timed, as well as demonstrated during his Tuesday lectures, once hypnosis or the application of some physical shock induced a simulation in the hysteric. In his last essay on hysteria he defended his approach, explaining: "We know nothing of its nature, nor about any lesions producing it. We know it only through its manifestations and are therefore only able to characterize it by its symptoms, for the more hysteria is subjective, the more it is necessary to make it objective in order to recognize it" (Micale 1990, 394). At this point it is useful to recall in detail how Charcot came to describe the phases of the hysteric attack, since I will later map both Stoker's vampirized heroines and Wagner's femme fatale Kundry onto this graph.

The beginning (*debut*) of an attack was marked by the painful symptoms of the hysterical aura that immediately preceded it, described by Charcot as follows: "lower abdominal pain, moving into the area of the stomach, then heart palpitations, the sensation of a hysterical lump in the throat, buzzing in the ears, beating and pounding in the temple, finally an impairment of vision. With the ensuing fainting spell the actual fit sets in."[3] The first phase, a period of agitation called epileptoid, or "*hystéro-épilepsie*" because it resembles an epileptic fit, comprised the first part of the attack itself, including cries, palor, loss of consciousness where the body would fall to the ground, and an ensuing rigidity of the muscles. In its perfect manifestation, lasting about four minutes, the hysteric patient would perform tonic convulsions— circular movements of the body—until she or he had become contorted into a ball, turning completely around its own axis, a convulsion of the body that would end in what Charcot called tetanus-paralysis of the entire body. This complete rigidity was then followed by clonic spastic convulsions. With both of these subphases Charcot emphasized the terrible distortion occurring in the body. The last part of this phase he determined was a stertorous breathing, with which the resolution of this phase set in.

In the second phase of the hysterical attack—a period of *grands mouvements*, of contortions and body dislocations that Charcot came to call the clown phase (*période clonique*)—the afflicted hysteric would exhibit an extraordinary expenditure of muscle power. In this phase Charcot thought to have detected eccentric body turnings and bizarre and grotesque body postures, marked by an unusual flexibility, mobility, fluidity, and sheer physical force; all of these gestures significantly differ from the body composure of the hysteric in her normal state. Although these dislocations were to a degree idiosyncratic to each patient, Charcot ultimately insisted on a constancy in movement: the circular curve in which the patient would bend completely in the back, so that only her head and her feet came to rest on the bed, while the protracted stomach formed the peak of the curve. These acrobatic movements—somersaults and a quick upward surge of the body—would be repeated several times; they were often introduced or interrupted by mechanical, piercing screams or hissing noises. Although Charcot designated this phase as being illogical, he nevertheless tried to interpret it, namely as a theatrical miming of passionate emotions such as anxiety or fear, in an embittered battle with an imaginary enemy or a fit of anger or hatred directed against oneself or against a stranger. Charcot emphasized the similarity in this phase between the hysteric and an animal, as though here the entire body had transformed into a dislocated foreign body.

The third phase of passionate agitation and attitudes was considered the most fascinating part of the hysteric attack, and here Charcot believed he recognized hallucinatory traits. According to his interpretation, during these passionate attitudes, the patient gives a very personal report of the stations in her psychic development, exhibiting emotionally laden, compelling gestures and articulating fragments of sentences. In other words, he understood the hysteric to be converting her psychic trauma and its symptoms into a personal drama, within which she finds herself enclosed or rather within, and in which she believes she is playing the main part, much as Freud would later call the phantasy a mise-en-scène of desire. Whether these performed hallucinations, were cast in a comic or a tragic mode, Charcot claimed, they were oblique representations of the passionate events and emotions from the patient's psychic reality—love scenes or fires, wars, revolutions, murderous acts, menacing gestures, amorous supplications, ecstasy—with the hysteric experiencing false sensory and mental images as true, with visions of animals and monsters calling forth actual fear or joy, tears, screams, or laughter. Charcot and his collaborators would record and transcribe the hysterics' verbal utterances and body gestures, in the hope of detecting the traumatic events that were being performed in these displayed hallucinations, but without using interpretation to resolve these phantasy scenes, as Freud later came to do. Instead, Charcot sought to construct a coherent, nosological narrative that would impose an order on what presented itself as utterly grotesque body and voice articulations; in it systematization would subject to the laws of a regulated pathology an evasive, psychosomatic illness and the resilient unruliness of the patient's exhibiting it.

The final phase of the grand hysterical fit, the period of delirium, marked the moment when, having traversed her passionate attitudes and gestures, the hysteric would slowly regain her consciousness though still remaining for a while in a state of melancholy and displaying loud crying and sobbing, lamentation, or laughter. While all four phases took about 15 minutes, the hysterical fit could appear in a sequence of twenty to two-hundred repetitions. For demonstration purposes, individual hysterics could have performed more than a thousand hysterical fits in the course of several years. Charcot's phantasm of nosological omnipotence is radically innovative, then, because in the course of this hysterical theatricality, the intimate life stories and phantasies of these young women were not only catalogued and represented as case histories in the publications of his Tuesday lectures but also quite literally reproduced for the benefit of the public by virtue of hypnosis or pressure on hysterogenic points. The somatic and hallucinatory reenactment of traumatic events could be mimed by the hysterics whenever Charcot needed them to perform during his Tuesday lectures. In other words, the hysterical attack not only allowed these patients to represent the scenes of their private theater but also emerged as a phantasmic site of infinite reiterability.

In his discussion Drinka notes that Charcot was the first psychiatrist to use image material in his lectures. He also emphasizes the spectrality of the Tuesday lectures, during which, after some introductory remarks on hysteria or hypnosis, Charcot would present the history of a particular patient by staging a dialogue with her.[4] Then, after Charcot had pressed on a hysterogenic zone or the patient had left the hall to be hypnotized by one of his assistants, she would suffer a hysterical fit. For the benefit of the audience, made up of other doctors and medical students, such writers as Henri Bergson, Emile Durkheim, Guy de Maupassant, and Edmond de Goncourt; journalists; artists; and actors including Sarah Bernhardt, the hysterics would then perform the four phases of the hysterical fit. Axel Munthe, a popular author of the time, describes this macabre spectacle in *The Story of San Michele*: "Some of them smelt with delight a bottle of ammonia when told it was rose water, others would eat a piece of charcoal when presented to them as chocolate. Another would crawl on all fours on the floor, barking furiously when told she was a dog, flap her arms as if trying to fly when turned into a pigeon, lift her skirts with a shriek of terror when a glove was thrown at her feet with a suggestion of being a snake. Another would walk with a top hat in her arms rocking it to and fro and kissing it tenderly when she was told it was her baby" (1930, 296). For their expert and endlessly repeatable performances of hysterical stigmata and the four phases of the hysteric attack these women won fame, attention, and notoriety in Paris and the international world of medicine. Charcot's innovation, one could say, was that he gave life, or rather body, to a psychosomatic disturbance, and this revivification fed off the aptitude, on the part of the actresses, to perform their deformities, their contortions, paralyses, and hallucinations—their language of hysteria—as a public spectacle.

Thus, Drinka suggests, "Although he thought he was using the tools of a neurologist, Charcot was also an incipient psychologist and a bit of a showman. While he was certainly aware that his performances were theatrical, he was not altogether sure whether the performance got in the way of science" (1984, 89). Indeed, many critics writing about Charcot after the event have emphasized that his elaborate demonstrations not only failed to convince many of his peers, but he and his collaborators also were victims of the hysterics, duped by their performances. Veith writes, "It seems never to have occurred to him that the patients might be acting out what they knew was expected of them; or that the repetition of these dramatic crises at the precise time of lectures and demonstrations before an appreciative audience of physicians and medical students may have been engineered by his assistants" (1965, 235). Similarly Henri Ellenberger describes the Salpêtrière as a "peculiar atmosphere of mutual suggestion developed between Charcot, his collaborators, and his patients" (1970, 98). Although this must remain conjecture, one can easily imagine that the patients styled their attacks according to the questions posed to them by the physicians, supporting and sustaining their desire by behaving the way they surmised these physicians, and above all the master Charcot, wanted them to behave, watching and learning from each other, becoming ever more dramatic as they saw the effect their performances had on the audience. Because of the uncanny correspondence between nosologist and medium Charcot in part accused his hysterics of simulating body disorders, while his colleagues in other clinics accused *him* of being a charlatan. And if, to a degree, Charcot used his patients as mediums for his nosological phantasy, manipulating them into offering a perfect representation of the phases and stigmata of hysteria to prove the accuracy of his nosological graphs, the hysterics also manipulated their interpellator, making him part of their performances, the medium for discovering ever new transformations for hysteric symptoms. The vanity that Charcot accused his hysterics of, thus inevitably ricocheted back; it was precisely his egoistic phantasm of omnipotence that made him susceptible to the hysterics' brilliant strategy of deception, creating a scene in which analyst and patient come to instrumentalize each other and mutually support the implicated mise-en-scène of desire.

Yet, as I have argued earlier (see Anton Mesmer's relation to Maria-Theresa Paradis), we cannot ultimately decide this case because the only transcripts we have are those composed by Charcot and his colleagues. Whether Drinka is correct in postulating that Charcot was oblivious to the transference and countertransference at stake in a medical situation in which the patients of the Salpêtrière were often young, working-class women, while the doctors there were often ambitious men, usually of the upper-middle classes or whether he, in fact, himself falls prey to the novelistic manner in which an author like Munthe paints the Salpêtrière, cannot really be the point. Rather, the aspect of Charcot's meticulous description, mapping, and demonstration of the somatic grammar of hysteria is at stake, which has most resiliently survived in both our cultural image repertoire and our critical discourse; it worked by linking a mysterious, elusive neurosis with an unruly feminine body calling forth constraint, be this literally in the sense of terminating a hysterical attack or figurally in the sense of organizing the grotesque and seemingly nonsensical hysteric poses into a coherent graph and narrative of psychosomatic disturbance.

Thus, feminist critic Martha Noel Evans argues that, as was the case for many physicians before him, Charcot's presentation of hysteria must be understood as dealing both with an actual disorder and a construct, with a pathology and a cultural statement about gender. Reflecting both his professional history and the politics of his times, Charcot's grammar of hysteria, Evans suggests, articulates a cultural malaise over changing gender roles whose aim was to pathologize those aspects of femininity that fell outside normative rules: "While hysterics were represented, on the one hand, as malleable, vain, suggestible epitomes of femininity, they were, on the other, perceived as willful, troublemaking, unladylike, virile creatures whose attempts at self-assertion were interpreted as resistance to the male authorities taking care of them" (1991, 40). Thus, if the hysteric fit was seen as a representation of sexualized manipulative power on the part of the patient, the inextricable counterpart to the equation is that it was publically reproduced so as to confirm the mastery of the physician. One of Charcot's students and colleagues, Georges Gilles de la Tourette, wrote of a patient at the Salpêtrière: "From the moment she is hypnotized she belongs to us" (Evans 1991, 37).

Even more critically, Janet Beizer speaks of Charcot's patients as ventriloquized bodies, so as to emphasize that his representations of hysteria repressed the woman's speech in order for it "to be expressed as inarticulate body language, which must then be dubbed by a male narrator" (1994, 9). Her most poignant examples for this dialectic are the dermatoglyphic depictions "dermographism" in the *Nouvelle Iconographie de la Salpêtrière*, where the emotional impressionability of the hysteric was visually rendered as a predisposition to an immune reaction of the skin that allowed physicians to etch words or patterns onto the arms, chest, or back of the patient, quite literally turning the body into a blank pad ready to be inscribed by the physician's message. From this she draws the general conclusion that in reading the hysterical body one is actually reading someone else's superimposed text. It is only the master text, which is to say, Charcot's labels and descriptions of the otherwise nonsemiotic, hysterical body, that makes it signify—even as the hysteric's narrative can never be read outside the frame of this mediating master text. Indeed, Georges Didi-Huberman (1984) considers these dermatoglyphic etchings on the bodies of anesthetized hysterics as analogous to hypnosis, in which physicians sought to produce and reproduce symptoms, with the hysterics as the mediums for messages they had induced in them.

I prefer to explore this visualization of the language of hysteria as the framing of the hysteric body in neither as totalizing nor as stable a manner as Beizer suggests, so as to shift my critical gaze to the issue of how the hysterical articulation undercuts the very framing her performance also calls forth. Nevertheless, Beizer's reading of Charcot's imprinting of the hysterical body as palimpsest leads to a conclusion supporting my own claim that the sexualization of this psychosomatic disturbance should be seen as a screen technique. For she, too, sees the gendered encoding of the hysteric as a "superimposed text that attempts to suppress the sentence, that originary (and doubtless final) text. For the message of a body semiotic in and by itself—whatever the sex—is death" (1994, 29). Indeed, the skin of the hysteric is only apparently an unmarked pad, as I have argued previously, given that the navel always signifies that the body has already been etched by traces of mutability and mortality that can be repressed but never extinguished. Writing dermographically on the hysteric body, or inscribing this body into a fixed and regulated graph, thus, also articulates an anxiety on the part of physicians not only in response to a malaise of gender roles but also in relation to a malaise about the traumatic knowledge of their own inevitable fallibility in the face of death. While Beizer rightly focuses on the fact that such a reinscription of the hysteric body serves to alleviate any anxiety about mortality because it uses a body explicitly speaking its frailty to produce one that bears the apotropaic message of the physician's mastery over body vulnerability, I would simply add that this in itself is a gesture fraught with ambivalence. To use a sexualization of the body to efface its traces of mortality is a strategy that unwittingly acknowledges what it seeks to deny.

Charcot's ambivalence about the value of offering a gendered representation of hysteria emerges as particularly intriguing, given that even as he rejected a sexual pathogenesis for hysteria throughout his career, emphasizing instead the importance of traumatic shock, he reinscribed the sexual, as Stephen Heath notes, when he catalogued the hysteric's body gestures along the lines of female stereotypes, labeling their passionate attitudes with subtitles such as "appeal," "amorous supplication," "eroticism," and "ecstasy," with everything coming down to "the genital thing."

Heath rightly argues that "to explain hysteria by 'the problem of sexual identity' is to miss and to contain the struggle it represents, the resistance it marks against that assumption of identity" (1978, 47). Indeed, the resilience of hysteria as a symptom and as a medical category lies in its conflating a refusal to decide between masculinity and femininity with an oscillation between proving the law of sexual identity and protesting against the oppression of that very same law.

Yet Mark Micale, in his work on male hysteria, emphasizes that while Charcot and his collaborators saw and perpetrated a sexual component in hysteria supporting the cultural stereotypes of their time—linking hysteria with nymphomania and with deceitful and treacherous sexual behavior and using photographs and descriptive prose to record "the erotic misbehaviour of their female hysterical patients in loving and lurid detail"—on the theoretical level they "demonstrated an almost wilful refusal to recognize the possible sexual dimensions of the disorder" (1990, 392). Micale meticu-

Planche XXI.

ATTITUDES PASSIONNELLES

ÉROTISME

Photographs of Augustine's "passionate attitudes" from *Iconographie photographique de la Salpêtrière*: eroticism, amorous supplication, menace, ecstasy.

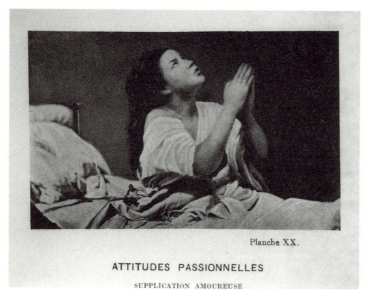

Planche XX.

ATTITUDES PASSIONNELLES

SUPPLICATION AMOUREUSE

Planche XVIII.

ATTITUDES PASSIONNELLES

MENACE

Planche XXII.

ATTITUDES PASSIONNELLES

EXTASE (1876).

lously reconstructs a *tableau clinique* of hysteria for Charcot's male patients, including anesthesias and hyperesthesias; exaggerations of sensibility to touch, temperature, and electricity; abnormalities of the five senses; paralyses and loss of muscular ability; dizziness; headaches; fevers; chest palpitations and chest pains; and language disorders, occurring most often in association with a traumatic physical incident or with an actual injury to the brain, spinal cord, nerves, or muscles. Indeed, the hysterical attacks these traumatized male patients exhibited followed the same pattern as those of the female patients. Even the hysterogenic points that Charcot would press in his female hysterics had anatomical analogues, so that Charcot would apply pressure to the groin and the testes of his male patients whenever he wanted to arrest or provoke a hysterical attack. From this Micale draws two significant conclusions. On the one hand, "Charcot posited a primary constitutional origin for hysteria in both sexes," whose basic design was identical for men and women. On the other hand, "Charcot, knowingly or unknowingly, formulated for the two sexes an essentially separate set of secondary causal factors that were consonant with prevailing notions of masculine and feminine natures. Plainly stated, women in his writings fell ill due to their vulnerable emotional natures and inability to control their feelings, while men got sick from working, drinking, and fornicating too much. Hysterical women suffered from an excess of 'feminine' behaviours, hysterical men an excess of 'masculine' behaviours" (406).

Furthermore, regardless of gender, Charcot understood hysteria as being triggered by an experience of psychic or physical shock, whether this was confined in the case of the women to domestic traumatic events, such as marital turmoil, unrequited love, superstitious fear, or death of a family member or, in the case of male hysterics, this was a response of depression to traumatic events in the workplace. In other words, even if a female hysteric would display an array of gestures ranging from fear or anxiety to pleasure or religious enthusiasm, whereas a male hysteric would display somber, melancholic, or discouraged gestures, in both cases their abundant or grotesque psychosomatic self-display revolved around their bodies' performing the radical nothing that experiences of loss entail. Thus, Micale concludes, "The most striking feature of Charcot's commentary on the disorder in men concerns not the phenomenon of difference but sameness . . . accomplished through the transposition, at times with remarkable anatomical literalness, of a very old and gynocentric model of sickness onto members of the male population" (408–409). Nevertheless, one aspect vexes this gender liberalization of the medical discourse on hysteria: namely, that the predominant visual representation of hysteria not only involved female rather than male hysterics, but that it also had recourse to the most gender-stereotyped images of the nineteenth century. Given that above all this visualization of hysteria came to have such an influence on readers of Charcot, it appears fruitful to further explore the scene of this spectacle, which so resourcefully mingled the histrionic with the scientific.

In the lecture hall of the Salpêtrière, the stage on which the public performances of the phases of hysteria were performed was literally framed by two paintings. On the one end of the hall hung Robert Fleury's painting of Pinel liberating the insane at the Salpêtrière, while on the opposite wall was the lithograph by Brouillet depicting Charcot lecturing to a group of physicians, with the unconscious body of a young hysteric draped over his left arm as the object of his analysis facing them (Showalter 1985, 149). Significantly, in this painted version of Charcot's lecture scene, while the audience is faced with a living performance of hysteria, their backs are turned to yet another representation of hysteria, namely a graphic rendition by Paul Richer of the hysteric's *arc de cercle*. During the Tuesday lectures in the amphitheater of the Salpêtrière, then, the hysterics performed within a space framed by three images of hysteria, three representations of their hysteric gestures (as these had already been transcribed and transmitted by the prevalent cultural image repertoire): first an image of the past on which their self-expression fed, the dramatic contortions of the possessed body tearing at its clothes, writhing on the dirty ground (Fleury); second, an image of the present they were in the process of enacting, the passively willing patient of the master, with no will of her own (Brouillet); and third, an image anticipating the future of this self-presentation, a curved body already transformed into the somatic alphabet Charcot and his collaborators were in the process of creating. One could speculate that to the young women called on to perform in relation to them, these representations must have served both as a warning and an invitation to imitation. For over the exhibited histrionic bodies of the hypnotized hysterics the three installed visual paradigms seem to have come to be knotted together. Indeed, as Gilman speculates, the hysterics at the Salpêtrière probably "learned from the representations of the hysteric how to appear as a hysteric" (1993a, 346). Showalter notes, "Charcot's hospital became an environment in which female hysteria was perpetually presented, represented, and reproduced" (1985, 150).

The troubling enmeshment that thus emerged from Charcot's performances at the Salpêtrière implies a complex network of mutual complicity that cannot adequately be subsumed under such terms as malingering or deception—be it Charcot's theory that is considered fraudulent or the hysteric's simulation accused of being mimickry. Rather Charcot, along with the more standard practice of recording his patients' symptoms on a daily or weekly basis, used inanimate visual imagery to reproduce the body language of his patients (photos and gravures made from photographs) as demonstration and documentation of his theory of hysteria. At the same time, however, he did so within the context of an inherited western repertoire of images—Pinel's painting of liberating the insane as well as a wide iconography of the feminine body, displaying moments of ecstasy, desire, seduction, passivity, or paralysis. At this time, as Didi-Huberman (1982, 59) notes, the police began to collect mug shots and fingerprints; the clinic as site for engendering, recording, and storing representations of a psychosomatic pathology thus emerges somewhat like a cross between the police station and the Ecole des Beaux Arts. Finally, the images that Charcot's collaborators produced (the book, *Les démoniaque dans l'art*, he published with Paul Richer on artistic renditions of demon possession as well as Bourneville's and Régnard's three volumes of the *Iconographie photographique de la Salpetrière*) came to influence, among many others, the sensationalist novelist Stoker (as I will discuss later in this chapter) and poets such as the surrealists Breton and Aragon who chose to celebrate the fiftieth anniversary of hysteria, explaining in their manifesto (with which this chapter begins) that they love nothing more than the young hysterics, contorted in ecstasy and exhibiting sexual passion. As Carroy-Thirard puts it, Charcot's hysteric is installed at the intersection of multiple scenes, with scientific, religious, and aesthetic representations knotted together over the debate between what is a real expression of psychic pain and what is artifice. Yet, in the midst of Charcot's grand effort at objectification, the hysteric continues to be an ambiguous concept depicted in the image of her heroes and heroines, be they protagonists of novels, paintings, or medical texts (1982, 304).

III

Perhaps more than any other critic, Georges Didi-Huberman has interrogated the way Charcot's rediscovery of hysteria feeds off an extraordinary complicity between doctor and patient, performing a relationship of mutually dependent desires, gazes, and knowledge. Though Charcot's clinical experiments and his spectacular presentations of the hysteric symptomology supported his innovation, Didi-Huberman claims it is above all the photographic situation that came to crystallize so ideally the connection between hysterical phantasms (convoked by hypnosis) and phantasms of knowledge (convoked as a mise-en-scène whose theme was medical experimentation). For the photographic work of the Salpêtrière served to instill a reciprocity of fascination. Doctors, insatiably seeking images of hysteria (be these live performances or photographic representations) and hysteric patients, complying with this spectacle, outmatching each other with the theatricality of their body poses, came together to stage a scene where hysterical suffering could be invented and fabricated as an art form, both as a spectacle and as an image. This complex performance was meant to sustain the phantasy that by making the intimacy of pain visible and touchable, by breaking open the surface of the hysteric's body to decipher what was invisible, one could master an ineffable and elusive anguish. As he explores this grand optic machinery, however, Didi-Huberman, always returns to the issue of the violence inscribed in the act of seeing, in the act of provoking regulated visibility, in the act of turning the patient into a readable object so as to transform the symptom into a sign: that is, the violence contained in the act of experimenting with the body in service of a nosological *idée fixe*. Any classification of the disorder and multiplicity of hysterical performance into a visual grammar, into an alphabet of the visibility of the body, Didi-Huberman notes, can succeed only at the cost of the afflicted patient, even if such a nosological project also proves to be a resourceful strategy for catching what has always been considered protean, namely the foreign body of hysteria.

Concerned not with the intimate narrative of the pathological history but rather with the surface form, the figurative possibility of generalizing a specific case into a clinical tableau, Charcot was primarily involved with recording the *hystérikè*—what is always delayed and intermittent (Didi-Huberman 1982, 108). At the same time he was wont to defend himself against charges that he was implicated in the hysterical forms he reproduced. In a lecture in 1887 Charcot explains, "It seems that hystero-epilepsy only exists in France and I could even say, as it has sometimes been said, that it only exists at the Salpêtrière, as if I had created it by the force of my will. It would be truly marvelous if I were thus able to create illnesses at the pleasure of my whim and my caprice. But as for the truth, I am absolutely only the photographer; I register what I see" (Didi-Huberman, 32). Yet, ironically, even as the medium of photography implies a verifiable referent, a sure and just image, Charcot's usage of labels makes clear that these representations designate a concept in which the referent, the concrete hysterical body, functions as an attribute, signifying not merely its own story but rather always also Charcot's own infatuation with the nosological image.[5] In a manner that will be significant for my reading of Stoker's *Dracula*, Charcot's medical photography had recourse to a seeming permanence of images so as to support the phantasm of a faithful memory, a durable and transmissible trace. Yet Didi-Huberman highlights the paradox of this nosological project: that the traumatic knowledge at stake escapes itself, despite itself, even as the object of this knowledge—the hysteric host with her symptoms—remains photographically fixed to the field of vision. Because hysteria offers an extraordinary abundance of symptoms that pertain to nothing, the aporia of Charcot's spectacular evidence involves a symptomatic visibility, which can be nothing but representation, the masquerade of a real organic symptom, which is rendered visible as proof it exists.

A paradoxical situation emerged out of this scene of mutual representative complicity, with the physician requiring the poses of the patient to confirm his scientific text and the patient, accepting this desire, performing the symptoms the physicians sought to discover so as to remain in the asylum. In the same measure that the hysteric allowed herself to be reinvented incessantly, transformed into images, her pain increased. This led Didi-Huberman not only to interrogate the moment when submissive consent turns into hatred, but also to explore what he calls the blood of the images (*sang des images*). He draws our attention to the disturbing fact that these representations of the body in pain, meant to confirm and satisfy a physician's notion of hysteria, also point to a disturbance that recedes from any attempt at representational recuperation, that thwarts any codified registration, and that matters because it insists on voicing itself in the register of the real. It is precisely in the biography of Augustine, the young woman most often depicted in the photographs of Bourneville's and Régnard's *Iconographie photographique de la Salpêtrière* and reproduced by Aragon and Breton in their surrealist manifesto, that Didi-Huberman locates the transformation of image into real pain. Particularly in relation to her case he speaks of an asymmetric complicity, where a supposed medical knowledge, perverted in its effort to impose a fictional structure onto a psychosomatic disturbance— roles, hypnotic repetitions, clinical protocols—is brought face-to-face with the hysteric's unyielding anguish at her inevitable, yet also inaccessible, traumatic knowledge (1982, 245).

In the second volume of the *Iconographie photographique de la Salpêtrière*, Bourneville and Régnard offer a detailed description of Augustine's case history, covering a year and a half of her stay at the clinic. They begin by recording the family situation and the attacks of anesthesia and paralysis she had experienced since the age of thirteen, only to follow this report by a seemingly exact record of her treatment after she had entered the Salpêtrière two years later. In their protocol they meticulously describe and date any changes in her body functions, registering her digestive functions, her menstruation, her breathing, her temperature, and her diverse hysterical symptoms, including loss of consciousness and paralysis. They offer transcripts of her conversations with imaginative creatures, which they describe as "her Invisible Ones" (1878, 150), calling the flow of narrative she presents a "chattering" (*bavardage*), a "veritable delirium of words" (148). Later in the transcript they also record the phases of her hysterical attack as well as the hallucinations she has while in a delirium, sometimes self-induced and at other times induced by ether inhalations.

In the *antecedents* to this medical protocol, the authors of the *Iconographie* offer the description of a combination of several traumatic events that might explain the hysterical symptoms that initially brought Augustine to a convalescent home and then in 1875 to the Salpêtrière; her diurnal and nocturnal hysterical attacks, which would begin with pains in the stomach, followed by cries, jumping on her bed, abundant tears, and a paralysis of her left side, making it impossible for her to move both arms and legs. What emerges from the narrative of her previous family history is that while she was a student at a religious school, she would often visit the wife of a painter. During these visits she not only repeatedly witnessed the drunken husband beating his wife, but was herself also assaulted. During the same period, while she was on vacation in Paris, she met Mr. C., her mother's employer and, as she found out later, her lover. Her mother forced her to kiss him and asked her to call him father. After she returned to Paris permanently after her schooling, she was placed in Mr. C.'s home, under the pretext of teaching his children how to sing and sew. Here she was visited at night by Mr. C. who, after two failed atttempts, finally raped her: "After having made all sorts of promises shine before her eyes, offering her beautiful gowns etc., seeing that she didn't want to cede, threatened her with a razor; taking advantage of her fright, he made her drink a liqueur, undressed her and threw her on the bed, and had complete relations" (126). After this violation, Augustine began to lose blood, suffered from genital pains, and couldn't walk, symptoms her mother attributed to the beginning of menstruation. Having returned to her parents' home, Augustine soon thereafter began having her first hysterical attacks, involving nocturnal scenes of fear and anguish that continued for a month and a half. Somewhat later, after she encountered Mr. C. on the street and he threatened her, she presented even more violent attacks. Then, while she was working as a chambermaid, her brother introduced her to two of his friends with whom she had sexual relations. This ultimately led to violent discussions with her family members, in the course of which it transpired that her mother had been the mistress of C. and that she had procured her daughter for him, and she also discovered that her brother was probably an illegitimate child. At this point Augustine's attacks became so much more frequent that her mother delivered her to the Salpêtrière.

Without going into the details of the delirious accounts Augustine offered of these events while at the Salpêtrière, I will briefly name some of her symptoms, because they uncannily resonate with those Stoker describes for his vampirized characters. As Daphne de Marneffe notes, the common theme is articulating the traumatic experience of abandonment. Augustine's hallucinations are "riddled with references to her mother who betrayed her, her father who did not protect her, her employer who raped her, and her brother who procured her for his friends. She dwells repeatedly, incessantly, on her own blamelessness, articulating her efforts to fend off unwelcome advances and to protect herself from pregnancy" (1991, 87). Though Augustine alternates between gay and sad hallucinations, her loss of consciousness is more often accompanied by visions of men with knives threatening to kill her or trying to put snakes in her stomach, of rats attacking her, of bad blood on her body. During these scenes of passion she repeatedly declares that someone is hurting her, calls out for help to her father, accuses her mother, and asks that the animals menacing her be taken away, and most often she ends her scenes by enacting a defense against her phantasized aggressors. In a particularly vibrant hallucinatory scene she accuses her aggressor Mr. C. of suffocating her with his grip on her throat and of her scarf suffocating her, and clenches her teeth, asserting that she will not drink.

The beginning of an attack is often marked by irregular breathing and a sense of oppression and anxiety; after her attacks Augustine often has nightmares, which she will not describe to her physicians. The authors of the *Iconographie* reencode the fact that Augustine is the host for a traumatic knowledge she is only partially cognizant of—one she could never discuss with her parents and instead converted into hysterical symptoms that obliquely perform her sense of fallibility, vulnerability, and abandonment— a narrative about secular forms of demon possession. Precisely because her

hallucinations are interpreted figuratively rather than psychologically (as
manifesting the presence of diabolic, imaginary creatures rather than as
semiotic transformations of traumatic knowledge) the authors remain inat-
tentive to the specific details her narratives actually conveyed. In their protocol she emerges as a hybrid medium, on the manifest level a cipher for Charcot's nosological phantasies about a schematized language of the hysterical
attack as well as traditional aesthetic representations of demon possession.
But on a more submerged level, latent because it was not interpreted by her
chroniclers, the urgency of Augustine's anguish remains as a trace, a foreign
body whose voice we sense precisely because it marks the gap in knowledge
in Charcot's grand representational design. As de Marneffe argues, while
zealously presenting a chronical of hysteria Charcot and his collaborators
staunchly refused to interpret the wealth of verbal information they recorded, unable to admit that these women could be "tellers of truth and
possessors of knowledge." As a result, they were not only "unable to see the
ways in which the women patient's own subjective desires affected the picture they were constructing," but also unable to take account of the role
their own subjectivity played (1991, 105).

Given that the chroniclers and photographers of the Salpêtrière privileged
the seemingly objectifying function of vision over the seemingly subjective
function of interpreting a spoken text, Augustine instead became as famous
as she did not because of the horrific family romance she had to tell but
rather because she had the unique acting ability to time her hysterical performances to precisely the sequences Charcot required and to divide them into
scenes, acts, living images, and pauses. On short notice she could perform
stigmata and hallucinations, articulating her diverse psychic woundings; in
these performances and reproductions of the hysterical attack the pathological merges, as Didi-Huberman insists, with artistic genius. Whether Augustine appeared in the amphitheater of the clinic or holding the required pose
for minutes before a camera, she did so in response to her physician's desire
as much as to the conditions imposed by the staging or the photographic
setting. These photographs thus signify far more than their labels (menace,
appeal, amorous supplication, eroticism, ecstasy, or mockery) indicate; indeed they simultaneously construct and destabilize the dialectic Beizer refers
to when she criticizes Charcot for ventriloquizing the hysteric's body. For in
these images Augustine is not simply spoken by Charcot: she is also the
medium of their mutually implicated desire and the mistress of a brilliant
acting technique. At the same time, these images also transform a concrete
case of hysteria into a figure of spectacle, a nosological cipher, with Charcot
visualizing and staging, rather than interpreting, her hallucinations—re-
processing rather than treating hysteria (Didi-Huberman 1982, 216). Significantly, in the clinical protocols that present Augustine's case, the authors of
the *Iconographie* give her various names, "Augustine" and "Louise," and
simply "X . . . ," "L . . . ," or "G . . . ." One could say that these representations knot various factors together as Charcot sought to catch an elusive

neurosis and render it visible in a series of images; as he sought to convert the enigma of someone's suffering into labels such as "hystéro-épilepsie"; as he sought to stage the hysteric's resilient and resourceful alternation between normalcy and a self-abandonment to the somatic staging of stigmata and symptoms—followed by a state of *belle indifférence*, with the hysteric apparently cleansed of all affect and anxiety, only to be revisited minutes later once again by the vile attack.

What these images recorded is, first, the hysterical attack in all its mutability as it takes over the patient's body, allowing her to articulate traces of an inaccessible traumatic knowledge by virtue of conversion. Second, we can intuit the narcissistic satisfaction for someone like Augustine, who was able to counterbalance her traumatic narcissistic woundings, given that she could procure the recognition of her physicians by staging her hysterical attack. As de Marneffe notes, "The doctor's interpretation was that her desire for attention and self-display were typical hysterical signs; yet for the patient who had suffered severe trauma in the spheres of love and loyalty, the treatment of her illness and the 'doctoring' of her photographs may both have been expressions of the attention and care she had been deprived of in the past" (1991, 90). Finally, these images represent the narcissistically informed desire on the part of the physicians to produce an image of hysteria, a desire that was so strong that they not only fell prey to the mimetic power of their patients but indeed also incited symptoms by simulation and inspired the production of new ones. In this strange circuit of mutual fascination it becomes impossible to distinguish between the agent and the object of manipulation, for even as the hysteric Augustine is coerced into performing the desired text of her master, Charcot and his colleagues wish to be duped into believing this performance is a true visualization of hysteria. Furthermore, the image itself is manipulated—not the objective shot of a particular moment but the subjective result of intricate staging. One could say that in this representational scene Charcot's invention of hysteria confronts Augustine's real language of trauma and seeks to subsume it, but is also consumed by it.

In other words, if Charcot used his demonstrations as well as the medium of photography to visualize this elusive psychosomatic disorder within clearly regulated schemata, what emerges in the course of his work is not merely a staging of his own phantasm of omnipotence but also a self-perpetuating series of oblique self-representations of his model. In the same gesture that Charcot uses for the mode of visualization, so as to endow hysteria with an objective foundation, he is forced to admit to himself that he remains within the realm of simulation; as Didi-Huberman notes, Charcot invented a theater against the theatricality of hysteria so as to denounce it as simulation and sinful excess (240). Augustine simulates real traumatic traces and real somatic pain in these representations (in the sense that she performs these in a quasi-altered mode), namely, *as* hallucinations or attacks of delirium. But she also simulates her attack in the sense that she can perform her symptoms whenever she is called on to do so for a given audience. Further-more, her simulation is compiled like a patchwork of an array of narratives taken from romance plots—gestures mimicking the iconography of visual representations of possession with modes of theatrical acting popular at the time. As though she were a postmodern subject *avant la lettre,* Augustine seems to not only function as the medium for a culturally given iconography that speaks through her but she also knots together the phantomatic pres-ences of two other scenes, serving as the medium for Charcot's phantasy of a standard, universal formula of hysteria as well as the medium for a mes-sage emitting from her unconscious. In the protocols and visual recordings of her at the Salpêtrière, Augustine appears to alternate representing inti-mate scenes from her own biography and imitating foreign narratives and gestures imposed on her from outside, determined by others. Thus my point is that far from being merely ventriloquized, Augustine articulates precisely this hybrid self-representation, the traumatic knowledge at the kernel of her own psyche and her suffering from reminiscences and traumatic woundings. The aporia is such that her abundant hysterical noise revolves around an enigmatic and elusive nothing, a pain that is always necessarily absent from the performance of hysteria and from the images produced and fabricated by Charcot, even as this nothing can find its articulation only in such an oblique performance.

In discussing the clinic as a stage for a spectacle of the hysterical malady, where the articulation of actual psychic anguish is inextricably crossed with the simulation of assumed poses, it is crucial, then, that Augustine was will-ing to act, as Didi-Huberman terms it, as the star mannequin exhibiting any pose her master required, as a living work of art in Charcot's imaginary museum, the living image of a nosological concept—and this had repercus-sions on her psychic state. For example, during a period when she was pho-tographed repeatedly, Augustine developed a curious symptom: she saw only in black-and-white (Didi-Huberman 1982, 108). Whenever she re-belled against the regime of the clinic, showing phases of violence, she would be anesthetized with chloroform or ether and locked into a cell for solitary confinement. For Didi-Huberman, plate XXV, depicting Augustine miming the gesture of crucifixion, can also be read as the paradigmatic representa-tion of the way the hysteric sacrificed herself by converting her body into a histrionic image—to the image and in the image of a nosological narrative—where her desire for recognition by the interpellated Other, the master physi-cian, finds its correspondence in Charcot's desire for knowledge.

Augustine's story nevertheless ends on a curiously subversive note. In using the medium of mimesis to thwart her master with his own devices, she employed the acting ability, which had allowed her to become one of the stars of the Salpêtrière, for her own liberation. Dressed as a man she simply walked out of the clinic in which she had been living since her fifteenth birthday only to disappear completely (Didi-Huberman, 269). Her later life is not documented, as though the only possible representations of

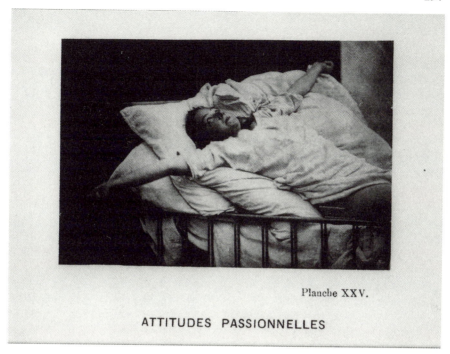

Planche XXV.

ATTITUDES PASSIONNELLES

Augustine miming crucifixion.

her were the strange distortions and transformations of the self exhibited during her hysterical performances. In her passionate attitudes she played roles—the seductress, the stigmatized or crucified martyr, the mocker, the victim—with her private pain not only inextricably knotted together with the acting convention and visual iconography of popular literature during her time, but indeed only finding articulation through this representational dislocation.

Her public performance of intimate scenes of trauma raises issues crucial to the postmodern debate: to what extent is the subject only the sum of the cultural codes and laws inscribed onto it? How much of one's self-fashioning is an act of integrity and how far does the subject merely reiterate the texts that have been grafted onto it by culture? Augustine's case opens up an even more troubling question: in what sense does the hysteric, sustaining and integrating the father's desire, performing ad infinitum and ad absurdum the representation Charcot sought, point to the way she irrevocably materializes at her body the phantasies of femininity that constrain her, even as this representational gesture is the only way to articulate what is most intimate—her psychic trauma? The reproduction of her public performance became the interface between an articulation of her own psychic foreign body, the foreign body of already existing cultural iconography (woman as Christ, the ecstatic martyr as seductress, the impulsive, irrational creature)

Planche XIV.

HYSTÉRO-ÉPILEPSIE

ÉTAT NORMAL

Augustine at the clinic in her "normal state."

and of Charcot's phantasy of a coherent language of hysteria. That is to say, over the body of the hysteric woman, an image repertoire came to be confirmed and a new one invented. At the same time there are significantly no images of the "normal" Augustine existing successfully outside the confines of the Salpêtrière and outside Charcot's graph of hysterical gestures. Ironically, then, at the limit of nosological classification the hysteric also supplies medical discourse with one of its most resilient texts: the narrative of the possessed woman as a condensed representation for the desire of the Other, engendered in and through representation, be this figure of alterity her cultural image repertoire, her interpellating spectators, or the foreign body of intimate traumatic knowledge.

Of course, many critics have commented that whereas the voice is significantly absent from the photographic representations produced by Charcot, Freud's radical innovation is that he privileged hearing over seeing (Heath 1978, 58). As Jacqueline Rose notes, "Freud's work on hysteria started precisely with a rejection of simply mapping the symptoms onto the body," making of hysteria a language "whose relation to the body was decentered, since if the body spoke it was precisely because there was something called the unconscious that could not" (Rose 1986, 38).[6] The consequences of Freud's challenge to Charcot, which rejected visuality and empiricism, Lisa Cartwright notes, is that "By the mid-twentieth century, sight and the body's surface appearance would no longer be regarded as reliable indicators of mental pathology; speech and audition would overtake them in the sensory hierarchy of psychoanalysis" (1995, 50). Though it is undoubtedly true that clinical photography as evidence of organic pathology has become outmoded, art historian Barbara Maria Stafford (1991) suggests that as we are once more becoming a predominantly visual-based culture, imaging the invisible body interior will again emerge as an increasingly pressing issue. I want, therefore, to ask why the images of Augustine not only had such a powerful influence on Charcot's contemporaries, such as Stoker, Zola, and Wagner, but also why they continue to harbor such a strangely compelling fascination for us. Viewing these representations of anguish and self-display quite self-consciously from within our postmodern world, I suggest that although Freud rightly rejects Charcot's visual-based empiricism because it manifestly denied the voice of the afflicted patient, something is articulated in this visualized silencing that any direct speech would, in turn, efface.

In other words, another dimension is at stake; hence the question, how stable in meaning are such representations as those of Augustine that supposedly signify contracture, and doesn't their resilience lie precisely in this inevitable indeterminacy?

Even if Charcot seeks to convince us that we must read the photographic representations of Augustine as examples of the five phases of hysteria he invented, could we not also read this particular series of portraits as rendering a different narrative—detached from, though also running parallel to, the subtitles signifying the nosological interpretation Charcot intended: "*debut*," "*tetanism*," or "*cri*"? Read against the grain, the portraits form a sequence documenting a young woman's physical pain and psychic anguish, as well as her ability to convert these into a self-performance, not only in the sense of the hysterical attack that was incessantly produced and reproduced. Rather, this photographic series also documents the articulation of this painful self-representation as something that falls away from the frame and formulas set by Charcot, as something that cannot be caught within his narrative and visual graph, thus subverting the entire interpretive nosological system in the same moment it is called on to establish and validate it. These images, following Charcot's own dictum, are themselves hysterical because they are much ado about nothing, a series of plates registering illogical, gro-

Planche XXIX.

HYSTÉRO-ÉPILEPSIE

CONTRACTURE

Augustine displaying "contracture" and the "beginning of the attack."

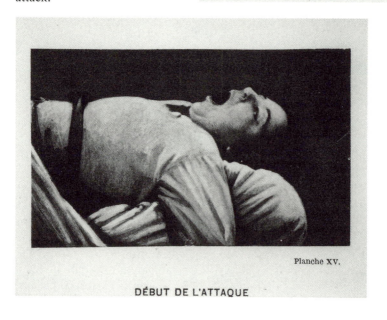

Planche XV.

DÉBUT DE L'ATTAQUE

tesque, but also beautiful postures that, unlike the claim made by their subtitles, show us nothing of the hysteric's disturbance, no etiology, no malfunction of the body, and no solution to organic or psychic distress. In the midst of the abundant presence of performed visuality, knowledge fails and Augustine's hysteria can be neither schematized nor treated. It remains unrepresentable, undescribable, unreproducible, and incurable even as it engenders such a plethora of images.

Read in this way, these photographs contain what Roland Barthes designates as an image's *punctum*, a detail that pierces the viewer and opens up the image, defying the closure any labeling implies. The fascination of these images for me lies less in the imitated pathos (the meaning Charcot wishes to impose on these photographs), interpretations that fit the frame of his narrative about the hysteric's life of passion. Rather, what violently impresses me as viewer is the way in which a traumatic pain that traverses these images cannot be caught up and contained within a coherent interpretation but nevertheless insists on inhabiting this series of portraits. This oblique representation of agony results because for a hysteric like Augustine, the simulation of externally prescribed poses of hysteric symptoms, though evidence of her spectacular performative skill, is never only a representational game but rather also a real pain, the return of traces of traumatic knowledge. As I have already discussed, the indeterminable traumatic pain came to transform itself in the course of her self-representations, in part becoming more intensive or more dramatic in the course of its repeated representation and reproduction; it literally rendered fluid the boundary between self and image. It was undoubtedly also heightened by of the fact that Charcot's attempts to capture the hysteric's symptoms within his master narrative of the four phases of grand hysteria completely fail to explain both her psychic distress and somatic disturbance.

What these images broadcast even as they document Charcot's phantasmic invention of a grammar of hysteria is a message about self-representation: the hysteric negotiates the public display of an intimate psychic truth with its concealment. While Charcot stages the hysteric Augustine so as to seemingly discover a formalized and codified language of hysteria, his project is nourished by the imitation of an already existing image repertoire of states of ecstasy and possession, so that his reproductions are no more objective than previous artistic representations of women possessed by the spirit of another. In other words, the cost of visualizing and objectifying is not simply that it silences the hysteric performer but also that it cruelly delineates the limits of the empiricist medical enterprise. The interlacing of desires, which is so superlatively reproduced by virtue of photographic reproduction, ultimately renders public the murky interface between two other scenes, hidden from and yet also resolutely informing the scene of Augustine's duplicitous performance, addressing and putting into question in one and the same gesture her interpellator's authority. For knotted together in the photographic representations of these poses is the "other scene" of the hysteric's unconscious, whose message is broadcast in converted form through her hysterical symptoms and the other scene of Charcot's image repertoire, which she equally converts into her hysterical attitudes of passion and pain.

If, as Stavros Mentzos claims for hysteric histrionics, "the knowledge producing psychic pain, fear or guilt, is not directly disclosed, even though in a certain sense it is indirectly articulated" (1993, 130), these images may actually be less contained than they seem, themselves hysterically resonating with another, strangely encrypted, foreign voice. As Luce Irigaray argues, reiteration if performed self-consciously can also serve as an affirmative way of calling certain givens into question: "To play with mimesis is thus, for a woman, to try to recover the place of her exploitation by discourse, without allowing herself simply to be reduced to it. It means to resubmit herself— inasmuch as she is on the side of 'perceptible,' of 'matter'—to 'ideas,' in particular to ideas about herself, that are elaborated in/by masculine logic, but so as to make 'visible,' by an effect of playful repetition, what was supposed to remain invisible: the cover-up of a possible operation of the feminine in language. It also means to 'unveil' the fact that, if women are such good mimics, it is because they are not simply reabsorbed into this function" (1974, 76).[7]

Along these lines, a re-viewing of these images, meant as a critical playing with mimesis, might revitalize Augustine's transformation of her traumatic knowledge as much as it might serve to merely perpetuate the appropriation we have come to associate with them. Furthermore, even if it is true, as Jacqueline Rose notes, that Freud's shift from a neurological to a psychological treatment of hysteria meant that the hysterical woman "instead of just being looked at or examined" was now allowed to speak (1986, 98), the question remains whether the Freudian case history doesn't also work in part by virtue of ventriloquy. In the next chapter I will return to the issue I raised in the introduction, namely, that the interpretive narratives Freud ultimately constructs out of the verbal information his patients gave him are as much endowed with his own phantasies of what so-called normalcy entails as are the nosological narrative Charcot develops through his labeled photographs and graphs. In other words, in the transcripts Freud produces, as he listens to what the hysteric tells him rather than watching her poses and gestures, something still is missing, not merely because visual self-display is so crucially part of the language of hysteria, but because *to miss something* is endemic to the structure of the hysteric's discourse and the exchange she sets up with her interpellator.

Before turning to two cultural reworkings of Charcot's iconography of hysteria—both tales about possession and salvation—I want to draw out some of the theoretical implications emerging from this elaborate staging and recording of the complex exchange of desire circulating between the hysteric and her physician. Arguing that a crisis in the individual's relation to alterity can play itself out, either culturally (in the form of spiritual possession) or organically (in the form of hysterical conversion), Jean-Michel Oughourlian analyzes the differences between these two modes of expressing one's relation to a foreign body of knowledge inhabiting the subject. Although Charcot's interpretation of hysteria repeatedly invokes the iconography of possession, Oughourlian's distinction is particularly useful for my reading of Stoker's *Dracula*, given that I will explore how this text pits a medical discourse against a supernatural one within a multivoice narrative, in which various afflicted characters seek a coherent explanation for their experience of trauma.

Oughourlian argues that, in contrast to possession, enacting a subjection before the Other, hysteria stages a revolt, a contest, an insurrection against the Other, who is perceived as a rival. This constant competition and outmatching of the Other allows the hysteric to insist on the priority of her desire before any desire of the Other, even though in contesting the desire of the Other she does not put into question its existence. Accordingly, while possession represents a *mechanism of salvation*, an incarnation of collective belief with submission leading to a cure, hysteria represents a *pathogenic mechanism*, the persistence of private conflicts and disorders. Furthermore, while possession manifests identification with the Other as a way of avoiding conflict, hysteria stages the inverse, proving itself to be the mimetic malady par excellence precisely because it insists on the impossibility of identification as mimetic therapy. Thus whereas possession implies renouncing one's proper desire, "substituting one's claim to and satisfaction of a desire supposedly one's own to the possession by a desire of the Other, to a cultural entity which represents alterity," hysteria enacts "the impossibility of renouncing one's claims on desire, relentlessly affirming against everyone, and at all costs, the appropriateness and precedence of one's proper desire" (1982, 229). Against submission the hysteric stages conflict, in a scene where she is spectator and plays a double role, hers and that of the Other. Staging a doubling of her personality, the hysteric takes possession of the Other, rather than being possessed by the Other, experiences dissociation as a splitting of the self, rather than abandoning herself entirely by unifying with alterity. Like Lucien Israël, for whom hysteria is first and foremost a form of communication with the Other, Oughourlian concedes that hysteria is less a malady than a particular expressive mode of playing with an acknowledgment (*'méconnaissance*) that a relation to alterity is central to all subject formation. Rather than fully recognizing this relation, accepting the desire of the Other as her own, the hysteric in her attacks and hallucinations dissimulates this relation, "by representing this dialectic of desire either as a form of rivalry, miming a combat, in the course of which she attacks or defends herself, or as desire realized, as the epiphany of desire, miming coition or at times mystic ecstasy" (1982, 236). In this dialectic, according to Oughourlian, it is ultimately the hysteric's desire that makes a part of her self appear like a foreign body, so as to represent the Other and through this transformation to master alterity.

In her effort to gain possession of alterity, however, the hysteric, also mimics the physician seeking to master the enigmatic symptoms that riddle her body. Even as the hysteric appeals to the physician to offer her the knowledge she requires to cure her disorder, her symptoms cannot be mastered: they resist the very narrative they also generate. Following Jacques Lacan, Gérard Wajeman thus claims that "the speaking subject is hysterical as such" (1988, 11) because, given that her discourse emerges as a question addressed to the Other, she empowers the Other to tell her who she is, and thereby "reveals the subject's symbolic dependence" on an interpellator. At the same time, "No answer settles the hysteric's question; all answers fail to master their object, none can silence the hysteric . . . and yet the two aspects are linked: the failure of knowledge incessantly fuels the riddle, and hence the production of knowledge" (15). In other words, even as the hysteric begins by empowering her interpellator, by acceding that she is what his knowledge states she is (be this witch, saint, seductress, or patient), the persistence of her protean symptoms articulate that she is entirely and precisely what the interpellator cannot say. As Wajeman puts it, "Pushing man towards knowledge (*pousse-à-savoir*), she also pushes him towards failure (*pousse-au-manque*): the man involved with her always finds himself stupid (*manque-à-savoir*)" (19).

The subject is then fundamentally hysterical in the sense that she demands to be recognized as an effect of her discursive exchange with an interpellating Other, even as she knows that the only true answer to the questions, underlying her symptoms—What is the cause of my disorder? What is this discontent called hysteria?—is to not answer them, refusing to fabricate new interpretive narratives because the traumatic knowledge that inhabits the hysterical subject, as this is enacted by her symptoms, is really unknowable. The only true answer, thus Wajeman, is a silence that lets the enigmatic symptoms speak, a pregnant silence (to which I will return in my discussion of Wagner's Kundry). To claim that the subject is fundamentally hysterical implies acknowledging that rather than our making sense of the world, the world makes sense of us but does so only because we ask it to. Silencing these necessary and satisfying interpretations, letting the symptoms speak, I have argued, might allow us to hear Augustine's voice, so manifestly silenced by the knowledge about hysteria that Charcot's nosology produced. As I turn now to two narratives that explore the toxic side effect of Charcot's empirical project, in which the hysteric's possession of a foreign knowledge is resolved by means of an imposed mechanism of salvation fatal to the hysterical subject, ultimately at stake is this resilient, resonant, silence.

IV

Jan Goldstein has argued that Charcot's meticulous assertion of a hysteric-demoniac equation should be seen as a politicized diagnosis, using a scientific world view to support a republican politics of anticlericalism, for the "redefinition of the supernatural as the natural *pathological*" was not only secularizing in impact and intent but also had "the effect of debunking religion" (1982, 236). However, because in reiterating religious meaning within the terms of an empirical nosological project Charcot and his colleagues drew on this traditional iconography, their positivist rigor only manifestly served to put into question a clerical world view. Reading Bram Stoker's *Dracula* as a fictional reiteration of the Charcotian project, I want to speculate that with it the belief in the miraculous and the supernatural, which a scientific project like Charcot's sought to screen out, reemerges as the toxic side effect of this empirically based anticlericalism.[8] As Terry Castle suggests for the late Enlightenment, the nineteenth-century positivist project, too, inevitably produced a new fascination with the uncanny, superstition, and mysticism, and that can be traced in another "scientific" discussion, which even more clearly informs Stoker's narrative about vampirism—namely, the spiritualist debate.[9] As Sonu Shamdasani notes for the work of Théodore Flournoy, "Nineteenth-century spiritualism arose out of the erosion of Christianity through the rise of secularization and the concomitant concern for personal immortality and the postmortem survival of the soul" (1994, xlix). Flournoy was concerned with explaining the emergence of secondary personalities in states of dissociation, the hallucinations, somnambulism, catalepsy, and trances his favorite medium, Hélène Smith, performed: "all the classical hysterical phenomena," as he wrote to William James in 1894 (Shamdasani, xix). He came to discuss the extraordinary revelations obtained in séances as manifestations of cryptomnesia. Wishing to disprove the supernatural origin for multiple personality disorders, Flournoy argued that the medium's memory of prior states in actuality represented a hidden, forgotten memory (cryptomnesia) that, after having undergone a process of unconscious elaboration, would resurface as a cross between phantasizing and remembering buried knowledge.

Because Flournoy's notion of preserved, encrypted knowledge not only resembles, as Shamdasani notes, "a curious grafting of the notion of metempsychosis onto an early Breuer-Freud model of trauma and catharsis," but also offers a late-nineteenth-century version of Nicolas Abraham's theories of the phantom as objectifying a gap in knowledge, I want to use this debate as the other medical intertext for my reading of Stoker's *Dracula*. The argument I will present is that Stoker produced a fictional account of a cultural crisis in epistemology, when an empirical model was initially pitted against a supernatural worldview. In the face of an unsolvable nosological enigma such as hysteria posed, however, this positivist worldview ultimately came to reinvoke the very visionary model it was meant to displace, just as Freud, some fifty years later, would recommend turning to the poets for the knowledge about femininity that lay beyond the parameters of his psychoanalytic discourse. *Dracula* (1897), I would argue, represents a hysterical, phantasy romance revolving around cryptomnesia, with vampirization serving as the mythopoetic code used to explain how subjects, afflicted by traumatic events, convert a sense of abandonment and uncertainty in symbolic investiture into scenes of possession by alterity.[10] Like Flaubert, in other words, Stoker proves himself to be an adept rewriter of the contemporary medical literature on the vexing question hysteria continues to pose: how to represent the body and the mind. Only for his text, the issue is no longer a malady of imagination, with abundant phantasy work about nothing, but rather cryptomnesia, where an excessive possession by a figure of alterity, recoded as a demonic spirit, ultimately transpires into nothing.

This strangely resilient novel begins with a transcription of Jonathan Harker's journal, kept in shorthand, describing his journey from Munich to Castle Dracula in the Transylvanian mountains. Here he arrives on St. George's Day, when at midnight, as one of the peasants explains to him, "All the evil things in the world will have full sway" (12). Once he has entered the castle, he begins to develop the idée fixe that his host, the Count, is in fact a supernatural creature: his image does not reflect in mirrors, his breath is rank, he is able to crawl down the castle wall facedown, and his cloak transforms into the great wings of a bat. Jonathan ultimately comes to believe that he is a prisoner in the castle, which appears to him to be a crypt harboring many memories. Like many gothic heroes before him, he begins to explore this strange site, only to discover figures from past events he has imagined—but whose knowledge he actually lacks—objectified in the phantomatic appearance of three young ladies who seek to seduce him by biting into his neck with their sharp teeth. Finally he sees the Count himself lying in his coffin, "as if his youth had been half renewed. . . . It seemed as if the whole awful creature were simply gorged with blood; he lay like a filthy leech, exhausted with his repletion" (71). Initially Jonathan responds to these strange events by losing consciousness, then by sensing his brain is on fire, until his anxiety leads to such melancholic depression that he imagines his own suicide. Planning to escape by scaling the castle wall, he notes that the precipice is steep and high and phantasizes that to give himself up to God's mercy and die at the foot of the castle is better than to surrender to the phantom figures of evil.

Under the influence of the generic laws of sensational literature, we as readers are initially willing to trust Jonathan's narrative as a plausible account of supernatural events. However, once one focuses instead on the textual signals Stoker scatters among the pages of his text that support a more skeptical reading, a different narrative emerges. Jonathan himself at one point admits that the entire account arises from his own delusions and thinks, "There is but one thing to hope for: that I may not go mad, if, indeed, I be not mad already" (51). In the letter Sister Agatha writes to Jonathan's bride Mina, she not only informs her that Jonathan Harker has been under care in a hospital in Buda-Pesth for almost two months, suffering from a violent brain fever, but also suggests that his account of the supernatural events are in fact hallucinations: "He has had some fearful shock . . . and in his delirium his ravings have been dreadful; of wolves and poison and blood; of ghosts and demons" (131–132). Once she has read the

passages in his journal, Mina herself initially doubts the reality of these hallucinations, explaining, "How he must have suffered, whether it be true or
only imagination. I wonder if there is any truth in it at all. Did he get his
brain fever, and then write all those terrible things; or had he some cause for
it all?" (231)

If, then, we follow Mina's initial response and read the text against its
generic grain, Jonathan emerges as a paradigm of Charcot's male hysteria.
From Sister Agatha's letter we discover that the shock he experienced is connected to railway travel ("He came in the train from Klausenburg"); between 1880 and 1910 railways were considered primarily responsible for
mental shock, leading doctors, in fact, to call traumatic neurosis *railway
spine* (Drinka 1984, 119). As part of his hallucinatory delusions, the Count
and the three woman appear as phantoms to Jonathan; still, they could actually be objectifying the gap in conscious knowledge he has in relation to this
traumatic experience. They could indeed be his hysterical transformation of
the physician and nurses watching him. In other words, it could just as easily
be the hospital in Buda-Pesth in which he finds himself locked in a room, his
clothes, portmanteau, and all writing materials taken from him during his
treatment. The scene of villainous incarceration in a castle where he believes
himself to be deprived of "all that might be useful to me were I once outside
the castle" (60) could, in fact, be his hysterical phantasy's reworking of the
hospital. Following this conjecture, one might surmise that in the most dramatic of his hallucinations Jonathan, wandering one night through the castle
to sleep in a chamber where he imagines "old ladies had sat and sung and
lived sweet lives whilst their gentle breasts were sad for their menfold away
in the midst of remorseless wars" (52), transforms the sisters taking care of
him into women vying with the physician-qua-Count over who is to possess
him. He might be convinced that they are waiting "to suck my blood" (57),
because at the acme of this delusion he believes he hears "a gasp and a low
wail, as of a half-smothered child." As I have already shown with Radcliffe's
gothic romance, approaching in phantasy the kernel of traumatic knowledge, the hysteric is flooded with such enjoyment that a loss in consciousness
ensues. Jonathan records, "Horror overcame me, and I sank down unconscious." Indeed, this dramatic encounter with three supposed women vampires can be read as a hysterical attack, following the trajectory of Charcot's
graph. The attack begins with a "sense of sleep upon him," the aura bringing
with it autohypnosis. Then, a scene of passionate attitudes follows in which
Jonathan hallucinates a combat with creatures menacing him. At the height
of his conflict he loses consciousness, only to awake, as Charcot's patients
would have, with amnesia, unable to remember who undressed him and
brought him to bed. In the following pages of his diary he repeatedly returns
to this hysterical phantasy that three women are seeking to consume him,
describing scenes of hypnotically induced visions ("I was becoming hypnotized! Quicker and quicker danced the dust, and the moonbeams seemed to
quiver as they went by me into the mass of gloom beyond . . . gathered till

they seemed to take dim phantom shapes") (63) that induce a fit during which he screams, like Charcot's description of the hysteric's *cri*. Recalling a patient like Augustine, he also describes nocturnal visions that call forth anxiety: "It has always been at night-time that I have been molested or threatened, or in some way in danger or in fear" (65).

When Mina goes to marry Jonathan in the hospital in Buda-Pesth, she corroborates the nurse's diagnosis that Jonathan has experienced a shock, leading to a brain fever whose traces "do not lightly die away" (132), and that he has no sense of time, mixing up not only the month but also the year. Significantly, on their wedding day Jonathan entrusts her with his journal, containing "the secret" to his mental illness, asking her to read it but never let him know about it unless some "solemn duty" should require him to remember these traumatic events. Rather than consuming her marriage with Jonathan, who only periodically wakes up from his bouts of fatigue, Mina spends her wedding night instead producing not a baby but a cryptonymic body, shielding but also preserving this testimony of Jonathan's traumatic knowledge. She wraps the journal in white paper, ties it with a pale blue ribbon, and seals it: "Over the knot with sealing-wax, and for my seal I used my wedding ring. Then I kissed it and showed it to my husband, and told him that I would keep it so, and then it would be an outward and visible sign for us all our lives that we trusted each other; that I would never open it unless it were for his own dear sake or for the sake of some stern duty" (139).

In other words, this manuscript of hallucinatory writing, of which it is not clear whether it is the result of a traumatic shock or whether it is the source of Jonathan's present illness, symbolically marks the conjugation between man and wife that is not fulfilled by the body. Later, when Jonathan believes to recognize the Count in the figure of a tall, thin man he encounters on a street in London, he has yet another hysterical attack. Mina notes that after falling into a hypnotic state and then into sleep, he awakes with amnesia, "as in his illness he had forgotten all that this episode had reminded him of" and, now anxious about this "lapsing into forgetfulness" (225), she decides to open the parcel and find out what is written there so as to find the origin of her husband's hysteria. Cutting the sealed knot, one could say, is one of the navel scenes of *Dracula*, for in this act of parturition Mina gives birth to the traumatic knowledge whose transcription she had initially encrypted in the parcel while Jonathan's amnesia had served to shield him from it. As a result of reading this text she will enter into his hysterical delusions, indeed literally rewrite at her own body the hallucinations he had experienced previously. Furthermore, in making this knowledge publicly visible, Mina also supports the mass hysteria orchestrated by Van Helsing, as I will argue later, whose solution is the birth of her child and the destruction of all objective evidence for any truth behind the collective delusion to which Jonathan's text gave rise. In other words, Stoker's entire narrative is framed within a hallucinatory text, encrypted on one side of and then reborn on the other side of the birth of Mina's son, whose name knots together all the men infected by Jonathan's hysteria.

While Jonathan's journal is also hysterical in the rhetorical sense, tracing the *hystérikè* (what is belated, delayed, and intermittent) but not the origin of the traumatic experience, both Jonathan and Mina offer clues for his hysterical outbreak. Describing his arrival at the Castle, he initially wonders, "Was this a customary incident in the life of a solicitor's clerk sent out to explain the purchase of a London estate to a foreigner?" only to correct himself: "I am now a full-blown solicitor!" (25) From this one could surmise that whatever event may have triggered the experience of traumatic shock in Jonathan, his hysterical delusions also articulate his uncertainty about his symbolic mandate, about his becoming partner to Mr. Hawkins. The hysterical phantasy, casting Dracula as his master who can hypnotize him, carry him from one room to the next, undress him, deprive him of his possessions, and control his mobility, reworks his uncertainty about symbolic investiture. Significantly, the attack in London, when Jonathan believes he recognizes the Count, occurs just after he and Mina have been to the funeral of his superior and then partner, Mr. Hawkins. Indeed, Mina obliquely notes the connection in her account of this attack: "Jonathan a solicitor, a partner, rich, master of his business, Mr Hawkins dead and buried, and Jonathan with another attack that may harm him" (222). The attack, one could say, converts a sense of abandonment, called forth by the death of his paternal partner, into a hysterical hallucination where the gap this loss engenders is filled by a phantom figure of demonic mastery. The hysterical fit Jonathan enacts satisfies two, contradictory desires. On the one hand, the reappearance of the Count counteracts the loss of a paternal figure, supporting the phantasy that he is not without a master, while, on the other hand, recalling phantasy scenes in which he was vulnerable and passive, it is also an antidote to his anxiety about the "responsibity about his new position" (231) now that he is the sole master of his law firm. As Mina explains to Lucy, "He says the amount of responsibility which [the death of Hawkins] puts upon him makes him nervous. He begins to doubt himself. . . . It is here that the grave shock that he experienced tells upon him the most" (204).

Only after Van Helsing enters the scene as a surrogate paternal figure, offering Jonathan as antidote to his psychosomatic distress the mythopoetic narrative of vampiric infection and salvation from this contagion, can he be cured of his hysterical symptoms. Van Helsing's treatment consists of disbanding the hysterical oscillation between belief and dissimulation by assuring Jonathan that his delusions are in fact true. As Mina notes, "It may be that it is the doubt which haunts him; that when the doubt is removed, no matter which—waking or dreaming—may prove the truth, he will be more satisfied and better able to bear the shock" (234). Accepting the notion of demon possession, as Oughourlian notes, implies an identification with the Other, an incarnation of collective belief that avoids conflict. In other words, if Jonathan's hysteria was in part a response to his uncertainty about taking on the responsibility as a solicitor and accepting the conflict this would entail, submitting himself to Van Helsing's vampire phantasy means relinquishing not only his claim to his desire but also all responsibility for the individual traumatic knowledge within his psychic topology. Mina, in turn, also prefers to believe in Van Helsing's vampire phantasy, and with it in Jonathan's supernatural contagion, to avoid confronting the far more disturbing knowledge that Jonathan's psyche is irrevocably wounded, that his health is vulnerable, that his position as solicitor is fallible, and that, to boot, the etiology for his hysterical distress is inaccessible. The cost, as I will show, is borne by Mina, for even as Van Helsing and his followers seek to deny the reality of an illness whose origin they cannot locate and whose resilient mobility incites doubt by recording all symptoms and then transforming the hysterical conversion of traumatic impact into a narrative about demonic possession, they themselves fall prey to its very language. Indeed, with her first confession to the master physician Van Helsing, Mina's own attacks begin: "The whole thing seemed to overwhelm me in a rush. . . . The whole fearful mystery of his diary, and the fear that has been brooding over me ever since, all came in a tumult. I suppose I was hysterical, for I threw myself on my knees and held up my hands to him, and implored him to make my husband well again" (238).

Before turning to Mina, and with her to the resolution of Stoker's narrative, however, I want to explore the two scenes of hysterical delusion that follow chronologically after Jonathan's journal, namely, the vampirization of the bride Lucy Westenra and of John Renfield, an inmate in Seward's lunatic asylum. Of all the characters, Lucy is perhaps the most obviously modeled on the notions of hysteria prevalent in Stoker's age. Though she is drawn as the ideal Victorian bride, skillfully playing with the attention of her suitors until she has procured a proposal from Arthur Holmwood, this image of ideal womanhood is marred by her also appearing excitable, restless, and uneasy with an undefined anguish; highly suggestible she is as well, feeling influences more acutely than others. As evidenced by her sleepwalking, she splits herself into a conscious person by day and a second personality by night, when, as Mina notes, "Even in her sleep she seems to be watching me" (98). During one of her nocturnal attacks of somnambulance, Lucy walks to the churchyard, where Mina finds her in a fit, gasping for breath. If she is impatient against anything impeding her sleepwalking during these *conditions seconds*, once awakened she is obedient and seeks to disclaim her trance behavior. The diurnal counterpart to these nocturnal fits of "gasping as if for air" and seeking to break out of the confines of her bedroom is a languid lethargy, anemia, and somatic exhaustion. Like the patients in the Salpêtrière, Lucy has hallucinatory visions—of a bat coming to her window or of a creature with great eyes burning like flames approaching her—during which she falls into a half-dreamy state; when she is awakened from her trance, she exhibits the melancholic delirium Charcot designates as the end of a hysterical attack. Indeed, the account she gives of the traumatic experience of sleepwalking to the cemetery closely follows the symptoms Charcot proposes for the beginning of the hysterical attack—a sense of oppression followed by audio visual hallucinations, a buzzing in the ear, ending in a fainting spell, and the fit and momentary anesthesia from which Lucy awakes with amnesia.

> "I only wanted to be here in this spot—I don't know why, for I was afraid of something—I don't know what. I remember, though I suppose I was asleep, passing through the streets and over the bridge. . . . I heard a lot of dogs howling—the whole town seemed as if it must be full of dogs all howling at once. . . . I have a vague memory of something long and dark with red eyes, . . . and something very sweet and very bitter all around me at once; and then I seemed sinking into deep green water, and there was a singing in my ears . . . and then everything seemed passing away from me; my soul seemed to go out from my body and float about the air . . . and then there was a sort of agonizing feeling, as if I were in an earthquake, and I came back and found you shaking my body. I saw you do it before I felt you." (129–130)

Even the two little red points Mina discovers on her throat can be seen as hysterical stigmata, the dermographic sign registering the presence of a foreign body of unresolved knowledge wandering through her psychic topology, for which Count Dracula serves as the externalized phantom objectification.

Mina's response to Lucy's psychosomatic disorder is to lock her friend into her room at night and fasten the windows, much as Jonathan was locked in his room after wandering through castle Dracula and as John Renfield finds himself locked in whenever he seeks to escape John Seward's asylum. Furthermore, Mina chooses to read Lucy's hysterical stigmata as conversions of her unsatisfied sexual desire; although she has accepted Arthur's proposal of marriage, the wedding ceremony has been delayed until his father will have regained his health (though in fact he will die within weeks of this nocturnal attack). Mina's interpretation is supported by the fact that once Arthur is with her, Lucy gives up walking in her sleep. Of course, a classic feminist reading would rightly argue that Lucy's anxious excitability could be read as her uncertainty about her symbolic investiture or about what the condition of matrimony will mean, much as the nocturnal gasping for air and somnambulant wandering could be construed as an expression of her anticipation that the Victorian marriage might prove to be an oppressive confinement.

Yet John Seward, who diagnoses Lucy's complaint as "difficulty in breathing satisfactorily at times, and of heavy, lethargic sleep, with dreams that frighten her, but regarding which she can remember nothing" (147), ultimately comes to the conclusion that this must be because he can find no organic disorders (though bloodless, she does not show the usual anemic signs). He also notes that sleepwalking is an old habit she had as a child and had inherited from her dead father, who "would get up in the night and dress himself and go out, if he were not stopped" (97). The current outbreak of hysterical symptoms, one can deduce, belatedly articulates an earlier experience of trauma, for which the text offers neither an explanation nor a solution. Insofar as Dracula's presence is registered by the return of this hysterical symptom, he functions as a phantom who objectifies a gap in knowledge, namely, the traumatic impressions handed down to Lucy by her father, which were already cryptomnic traces for him, rather than a secret that could be uncovered. Furthermore, as I will discuss in relation to Freud's presentation of the case of Elizabeth v. R., if the fact that Lucy only walks in her sleep when she is alone means that the outbreak of hysteria is associated with the absence of her groom, it is also connected with the knowledge of impending death. The somnambulant Lucy imitating her dead father and, in her extreme suggestibility, responding to a premonition that her future father-in-law will not live much longer. Moreover, as Seward notes, she is also aware that her mother is fatally ill, so that the outbreak of her hysterical symptoms can be read as a more general conversion of her anxiety about vulnerability and abandonment. It broadcasts her unconscious recognition that, in fact, the symbolic family bonds she has or is about to form are highly precarious. Her stigmata, the languor, fatigue, and bloodlessness, could also be a physical simulation of the death she realizes is encroaching upon her mother's body. As with Jonathan and Mina, Van Helsing is meant to fill the gap in Lucy's family situation, to assume the position of paternal authority she lacks. However, if we recall Burton's astonished admission that he has no right to speak about sexual abstinence in connection with the "nun's and maid's and widow's melancholy," because he also leads the monastic life of a bachelor, Van Helsing emerges as an equally unlikely representative of paternal authority: "He has no wife nor daughter" (150).

With the third vampirized character, John Renfield, the "zoophagous (life-eating) maniac" (95), Stoker completes his intricate network of figural analogies, as though he were offering several modalities of the exchange between hysteric patient and interpellator. Like Lucy, Renfield restlessly awaits for the arrival of someone whom he, in counterdistinction to the others, explicitly calls Master, evoking in the attendants the thought that he, like Charcot's hysterics, has been seized by "religious mania" (132). Like Lucy he also appears to be utterly suggestible, behaving as though he were under the influence of an undetermined force. At the same time he is surveilled by John Seward, who also records all changes in his symptoms (much as Lucy is locked in and watched by Mina, who is equally eager to record any changes in the composure of her friend). Like Jonathan and Mina, Seward keeps a notebook "in which he is always jotting down something" (94), recording—as they do—the delusory systematization of events that are meant to lead to salvation, though in his case they pertain to the animals he feeds and then feeds upon. Furthermore, Renfield, whose delusory phantasy it is to absorb as many lives as he can, offers an inversion of Jonathan, whose delusion staged the desire to be consumed by three women and their master—and it reflects Lucy, whose clandestine phantasy is to consume all the men around her (as she jokingly confesses to Mina, "Why can't they let a girl marry three men, or as many as want her") (81). Finally, like Lucy, Renfield splits into two personalities, one exhibiting a docility, a pleading softness whenever he seeks favors from his master physician Seward, the other fiercely violent, speaking during his paroxysms of rage (like Charcot's Augustine) to an invisible master, explaining in his hallucinations that he will be his faithful slave, that he is awaiting his commands. Furthermore, as Charcot noted with the epileptoid phase of the hysterical attack, Renfield also exhibits an astonishing strength and displays physical contortions during these fits, appearing "more like a wild beast than a man" (135). Like Lucy, who oscillates between languor at day and attacks of sleepwalking at night, he performs a similar shift of symptoms. During the day he exhibits violent paroxyms accompanied by appalling screams, which last until he is so exhausted that he swoons into a sort of coma; at night he falls into a prolonged, lethargic melancholy that might continue into the day and last for more than a week, especially when he imagines that his master has abandoned him. Later in the novel, it seems to Seward as though John Renfield's reason momentarily had been fully restored. Yet within minutes the patient moves from normalcy to performing a frantic attack in which he throws himself on his knees, staging a passionate attitude (similar to those photographed by Régnard), which Seward explicitly diagnoses as a hysterical outburst: "He held up his hands, wringing them in plaintive supplication, and poured forth a torrent of entreaty, with the tears rolling down his cheeks and his whole face and form expressive of the deepest emotion" (317).

Once Van Helsing arrives, a hysterical recording of events—writing into journals and then transcribing onto phonographs or typing out these handwritten manuscripts—is pitted against the language of hysteria that writes itself on the body of the afflicted subject, notably Lucy's languid bloodlessness and Renfield's epileptic fits. Stoker's *Dracula* thus imitates the plurality of voices so typical of the hysterical hallucination, which knots together many personalities into one articulation. On the other hand it also imitates the genre of the medical protocol, using the exact dating and recording one could find in Régnard's and Bourneville's *Iconographie*. As Van Helsing counsels his late pupil John Seward, knowledge is stronger than memory, and recording everything, including doubts and surmises, is meant to counteract memories that are ultimately weaker and thus untrustworthy. In other words, replacing memory traces by positivist protocols that seemingly register everything is meant to counteract hysteria, the malady of reminiscences, in which memory can *not* be controlled but rather returns traumatically in bits and pieces, as the foreign body of cryptomnesiac knowledge.

Indeed, when Lucy recounts the hallucinatory visions of nocturnal assault (which will later be converted by Van Helsing into the scenario of Count Dracula, coming to feed upon the blood of Arthur's bride), this phantasy can be read not only as a sexualized mise-en-scène of desire but also as the imaginary figuration of her sense that she is being exhausted by a nocturnal psychic struggle, her unconscious actively haunting her with messages that broadcast to her the legacy of traumatic knowledge she has encrypted in her psychic topology. Within this struggle against reminiscenses that cannot be regulated, Lucy's body becomes the medium for two forces of alterity vying with each other for mastery. Like Augustine, she describes her symptoms such as nightmares and noises that frighten her out of her wits: "The flapping against the windows, the distant voices which seemed so close to me, the harsh sounds that came from I know not where and commanded me to do I know not what" (176). On the other hand, Van Helsing casts himself as a Sarastro-like figure of the transcendent agency of superego guilt, who, in Slavoj Žižek's words, plays cat and mouse with those at his command, concealing information and letting them grope around and make blind guesses; ultimately he insists on total obedience. As he explains to Arthur, "I shall want you to trust when you cannot—and may not—and must not yet understand. But the time will come when your trust shall be whole and complete in me, and when you shall understand as though the sunlight himself shone through. Then you shall bless me from first to last" (220). While the band of men ultimately gives in to this dictate, Lucy's language of hysteria is more resistant to the end. Even as she resists full identification with the foreign body of traumatic knowledge she acknowledges in her trance state, having amnesia about these hysterical attacks once she wakes up, she also resists full identification with the figures representing paternal authority. Tricking John Seward, who is supposed to watch over her, into falling asleep so that he will not prevent the hysterical attack from occurring is one of several examples of her enacting the aporia that the very phallus she leans on for support—feeling secure in Van Helsing's presence, appealing to Seward to cure her—is also irrevocably fallible. When Van Helsing and Seward check up on her, she is again horribly white and wan.

That Lucy's vampirization can be read as her hysterical performance of the traumatic impact of mortality is perhaps most convincingly supported by the scene that precipitates her own demise, putting closure on the sequence of hysterical stigmata that began when she walked to the cemetery in her sleep. In her memorandum about this fatal night Lucy begins by recording her sense of exhaustion and her fear of sleep, as this anguish, recalling Charcot's stage of the hysterical aura, translates into strange sounds (the howl of a dog) and visions (a big bat at her window) that oppress her and make her lament the solitude. Her mother appears, seemingly uneasy about her daughter's health. Yet what she ultimately enacts is a concrete manifestation of her daughter's earlier anxiety about abandonment. As they lie in bed, embracing each other, Lucy, who anticipates her mother's demise, seems to hear flapping and buffeting at the window, at the same time that she also hears her mother's "poor dear heart still beating terribly." Uncannily resonating with Freud's and Breuer's description of their patients' experiences at the deathbed of their parents, in Lucy's hysterical hallucination the struggle of death that her mother's body enacts is externalized, in a vision of an outside assault. In other words, she simultaneously imagines a crash at the window and the head of a great, gaunt, grey wolf appearing, and she hears her mother cry out in fright and sees her clutch wildly at anything nearby as she points toward the window before dying of a heart attack: "There was a strange and horrible gurgling in her throat; then she fell over, as if struck with lightning, and her head hit my forehead and made me dizzy" (186). At this point, having arrived at the high point in her own anxiety attack, Lucy has a vision of a myriad of little specks blowing in through what she perceives as a broken window. Imitating her mother's body, whose heart had ceased to beat, she experiences anesthesia and loses consciousness altogether, now somatically enacting the traumatic gap in her consciousness engendered by anxiety. In the second part of this horrific death scene, Lucy records how, having regained consciousness, she called out to her maids who then helped her lay her mother on the bed and cover her with a sheet. She tells them to drink a glass of wine to calm their nerves, but they partake instead of the laudanum the physician had prescribed for her mother, and Lucy finds them asleep on the dining-room floor. Now utterly alone with her dead mother, unable to leave the house, feeling both abandoned and vulnerable to the highest degree, Lucy is overwhelmed by the realization of precisely the scene of traumatic loss that her hysterical stigmata have been anticipating. Repeating Jonathan's melancholic despair, the last person she addresses in her memorandum is her bridegroom, Arthur, declaring that she feels she must follow her mother into death ("My dear mother gone! It is time that I go too") and appealing to God to help her on this journey. What is significant about this memorandum is that at no point does she describe Dracula's incursion but rather only her hallucinatory response to the trauma of abandonment before death. The next morning Seward and Van Helsing find her cataleptic and unconscious, lying next to her mother's corpse, much as Geneviève had been found unconscious at the grave of her dead lover.

The blood transfusions Van Helsing prescribes serve as a metaphor for the way the hysteric drains her interpellators. Seward not only notes that he himself seems to be imitating Lucy's fatigue in the form of a "numbness which marks cerebral exhaustion" (165), but also explains that he cannot afford to lose blood because he is overexcited and weary, requiring rest (184); Van Helsing comments that they need new donors because those who have already given blood are exhausted. Furthermore, as though recoding the ancient medical notion that hysteria marks the wandering of a dissatisfied uterus, giving Lucy blood is also a way of feeding a desirous uterus—a horrific reversion of the "penis normalis five times a day" Freud will prescribe to his hysteric patients. Despite Van Helsing's treatment, Lucy continues to waver to the end between the two figurations of alterity, refusing (in the terms suggested by Oughourlian) to cede her desire to the Other, be this the foreign body of traumatic knowledge haunting her or Van Helsing's mythopoetic phantasy of demon possession. Instead, after the fatal anxiety attack, waking from her amnesia she initially gives Van Helsing the memorandum describing her hallucinations. Toward dusk, however, her *condition second* takes over, and in trance she destroys her confession: "She took the paper from her breast and tore it in two. Van Helsing stepped over and took the pieces from her. All the same, however, she went on with the action of tearing, as though the material were still in her hands; finally she lifted her hands and opened them as though scattering the fragments" (198). Similarly, in her conscious state she supports Van Helsing's curative process, pressing the garlic flowers close to her, but in her lethargic state (marked by the stertorous breathing that marks the end of the first phase in Charcot's graph of hysteria) she undermines his dictate, pushing the flowers away from her, and repeating both actions many times as she moves back and forth between spells of sleeping and waking (207).

It is only once Lucy has so mysteriously died that Van Helsing offers the survivors an interpretation of the strange events that have occurred, giving the name *vampire* to the presence of a foreign body provoking hysterical symptoms and attacks in Jonathan, Lucy, and Renfield. He is rearticulating a medical condition, for which no lesions can be found, in the iconography of supernatural belief. Indeed, in this skeptical reading of *Dracula* I would propose that the vampire figure Count Dracula whom Van Helsing invokes is a phantom objectifying a gap in his knowledge as physician, namely, that he can find no organic lesions to explain Lucy's fatal blood loss. Onto this gap, cruelly pointing to his fallibility as physician, he grafts what I suggest calling the horrific inversion of the hysteric's family romance, which involves an uncertainty about symbolic investiture—a vampire romance—in turn involving symbolic fallibility. With this he infects the other members of the community, staging an inversion of the contagion of traumatic knowledge with which they have been afflicted.

However, as I have argued, the dialectic structuring the exchange between the hysteric and her interpellator inevitably has the former drawing the latter into her mise-en-scène of desire. In Stoker's narrative even as Van Helsing casts himself as the omnipotent figure of paternal authority, he is fallible in that his knowledge of hysteria is incapable of finding a solution to this disorder. He is also inconsistent in that he responds to the gap in knowledge the hysteric Lucy confronts him with by producing a hysterization of his own. While Mina's entry from 22 September records how Jonathan responds to the funeral of Mr. Hawkings with a hysterical attack on a street in London, hallucinating the return of the man he had cast as cruel master in his prior delusions, on the same day Dr. Seward records the following scene in his diary. The moment he and Van Helsing are alone in the carriage taking them away from the double burial of Lucy and her mother, the latter gives way "to a regular fit of hysterics." Seward adds, "He has denied to me since that it was hysterics, and insisted that it was only his sense of humour asserting itself under the very terrible conditions. He laughed till he cried . . . and then he cried till he laughed again; and laughed and cried together, just as a woman does. I tried to be stern with him, as one is to a woman under the circumstances; but it had no effect" (225).

An ironic ambivalence subtends the last phase of the novel as Van Helsing masterminds a mass hysteria manifestly aimed at pitting against the symptoms of hysteria, whose stigmata ceaselessly hover between simulation and real, a mythopoetic narrative assuring the afflicted that their delusions are true. Mina is willing to enter into Van Helsing's master plot because it is more reassuring for her to believe in the existence of a demonic monster (241) than in the falliblity of her husband. Similarly, Jonathan is cured by Van Helsing because to trust in his vampire romance means removing the doubt his hysteric attacks had induced in him, forcing him to acknowledge the coexistence of a vulnerable and an empowered aspect of his self. With the support of this mythopoetic phantasy, Jonathan can now trust his own senses, even if the evidence they broadcast to him appears to run contrary to normalcy. "I *was* ill, I *have* had a shock; but you have cured me," he explains to Van Helsing (243), because he can now seemingly remove the sense of psychic duplicity, acknowledging only the one, hallucinatory aspect of himself. However, even as the various characters submit themselves to Van Helsing's belief in the existence of vampires, so as to remove the trace of doubt in psychic unity and the uncertainty in symbolic investiture that the presence of a foreign body in their midst called forth, the only proof they rely on is the recordings of subjective impressions, which raise nothing but doubt in those who read them but who did not take part in the events they describe. In an uncanny imitation of Charcot's project of producing protocols and graphs of hysteria, the fictional Van Helsing and his collaborators meticulously record all events they witness, transcribe and circulate these recordings, and in the process both influence and outmatch each other. In effect they perform all three parts of the scenario enacted during Charcot's *leçons de mardi*—the surveying clinician, the surveyed hysteric, and the audience; indeed, they blur the boundaries between these various figures.

It is at this point in the novel that the last, and for my reading the most significant, dead father is invoked. Trying to overcome the resistance John Seward shows at believing that the bat that bit Lucy could be a figuration of the mythopoetic "Un-Dead," Van Helsing asks him whether he believes in corporeal transference, astral bodies, or materialization. Only, however, when he brings up the notion of hypnotism, does Seward agree, explaining, "Yes. . . . Charcot has proved that pretty well." To this Van Helsing responds by commemorating the loss of his symbolic father: "And of course then you understand how it act and can follow the mind of the great Charcot—alas that he is no more!—into the very soul of the patient that he influence" (247). Seward continues to display doubt at Van Helsing's project, self-consciously aware that only those fired in imagination and willing to believe can support what otherwise seems a delusion. Indeed, after his first visit to Lucy's crypt he wonders if his mind has not in some way become unhinged, arguing that the Professor is "so abnormally clever that if he went off his head he would carry out his intent with regard to some fixed idea in a wonderful way" (262).[11] Precisely through Seward's insistent resistance Stoker thus builds into his narrative those textual details that support the skeptical reading I am proposing. Yet, nevertheless, Seward also supports Van Helsing in the collective performance of a phantasmic scene that demonstrates how much his old teacher, haunted by the dead Charcot and the cross between medical and supernatural knowledge his nosological project had come to represent, transforms identification into a mimetic rearticulation staging the toxic side effects of the dead master's lesson. In other words, uncertain of his symbolic investiture and faced with a gap in knowledge, Van Helsing appeals to his dead symbolic father, even as he invokes the phantom figure Count Dracula to fill this double gap.

In what I propose as the second navel scene of *Dracula*, functioning analogously to the one in which Mina cut open the sealed knot of the parcel containing Jonathan's journal and thus gave a second birth to this collection of hallucinatory texts, Van Helsing insists on breaking open the crypt containing Lucy's corpse, itself a somatic text onto which the hallucinations and stigmata of hysteria have inscribed their signs. In what I suggest calling a grand scenario of Charcot's vampires, Van Helsing, imitating his dead master, restages a scene where, with the help of a medium, he convinces his audience of the truth of his theory. What he offers is an uncanny inversion of the leçons de mardi, given that it occurs at night, with the amphitheater now transformed into a cemetery. And although the retracing of Charcot's grand cycle of the hystericized body is fairly precise, rather than presenting a hypnotized woman, Van Helsing uses the vampirized corpse as his object of demonstration. Like Charcot, Van Helsing is a showman of sorts, first presenting an empty coffin to Seward and then, several hours later, showing him Lucy in her coffin, seemingly preserved just as she had been the night before the funeral. Also like Charcot who used hypnosis to get his patients to perform the stigmata and phases of hysteria, Charcot's phantom, Dracula, also hypnotizes his victims before biting them, and Van Helsing requires the hypnotized Lucy to demonstrate his cure of vampirization. He explains to his audience that because "in trance she died, and in trance she is Un-Dead" he must also kill her while she is in this other state.

Like Charcot's hypnotic medium, then, the Un-Dead Lucy is called on to perform a scene demonstrating that she is the host for a foreign body. Similarly, like Charcot, Van Helsing has a power of persuasion that rests on his deployment of a *visual* spectacle. He requires a medium performing the gestures of the Un-Dead to prove his theory about the existence of vampires, as he also requires an audience willing to be fascinated and then taken in by this spectacle. For Van Helsing is not satisfied simply by asking John Seward to assist him in his plan to mutilate the corpse, cutting off Lucy's head and driving a stake through her heart. Rather, he insists that all three suitors must watch as he provokes and then terminates Lucy's vampire attack. Before their eyes, he lays pieces of holy wafer, rolled into strips, into the crevices along the door of the crypt, "so that the Un-Dead may not enter."[12] Then, again like Charcot's hypnotized hysterics, Lucy appears on the scene, transfigured: "The sweetness was turned to adamantine heartless cruelty and the purity to voluptuous wantonness" (271). As Charcot's nosological phantasy comes to be rearticulated in the guise of Van Helsing's vampire romance, the hysterical medium first traverses a phase of animal-like behavior, snarling at her spectators and growling over the child she had clutched strenuously to her breast, only to perform an array of passionate attitudes, shifting from voluptuous seduction (speaking to her bridegroom in "diabolically sweet tones") to the expression of malicious aggression as she recoils from Van Helsing's golden crucifix, imagining it to be a threatening instrument. Though this part of the vampire attack ends in a moment of magical transfiguration (the corporeal Lucy passes through a blade-like interstice in the crypt door, offering yet more visual proof for Van Helsing's supernatural theories) the full hysterical or vampirical attack ends with the horrific inversion of the method Charcot had developed to restrain the hysterical attack. Rather than thrusting his fist into the abdominal area of the afflicted Lucy, Van Helsing commands Arther to thrust a stake into her body with all his might. After this assault Lucy's face is now "of unequalled sweetness and purity," with "traces of care and pain and waste," like the hysteric who after her attack has terminated exhibited a melancholic serenity.

One could speculate that the staking of Lucy stages a hallucinatory mise-en-scène of desire, where the stigmata of vampirization can be cured by imposing on the afflicted body the symbolic phallus, whose impotence vampirization had repeatedly articulated. For Stoker's vampirization is not only modeled on hysteria in the sense that it records the presence of a foreign body but, more crucially, this affliction constantly challenges and indeed thwarts the power of the physician. The phantasy at stake, to invoke Freud's formula, fulfills a double wish: not only that such a symbolic endowment could be successful but also that what Lucy suffers from should be the lack of the phallus. For like the hysteric, the vampirized Lucy, articulating at her body the ineluctable traces of her own mortality and vulnerability as well as the fallibility of the paternal figures of authority around her, broadcasts a message about phallic disillusionment. She knows that to have the phallus, to be symbolically empowered, is an illusion, at the same time that she is willing to sustain a complex system of phantasies that a body might be cleansed of all traces of mutability and there might be an infallible paternal figure, an intact family unit. While she vacillates between supporting a trust in the phallus and recognizing the illusion of believing in phallic empowerment, the men staking her seek to obliterate this disillusionment in the same way they seek to efface the doubt raised by psychic discontent. Of course, the repressed knowledge of human impotence returns as a hallucination in the real and the gap, about which the hysteric makes so much ado and so resourcefully embellishes its margins, is filled with a phantom figure—the vampirized bride. The staking of Lucy thus represents the successful fulfillment of a wish insofar as it supports the phantasy that the infected body can be cleansed, that the dissatisfied bride can be appeased, and that paternal authority can be restored. But seen as a whole, Stoker's *Dracula* dismantles the very certainty Van Helsing's vampire narrative produces, because the text illustrates that such recuperation is only possible as a hallucinatory delusion.

Marking the turning point of the novel, Van Helsing, having offered his own hysterical simulation of his master Charcot's phantasm of omnipotence, shifts from cleansing the infected body or from reanchoring the uterus in its proper place to destroying the source of the infection. He moves from using his stake to erase the traces of traumatic knowledge, which the presence of this foreign body called forth in its hysteric victim, to effacing the wandering foreign body itself so as to again screen out the traumatic gap in knowledge this phantom objectifies. In this last phase of Van Helsing's grand hysteria, Seward continues to waver between trusting his old master and entertaining doubts about his project, noting, "I sometimes think we must be all mad and that we shall wake to insanity in strait-waistcoats" (351). Jonathan, in turn, by fully accepting Van Helsing's mythopoetic phantasy of salvation from supernatural evil, far from experiencing the belated effects of his prior traumatization, is (in Mina's words) more resolute than ever before, stronger and full of volcanic energy. While he believes himself purified, however, it is Mina who will use the language of hysteria to articulate an inherited traumatic knowledge. The difference is that hers is a malady of representation more clearly engendered by the reading of the others' texts, in which the hallucinations and stigmata elicited by the vampiric presence had already been described. Indeed, Mina locates the beginning of her hysterical symptoms—her sense of powerlessness although she is not "of a fainting disposition," feeling that her brain is all in a whirl, being the victim of crying fits she has never had before—in her reading about Lucy's terrible death, and she explicitly links this to what she has read about Jonathan's experiences in Transylvania. What makes her susceptible to vampirization is that she has inherited the doubt Jonathan has cast off: "As it was, I didn't know what to believe" (287).[13] Although all the characters seem to feed their hysterical compilation of records about the uncanny presence of a foreign body in their midst with the traditional vampire lore Van Helsing finally recalls for them, just as Charcot used the iconography of demon possession, Mina begins to somatically imitate these transmitted narratives once Van Helsing and his collaborators exclude her from their hunting plans. Indeed, the first scene of being vampirically infected that she records begins with the sentence, "It is strange to me to be kept in the dark," as though the hysterical attack she is about to describe were her means of articulating her sense of being abandoned and uncertain about her symbolic investiture as Jonathan's wife.

The attack itself follows along the pattern described by Lucy, beginning with the onset of a hysteric aura; Mina hears "the sudden barking of the dogs and a lot of queer sounds, like praying on a very tumultuous scale" and has a vision of white mist creeping across the grass. Finding "a lethargy creeping over me" she falls into her trance from which she wakes with amnesia; "I must have fallen asleep, for, except dreams, I do not remember anything until the morning when Jonathan woke me" (332). As she continues recording her dream hallucination, she self-consciously draws parallels to her own visions and those she has read about. The pillar of cloud whirling in her room, corresponding to a mental state in which "things began to whirl through my brain," evokes first a Biblical reference from Exod. 13: 21–2—"a pillar of cloud by day and of fire by night"—only to transform into a creature of whom Mina writes that it "seemed to shine on me through the fog like two red eyes, such as Lucy told me of in her momentary mental wanderings when, on the cliff, the dying sunlight struck the windows of St Mary's Church." This realization leads to an anxiety attack, imitating Jonathan's loss of consciousness, once the intensity of traumatic enjoyment becomes unbearable: "Suddenly the horror burst upon me that it was thus that Jonathan had seen those awful women growing into reality through the whirling mist in the moonlight, and in my dream I must have fainted, for all became black darkness." This gap in consciousness is then objectified in the phantom face of Dracula, "a livid white face bending over me out of the mist." Her various states of consciousness are so fluid that Mina is uncertain whether this phantom figure, apart from being her reformulation of the figure who used to haunt her husband, might not have been Jonathan himself. Describing how she woke up, she notes, "It took me an effort and a little time to realize where I was, and that it was Jonathan who was bending over me" (332). Finally, Mina imitates Jonathan's journal, like him noting that such dreams could "unseat one's reason if there were too much of them." The hysterical symptoms she exhibits after this first attack are hypersensitivity and suggestibility, as well as a lethargy coupled with a fear of sleep.[14]

Because all of Van Helsing's collaborators at this point had read each others' hallucinatory transcripts, they all are infected by the presence of the foreign body among them. Unlike Jonathan's and Lucy's hysterical attacks, which had been recorded clandestinely and could only belatedly affect the others, Mina's attacks blur the boundary between her hysterical visions and the hallucinations that Van Helsing and his crew experienced. This mutual implication becomes apparent in a phantasy scene, which also includes the one character whose madness is certain, John Renfield. He was found one morning with terrible injuries, and after undergoing surgery Renfield describes a hallucination beginning with a scene of male rape of the patient (much as Mr. C. had done with Augustine), the intruding figure seducing by "promising me things—not in words but by doing them," conjuring up a multitude of rats for him to feed on. Both the desire for and the struggle against this intruder is then reencoded, however, in the language of a religious phantasy, with Renfield beckoning his assailant, "Come in, Lord and Master!" only to end by describing his futile struggle against this assailant whom he imagines has also attacked Mina (360).

In Seward's journal what immediately follows this record of Renfield's hallucination is the scene where he and three collaborators witness the Count forcing Mina down on his bosom, holding her to the open wound in his breast, and compelling her to drink, while her husband lies in a heavy stupor on the bed. Influenced both by Renfield's story and old medical texts describing how witches copulated with the devil, one might conjecture that the physicians and their collaborators enter into a collective hallucination about Mina's drinking demon blood, which she, seeking to support the paternal authority of Van Helsing, also accepts as the truth when she is later coerced into a confession. With Van Helsing holding one of her hands and "the other hand locked in that of her husband" (368), she offers them "her terrible story" cast in the mythopoetic language about vampirism that has been suggested to her, hysterically simulating in her narrative the scene of demonic possession they wish her to confirm. In contrast to the first attack, which Mina simply recorded through her impressions, she now embellishes each stage with interpretive details aimed at supporting the wishes of her interpellator. First she describes the phantasies that had precipitated her anxiety, "all of them connected with death, and vampires; with blood, and pain, and trouble." The onset of her terror is accompanied with a vision of white mist similar to the one she had previously experienced. Realizing that Jonathan, in bed with her, is sleeping so soundly that she can't wake him, she recasts her sense of utter abandonment (obliquely recalling Lucy in bed with her dead mother) into a phantasy of a tall, thin man in black standing before her. Though she confesses, "I knew him at once from the description of the others," this admission could also be read to mean "I imagined him in imitation of the description given by the others." Her narrative culminates in her description of how, after a momentary heart failure, she falls into paralysis, again recoding a disempowering experience of a foreign body of traumatic knowledge entering the demonic scene her listeners have told her about witnessing, namely, the phantasy of being fed upon and then feeding on this foreign body.[15]

Ultimately, Van Helsing's project of salvation becomes a rivalry in writing. On the one hand, he and his collaborators interpret Mina's hysterical symptoms and stigmata, like Jonathan's and Lucy's before her, as manifestations of demonic writing. On the other hand, they also pit their own transcriptions of the events against their phantasy that Mina is now Dracula's medium, not only infected by his blood but also speaking his commands. As Jonathan notes, recording is an antidote to madness: "I must keep writing at every chance, for I dare not stop to think" (372). Their writing itself, however, also has recourse to Mina's body, such as when Van Helsing touches her forehead with a piece of sacred wafer, searing a mark into her skin to stigmatize her as unclean. Through this image Stoker recalls the dermographic experiments undertaken by Charcot's colleagues, the word Satan being written on the anesthetized skin of a patient's naked back. Finally, Van Helsing and his crew also have recourse to hypnosis, transforming Mina into a two-way medium. She helps them sight the Count by giving them indications of his whereabouts, a horrific inversion of the patient's helping the physician locate the possible lesions of her discomfort. At the same time, however, she signals to them that the foreign body within her is cognizant of their plans and willing to alter his return route to Castle Dracula so as to evade them, which in turn can be read as an analogy to the hysteric's protean symptoms's assuming new shapes as they outmatch the intelligence of their interpellator and keep receding from his grasp. However, whereas Charcot sought to discern and graph the site of hysterical body gestures and attitudes, Van Helsing concern is with designating the site of evil and eradicating it.

As with Lucy and many of Freud's and Breuer's patients at the time that Stoker's *Dracula* appeared, Mina's normal self emerges at sunrise and sunset. During the day she exhibits extensive bouts of lethargy (which Charcot called a *sommeil hystérique*), lasting perhaps for weeks, while at night she exhibits hysterical fits, when she acts out their collective phantasy that she is poisoned, that the demon inside her will destroy her, and that he is calling and giving her orders. During phases of hypnosis, Mina performs her version of passionate attitudes, simulating the voice, gestures, and sensations of the alterity figure seemingly in possession of her, such as the scene where she mimes how Dracula's coffin is brought to light after having been stowed away under the deck of the ship transporting it to Transylvania (442).[16] And like Charcot, Van Helsing must admit the limit to the hysteric medium's trustworthiness; he notes, "It seems to me that her imagination is beginning to work. Whilst she has been in the trance hitherto she has confined herself to the simplest of facts. If this goes on it may ultimately mislead us" (444). Leading them to Count Dracula's castle, Mina engenders their collective retracing of the track Jonathan described in his journal, even though the reliability of this narrative remains contested to the end. When they finally arrive at the site which had functioned as the externalized stage of his traumatic mise-en-scène of desire, the other participants of this hallucination return in the real. As if hysterically imitating Jonathan's hallucinations, Van Helsing notes in his memorandum, "It was as though my memories of all Jonathan's horrid experience were befooling me; for the snow flakes and the mist began to wheel and circle round, till I could get as though a shadowy glimpse of those women that would have kissed him" (471), and, following these phantom creatures into Castle Dracula, he destroys them. With all the actors in Van Helsing's vampire romance converging on one spot, the master figure in Jonathan's narrative can also finally materialize. As the sun is about to set, Jonathan's great knife shears through the throat of the Count lying within the box, while Quincey Morris plunges his bowie knife into the heart. This moment of supposed salvation is jarring, however, because once staked, far from offering a corporeal image of purification, the phantom crumbles into dust. In other words, as Van Helsing and his collaborators wake up from their collective delusion, they face a complete lack of visual proof for the existence of this foreign body. Not only has his externalized form "passed from our sight," but the trace of its inscription on Mina's body is also gone.

Although Van Helsing initially calls this a moment of triumph—"the curse has passed away" (485), the novel ends by noting that a year after the events even the participants begin to doubt their hallucinations: "It was almost impossible to believe that the things which we had seen with our own eyes and heard with our own ears were living truths. Every trace of all that had been was blotted out" (486). Furthermore they recognize their transcripts lack authentic documentation: "nothing but a mass of type-writing" (486), which no one would accept as proof of their wild story. In other words, the representations they are left with install not the physician's cure but rather the hysteric's much ado about a discontent whose reference point, whose organic lesion, whose origin remains inevitably inaccessible. The re-anchoring of a foreign body, which began by causing Jonathan's mind to wander and then, as part of a complex exchange of mutual desires and contagious phantasies, came to infect all those connected with him, thus plays itself out in two final moments of parturition. Mina achieves the motherhood initially denied her, owing to her husband's incapacitation, a motherhood that, according to the medical discourses of the time, is the best antidote to hysteria. She gives birth to a boy whose "bundle of names links all our little band of men together," but who is called Quincey because his birthday is the same day that Quincey Morris died. In his note Jonathan elegantly elides the fact that his son's birthday commemorates the day they believe to have destroyed a vampire, thus functioning as an omphalos for both dead bodies. The second parturition, the text at the beginning of Mina's motherhood and engendering the events leading to the birth of her son, is the record of her husband's delirium. While her marriage could initially not be consummated, this text had inflamed her imagination, and, by analogy, it should also have inflamed us as readers. At the end of *Dracula* we, too, are hystericized, teetering between a purely positivist explanation of the strange events—which misses the fascination and the desire evoked by the presence of a phantasmic foreign body—and a delusional phantasy—which in turn misses that this foreign body broadcasts a message about the traumatic impact of vulnerability and fallibility by instead translating it into a supernatural narrative about demon possession.

Henri Ellenberger was one of the first historians of psychology to recognize the importance of Flournoy's exploration into the mythopoetic unconscious. Vindicating this forgotten psychologist, he argues, "Today, we seldom hear of the mythopoetic unconscious. What psychoanalysts call fantasies represent a minute part of mythopoetic manifestations. We have lost sight of the importance of this terrible power—a power that fathered epidemics of demonism, collective psychoses among witches, revelations of spiritualists, the so-called reincarnation of mediums, automatic writing, the mirages that lured generations of hypnotists, and the profuse literature of the subliminal imagination" (1973, 56). This fascination for the subliminal unconscious resonates in such sensationalist literature as *Dracula*, whose continued fascination is documented in the countless novelistic and cinematic rewritings that have populated the image repertoire of the twentieth century. But it also uncannily resonates in phantasies of totalitarian salvation (*Heil*), for whose resilience the twentieth century has come to be representative as well.

V

Nietzsche, in his polemical argument against Richard Wagner, whom he saw as a décadent representing the most intimate language of modernity, voiced his discomfort with the damaging infection emanating from this music, invoking hysteria as the psychosomatic disorder that had come to stand for modernity. Mocking Wagner's moral and religious themes of salvation and grace as false pretenses, entering the register of what can only remain unknowable, of transgressing the line demarcating all systems of representation (and insisting that for a philosopher such a move is always *de mauvais fois*), Nietzsche claims, "Wagner's art is sick (*krank*). The problems he stages—all of them problems of hysterics—the convulsiveness of his affect, his overexcited sensibility (*überreizte Sensibilität*), his taste, which requires ever more spice, his instability, which he transforms (*verkleidet*) into principles, and not least of all his choice of heroes and heroines, seen as physiological types (—a museum of pathology! [*eine Kranken-Galerie*]): All this taken together produces a syndrome that leaves no doubt. *Wagner est une névrose*" (1888, 22).

This most enigmatic of all psychosomatic disturbances is to Nietzsche such a useful trope for modernity because the hysteric uses her nervous illness, her "belatedness and overexcitedness" (22), as stimulation. Emerging from a state of utter exhaustion, symptomatic for Nietzsche of this historical moment, she also exhibits a protean ability to take on many roles even as these are self-consciously presented as simulations, deceptions of what is true. The hysteric fascinates her audience (her peers, analysts, and doctors) because of the violence of a body language, which appears particularly urgent given that it always uses pain and incapacitation as its ultimate point of reference. She also fascinates, however, because her symptoms are artificial and have no organic lesions. The artifice is further supported by virtue of the *belle indifférence* she maintains toward each role, carelessly shifting from one painful symptom to the next. Applying this medical discourse to Wagner's operas, Nietzsche argues that we find seductively merged in them three stimulating gestures of hysteria: "the brutal, the artificial, and the innocent (idiotic)." They reenliven the most exhausted, calling the half dead back to life, but in doing so, they not only perform hysteria but more importantly hystericize the audience as well. As though he were speaking of Charcot, Nietzsche claims that Wagner "is the master of hypnotic tricks" (23).

For Nietzsche the "hystericism" (27) staged by Wagner ultimately involves a language of music that explicitly *acts*, developing more and more into a talent at deception, with exaltation and exuberance pushed back into the smallest structures to meet listlessness—"Everywhere paralysis, drudgery, numbness or animosity and chaos." But its acting must be seen as artifice, devoid of life, where hallucination, pathos, and an unremitting persistence of extreme feelings aim at effect, not truth. Nietzsche concludes, "He is after effects, he wants nothing but the effect [*er will Nichts als die Wirkung*]. . . . Wagner's music is never true.—But one takes it to be so: and that is as it should be" (31). Given that wanting nothing but the effect (which one considers to be true) is, after all, just another way of calling the histrionics and somatizations typical of hysteria much ado about nothing, it is not surprising that Nietzsche reduces all Wagnerian heroes and heroines to Flaubert's Emma Bovary, perhaps the greatest hysteric of 19th century literature. Emma so passionately and fatefully lives her pathological imagination by trying to materialize at her body the texts she has read—taking for truth what is merely artifice, a representation, a deception—what Pierre Janet has called living a maladie par représentation.

If we take Nietzsche's claim seriously, by mapping it onto the medical discourse coterminously with his polemic—namely, Charcot's conviction that the hysteric's performance masquerades effect as truth even as it seductively draws her audience ineluctably into the play of her grand emotions and passionate attitudes—two points must be stressed. The hysteric offers representations of the self that she is convinced are absolutely true at any given moment, even though the overabundance of roles and easy convertibility of one symptom to another (the refusal to privilege any one of them), imply that all her symptoms are artifice (much ado): her performance disturbs the clear opposition of truth and simulation. As one of Charcot's students, Dubois, wrote, "The hysteric is an actress on stage, a comedian; but one must never reproach her, because she does not know what she plays; she sincerely believes in the reality of the situations" (cited in Trillat 1986, 163). As I have been arguing throughout, precisely because it eludes any definitive nosology, hysteria irritatingly broadcasts the fallibility of any medical discourse seeking to find a cure for the vicissitudes and transformations of the body. It performs the limits of the very medical discourse that constructs it, pointing to an undefinable, inevitable, and yet inaccessible phenomenon at the ground of all nosological classification. Invoking *Hysterismus* as the label for Wagner's music drama obsessively concerned with salvation (*Heil*), cure (*Heilung*), and redemption (*Erlösung*) may not serve merely to claim it as the symptomatic illness of a particular historical moment. Rather, it may also point to a resilient contradiction at the very core of his work: namely, it is necessarily performative, deconstructing the very phantasy of healing it seeks to enact, pointing to the fallibility of its very pathos. Nevertheless, to speak of Wagner as a seductive master of hypnosis troubles the relation between hysteric and physician. Not only does it point out that any interlocutor is drawn into the hallucinatory space of the hysteric, so that any speaking about hysteria is necessarily tainted (infection, so to speak, unavoidable). It also asks us to recall that hypnosis was the method Charcot favored for encouraging his patients to speak and perform a truth not available to their conscious selves. Given that Hysterismus thus also means rendering visible and vocal an intimate truth, communicating with an unknown site of which our conscious activity is but a feeble reflection (Israël, 1976), broadcasting a message about woundedness—be it the fallibility of paternal law and social bonds or the mutability and vulnerability of the body—there may be a cure found in Wagner's art that has nothing to do with any mythic or phantasmic notions of redemption (Heil), even as its articulation requires a mythopoetic scenario.

One might well want to hold onto Nietzsche's insistence that the realm of salvation is *hors langue*, therefore, and should not be performed, since any rendition of it is a deceptive artifice, and not fall behind this realization by postulating that a truth exists in music, located beyond its representations and its effects. On the other hand, it may be equally critical to acknowledge the human desire for a belief beyond symbolic codes or any narcissistically informed phantasies: the desire to return to a register of experience that Freud designated as originary trauma [*Urtrauma*] and which Lacan returns to in his discussion of jouissance, even if this can never be fully captured by any system of representation. Proposing, as in the case of *Dracula*, a skeptical reading against the grain of a text's manifest program, I am advocating a critical gesture, admittedly a tricky one, itself hysterical in that it embraces a deceptive and protean rhetoric. My interest in a critical reiteration of Wagner's Hysterismus is that, especially after the devastating consequences of a cultural phenomenon one could call Wagnerism, one cannot afford to overlook a deep need for phantasms of totalizing grace, for a subjection before alterity (which Oughourlian aligns with possession), even though giving into this need—without any trace of irony and without hysterically contesting such a subjection—is, I will argue, a move to psychosis. I would speculate that if one reads Nietzsche on Wagner concomitantly with *Parsifal*, the figure of Hysterismus may gain a critical resonance, proving Nietzsche's claim is uncannily to the point, though perhaps for different reasons than he intended. The crux may be whether, in these narratives of salvation (Heilung qua Heil), the performer of an overpowering and overdetermined gesture of extreme feeling [*extremen Gefühls*] knows it is only an effect [*Wirkung*], even as the performance assumes a complicity with its audience that goes along with the pretense of truth, or whether one is taken in by the language of hysteria, projecting truth where there is only much ado. At stake is whether the boundary between appearance and truth is perpetually renegotiated or whether it is ultimately abolished, with hallucinations finally inundating the psychic apparatus to such a degree that cultural laws and private phantasies fail before this flood of traumatic enjoyment. A critical reiteration of Wagner's last and most sacred opera, *Parsifal*, may well involve exploring how our enjoyment of its operatic text negotiates precisely this duplicitous approach.

The artful pretense that allows opera divas to move from one assumed identity to another, apparently indifferent to any psychic reality, leads Catherine Clément in her book on women and opera to compare them with hysterics who articulate their repressed traumatic knowledge in numerous ways: in symptoms characterized as masquerade or histrionic lie, emotional instability, and lability; in an egocentrism easily dependent on others, open to the suggestibility of the hypnotist but also in line with their emotional vacillation; and in the form of a *belle indifference* resistant to misfortune and pain. Beaten, tortured, and vanquished one day, the hysteric is recomposed the next, ready to produce a new symptom; like her, the diva who in one moment cries seemingly real tears and suffers with the force of her entire body, rises after her aria, smiling, once again the aloof performer. As Clément suggests, hysteria functions by seducing and allowing for identification, all the while it also helps one find one's bearing by leaning on vain images of plenitude and security, only in the right moment to reveal their fallibilty and to scream (1979, 69). Many operatic heroines, from Gioacchino Rossini's Rosina to Alban Berg's Lulu—and Wagner's Kundry— laugh violently and uncontrollably at the fallible representatives of paternal potency, disconcerting and confusing the very symbolic order they also support. Indeed, Kundry is explicitly cast as a female variant of the Wandering Jew, doomed to wander the earth and assume different roles precisely because she laughed at Christ in his pain, even as it is *her* horrific scream that accompanies the collapse of Klingsor's magic garden at the end of act 2. Yet Clément's point is not to emphasize the victimization but rather the subversion contained in the outburst of the feminine voice. For her the crucial analogy between the hysteric and the opera diva pertains because each is indifferent to her pain, each can incite further stagings of pain and death without ultimately killing a central point of resistance in their psychic make-ups. Suffering and recuperating, both enact the dialectic of undoing and victory, and because they endlessly die only to be resurrected again, they manifest, for Clément, the power of the feminine voice to disconcert the very paternal discourse that also constrains it.[17]

Interested in the function of the hysteric not as a figure of disturbing feminine power but rather as a symptom of the masculine discourse by which she finds herself interpellated, Slavoj Žižek also points out the analogy to other Wagnerian characters: in Harry Kupher's interpretation, the wandering Dutchman is staged as though he were Senta's hysterical vision, confirming her phantasy of being a redeemer, and in Jean-Pierre Ponelle's interpretation Isolde's arrival and death is staged as the hallucination of the dying Tristan. Yet for Žižek, also, Kundry is the paradigmatic example of the hysterical woman who demands from the other precisely to resist her conquest. Taking symptom to mean an "answer without its question" (1993, 185), a compromise formation, owing to which "the subject gets back, in the form of a ciphered, unrecognized message, the truth about his desire, the truth that he betrayed or was not able to confront" (187), Žižek offers two possible readings of Wagner's heroine. The more conventional one uses Lacan's thesis that woman is a symptom of man, existing only insofar as she is a materialization of his Sin, to suggest one formula for healing—purifying one's desire is coterminous with the abolishing of one's symptom, that is, with disolving hysteria: "When Parsifal purifies his desire and rejects Kundry, she loses her speech, changes into a mute shadow, and finally drops dead. She existed only insofar as she attracted the male gaze" (187).

The second, more radical reading inverts this formula to suggest that it could just as well be the subject, not the hysteric, who loses its ground when the symptom is dissolved: one could also say that "man exists only through woman qua his symptom" (188). If Kundry's hysteria stems from her demanding that Parsifal refuse her demand, she redeems him by renouncing phallic enjoyment, rather than, as the conventional reading suggests, being redeemed by Parsifal as he overcomes his phallicity. The seminal aspect Žižek insists on, however, is that in redeeming Parsifal, Kundry also feminizes him or, as I will argue, hystericizes him so that her kiss produces in him a hallucinatory somatization of Amfortas's wound in his own body. Kundry's function as hysteric thus lies in giving Parsifal knowledge about the fact that he might well be the counterpoint to the wounded Amfortas, but also recognizing his femininity as a "saintly ascetic jouissance beyond the phallus." (189) But, as Žižek also notes, it is precisely this radical questioning of phallicity that Wagner ultimately could not confront. The avoidance of what I suggest calling Parsifal's full hysterization—pretending to be the redeemer even as he knows this can never be a truth—is one way to explain the sudden change in register that gives *Parsifal* an exceptional status among Wagner's operas: "the sudden reversal into fairytale bliss and, accompanying it, the initiatory dimension" (277).[18]

Mapping Wagner's text, revolving as it does around a wound that will not heal and a phantasmic enactment of redemption, onto Charcot's discourse of hysteria is particularly resonant in that this psychosomatic disturbance employs a grand, protean, and resourceful register of effects to broadcast its message of vulnerability and fallibility. My principal intent, however, is to focus on the way Wagner's Hysterismus may mean insisting precisely on the nonviability of any totalizing cure, on the impossibility of untainted truth in representation. For in the figure of Kundry, the most explicitly hysterical figure in the opera, Wagner offers us a voice that interrogates and dismantles the very phantasy of salvation he seeks to construct.[19]

Oscillating between various roles, with no apparent will of her own, giving to each of her peers—Gurnemanz, Klingsor, and Parsifal respectively—the message they need, she supports the paternal desire of the knighthood. She appears in the guise of the wild pagan and then the penitent sinner, the desire of the magician in the guise of a medium without a will, and then seductress, and Parsifal's desire to know his origins and his destiny, first in her role as surrogate mother and then in her imitation of Mary Magdalena. Like Geneviève and Augustine, she can perform each and every part her interpellator requires of her, can shift effortlessly between the saint and the seductress; between the one who mocks Christ, the one who imitates his stigmata, and the one who begs for salvation from her pains. But in true hysterical fashion, given that she is a wandering foreign body and the interface between the various worlds, who knots together the respective phantasies without limiting herself to any one of them, she has an excess of knowledge, which shows up the inconsistency of each single phantasy scene.[20] If, as Žižek argues, the symbolic itself opens up the wound it professes to heal, then the hysteric Kundry emerges as its most reliable representative, for she radically insists on questioning the possibility of closure, keeping the wound open against any protective fiction of *Heil*. Not only does she play a double game, serving more than one master, her services are also always incomplete: she brings a balsam to Amfortas though she knows it cannot cure him, indeed she insists, "ich helfe nie" ["I never help"] (act 1), "nie tue ich Gutes—nur Ruhe will ich" ["I never do good—I want only peace"] and later merely concedes, "dienen . . . dienen" ["to serve . . . to serve"] (act 2). Equally she supports Klingsor's desire to wound Parsifal, while the knowledge she gives the "reine Tor" (innocent fool) in the course of her seduction only serves to bring about the total collapse of Klingsor's magic world of romantic phantasies once Parsifal has become master of the spear.

This excess knowledge, which lets her function beyond any one paternal mandate of symbolic authority, harks back to what one could call her originary scene of traumatic knowledge, when she laughed at Christ's wound and he smote her with his gaze. I suggest that this laugh is the core wound of Wagner's *Hysterismus*, symptomized after the event in Kundry's truncated language and body movements as well as in the repetition compulsion, which forces her to keep open the psychic wound that Christ's gaze inflicted on her by endlessly seducing men in a search for the one who will refuse her demand. Such the aporia is that even as she seeks a knight who will successfully resist her fascination, she finds that her seductive powers merely prove to each proud knight the fallibility he wishes to deny, so that she is forced to repeat her fateful laugh, mocking each knight's wound once it has been made external. Her mocking screams, her utterances of fatigue and despair, but above all her hysterical laughter perform the *hystérikè*, always delayed and intermittent—what Nietzsche calls Wagner's "*Spätheit und Überreitztheit*." Most crucially, however, her laugh histrionically demarcates the psychic gap over which all of Kundry's grand emotions are played out, a gap that resonates in her gasp and then silence as she recalls the memory traces of her primal scene of trauma during her confession to Parsifal in act 2. After she has explained her seeing him and laughing ("Ich sah Ihn—Ihn—und—lachte!), Wagner inserts a full orchestral break, with a fermata over the bar to indicate a sustained pause, completely arresting all movement, sound, and rhythm. It is a quite literally breathtaking silence amid this otherwise over-abundant sound. My point, however, is that having come as close as she can to her traumatic knowledge, Kundry does not fall silent. Rather she articulates this traumatic knowledge obliquely, as a gap in music, as the nothing about which her histrionic performances and all her hysterical stigmata revolve. Moving away from this recognition, her voice starts up again ("again very slowly" is Wagner's direction), cautiously breathing the explanation that also once again misses her pain, anguish, and desire: "da traf mich—sein Blick" ("Then his gaze—smote me"). As the orchestra gains in tempo and passion (Wagner writes "quick, invigorating, very passionately") Kundry once more embarks on a hysterical self-presentation, the woman in despair, seeking in every potential lover she meets a repetition of the man who wounded her, and she continues her histrionics through the end of the second act, again covering the gap in her vocal utterance with a narrative, which now, however, resonates with the traumatic silence. On the narrative level, the wound Kundry inflicts on the Grail community only can be resolved ultimately by foreclosing this representative of difference, who is responsible for Amfortas's bleeding wound (as she was meant to be the agent Klingsor sought to use to disempower Parsifal). During act 3, when she is on stage but virtually emits nothing more than sighs and screams, her voice finally falls silent as she sinks lifeless to the ground, her gaze fastened on Parsifal, and the Grail community's hallucinatory performance of Heil finds its fulfillment.

About the cry Kundry utters and the silence that engulfs her after she has flung herself to the ground, while above their mutual heads Parsifal uses the spear he has regained from Klingsor to make the sign of the cross (a gesture uncannily recalling the vampire Lucy receding from Van Helsing's garlic and holy wafers), Michel Poizat has written the following: "The truth of the vocal object, this beyond or this hither of speech and even of the cry, is silence, the fixed point around which the trajectory of the quest that structures opera ceaselessly revolves, the abyss in which the fantasy dissolves like Klingsor's castle and enchanted garden, like Kundry herself after she has hurled her final cry, leaving the listener gasping in the face of the 'discovery' of this emptiness" (1986, 191). He concludes that the fascination of such an opera as Parsifal might be its double movement, bringing forth the spoken word at the same time that it yields to "the sonorous real in all its continuity." It inserts an unnameable silence," he argues, "into a system that makes it acceptable, that signifies its call but denies it even as it recognizes it, in the nostalgic yearning to dissolve into it and disappear" (192). On the level of the libretto, Parsifal's redemption marks the illusory and deadly retrieval of this absolute jouissance, the sonorous real heralding the recovery of a primordial union of plenitude and integrity (Heil) before differentiation, tension, and symbolic castration. This retrieval is fatal because it requires the silence and death of Kundry. Moreover, in renouncing desire, it is aimed at repressing or denying that to be a speaking subject, a subject of culture, means acknowledging the renunciation of abundant presence, or as Poizat puts it, "forgetting that in the death of desire it is the death instinct that ultimately is played out" (195). Finally, it is fatal because Wagner "deceives himself or his audience by making us believe that that recovery is possible" (198).

Adding to Poizat's discussion of the two levels structuring Wagner's opera, I would simply insist that there is a third effect of silence, resiliently resisting Parsifal's phantasm that absolute jouissance, a primordial presence, a tensionless state of existence can be retrieved: namely, Kundry's hysterical laughter, broadcasting her traumatic knowledge that we are irrevocably wounded, smote by the gaze of the Other, sustained by a belief in salvation but also by the conviction that satisfaction of desire is necessarily impossible. If the tension between two effects of silence, as these are designated by Poizat, structures the dialectic of Wagner's narrative, producing narratives about recovering a state before symbolic castration, then, I would add, the navel of Wagner's ambivalent phantasy, organizing its structure and constituting the cause of its effect, is the full orchestral break, which supports Kundry's traumatic recognition of the source of her woundedness, the very condition of her existence. Wagner's Hysterismus, I would claim, consists in a traumatic disturbance remaining, resonating within the drive toward salvation from narrative, from history, and ultimately from all tonality, a silence demarcated on both sides by traumatic hysterical laughter, which can never be resolved.

Kundry's laughter is as duplicitous as Wagner's phantasmic scenario. By laughing at Christ the symbol, she mocks the fallibility of a symbolic order that seeks to stabilize itself by turning a wounded body into the icon of its own narrative of salvation. On the other hand, this laugh could be read as a traumatic acknowledgment of her own mortal woundedness. For could it not be the gaze of the *man* in pain, not the symbol, speaking not of salvation but of mutability, that touches her so ineluctably? Her hysterical laugh thus speaks of the knowledge that no representation can adequately render an originary traumatic experience of vulnerability, and thus the fallibility of any protective fiction claiming redemption, a disconcerting knowledge that the wound must be kept open because the originary traumatic impact cannot be healed. Thus, even as her hysterical performance supports the phantasies of her respective peers—Gurnemanz's dream that the knighthood will be redeemed, Klingsor's delusion that he will become the sole master of the grail, Parsifal's phantasy that he can fulfill the destiny of Christ—it also broadcasts the diametrically opposed message as well. For it enacts excess knowledge to illustrate that no knowledge can be true in a totalizing sense, given that it can repeat but not return to the originary wound that subtends and engenders all narratives of salvation. If Kundry's first laugh meant uniting with Christ in his pain, enjoying his wound, the belated series of laughs are symptoms for this penetration beyond phallicity, saying that this gaze has wounded her, asking to be healed but knowing this originary shock can neither be recuperated from nor undone.

Wagner's Kundry, functioning as the navel of Wagner's operatic phantasy and knotting together the various protective fictions with a beautiful indifference to the resolution of each, is yet another uncanny Charcotian vampire, with Wagner's *Kranken-Galerie* feeding off the iconography of hysteria that Charcot installed in his living museum of pathology at the Salpêtrière. In the course of the opera Kundry is repeatedly introduced as a body without will, speaking the desires of those who animate her. In act 1 she is compared to a wild animal, running onto the stage in a fit of spastic motions only to fall into a cataleptic, death-like paralysis. In this trance she enacts, with tormented agitated body gestures, the tale of Amfortas's wounding, which Gurnemanz narrates to his fellow men, as though she were his medium, both confirming the tale of how their community fell into disarray and symptomizing the discontent, the difference, indeed the fissure that subtends this social structure—broadcasting a message about its vulnerability. In a sense, by succumbing to Kundry's seduction, Amfortas was himself hystericized, the wound that will not heal serving as a symptom not only of the irrevocable mutability of his body but more so that the cultural order he represents is fallible. At the same time, in the gesture of a maladie par représentation, he reenacts the wounding of Christ, staging himself as an embodiment of the holy icon. If Kundry has more knowledge than Gurnemanz, symptomizing in her restlessness that she knows the hidden truth of Amfortas's suffering, she also turns into Parsifal's medium, broadcasting to him a truth about his origins, but one whose message involves human loss: the death of his mother. One could call the ceremony ending act 1 a hysterical performance of mutability, exhaustion, and the wish for traumatic enjoyment. It is enacted in the triangulation of Kundry, a paralyzed body seeking the quiet of death and speaking from another site, her unconscious; Titurel, a living dead speaking from an open grave; and Amfortas, seeking death, suffering at the sight of the grail that enraptures the other members of the community, falling (like Kundry) into a hypnotic trance as he hallucinates his deliverance. All three phantasmically celebrate the very wound they seek to dissolve. Smitten by the sight of this overdetermined and overabundant spectacle of vulnerability, Parsifal, too, is hystericized. Struck dumb, enraptured, he is drawn into Kundry's hypnotic, mimetic gesturing. At the height of Amfortas's lament he suffers a convulsive heart attack, followed by paralysis; now, like her, a medium, he represents in his body the desire of the Other, namely, Amfortas's anguish.

At the beginning of act 2 Kundry is again revived from a deathlike trance, and once more recalling the performances of Charcot's hysterics, she wails, wimpers, and writhes in seemingly meaningless contortions of the body as Klingsor reminds her of her complicity in the wounding of Amfortas. In the duplicitous mixture of ecstatic laughter and convulsive lament, she acknowledges the desire and the fear that Parsifal, too, will only confirm the message of fallibility it is her curse to proclaim. Indeed, Klingsor coerces Kundry to perform the role of fascinating temptress so that the innocent fool, submitting to her charm, will come under his power, much as Charcot stages the passionate attitudes of his hysterics so as to fascinate his Parisian audience and as Van Helsing stages the vampirized Lucy to convince Arthur and his friends to believe and trust in his vampire phantasy. Once Kundry has reemerged in the guise of fatal temptress (now a young woman of great beauty, completely transformed, dressed in a phantastic costume of Arabian style), it is crucial for the seduction scene, however, that her narrative layer various protective fictions over the psychic and vocal gaps amid her enjoyment of Christ's pain, and that these protective fictions, directed at her interpellator Parsifal, negotiate this traumatic knowledge by addressing and shielding it.

The first attitude she performs, in trying to seduce Parsifal by presenting him with a mise-en-scène of his desire, involves his phantasy of origin, a version of Freud's family romance. Calling out to Parsifal the name his mother had given him, she tells a story about Herzeleide's maternal love for her son ("ich sah das Kind an seiner Mutter Brust") ["I saw the child at its mother's breast"], the death of his father Gamuret, and how his mother sought to protect her son by keeping him ignorant of the family legacy, away from arms and combat. The story she tells, however, discloses more than the fact that in Parsifal's family the position of a paternal figure of authority is empty. Rather, the memory she invokes for Parsifal is inextricably interwoven with his sense of guilt. For Kundry offers him a representation of the anguish of his mother, who, having waited in vain for her son to return, is rendered silent by lament, eaten up by grief ("bis ihr verstummt' die Klage, der Gram ihr zehrte den Schmerz") ["until her lament fell silent, her sorrow ate at her anguish"], and ultimately asking for death to deliver her from abandonment. In calling forth, as medium, the phantom of the dead mother, Kundry also serves to undo Parsifal's amnesia, engendering an acknowledgment of difference, the pain of loss, the lack of plenitude, the traumatic knowledge that his mother tried to keep from him, which he unwittingly inflicted on her. Parsifal ruefully explains, "My mother, my mother I was able to forget. Ah, what else have I forgotten," initially willing to follow his guide Kundry in her effort to convey to him the message about traumatic knowledge that his "dumb foolish innocence" (dumpfe Torheit) has allowed him to deny.

In a second attitude, she moves from invoking both maternal love and the death of Herzeleide to taking on the role of teacher, seeking to initiate Parsifal into the rites of heterosexual love ("als Muttersegens letzten Gruß, der Liebe—ersten Kuß") ["as the last greeting of maternal blessing, love's—first kiss"]. Yet the kiss she offers, and herein lies the hysterical duplicity of Wagner's libretto, serves two purposes. On the one hand, the sexual knowledge it conveys would stain Parsifal, engendering, were he to follow this beckoning call, a fall into mortal sin and fallibility, in imitation of Amfortas; it would infect him with desire, which by definition is always unsatisfiable. On the other hand, it functions as a new *protective* phantasy of tainted sexuality, removing Parsifal from confronting the traumatic knowledge of human lack at the center of all phantasies of redemption, namely, the death of his parents and his amnesia about this abandonment.[21]

The peripeteia—when Kundry's kiss awakens in Parsifal a hysterical identification with Amfortas's wound and the knowledge of its origin, somatizing the Other's pain in his own body—thus stages the rivalry between sexual and traumatic knowledge, between a physical penetration and a penetration by the Other's, gaze, where the former is a protective-though-wounding screen phantasy for the latter. Parsifal believes he now recognizes what is actually only one aspect of Kundry's protean faces of seduction. He sees the temptress, responsible for Amfortas's implenitude, but she has also become the medium through which he can hear not only the anguish of Amfortas but, more crucially, of Christ ["des Heiland's Klage"]; in his identification with this double pain, he merges the two figures into one. At this point in her hysterical self-display, Kundry shifts from being the maternal nourisher and teacher to the helpless subordinate, willing to make a confession to Parsifal as part of her wish that he might emerge as her savior.

In her plea for redemption, offering the mirror inversion of the role of redeemer, which Parsifal has come to fashion for himself, Kundry finally comes closest to the actual demarcation point of her hysterical performance, reenacting her scene of traumatic infliction and ending with a horrific gasp as she realizes the full impact of her laugh. Ironically this is the one moment of true utterance, even if Kundry after having fallen silent returns to her hysterical seduction of Parsifal. The final phantasy scenario she enacts for him feeds off her traumatic recognition, claiming that were she to fuse with him in erotic unity, his love could redeem her: "Allow me to love you, divine one, then you will redeme me." Not only is this the exact inversion of her second attitude, exchanging the role of the teacher who is able to instruct the novice in the secrets of love for that of the lowly penitent, dependent on Parsifal's bestowing his love on her. This imitation of Mary Magdalena is neither Kundry's true nor final self-representation, but merely another of her many self-performances. While Parsifal privileges this guise, because it supports his phantasy that he could be a true imitation of Christ, Kundry at each stage of her seductive performance not only believes in what she simultaneously knows is also a pretense, but also can shift roles whenever the situation requires a new attitude. Just before she calls out to Klingsor to help her, for example, and he, having thrust his spear at Parsifal, finds that his opponent has caught the weapon and is now fully empowered, she confronts the innocent fool with one final passionate attitude. Continuing to plead with him that his love might be her salvation, she supports the demand by revealing that it had been her kiss that gave him the power to be possessed by the pain of both Amfortas and Christ: "So war es mein Kuß, der welthellsichtig dich machte?" ("Thus it was my kiss that made you a visionary?").

While Kundry's much-ado revolves around the unresolvable and unrecuperable traumatic experience of being smitten by Christ's gaze, Parsifal's is an identification with the wound of the Other as mimetic representation of Christ's wound. Both are sustained by the desire for Christ, but Kundry's seductions and hypnotic utterances aim at a second confrontation with the gaze that smote her, even though this gesture defers, reveals and conceals because it knows that the psychic gap irrevocably demarcates all trauma from representation. Hers is the gesture of contesting and insurrection with her interpellator, which Oughourlian sees as the mark of hysteria, accepting a dependence on the Other yet refusing to relinquish her desire to the representative of alterity. Parsifal's hysterization, in contrast, transforms into a psychotic hallucination as he believes that the identification with Amfortas's wound (thus the repetition of Christ's suffering) forecloses the dislocation all representation is informed by, identifying with the desire of the Other and subjecting himself to alterity. As Parsifal strikes a cross in the air with Klingsor's spear, defiantly abandoning Kundry, he moves beyond what Freud repeatedly calls the hysteric's neglect of the distinction between phantasy and reality—and what Nietzsche calls wanting nothing but the effect, which one takes to be the truth. He has moved to a level where the boundary between phantasy and reality is abolished; he literally embodies hallucinations, no longer negotiating between belief in the representation and recognition that it is merely effect but now convinced he is the representation. If Kundry's hysterical gesture of seeking a fusion with the Other screens the traumatic impact of being smitten by the gaze of radical alterity and then abandoned (in her psychic vulnerability) by a protective fiction of love that repeats the family romance, Parsifal's psychotic gesture of fusion screens all traumatic woundedness with recourse to the delusion of having become one with the wound, repeating and dissolving it in one and the same gesture.

At the end of the opera, even if what is achieved is a seeming erasure of difference, both the libretto and the score are structured by an opposition between Kundry's continued hysterical play and Parsifal's enraptured longing for a transparent identification with Amfortas's suffering and salvation as the fulfillment of a mythic text he chooses over the family and seduction romance Kundry offers. Even though the libretto pits Kundry's representation of sin against Parsifal's desire to circumvent sin, pits her chromaticism against his striving for the pure, diatonic leitmotiv, both gestures respond to and screen the total gap in sound and text after Kundry's recollection of her laughter at Christ's anguish. So that, although one could interpret her silence at the end of act 2 as signifying that she has given into Parsifal's delusion, one could also read it as her recognition that he, too, cannot fulfill her desire—because it is an impossible one to fulfill, because one can never return to an originary scene of traumatic impact, because one is doomed to wander as a foreign body cast in many roles and incessantly coming back without ever filling the psychic gap, because one can only repeat its impact, holding onto the intermittence and delay of the hystérikè, laughing that strange mixture of mockery and knowledge.

Even in Act 3 Kundry continues to perform the hysteric's gestures. Once more she is initially in a state of paralysis, and as Gurnemanz resuscitates her, she wakes up screaming, only to perform for him his desire that this be the holy day he has been waiting for. In the costume of a penitent, her gestures no longer those of a wild animal but rather serene and dignified, she enacts one last screen phantasy, a religious modulation of the secular family romance she presented to Parsifal in the prior act. Together with Gurnemanz she supports Parsifal's phantasy that he is about to fulfill the destiny of the wounded knighthood, that he is the uninjured father and king who will take the place of the dead Titurel and the wounded Amfortas as guard of the grail. The final ceremony of salvation celebrates a collective entrance into total delusion, the fusion of Amfortas's blood on the spear that smote him with Christ's blood.

As part of my rearticulation of Wagner's Hysterismus I would speculate that the significance of Kundry's falling silent before the completion of Wagner's leitmotiv is that this ultimate exhaustion is one last effort at symptomizing the Other's desire. This last vocal break in tonality, I suggest, signifies her discontent at the new, albeit psychotic, paternal mandate of symbolic authority. For could we not reverse the conventional causality and say that her corpse, lying next to Titurel and replacing the wounded body of Amfortas, does not signify the fact that in dying she is redeemed? Rather, it signifies the fact that the members of the Grail community have now eliminated the foreign body in their midst and thus overcome the last moment of tension and life-sustaining strife. There is no longer anyone to laugh at insignias of phallicity, playing to each and thus overdetermining them, interrogating their fallibility. The way seems unbarred to a salvation that obliterates all differences. In contrast to Stoker's hearty band of vampire hunters, Wagner's Grail community does not wake up from its hallucinatory delusion.

But must we as viewers comply with this narrative solution? I suggest we need not, which brings me back to Nietzsche's Hysterismus. If we see Kundry as our point of identification for this play of grand emotions, which seems to be true even though this play seeks nothing but effects, she then is the navel and symptom of a grand phantasy scenario that discloses the very Heilung or Erlösung (cure, redemption) it evokes. If one of Wagner's phantasies enacts the wound being healed only by the spear that smote it (a phantasy I call a psychotic foreclosure of difference) his other phantasy stages that the one who professes to heal the wound also engenders it (the latter I would call the hysteric's resilient and resourceful enactment of hystérikè that includes a knowledge of traumatic enjoyment even as it preserves the protective demarcation of a psychic gap). If Wagner's Hysterismus can be located in his leaving these two phantasies side by side, unresolved, and vying for dominance, his character may well show in making it our responsibility to choose which one to privilege.

VI

Commenting on Lacan's dictum that the subject is by definition a hysteric, Žižek notes that hysteria should be understood as a complex strategy, a "radically ambiguous protest against the Master's interpellation which simultaneously bears witness to the fact that the hysterical subject needs a Master, cannot do without a Master, so that there is no simple and direct way out" (1996, 164). Because the subject exists only insofar as it is the object of an interpellating Other's desire, its existence involves asking what this Other desires and how to comply with this desire. Confronted with a representative of alterity, the hysteric subject needs to believe that this impenetrable Other wants something from her but that she can also never be certain what that something actually is. In other words, the hysteric subject performs a protean array of self-representations to assure herself that there is an Other willing to be fascinated by this enactment, that her articulations are acknowledged by an addressee. On the other hand, the versatility with which the hysteric transforms the outward appearance of the self-representation also serves to test the Other's desire, in an endless search for the one role that will satisfy, knowing full well that this is neither possible nor viable, since to find and then assume the perfect role would be tantamount to transforming a life-sustaining interrogation into a reifying subjection.

As Žižek notes, "On the one hand hysteria is secondary, a reaction against interpellation, a failed interpellation, a rejection of the identity imposed on the subject by the predominant form of interpellation, a questioning of this identity ('Am I really what you're saying I am?'); at another, more fundamental level, however, hysteria is primary; it articulates the radical, constitutive uncertainty as to what, as an object, I am for the other (1996, 165). To say that the subject as such is hysterical, Žižek concludes, means that the subject's existence depends on a resistance to interpellation, on an acknowledgment that it can never fully recognize itself in the interpellative call, on an acceptance that interpellation ultimately fails precisely because the figure bestowing symbolic authority is fallible and inconsistent. The subject is hysterical insofar as she maintains a minimal of inner distance toward the apparatuses and rituals from which ideology acquires material existence," a distance toward the very master's voice it also demands. Yet even as the hysteric subject insists, "I am not that which the Other desires me to be for him," and performs a variety of roles to sustain his fascination, she also knows that no kernel of the self existed before the process of interpellation.

To pick up a theoretical point made in chapter 3, insofar as the subject harbors an encrypted secret knowledge in her psychic topology, forming the kernel or navel of all phantasy identity and work, this so-called originary scene is not to be understood as a primordial truth preceding representation but rather as the first of a plethora of protective fictions that shield from the gap remaining even after phantasmic space has been traversed. Just as important, however, the interpellator is not only tainted by his exchange with the hysteric but also left to deal with the remains once she has abandoned him for a new phantasmic exchange. After all, Maria Theresa von Paradis went on to become one of the most accomplished pianists of her time, while Anton Mesmer lost his reputation as physician in Vienna. Augustine simply walked out of the Salpêtrière, but Jean-Martin Charcot was left to defend himself against charges leveled by the medical community that he was either the victim of hysterical deceit or himself a charlatan. And Dora, having listened to Freud's interpretation of her second dream "without any of her usual contradictions," as Freud notes, "seemed to be moved, said good-by to him very warmly, with the heartiest wishes for the New Year, and came no more" (1905, 109), leaving Freud with the fragments of this analysis of hysteria and provoking him to abandon entirely the project of solving hysteria. In the next part of hysterical case histories I will continue to explore, then, the way the hysteric, while insisting on her need for the illusion of paternal authority, nevertheless also contests her interpellator's infallibility, maintaining—both with and against the symbolic investiture he represents—a knowledge about the very void that remains beyond all imaginary phantasms and all ideological identification.

_____ **PART THREE**

▶ HYSTERIA'S CASE HISTORIES

CHAPTER 5

Turnings of Nostalgia: Sigmund Freud, Karl Jaspers, Pierre Janet

> Above all, the hysteric is someone who has a story, an *histoire*, and whose
> story is told by science. Hysteria is no longer a question of the wandering
> womb; it is a question of the wandering story, and of whether that story
> belongs to the hysteric, the doctor, the historian, or the critic.
>
> —*Elaine Showalter*

I

MAX SCHUR (1972) was the first to recount what is perhaps the most controversial episode in Freud's work on hysteria—the near fatal operation that his
friend Wilhelm Fliess, the nose and throat specialist from Berlin, had performed on one of his first hysteric patients, Emma Eckstein. In the biography
Freud. Living and Dying, Schur points out three themes that were knotted
together in Freud's depiction of these events, which dominated his correspondence with Fliess during March and April 1895. Of these themes the
first was the way Eckstein's anguish, both organic pain and psychic distress,
frustrated Freud and spurred his theories of the etiology of hysterical disturbances; the second was the way her illness mirrors his own cardiac disorders; and the last was the ambivalent, homoerotic desire that played itself
out as Freud, initially exonerating Fliess, ultimately used this episode to
withdraw from his friend's influence. In their account of *Freud's Women*,
John Forrester and Lisa Appignanesi (who consider Freud's treatment of
Emma to be the primal scene of psychoanalysis) redressed the inattention
paid to the third figure in the controversial scenario, the hysteric patient
herself. Having uncovered Emma Eckstein's own biography, they attribute
seminal importance to this episode not only because it came to engender
Freud's discovery of the importance of phantasy work and psychic reality,
but also because it inaugurated a legacy between analyst and patient that
would prove far more substantial than the bond between the two physicians.
Born into a well-known, bourgeois Viennese family on 28 January 1865,
Emma Eckstein entered into analysis with Freud when she was about thirty.
After three years of treatment she became an analyst herself, working mainly
in the area of sexual and social hygiene. She also explored how "daydreams,
those 'parasitic plants,' invaded the life of young girls," in this work "describing a characteristic feature of the girlhood not only of herself, but of

many others of her era who would enter psychoanalysis" (Appignanesi and Forrester 1992, 138). If Freud, as I have already argued in relation to his specimen dream of Irma's injection, needed to identify with his hysteric patients to solve not only his own hysteria but also to discover the workings of the unconscious, the outcome of Emma Eckstein's story illustrates a parallel transition. The hysteric uses her own malady of and by representation to become an adept analyst of imaginations gone awry in others.

Freud's representation of this episode, however, also uncannily resonates with the iconography of demon possession that had not only haunted the work of his teacher, Jean-Martin Charcot, but also of sensationalists like Bram Stoker, who recast the work of alienists, or psychiatrists, in the genre of horror fiction. In December 1894 Freud asked Fliess to examine Emma Eckstein for any pathology of the turbinate bones and sinuses, hoping to find an organic lesion that would allow him to explain her hysterical abdominal symptoms, given that his friend had written extensively on the interconnection between the pathology of the nose and sexual genitalia. Fliess diagnosed a pathological disturbance, suggested the surgical removal of the afflicted parts of the nose with the local application of cocaine as a form of anesthesia and came to Vienna to perform the operation himself, but did not stay long enough to attend to her aftercare. At the same time, he used his visit to Vienna to examine Freud's nose and cauterize his turbinal bones (Schur 1972, 80). Following surgery, however, Emma's pain persisted, and she exhibited fetid secretions and some bleeding. Freud, after initially attributing her complaint to her hysteria, decided to call in another specialist.

In his letter to Fliess from 4 March, he offers a first report, explaining that "Eckstein's condition is still unsatisfactory" and describing the persistence of her swelling, her massive hemorrhage the day before, his inability to irrigate the nose, and the increase in pain and visible edema. Although Gersuny, whom he had consulted on the case, had threatened to break the turbinal bone, Freud nevertheless also turns to his friend with the plea, "Please send me your authoritative advice. I am not looking forward to new surgery on this girl," only to add, "Something more pleasant after all this." Moving rapidly from an actual situation of physical anguish to the *Studies on Hysteria*, Freud explains that he is in the process of putting together with Josef Breuer his essay on the theories of hysteria. "Breuer cites nasal headaches and the elimination of intercostal pains via the nose as an illustration of effects operating at a distance from the organ affected. I congratulate you" (1985, 114–116). Shifting from one authority figure, the surgeon Gersuny, to another, his collaborator Breuer, Freud is still able at this point to screen out any doubt in his alliance with Fliess and the appropriateness of his work.

However, by enclosing a "case history" with this letter, of which he is the object, Freud fashions for himself a second role, suggesting an identification between himself and Eckstein in relation to Fliess as surgeon. Like hers, the symptoms he discovers in himself involve a persistence of pain as well as a continual discharge of pus and scabs, but also "pain in the heart region, atactic pulse, and beautiful insufficiency (*Insuffizienz*)." As he continues to describe his state of physical weakness and confusion, it is Freud who emerges as the hysteric, infatuated with an image of self-expenditure: "Today, for example, I arrived someplace, found the carriage of the [other] consultant already waiting at the door, ran up the stairs, and once upstairs was unable to talk for five minutes and had to admit that I was ill, and so forth. . . . This morning I once again wanted to die (relatively) young." At the same time Freud takes pleasure in relating to Fliess that his symptoms confirm their mutual nosological phantasy about the relation between noses and other organic disorders, writing him, "Though not designed to make one feel at ease, this information affords some pleasure because it emphasizes once again that the condition of the heart depends upon the condition of the nose." Indeed, following Madelon Sprengnether who suggests one read Freud's letters to Fliess as "love letters" (1990, 28), the romance with Fliess comes to support the phantasy scenarios Freud is in the process of working through hysterically in his own body—his anxiety about his own impending death as well as his aspiration to outmatch his teacher Charcot and solve the enigma of hysteria. These scenarios require an interpellator, namely Fliess, even as they need to be recorded in correspondence. Freud ends this first letter with the injunction, "But that is no reason for you to come. I shall instead report to you faithfully" (1985, 116). There are, then, two patients about whom Fliess, operating from a distance in Berlin, will receive letters in the following weeks, and the narrative that emerges not only blurs the boundary between patient and analyst but oscillates between obliquely accusing Fliess of inducing pain and discomfort in his colleague and extensively describing Emma Eckstein's physical and mental anguish. In other words, Freud wants to support the desire and authority of the friend he appeals to even as, in imitation of the hysteric, he uses her case to dismantle Fliess's infallibility as physician.

The seminal letter (1985, 116–119), written four days later, which describes the full import of Fliess's incompetence, presents a scenario infused with the iconography I have been tracing for the representations of vampirism—profuse yet inexplicable swelling and bleeding that are apparently ceaseless, men operating on a pallid, passive feminine body that seems initially to be guilty but is ultimately proved blameless, once her physical disturbance is shown to be the result of the presence of a foreign body. Explaining to Fliess that he now finally sees his way clearly and thus can give a report that will wound [*kränken*] his friend as much as it did him, he presents the following scene: "I asked Rosanes to meet me. He did so at noon. There still was moderate bleeding from the nose and mouth; the fetid odor was very bad. Rosanes cleaned the area surrounding the opening, removed some sticky blood clots, and suddenly pulled at something like a thread, kept on pulling. Before either of us had time to think, at least half a meter of gauze had been removed from the cavity. The next moment came a flood of blood. The patient turned white, her eyes bulged, and she had no pulse. Immediately thereafter, however, he again packed the cavity with fresh iodoform gauze and the hemorrhage stopped. It lasted about half a minute, but this was enough to make the poor creature, whom by then we had lying flat, unrecognizable. In the meantime—that is, afterward—something else happened. At the moment the foreign body came out and everything became clear to me—and I immediately afterward was confronted by the sight of the patient—I felt sick. After she had been packed, I fled to the next room, drank a bottle of water, and felt miserable. The brave Doktorin then brought me a small glass of cognac and I became myself again." Once the operation has been repeated, this time under the direction of Gersuny, however, Emma Eckstein begins to recover. Freud continues in his narrative to his friend, "Since then she has been out of danger, naturally very pale, and miserable with fresh pain and swelling. She had not lost consciousness during the massive hemorrhage; when I returned to the room somewhat shaky, she greeted me with the condescending remark, 'So this is the strong sex.' "

Given the twofold subtext to this scenario—Freud's own hysteric identification with Emma and his ambivalent romance with Fliess—it is quite remarkable that the exoneration of all the involved figures should result from Freud's feeling compelled to explain his sudden flight from the spectacle of a profusely bleeding wound. For the injury that the persistence of Emma Eckstein's pain had posed to his self-esteem as physician finds its acme at the moment when everything becomes clear to him because he sees the bloody gauze extracted from her nose, feels nausea, and is only able to recover his self-composure after absenting himself from this overdetermined scene of trauma. He begins by asserting his own fortitude, "I do not believe it was the blood that overwhelmed me—at that moment strong emotions were welling up in me," only to list a plethora of thoughts that might excuse his flight. The first addresses the fuzzy interface between organic and psychic illness, which will emerge as the linchpin not only of his discussion of Emma Eckstein but also of the *Studies on Hysteria* he is writing: "So we had done her an injustice; she was not at all abnormal, rather, a piece of iodoform gauze had gotten torn off as you were removing it and stayed in for fourteen days, preventing healing; at the end it tore off and provoked the bleeding." The second thought addresses his hysterical ambivalence toward his friend, wavering between an almost frantic assurance of esteem and an oblique reproach articulated in comments that are only manifestly self-critical: "That this mishap should have happened to you; . . . how wrong I was to urge you to operate in a foreign city. . . . How my intention to do my best for this poor girl was insidiously thwarted and resulted in endangering her life." Indeed, even as Freud purports to reassure his friend, one cannot help sensing a strangely sadistic pleasure as he continues, "I really should not have tormented you here, but I had every reason to entrust you with such a matter and more." Freud insists that his integrity as a physician is unblemished

("You did it as well as one can do it"). Still, in denying that there are grounds for reproaches ("Of course, no one is blaming you, nor would I know why they should"), he seems to obliquely evoke precisely this criticism, knowing full well that any court would have sentenced Fliess for malpractice. Furthermore, Freud concludes in relation to Emma Eckstein that, "nothing remains but heartfelt compassion for my child of sorrows," but he admits that he had shied away from writing this letter—from describing the traumatic scene of horror but also from reassuring his friend. He excuses his delay with the assertion that "it was not necessary for me to reaffirm my trust in you once again." Indeed, while he so lavishly shares with Fliess the depiction of what the other can only perceive as a shameful scene, he refuses to entrust him with his newest theoretical discoveries until "we have Eckstein off our minds."

Freud ultimately uses his momentary mental confusion to introduce the last step in this complex narrative of exoneration and blame. For once he has worked through the knot of strong emotions that welled up in him simultaneously at the sight of Emma Eckstein's bleeding body, he finally arrives at a figure whom he can blame directly: "I was not sufficiently clear at that time to think of immediately reproaching Rosanes. It only occurred to me ten minutes later that he should immediately have thought, There is something inside; I shall not pull it out lest there be a hemorrhage. . . . But he was just as surprised as I was." In the midst of all this self-vindication, one must not lose sight of the fact that the foreign body inside Emma Eckstein's nose was not only put there by the physician Fliess but also forgotten, so that the horrific scene Freud describes in fact involves the traumatic recognition that occurs when, belatedly and under the surveillance of a more reliable representative of the medical establishment, what has been forgotten returns.[1] Yet Freud's own hysteria is not supported by this gesture of the *hystérikè*, the continual delay in recognition and action. Rather, the momentary loss of mental clarity suggests a final, hysterical identification with Emma, lying helplessly prostrate with something welling up out of her nose while she was fully conscious of the horrific event. In addition to the complex emotions of guilt overwhelming him at the sight of his patient's body in pain, could his flight from this ghastly spectacle not also be read as a psychosomatic articulation of Freud's need to detach himself from an unbearable proximity to the traumatic enjoyment that threatened to engulf him, seeing in Emma Eckstein's wound a somatic inversion of the *Insuffizienz* he was himself enjoying, owing to his own heart condition?

Schur presents this episode as an example of how Freud, fully aware of Fliess's guilt, nevertheless also needed his friend "because he was in the midst of momentous discoveries and decisions about the direction his work was to take. Moreover, he was not yet quite secure about his own health" (1972, 81). Indeed, as Freud documents Emma Eckstein's recovery, he continues to record his own symptoms, so that by describing his patient's anguish after the unsuccessful surgery on her nose, he is able to articulate indi-

248

rectly his doubts about whether Fliess was correct in assigning such a central role to nasal pathology in the treatment of his own cardiac symptoms. As Schur notes, the "letter written on April 20th, 1895 clearly indicated the meshing of the Emma affair with both Freud's own health problems and the complex manifestations of his ambivalence conflict concerning Fliess" (82). I would simply add that it also uncannily resonates with the image of the vampirized Lucy, so irritatingly bloodless. While Freud pretends to be offended that Fliess deems it necessary "to have a testimonial certificate from Gersuny" for his rehabilitation, insisting instead, "I wanted to pour forth my tale of woe and perhaps obtain your advice concerning E., not reproach you with anything," he also begins to voice his doubts about his friend's diagnosis. Of his own ailment he explains, "I would like you to continue to be right—that the nose may have a large share in it and the heart a small one." Nevertheless he not only adds "in view of the pulse and the insufficiency I frequently believe the opposite," but also declines Fliess's request to visit Berlin, explaining that owing to his financial situation "I am not sufficiently demoralized to take your suggestion of sparing me the loss [of 1,000 to 1,500 florins]. Furthermore, I think I do not have to" (1985, 126). This refusal to take the other physician's advice will soon thereafter be mirrored in the patient Irma in his specimen dream, who in turn refuses Freud's solution. In the letter, however, it is presented explicitly in analogy to Freud's rejection of Fliess's recommendations for Eckstein's treatment.[2] Contradicting his friend's advice that they might have waited with the second operation, he explains, "At close range many things look different—for instance, the hemorrhages. I can confirm that in their case there could be no question of biding one's time. There was bleeding as though from the carotid artery, within half a minute she again would have bled to death (exsanguis)." Freud adds "the packing was gently and gradually removed. . . . She is in the clear [sie ist jetzt frei]" (125).

In ensuing letters he continues to call Fliess "Dear Magician" (126), showing signs of agitation that he is not writing back ("You seem to be angry when you cloak yourself so assiduously in silence" (126), and clear relief when his beloved friend finally responds. Yet as Schur argues, "He was also showing much more independence by refusing to undergo any radical procedures—perhaps with Emma's complications in mind" (83). At the same time he continues to offer a double report of his own recuperation and that of their mutual patient, invoking a parallel not only between her hysterical dysfunction of the legs and his cardiac disorder but also between her blood and his pus. On 26 April he writes, "Something strange but not unpleasant has happened to me. I put a noticeable end to the last horrible attack with cocaine; since then things have been fine and a great amount of pus is coming out. . . . She, too, my tormentor and yours [Quälgeist], now appears to be doing well" (127). One day later, complaining about the distance between them and his own horror at writing too many letters, he notes, "Since the last cocainization three circumstances have continued to coincide: (1) I feel well; (2) I am discharging ample amounts of pus; (3) I am feeling *very* well" (127). In the other patient, however, the excretion of body fluids has the opposite effect: "Eckstein once *again* is in pain; will she be bleeding next?" (128). Finally, on 25 May Freud confirms their mutual convalescence. Of their patient he notes "Emma E. is finally doing very well and I have succeeded in once more alleviating her weakness in walking, which also set in again," while of himself he records, "I discharged exceedingly ample amounts of pus and all the while felt splendid; now the secretion has nearly dried up and I am still feeling very well" (130).

What is striking about this double cure, however, is not only that it occurred while Fliess remained at a distance in Berlin but rather that the "ideas about the nose" (130), which Freud had been chronicling at his own body refute Fliess's theory. They also trace precisely the pattern Freud will develop in letters to his friend about the delayed reaction that traumatic impressions produce in the psyche. While Fliess had argued that Freud's transferred or distant symptoms [*Fernsymptome*] were caused by the congestion and flow of pus as well as swelling in the nose, Freud now claims these merely produced local symptoms and headaches. The distant symptoms— the hysterical symptoms working by virtue of a curious sympathy between the organs, namely Emma Eckstein's abdominal pains or his cardiac disorder—have a different point of origin according to his new theory: "For the distant symptoms I would like to hold responsible only a special state of excitation (*Reizzustand*) in the nerve endings (such as we may suppose, for example, in the case of scars [*Narben*]). . . . This condition of the tissue, which develops *after* the flow of pus, infectious swelling, and so forth, is, I believe, the cause of the distant effects (*Fernwirkungen*) and develops, through accommodation (*Entgegenkommen*) on the part of the organs concerned, into the distant suffering of the various organs (*Organfernleiden*)" (130). As I discussed in the introduction, in a letter he sent to Fliess in January 1896, Freud argues that hysterical symptoms, presupposing a primary experience of trauma, were seen to reenact not the traumatic event itself but rather the boundary idea (*Grenzvorstellung*) that formed as a result of an excessive expression of anxious excitation (*Schreckäusserung*): the scar that formed over the gap in the psyche as its aftereffect.

In the letters written in between Emma's first accident at the hands of Fliess and her ultimate recovery, Freud records his own traumatic shock ("I am deeply shaken") over the possibly fatal outcome of this "operation that was purported to be harmless" (124), given that like the vampirized women in Stoker's *Dracula*, Emma continued to hover between life and death for weeks, having hemorrhages and requiring packing, so that the danger of infection was always present. At the same time, seeking to exonerate himself and his friend, he develops his theory about the etiology of hysteria, whereby the horrific organic disturbance, namely Eckstein's apparently inexplicable, incessant bleeding, can be seen after all as the belated articulation of psychic distress and phantasy work. Not the physicians but rather the hysteric patient emerges as the true engenderess of her own discomfort. Finally, against the background of a growing sense of guilt toward his patient and a growing distrust of the medical ability of his friend, Freud uses this correspondence to confirm their triadic bond.

On 13 March he writes to Fliess, "It is a shame that both of us suffer from so much illness when we have so much ahead of us. . . . Things are finally going well with Eckstein, as they could have without the detour three weeks ago. It does speak well for her that she did not change her attitude toward either of us; she honors your memory beyond the undesired accident" (119). Two days later, in turn, he not only continues to describe his own physical ailment but finds a psychic correspondence in his patient, using both as oblique criticisms of the surgeon they have in common so as to ultimately emerge as the more reliable physician: "Surgically, Eckstein will soon be well, now the nervous effects of the incident are starting: hysterical attacks at night and similar symptoms that I must start to work on." Even as he insists, "It is now about time you forgave yourself the minimal oversight, as Breuer called it," he also adds, "How have I been? . . . infamously miserable. Since yesterday evening it has abated; I am again a human being with human feelings. . . . It has not been this bad for a long time. The suppuration is now quite inconsiderable; the whole business started with a scab, which came out while you were still present" (120). Five days later, however, to explain why he delayed sending his letter, Freud reports that while he suddenly feels very good again, Emma Eckstein has taken a turn for the worse, once more exhibiting pain and swelling, for which the organic lesion remains unknown. After another hemorrhage attack, she had been packed, but when the packing was removed, a renewed hemorrhage occurred, "so that she almost died. Since then she has been lying in bed again, tightly packed and totally miserable. . . . In my thoughts I have given up hope for the poor girl and am inconsolable that I involved you and created such a distressing affair for you. I also feel very sorry for her; I had beome very fond of her" (121).

One is again compelled to associate to the vampirized Lucy, upsetting her perplexed physician with the riddle her body poses—where all the blood of four strong men they infused into her veins could have gone. Given that Freud cannot explain what is inducing all the bleeding, he becomes increasingly hystericized by Emma Eckstein's persistent anguish—his own heart and nose problems continue to develop in sympathetic correspondence with hers. At the same time, his phantasy that she is already of the dead proves to be a hysterical reworking of his sense of failure as a nosologist, and also of his anxiety that his own death might be imminent. Indeed, he is forced in the next letter to admit that after the operation had been undertaken, the surgeon Gussenbauer discovered, "It was nothing, and nothing was done. . . . [Gussenbauer] supposes the bleeding was only from granulation tissue; . . . I am glad that none of the bad expectations has materialized" (122). In other words, the hysterical much ado about nothing, to which Freud will later attribute Emma Eckstein's bleeding, articulates his own hysterical exaggeration, in the course of which he casts the hemorrhaging woman as a bride of death, only later to recode this as her phantasy of being possessed by the demons of repressed traumas. Whenever she seems to be recuperating, Freud notes that "Of course, she is beginning with the new production of hysterias from this past period, which are then dissolved by me." Insofar as these symptoms directly respond to a concrete retraumatization—namely the physicial and psychic shock to Emma induced by Fliess's oversight—the origin for these hysterias can quite unequivocally be located in their falliblity as physicians. To screen this fact, however, Freud once more shifts his attention to their persisting physical anguish and his traumatization. Of Fliess he writes, "I also must accept that you are not yet feeling well; I hope this will not be for long. I think you will soon have worked your way out of it," while of himself he claims, "My own condition is not especially bad, but keeps me out of sorts. A pulse so irregular does seem to preclude well-being; the motoric insufficiency has again been intolerable for several days" (122). Indeed, the strange identification between Freud and Eckstein seems such that at least when she recovers her health, he loses his strength. On 2 April he writes, "These past few days I have really felt outrageously indifferent. Writing has been difficult for me—times in which I am not bearable, the most minute intimations of fluctuating mood changes. Now I am my old self again, also vigorous of heart." At the same time he interprets this incapacitation as the psychosomatic response both to Fliess's absence and to Eckstein's recovery: "Altogether I miss you very much. Am I really the same person who was overflowing with ideas and projects as long as you were within reach? When I sit down at the desk in the evening, I often do not know *what* I should work on. She, Eckstein is doing well" (122).

Once a new attack of hemorrhaging sets in, Emma Eckstein (like the vampirized Lucy), is presented as someone draining the energies of her physician. On 11 April Freud begins his letter with a note of despair, "Gloomy times, unbelievably gloomy. Above all, this Eckstein affair, which is rapidly moving toward a bad ending," describing the last reenactment of the traumatic scene with which the entire episode began. With the packing in place, Eckstein had begun to bleed and continued to do so for several days, and when the physicians tried to remove the packing to investigate the cavity, "there was a new, life-threatening hemorrhage, which I witnessed. It did not spurt, it surged. Something like a fluid level rising extraordinarily rapidly, and then overflowing everything." Once more emphasizing that the cause remained elusive, Freud surmises, "It must have been a large vessel, but which one and from where?" only to return to a visualization of the gap in knowledge with which Emma confronts these physicians: "Of course, nothing could be seen and it was a relief to have the packing back in again." He continues to pursue the parallel between her and his near fatal conditions, given that both perform the hystérikè of intermittent bouts of somatic disturbances. He responds belatedly to a scene where her gaze bore into him as he watched her profusely bleeding wound, only to turn away for fear of losing himself in this traumatizing spectacle. About Emma Eckstein he writes, "Add to this the pain, the morphine, the demoralization caused by the obvious medical helplessness, and the tinge of danger, and you will be able to picture the state the poor girl is in," while about himself he notes, "I do not know whether I should hold this depressing business exclusively responsible for the fact that the condition of my heart remains so much below par for this year of illness. After an interruption of several months, I started to take strophantus again" (124).

Sprengnether suggests that "Freud's reactions to Eckstein's bleeding appear as a series of shock waves that set the course of his future theorizing," (1990, 37) at the end of which he will not only have exonerated Fliess but also detached himself from his friend's ideas. Returning, once her life was no longer in danger, to the hypothesis that Emma's bleedings are psychic in origin, he will ultimately deprive them of their traumatic effect and reintegrate them instead into the sexually encoded Oedipal paradigm. In other words, in one and the same gesture Freud was able to dissociate himself from the very feminization this horrific episode allowed him to articulate for himself: moving in relation to Fliess from the position of patient to one of master analyst and, in relation to Eckstein, from an identification with her vulnerability and its traumatic traces, as these became articulated in the hystérikè of delayed and intermittent somatic attacks, to a reencoding of this scene within a gendered paradigm that redrew a clear boundary between the female patient and the male analyst.

As Appignanesi and Forrester rightly assert, however, to read Emma only as an intermediary or victim in a story "which is essentially a tale of two doctors," as this moves from trust, idealization, and transference to gradual disillusionment, "eliminates the feminine in favour of Freud's relationship to the male friends, colleagues and authorities. And this elimination of the feminine actually conceals a more important elimination: that of the patient" (1992, 120). Focusing simultaneously on the hysterical identification and transference between analyst and patient, as well as on the homoerotic bond between the two physicians, indeed opens up another story, which could perhaps be called the originary traumatic scene of psychoanalysis. For this scenario stages Freud's shift from the seduction theory, in which he referred to actual scenes of misuse, to his notion of psychic reality, in which he came to believe in the mind's ability to fashion scenes of abuse so as to articulate traces of traumatic knowledge that are only indirectly available to representation: that is, the scars of trauma and not the events themselves.

About one year after pleading with his dear magician not to be angry with him for not coming to Berlin to undergo more surgery, Freud records his new conjecture about their patient's hemorrhages, hoping to afford pleasure to the addressee of the letter: "I shall be able to prove to you that you were right, that her episodes of bleeding were hysterical, were occasioned by longing (*Sehnsucht*), and probably occurred at the sexually relevant times"

(1985, 183). The scenario Freud offers Fliess in the following letter shows ever more uncanny parallels to Van Helsing's attempt to fill his gap in knowledge with a phantom figure, only in this case Freud casts himself in the role of the desired agent of seduction. At the same time it evokes the configuration of the hysteric as malingerer, simulating somatic disturbances under the influence of suggestion so as to obliquely articulate an erotic phantasy in which being penetrated by a foreign body and bleeding, owing to a longing for this foreign body, come to mutually represent each other. Freud begins by asserting, "She had always been a bleeder, when cutting herself and in similar circumstances; as a child she suffered from severe nosebleeds; during the years when she was not yet menstruating, she had headaches which were interpreted to her as malingering and which in truth had been generated by suggestion; for this reason she joyously welcomed her severe menstrual bleeding as proof that her illness was genuine, a proof that was also recognized as such by others."

Above all, Freud returns to the notion of hysteria as *hystérikè*, where a delayed and intermittent realization of desire points back to a previous event. For in his interpretation he links her persistent bleeding not only to the traumatic scene when Rosanes extracted the bloody gauze from her nose but also to earlier sexual desire in connection with a bleeding nose: "She described a scene from the age of fifteen, in which she suddenly began to bleed from the nose when she had the wish to be treated by a certain young doctor who was present (and who also appeared in the dream). When she saw how affected I was by her first hemorrhage while she was in the hands of Rosanes, she experienced this as the realization of an old wish to be loved in her illness, and in spite of the danger during the succeeding hours she felt happy as never before. Then, in the sanatorium, she became restless during the night because of an unconscious wish (*Sehnsuchtsabsicht*) to entice me to go there; since I did not come during the night, she renewed the bleedings, as an unfailing means of rearousing my affection. She bled spontaneously three times and each bleeding lasted for four days, which must have some significance" (1985, 186). Despite its cruel inattention to Emma Eckstein's very real mistreatment (a so-called oversight) at the hands of her physician, which for several weeks threatened fatal results, Freud's interpretation is also a brilliant tour de force. The nocturnal bleeding, a somatic reiteration of the traumatic remains of the operation inflicted on her, is here transformed into a protective fiction about unrequited sexual desire. This narrative shift exonerates Freud, not only because the phantasy no longer involves a physical vulnerability that is also his own, but because it revolves around the love for a physician. Above all it shows him to be merely the aftereffect, the belated representation of an early object of desire. With a narrative offering a coherent solution to the terrible enigma that had haunted him in the previous year (and at the very least hindered alleviation of his own heart disorder), Freud concludes on 4 June, "Her story is becoming even clearer; there is no doubt that her hemorrhages were due to wishes (*Wunschblutungen*); she has had several similar incidents, among them actual (*direkte*) simulations, in her childhood. Your nose has once again smelled things correctly. Incidently, she is doing exceedingly well" (192).

After the apparent solution of the Eckstein episode Freud continues to use his correspondence with Fliess to test the ideas he is about to publish in his *Studies in Hysteria*. At the same time he records the critical shift in his theorizing about the relation between traumatic impressions and somatic aftereffects that will result in the birth of psychoanalysis. At the very begining of his work with hysterics Freud had suggested to Fliess that the origin of this neurosis was not only sexual in nature, but that the trauma could also be traced back to an actual moment of seduction and misuse by a perverse father or other relative. In the course of building his theory, however (recalling Charcot's analogy between the hysterical fit and demonic possession), he began to see Eckstein's story as part of this cultural iconography. On 17 January 1897 he writes to Fliess, "Incidentally, the cruelties [of those possessed by the devil] make it possible to understand some symptoms of hysteria that until now have been obscure. The pins which make their appearance in the oddest ways; the sewing needles on account of which the poor things let their breasts be mutilated and which are not visible by X-ray, though they can no doubt be found in their seduction stories!" Inserted in parentheses he adds, "(Eckstein has a scene where the diabolus sticks needles into her fingers and then places a candy on each drop of blood. As far as the [that] blood is concerned, you are completely without blame!)" (225).

By interpolating Emma Eckstein's actual scene of anguish into the literature of possession, Freud offers a significant reversal of her story, transforming a scene of two physicians extracting a foreign body they have introduced into her nose, thereby inducing weeks of hemorrhaging, to one in which a demon draws her blood. Moreover, he privileges the phantasmic recreations of an initial seduction, the scenes Emma hysterically produced after the event, reencoded within the vocabulary of her image repertoire. Freud can therefore argue not only that the originary trauma had nothing to do with Fliess, given that it has to do with seduction by a figure of alterity ("as far as the blood is concerned, you are completely without blame"). Rather, by privileging psychic realities (the scenes in one's psychic topology) over somatic realities (the actual somatic attacks of pain), Freud is able to define hysteria as a pathological fusion of remembrance and phantasy. In his "Architecture of Hysteria," inserted into a letter of 2 May 1897, Freud notes that the aim of hysteria is to reach primal scenes of traumatic sexuality. This is usually achieved not directly, however, but "only by a detour via phantasies. For phantasies are psychic facades produced in order to bar access to these memories. Phantasies simultaneously serve the tendency toward refining the memories, toward sublimating them." In the architecture Freud proposes for the psychic topology of the hysteric, primal scenes of traumatic knowledge are thus not only demarcated by memories but also constantly reworked belatedly, as he adds, "by means of things that are *heard*, and utilized *subsequently*, and thus combine things experienced and heard, past events (from the history of parents and ancestors), and things that have been seen by oneself" (1892–1899, 240). Furthermore, because Freud became convinced that there are no markers for reality (*Realitätszeichen*) in the unconscious, he also postulated that one could not distinguish between truth and fiction once it has been cathected with affect. Like the *Organfernleiden* Fliess is researching, hysteria, though aimed at a primal scene of traumatic sexuality and called forth by actual traumatic events, acts primarily on the *stage* of psychic reality. What the analyst must redress is not the actual events but the way they have been reformulated in phantasy. This is not to say that actual traumatic experiences did not occur, nor that they had no significance for psychic processes. Rather, Freud's compelling insight consists in his insistence that precisely because hysterical phantasy blurs the boundary between what is true and what is fiction, between what has been experienced and what has been transmitted as a story—precisely because there may be nothing to see inside Emma's nose or Irma's throat, no one event to locate as the point of origin for all subsequent scenes—it is the phantasies one must take seriously. They produce real, psychosomatic anguish and they are the only traces of traumatic knowledge available for readjustment, both to the patient and to the analyst.

In his controversial analysis of the Freud-Fliess correspondence, Jeffrey Moussaieff Masson (1984) has argued that Freud's abandonment of the seduction theory, (which favors the phantasy of seduction over the reality of parental abuse of children), must be seen in light of his effort to exonerate Fliess and to dissociate himself from Emma Eckstein's physical and mental anguish. Though this interpretation is undoubtedly valid, it sheds light on only part of the story. For, as Appignanesi and Forrester demonstrate in their counternarrative, Emma cannot be reduced to the figure of victim in a homoerotic bond between two ailing physicians sharing a cocaine habit and developing a theory about the etiology of hysteria that will distance themselves from any responsibility for a nearly fatal operation. Rather, she came to actively further the psychoanalytic project in two ways: provoking Freud's sense of fallibility while also eagerly collaborating with his analytic cure.

It was Emma Eckstein who supplied Freud with the material that would allow him to theorize the hystérikè of hysteric symptomatology. In his *Project for a Scientific Psychology* he recalls how Emma was, at the time, subject to "a compulsion of not being able to go into shops *alone*. As a reason for this, [she produced] a memory from the time when she was twelve years old (shortly after puberty). She went into a shop to buy something, saw the two shop assistants (one of whom she can remember) laughing together, and ran away in some kind of *affect of fright (Schreckaffekt)*. In connection with this, she was led to recall that the two of them were laughing at her clothes and that one of them had pleased her sexually" (1895, 353). As Freud probes further, he discovers a second memory, which Emma denies having had in mind during the first recounted scene: "On two occasions when she was a child of eight she had gone into a small shop to buy some sweets, and the shopkeeper had grabbed at her genitals through her clothes. In spite of the first experience she had gone there a second time; after the second time she stayed away" (354). On the basis of this revelation, Freud discovers that a repressed memory can become traumatic by virtue of deferred action and belated reencoding: "Here we have the case of a memory arousing an affect which it did not arouse as an experience, because in the meantime the change brought about in puberty had made possible a different understanding of what was remembered" (356).

Emma's hysterical body is thus not only the site in which the fusion of an organic disturbance and psychosomatic simulation produce an inexplicable hemorrhage. Rather, her hysterical symptoms also perform for Freud the murky knot of phantasies and realities of seduction, of remembered and imaginatively reworked scenes, of desire being aimed not only at a state of pleasure, which could fill the sense of something lacking, but also at the return to a prior scene of trauma. As Appignanesi and Forrester note, initially "Emma's case was crystal-clear in terms of her attempted 'seduction' by the shopkeeper. But a year after Emma had nearly bled to death because of Fliess's error, Freud was finding a history of bleeding in her case, turning the dramatic events of her 'bleeding scene' to psychoanalytic use" (1992, 136). The traumatic experience of a bungled operation came by deferred action to uncover repressed material, which referred not only to her earlier experiences of bleeding and transference of desire onto a physician meant to cure her fallible body. It also produced a link between the memory of the shopkeeper's assault with inherited images of being assaulted by a demonic figure. In other words, the episode reveals how belatedness is not only the key to hysterical language, but also inscribed from the very beginning into the psychoanalytic project itself.

On the other hand, as Appignanesi and Forrester note, Emma Eckstein not only taught Freud about "the no-man's land between fantasy and memory, resonating with sadistic acts and fantasies of a former historical epoch," but rather also demonstrated to him how, in addition to his own writing and lecturing, his ideas and techniques would be perpetuated: "Just as Freud entered his self-analysis, discovering that he could only help his patients when he made himself a patient, when he attempted to heal his own neurosis, it was as if the inverted mirroring process was taking place in Emma: she got up off the couch and started to treat other neurotic patients" (1992, 138).[3] Significantly, Freud's last mention of her to Fliess pits the dutiful daughter against the irresponsible friend. On 12 December 1897 Freud writes, "My confidence in paternal aetiology has risen greatly. Eckstein deliberately treated her patient in such a manner as not to give her the slightest hint of what would emerge from the unconscious and in the process obtained from her, among other things, the identical scenes with the father. Incidentally, the young girl is doing very well" (1985, 286).

II

In the past chapters I have repeatedly invoked the fact that Freud discovered the unconscious and invented psychoanalysis, after having watched the working-class hysterics perform in Charcot's Salpêtrière, by discoursing with the bourgeois, hysteric patients who came to see him in his Viennese practice. I will now map this inaugural moment—Freud's very early work on hysteria and its traumatic etiology, as he recorded this in his letters to Fliess, in preliminary remarks to his *Studies on Hysteria* (1895) written with Breuer, and in the *Five Lectures on Psycho-Analysis* (1909) he gave at Clark University in Massachusetts—onto two other projects that were contemporary with his. These projects also explore how a psychosomatic reenactment of earlier traumatic experiences produces symptoms, which ultimately dismember precisely the notion of an intact family the patient seeks to sustain. The first is Karl Jasper's dissertation *Nostalgia and Crime (Heimweh und Verbrechen)* (1909), in which he studied young women for whom the loss of their home and family came to recall prior experiences of trauma to such a degree that they initially used phantasy work to convert their anxiety into psychosomatic disturbances, but ultimately committed acts of violence. In contrast to Freud's bourgeois women, who suffered from mental overexcitation and psychophysical fatigue, Jasper's cases involve working-class servant girls who commit arson and murder in their new homes. Furthermore, his dissertation records and evaluates the archives of forensic medicine compiled by the psychiatrists who had been asked to treat these criminal women, rather than transcribing and interpreting information given to him firsthand, as Freud did.

There are, nevertheless, some resonant parallels between the hysteric, incapacitated by her psychosomatic illness and draining her peers with her insufficiency, and the nostalgic, confined in an asylum, away from her family, because she has committed arson or child-murder (recalling the phantasy of *Heil* enacted by Wagner's Grail family). Both Freud and Jaspers note that the women whose cases they chose to study at the onset of their psychoanalytic projects pose a fascinating and tantalizing enigma that revolves around the issue of a foreign body introduced into the familiar or emerging from the familiar, only to unsettle it in the process. In his *Project for a Scientific Psychology*, for example, Freud writes, "Hysterical, excessively intense ideas strike us, on the contrary, by their oddity; they are ideas which in other people have no consequences and of whose importance we can make nothing. They appear to us as intruders and usurpers, and accordingly as ridiculous" (1895, 348). Then again, in the first of his *Five Lectures on Psychoanalysis* he explicitly addresses the fallibility of the analyst when faced with hysteria: "All his knowledge—his training in anatomy, in physiology and in pathology—leaves him in the lurch when he is confronted by the details of hysterical phenomena. He cannot understand hysteria, and in the face of it he is himself a layman. . . . He regards them as people who are transgressing the laws of his science—like heretics in the eyes of the orthodox" (1909, 12). Jaspers also begins his study with the statement of theoretical bafflement and helplessness: "For a long time now we have been interested in crimes (murder and arson) that have been performed with unbelievable cruelty and brutality, whose perpetrators, however, are delicate creatures, young and good-natured prepubescent and pubescent girls. The contradiction between act and actress, the lack of motive and thus the enigmatic and incomprehensible aspect of these events, elicit either sympathies or disgust" (1909, 1). Because there seems to be no binding connection between these innocent girls and their monstrous criminal acts, they pose a hermeneutic task to forensic medicine, which ultimately remains incomprehensible and unsolvable, much as the lack of organic lesions and the obvious overdetermination of hysterical symptoms led Freud repeatedly to designate hysteria as "the puzzling leap from the mental to the physical" (1917, 258).

The other psychological project I propose as a mapping for Freud's early work on hysteria comes from Pierre Janet, not only perhaps Charcot's most able student but also someone who explored the traumatic experiences at the navel of his patient's hysterical symptoms. Indeed he repeatedly castigated his Viennese colleague for emphasizing sex, because many of his patients were afflicted by nonsexual trauma. Yet, like Freud's hysterics, Janet's also proved to be haunted by memory traces, which he calls *idée fixe*, causing cerebral exhaustion, a weakening of the faculty of psychological synthesis (*abulia*), and the tendency to a complete and permanent division of the personality. I will, therefore, read these three collections of case studies as explorations into disturbances of the family romance, interrogating its very premises. For the symptoms of these hysterics and nostalgics dismantle our notions of the family by staging the wandering of a foreign body, the agonistic persistence of an idée fixe harking back to a traumatic knowledge that cannot be contained. Even as the manifest aim of their phantasy work is to restore a situation of unmarred plenitude and protection connected with the idea of a home, what these hysterics and nostalgics so compellingly illustrate is that familiarity is inevitably inscribed with traumatic difference.

Indeed, the dialectic of foreign and familiar plays out quite explicitly in all three sets of case histories. In their discussions of hysteria, Freud and Breuer argue that "psychical trauma or more precisely the memory of the trauma—acts like a foreign body which long after its entry must continue to be regarded as an agent that is still at work" (1893–95, 290). Pierre Janet in turn suggests that the hysterics' inability to synthesize divergent aspects of their selves "favours the formation of certain parasitic ideas which develop completely and in isolation under the shelter of the control of the personal consciousness," such that the idée fixe engenders "mental disintegration characterised by a tendency towards the permanent and complete undoubling (*dédoublement*) of the personality" (1894, 528). Finally, Jaspers presents the stories of patients who are quite literally foreign bodies in a surrogate family; their home has become foreign to them, retrievable only through memories of the lost familiarity that haunt them. In all cases the crucial point, however, is that the foreign uncannily emerges as the very navel of what is considered to be familiar. As Breuer notes at the end of his theoretical discussion, "The split-off mind is the devil with which the unsophisticated observation of early superstitious times believed that these patients were possessed. It is true that a spirit alien to the patient's waking consciousness holds sway in him; but the spirit is not in fact an alien one, but a part of his own" (Freud, 1893–95, 250).

In turning to a more detailed discussion of Freud's and Breuer's *Studies on Hysteria*, I am returning to issues I raised in the introduction in relation to a discussion of the traumatic etiology of symptom formation. For as I had already suggested, if Freud and Breuer initially claim that all hysterical symptoms are determined by mnemonic traces of traumatic experiences, the question emerges whether a primary scene of trauma can be retrieved. In early drafts on the architecture of hysteria, Freud in fact suggests that traumatization involves a process in which excessive anxiety in the face of an accident—an event of physical or psychic injury—is followed by a gap in the psyche. The hysterical symptom, functioning as the navel marking a complex knot of psychic woundings, occurs after the event, in response not to the actual trauma but to a psychic *representation* of this occurrence, to a memory trace, while the *Urtrauma* remains unrepresentable and inaccessible. These memories, furthermore, must be seen as protective fictions (*Schutzdichtungen*), inventions that reformulate traumatic knowledge into viable phantasies and symptoms, even while they seal the gap, shielding from the self-expenditure that any full enjoyment of this traumatic kernel would entail. Yet my point throughout has also been that the hysteric's mnemonic fictions preserve and encrypt the traces of this traumatic knowledge, rather than symbolizing it, so as to relinquish or repress these remains.

Therefore, I want to recall the issue of delayed and intermittent representation that inevitably accompanies any discussion of trauma. Cathy Caruth notes, "In its general definition, trauma is described as the response to an unexpected or overwhelming violent event or events that are not fully grasped as they occur, but return later in repeated flashbacks, nightmares, and other repetitive phenomena" (1996, 91). Owing to this, traumatic experience always involves a certain paradox: "The most direct seeing of a violent event may occur as an absolute inability to know it; that immediacy, paradoxically, may take the form of belatedness. The repetitions of the traumatic event—which remain unavailable to consciousness but intrude repeatedly on sight—thus suggest a larger relation to the event that extends beyond what can simply be seen or what can be known, and is inextricably tied up with the belatedness and incomprehensibility that remain at the heart of this repetitive seeing" (92). The hysteric, one could say, enacts an interminable negotiation between Urtrauma and its vicissitudes, performing an abundant hystérikè, which takes the form of memories, screen-memories, phantasies, and protective fictions, and thereby preserves the resilience of the initial trauma. At the same time, I have also insisted that the analytic narratives, meant to serve as a solution to the hysterical symptom, inevitably function analogously to these protective fictions, interlaced by a mutually implicated desire, and moreover themselves repeating the hysterical performance. Like it, they remain on the level of representations, retouching the after-pressures (*Nachdrängen*) without ultimately touching the Urtrauma.[4]

In their introductory chapter to *Studies on Hysteria*, Freud and Breuer argue that the hysteric is genuinely unable to recall the originating cause of her symptoms, and indeed has no conscious knowledge of the causality between a prior event and her current pathology. This connection can be made visible to her only once the patient, in the course of hypnosis, produces memory traces from the time when the symptom was originally formed. Two points are, nevertheless, stressed from the start in this discussion of hysteria's traumatic etiology. For one, while any experience that calls up distressing affects, such as fright, anxiety, shame, or physical pain, could potentially operate as a traumatic impulse, whether it actually does so depends on the predisposition of the afflicted patient. For another, this traumatic impact only becomes pathological once it is remembered—that is to say, reactivated by a second event. The cathartic method they propose as a cure of hysteria thus works with the presupposition that once the connection between a precipitating trauma and its symptoms, which are ostensibly spontaneous but in fact represent a deferred action, has been established, both can be resolved. From this Breuer and Freud discovered what became the theoretic kernel of psychoanalytical work: "that each individual hysterical symptom immediately and permanently disappeared when we had succeeded in bringing clearly to light the memory of the event by which it was provoked and in arousing its accompanying affect, and when the patient had described that event in the greatest possible detail and had put the affect into words" (1893–95, 6).

In other words a traumatic impression that, once reactivated, calls forth a chain of symptoms can be undone by tracing these symptoms back to mnemonic representations of the originary event, or rather, once the affect connected with the traumatic moment, which had been preserved though unbound to any one psychic representation (indeed wandering within the psychic topology), is linked back to a narrative about this event. Thus traumatic impact and memory come to be inextricably meshed in Freud's early formulations. On the one hand he claims that "Every hysteria can be looked upon as traumatic hysteria in the sense of implying a psychical trauma and that every hysterical phenomenon is determined by the nature of the trauma," so that "Hysterical patients suffer from incompletely abreacted psychical traumas" (1893–95, 34). On the other hand, as I have already cited, the core formula for hysteria that Breuer and Freud ultimately propose is that "hysterics suffer mainly from reminiscences" (7). Their symptoms enact memories that are residues of traumatic experiences, representing these as mnemic symbols, because a reaction to the wounding experience had initially been suppressed. Because it was never sufficiently abreacted, the affect remains attached to the memory and, having become pathological, haunts the afflicted patient who unwittingly preserves the past event, rather than relinquishing it.

Uncannily resonating the iconography of vampire lore, Breuer and Freud draw two conclusions from their discovery of a foreign body of nonab-reacted, traumatic reminiscences encrypted in the psychic topology of their patients. First, the memories that have become the determinants of hysterical phenomena persist for a long time with astonishing freshness and with the whole of their affective strength preserved, much like the revenant vampire feeds on the blood of its victim, exhausting it in the process. Second, these parasitic memories are not at the hysteric's conscious disposal; indeed they are completely absent from the patient's memory while she is in a normal psychiological state. The presence of traumatic reminiscences within the psychic topography of the afflicted patient are thus seen to operate with a splitting of consciousness into a normal and a hypnoid state—a double con-science, similar to the one described by both Charcot and Stoker. For Breuer and Freud emphasize that "Among hysterics may be found people of the clearest intellect, strongest will, greatest character and highest critical power" who, in their hypnoid states, are insane "as we all are in dreams." Unlike normal dream psychoses, which "have no effect upon our waking state, the phantasy material formed during hypnoid states, when the *condition seconde* is powerful, not only dictate the behavior of this second state, but also "intrude into waking life in the form of hysterical symptoms" (1893–95, 13). In other words, these phantasmic foreign bodies gain control over somatic innervation, which can result in intermittent, acute hysterical attacks during which the patient is susceptible to hypnoid states and re-newed visitations of these traumatic impressions. What determines the hys-teric subject therefore, is not her double consciousness, which Freud and Breuer see as a universal human trait, but rather the uncontrolled blurring of the boundary between these two states.

The psychoanalytic cure, then, is aimed at redressing the missed opportu-nity for abreaction, in the course of which a reenactment of past events is meant to take away the power of the encrypted, traumatic reminiscence by virtue of transforming affect into words. However, given that these patho-genic reminiscences do not arise while the hysteric is in a normal state but rather during her abnormal state of hypnoid consciousness, any recollection of the operative psychical traumas can also only be called forth while the patient is hypnotized. In other words, if a predisposition toward hypnoid states can be seen as encouraging the production of hysterical symptoms, the analytic cure uses hypnosis to cure this disorder. The analyst seeks to enlist the help of precisely the double conscience that is also the precondition for the illness. Furthermore, while this condition seconde is the state during which pathogenic phantasies are produced, it also functions as the link to

the residues of traumatic knowledge, from which the so-called normal consciousness is completely severed. The hysteric performs her pathogenic reminiscences, offering to her analyst material that will allow him to reconstruct
past traumatic scenarios, while she is in a trance state, experiencing amnesia
as she returns from the hypnoid to the normal consciousness. The hysterical
symptom, functioning as a parasitic foreign body, touches on the psychic
gap that delineates all traumatic knowledge from any direct or immediate
representation. But it also requires a gap in the memory. The brilliant but
controversial moment in Freud's and Breuer's cathartic method, I would
argue, lies in their almost magical belief that filling up this gap could also
imply the removal of both the conditions that led to producing the symptom
and the traumatic core itself: that there should be a hidden secret, ready to
be disclosed. At the end of their preliminary communication they explain
that psychotherapeutic procedure "brings to an end the operative force of
the idea which was not abreacted in the first instance, by allowing its stran-
gulated affect to find a way out through speech; and it subjects it to associa-
tive correction by introducing it into normal consciousness (under light hypnosis) or by removing it through the physician's suggestion, as is done in
somnambulism accompanied by amnesia" (1893–95, 17).

III

I now turn to some of the case histories themselves to show both the compelling force, but also the limitations, of this belief in the infallibility of a coherent analytic narrative, especially so when privileging the sexually encoded
family romance becomes screening representations of traumatic impressions. In the first case history in *Studies in Hysteria*, perhaps the most poignant aspects of Anna O.'s incapacitation is that, triggered by her father's
mortal illness and this intellectually vital girl's having been forced to limit
her imaginative activity to daydreaming, she developed a peculiar psychosis.
In the course of nursing her dying father, Anna herself fell ill, exhibiting
anorexia, anemia, nervous coughing, impaired vision, a functional disorder
of her speech, and paralyses of the body. Above all, Breuer noted her proclivity toward somnambulism in the afternoon, followed by a self-induced
hypnoid state in the early evening and great liveliness during the rest of the
evening. Breuer came to interpret this behavioral pattern as a simulation of
the daughter's nursing her father, sleeping in the afternoon, and waking at
night. This hysteric double consciousness, however, also indicated that she
was living two entirely distinct mental states—one melancholic, anxious,
but normal; the other, a hallucinatory condition seconde. Throughout the
day she would have intermittent *absences*, whose content she would not be
able to recall once she had regained her conscious self, during which she
would be abusive toward others as well as herself. As Breuer notes, "At
moments when her mind was quite clear she would complain of the pro-

found darkness in her head, of not being able to think, of becoming blind and deaf, of having two selves, a real one and an evil one which forced her to behave badly" (1893–95, 24).

When her adored father died, whom, owing to her illness, she had seen only intermittently and for short periods, this event inflicted on her "the most severe psychical trauma that she could possibly have experienced" (26). Her psychosomatic disturbances, her absences, and her self-induced hypnosis continued after she had initially simulated his death more directly; she went for days and nights without sleep or nourishment and made numerous attempts at suicide. Breuer, however, soon discovered that if during her hypnoid state she was able to narrate the hallucinations she had during the day, "she would wake up clear in mind, calm and cheerful" (27). In other words, during her so-called conscious state, the diverse symptoms of body incapacitation came to articulate, in the manner of conversion, the phantasy scenes she would mentally enact in her "private theater" during her hallucinatory absences. Giving utterance to all her hallucinations, what she called chimney sweeping, came to relieve her of the residue of traumatic material haunting her psychic topology. On the other hand, if she did not convert the phantasies she produced during her absences into narratives reproducing the event that had called forth a particular symptom, she would be left tormented. Breuer treats these pathogenic ideational complexes like a foreign body, speaking of them in terms of something that remains stuck inside her, while "the treatment, too, works like the removal of a foreign body from the living tissue" (290). Indeed, in what one could read as a surgical gesture, but also an imitation of religious confession, Breuer says of each pathological reminiscence that they "talked it off."

One of the most striking aspects of Anna's double consciousness was that it entailed a layering of temporal moments. For a phase during the treatment she was living in two, separate time frames, consciously in the winter of 1881–82, the year of her father's death, but in her condition seconde, however, in the previous year. From this Breuer ultimately deduces that what had initially provoked her sequence of hysteric symptoms was some fright she had experienced while nursing her father. Two memory traces Anna offers to Breuer after considerable resistance illustrate her identification with her father's dying. The first involved a hallucination she had while nursing him, when "she had seen him with a death's head"; the second was a hallucination that occurred while she was visiting her relatives. She had come into a room and, "seen her pale face reflected in a mirror hanging opposite the door; but it was not herself that she saw but her father with a death's head" (1893–95, 37). Indeed, all her symptoms, the physical incapacitations and the hallucinatory scenes, ultimately proved to revolve around a primal scene of mortality—the anxiety about nursing her dying father and her own disempowerment before death. This anxiety culminated in a nocturnal scene, with Anna, "sitting at the bedside with her right arm over the back of her chair," fell into a waking dream and "saw a black snake coming toward the sick man from the wall to bite him." During this scene she not only experienced her own inability to fend off this agent of death: "She tried to keep the snake off, but it was as though she was paralysed." Furthermore, she appears to transform her body into a medium of death itself; her right arm "had become anaesthetic and paretic; and when she looked at it the fingers turned into little snakes with death's heads" (38). The whistle of the train bringing the doctor broke the spell, but even his arrival could not undo the terror she had experienced. What is crucial about this case is that an affect of anxiety and dread about the impending loss of the paternal figure of authority, meant to secure a stability in her social world, actually transformed Anna O.'s habitual daydreaming into a hallucinatory absence or double conscience. Precisely this proximity to the traumatic scene of another's self-expenditure rendered visible the latent split of the self, the workings of the unconscious as another scene, broadcasting a message about vulnerability and fallibility that thwarted her fantasies of being able to unconditionally and indefinitely rely on a paternal figure of authority.

Working with the notion that hysteria as a malady of simulated representation, Breuer is able to interpret his patient's hysterical symptoms as repetitions of the different details of this noctural scenario of traumatic impressions. Whenever she encountered objects that reminded her of snakes, a contracture of the right arm would occur: for her this visual impression had come to call forth the affect of the originary hallucination. Her autohypnotic absences were interpreted by Breuer as conversions of the gesture of waiting for the doctor to arrive; her inability to eat was a conversion of the sense of nausea at her father's decline; and her impairment of vision, a repetition of the moments when her eyes were filled with tears. Breuer ultimately gets his hallucinatory patient to literally reenact this originary primal scene of mortality: "On the last day—by the help of re-arranging the room so as to resemble her father's sickroom—she reproduced the terrifying hallucination which I have described above and which constituted the root of her whole illness." With this second reenactment of the horrific scene, now not just as a verbal rendition but also as a concrete performance, parturition is achieved. Anna appears to be free "from the innumerable disturbances which she had previously exhibited."

What intrigues Breuer most about Anna O. then, is, the way she exhibited a split in consciousness because the "the absence of adequate intellectual occupation left her with an unemployed surplus of mental liveliness and energy" (41), leading first to daydreaming and then to autohypnosis and psychic absences. Indeed, Breuer exhibits astonishment at the complete discrepancy between Anna's two psychic states, much as Van Helsing and his crew are surprised at the coexistence of purity and lascivity in the vampirized Lucy. It was especially noticeable, he explains "how much the products of her 'bad self,' as she herself called it, affected her moral habit of mind," so that while in the second condition she would emerge as "a hysteric of the malicious type—refractory, lazy, disagreeable, and ill-natured," but once these stimuli had been removed, "her true character, which was the opposite of all these, always reappeared at once." Breuer also notes, "Though her two states were thus sharply separated, not only did the secondary state intrude into the first one, but . . . a clear-sighted and calm observer sat, as she put it, in a corner of her brain and looked on at all the mad business" (46).

What Breuer significantly chooses not to emphasize, however, is that Anna O.'s hallucinatory autohypnosis, even if it results from her proclivity toward daydreaming, came to the fore in response to a very real event: her father's demise and her empathic identification with his dying body. Thus the crucial oscillation is not only between a melancholic and a malicious hysteric but also between a caretaker, who seeks to preserve life, and a hallucinator, embracing death. Indeed, Breuer further notes that the hysteric is most true to herself while in her hypnotic state, given that in the normal state, which he chooses to call her "true character," she actually has no access to her memories and to the traumatic impressions so fundamental to her subjectivity. Taking this a step further, one could speculate that the hysteric is actually closer to the truth of her situation as a daughter positioned within a given family bond when she recognizes the inevitable threat of implenitude, loss, and abandonment. And it is this truth that she comes to articulate by imitating her father's dying in the form of her own body incapacitation, after the horrible event she has anticipated actually sets in. In other words, the language of hysteria that Anna O. performs for Breuer is significant not only because it involves overabundant phantasies, engendering an oscillation between two mental states, but because the contradiction of personality, splicing an incapacitation of the body with mental clarity and hallucinatory visions, is a reworking of the traumatic knowledge of human mortality.[5]

Emmy von N. is another highly suggestive hypnotic subject who exhibits the same split in personality as Anna O., and with it intermittent hallucinations of terror that come and go very suddenly, followed by amnesia. In her case also the series of traumatic precipitating causes, which her hysterical symptoms make so much ado about, are death-related. In hypnosis she tells Freud about her first fainting fit, as well as the spasms she had when she was five and her siblings often threw dead animals at her. Then at seven, she felt anxious when she unexpectedly saw her sister in a coffin; by the next year her brother was often terrifying her by dressing up as a ghost; at nine, she saw her aunt in a coffin, the corpse's jaw suddenly dropping. She continues her list of anxiety-inducing memories, describing the hallucinations she had during the period she was nursing her tubercular brother and her fright at finding her mother unconscious from a stroke and, four years later, finding her dead. The traumatic event that produced the most-lasting effect, finally, was the sudden death of her husband, which ultimately triggered the hysterical attacks that brought her to Freud: "As she was lying in bed after her second confinement, her husband, who had been sitting at breakfast at a small table beside her bed, reading a newspaper, had got up all at once, looked at her so strangely, taken a few paces forward and then fallen down dead" (60).

During hypnosis, Freud asks Emmy v. N. to recall the plethora of scenes that her hysterical symptoms represent in converted form, only to continue using suggestion so as to wipe away "these pictures, so that she is no longer able to see them before her" (1893–95, 53). In other words, like a surgeon, he eradicates each one of the impressions that are haunting her, and even the affect of fright connected with them. One could say he pits an extinction of all memory traces against her vivid abundance of reminiscences, as though he were rewriting her past for her: "I made it impossible for her to see any of these melancholy things again, not only by wiping out her memories of them in their plastic form but by removing her whole recollection of them, as though they had never been present in her mind" (61). He performs a form of parturition not unlike Van Helsing's, giving birth to a woman seemingly purified of the traces of traumatic knowledge haunting her. This radical obliteration, however, involves a dialectic whose pathogenic reminiscences, provoking gaps in consciousness, are replaced by gaps in memory. With satisfaction he notes, "She made her complaints about gaps in her memory 'especially about the most important events,' from which I concluded that the work I had done two years previously had been thoroughly effective and lasting" (84).

Freud uses his theoretical discussion of the case to develop his notion of hysteric conversion. Emmy v. N.'s case thus serves as the specimen example for his claim that hysteria converts residues of traumatic events that have not been discharged by abreaction or thought-activity into chronic somatic symptoms. At the same time, however, her case is also meant to offer proof of his claim about the sexual etiology of hysteria, and it strikes me as significant that precisely at this point in his analytic narrative Freud introduces theoretical material, rather than relying on the psychic material that has been presented to him by the patient herself. For, seeking to explain the persistence of her phobias, he suggests that while psychical factors, harking back to traumatic events, account for the choice of her phobias, "It is necessary, I think, to *adduce* a neurotic factor to account for this persistence—the fact that the patient had been living for years in a state of sexual abstinence" (88). Freud thus concludes that two psychic moments came together to produce her hysteria. One was that distressing affects attached to her traumatic experiences of mortality had remained unresolved in her psychic apparatus and produced symptoms, which stood as overdetermined somatic symbols for these remains, with each symptom the nodal point for many traumatic moments. On the other hand, he locates her proclivity to hysteria in the abundantly lively activity of her memory, which allowed her to live the past with the same intensity as the present, indeed to preserve and commemorate the past, refusing to relinquish it. His cure consists in exhausting precisely this "accessible stock of pathological memories."

The analytic solution he proposes, however, raises several questions. For example, it remains unclear whether, by wiping out her pathogenic memory traces, Freud ever came to resolve the traumatic kernel, or whether he simply retouched the effects of this resilient source of unconscious knowledge, when he used hypnosis to rewrite the content and affects that would populate her memory. During analysis Freud could fight against his patients pathological ideas, both by "suggesting the symptom away *in statu nascendi*" and by "resolving the affect by abreaction," but the therapeutic success, though considerable, was not a lasting one. As he is forced to admit, once Emmy v. N. left him, her symptoms simply reappeared under the impact of fresh traumas. The explanation he offers both for the etiology and persistence of her hysterical symptoms addresses three factors: her severe neuropathic heredity, the great number of traumatic experiences in her life, and the lively activity of her memory, which "brought now one and now another of these traumas to the surface of her mind" (102). Searching for an explanation for why she retained these distressing affects, Freud, considering a hereditary disposition to be an insufficient answer, points instead to her mental solitude and her isolation within her family. Given the failure of his cure, however, Freud is forced to admit that circumstances of life and natural disposition also offer only a partial explanation for the mechanism of retaining large sums of excitation. So he deftly inserts into the gap in his knowledge an additional factor, which never actually emerged from Emmy v. N.'s own narrative. "It has also struck me," he notes, "that amongst all the intimate information given me by the patient there was a complete absence of the sexual element, which is, after all, more liable than any other to provide occasion for traumas." Because his own theorization has convinced him that an exhaustive explanation is possible only if it includes sexuality as the agent provocateur in the mental life of the hysteric, he turns his failure at finding a solution to Emmy v. N.'s illness into the result of her reticence. Without any proof to sustain his hypothesis, indeed much like the vampire hunters who ultimately must have recourse to faith, he adds, "It is impossible that her excitations in this field can have left no traces whatever; what I was allowed to hear was no doubt an *editio in usum delphini* [a bowdlerized edition] of her life-story" (103).

My point is not to deny the importance of sexual needs and their powerful influence on the development of neurosis but rather to recognize the fact that by seeking a sexual etiology so as to offer an "exhaustive explanation" Freud goes far afield of what Emmy v. N. was actually telling him. My own speculation is that listening to her recollection could lead to a different interpretive narrative, one that actually privileges the death-related traumatic experiences and the many instances of abandonment that broadcast her social vulnerability and disappointed any sense of family plenitude as the resilient and ineffaceable center of all her hysteric conversions. Furthermore, the fact that Freud was unable to complete his cure—that once he was no longer present to retouch her memory, the archive of traumatic knowledge

Emmy v. N. had encrypted in her mental topology simply grew as luxuri-ously abundant as before—could articulate something other than that what had been missing from his analysis was the sexual element. For this resilient regeneration of her haunting reminiscences might in fact be broadcasting that any reworking or abolishing of memory traces never touches the trau-matic kernel. Analytic success, in other words, might well involve accepting that no explanation can be exhaustive, that despite whatever theoretical framing one chooses to privilege to contain the affective foreign bodies that have attached themselves to memory traces, their impact will persist.

The last case I will discuss, the case of Elisabeth von R., is also the "first full-length analysis" (139) undertaken by Freud, and one is compelled to wonder whether he was able to find a solution to this case of hysteria be-cause her story could be interpolated into the theory romance of a sexual etiology of hysteria, which Freud so desperately wanted to prove. Indeed, as Mary Jacobus notes, the case of Elisabeth v. R., relying so heavily on the "romantic smoke screen of her doomed love for her brother-in-law," could be seen as an instance where "Freud displaces displacement itself from one story to another, smuggling the incestuous Oedipal plot ("*sentimenti illeciti*") into the sickroom" (1986, 227). In this case, also, Freud discovers a proclivity toward dissociation and toward a somatic dysfunction; paraly-sis and pain, especially in the legs, came to produce severe difficulties in walking. Using hypnosis or inducing a hypnotic-like state, Freud worked by eliciting his patient's confession about events that were known to her, only to penetrate into ever deeper layers of her memory whenever "some train of thought remained obscure or some link in the causal chain seemed to be missing" (139).

In the case of Elisabeth von R., Freud explains, the presence of traumatic material is treated as "only a secret and not a foreign body" (139), because the patient was conscious of the basis of her illness, though once again we find that the traumatic moments triggering her psychic impasse encompass scenes of mortality: nursing her father, who was suffering from a pulmonary edema and chronic infection of the heart, as well as the death of her married sister after confinement, also owing to a cardiac disorder. These deaths pro-voked so strong an anxiety in Elisabeth, precisely because they made it pain-fully clear that her entire aspiration for happiness had proved untenable. Not only was her ambition to become a professional musician thwarted, but she was brought face-to-face with her helplessness at the destruction of fam-ily bonds. This case is significant above all, however, because, in this story of hysteric invalidism, Freud excavates the crucial element of the daughter's helplessness and her sense of abandonment. As he works through her patho-genic memories—involving her guilt at her father's and her sister's deaths, as they stand in conflict with her desire for public success, family renown, a stable family unit, and a marriage that would not be degrading to her sense of self as a strong-minded woman—a narrative emerges running counter to (though also sustaining) the romance Freud ultimately privileges. Faced with her father's dying, Elisabeth experienced the traumatic acknowledgment of the fundamental solitude of the subject, that is, not only the vulnerability of her mutable body but also of the entire social system of the bourgeois family at the base of her aspirations. Her hysteric symptoms, the staged incapacitation of her body, signified that she chose to have recourse to a phantasy meant to fill this gap, this radical negativity, namely, the phantasy of a happy resolution in marriage of her romance plot. For both the scenes involving the father's and the sister's dying, the sexual impasse that screens the impasse of mortality is Elisabeth's narrating her conflict between desiring a potential suitor and feeling guilty at her desire for this love: she feels she should exclusively take care of her father (in the first phase of her illness) and yet the man she desires in her phantasies is her sister's husband (in the second phase of her illness).

In Freud's rendition of the happy end this analysis finally produced, the seminal peripeteia occurred when he discovered that his patient's pains always radiated from a particular area of the right thigh and were most painful there, because "it was in this place that her father used to rest his leg every morning, while she renewed the bandage round it." Furthermore, her hysterical body language proved to be such that "her painful legs began to 'join in the conversation' during our analyses" (1893–95, 148). Whenever memories pertaining to the illness and death of her father came up, the right leg would cause pain, whenever memories pertaining to the dead sister and her brother-in-law came up, the left leg would be in pain, and in each case the pain would persist until the relevant material had been talked through. Indeed, it was Elisabeth v. R. who taught Freud that her body disorders were in fact somatic conversions of a symbolic expression of thoughts too distressing to be articulated directly. Significantly, these somatically converted thoughts in all cases revolved around the sense of fallibility and vulnerability. Her dysfunction in muscular coordination when standing (astasia) or walking (abasia) came to articulate her sense of isolation: she found it painful "standing alone" and felt helpless about her failure to establish a new life for her family—she could not "take a single step forward" (152). Confronted with these two talking legs, Freud develops two plots, the first a mourning plot involving Elisabeth's response to the illness and death of her father, the second a bridal plot, involving the death of her sister and her desire for her brother-in-law. Interpreting her astasia-abasia as the symptomatic nodal point between two deathbed scenes, Freud develops a narrative in which, on the one hand, Elisabeth felt guilty because she had spent the evening with a suitor while her father grew gravely ill, while, on the other hand, she felt elated at the death of her sister. He explains, "At that moment of dreadful certainty that her beloved sister was dead without bidding them farewell and without her having eased her last days with her care—at that very moment another thought had shot through Elisabeth's mind, and now forced itself irresistibly upon her once more, like a flash of lightning in the dark: 'Now he is free again and I can be his wife'" (156).

One could speculate instead that perhaps it is Freud himself for whom an irresistible thought suddenly produces clarity in the midst of therapeutic obscurity. For he continues in his narrative, blurring the boundary between the realization he is attributing belatedly to his patient and his own moment of recognition: "Everything was now clear. The analyst's labours were richly rewarded. The concepts of the 'fending off' of an incompatible idea, of the genesis of hysterical symptoms through the conversion of psychical excitations into something physical and the formation of a separate psychical group through the act of will which led to the fending-off—all these things were, in that moment, brought before my eyes in concrete form." From this interpretation, exhibiting a leap of faith that is comparable to his hysteric's leap into their phantasy scenarios, he ascertains, "thus and in no other way had things come about in the present case" (157). Her hysteric dysfunction of the legs, he concludes, is first and foremost a conversion of the guilt she felt for desiring her sister's husband, while the experience of watching at the deathbed of her father was, by virtue of deferred action, a catalyst for the persistence of these hysterical symptoms. The motive for her hysteria was defense; the mechanism, conversion; the catalyst, the conflict between her duty toward her dying family members and her erotic desire that obliquely sought their deaths—namely, the phantasy of abandoning her father in favor of her suitor and of obliterating her sister to marry her brother-in-law.

I want to make a twofold point, and here I suggest one may begin rethinking Freud's interpretation of this case study. The core traumatic impact could well be the recognition of vulnerability in the very fundamental sense that it grounds all subjectivity. The trauma that persisted in haunting Elisabeth v. R. can be seen as harking back to prior experiences of passivity, of helplessness, of being unprepared and unequipped for dealing with exterior excitations. As Jacqueline Lubtchansky argues, in moments of psychic vulnerability, such external excitations are overwhelming enough to break any mechanism of self-protection, so that it is the mechanical violence exercised by trauma that liberates a quantum of sexual excitation (1973, 132f.). It is this second wave of excitation, metonymically contiguous with the initial vast rupture of the defense barrier, which is given a screen phantasy, namely, the mitigating phantasy of an intact family, or an adequate husband, even as the hysteric knows of the lack that her phantasies seek to screen off. Freud himself, after all, defines screen memories as the gesture of a psychic compromise, where a repressed traumatic knowledge is replaced by a contiguous desire.

To maintain the phantasy of returning to the situation of the intact home that had never in fact existed, however, the phantasy of a functional family, the hysteric Elisabeth v. R., one might argue, does violence to her body by transforming herself into an invalid. Though she obviously creates a new impasse—in this position of incapacitation she cannot even begin to take on responsibility for recreating the severed family bonds—the satisfaction becomes the original trauma's being successfully shielded off. It is brilliantly telling that Freud himself ultimately holds onto this romance, this screen narrative. Having given her the interpretation of her psychic distress that best complements his own interpretive desires—namely, that the secret she has been fending off is her love for her brother-in-law, because it is radically incompatible with her love for her sister—he has found a solution to her case and reassures both himself and Elisabeth herself that she is cured.

I want to call this an analytic, screen narrative because it remains arrested at the level of representations, falling short, in fact, of addressing the traumatic impact of the recognition of vulnerability and fallibility at the ground of all memory and fantasy work (as well as all symptom formation). It leaves quite intact, however, the impact of rupture that causes belated anxiety about having lost a love object, a protective shell, all of which is so alive in the unconscious, as Lubtchansky puts it, like a presence more present than anything materially present (1973, 384), which crystallizes and takes psychosomatic shape owing to phantasies of seduction and romantic desire. Furthermore, the fact that Freud watches Elizabeth whirl past in lively dance at a private ball one evening, could as much attest to the resilience of her newly acquired protective fiction as to his analytic cure. After all, we could also read this as the final gesture of the happy or successful hysteric, whirling over radical negativity rather than reenacting it at her incapacitated body.

IV

In a passage from the first of his five lectures on psychoanalysis, Freud compares "the Monument" commemorating the Great Fire of 1666 in London with hysterical symptoms as mnemic symbols: "Up to a point the comparison seems justifiable . . . but . . . what should we think of a Londoner who sheds tears before the Monument that commemorates the reduction of his beloved metropolis to ashes although it has long since risen again in far greater brilliance? Yet every single hysteric and neurotic behaves like [this] unpractical Londoner. Not only do they remember painful experiences of the remote past, but they still cling to them emotionally; they cannot get free of the past and for its sake they neglect what is real and immediate. This fixation of mental life to pathogenic traumas is one of the most significant and practically important characteristics of neurosis" (1909, 17). In Karl Jaspers's *Nostalgia and Crime*, one turns to case studies where the fixation of mental life to pathogenic traumas, the suffering from reminiscences, takes a horrific turn. However, read in conjunction, a fascinating analogy emerges between these two case studies, for what in Freud's discussion of hysteria is internalized, the foreign body wandering through the psychic apparatus to unsettle it from within, in Jaspers' text becomes externalized. In these cases the family romance is dramatically dismembered when the young woman servant finds herself displaced from her familiar geography, literally made foreign, wandering through an unfamiliar symbolic space (a new village, a new family) and unsettling it, only to find herself confronted with her internal split, her psychic extimacy, as Lacan terms it, broadcasting to her that the intimate is Other, like a foreign body, a parasite.

So as to concretize the theoretical analogy I am exploring, it will be necessary to recall the story of one of Jaspers's case histories in depth. One night, in a small German village, about 1906, the fourteen-year-old Apollonia S. slips from her bedroom and takes the little baby boy, whom she has been employed to care for, from his cradle and carries him to the river bank. From a bridge she throws him into the water. Without turning around, she returns to her bedroom and undresses; once the father has awakened to find his son gone, she takes part in the search for the lost child. The police suspect only the parents and arrest them, but Apollonia breaks down and offers her confession three days later. She tells the police where they can find the corpse, explains that she is well aware of having transgressed a moral forbiddance, but explains that she wanted under all circumstances to return home. What emerges in the course of her psychiatric surveillance—and Jaspers shows that this is one of hundreds of such cases to be found in the medical literature about nostalgia since the eighteenth-century—is the contradiction between a shy, helpful, hardworking girl who had been the main caretaker of her younger siblings in her own home, and one who, sent away to work for strangers, falls into a state of pathological nostalgia, oscillating between psychic catharsis (eating disturbance, passivity, reclusivity) and (once she realizes her parents will not allow her to return home) the exertion of brutality and violence.

Like many other subjects discussed by Jaspers, Apollonia S. was not morally degenerate; indeed, she was fully aware of having committed a crime, so that the final explanation he offered is nostalgic depression, which—and therein lies the connection to the language of hysteria—placed her into a condition seconde. As though in a hypnoid state, she thoroughly dissociated herself from her current surroundings and their moral codes, driven exclusively by a protective phantasy of an intact home she wanted to return to. Owing to a split of consciousness, this otherwise gentle and obedient girl was able to perform a monstrous crime—the murder of a child. Here, then, we have a story of reminiscences that have become pathogenic, even though at first the two instances of psychically distressing memory work seem to be counterimages. While the hysteric suffers from painful memories, whose conflictual affect she would like to shed but cannot because a proper abreaction has not occurred, the nostalgic suffers from pleasurable memories she would like to reenact, but which she cannot because she has been displaced from the one site promising such a satisfying fulfillment.

By holding onto overabundant memories, however, the nostalgic (like the hysteric) raises two questions. First, what is the status of the situation or condition of promised satisfaction or shelter the nostalgic yearns for, given that in her case one could speak of the "unreal character of neurotic satisfaction and the neglect of the distinction between phantasy and reality" (1917, 375) that Freud designates as one of the main traits of hysteria? Second, if we accept that this mnemic symbol of a site of protection could be a screen memory, responding to and resolving a far more fundamental traumatic impression of fallibility and vulnerability, the object toward which the desire of the nostalgic is aimed becomes problematic. For the absences so common to the hysterical attacks Freud observed, are found also in the cases of pathological nostalgia Jaspers relates. Though Freud seeks to link these lapses of consciousness during the hysterical attack to the climax of intense sexual satisfaction, his description of the mechanism of the hypnoid states, the absences during daydreams, suggests another form of enjoyment. "All the subject's attention is concentrated to begin with on the course of the process of satisfaction," he argues. "With the occurrence of the satisfaction, the whole of this cathexis of attention is suddenly removed, so that there ensues a momentary void in her consciousness. This gap in consciousness (*Bewußtseinsleere*), which might be termed a physiological one, is then widened in the service of repression, till it can swallow up everything that the repressing agency rejects" (1909b, 234). In other words, at the limit of phantasmic satisfaction, when daydreams, entirely superseding any experience of reality, offer complete pleasure, we do not find any sense of closure or plenitude but rather the experience of a gap in consciousness, widening to such a degree that the hysteric is no longer in her phantasy scene but rather in a site beyond representation. Read against Freud's discussion of the psychic gap that demarcates all represssion and phantasy work from the originating trauma, one might ask whether these girls have absences once they have traversed the satisfying and reassuring phantasy scene of protection and plenitude, and whether they end up enacting a return to the source of the traumatic impressions that lived on as foreign bodies in their psychic apparatus. Having traversed the phantasy, then, do they actually return to the destructive enjoyment of utter vulnerability, helplessness, and lack found at the heart of the family?

Without going into the details of Jaspers's case studies, one can, nevertheless, isolate the following points. The troubling question raised by these cases of violence engendered by pathological nostalgia concerns the status of concepts such as home or family—once we see that the loss of a familiar geography or social space can induce such an extreme psychic liability, such an excessive neglect of the distinction between phantasy and reality that all moral judgment fails and the eruption of violence ensues. Summarizing and evaluating medical discourses on pathological nostalgia, Jaspers speaks (much in the vein of Pierre Janet) of *idées fixes*. The conjunction of crime and nostalgia suggests a disturbance in the imaginative capabilities of the young women. Because all vital powers have been cathected onto an idea, namely, the idealized concept of home and an obsessive notion of returning to this place, the register of the body and mind begin to collapse into each other.

The psychic imbalance of energy, a jamming whose somatic corollary is the paralysis of the body, can only be cured if the fixed ideas can once again be made fluid. Having recourse to an act of violence, outside all categories of representation, seems to bring about such a way out of the psychic impasse, even as it also uncannily seems to suggest that it might well be the far more archaic desire for the originary traumatic enjoyment that subtends phantasies of protection and plenitude. The most obvious parallel between Jasper's nostalgics and Freud's hysterics is that both are illnesses of the imagination. To be more precise, while hysterics suffer from too lively an imagination, nostalgics seem to suffer from their imaginations not being flexible enough to encompass a change in geography.[6]

To stay with the similarities, however, one can say that nostalgia, like the hysteric's undefined longing, turns the body into the medium of psychic language even as it also provokes momentary absences from lived reality. While the hysteric produces parodies of the concepts of femininity against which she revolts—her paralysis and speechlessness as an exaggerated mimicry of late-nineteenth-century notions of ideal womanhood—the nostalgic produces idealizations of a lost homeland to compensate for her sense of not belonging. Yet both protective phantasies function along the lines of what Freud called the family romance of neurotic phantasy life. Whether the imagined scenarios enact ambitious wishes that elevate the subject's personality by endowing him or her with a more prestigious family than he or she has in reality or whether the scenarios revolve around a geographical and social space that is more elevated than the one the nostalgic finds herself in, in all cases a twofold message is being articulated.

On the one hand, substituting any lived reality with a phantasized family or home that is more elevated, more adequate, or more satisfying is manifestly an act of reinventing the past along the lines of all-too-familiar narratives of a protective house, loving parents, and the first blissful presence of objects of affectionate feelings (Freud 1908, 148). On the other hand, the more latent message broadcasts the ineluctable sense of abandonment from any protective home unit, and concomitantly, the fallibility of any such family romances. Again, what is compelling are the connections to hysteric memories. Faced with a psychic crisis that threatens to call up past trauma, these nostalgic phantasies produce images of happiness, plenitude, and intactness that are coded as having been lost, when, in fact, they always had the status of protective phantasies. They shield not only from any real memory, but also from the psychic gap that demarcates trauma from all representation. At the same time, if we recall that Freud had insisted that hysteric phantasies are made up in part from "things heard by children at an early age and only understood later" (1892–99, 244) one could speculate whether the violence enacted in these foreign homes by servant girls, detached from their home and family, do not uncannily resonate with the brutality depicted in the fairy tales the Grimm brothers began collecting at the onset of the nineteenth century, tales these girls would have heard from early childhood on. However, whereas the children in fairy tales, who have been the object of abuse by surrogate parents, ultimately strike back at these disappointing parents, only to reaffirm the intact family unit at the end of their trials, the servant girls in Jaspers's case histories reenact parental abuse by representation, destroying the home of the surrogate parents, but above all attacking the bodies of the children that resemble them most, abandoned to the care of a surrogate parent.[7]

Jaspers attempts to solve the contradiction they pose by highlighting the childlike disposition of the nostalgic criminal. In his analysis of the cases he argues that a child who has not yet learned to draw the boundary between self and surroundings (such that his or her identity is still entirely bound up with this intimate living space), violently separated from the familiar geography, will lose all psychic support. The child cannot yet emotionally substitute the foreign for the familiar. In so doing, however, he implicitly works with the notion of an intact home. I want to suggest, much along the lines of Freud's very early work on hysteria (i.e., the work prior to his repudiation of the traumatic etiology of hysteria), that perhaps precisely this tacit presupposition is at stake. It may, in fact, be the lost home that is itself the site of discontent. The perturbing inability on the part of these girls to draw a boundary between pathogenic phantasies and lived reality would then not be a divergence from but a continuation of the fact that the concept of a happy home was always already a screen phantasy, placed over a recognition of lack in the home, and perhaps even violence as its vanishing point. In the most obvious sense, these families could not have been an entirely intact social unit, given the economic situation that forced them to send their children into service with strangers in the first place. But in addition, even before these nostalgic girls became servants, they were surrogate mothers in their own homes, and thus representatives for a maternal lack at the very hearth they subsquently phantasize as being the site of protection and plenitude.

Given that these murdering servant girls can be seen as performing the maternal function gone awry, it is useful to recall Michèle Montrelay's discussion of the way the maternal body harks back to a time of chaotic intimacy, of a continuous expanse of proximity and unbearable plenitude, where what threatens the subject is a missing difference and lack. To become a mother, Montrelay argues, always involves anxiety, because "this body, so close, which she has to occupy, is an object in excess which must be 'lost,' that is to say, repressed, in order to be symbolized" (1977, 237). With Jaspers's murdering nannies it is as if, recovering themselves as the tantalizing and threatening maternal body, all repression was relinquished for a moment, and they came instead to enact the powerful but also destructive scene of chaotic intimacy. In a similar vein Julia Kristeva notes in her discussion of female melancholia that matricide is the vital necessity for any individuation. "The feminine as image of death," so prevalent in our cultural image repertoire, according to her, is not only "a screen for my fear of castration, but also an imaginary safety catch for the matricidal drive that, without such a representation, would pulverize me into melancholia if it did not drive me to crime." The psychic logic, she adds, is as follows: "No, it is She who is death-bearing, therefore I do not kill myself in order to kill her but I attack her, harass her, represent her. . . ." (1987, 28). What the criminal servant girls enact is precisely the destruction of the subject, which the matricidal drive is meant to prevent. Infanticide in these cases emerges as the moment when matricide fails, when a return to the dangerous proximity of the maternal body translates first into melancholia and then into a destruction of the child. Only in these cases that Jaspers reports the child, who is ultimately the object of this violence, has been displaced from the servant girl to the so uncannily familiar foreign baby.

My point is that the traumatic experience these nostalgics found reinvoked, to which they responded first somatically and then through acts of violence forced on them a return of the familiar. Again, it is useful to recall the language with which Freud so skillfully distinguishes between anxiety and fear. In his "Supplementary Remarks on Anxiety" he argues that neurotic fear pertains to a manifestly unknown danger; it has a quality of indefiniteness (*Unbestimmtheit*) and a lack of object (*Objektlosigkeit*). Yet on closer scrutiny, Freud believes to discover precisely the duplicitous configuration of intimate foreignness he had begun with in his early work on hysteria. He discerns a psychic sequence that leads from anxiety, back to events of real danger, only to end with the scene of helplessness he calls trauma: "Anxiety is, therefore, on the one hand an expectation of a trauma, and on the other a repetition of it in a mitigated form" (1926, 165).

In one and the same gesture, anxiety harks back to the all too intimate, but radically unmitigative, difference at the source of all phantasies of recuperation, even as it produces the protective fiction of a surmountable moment of danger. While the expectation touches on the desire for the archaic enjoyment that trauma harbors, the repetition of a protective phantasy scene of trauma renders this destructive desire bearable. For Freud claims that a situation of danger is in fact the recognized, remembered, and expected situation of helplessness that resonates with the impact the originary trauma produced in the psychic apparatus, a trauma that is irrevocable and irreducible. It wanders in the body; it has a latent presence even if, or precisely because, it is not accessible to representation. The body forgets nothing, acts out what we have no power over, thwarts all our phantasies of power—and just when the language of representation fails, the body acts, confronting the subject with its own extimacy, flooding the symbolic space, the foreign geography, with material of the parasitical intimacy that Lacan calls the register of the real. Treating it like any other symptom, and thus assuming that its displacement must serve some wish fulfillment, Freud, of course, seeks to highlight the psychic gain to be had from anxiety. If anxiety is the original reaction to the vulnerability experienced during a traumatic event, its later reproduction serves to turn impotence into mastery: "The ego, which experienced the trauma passively, now repeats it actively in a weaker version, in the hope of being able itself to direct its course (1926, 167). Yet the point to emphasize is that, whatever phantasmic mastery a reproduction of anxiety may afford, this is a screen phantasy, ineluctably tainted with the stain of fallibility.

I would speculate, therefore, in the case histories Jaspers presents, the fact that the nostalgic girls were forcibly separated from their so-called happy homes, expelled from the protective emotional warmth of the family hearth is not at stake. Rather, separated from a familiar environment, and in a new context supposedly entirely foreign to them, they unexpectedly found themselves confronting something all too familiar—the anxiety (of lack and fallibility) they always had known, but which they had mitigated with phantasies of a happy home and a satisfying homeland. Embellishing Jaspers, I would suggest that it was not indifference toward the child at all, but rather the contrary that provoked them to resort to infanticide. For it is entirely possible that these nostalgics discovered in the children they were to care for a double of their own situation of abandonment: thus they were enacting on the representatives of their own childish helplessness precisely the same scene of violence, whose victims they believed themselves to be in their psychic reality. To use Freud's terminology, the foreign home became a dangerous situation for them because it transpired to be a recognized, remembered, expected situation of all-too-familiar familial helplessness.

I want to suggest that reading Jaspers's text in conjunction with Freud's work on trauma and hysteria leaves us with not simply the appeal to rethink the connection between nostalgia and crime, but more importantly the question of violence written into any phantasy of home and homeland. The hysteric uses her body to articulate the difference at the heart of the bourgeois family, and in her refusal to undertake the so-called normal Oedipal journey, engages with the paternal metaphor, supporting the father's desire, even as she makes what is latent manifest, namely the violence, sacrifice, and incest on which the bourgeois family is founded. So, too, the nostalgic may unwittingly bespeak our need to rethink such categories as home, nation, and ethnicity when we discover that a loss of these phantasies can erupt in brutal violence, in a blindness toward the foreign because it is translated into an experience of the all too familiar. The message to read—if we accept these case histories as cultural symptoms—may relate to an acceptance of the vulnerability or fallibility of such concepts as family and home, of the fact that they can never adequately fill the psychic gap demarcating trauma from its representation. In the cases of both pathological reminiscences and phantasies, what is somatized is violence at the heart of the family romance and the romance of geographic belonging—be this the death of the father, entailing both the loss of a privileged object of affection and (the threat of a disruption of) the family bonds in the case of the hysteric staging a battle at her body to destabilize the family or be this the loss of a familiar geography in the case of the nostalgic staging a battle against the unfamiliar social space. Both react by constructing protective phantasies of the intact family or the intact homeland meant to compensate not just lack but, above all, traumatic impact.

As Renata Salecl notes, "A country is always already a kind of fiction: a country is not only 'a piece of land,' but a narration about the land." She not only argues that in psychoanalytic terms any notion of a country or homeland must be seen as a phantasy. Rather, she adds that since phantasy refers to the way subjects "structure their desire around some traumatic element that cannot be symbolized," thereby giving consistency to social reality, this reality in turn must be seen as being "traversed by some fundamental impossibility, by an 'antagonism' which prevents reality from being fully symbolized." Filling out an empty place of reality, phantasy functions "as a scenario that conceals the ultimate inconsistency of society" (1994, 15). For the murderous nostalgic, the home romance gone so violently awry could be seen in analogy to the hysteric, using her family romance to conceal the inconsistency in paternal authority, even as she also enacts the fallibility of the dead father by imitating him in the diverse language of body incapacitation. For the nostalgic also employs a phantasy of intact plenitude to fill out an empty place in lived social reality, but to such an excess that what she ultimately enacts is the antagonism at the heart of the home—its internal, uncanny difference.

What returns for the nostalgic girls who find themselves in an unfamiliar world is an entirely familiar traumatization, leading back directly to the discontent at the core of the home they had left (which, owing to their crimes, they will never return), as well as to a recognition that violence and crime were already written into any concept of home and any contingent longing, desire, or object of phantasy. While Freud insists that phantasy repairs trauma, Jaspers disturbingly implies that it also produces violence. In fact, one could argue that these servant girls, like Freud's Elisabeth v. R., are ultimately successful. Having committed arson and murder, they no longer need to return home, as though the accute danger to their psychic survival had from the start not been the absence but rather the unbearable presence of too much home, the chaotic proximity connected with this social maternal space. Having traversed their phantasy, only to perform an act of incomprehensible violence, these girls successfully reassured themselves of the loss that is coterminous with sustaining individuation. Now prevented forever from returning home from their exile, they can sustain the precarious phantasy of intactness without running the risk of a fatal implosion. For within psychoanalytic terms, not the loss, but rather the extraordinary attraction of the home is what threatens the subject.

V

In his conclusion to *The Mental State of Hystericals*, Pierre Janet noted nostalgically, "The word 'hysteria' should be preserved, although its primitive meaning has much changed. It would be very difficult to modify it nowadays, and truly it has so great and beautiful a history that it would be painful to give it up" (1894, 527). In his own writings, based on the premise that "every hysterical attack is also a psychological event" (1894, 2), he had come to offer what he considered to be a consistent and coherent pattern for this mental disorder that had, for so many centuries, appeared to be protean and illogical. To differentiate hysteria from all other mental disturbances, he worked with the distinction between "accidents," on the one hand, considered to be contingent symptoms produced as a result of subconscious *idées fixe*, and stigmata, on the other hand, or negative symptoms considered to be the expression of basic disturbances and the result of a narrowing of the field of consciousness. For Henri Ellenberger, the novelty of Janet's work can be located in his discovery of precisely these subconscious fixed ideas and their pathogenic role. While, according to Janet, their cause was usually a traumatic event, he interpreted their persistence as an indication that the frightening impression had become subconscious. Two psychic topologies then came to exist simultaneously: on the conscious level, traumatic impressions were replaced by symptoms; on the subconscious level, pathogenic fixed ideas served to encrypt the distressing trauma that could not be articulated directly. Furthermore, this malady by representation was in part connected to a narrowing of the field of consciousness, in part, however, to a mental weakness resulting from either a hereditary predisposition or harsh living conditions. (Ellenberger 1970, 373). The belle indifference, for which the hysteric had come to be so renown in the course of Charcot's teaching, was in turn reinterpreted by Janet as an indication of the existence of these split parts of the personality, where the conscious mental state had become completely abandoned by the subconscious. Janet maintained that because these subconscious fixed ideas were endowed with an autonomous life and development, they existed completely independently of the other personality, so that the hysteric was beautifully ignorant of the division of her mental state. "The hysterical personality cannot perceive all the phenomena" he argued, "it definitively sacrifices some of them. It is a kind of autotomia, and the abandoned phenomena develop independently without the subject being aware of them" (Ellenberger 1970, 375). In contrast to the longstanding prejudice of elusiveness, Janet's nosology thus cast hysteria as an extremely predictable and repetitious malady, for he claimed that "early in the course of the disease patients organized their fixed ideas and their resulting manifestations; they tended to organize their emotional patterns, their movements, and their ideas—whether borrowed or their own—and to weave them all together to transform them more or less through a kind of subconscious meditation" (1965, 251). Far from being too mobile, the hysteric was acutally too static, excessively absorbed by her subconscious fixed ideas, autonomously self-contained and indifferent to her actual surroundings.

The other seminal distinction between Janet's work and that of his contemporaries, as Ilza Veith points out, was that he sought above all to dismiss as absurd the role of the uterus and, concomitantly, refused to accept the hypereroticism of hysterical patients. From the study of hundreds of cases he claimed to have found "that such erotic disposition does exist in hysteria but only to the same degree as do all other fixed ideas," and that in general hysterics are "not any more erotic than normal persons" (1965, 251).[8] Indeed, all the characteristics normally attributed to an exaggerated sexual preoccupation—fickleness, simulation, mendacity, and histrionics—were read by Janet in relation to the indifference and forgetfulness toward prior roles and attachments, resulting form the fact that the *idée fixe* quite literally ate at the emotion and the intelligence of the afflicted patient. As Martha Evans argues, "Janet's refusal to associate femininity with a proclivity to hysteria reflected an effort to liberate psychiatry from the narrow gender-based interpretations of mental life common in his day. His universalization of the etiology of hysteria thus represented a significant move away from the conservative equation of femininity with emotional weakness and instability" (1991, 62). Indeed, he differed with his former colleague Freud most radically in that for him the content of the fixed idea's provoking hysteria did not have to be of any particular nature, but rather could simply be the result of a distressing experience or of the sense of incompleteness and inadequacy. As Evans adds, Freud's theories, according to Janet "represented an unfortunate retrogression to the old equation of hysteria with frustrated sexual urges" (62).[9]

Throughout his work Janet remained attached to the schema of a doubled personality (*dédoublement*); he also privileged not the content of the parasitic idea but rather the structural effects that emerged as the subconscious came to be invaded and indeed taken over by psychic foreign bodies, by the all-encompassing idée fixe. This doubling of the personality, for which dissociation and a shrinking of the field of consciousness served as symptoms, was conceived as the immediate consequence of a fallibility, on the part of the afflicted patients, toward psychic synthesis. Retaining throughout his work a belief in the traumatic etiology of hysteria, Janet tended to privilege physical shocks as the catalysts for hysterical accidents (be these chronic diseases, infections, organic diseases of the nervous system or any forms of intoxication), but he also recognized experiences of moral shocks and painful emotions. What these "provocative agents" had in common, however, was that they could "weaken the organism and increase the depression of the nervous system" (1893, 526).

I have chosen to conclude this chapter with a discussion of Janet's work above all, however, because the cure for hysteria he proposed, I would suggest, was itself a form of hysteria. For the basic premise underlying his treatment was the notion that even if a consciousness induced belatedly by the analyst is actually false, it may still be viable, indeed far more so than the hysterical symptoms, obliquely standing in for particular traumatic impressions. As Ellenberger notes, while aiming his therapy at the subconscious fixed ideas, Janet nevertheless insisted that simply bringing them into consciousness was insufficient; this process merely transformed a hysterical idea into a conscious fixed obsession. Instead, he was convinced that "Fixed ideas must be destroyed by means of dissociation and modulation. Obviously, since the fixed idea is itself a part of the whole illness, its removal has to be supplemented by a synthesizing treatment in the form of reeducation or other forms of mental training" (1970, 373).

In other words, rather than recalling the traumatic events, which the hysterical attack was standing in for, to resolve the attack by making the afflicted patient recognize what she had sought to repress, the discovery and dissolution of the subconscious idées fixe proposed by Janet, instead involved the implantation of new stories, so that a contingent shock would come to be mitigated by virtue of rewriting the old memory traces that had become fixed in the subconscious. Indeed, echoing Janet's dictum that "psychoanalysis is, above all, a philosophy" (1914–15, 185), Ian Hacking sees the French physican and his Viennese colleague as the antagonists in a contest, with Janet assuming the role of an excellent healer and Sigmund Freud cast as the almost tragic figure, motivated by the search for ideal truth: "not truth about the life of this or that patient, not truth about family life in turn-of-the-century Vienna, but a higher theoretical Truth about the psyche" (1995, 196). According to Hacking, by using suggestion and hypnosis Janet "dealt with traumatically caused neuroses by convincing the patient that the trauma had never happened" (195). The magic act his therapy performed consisted in the fact that hypnotically induced falsehoods would cause the disappearance of many of the hysterical symptoms. Janet would cure his patients by telling them a so-called lie and getting them to take these false memory traces as truth. In counterdistinction, Freud's patients "had to face up to the truth—as he saw it." Hacking speculates that Freud often deluded himself, "thanks to his resolute dedication to theory," so that many patients came to believe things about themselves that were false, "things that were often so bizarre that only the most devout theorizer could propose them in the first place." The crucial difference for Hacking, however, is that Freud never "got his patients to believe what he himself knew to be lies. Janet fooled his patients; Freud fooled himself" (196). Of course, my own point throughout has been that the language of hysteria defies the distinction between truth and lie, ceaselessly performing that psychic truths can be articulated only as deceptions and that the analyst, purporting to seek a truth, ultimately desires to be deceived.

One of the most spectacular case histories for Janet's belief that traumatic experiences could be adjusted is that of Mme. D., a patient he began to treat under Charcot's supervision at the Salpêtrière. In Calais, on 28 August 1891, the thirty-four-year-old seamstress experienced a hysterical anxiety attack. As Janet notes, her family certainly presented some hereditary antecedents; she was of nervous temperament and easily excitable, she sometimes spoke in her sleep, often felt overwhelmed, and suffered from the slightest emotional upheaval. Thus she was a perfect victim for the lugubrious joke a stranger decided to play on her. As she later explained, she was sitting alone in her room, working at her sewing machine when she suddenly saw the door open. A person she had never seen before approached her and said abruptly, "Madame D. . . . Prepare a bed. Your dead husband is about to be brought to you." She did not move but instead started to cry, resting her head on her machine; he added, "Do not cry so much and go upstairs to prepare the bed." After this remark he supposedly left her to her despair. The neighbors, hearing Mme. D.'s shrieks and moans, tried to first quiet her and then, fetching her husband, a carpenter who had been away at work while the "accident" occurred, called out to her, "Calm yourself, here he is." She, in turn, thinking they were actually bringing her husband's corpse, fell into a convulsive hysterical attack that lasted some forty-eight hours, with intermittent bouts of delirium. During her hallucinations she would incessantly return to the traumatic event, recalling the stranger and his distressing words, deploring the death of her husband, and bemoaning her fate.

After two days Mme. D. grew calm again, only then exhibiting a retroactive amnesia for some six weeks; she could remember nothing that had happened to her between 14 July and the fateful event. At the same time, from this period on she also had anterograde amnesia and could no longer form any memory whatever; she was unable to remember what was said to her or what she was supposed to do in the course of the day. All impressions would pass over her without leaving any lasting traces, whether of insignificant daily events or more dramatic events, such as a short trip she took with her family or her pain after having been bitten by a dog. At the same time she had perfect control over her movements and her language, indeed she could also perfectly recount events of her past that had occurred prior to the day of her traumatic accident. With the help of a notebook into which she would record the most minute instructions to herself, she was able to continue with her domestic chores.

Soon after her husband had delivered her to the Salpêtrière, however, Charcot discovered that she would speak at night; in a hypnoid state she would recount all the events she seemed to have forgotten during the day. Once she had been handed over to Janet, he began to devise a method for retrieving the lost memories that obviously still existed in her subconscious. Along with hypnosis, he used automatic writing and automatic talking, carried on while she was seemingly distracted by someone talking to her, to explore her forgotten memories. Assuming that her amnesia was the result of her psychic trauma he then undertook to dissolve her fixed ideas about the scene with the stranger that continued to haunt her subconscious and resurface at night (while during the day they had destroyed her ability to synthesize new data in her consciousness). Over several days, using hypnosis, Janet was able to modify her fixed ideas. As he explains in his report, "Mme. D. still dreams, but the man who appears now terrifies her far less because he has been transformed. He has taken on my own shape, and, instead of his terrifying sentence, he simply says, "Mme. D., prepare a bed, because I desire to sleep at your home in C." Although rewriting the parasitic, fixed idea, modifying the hallucination into a common occurrence, had been difficult, Janet concludes that his patient soon recovered her ability to remember, despite some initial physiological side effects. As her memory traces returned, Mme. D. suffered from violent headaches, vertigo, and even deliria when a particularly important set of reminiscences came back into her possession, as though she were going through a scene of parturition. All these symptoms, however, disappeared once she had definitively regained her lost memories—with, of course, the dramatic adjustment of the one distressing scene. Though Mme. D. was never fully cured of her anterograde amnesia, forgetting in the course of the night what had happened the previous day and then maintaining this amnesia for three weeks, she was nevertheless discharged from the Salpêtrière and allowed to return to her family (1893, 170f.).

As Janet notes in an article on psychoanalysis presented at the International Congress of Medicine in London in 1913, both his psychological analysis and Freud's psychoanalysis take as their starting point "the study of the traumatic memory in neuroses" (1914–15, 19). Psychoanalysis, Janet argues, attaches great importance "to the discovery of the traumatic memory," but contents itself with this first part of the process. It presupposes that bringing traumatic memories "to the light of day, should be sufficient; the patient is cured when he becomes conscious of this memory of the sexual perturbation that he experienced during his early infancy, and which he unfortunately had repressed into the subconscious." Admitting that treatment must in part consist of searching for a traumatic memory, "which is apparently forgotten and buried in the subconscious, and leading the subject to give clear expression to this memory," Janet, in turn, emphasizes in his own therapeutic work the idea that what makes a memory traumatic is that the afflicted patient has not been able to adapt herself to the difficult situation it evokes. The physician's part, therefore, consists not only "in discovering what this situation is, but in aiding the patient to adapt himself to it and to adjust it in some way" (1914–15, 182). Learning from the resilience of hysterical symptoms, Janet proposes a cure that acknowledges the life-sustaining power that can be attributed to fictions of the self. As though he knew that the traumatic kernel could never be resolved, Janet contented himself with restoring its after-pressures, converting a traumatizing into a soothing idée fixe. While Jaspers's servant girls had committed radical acts of violence to sustain the precarious phantasy of an intact home, his patients could find reassurance even in their invulnerability once he had got them, however unwittingly, to accept as truths the retouched memories, where scenes of abuse and abandonment had been transformed into scenes of plenitude and protection.

The most compelling example of the way hysterical delusion might well be a model for the successful adjustment to trauma is undoubtedly that of Madeleine, the protagonist of Janet's last book, *De l'angoisse à l'extase* (1926). I will end my discussion of wandering foreign bodies and hysterical phantasy work with Madeleine's case history, because, having rewritten her family situation in the key of religious delirium, she was not only successfully treated by Janet but also taught her physician that anguish is the mirror inversion of ecstasy, that the torturous despair of doubt and the joys of consolation are inseparable. Janet, who came to treat her in the late 1890s at the Salpêtrière, was particularly intrigued by her strange symptoms. For weeks on end, she would walk only on her toes, explaining that walking in this way was a sign of God's love for her. In part this related to Christ's suffering on the cross, with his legs twisted in a similar manner. Her stigma, however, also related to the assumption of the Virgin Mary, whom Madeleine hoped to imitate. Walking on tiptoe meant she herself was on the verge of being taken into heaven before actual demise, with her body fully intact. Given the importance Janet placed on hereditary disposition, he pointed out (though not until the very end of his presentation of her case) certain factors about her childhood, such as the fact that the mother had died of a brain hemorrhage when Madelaine was a small child. Furthermore, he was inclined to attribute her tiptoeing in part to her hereditary predisposition to faulty nerves: she had always had difficulties walking, running, and climbing; furthermore, she had been an insomniac and prone to violent trembling, and afraid of storms, railways, and automobiles, all of which had produced nervous crises and periods of catalepsy during childhood. Her symptom of walking on tiptoe, as well as her transfixion, however, was ultimately conceived by Janet as the working of an idée fixe in her subconscious, whose origin was a mixture of traumatic experiences during childhood and the genetic weakness of her limbs. Yet Madeleine resiliently countered his interpretation, insisting to the end that no traumatization preceded the appearance of her stigmata, but rather that they resulted of her miraculous identification with divinity. Thus Janet was forced to enter into her hallucinatory game, interrogating but also sustaining the religious encoding she gave of her symptoms. For a reader of Janet's text, these delusions are especially intriguing because at a time when psychiatry had come to challenge French clericism, as Jan Goldstein (1982) has argued, Madeleine's stigmata and hallucinations had recourse to the iconography attached to Catholic saints—though in the process she came to transform this public-image repertoire into a personal family romance.

Not unlike many devout Catholic women of the French bourgeoisie, indeed not unlike Emma Bovary, Madeleine cherished the phantasy early on that she wanted to sacrifice her life to God. But, somewhat more radically than her peers, she did not express her discontent at the constraints imposed by her family in the form of an invalidism and incapacitation, practiced by Freud's Viennese patients. Rather, she decided to leave her family when she was eighteen, disgusted at their worldy ease and plenitude. She decided to live a life of misery and self-sacrifice, spent in nursing the poor. Unlike the servant girls described by Jaspers, she chose to leave home of her own accord to work as a governess to a family in Darmstadt. However she, too, came to articulate the difference that inhabits the very heart of the home. For after a short period working as a governess, she decided that she wanted not only to dispossess herself of her home but also of all belongings. In order to fulfill this family romance, which ironically consisted in dissolving all family bonds and transforming herself into a completely free-floating foreign body, she left for Paris, cut off all ties to her family, and indeed cast off her real name and called herself Madeleine, in imitation of Mary Magdalena. While caring for the poor, she was repeatedly arrested for vagrancy, swindling, begging, and prostitution, though she never stayed long in prison. She continued to dedicate her life to taking care of the impoverished women in the streets of Paris until her own physical exhaustion forced her to go to a hospital. After several transitions she finally arrived in Janet's ward, where she was to stay until her release in 1902.

Early in his observations, Janet noted a curious dialectic. On the one hand Madeleine exhibited somatic anesthesia and wounds on her feet and hands that recalled the stigmata of Christian saints. Above all, she would somatically reenact an imitation of Christ's crucifixion. While walking across the room, she would suddenly stand transfixed in ecstasy, remaining motionless for up to twenty-four hours, neither eating, sleeping, nor responding to questions. The counterpart to this indifference to the world and her motoric inertia, was, in turn, a remarkable spiritual activity, which to Madeleine appeared rich and beautiful. Seeking to share with Janet what her state of ecstasy was like, she would relate, "No, the state I enter into is not a sleep, ordinary sleep is a kind of cessation of the spiritual life so as to sustain the animal life. . . . My state is the complete opposite; it is the domination of the spirit over the body, which ceases to act so as to give more room to the soul to be able to think, to contemplate and to love. . . . It is a suspension of the meaning of life, as though I no longer had a body, no longer had any members, there is nothing but spirit which lives intensely. . . . I am as though I were dead to all that is around me, only my body is here and my spirit and my heart glide among immense horizons where they flounder and lose themselves deliciously" (1926, 60).

These ecstatic transfixions, one could say, functioned as the somatization of her desire to abandon all sense of a worldly home, enacting at her body how, by virtue of abundant dissociation, the discontented foreign body can wander ceaseless and resiliently among celestial spheres. As Janet notes, an important characteristic of asthenic and abulic disorders is a discontent with the "world which presents itself as real. The world is too complicated, it causes us too many deceptions and sufferings, it demands actions that appear to be too massive and too costly" (347). This is, of course, yet another version of the hysteric's much ado about nothing, for Janet finds that the suppression of all interest in the world is often the somatization of a sentiment of a gap in one's life (*sentiment du vide*). Psychasthenic patients will often complain they are indifferent to everything: nothing interests them, so why do one thing rather than another? They say, "Nothing tempts me, nothing disgusts me." However, if one reformulates this to uncover a denied idea, what they in fact articulate is the following: "It is the nothing, the gap demarcating traumatic knowledge from all life-sustaining narcissistic phantasies of plenitude, protection, and integrity, that is so dangerously appealing that anxiety and doubt incapacitate me, thus allowing me to imitate what I cannot enjoy."

In the case of Madeleine, however, this gap, this nothing of which she was so painfully cognizant, also came to be screened by a resilient protective fiction, in which she fashioned for herself a complex, holy family romance, learning to preserve her precarious phantasma of an intact home of plenitude by displacing it into the celestial realm. She either wrote to Janet almost daily about her interpolation within the divine family, whenever her periods of anesthetized ecstasy were suspended or recounted these hallucinations to him while in her ecstatic states, offering him the role of Joseph in her private theater, fully able to oscillate between addressing God and addressing Janet as her two significant interpellators. In these visions she was at times consumed in pure union with God. Then again, at times she imagined herself to be the baby Jesus confined inside the Virgin Mary's uterus, reenacting his birth, while at other times she was the Virgin Mary herself, feeling the movements of the baby of God in her stomach. At still other times she would be nursing God with her milk, only to revert rapidly to a scene in which she was pregnant with God's child. Then again she would be Jesus Christ himself, imitating his passion in the olive shrine or hanging, like him, crucified on the cross. At the height of her ecstatic happiness, as Janet notes, she performed a constant change in decor and roles, in a personal drama in which she identified herself with all three members of the holy family and their physical sufferings—be these the gestations of Mary or the crucifixion of Christ. Despite all the versatility and changeability of these visions, in other words, they all revolved around "important acts about the relation between filiation and maternity between God and Madeleine" (67). Indeed so luxuriously abundant was her phantasy that Madeleine, who in reality led a modest and chaste life, in her religious delirium "brutally" offered Janet a scenario "in which she was not only the daughter of God, the mother of God, but furthermore the mistress of God, or, if one likes, the wife of God, and that she was completely cognizant of this." She renders this hallucination in the following ecstatic language: "My whole being is inebriated by divine kisses. Oh! If I could only communicate what I am feeling. . . . I have just passed a night of love and madness, yes it is true, God is driving me mad with love. . . . The waves of tenderness that inundate me do not allow me to believe I am dreaming, I sense that I actually love God" (67). Yet the contradictions Madeleine performed in the course of her complex, holy family romance were such that, on the one hand, her God was omnipotent and invisible, while on the other hand he was totally at her phantasmatic disposal: "In reality God is not just what he wishes to be, he is what Madeleine wants: he is in love, if she is so disposed, he is professor and philospher when she is willing to listen or rather to discourse" (418). If we recognize that Janet, conceding that "God plays the role of director in cases of psychasthenia" (419), accepts his supporting role of Joseph, we also see how much more self-effacing and humble is his magic act of reworking the fixed ideas of his patients in comparison with the spectacular showmanship of his teacher Charcot.

The other aspect of Madeleine's case that fascinated Janet was the way she oscillated between states of beatitude, during which she insisted that her joy was so extreme that she never wanted to be delivered of this delirium, and periods of melancholic torture, of grave despair and self-doubt. The moment of transition between these two states came very often to be marked by phantasies of suicide: "At the last degree of suffering a change of tone would arise in her sentiments. One could watch the appearance of the thought of death considered to be a return to nothingness; when Madeleine spoke of death a lot, and began desiring it, these expressions which made her think of the idea of suicide would also announce the approach of a period of ecstasy" (165).[10] The interpretation Janet finally reaches for this case history is that this patient, unable to sustain amorous relations in her actual social sphere, came to realize the love she so vehemently aspired to in her delirium: "While at times this delirium was directed at a terrestrial person . . . ordinarily this was still too insufficient, because it quickly led to difficulties and doubts and Madeleine could only repose herself fully in a satisfying love by taking God himself as the object of this love" (426). To love God was her successful idée fixe, the fiction most likely to protect her from psychasthenic anxiety, obsession, and doubt. Madeleine's story is so compelling for me because she enacted on her own terms what Janet proposed as a viable cure for hysteria—rewriting reminiscences and a traumatic knowledge about the fallibility and vulnerability of worldly existence into satisfying fictions one can live by. If only a union with God could offer this woman of radical doubts a satisfying and sustaining phantasy of love, was she not also articulating, more than her inability to sustain worldly bonds, the traumatic truth the hysteric daughter seeks to broadcast to her family: namely, that all worldly paternal figures of authority are inevitably fallible, unreliable, and inconsistent? Tempted by her doubts, her uncertainty, her relentless interrogations, and her equally obsessive manner of indefinitely interpreting all things around her (75), she may well have given voice to a truth about the radical vulnerability of human existence, a message too traumatizing to her worldly peers, however, to be sustained without their own analytic, protective fictions.

In the course of listening to Madeleine's visions, trying to reencode her religious ecstasy in the pragmatic and positivistic language of psychiatry, Janet was ultimately able to provoke a state in which both her ecstasies and her agonies grew so less frequent that she could be discharged. She went to live with her sister, but continued to write to Janet until her death, owing to a heart ailment, in 1918 at the age of sixty-three. Drinka argues that Janet, classifying Madeleine as a psychasthenic, (i.e., suffering from a loss of psychic strength) and interpreting her love for Christ as an expression of amorous delirium, "secularized this would-be saint." He does concede that Janet's treatment of Madeleine was marvelous, precisely because the physician believed he could talk this madwoman out of her madness and was convinced that his beliefs were truer than hers, "that his logic was more compelling than her transcendental visions" (1984, 355). Yet I would counter with another interpretation, namely, that Janet's treatment of Madeleine is miraculous for a different reason. For rather than rigidly imposing his theory about psychasthenia onto the stories she was telling him, the aging psychologist was willing to acknowledge his own implenitude. By assuming the position of intermediary, and at best midwife, accepting that he was Joseph, the privileged audience for whom the divine triad performs its act, Janet made it possible for a dialogue between physician and patient to take hold. In other words, relinquishing the role of a supposedly infallible paternal figure of authority, he ultimately emerged as a fully reliable interpellator, such that Madeleine could not play through the ambivalence so characteristic of hysteria—in the course of which the patient sustains the father's desire even as she is compelled to prove to him the inconsistency in his power and demands. Instead, she allowed Janet to convince her that, in contrast to her dramatic oscillation between an excess of anguish and an abundance of ecstasy, psychic equilibrium might not be so very unsatisfying, especially once one accepts it as a hysteric's compromise, not a state of psychic truth.

In his closing statement, Janet compellingly illustrates the parity that had come to characterize their strange interaction, for while he was able to train Madeleine to sustain indefinitely the mundane period of psychic balance between despair and delusory joy, he learned from her the curative power of these very religious delusions that came to fashion a divine family romance, to preserve the phantasma of intactness by ensuring that it would never be fulfilled. If these religious ideas "provoke doubts and fears," he admits, they "also bring about consolations and hopes and certainly they can be used to successfully ward off the melancholic's sense of abandonment and despair." Although with certain afflicted patients religious ideas can be dangerous, he adds, "In the life of Madeleine their influence . . . doesn't seem to me to have been pernicious; it may perhaps have prevented a vulnerable person from falling into the real depths of psychic estrangement" (1926, 476). The crucial point, I suggest, lies in the fact that Madeleine was able to split herself between her divine family romance and a knowledge of the fallibility of the world, fully convinced that both states were true. But it was also her luck that she was able to convey her unavoidable oscillation between traumatic knowledge and protective fictions to an interpellator, who was willing to acknowledge that the psychic contradiction she so persistently performed was precisely also her psychic truth.

Anne Sexton's Business of Writing Suicide

> The great theme is not Romeo and Juliet. . . . The great theme we all share
> is that of becoming ourselves, of overcoming our father and mother, of
> assuming our identities somehow.
>
> —*Anne Sexton*

I

ADRIENNE RICH began her commemorative address, delivered in memory of
Anne Sexton at City College in New York in 1974, with the strong statement
"Anne Sexton was a poet and a suicide." She continued by offering her own
counterstance: "Many women writers, learning of her death, have been trying to reconcile our feelings about her, her poetry, her suicide at forty-five,
with the lives we are trying to stay alive in. We have had enough suicidal
women poets, enough suicidal women, enough of self-destructiveness as the
sole form of violence permitted to women" (1974, 122). While I fully agree
with Rich that women should explore expressions of violence other than
those turned solely against themselves and that an attraction to death should
not be considered the privileged mode of the female poetic voice, I also believe that we may not yet have paid enough critical attention to the interface
of suicide and poetry, especially when it comes to the issue of women writing
and performing in public spaces. In response to the outrage that arose when
the press discovered that Anne Sexton's therapist, Dr. Martin T. Orne, had
released the taped recordings of his sessions with the poet to Linda Gray
Sexton, for use in the biography she had commissioned, the daughter confirmed, "My mother was a dramatic woman, an actress, a publicity hound
and wise in the way of business" (Linda Gray Sexton 1991, 20). I want,
therefore, to reflect about Anne Sexton as a public figure, as a woman whose
business was poetry and suicide, in order to explore the contradictions, the
eccentric disregard of propriety, the anguish, the fatality, but also the resilient power contained in the strange equation of poetry and suicide.

Anne Sexton is most commonly thought of in tandem with Sylvia Plath,
given that together they made it their business to repeatedly invoke their
own suicide attempts and their fascination with and desire for death in both
their work and discussion of each other. Indeed, in her article "The Barfly
Ought to Sing" Anne Sexton describes how she, Sylvia Plath, and George
Starbuck used to go drinking together in the lounge-bar of the Boston Ritz
after their poetry workshops with Robert Lowell, talking at length about

their first suicide attempts, "as if death made each of us a little more real at the moment. . . . We talked death and this was life for us, lasting in spite of us, or better, because of us, our intent eyes, our fingers clutching the glass, three pairs of eyes fixed on someone's—each one's gossip" (1966, 90). For Sexton, however, using poetry to turn an experience of death and a desire for death into one's business meant thriving on an aporia. For even as she describes the burned-up, quasi-erotic intensity with which they talked death, she insists that "Suicide is, after all, the opposite of the poem. Sylvia and I often talked opposites" (1966, 90).

In her biography of Anne Sexton, Diane Wood Middlebrook introduces a provocative new element into the equation that Adrianne Rich offers of suicide and the poet—Sexton's public performance of the stellar female poet. For throughout her compelling presentation of Anne Sexton's life, Middlebrook suggests that the transformation of frustrated, indeed mad, suburban middle-class housewife into successful poet (for which this biography has become so famous within the archives of twentieth-century women's writing) was sustained precisely by the fact that the poet herself actively worked at fashioning herself into a marketable image (1992, 401ff.). During the fourteen years that she published and presented her poetry, starting with *To Bedlam and Part Way Back* (1960), Anne Sexton earned almost all of the important awards available to American poets, including the Pulitzer and the Shelley prizes. She saw her play *Mercy Street* produced off-Broadway; was published in major literary and mass-market magazines and newspapers, including *Esquire* and the *New York Times*; and became a regular contributor to the *New Yorker*. At the end of her life she was among the best-paid poetry performers in America, monitoring the fees offered to James Dickey so as to set her own fees. To the hilt a creature of contradiction, she would launch her complaint at the misery of American middle-class women, even as she would insist on doing so in the elegant attire, gesture, and style of precisely this class. Similarly, she could live the contradiction of presenting her poem "Little Girl, My Stringbean, My Lovely Woman" at a read-in against the Vietnam War at Harvard in 1966 and, in what now seems to be incompatible, also writing her poem "Moon Song, Woman Song" for a commemorative ceremony, honoring the Apollo Moon Landing in 1969.

Middlebrook describes her as both a shrewd businesswoman and a successful teacher who was offered honorary doctorates from several American universities and who rose to the rank of professor at Boston University even though her education had been skimpy. Particularly intriguing about her, of course, is the fact that she was able to conduct this business as poet even while she was suffering from a mental disorder that, eluding diagnosis, could not be cured and whose symptoms were suicidal self-hatred and addiction to alcohol and pills. A split ran through Anne Sexton's personality such that even as she seemed to lose control over her psychic behavior, falling into trances or epileptic fits at home, in the midst of her family, she still was an expert at selling herself and her work to the public, perfectly adept at producing calculated radio and magazine interviews, completely poised when she encouraged herself to be photographed or when she had recordings and films made of her readings. Middlebrook confesses that she initially hesitated to accepting Linda Gray Sexton's offer that she become her mother's official biographer; she did not like Sexton's public persona. At the same time she admits that the compelling force and resonance of Anne Sexton's writings, indeed her legacy, relied heavily on the power her physical presence had on her audience, an aura that has been preserved beyond her death in the many photographic and sound recordings of her highly stylized manner of self-presentation (1991, xx).

To view Anne Sexton as a cultural phenomenon, as I suggest we could, means addressing the fact that she was one of the first American women writers to perfect the writing and presentation of poetry as a performance that would appeal even to poetry-avoiders. Over and beyond the controversy her writings provoked, what has entered into public memory is her physical beauty, and along with it the flamboyant and provocative, almost exhibitionist manner so perfectly controlled, with which, in Maxine Kumin's words "she bared her liver to the eagle in public readings where almost invariably there was standing room only. . . . Her presence on the platform dazzled with its staginess, its props of water glass, cigarettes, and ashtray. She used pregnant pauses, husky whispers, pseudoshouts to calculated effect. A Sexton audience might hiss its displeasure or deliver a standing ovation. It did not doze off during a reading" (1981, xxi). In an article published in the *American Poetry Review* and entitled "The Freak Show," Sexton articulates all the contradictions inherent in a public staging of intimate poetic expression, all the while skillfully leaving her own position opaque. She explains that she writes for an audience of one, that perfect reader who understands and loves, but she realizes that the moment she performs her poetry, she turns into a freak, an actor, a clown, an oddball. The act of performance emphasizes what is implicit to all intimate poetry: that writing turns the intimate into something exterior, draws a boundary between experience or feeling and expression, creates a distance between the speaker and the persona or self-representation articulating the speaker in the process of poetic transformation. But in so doing, the *self-conscious* performance in fact implicitly uncovers this underlying contradiction. "Poetry is for us poets the handwriting on the tablet of the soul. It is the most private, deepest, most precious part of us. Yet somehow in this poetry biz, as one of my students calls it, we are asked to make a show of it" (1973, 35).

What I find so compelling in Anne Sexton as public performer of femininity is the fact that, in the course of her extravagant, flamboyant, mannered self-presentation, she seems cannily to have staged a psychoanalytic and a deconstructive truth: that the most interior part of the psyche, according to Jacques Lacan, has a quality of being Other, of being like a parasitic foreign body, which (see the introduction) he calls *extimacy* (Miller, 1988).

In other words, her performances of her poetry externalize the fact that as a woman, born and raised in a particular cultural space, she is performatively constructed by a particular discourse and a particular psychic makeup. If we further recall that linguistic speech-act theory designates the performative as an utterance that constitutes some act, especially the act described by the verb of a sentence, Anne Sexton's gesture of presenting herself other than she is, as an actress, speaking lines she has constructed for herself, recasting sentences or stories handed down to her by her relatives or lines that have come to her by inspiration—but in all cases lines that are explicitly marked as not being natural—she insists that the act of self-representation is the verb of her public performance. She seems to say, "I am a performance, indeed, I am only *as a performance*, as the knotting together of languages that have determined me—be it the forbiddances of my parents, the cultural texts they have endowed me with (the family romances they lived by); be it the constraints and phantasmas of the culture I was educated in (its fairy tales and myths); be it my unconscious, that speaks to me a knowledge I have no direct access to." Indeed Sexton was quite vocal about the alterity of the unconscious, explaining in an interview with Barbara Kevles, "Sometimes, my doctors tell me that I understand something in a poem that I haven't integrated into my life. . . . The poetry is often more advanced, in terms of my unconscious, than I am. Poetry, after all, milks the unconscious. The unconscious is there to feed it little images, little symbols, the answers, the insights I know not of" (Sexton 1974, 85). Later I will return to the notion that intimate psychic truth was conceived by Sexton as radically Other, when I will develop a set of analogies between her psychic disturbances, therapy, and creative acts. At this point I simply want to emphasize that in the case of Anne Sexton the issue of the female poet's public self-display is twofold, and it is above all this duplicitous doubleness, this splitting of the poet into substance and performance of poetic speech, which makes her such a compelling case for any discussion of the equation of the suicide and the poet.

Like Robert Lowell and W. D. Snodgrass (though perhaps more boldly so) Sexton wrote so-called confessional poetry about intimate aspects of the feminine condition—her psychic lability and the madness that came to take possession of her; her own transgressive sexual desires, such as incest or adultery; her ambivalence about motherhood; and explicit descriptions of the female body, including the infamous celebration of her uterus and her poems on menstruation, abortion, masturbation, and drug and alcohol addiction. Indeed, much as Michel Foucault discussed, her poetic confessions broadcast a family complaint about the unhappy alliance between kinship and sexuality at the very heart of the the home. The designation "confessional poetry" is in a sense particularly fitting for the work of Anne Sexton, who was born on 9 November 1928 in Newton, Massachusetts, as the youngest of three daughters and who spent most of her life in the well-to-do suburbs of Boston. For although Sexton left the Roman Catholic church

early in her life, her poetry invokes the convention of confession as prepara-
tion for religious absolution. At the same time, the aim of her confessions is
not only the avowal of her most intimate feelings but also her interest in
rendering palpable the more painful aspects of the female experience in all its
horrific intensity. Her passionate family broadcast dismantles the sexualized
kinship alliances inherent in the bourgeois family, even while she is fully
aware of the necessity for this sociopsychic configuration. Anne Sexton
could persuade her audience of the validity of her complaint precisely because she came to transform her own anguish and passion into a resilient
and versatile public display. In her first collection of poems from 1960, *To
Bedlam and Part Way Back* (Sexton, 1981), she describes her psychic breakdown, her stay in an insane asylum, her therapy as a confrontation with the
traumatic impressions of the past that have taken possession of her as
though they were demons, and finally her attempt, after returning from the
clinic, to find a new place for herself in her family.

Many of the most forceful poems she wrote after the success of her poetic
debut deal with her place within the family, which takes on such an ambivalent shape because her anguish and sense of abandonment inevitably become
enmeshed with the proud recognition of her heritage. In her repeated reenactment of her family romance, which she explored and dismantled in one
and the same gesture, the principal players in the parental generation are the
father, Ralph Harvey, son of a banker and owner of a wool factory; the
mother, Mary Gray, daughter of a newspaper editor in Maine, who wanted
herself to become an author but was forced to give up her ambition after her
marriage; and the great-aunt Nana Ladd Dingley, known as "Nana," who,
living with the Harveys, was Anne's only confidante during her adolescent
years. When Anne was thirteen, Nana was sent away to a nursing home due
to her psychic instability. For the rest of her life Anne felt guilty about this
expulsion, even while she sensed that her great aunt had imparted to her the
legacy of psychic disorder. Accordingly, Anne Sexton's poems revolve
around phantasy scenarios that enact traumatic impressions of her childhood: the sexual abuse inflicted on her by the father; the madness, departure,
and death of the beloved great-aunt; the desire to be recognized by her dom-
ineering mother and the consuming anger she harbored toward her. These
are then repeated in scenarios involving the second generation: Anne as
daughter, wife, and mother, driven by a desire to please, fascinate, and
achieve public recognition; on the other hand, Anne haunted by a desire for
erotic self-expenditure and death, overwhelmed and terrified by the experience of motherhood, unable to live up to the feminine ideal of post–World
War II bourgeois America. This poetic confession of her discontent with the
family, furthermore, was continually framed by actual traumatic experiences of self-destruction. On her birthday in 1956 she untertook her first
suicide attempt, inaugurating almost twenty years of psychotherapy during
which she learned to hear the voice of her unconscious and transform it into
poetic articulations, even while she was never fully able to eradicate her deep
depressions and suicidal tendencies. As Diane Middlebrook argues, "The

most characteristic narrative voice of Sexton's poetry is searingly personal and is not dissociated from the author; in fact, it is possible to piece together in Sexton's work a continuous narrative about a character named 'Anne.' Born into privilege, she is cursed from infancy with fears that mature into a desire to die. 'Anne' appears as girl, young wife, emerging and mature artist, and as a broken woman whose rage is directed against herself" (1988, xiii). Yet I would add that Sexton's work is also a continuous narrative about her relation to a figure called "father" representing paternal authority, a figure of alterity, the daughter's interpellator to whom she addresses her question of identity, whom she requires to negotiate any decision as to whether she is masculine or feminine, alive or dead, creative or destructive. This persona at times appears as "Daddy" in the poems about incest and parental abuse, but also about paternal love and her longing to be that which fills the lack in paternal desire; especially in the cycle "Death of the Fathers" he appears as her teacher, who supports or critiques her confessional style. The figure of parental authority also appears in the guise of the therapist to whom, as in "Anne, Flee on Your Donkey," she addresses her complaint and despair about her madness, and he also appears in the guise of the lover or husband to whom she addresses her desire and anxiety about sexuality and love. Finally, in those poems where she moves from private phantasy scenarios to a reiteration of her public's image repertoire, the mythopoetic paternal figure is drawn as the king, in her book of fairy tales, or, in her late religious poetry, in the shape of God.

Anne Sexton's resilience as a poet resided in the fact that her body was not only the thematic subject of her poetry, but also its poetic medium: a self-conscious vehicle for her self-display, on a par with her words. And it is precisely because of the way she explicitly staged her presence within public space that Sexton is, in fact, quite different from the other women poets politically committed to the situation of women in the 1960s and early 1970s, including Maxine Kumin, Adrienne Rich, or Muriel Rukeyser. In a sense, her performances worked in two directions. On the one hand, to invoke Teresa de Lauretis (1984), she sought to enact the contradiction that any female self-representation, as long as it is informed by prevalent cultural expectations of femininity—indeed inscribed by these patriarchal constructions—does not coincide with the reality of female experience. In so doing Sexton's public self-representations performed the terms of the production of woman as text, as image, but by virtue of her performance they also came to exceed the constraints or inadequacy this transformation implies. Instead, her performances offered a jarring spectacle that both invited identification and defied it: as I have already quoted, they would elicit the hiss of displeasure or the delivery of a standing ovation (or both). On the other hand, her performances also staged the performative quality of gender, the parody of femininity as described by Judith Butler (1990), who argues that when a female subject assumes a particular gender position within a given cultural space, it is a performance, constituted by what must be dislocated in order for this position to hold. The female subject, she maintains, is constructed through a series of exclusions and choices. The speaking and spoken persona, is not simply situated in an identity, autonomous and original. Rather, the subject is constituted through the discursive position that she chooses in order to define herself, as well as through the family relations that determine her formation. In other words, the subject is constituted performatively; there is no easy equation between a female subject and its articulation, no transparent coincidence between the woman Anne Sexton and her self-representations, her public persona. Her truth is a foreign body inhabiting her, speaking from within but finding articulation only through externalizations that are no longer true renditions of the female condition because they are representations, even while they are only true because the act of public performance performs them as truths.

In the coda to the second edition of her biography of Anne Sexton, Diane Middlebrook (1992) suggestively argues that we could see this poet as a precursor of the generation of women performance artists that emerged in the 1980s, artists such as Laurie Anderson, Patti Smith, P. J. Harvey, or Madonna—and I would add, in the medium of visual arts, Cindy Sherman, Nan Goldin, or Orlane. In her insistence on exploring women's power within the public space through a highly contrived performance of femininity, Anne Sexton oscillates, using her body as the site in which to perform those images of femininity privileged by a particular culture, even as the self-consciousness inherent in this pose discloses the presuppositions of the implicit ideology. At the same time she illustrates, perhaps more poignantly and fatefully than the generation of performance artists that comes after her, how the act of public performance, exhilarating as it may be, also implies being subsumed by, indeed depleted by, this transformation of the woman speaking about her body into the feminine body as medium of its own self-expression. In her interview with Barbara Kevles, Anne Sexton also explains how public readings consume three weeks: "A week before it happens, the nervousness begins and it builds up to the night of the reading, when the poet in you changes into a performer. Readings take so much out of you, because they are a reliving of the experience, that is, they are happening all over again. I am an actress in my own autobiographical play." (1974, 109) In other words, in the act of performance the poet and the suicide conflate because the speaking woman transforms into an image of herself, repeating an intimate scene but at another site, at another temporal moment, no longer authentic. While Sexton always understood writing poetry as the movement through death into a new life, "Inherent in the process is a rebirth of a sense of self, each time stripping away a dead self" (1974, 86), her performances augment this dialectic by staging a willful splitting into self and representation of the self, staging the performative constitution of the female poet, insisting that her existence is *as* an actress, *on* a stage, *in* a play scripted by her life.

A seminal difference between Sexton and her performing daughters, one could argue, is that the second generation performs femininity within and in explicit reference to a cultural context informed by twenty years of feminist theories' dismantling the presuppositions underlying traditional gender constructions. To speak of self-conscious staging in the case of Anne Sexton implies something far less self-assured. Though her gestures were also calculated, controlled, and self-reflexive, they did not come from the position of one who could ironically distance herself from the discourse that constructed her, but rather from one who could only make explicit her implication within this discourse. In her gesture of making her intimacy external (without, however, being able to extract herself from its fatality) Anne Sexton, one could say, performed the constraints of the discourse within which she was formed. Yet it seems poignant that both generations of performance artists share sex, violence, mental illness, humor, and passionate spirituality as themes, as they also share their performing poetry that publicaly articulates female intimacies.

Above all, they share the fact that they make explicit the distance between the female poet, her body and voice articulating this poetry, and the poetic text itself. They quite explicitly insist that they are not making a confession but playing at confessing. One could add that their gestures are hysteric mimesis, in accordance with what Sarah Kofman (1980) has called the affirmative Woman, split between denying and affirming her construction as Woman, as a cultural text, a gendered construction. They can be seen as affirming femininity—a parody that accepts and deconstructs the feminine—because they oscillate between the gesture of incarnating a woman's truth and incarnating a deception of her truth, performing the reconciliation of incompatible attitudes toward lack and integrity, toward lying and telling the truth about one's intimacy. As Sexton articulates this affirmative duplicity, "Many of my poems are true, line by line, altering a few facts to get the story at its heart. . . . Each poem has its own truth. . . . But then poetic truth is not necessarily autobiographical. It is truth that goes beyond the immediate self, another life. I don't adhere to literal facts all the time; I make them up whenever needed." (1974, 103). In other words, what Sexton shares with her performing daughters is that she seems to be telling the audience in one and the same gesture, You think you see a woman in all her intimacy confessing to you her private desires, phantasies, and anxieties; you do, but what you also see is her performing a representation of this woman. What you are also presented with is a text of feminine intimacy, a duplicitous representation of the feminine confession, in fact a self-conscious performance of the fact that we are performatively constructed according to the stories we are taught and the stories we live by.

II

Taking a cue from Middlebrook, I would suggest that Anne Sexton's publicly staged performances of the female confession and the female complaint allow us to theorize what is a truly spectacular contradiction in Anne Sextons's biography: namely, her alternating public success and psychic disturbance. She continually renegotiated the exchange between psychic illness as a result of the postwar bourgeois feminine condition and its therapeutic rearticulation through analysis and art. It is quite significant that Anne Sexton was diagnosed as a hysteric, giving voice to her dissatisfaction with her roles as daughter and mother through this illness by representation, where physical symptoms stand in for a disorder that cannot be located in the body, where the disorder is itself performative. The production of her hysterical symptoms—be they loss of consciousness, speaking in different voices, loss of control over body functions—were themselves the only possible articulation of the psychic disturbance, but a disturbance that came to use the language of the body when it could no longer resort exclusively to symbolic language. Like the patients of Charcot, Freud, and Janet, Sexton was haunted by memories and stories she had encrypted and could not shed, texts occupying her body as though it were their host, using her body to speak their alterity. At the same time, her hysterical symptoms also complied with the definition of the hysteric subject I have been working with—namely, that there is a noncoincidence between her self-representations and the being she really is, such that she not only plays roles but also her existence resides in the performance of these roles (Mentzos, 1980). The issue for Sexton was not whether there is a true kernel of the self, which the hysteric is oblivious to or keeps hidden in the course of her public display. Rather it was that public display was the only way she could articulate her true self, albeit knowing she was giving a performance. In my discussion of the spectacular performances of such young hysterics as Augustine in Charcot's amphitheater during his Tuesday lectures or the case histories told by Freud and Breuer in their *Studies on Hysteria* (1893–95), I had emphasized that hysteric self-display always meant the public staging of an intimate trauma and intimate phantasies, a presentation of the self as "an actress in an autobiographical play" (Sexton 1974, 109). And it is here that the analogy between hysteria and Sexton's art of performance begins to unfold. Like the classic hysteric, she seems to have fallen into a sort of trance, both when she spoke during her interviews and when she performed her poetry in lecture theaters; she, too, articulated traumatic truths by having recourse to other, foreign, *extimate personas*. Sexton related, "It's a little mad, but I believe I am many people. When I am writing a poem, I feel I am the person who should have written it. Many times I assume these guises. . . . Sometimes I become someone else and when I do, I believe, even in moments when I'm not writing the poem, that I am that person" (1974, 193f.).

Sexton's public performances are compelling in the way they ask us to consider how giving voice to alterity is a gesture both sincere and contrived, how she may have shown no regard for the private (as some have accused her) by turning all intimacy into a public self-display, but how this confession was always also presented as an assumed role, a resourceful ruse. My point is not to belabor what seems obvious: that the spontaneity of confessional poetry is highly artificial, that the seemingly private is presented in an inextricably public guise, or that the seemingly autobiographical is the result of extreme artifice. As Sexton says, "I use the personal when I am applying a mask to my face" (quoted in Pollitt 1991, 21). Rather, I want to suggest that a fruitful alignment can be made between hysteria and feminine performance. For both the hysteric and the performance artist stage a scene in which the woman being spoken of is someone other than the one speaking. They negotiate the issue of private and public, of the intimate being confessed and openly exhibited, precisely because to undertake an autobiographic performance always contains a contradiction; the act of performing or of representing undermines any easy assumptions of authenticity inherent in autobiography. Put apodictically, the public performance is a hysterical gesture, even while hysteria articulates the split between a seemingly controlled, public self-representation and the disturbances underlying and subverting any fixed notion of self-representation. Thus, when we consider Middlebrook's assessment that the horizon or storyline of much of Sexton's poetry is "of course, autobiographical, focused on Sexton's attraction to death" (1985, 313) alongside Sexton's own insistence that "suicide is the opposite of the poem" (1966, 90), we are quite literally at the aporetic kernel of her stellar self-performance.

Sexton did not like to call herself a confessional poet, even though she wrote to Stanley Kunitz in 1970, "Now I say that I'm the only confessional poet. No matter how hard you work at it, your own voice shows through" (Sexton and Ames 1979, 372). She preferred to be thought of as a storyteller, and, as Middlebrook points out, she always claimed that her career as a poet had the shape of a story, which opened not with the event of writing her first poem but with "the suicide attempt that separated her from a former life" (1984, 7). In an interview with Barbara Kevles she offered a narrative of this splitting and transformation of herself: "Until I was twenty-eight I had a kind of buried self who didn't know she could do anything but make white sauce and diaper babies. I didn't know I had any creative depths. I was a victim of the American Dream, the bourgeois, middle-class dream. All I wanted was a little piece of life, to be married, to have children. I thought the nightmares, the visions, the demons would go away if there was enough love to put them down. I was trying my damnedest to lead a conventional life, for that was how I was brought up, and it was what my husband wanted of me. But one can't build little white picket fences to keep nightmares out. The surface cracked when I was about twenty-eight. I had a psychotic break and tried to kill myself" (1974, 84). The story of her transformation, however, illustrates that lurking under the surface normality were not only the psychic demons that caused this discontented daughter to suffer throughout her life from psychic disorder. Rather, her creative potential also had its roots here, so that her suicide attempt was a kind of rebirth at the age of twenty-nine, the begining of a fairy-tale-like transformation, allowing her to oscillate so productively but also so precariously between destruction and creativity.

She once wrote to a student, "Poetry led me by the hand out of madness. I am hoping I can show others that route" (Sexton and Ames 1979, 335).

If we splice the metaphor Sexton offers of a surface that cracks only to allow madness and suicidal desire to emerge, with the argument Judith Butler makes about the performative aspect of the gendered subject, we can interpret Sexton's psychotic break as an indication of the return of what had to be dislocated or excluded for the construction of the American, middle-class, bourgeois housewife to take place and to hold. Indeed, the cracking of the surface, the psychotic break, could be read as yet another metaphor for the trope established within classic medical discourse on hysteria, namely the image of the breaking away of the uterus. In the case of Anne Sexton, as the somatic initiation of disruptive dislocation, this cracking, this breaking loose, took on four performative modes. The first scene encompassed the various expressions of madness: in her case, particularly hallucinations, suicidal tendencies, a split into multiple identities, and a tendency to fall into a self-induced trance and become unresponsive. As Orne suggests, "It seemed likely that she used some of the trance episodes to play the role of dying, which perhaps helped her not to suicide" (Middlebrook 1991, xvii). In these trances, she exhibited the classic symptoms of hysteria—a chameleon-like ability to adopt any symptom, concomitant with profound dissociation and lesions of memory. The second scene was of psychoanalysis; while in a trance, Sexton would take on several personas, invent roles for herself, and create narratives about past traumas that were not representations of actual events but fictitious versions: She would speak from another place, indeed give herself over to her unconscious so completely, to the Other truth, the alterity within her psychic apparatus, that at the end of her sessions she would become entirely unconscious. Owing to this, her therapist decided to tape their sessions and asked her to transcribe them, so as to get her to recollect what had passed and what her state of dissociation had demanded she repress. The third scene was that of writing, which Sexton herself likened to a trance-like or a death-like state. Here we see the resonant analogies emerge. Her therapist had encouraged her to write poetry, arguing that in the act of creation she would discover truths about herself that were not available to her conscious self, at the same time that her poetry might help others. Yet the trance-like state, the little deaths she experienced while writing, of course, also came to hark back and mirror her psychic illness, her fascination with playing death. Then, too, in the state of writing she could repeat both the role playing that characterized her hysteria and the production of explanatory fictions and personas within her therapy sessions. The last scene was her performance of her poetic writings, whose themes were madness and a fascination with death, with taking on roles, with therapy, and writing, imitating once more her dissociation, only now using it fruitfully for her public self-display.

What we have learned from feminist scholarship on hysteria is that in most cases the hysteric's symptoms—inertia, overexcitation, role playing, and motoric, functional disorders—in fact signal a recourse to body language so as to address the stifling social situation of women, the disillusionment of youthful hopes (Smith-Rosenberg, 1985). Mapping this social issue onto the pattern of hysterical performance delineated so far, we can embellish the four modalities. Anne Sexton's hysterical disorders can be read as symptoms for all that was wrong in her culture's relation to feminine subjectivity; in fact, they perform the daughter's discontent with these constraints. Her dissociations, her chameleon-like ability to take on any illness, and her role playing can be seen as a desperate somatic parody of what was expected of the suburban housewife and mother at the time: the vacuous smile, perfect poise, and total submission to the bourgeois myth of domestic bliss, integrity, and harmony (Middlebrook 1991, 40). Her confessional poetry then came to repeat, by making completely public, this illness that for many women grew out of the restricted roles postwar, American culture offered them. The performative quality of Anne Sexton's public self-display thus put closure on the psychotic break in the shell of middle-class normalcy by working with two aspects of hysteria. For in one and the same gesture, her performance of hysteria came to serve both as a symptom of her discontent in relation to the discursive constitution of the feminine subject whose body she found herself emplaced in, and as a critical, albeit sometimes utterly self-destructive, display of this discontent.

In light of Catherine Clément's (1979) comparison between performers and hysterics, which highlights the way both share the gesture of superlative simulacrums, of pretense, of pure appearance, I find it significant that Anne Sexton should have been diagnosed as a classic hysteric. As Clément notes, both performers and hysterics reconstitute themselves daily in the spectacle of the roles they play, with life assuming the status of an intermission between performances; both move from one assumed identity to another, apparently indifferent to any psychic reality. Because each is indifferent to her pain, both hysteric and performer can incite further stagings of pain and death-like states without ultimately killing a central point of resistance in their psychic makeup. Given that Anne Sexton embodies both the hysteric and the performer, her case allows us to explore the mutual implication of these two gestures, for the biographical narrative she privileged runs along the following pattern. Initiating everything was the break through of traces of traumatic knowledge, the psychotic break with her existence as a suburban housewife, and an incursion of real psychic distress that served to disclose her previous identity as having been an illusory falsity, a lie, and a mask. In therapy, Sexton had recourse to several so-called false personas as means by which to give figure to these traumatic traces, only to discover that they were "truth crimes," "lies" she had been treating as "memories," her public self revolving so brilliantly around nothing. This hysterical performance of roles led her to fear: "I am nothing, if not an actress off the stage. In fact, it comes down to the terrible truth that there is no true part of me. . . . I suspect that I have no self so I produce a different one for different people.

I don't believe me, and I seem forced to constantly establish long fake and various personalities" (quoted in Middlebrook 1991, 62f.).

Yet the sense that she was a "total lie," which can be seen as her performative response to the lies she had been told about the intact plenitude and protection inherent in a bourgeois family—lies meant to eclipse all violence, anguish, and destruction from the privileged image of the family—found its inversion in her transforming the disempowered assumption of domestic roles and the display of a plethora of selves from the therapy setting into writing and performing her poetry. The destructive hysteria of her day-to-day existence became a constructive hysteria once she actively used these masks and lies to consciously create and perform personas: "Only in that funny trance can I believe myself, or feel my feeling," she noted about writing. "It is the split self, it seems to me, that is the mad woman. When writing you make a new reality and become whole. . . . It is like lying on the analyst's couch, reenacting a private terror, and the creative mind is the analyst who gives pattern and meaning to what the persona sees as only incoherent experience" (quoted in Middlebrook 1991, 64). Poetry and its performance made these lies, these masks, fruitful rather than pernicious, precisely by opening them to the public. "Think I am a poet? false—someone else writes—I am a person selling poetry" (quoted in Middlebrook 1991, 63). My point, then, is not that writing, selling her confessions, and transforming her sense of being an actress *off* the stage into an actress *in* her own autobiographical play allowed Sexton to achieve a satisfying wholeness. Rather, it is to emphasize the performative that structures all four of Sexton's modes— the discontented housewife, the dissociated analysand, the tranced writer, and the staged self-displayer. Each modality is a masking and unmasking of the fact that femininity is structured by the discourse in which a woman finds herself emplaced. At the same time I want to hold onto the fact that each modality of the self-lie also performs the presence, albeit as an obscene underside, of traces of traumatic knowledge, which at first are entirely repressed, then articulated obliquely in the truth-crimes in therapy, and finally made fully extimate in the tropes and phantasy scenes of her poetry, as well as in the personas of her public readings. For until the end Anne Sexton also insisted, "I'm hunting for the truth. . . . Behind everything that happens to you, every act, there is another truth, a secret life" (quoted in Ostriker 1982, 274), knowing full well that she would only have access to this encrypted, traumatic truth once she had transformed it into a representation.

The point about hysteria is, of course, that it jars; it performs contradictions such as those between confession and control, intimacy and extravagance, mental breakdown and public success, but flaunts its candor and contrivance so excessively that it appears in bad taste. I would speculate that this is precisely why people disliked Anne Sexton. By performing the disease of her culture to its utmost extreme, to its turning point, she created unease in her audience. The hysteric, thus her message, will not be contained: she not only makes public her private traumas but also performs them as contradictions. Robert Lowell's disparaging comment, "She became meager and exaggerated. Many of her most embarrassing poems would have been fascinating if someone had put them in quotes, as the presentation of some character, not the author" (1978, 71) unwittingly hits the mark. Under the auspices of her hysterical performances, her poetry was always meant to be seen in quotation marks. As Alicia Ostriker (1982) notes, her power as a poet lay precisely in her eccentricity (making external with force what is conventionally kept internal), in her insistence on emotional intimacy, on unresignedness, and in her explicit discussion of the female body against the poetic reticence and good taste traditionally valorized within the archives of modern poetry—even if this meant that she was a dazzling but not a "fine" artist.

In a sense this flaunting of contradiction goes to the heart of the matter: that the hysteric must keep open the question of identity, oscillating between various self-fashionings, celebrating and affirming each through her performances. She must remain not only alive to creation, as Diana Hume George notes, but also to the lived truth of terror, with panic always rumbling underneath joy (1987, 163). As Jacques Lacan argues in his discussion of Freud's case study on Dora (1951), the hysteric places herself in relation to a figure of paternity, sustaining his desire even as she ceaselessly questions the authority of his power. In Anne Sexton's poems the figure of father appears as both desirable and abusive, supportive and destructive, while her position before this paternal authority remains contradictory, both accepting that the question of her existence can only be articulated in relation to her interpellator and perpetually renegotiating her relation to the Other. This exchange uses phantasy scenarios to perform the question "What am I?" and, as Jacques Lacan notes in his article on a possible treatment of psychosis (1966, 549), will bathe the hysteric, support her, invade her, or tear her apart, as articulated in the various symptoms she produces. With Anne Sexton this exchange was staged in the repeated enactment of psychic disorder, in the dialogue with her therapist, in her poetry, and in her public performance of this autobiographical play. The point to remember, however, is that this resilient, creative, but also destructive, dialogue is not only addressed toward the Other but also articulates psychic alterity. The fact that Anne Sexton repeatedly staged her existence as the impossibility of deciding once and for all to be feminine or masculine, to live or die, is crucial to the enmeshment of hysteria and performance, because unwittingly she knew that all her hysterical roles revolved not around a stable self-kernel but around the nothing of a traumatic knowledge, as inevitable as it is inaccessible. In the light, then, of the autobiographical play, which she staged in public auditoriums as well as in the homes of her family and her friends, her epigraph to the collection *Live or Die*, taken from an early draft of Saul Bellow's *Herzog* ("Don't cry, you idiot! Live or die, but don't poison everything") can only be understood as the supremely ironic inversion of her insistence, "I talk of the life/death cycle of the body (1974, 109). For even as her hysterical optimism allowed her to hold onto a belief in the existence of a human condition in which death can happily be severed from life, this hope could only be the frame for poetic dialogues and scenarios insisting that the trace of mortality's infection and the poison of this traumatic knowledge is ineluctable.

Thus one must inevitably return to the issue that Anne Sexton was a poet and a suicide, that her act of performing intimacy made suicide the opposite of the poem even as the horizon of the poem remained her attraction to death. For as poetry became her business, she learned to transform both the female complaint and the critique of her cultural construction, initially performed as an illness in her body, into a stardom we might interpret as a second-degree performance of the female complaint. In the course of her career, the poetic lament given voice through writing and staging was supported by another favored narrative, as powerful as the story of the psychotic break in the shell of supposed middle-class plenitude and intactness: namely, her favorite palindrome, "Rats live on no evil star" (Kumin 1981), which she had seen on the side of an Irish barn and had wanted carved on her gravestone. In the uncollected poem, "An Obsessive Combination of Ontological Inscape, Trickery and Love" she wrote "Busy, with an idea for a code, I write / signals hurrying from left to right, / or right to left, by obscure routes, / [. . .] until, suddenly, RATS / can amazingly and funnily become STAR" (reprinted as an epigraph in Colburn 1985). In a letter to her analyst she plays with the same concept "If I write RATS and discover that rats reads STAR backwards, and amazingly STAR is wonderful and good because I found it in rats, then is star untrue? . . . I don't really believe the poem, but the name is surely mine so I must belong to the poem. So I must be real. . . . When you say "words mean nothing" then it means that the real me is nothing. All I am is the trick of words writing themselves" (quoted in Middlebrook 1991, 82).

This palindrome brilliantly summarizes her sense that she existed precisely as the psychic staging of an incessant and resilient exchange between her sick self, riddled by the traumatic impressions of the past and possessed by the unhappiness of her family legacy, and its transformation into a splendid, publicly successful, and fortunate poetic self-construction. The entire trajectory of her poetic career is structured by a recurrent pattern, in which her public success was never more than the precarious inversion of her psychic disorder. In the poem "Rowing," Sexton invokes a "gnawing pestilential rat inside me" which she feels she must get rid of, offering a trope for what she wishes to cast off (for that intimate alterity Jacques Lacan calls extimacy, for the foreign body of archaic, destructive jouissance), which she was initially able to contain by translating it into various hysteric symptoms, but which ultimately broke the shell in the form of suicidal wishes. Through the experience of therapy cum poetry writing she fashioned herself into a multifarious persona called Anne, hysterically oscillating between an unbearable but true alterity and the bearable versions of her self she could live

with, negotiating her constant performative recasting of the self and its obscene underside—the knowledge that "the real me is nothing." In other
words, her career could only be staged amidst her proclivity for self-destruction, without ever eradicating the transgression inherent in successful public
self-display. The omphallic center of her career's narrative that began with
her suicide, tracing a trajectory from mad housewife through analysand to
public star only to end once more in suicide, is marked by the equally persistent reemergence of the rat—the horrifying, enticing foreign body of traumatic truth broadcasting that implenitude and fallibility are unavoidable
and somatically voicing this message in her psychotic breaks, trances, hallucinations, anger, or physical incapacitation. The star coming out of, implicated by but also transforming, the rat is merely the hysteric's most successful and satisfying protective fiction. Thus Sexton confidently writes in her
poem "The Black Art," "My friend, my friend, I was born / Doing reference
work in sin, and born / Confessing it. This is what poems are: / With mercy /
For the greedy, / They are the tongue's wrangle / The world's pottage, the
rat's star." However, the point of Lacan's notion of extimacy—so perfected
in the hysteric's performance—is that one can only oscillate between the rat
and the star, and use the rat's dislocation (hysteria's wandering uterus) to
produce stellar reversions of the self, but never truly sever the two.

   To illustrate how Anne Sexton's hysterical performances of the self used
the act of confession to transform private, intimate disturbances into a public broadcast of her discontent, I will focus on two collections of poetry. In
a first step I will discuss her reiteration of the collective image repertoire of
domestic fairy tales, in which the traditional family romance is rewritten to
disclose the paternal violence inherent in kinship structures. In a second step
I will present the far more explicitly autobiographical early collections, *To
Bedlam and Part Way Back* and *All My Pretty Ones*, in which Sexton rewrites her biographical family romance so as to disclose how the dead haunt
any self-fashioning of the daughter.

III

Paul Brooks at Houghton Mifflin had initially entertained some doubts
about publishing the seventeen Grimm fairy tales Anne Sexton had gathered
together under the title *Transformations*. Their raucous humor, seemingly
so untypical of her style, made him feel ill at ease. In a letter addressing his
misgivings, however, Sexton insists on a continuity in poetic voice: "I realize
that the 'Transformations' are a departure from my usual style. I would say
that they lack the intensity and perhaps some of the confessional force of my
previous work. I wrote them because . . . it made me happy. . . . I would like
my readers to see this side of me, and it is not in every case the lighter side.
Some of the poems are grim. In fact I don't know how to typify them except
to agree that I have made them very contemporary. It would further be a lie

to say they weren't about me, because they are just as much about me as my other poetry" (Sexton and Ames 1979, 362). Anne Sexton's sense that a complaint lodged against the family could well be couched in the language of fairy tales proved astute, for she sold more copies of the hard-cover edition of *Transformations* than of any other volume of poetry. The collection is dedicated to her daughter Linda, "who reads Hesse and drinks clam chowder" (Sexton 1981, 221); because she continually talked about the stories she found in her torn blue volume of Grimm *Fairy Tales*, her mother decided to read this archive of traditional family romances against the grain. This hysterical reiteration, however, aims at interrogating the gender roles these familiar stories proclaim so as to uncover the toxic side effects of the happy end in marriage—the constraint and renunciation inherent in heterosexual couple formations, as well as the paternal violence inherent in the law of bourgeois family alliances. In an interview with Al Poulin for *American Poets* she explained, "Sometimes my daughter would suggest 'read this or that, try this one' or something, . . . and if I got, as I was reading it, some unconscious message that I had something to say, what I had fun with were the prefatory things, I mean that's where I got my great kicks, where I expressed whatever it evoked in me—and it had to evoke something in me or I couldn't do it" (Colburn 1985, 145).

Certainly the most compelling voice in these transformations is the speaker, who presents herself in the first poem, "The Golden Key" (223–4), as "a middle-aged witch" and asks her seven listeners to remember the stories they were told in their childhood. As she revisits the familiar fairy tales, she is accompanied by a seven-year-old boy ("each of us") who has found a golden key, one could say a deconstructive tool, which empowers the curious, critical reader to interrogate the archive of cultural texts that which have been instrumental in her or his discursive formation. The rhetorical stance that the bewitching speaker Anne assumes from the start thus mirrors the thematic argument of the stories she is about to tell. For if each fairy tale in some sense revolves around the change from misfortune to luck—from vulnerablity to strength and infallibility, loss to gain, distress to happiness— her hysterical mimicry of these familiar tales serves to dismantle the presuppositions within this treasure of western mythopoetics by offering agency to the feminine voice framing each poem, even while on the content level the tales this witch tells revolve around feminine submission and confinement. The golden key of her hysterical revision not only resuscitates these old stories that haunt us like phantoms, therefore, but it also dislocates them from their fixed position in our remembered image repertoire, making them wander hysterically. Uncovering clandestine meanings we have chosen to disregard, the witch Anne demonstrates that the essential truths these tales proclaim about kinship alliances are actually necessary cultural constructions. Uncannily differing with our memory of these stories, the witch Anne lets us discover that the harmony of marital happiness is always marred, that the lover can often be a murderer, and that children are not innocent of destructive enjoyment (far from being able to disclaim their parental legacy, namely, their congenital psychic and physical stains, they can merely repeat the transgressions inherent in the family structure).

In these transformations, Anne's complaint, then, is launched against a traditional understanding of the bourgeois family, which, according to Michel Foucault, restricts the deployment of bodily pleasures and the vicissitudes of sexuality, making the exclusion of all that diverges from the norm (that is in excess of) its founding principle. In the course of this delimitation the female body is reduced to a stake within the paternal system of exchange, meant to secure the succession of one generation to the next, to sustain the bourgeois family and irrevocably inscribe the difference between femininity and masculinity. But Sexton's complaint is ultimately launched at the fact that, in the course of a sexualization of kinship alliances that came to inform the bourgeois family at the end of the eighteenth century, incest emerges as the clandestine, resiliently upheld, transgressive core of this system of exchange. As Foucault notes, it transpired into "an object of obsession and attraction, a dreadful secret and an indispensable pivot. It is manifested as a thing that is strictly forbidden in the family insofar as the latter functions as a deployment of alliance; but it is also a thing that is continuously demanded in order for the family to be a hotbed of constant sexual incitement" (1976, 109). Thus Sexton's hysterical mimicry does not merely reenact traditional fairy stories in contemporary guises. Rather, her interrogative rearticulation illustrates that these stories can be used as symptoms, both broadcasting in an oblique language her discontent with the cultural image repertoire she has inherited and transmitting a confession of her discontent with her position as daughter (and calling on her readers to follow her in this dissent). The protagonists of these family romances seek to liberate themselves from given family constraints, to be reborn into a more satisfying family bond. Yet as each tale closes, we are forced to recognize that the repetition of family secrets is inevitable, that the traces of traumatic knowledge are inextinguishable, and that above all the condition of constraint is inescapable. To the extent that the hysteric witch Anne sustains the public law of paternal authority by offering the happy end required by the fairy tale genre, her framing comments belaugh and belie any easy reliance on the plenitude and infalliblity of marriage. Instead, using the voice of black humor, she broadcasts a confession and complaint, insisting that complete happiness is a protective fiction—desirable but unattainable because horrific psychic woundings lie just beneath the surface of any such configuration, waiting to break open the happy shell. Read against the grain, these mythopoetic narratives not only offer public stories of cultural constraint and familial restrictions but also transform only too readily into tales about private trauma. Along the lines of Sexton's favorite palindrome, the hysterical mimicry performed by the witch Anne resuscitates the dead texts of the past only to call our attention to the rats that lurk in the intimate kernel of fairy-tale fortune.

For example, "Anne" recasts the narrative of "Twelve Dancing Princesses" (276–281), to dismantle the harmony supposedly contained in the romantic, happy ending. Marriage emerges as an initiation ritual that curtails any unrestrained enjoyment of bodily pleasures, that forbids nocturnal excesses. She begins her narrative frame with the question, "If you danced from midnight / to six A.M. who would understand," comparing the ecstatic brides of the tale to a runaway boy, a clandestine adulteress, the passengers on a nocturnal flight, the amnesiac, the drunken poet, the insomniac, and the night nurse. Their activity must be controlled if the diurnal economy of reasonable order, which the king's authority represents, is to be preserved and secured against its inherent nocturnal transgressions. For the message this fairy tale proclaims is that in order to become adult women, the princesses must be deprived of the dancing shoes that came to signify their disobedience, or their escape from the bedchamber, whose door the king had locked and bolted: "The princesses were torn from / their night life like a baby from a pacifier." Recuperated into the behavioral codes of the bourgeois family, they can only elegiacally mourn this prior freedom, the lost intensification of the body that exceeds the confines of paternal law. At the wedding of the eldest sister they seem utterly depleted: "Now the runaways would run no more and never / again would their hair be tangled into diamonds, / never again their shoes worn down to a laugh, / never the bed falling down into purgatory / to let them climb in after / with their Lucifer kicking."

Whereas in this interrogation of the bourgeois marriage solution the poetic persona "Anne" sympathizes with the castrated princesses, in "Snow White and the Seven Dwarfs" (224–229) she aims to critique the figure of the complicitous bride. The heroine who is usually thought of as a paragon of femininity, emerges as a dumb puppet without a will of her own, representing nothing but a patchwork of existing cliches about beauty: "The virgin is a lovely number." Indeed, she is as indifferent to her mother's command as she is to her husband's desire, mechanically opening her eyes "to say; / Good Day Mama," and shutting them again, "for the thrust / of the unicorn." But the issue of automatization thus brought into play does not only refer to the fact that all stories inevitably circulate the same stereotypes of marital discontent while portraying the good, unsoiled, white bride protecting herself against the murderous jealousy of a stepmother so as to procure a successful passage from one generation to the next while still supporting paternal authority. Equally inevitable, the daughter, complying with the beauty myth of her cultural code, learns to imitate the queen's narcissistic love of her own beauty, which is fatal because it can tolerate no rivals but repeats the murderous impulse of this transgressive stepmother. Thus, although the wicked queen is punished for vanity—"Beauty is a simple passion"—she is, in fact, replaced by a stepdaughter who repeats the faults of her predecessor: "Meanwhile Snow White held court, / rolling her china-blue doll eyes open and shut / and sometimes referring to her mirror / as women do." For what guarantee do we have that if, when the wicked queen looked in the mirror, "Pride pumped in her like poison," this infection has not been transmitted to Snow White along with her new role as queen?

A similar dismantling gesture is performed by the laughing witch Anne in "The White Snake" (229–232). Here the sadistic bride is fully sanctioned as a representative of the bourgeois marriage code: "The local princess was having a contest. / A common way for princesses to marry. / Fifty men had perished, / gargling the sea like soup." Only the servant who has eaten of the white snake and, in the language of hysteria, now hallucinates clandestine messages ("he heard the animals / in all their voices speak. / Thus the aura came over him. / He was inside") can successfully enter into her desire. Yet once he returns with the apple of life, explaining "Here is what you hunger for," only to discover that their bodies can also meet "over such a dish / His tongue lay in her mouth / as delicately as the white snake," we begin to suspect that the princess desires in the marriage bond not a romantic partner but rather a pledge—the apple of life—to prove that her lover has engaged with her destructive enjoyment, entered into a competition pitting life against death. And if marriage can only be born of the proclamation and enforcement of this murderous law, its resolution also is not free of the traces of destruction. For if eating of the white snake allowed the groom to enter into a hallucination and decode voices of alterity, consuming the marriage bond enacts the entrance into a state where all voices of difference are dramatically erased: "They were placed in a box [. . .] and thus passed their days / living happily ever after— / A kind of coffin, / a kind of blue funk. / Is it not?"

Against such interrogations of the viability of the heterosexual couple, the witch Anne pits stories about love alliances that fall outside the kinship structures privileged by bourgeois culture, such as her transformation of the fairy tale "Rapunzel" (244–249). Rather than praising the marriage between the prince and Rapunzel, consummated only after long suffering, she nostalgically commemorates the love between two women, which occurs prior to heterosexual love and must be relinquished in its favor: "A woman / who loves a woman / is forever young." Because this kind of love can only be sustained as a hermetically sealed-off dyad, at the expense of excluding men, the fairy tale prescribes that the girl must learn to surmount this love and accept difference rather than sameness in her love object. She will live happily provided that the "mother-me-do" she played with the older woman "can be outgrown," for "The world, some say, / is made up of couples. / A rose must have a stem." Yet the hysteric witch Anne counters this traditional message by offering a series of images praising the nourishing tenderness acted out in homoerotic love, where, in the course of playing "mother-me-do" the younger girl is introduced to the language of sexuality and discovers the intensity of her own desires by touching an older copy of herself. At the same time this awakening is mutual, for the older woman is revivified by the touch of the young girl, remaining forever young herself by virtue of this pleasurable game. This exchange, however, must remain clandestine, a carefully kept secret, and mother Gothel admonishes Rapunzel, "Do not discover us." In contrast to "Anne's" heterosexual brides, who all appear to be paralyzed dolls eternally fixed into a prescribed position, or melancholic creatures whose living power has been spent, this love bond enacts a dynamic exchange, and significantly, it is the only scene of erotic enjoyment rendered in poetic detail: "They touch their delicate watches / one at a time. / They dance to the lute / two at a time. / They are as tender as bog moss. / They play mother-me-do / all day."

Yet the logic of fairy tales forbids a love where it is the older woman and not the father who locks the daughter in "to keep the boys away," where the maternal body is enjoyed with impunity because the father, who could invoke guilt, is entirely absent. For if, at the outset of the tale, the father is willing to exchange his daughter for the rampions growing in Mother Gothel's garden, because his wife believes she will die if she does not partake of this food, the daughter not only guarantees the survival of her natural mother but also comes to represent the rebirth of her surrogate mother, who gives her the name "Rapunzel, / another name for the life-giving rampion." From the start this exchange was marked by a threat of death to the maternal body, which could only be mitigated by losing the daughter, so that once Mother Gothel takes on the maternal position, she is forced to also imitate and pass on the beloved surrogate daughter to a son, thus assuring generational succession. In her revision, however, "Anne" radically differs with the traditional fairy tale solution; her poem does not end with the expected image of the happy bourgeois couple's proving that mother-me-do can be outgrown, at least by the daughter. Rather, her last lines sing of the distress of the abandoned Mother Gothel. True to the gesture of ambivalence in her notion of transformation, "Anne" depicts the depleted mother as victim of the marriage bond: "As for Mother Gothel, her heart shrank to the size of a pin / Never again to say: Hold me, my young dear." Still, the very last image of the poem pays tribute to the older woman's phantasy, sustained by this irrevocable loss and by her uncompromising love, which, in defiance of paternal law, refuses to be overcome. For in the act of imaginative recuperation, Mother Gothel is able to reinvoke her lost happiness, and in these short moments, as mourning crosses with hope, she effects her own resuscitation: "Only as she dreamt of the yellow hair / did moonlight sift into her mouth."

The most radical, but also most personal, reformulation of the familiar fairy tale stands at the end of *Transformations*. In the prologue to her poem "Briar Rose" (290–295) "Anne" explicitly offers a representation of the hysteric sustaining the desire of the father who also abuses her; of the girl falling into a trance and, in the course of her hallucination, using her body to articulate the foreign voices dictated to her by her unconscious; of the girl "stuck in the time machine" who conjures up images of the past during both her hysterical dissociation and her therapy and performs different roles until she finally alights on what she has encoded as her primal phantasy scene of trauma, the seduction of the father. However, given that in this liminal region between consciousness and unconsciousness, between past and present, her heroine is depicted as someone "speaking with the gift of tongues," Anne Sexton from the start also self-consciously addresses her own role as poet. For it is equally true of the author of these transformations that she performs different roles, having become the medium of other voices and other stories, and she lingers between past and present, crossing psychic discontent with poetic gift.

In contrast to the other poems, the revised summary of the actual Grimm fairy tale takes up less than half of the text, and supporting the associations raised in the prologue, "Anne's" retelling revolves around the bond between father and daughter. Because at her christening Briar Rose is endowed with the curse of premature death, the king contrives a complicated array of protective measures, which, however, prove to be tantamount to total appropriation of her being: "Each night the king / bit the hem of her gown / to keep her safe. / He fastened the moon up / with a safety pin / to give her perpetual light / He forced every male in the court / to scour his tongue with Bab-o / lest they poison the air she dwelt in. / Thus she dwelt in his odor. / rank as honeysuckle." Nevertheless, or perhaps because the paternal care stifles her, she pricks her finger "on a charred spining wheel" on her fifteenth birthday, and the entire court falls into a trance, "stuck in the time machine," until a prince, finding the tableau intact, kisses Briar Rose. And uncannily, or perhaps cannily, once the girl is resuscitated, she believes to recognize the father in the figure of her saviour: "She woke up crying. / Daddy! Daddy! / Presto! she's out of prison!" The marital happiness that ensues is not merely inscribed by this misrecognition, but also profoundly marred owing to her fear of sleep. For even while the Prince's kiss undoes the wicked fairy's curse, it cannot liberate Briar Rose from the anxiety-inducing knowledge of her vulnerability, which she associates with falling into any trancelike state. Though she can only articulate this anxiety obliquely, it revolves around the fear that in a state of dissociation she is completely at the disposal of the gaze and touch of her spectator.

"Anne" thus self-consciously transforms the story of Briar Rose into a cipher for the hysteric haunted by psychic demons, commanding herself, "I must not sleep / for while asleep I'm ninety / and think I'm dying." She is compared to the patient of a psychiatric clinic, so heavily drugged with medication that she appears to be a living dead: "I'm all shot up with Novocain. / This trance girl / is yours to do with. / You could lay her in a grave, / an awful package, and shovel dirt on her face / and she'd never call back: Hello there!" She is compared to the hysteric, hypnotized for use as a demonstration by her physician, with Sexton implicitly referring to Charcot's Tuesday lectures, when his collaborators would stick needles into anesthetized body parts of the patients to demonstrate that hysterical symptoms were pure simulations: "You can stick a needle / through my kneecap and I won't flinch." But Briar Rose also turns into a cipher for the fact that waking

up from the sleep of psychic oblivion may be more painful than anesthetiza-
tion and that psychosomatic disorder may be a satisfying protection against
the far more distressing acknowledgment of traumatic knowledge. After the
Prince has revitalized her with a kiss, she incessantly replays the same phantasy scenario, in which the vulnerability from her one-hundred-year slumber
conflates with another scene of helplessness. Her hysterical physical incapacitation thus can be decoded as symptomizing the scene of paternal incest:
"Daddy? / That's another kind of prison. / It's not the prince at all, / but my
father / drunkenly bent over my bed / circling the abyss like a shark, / my
father thick upon me / like some sleeping jellyfish."

In her interrogation of this familiar tale, the witch Anne thus reveals that
within the paternal code of kinship the prince inevitably emerges as a repetition of the father, the two positions being mutually exchangeable. Moreover, in the course of her poetic transformation the paternal figure of authority proves to be exchangeable with the obscene father, who really enjoys
his daughter. Briar Rose's trancelike immobility and dissociation are decoded as the psychosomatic representation of this sexualized scene of violence inherent in the structure of the bourgeois family. Against the traditional happy ending, "Anne" broadcasts that waking up into marriage may
prove to be a liberation from one form of imprisonment, namely, the father-
daughter incest, but it can never efface the daughter's anxiety. On the contrary, to wake up from the protection that her hysteric dissociation, imitating a living death, affords, inaugurates the return of her repressed traumatic
knowledge. The "coming out of prison" called forth by marriage, which is
significantly called a "life after death," provokes a new symptom, her insomnia. The horrific memory traces of prior traumatic impressions revolving around paternal violence and a psychosomatic enactment of living death
cannot be erased. Inherent in the process of transformation, they merely
keep returning in ever new shapes.

While Anne Sexton was negotiating with her editor at Houghton Mifflin,
hoping to appease his reservations about her fairy tale revisions, she wrote
to Kurt Vonnegut, asking for a supportive text: "I feel my transformations
need an introduction telling of the value of my (one could say) rape of them.
Maybe that's an incorrect phrase. I do something very modern to them. . . .
They are small, funny, and horrifying. Without quite meaning to I have
joined the black humorists. I don't know if you know my other work, but
humor was never a very prominent feature . . . terror, deformity, madness
and torture were my bag. But this little universe of Grimm is not that far
away. I think they end up being as wholly personal as my most intimate
poems, in a different language, a different rhythm, but coming strangely, for
all their story sound, from as deep a place" (Sexton and Ames 1979, 367).
She thus unremittingly stays true to her version of confessional poetry, in
which the professional show woman Anne Sexton, offering a public performance of intimate confessions that require the gesture of poetic transformation to recover submerged truths, intersects with the witch "Anne," who,

entrusted with familiar culture knowledge, preserves the heritage by rewriting it. Yet she also remains true to the ambivalence inherent in the gesture of transformation, crossing destruction with creativity, humor with horror, for the "dark, dark laughter" of these transformations merges the plenitude of protective fiction with the threat of nightmare visions. In the image of Briar Rose, waking up to find not the Prince but rather the incestuous father towering above her, we find not only the princess hysterically knotted together with the narrator of the tale, but also the witch persona with the poet Anne Sexton. With horror we realize that this is not just a dismemberment of a remembered childhood fairy tale, but rather also Anne Sexton's autobiographical recollection of earlier traumatic impressions, reawakened in the course of revisiting this familiar tale. And like her, we are hysterically caught in this double gesture, which allows familiar but seemingly forgotten knowledge to reappear so uncannily in our own phantasy scene, only to awaken us from our trance, forcing us to acknowledge that behind the protective phantasies of familiar fairy tales' fortunes lurks traumatic knowledge.

IV

In a sense all of Anne Sexton's poetry is driven by a desire to tear open again the seams meant to heal narcissistic wounds, not to simply accept psychic scars. Accordingly she chose as a motto for her first collection of poems a passage from a letter Schopenhauer wrote to Goethe in 1815: "It is the courage to make a clean breast of it in the face of every question that makes the philosopher. He must be like Sophocles's Oedipus, who, seeking enlightenment concerning his terrible fate, pursues his indefatigable enquiry, even when he divines that appalling horror awaits him in the answer. But most of us carry in our heart the Jocasta who begs Oedipus for God's sake not to inquire further." Starting with *To Bedlam and Part Way Back* Sexton repeatedly explores the question of whether one should uncover clandestine parental knowledge whose secrecy remains a precondition of the bourgeois family or whether an unmitigated exhibition of the violence and the transgression inherent in the cherished notions of an intact home represents an untenable offense against the decorum and loyalty one owes one's ancestors. Indeed, given that she places her writing from the very start under the aegis of the story of Oedipus, Sexton implies that the painful and tormenting question of one's heritage was one of the most compelling inspirations for her own poetic project. Much like Freud in his discussion of a phylogenetic endowment of phantasy (see chapter 3), she seems to appropriate from Sophocles' narrative the realization that the most resilient phantasies of our cultural image repertoire ultimately revolve around primal scenes of traumatically disempowering knowledge, whose truth is as inevitable as it is inaccessible. And as in Freud's work, which Sexton knew owing to her own psychoanalysis, the three originary phantasy scenes—interrogating the family legacy to discover one's individual fate, interrogating the imposition of castration to discover one's gender designation, and interogating the workings of seduction to discover one's sexuality—emerge as the seminal scenarios to which the persona "Anne" has recourse in her effort at solving the questions left unanswered by her parents. Scenes of phantasy, as I have been arguing, revolve around the question of birth, inauguration, and parturition; at stake, one could say, are three questions: Who am I in relation to my heritage? From where does the anatomy of my body originate? What are the initial motivations for my urges, my desires, my imaginations? Thus, even while all phantasy work is the deferred expression of a belated gaze, it refers to originary and originating scenes. What Sophocles' tragedy of Oedipus taught psychoanalysis, as well as those writing in its wake, is that the solution to these originary phantasies is staged as a scenario that revisits the beginning of the subjects' story. Yet this performance always also contains a countermovement; although the origin of phantasy emerges as a phantasy of origin, the subject posing the questions receives the longed-for answer only in the course of temporal dislocation, in the figure of the hystérikè, as a belated and intermittent message.

As I discussed in the introduction, Sophocles' enactment of his protagonist's phantasy of origin has Oedipus asking the messenger to tell him who his father and mother were without considering the costs of this knowledge. In her first collections of poetry Anne Sexton stages a similar dialogue, only she addresses an invisible messenger—be this a therapist, teacher, friend, family member, or an imagined reader. In her phantasies of origin, Sexton in turn, poses the questions, What is my relation to my parents? How can I take possession of my familial inheritance? How can I put the terrible legacy I have been endowed with to poetic use? In her poem "Old Dwarf Heart" (1981, 54–55) she calls the anatomic sign representing this ineffaceable trace of her parental legacy an "old ornament, old naked fist . . . mother, father, I'm made of." It is a physical wound that accompanies her everywhere ("Where I go, she goes"), harboring a treasure of knowledge about psychic anguish ("Good God, the things she knows! / And worse, the sores she holds"), which cannot be hidden ("Even if I put on seventy coats I could not cover you") and whose function is to broadcast to her a reminder of mutability in the very midst of experiences of plenitude, intactness, and romantic happiness: "When I lie down to love, / old dwarf heart shakes her head. / Like an imbecile she was born old. / Her eyes wobble as thirty-one thick folds / of skin open to glare at me on my flickering bed. / She knows the decay we're made of." Functioning as the somatic sign of an ineluctable legacy, knotting together the vicissitudes of body anatomy with the fate of the family genus, this old dwarf's heart, I suggest, is a metaphor for the navel, the knotted scar on the human body, commemorating the cut of the umbilical cord and the gift of mortal existence.

This knotting together of creation and destruction, of parturition and murder, both in Anne Sexton's biography and poetic confessions, is compelling because—beginning with the appearance of her first collection of poems through to her suicide fourteen years later—personal unhappiness remained inherent to her professional success. In the same month in which *To Bedlam and Part Way Back* appeared, Anne Sexton's father-in-law died in a car accident. Her mother had already died of cancer at Eastertime the year before and her father, three months after his wife. Sexton learned to pit a poetic reenactment against her sense of overwhelming despair in the face of so many losses. After the death of her mother she confessed in a letter to W. D. Snodgrass, "This letter is disjointed. I am slugged with tranquilizers today. My mother died last night. I have just returned from the undertaker's and viewing the body and picking out the gaudiest baroque (but cheapest) casket. And will leave here in a minute, with my sister to go down to Gloucester and pick up some pieces. De, I am going to lose myself—or else, the chance is that poetry will save me" (Sexton and Ames 1979, 66). After her father's funeral she formulated a similar association between death and art, writing to Snodgrass, "So now he is funeraled, cremated, and I have no parents left to run away to Calif. from. Some misty God has shoved me up the ladder and I am my own inheritor. . . . I am going to try and NOT write a poem about it. God damn morbid life I've been leading, that's all I can say. How can I write anything positive? My old gods are tumbled over like bowling pins. All is an emotional chaos. Poetry and poetry alone has saved my life" (1979, 81). She drew strength in her poetry from the loss of these familiar faces against which she could hurl her emotions, as well as from the guilt that overcame her because she was surrounded by the dead—"I seem to specialize in dead people. Guilt. Guilt etc." (1979, 115). In addition she learned to think of herself both as an heiress accepting a designated position within a particular family history and as a legator bequeathing her own legacy, cultivating the memory of her inherited knowledge and passing on her commemorative exhibition of family secrets.

But given that in her function as poet this daughter decided to write under the sign of Oedipus, the debt toward her parents came to consist less in erecting a protective family fiction, which would serve to resurrect the deceased in an idealized form. Rather, the debt this Oedipal daughter sought to pay off consisted of inquiring into the misfortune, abuse, and transgression inherent in the structure of her family. For Anne Sexton to become her own inheritor meant settling a plethora of psychic scores: not merely discharging herself of the death of her parents or simply working through the many psychic killings they had inflicted on her, but also confronting her own desire for death. As was so often the case in her life, any metaphoric scripting of the self as poet became strangely enmeshed with actual contingencies; after the opening of her father's will Anne Sexton and her sisters discovered that in order to maintain his extravagant life style Ralph Harvey had sold all his shares in the company. Anne's husband, Kajo, who had been working for his father-in-law for many years, was able to remain with the firm as director and traveling salesman, but the wealth the daughters had hoped to inherit was irrevocably lost. From her parents' belongings, Anne chose her mother's writing desk, her comprehensive library, her fur coat, and a ruby-and-diamond ring set in platinum, which she had fitted and then never took off. The more significant inheritance, however, consisted not in these material goods, but rather in the memories and associations, the unanswered questions, and the unhealed psychic wounds—to the poet daughter, an inexhaustible estate.

One should not overlook, however, that the poetic subject "Anne" not only fashioned herself in the image of Oedipus, who had been willing to face the most horrific truths about his origins and ready to take on the most traumatic knowledge. Rather, she was equally willing to recognize the validity, indeed the nobility, of Jocasta's choice: "But most of us carry in our heart the Jocasta who begs Oedipus for God's sake not to inquire further." (1981, 2). Jocasta in fact has a double function in Sophocles' *Oedipus Rex* (see the introduction). Initially she admonishes her husband to stop interrogating the messenger, hoping that the terrible family secret might remain unexposed so that the illusory stability of her marriage might be preserved, regardless of how precarious this bond actually is. But even before the messenger relays to Oedipus the truth about his origins, she turns away from her husband, returns to her bedchamber, and there hangs herself. By this act of suicide she courageously acknowledges her own guilt—at the precise moment when disclosure becomes inevitable of the traumatic knowledge she has clandestinely encrypted (without knowing its full import). Giving herself to death emerges as an act through which she finally takes full possession of the family inheritance that her silence has sought to avert, and in taking this possession she confronts the traumatic knowledge directly, suspending all symbolic or imaginary mediation.

Oedipus's initial response to the messenger's tale about his origins, as I have already argued, is not remorse but rather aggression. With his sword in hand he penetrates Jocasta's bedchamber, seeking to destroy the bodily site of his origin that also bore his children, so as to dispossess himself of the inherited guilt he has just been forced to confront. Only the sight of the corpse of the woman who was both his mother and his wife forces him to assume, at his own body, the responsibility for his fatal legacy. If, as I have speculated, he blinds himself in lieu of committing matricide, only this blindness leads to the necessary but traumatic insight that to accept the "mother, father I'm made of" inevitably also requires an acknowledgment of his own fallibility and vulnerability. Anyone embarking on an inquiry into the question of origins, descent, and transmission proves to be irrevocably caught in this circularity.

By placing her poetry under the aegis of the Oedipus story, Sexton thus also engages the position represented by Jocasta, for it was only the death of her parents, both literally and figuratively, that forced her to embark on her inquiry into the estate of family secrets. This double legacy meant shifting back and forth between an unrelenting interrogation of the traumatic truth screened over by her family romance and a clandestine acceptance of its forbidden, threatening knowledge. In either case, the vanishing point for this incessant oscillation was the gift of death. The message Sexton seems to have learned from Schopenhauer's reading of Sophocles is that to continue interrogating one's origins, to refuse to submit to the facticity of fate means giving death to the site of one's birth; mythopoetically rendered as murdering the field of progeneration. On the other hand to accept the sobering insight that the circumstances of one's birth are irrevocable ultimately leads to the act of giving death to oneself: rather than figuratively killing off one's site of origin, that is, literally returning to one's ancestors. For more than a decade Anne Sexton was able to live under the sign of Oedipus, repeatedly giving in to the urge to commit suicide, which she had come to encode as a maternal force, only at the last instant to keep this taste for self-expenditure at abeyance. With the help of therapy and poetry, her attacks of depression and hysteric hallucinations (which might be seen in analogy to Oedipus's mad act of self-blinding) ultimately led her to reconstruct the desired phantasies about her origin and her estate.

Indeed, the question of psychic inheritance, of "mother, father I'm made of," emerges as the thematic navel of Anne Sexton's first collections of poetry. In the course of her hysterical refusal to stop interrogating the inherited phantasies of origin her parents bestowed on her, exploring the traumatic knowledge encrypted within her psychic apparatus proved a viable alternative to the desire to fully enjoy this traumatic kernel by giving death to herself. Having embarked on this painful but edifying journey into a disclosure of family secrets, the daughter learned to accept the destiny of her body, its implenitude and mutability, as well as her psyche—the mental instability originating from or having been called forth by her parents. For "Anne," conducting her interrogation under the sign of Oedipus, to assume responsibility for this double inheritance, to enter into the symbolic mandate bestowed upon the daughter, meant launching a complaint at times about the way this parental legacy also functioned as a curtailment. For in seeking the origin of her desire, Sexton not only depicts her own fallibility but also illustrates how inadequate are the roles offered by conventional notions of the postwar bourgeois American family. To insist on a lack in the self, on something missing in the family, became coterminous with pointing out how her own desire was more: in excess of the culturally privileged roles of daughter, wife, mother, and author. In this surplus, however, the gesture of outmatching also threatened to tip over into its opposite. The uncanny inversion of having a surplus of desire, exceeding the mark of what is allowed, proves to be the psychic state of experiencing no desire. To be more than the role prescribed to the dutiful bourgeois daughter could, under certain circumstances, transform into being no one. In the semantic opposition between her kitchen, the hearth of the suburban home, whose restrictions she so fully and traumatically broke open after her first psychotic attack, and the insane asylum, whose shelter she would seek throughout her life—the privileged spatial dichotomy structuring her first collections of poems—the postwar American bourgeois family had become wholly uncanny.

If one understands Sexton's poetry as the confession of her family legacy, as a lament on the transgressions committed by her parents but also a complaint launched against the abuses and constraints conducted in the name of paternal authority and subtending its law, the fact that she was diagnosed as a hysteric by the physicians treating her harbors yet further resonance. For, as I argued in my interpretation of Freud's and Breuer's *Studies on Hysteria*, the hysteric proves to be the daughter who is more than daughter, who supports the desire of the father to excess, even while she radically interrogates his authority. In this fundamentally ambivalent gesture, the hysteric revolts against the father, questioning the image of daughter and wife his authority dictates, dismantling his truths as necessary but inconsistent constructions. Transgressing his prohibitions, she also seeks to save the father as support of her symbolic universe, even though she has recognized his fallibility and implenitude. For this reason I have insisted on the importance of the fact that, in the case histories Freud and Breuer presented, hysteric attacks should so often occur while the daughter watches over her dying father. For it is at such moments that the ambivalent attitude the hysteric harbors toward the paternal authority the father stands in for—the intactness of the family—is actually materialized. His demise not only forces the daughter to confront her own helplessness in the face of death but also the tear in the family structure, which was always present though often successfully screened by the protective fictions of home romances. Yet in the gap that opens up, as the hysteric is called on to recognize that the father is a mortal and fallible person, which is incompatible with a figure of paternal authority expected to guarantee the permanence and harmony of her social world, a desire for another interpellator surfaces. If, then, by virtue of dying, this desired agent of paternal interpellation fails, the hysteric finds herself compelled to resurrect the desired master at her own body. Having been taken into possession by the father who is missing, she broadcasts obliquely the traumatic message about the gap in the family, its inevitable perishability. Producing hysterical symptoms proves to be her only viable mode of articulating her discontent, yet she does so in a discourse that uses the language of the body precisely—because paternal language has failed. And if Freud ultimately came to call hysteria a malady of reminiscences, in which the subject is haunted by memory traces of traumatic events whose affect has not been sufficiently abreacted, Anne Sexton performs this limen between the living and the dead, between the actuality of the presence and an equally real phantomatic past, by sustaining her dialogue with the deceased as well as feeding her own urge toward death.

However (as I argued in my discussion of Freud), a further characteristic of hysteria is that the afflicted subject uses her body to repeat by proxy a prior traumatic experience, and in the course of this mimetic self-representation oscillates between various positions: recollection and recreation, masculine and feminine self-determination, a resurrection and resuscitation of the dead and a deanimation of the living. With the help of her histrionic display of intimate phantasy scenes, the hysteric "Anne," much like Emmy v. N., adorns the past, draws life from the dead. She brings clandestine knowledge to light and stages her own biography in relation to past traumas, to preserved memory traces, whose vanishing point is death. She insists on keeping these oppositions in motion, refusing to decide exclusively in favor of one or the other position. In a letter to her friend Lois Ames, Anne Sexton describes one of her suicide attempts as though this had offered her a way to resolve this indecision once and for all: "I've been in a mess, Lois, from bad to worse. . . . In July I tried—well, rather I took an overdose of pills and ended up in MGH being pumped out and with private nurses for 48 hours. Rather a stupid mess. Live or die, you fool, but don't mess with Mr. inbetween! Still, it wasn't a serious serious attempt or I would have succeeded. Part of me is live. But I forgot about the diet from death. I went on a binge" (1979, 297). However, her biography and poems insist on the gesture of the in-between, on the fact that her life depended on an oscillation between inquiring into the truth of her heritage and accepting the clandestine, encrypted traumatic knowledge inherent in its very structure. Her story as a poet and a suicide is compelling precisely because she was unable to decide between "Live or die," that she could not draw a boundary between the two, and instead broadcasted a message about death being the transgressive truth inherent in any protective fictions sustaining life. An affirmation of life can never be cleansed of the traces of death, such a discharge not even being desirable. "How does one live," she asks her friend Anne Clarke after the demise of her parents, "with the knowledge that death, their special death, is waiting silently in their body to overtake them at some undetermined time" (1979, 235).[1] And if her poem "Mother and Jack and the Rain" ends with the decision "to conjure up my daily bread, to endure, somehow to endure," (1981, 111), to avert her own urge toward death meant, above all, admitting to herself the ambivalence of life. At stake in Sexton's urgent confession is not an attempt to efface the traces of inherited traumatic knowledge, but rather an effort to undertake a psychic journey, and even though it begins with being possessed by tormenting phantoms of the past, its aim is the transformation of this distressing, inevitable inheritance into a poetically empowering possession.

In the last three poems of her first collection, *To Bedlam and Part Way Back* (1960), Sexton unfolds how her psychic breakdown and the trace of the death drive in her desire is inextricably knotted together with her inquiry into her family legacy, the transmission and transformation of this heritage, and the development of her poetic power. Even though her story is based on her treatment in a psychiatric clinic, she initially explores a psychoanalytic explanation for her distress, she readily augments this with a sociological and a spiritual mode of interpretation. In the poem addressed to her teacher John Holmes, "For John, who begs me not to enquire further" (1981, 34–

35), Sexton defends herself against his reproach that she should not exhibit her personal anguish and the transgressions of her family so unabashedly in her poems by pitting against this interdiction a poetic principle of the merciless gaze. What she discovers as she explores her pathogenic memory traces, her "narrow diary of the mind," may not be beautiful, but it offers "a certain sense of order," which inspires hope in her because it allows her to escape from the prison of her own madness—her "own selfish death" and her restricted life as a suburban housewife. The metaphor she creates to describe this painful but equally empowering journey into self-discovery is the comparison between her psychic apparatus and "an inverted bowl," damaged by her desire for self-expenditure and the concomitant self-interrogation, the imperfect surface now offering an awkward spectacle. Proudly she holds up to her skeptical teacher, and by implication to her readers, "my awkward bowl, / with all its cracked stars shining," as an emblem for the mad housewife, exhibiting the diary of her mind in her poetic confession. This uncanny structure resembles a "complicated lie," for even though the cracked bowl continues to look like the domestic object it once was, it can now no longer be used in the kitchen, just as "Anne" can never again assume the role of happy housewife after her first stay in a psychiatric clinic. Her restored identity only begins to unfold, along with the cracks that have emerged on the glass surface, and this conversion of destruction into discovery proves to be a form of communication. The story of her own anguish turns into a gift presented to her audience; in the act of poetic transformation her "cracked mirror," her "selfish death" emerges as "cracked stars shining."

Even though she realizes that most people would prefer to avert any knowledge about psychic lability and family fallibility, would prefer to construct a protective shield between themselves and this traumatic knowledge, begging the distraught and discontent hysteric daughter not to inquire further, "Anne" insists that this glass bowl, representing her "diary of the mind," could only shine after she had had the courage to look into the darkest spots in her psyche: "This is something I would never find / in a lovelier place." At the same time she also insists on the fluid boundary between "Anne" on the one hand, who, writing under the aegis of Oedipus, seeks to disclose the mystery of her psychic anguish and her interpellator John on the other, who, standing in the protective shade of Jocasta, seeks to evade this painful knowledge. Twice she notes that her kitchen—the site of both family constraints and family bonds that has become uncanny, owing to her madness and her poetic confession—merges with the kitchen of the very teacher who calls for restraint, that her face becomes his: "my kitchen, your kitchen / my face, your face." Apparently, whoever engages with the gift "Anne" offers can no longer protect her- or himself against its infection.

In the last two poems Sexton presents scenes from the cracked bowl of her psychic diary, constructing between herself, her daughter, and her mother a triadic configuration that hysterically revolves around transmission and transformation of a maternal legacy. She interprets maternal genealogy not as something to be located outside, but rather formulated under the aegis of the Oedipal dilemma; she actually explores what a feminine reiteration of this mythopoetic narrative might look like, in which the development of the girl's desires and anxieties, rather than merely marking the abnormal deviation from those of the boy, negotiates castration outside an economy based on sisterly envy. In "The Double Image" (35–42) she offers a triptych that is uncannily inscribed by death and regeneration. On the one hand she addresses her daughter, confessing her guilt, owing to her psychotic break, that she could not be together with her during the first years of her life. Torn between a desire for motherhood and a desire for death, driven by the voices of "ugly angels" in her head, she had come to prefer the old debt toward the dead, her traumatic enjoyment of self-expenditure. In exchange for the birth of a healthy daughter—"Life made you well and whole"—she also gave birth to herself as a psychic corpse, pledging her soul to the demons haunting her: "I let the witches take away my guilty soul." However, despite the lack and inadequacy of the mother from the start written into the life of her daughter Joyce, "Anne" also emphasizes the renewal, resulting from her fallibility, once again covering the trace of this transgression: "There was new snow after this."

Constructing the second side of the tryptich, "Anne" addresses her own mother, whose home in Gloucester she moved into after being released from the psychiatric clinic, rather than returning home to her daughter. This abode is encoded as a limenal site because "Anne," an adult woman, has returned to the house of her childhood and although she can bear being alive, she has not yet fully recoverd from her breakdown: "I lived like an angry guest, / a partly mended thing, an outgrown child." In her mother's home an uncanny redoubling of the self occurs. The mother turns into a reflection of the daughter, and in acknowledging this similarity, "Anne" not only can take possession of her mother but also learn to contain the maternal influence. This interrogation of the spiritual powers that have rendered a healthy maternity impossible—the mental witches calling for self-destruction, the family phantoms from the past returning—is condensed into the production of two portraits. At first the mother has her daughter painted, explaining that because she cannot forgive "Anne" her suicide, this portrait is meant to replace the daughter, irrevocably tainted by her act, with an unstained image. Fully in the tradition of gothic literature, however, an uncanny exchange sets in. On the one hand this portrait of the daughter, which the mother commissions instead of forgiving her transgression, transforms "Anne" into a cadaverous double—"holding my smile in place, till it grew formal"—as though the seemingly eternal aesthetic rendition were meant as an apotropaic charm against the vulnerability of the body and the lability of the psyche. For in this image of the daughter, "hung in the chill / north light, matching / me to keep me well," every trace of the threatening clandestine knowledge, which "Anne" by virtue of her suicide had brought to the surface, has successfully been effaced. On the other hand, owing to the similarity between mother and daughter, which emerges with particular force in this portrait, the power of death passes from the one to the other. In other words, even though it was meant to obliquely articulate the daughter's unforgivable transgression, in the course of commemorative recuperation the portrait becomes a harbinger for the death of the mother who commissioned it: "She turned from me as if death were catching / as if death transferred, / as if my dying had eaten inside of her." Anne now finds herself to be the nexus point between her two-year-old daughter, beginning to blossom, and her mother, dying of cancer, both reflections of herself, for she has also endowed her daughter with her physiognomy: "Unacquainted with my face, you wore it." The mother, in turn, had had a second portrait done, now of herself, and this, too, was meant as an accusation against the daughter. For it is painted under the influence of the cancer for which she holds her daughter responsible. Hung in the south light of the same room as the first portrait—"two portraits hang on opposite walls"—the two images come to mutually reflect each other. Her mother's smile "held in place" perfectly corresponds to Anne's smile "held in place," representing to the daughter "my mocking mirror, my overthrown / love, my first image."

Having returned to her own home, though still not yet healthy enough to have her daughter (who had been living with the other grandmother) return to her, "Anne" stages a meeting between the three generations of women. Together with her daughter ("my splendid stranger"), she visits her all-too-familiar mother. Under the auspices of the two portraits, "two ladies sitting in umber chairs,"—she performs a scene of parting and of receiving. For she can now recognize that the painter caught both women at a psychic turning point. The smile Anne holds in place signifies her hope for a new life—"all of me waiting in the eyes"—the portrait of the mother in contrast, signals her acceptance of death. Through this double image, "Anne" can acknowledge her mother as the first image she had of herself, even while she realizes that this first love is irrevocably lost, no longer accessible. However, given that her mother, infected with cancer, also stands in for the death she thinks she received from her daughter by way of the commissioned portrait, the painted image of the mother also commemorates "Anne's" surmounting of death: "that stony head of death I had outgrown." At this liminal site between reanimated bodies and their deanimated images, between regeneration and demise, in this hall of mirrors where the doubled woman stares at herself "as if she were petrified in time," the grandmother not only embraces her granddaughter. Rather, the daughter "Anne" can now take possession of her maternal inheritance and take leave from the enticing but destructive maternal presence.

While the bond to her mother, represented by these two portraits, signifies the debt she owes to death, her daughter's face, reflecting her own, signals that "Anne" also has a debt to life. Once more she conceives of herself as the knotting point between two claims addressed to her. Joyce, who is slowly learning to call "Anne" mother, functions as the mirror inversion of her own mother, dying of cancer. A narcissistic economy between two generations of women is preserved. For if "Anne" has to lose her first image to rid herself of the destructive witches haunting her mind, she requires a second image to accept living, and acknowledge her own maternity. In this phantasy scenario, rewriting the Oedipal family romance, the daughter, once she has settled the debt she owes her mother, finds that an inversion of this debt, directed at her own daughter, takes hold. Realizing that the triptych ultimately performs the interweaving between three generations of women, she concludes with a sentence, addressed to the daughter: "I made you to find me." In a letter to Anne Clarke at Christmas in 1964, Sexton describes her emotions at the deathbed of her mother: "I remember well being right beside my mother as she died, and trying to help her, to stay there, right there so she wouldn't have to walk the barrier alone [. . .] and I did. And then she was gone. She was in the nothingness. . . . Without me. Without herself! . . . Thus she made the transition from somethingness to nothingness . . . but what good was I? With all that love (longing) I couldn't stop the hours or the pain [. . . .] And now she is nothing. Except for me . . . for me she is a big something . . . a something I love and hate and still react and talk to. That is what keeps us alive. The living thing we leave behind" (1979, 229f.). This ambivalent inheritance, which she came into after the death of her mother, is also the theme of the last poem in *To Bedlam and Part Way Back*, where she presents yet another phantasy scenario revolving around being haunted by the maternal presence, seeking to free herself of this possession but knowing that her poetic power would also always feed on this legacy.

In "The Division in Parts" (1981, 42–46), "Anne" describes how she and her sisters divide up her mother's estate according to the dictates of her will, even though this bequest oppresses her, because her emotional mourning lags behind the symbolic death ritual in which the opening of the will marks the moment when the deceased withdraw from the living, leaving their possessions in the care of the survivors: "Your coat in my closet / your bright stones on my hand . . . settle on me like a debt." While her mother was still in the hospital, "Anne" was able to take part in her real suffering. But the actual loss initially calls forth an inability to feel sorrow because it entails an experience of trauma that suspends all ability to name emotions: "Time, that rearranger / of estates, equips / me with your garments, but not with grief." This discrepancy is highlighted by virtue of the fact that mourning her mother falls in the period of Easter. Confronted with her own helplessness in the face of this death, "Anne" finds the Christian ritual her mother had taught her equally inadequate: "I imitate / a memory of belief / that I do not own." Only belatedly and intermittently can the inherited estate—the maternal belongings and her reminiscences of the maternal presence—be filled with the affects of sorrow and grief. In this liminal period the crucified Christ becomes the paradigmatic trope for "Anne's" own psychic indecision. Because he stands for the belief that from self-sacrifice a love can be born that acknowledges the legacy of debt and anguish, "Anne" uses the image of Christ, waiting on the Cross, to transform her ambivalent feelings into a loving acceptance of her mother: "I must convert to love." Neither a pretense at normalcy, the nostalgic exploration of childhood memories, nor the attempt to ban these reminiscences by evoking ghosts proves to be an adequate form of mourning. To enter the estate bequeathed to her by her mother instead entails a hysterical gesture. "Anne" recognizes that she must both curse the phantomatic presence of her deceased mother and evoke it at the same time. Because her mother was the source of her own language—"my Lady of my first words"—the maternal spirit will continue to be the patron saint of her poetic performance: "You come, a brave ghost, to fix / in my mind without praise / or paradise / to make me your inheritor." This mother continues to watch over the estate of inherited knowledge, even while it takes her daughter "Anne" to transform it into poetic phantasies.

While Sexton was uncertain what she would call her second collection of poems, she played with the titles *The Survivor* or *The Truth the Dead Know*, for as she confessed to her friend Dennis Farrel, "It is mostly about the dead . . . and love . . . and sin . . . but mostly the dead" (1979, 137). The title she finally chose was suggested to her by another friend, who, as Sexton explained in an interview, expressed her condolences by referring to a citation from *Macbeth*: "Oh no, Anne, your mother in March and your father in June. All your pretty ones at once" (Colburn 1985, 43). By taking Macduff's words (who, having fallen prey to Macbeth's traumatic enjoyment of uncurbed destruction, had lost his entire family in one fell swoop) and making them her own, Anne Sexton no longer emphasized the self-certain power of the survivor, nor any truth bequeathed by ancestors, but rather the elegiac sorrow of the mourner.

The first poem in *All My Pretty Ones* marks the beginning of a series of dialogues with the dead and enactments of deathbed or murder scenarios that perform the hysteric's malady of reminiscences. Much along the lines of Emmy v. N., Sexton uses her poetry to scrupulously adorn her dead, leaving the coffin lids undone. At times she explicitly recalls her dead parents, as in the poem "All My Pretty Ones," in which, addressing her dead father, "Anne" describes how, in going through the belongings he left behind to discard these unwanted goods, her eyes are transfixed by the photos in an album. These images help her resurrect scenes from her father's past, much as reading her deceased mother's diary resuscitates her memories of the parents whose inheritor she has become. In this archive of memory traces, "this hoarded span," the parents do not appear as the immaculate figures of plenitude so commonly, according to Freud, configured in the family romance as an idealization of childhood. Nevertheless, preserving these memory traces allows "Anne" to overcome the sorrow of loss and use her own survival to articulate a love that lies beyond any guilt or anger she felt at having been abandoned.

In "The Operation" (56–59) she returns once more to the depiction given of her mother's suffering in "The Double Image," only now she relates the issue of infection to her own illness. While she was staying at a hospital with pneumonia, the doctors discovered a swelling in the abdominal area and recommended an operation, during which they removed a benign ovarian cyst and her appendix. Although Sexton recovered rapidly, she continued to harbor the fear that she had taken on her mother's cancer as a kind of returned gift, for she had allowed her mother to convince her that she had been responsible for the fatal ailment. Having returned to the question of inheritance, "Anne" not only describes how mother and daughter resemble each other, given that the doctors "equate my ills with hers / and decide to operate." Rather, she also equates the uterine site of her origin with that of a possible cancer. Her "most gentle house" transforms almost seamlessly into an "embryo of evil." As in the discourses of the hysterics Freud and Breuer describe in their *Studies*, various time periods conflate; while she is waiting for her own operation to take place, "Anne" remembers her hospital visits to her dying mother, during which she was forced to confront the merciless knowledge of her own mortality: "The historic thief is loose in my house." But while the spirit of death initially only haunted her home, it ultimately came to inhabit her very body—"fact: death too is in the egg"—as though her abdominal swelling were a hysterical symptomatization of the knowlege of death her dying mother bequeathed to her. Accordingly, her own operation is described as though it were a deathlike experience, and in this liminality the daughter returns to her mother, whose death she always associates with parturition: "I plunge down the backstair / calling mother at the dying door, / to rush back to my own skin, tied where it was torn." In this phantasy scenario, then, the daughter calls out for help to the maternal figure to whom she owes her life, at precisely the moment when she believes she must pay back this debt—"I thought I'd die." Yet this call quickly transforms into a recollection of her early childhood memories of a nurturing, protective maternal figure—"recalling mother, the sound of her / good morning, the odor of orange and jam." The encouraging maternal words resounding back to her from this protective fiction of a seemingly intact happy childhood —"and run along, Anne, and run along now"—are knotted together with a knowledge of her irrevocable implenitude; the torn body of the adult woman stitched together again but not fully mended, "Humpty Dumpty Anne" returning to normalcy, whose scarred body, like the navel of parturition, bears the trace of the cut. As in so many of Sexton's poems the inherent ambivalence of this poetic dialogue with the dead is preserved: it knots together a recollection of the dead and her own expectation that she might bear death—the past as site of happy protective and agonizing abuse; the future as a surmounting of psychic and bodily pain and a transmission of this traumatic knowledge.

In certain poems "Anne" discusses the presence of the dead among the living in more general terms. "A Curse against Elegies" (60–61) enacts a scenario in which an unidentified speaker insists that he is "tired of all the dead" and wants to leave the cemetery and forget the deceased because these ancestors do not care about the survivors: "The dead are bored with the whole thing." His addressee, however, much like the hysterics in Freud's and Breuer's *Studies*, continues to persist in her bond with the dead, stubbornly remaining in the graveyard, eagerly seeking out the faces of the deceased until her lover scornfully tells her, "Talk back to your old bad dreams." Mourning, thus the argument of Sexton's hysterical dialogue with the dead, feeds on the undecidability between an indifference toward the dead and their active commemoration; between the ability to conceive of oneself's being severed from one's ancestors', as being one's own inheritor and the recognition Anne Sexton had at her mother's deadbed—"What keeps us alive. The living thing we leave behind." In other poems, "Anne" celebrates her own desire for death. At times she offers vignettes, as in "Starry Night" (53–4) where she describes her phantasy that the night might suck her up like a great dragon, so that she would "split / from my life with no flag, / no belly, / no cry." Then again in "Old" (69) she phantasizes her death as the slow entrance into a trance state—"Death starts like a dream"—where scenes of the past are revived. Yet other poems appear like hysterical hallucinations, such as "The House" (71–75), in which the scene is a nightmare inversion of the family romance, recurring incessantly—"The same bad dream goes on"—and serves to interrogate the protection and intact happiness supposedly nourished at the hearth of the home. The house of her childhood has once again been rebuilt, the parents have been resurrected, particular episodes and the characters belonging to them have been revived. Once again the proximity to death is significant in this return to the scenes of the past. The childhood home functions as a trope for the psychic apparatus of the dreamer, emerging as a crypt and the site of nonabreacted memory scenes, where the dead are preserved and incorporated into the dreamer's psychic topography, like foreign bodies that feed on the mental energy of the surviving daughter. On the other hand, this recurring nightmare always ends with the utterance, "I wish I were dead." Hysterically blurring the distinction between the end and the beginning of mortal existence, the dream ultimately enacts a phantasy scenario where to imagine being dead proves coterminous with imagining a return to the encrypted archive of one's memory traces: "At thirty-five / she'll dream she's dead / or else she'll dream she's back." Both the act of receiving death and the act of effacing temporal differences emerge as an arresting of death, a moment of expectation, where the psychic apparatus (compared with a sitting house, a waiting machine) is suspended in its activities: "All day long [. . .], waiting to topple."

Poems such as "For God while Sleeping" (63–64) and "In the Deep Museum" (64–65), in turn, use hysterical hallucination to perform scenes in which the phantasizer is brought ever closer to the traumatic kernel at the navel of phantasy work. In the first of these two poems, "Anne" describes a dream in which she witnesses the crucifixtion of Christ, returning to the mythopoetic image that she had already used in the poems commemorating her mother's death. In this phantasy scene she rewrites the Christian iconography, not only emphasizing the anguish and pain of the dying man but, more importantly, the seediness of the spectators of the scene ("Everyone in this crowd needs a bath. / I am dresssed in rags"). Her hysterical invocation discloses the traditional idealization of this scene of death, for her Christ is no sublime icon, but rather simply a "skinny man" whose name she does not know, grinding his teeth, his diaper sagging. Far from being gloriously poised, as though about to embark on his flight beyond the heaviness of human existence, he is addressed by the dreamer as "hooked to your own weight / jolting toward death under your nameplate." Even for this figure of divinity, "Anne" seems to discover, death confirms rather than suspends the somatic and the symbolic debt: the weight of the body and the weight of the name one has been endowed with. In the second poem, which stands as an uncanny inversion of the first, "Anne" presents her hysterical identification with the dead Christ, performing a phantasy scene in which she is dead yet also conscious, fully cognizant of her own gradual disintegration. Indeed, both of these poems uncannily resonate with Madeleine's rewriting of the divine family romance. For, as was true for Pierre Janet's patient, "Anne's" hysterical versatility allows her to assume several roles, although the scene she rewrites, significantly, is not Christ's conception and parturition (Madeleine's identifying with the pregnant Mary carrying the divine child or phantasizing her presence in Mary's uterus). Instead of the birth "Anne's" hysterical reiteration of Christian mythopoetics takes the death of Christ—not the womb but rather his last abode, the tomb—as its focal point. She also has recourse to transmitted iconography, however, so as to dismantle the protective fiction it serves to construct. Rather than concentrating on Christ's resurrection, "Anne" identifies with Christ, describing the situation of being buried, with rats licking and knawing at one's limbs, their teeth testing him, taking the gift of his body, expediating the process of disintegration: "My ankles are a flute. I lose hips / and wrist." However, far from being terrible, this dissolution of the body, is a moment of traumatic enjoyment: "I bless this other death. Oh, not in air— / in dirt." Of course, like Madeleine's hallucination, this alternative representation of Christ's death, this mythic revision is an iconoclastic gesture. Audaciously "Anne," imagines herself to be the rotting body of Christ and proclaims "Far below The Cross, I correct its flaws." In contrast to Madeleine, whose core phantasy lay in imitating Mary's flawless assumption into heaven, "Anne" radically questions the Christian myth of God's son, taking upon himself the sins of mankind, only to return to his divine origins intact, with all wounds effaced. The traumatic truth she discerns at the navel of this image instead revolves around a conviction that the trace of frailty and fallibility can never be erased and that the more viable images commemorate these remains. She is fully in line with the language of the hysteric, whose aim is to save and sustain paternal law even while the excessive display of her discontent, of her difference with its pre-suppositions, also dismantles its authority by pointing to the clandestine transgression at its very core. In "Anne's" hallucination the monstrous mira-cle is not that this man, having taken death upon himself so as to save man-kind, should return, his body fully restored. Rather, the truly miraculous would be his utter disappearance, making his presence, like the traumatic knowledge accepted, inevitable and yet also inaccessible. Her poem ends with the disturbing message that to have corrected the flaws of the Cross means "We have kept the miracle. I will not be here." The traumatic truth of death is best rendered not as the protective representation of the sublime body of the resurrected Christ, leaving an empty tomb behind, but rather in a radical representation of the gap demarcating all trauma from its significa-tion, in the total effacement of the body of him who has enjoyed death, for in that marked absence—the preserved, empty crypt—his voice can fully resonate.

Finally, a hysteric's suffering from reminiscences is also celebrated in the closing poem of this collection. In "Letter Written During a January Northeaster" (89–92) the absence of "Anne's" lover calls forth an experi-ence of solitude that, in the language of the hystérikè, belatedly and intermit-tently recalls prior traumatizations. To fill the void that has suddenly opened amid her uneventful, everyday life, "Anne" writes letters to her lover, yet phantasy images of death unwittingly also arise like phantoms out of this gap, as do memory traces of deceased ancestors. In defiance of "Anne's" protective fiction of a happy, intact love, which by virtue of her correspon-dence she seeks to sustain in the absence of her lover, these dead come to haunt her with a broadcast of their traumatic knowledge. The first scene "Anne" describes to her absent lover is the cemetery covered with snow, her phantasy being that the dead rejoice at the fact that they will have no visi-tors. These dead, casually accepting their solitude, are invoked initially in contrast to her own desire for the return of her lover, and her own abode. Yet, even though she begins by asserting that she finds the snow and the silence oppressive because her home harbors the living, not the dead—"My window, which is not a grave / is dark with concentration"—in the course of the poem the boundary between the two sites becomes fluid as her home progressively grows to resemble that of her ancestors.

This process toward hysteria begins as she notes that a silence has fallen on her living quarters such that when she speaks, "My own voice shocks me." In the next move "Anne" records a suspension of time, the experience of a continuous, immutable presence, which causes her to no longer see any need to record the change in days of the week—"There is no other day but Monday." And while at the beginning of the poem her beloved still func-tioned as her privileged interpellator to whom she addresses her thoughts—"You are the only one / that I can bother with this matter"—his failure to respond to her letters brings about a hysterical shift in her consciousness: like the patients described by Freud, she begins to prefer the events and figures of the past to living in the present. After a series of associations to the nothingness encroaching on her conscious self, producing an enjoyment of self-expenditure—her pleasure at becoming "dead drunk," or at receiving the news about the death of twenty-eight men aboard a damaged radar tower—her physical catalepsy and anesthesia grow ever more acute, becoming the somatic symptoms of her psychic rigidity and immobility. In the same strophe in which she laments the absence of any response from her lover—"Dearest / where are your letters?"—which is to say, as she recognizes the inadequacy of this interpellator, she also hallucinates a phantom to fill this gap. The mailman, she claims in this last love letter (which, like Emma Bovary, she writes although she no longer has a lover to send it to) "is an impostor. / He is actually my grandfather." This uncanny messenger, rather than bringing letters from the absent lover she yearns for, delivers the message that while the recipient of her love is expendable, the clandestine traumatic knowledge of her ancestors will inevitably return. The poem—and with it Sexton's collection *All My Pretty Ones*, which is "mostly about the dead"—ends with a double disappearance. As she watches the mailman, transformed into her dead grandfather, floating "far off in the storm," she notes that, like hysterics, the dead can pick up their disguises, shake them off, and slowly pull down the shade, only to fade out "like an old movie." Yet with him her living interpellator vanishes as well: "Now he is gone / as you are gone / But he belongs to me like lost baggage." The lover, once he no longer responds to her performance of the self, can simply disappear from the scene of her phantasy work, from the treasure of images and the archive of memories. The representative of her dead ancestors, however, disguised as a mailman who came to deliver to her the truth the dead know, remains ineffaceably inscribed in her psychic topology even after his disappearance. He represents the trace, the stain, the remains, the encrypted legacy, a lost piece of possession, a debt to the dead that, as Oedipus and Jocasta come so fatefully to realize, one can never fully pay off.

V

Not only in Anne Sexton's poetry but also in her biography, a disquietingly contradictory note persists to the end. For if her business was the poetic transformation of her psychic rats into her public persona as star, and if her hysteric performance was her way of living, with being star the protection from the rats written into her psychic apparatus—if, as Maxine Kumin (1981, xxix) noted, her art was the apotropaic charm that screened her from the omphalic death baby we carry within us from the moment of birth—we can never forget that her business was also death. Much like the transformation of her contemporary Norma Jean Baker into Hollywood star Marilyn Monroe, or of the obese Maria Kalogeropoulos into the emaciated opera diva Maria Callas, meant recreating a discarded self as a glamorous performance of seduction, so too taking on other voices, existing as the performance of texts, for Anne Sexton implied a death of the self. Or rather, it meant recognizing that the self is always a plurality, constructed over nothingness, with the lure of a traumatic enjoyment of self-expenditure enticingly lurking beyond the performative gesture. So I therefore return one last time to the equation evoked by Adrienne Rich—to be a suicide and a poet—to insist that it is an impasse we cannot emphasize enough: it is not solvable. For if rats can amazingly write star, the danger of another reversal remains ready to strike back, with star suddenly and horribly transforming into rats.

Significantly, one gender distinction runs through Sexton's obsession with death. The father figure appears only as the *sexualized* version of the traces of death in her desire, the figure to whom she can address, in a gesture of intermittent deferral, her hysterical love for death by and in representation. To her friend Anne Clarke she once wrote, "When (to me) death takes you and puts you thru the wringer, it's a man, but when you kill yourself it's a woman (1979, 231). This feminization of suicide is, in turn, celebrated in "Wanting to Die": "Death's a sad bone; bruised; you'ld say / and yet she waits for me, year after year, to so delicately undo an old wound" (1981, 43). One is reminded of Mozart's Pamina, knife in hand, asked by her mother to kill her father, but threatening to kill herself to avoid her mother's curse and be allowed to return to her realm. However, as I have also been arguing, the hysteric must oscillate in her relation to paternal authority, must keep renegotiating how to exist in relation to the sexualization of kinship alliances as well as to the traumatic knowledge of transgression, fallibility, and vulnerability underlying this sexualization. Using her body to publicly perform poems about the hysterical language of the body as well as poems about her romance with death, Anne Sexton was able to maintain a life-sustaining psychic balance as long as she continued hysterically to row toward "father," who in her late religious poetry had come to take on the shape of God. Reiterating Oedipus, who seeking to discover the truth encrypted beneath the protective fictions of his childhood continues his inquiry even when he guesses "that appalling horror awaits him in the answer," Anne Sexton continued rowing, so as to keep alive against "the pestilential rat inside me," with a paternal interpellator crossing the equation between rats and star, preventing the two figures from collapsing into each other.

In the end, however, what makes hysteria both so resilient but perturbing is that there is no way out of the oscillations. Bringing the daughter's discontent into play, dismantling the presuppositions of the family romance on which it also depends, this discourse defies closure. While Freud was forced to realize that there is no adequate solution to a case history of hysteria, Anne Sexton also came to acknowledge that the only real alternative to "still rowing toward God" is to ultimately shift registers. But to move beyond hysteria meant a termination altogether of the awful rowing, in a scene where the romance with death transforms into a real encounter. If we recall once more Schopenhauer's reading of Oedipus, which serves as motto to *From Bedlam and Part Way Back*, one could say that Sexton came to fulfill both of the positions described there. On the one hand "Anne's" extended negotiation with "father" came to perform a hysterical reiteration of the Oedipal trajectory, sustained by relentless self-inquiry. On the other hand, however, the solution to this journey was a return to the maternal position, to Jocasta, significantly, who not only "begs Oedipus for God's sake not to inquire further," but whose act also consists in hanging herself once the family secret—the deployment of sexuality and kinship alliance in the form of incest and patricide—has been fully disclosed. After all, in the last image we have of Anne Sexton she is clad in her mother's fur coat, a vodka glass in her hand, slumped back on the seat of her car, finally giving in to those pestilential rats, to the death fumes of gas. One month before her forty-sixth birthday she chose a narrative beyond hysteria, the scene of suicide: another answer to the daughter's discontent.

"You Freud, Me Jane": Alfred Hitchcock's
Marnie, the Case History Revisited

> As she laughed I was aware of becoming involved in her laughter and being
> part of it, until her teeth were only accidental stars with a talent for squad-
> drill. I was drawn in by short gasps, inhaled at each momentary recovery,
> lost finally in the dark caverns of her throat, bruised by the ripple of unseen
> muscles. An elderly waiter with trembling hands was hurriedly spreading a
> pink and white checked cloth over the rusty green iron table, saying: "If
> the lady and gentleman wish to take their tea in the garden. . . ." I decided
> that if the shaking of her breast could be stopped, some of the fragments
> of the afternoon might be collected, and I concentrated my attention
> with careful subtlety to this end.
>
> —*T. S. Eliot*

I

IN HER COMMENT on T. S. Eliot's prose poem "Hysteria," which appeared
in his first book *Prufrock and Other Observations* (1917), Claire Kahane
suggests that it "announces in its very title its intention to appropriate a
pathological dislocation as a poetic subject. Erasing the line that distinguishes poetic form from prose, 'Hysteria' technically performs the obliteration of boundaries that threaten its speaker" (1995, 128), drawing the male
spectator into the very texture of the hysterical spectacle. Indeed, as Juliet
Mitchell claims, one could fruitfully see the hysteric as a creative artist of
sorts, telling tales and fabricating stories, "particularly for doctors who will
listen." Furthermore, because these stories are about psychic reality, seduction, and phantasy, psychoanalysis came to use the language of hysteria to
ground both a theory and a therapy of subjectivity on the question of who
tells the story and to whom it is directed (1984, 299).

Yet, as I have been arguing in the past chapters, the hysteric is fully aware
that the scenario she enacts involves not only playing games but also employing deceptions. Her desire, Anne Juranville argues, not only presents
itself as profoundly enigmatic. Rather, the hysteric is also a master in laying
false traces, never forgetting that she is herself implicated in the deception of
her interpellator. Even though she may define the rules of this game of desire
and may shine in the role she has cast for herself, she also hides herself in the

course of this game. As Juranville explains, on the one hand she evokes the desire of the Other by offering to him her performance of a scene revolving around nothing, staging sentences that declare her lack: I do not know . . . , I do not have . . . , I can not . . . , I am not . . .[1] Yet even though the desire of the Other fascinates her, the hysteric's discourse is ultimately aimed at avoidance. So as not to disappear in the lack she represents to her interpellator, she constitutes her desire as being unsatisfiable, preventing her desire from ever reaching its destination. Juranville formulates the aporia staged by the hysteric: "By pitting desire against desire she supports the desire of her masculine interpellator, which she uses to support herself. She finds her enjoyment in this nonsatisfaction of desire. Not, however, by acting as the object causing the Other's desire, but rather as the subject of her symptoms" (1987, 76). In other words, the hysteric's subjectivity is, in the course of her phantasy work, that she identifies with the symbolic father. She represents herself through a performance of paternal seduction, but to trick the representative of paternal authority her game addresses she dons the guise of femininity. As Juranville puts it, "When addressing a man, she plays the woman, when addressing someone in the maternal position, she 'acts the man'" (77).

In the course of this complex game of self-effacement, however, the hysteric self-consciously remains within the realm of dissimulation, betraying the very premise of deception her self-enactment is based on by performing her disbelief or mistrust in paternal truth. She paradoxically rejects what is mere appearance, since her negation of so-called normal femininity is aimed at interrogating precisely the discursive formations of gender within which she finds herself. Turning this self-dismantling masquerade of femininity and filiality into her symptom, the hysteric believes neither in the femininity nor the daughterdom she nevertheless awkwardly assumes. At the same time she also appropriates masculinity, so as to undermine the paternal authority she plays to, not least of all because amid all her doubt she holds onto the conviction that, as Juranville concludes, there is a "horizon of absolute femininity, beyond the phallus" (79) that plays itself out without any reference to phallic economy, but which still confirms her belief in the Other.

Because she was such an adept performer of what Regula Schindler calls the hysteric's "misappropriation of the paternal master narratives,"[2] no other hysteric appearing in Freud's writings has fascinated critics quite as much as Ida Bauer. Indeed, to recall once more Professor Blum's comment on the critics' response to Zelig's chameleon act, there appears to be nothing that has not been said about this case history.[3] This eighteen-year-old woman had been brought to Freud by her father in the winter of 1900 but decided to break off her analysis after only three session. In response to the wound she inflicted on his analytic authority, when she so staunchly refused to accept the interpretive solution he had come to offer her, and seeking to fill the gaps left by her sudden departure, Freud published his account of this case history five years later under the title *Fragments of an Analysis of a Case of Hysteria* (1905), giving her the name Dora. As he explains in the first part of his narrative, Dora suffered from difficulty in breathing, migrainelike headaches and a nervous cough, fatigue, lack of concentration, and an intermittent loss of voice. The year she went into analysis she had shown severe depressions, which had culminated first in a fainting attack after a moderately serious argument with her father and then a letter addressed to him, in which she threatened to take her life. Without great difficulty Freud recognizes her symptoms as being typical articulations of a minor case in hysteria, whose manifest cause appears to reside in her *"taedium vitae."*

Yet what intrigues him is that, for several reasons, Dora's speech is enigmatically fragmentary. Many neurotic patients leave "gaps unfilled, and riddles unanswered," with the connections, for the most part, incoherent and the sequence of different events, uncertain (1905, 16). In this particular case, however, he is acutely aware that Dora does not want to tell everything, that she knows more than she is willing to admit. Thus Freud's own reconstruction revolves around a point of indeterminacy, which cannot be solved because we have only his narration of the case yet which has inspired a host of critical rereadings. For when he records that Dora would often respond to his questions by saying "I do not know," what the reader cannot know for certain is whether Freud is right in claiming that her utterance signifies a lack in knowledge owing to represssion or whether she is merely playing a game with her analyst, tricking him into believing she lacks knowledge, seducing him by offering a fragmented story to support his hermeneutic desire to uncover latent meaning.

From what Dora and her father tell him, Freud is quickly able to reconstruct a family story of intrigue, mystery, secrets, clandestine and transgressive bonds, accusations, and deceptions. The father, who had contacted syphillis before entering into marriage, had engaged in a friendship with another couple, the K.'s. Frau K. had nursed him during one of his serious illnesses, Herr K. had repeatedly demonstrated kindness toward Dora, while the latter had taken care of the two small children of Herr and Frau K., indeed acting as a representative of their mother in her absence. In the course of analysis Freud discovers that Dora was not only fully aware of the affair between her father and Frau K., but that in the past she had actually helped them meet clandestinely. At the same time he also learns that to further their romantic interests, Dora's father and Frau K. had planned to give Dora to Herr K., analogous to the way her father had later decided to give Dora to Freud for analytic treatment. In the narrative of this case at least, Herr K. and Freud thus come to occupy the same position: namely, the man who is to receive Dora as a gift so that a clandestine affair, which is perfectly known to those involved, might remain covered up.

In the first two sessions, Freud discerns that Dora's *pétite hysterie*, as he calls it, revolves around two key scenes. The first occurred when Herr K., meeting her alone in the rooms of his store one day, suddenly pressed her to his body and kissed her on the lips. Dora never spoke to her parents about this event, but once she had related it to Freud, he (fully in line with his interest in finding an etiology of sexual trauma to her case of hysteria) explains, "This was surely just the situation to call up a distinct feeling of sexual excitement in a girl of fourteen who had never before been approached. But Dora had at that moment a violent feeling of disgust. . . . I should without question consider a person hysterical in whom an occasion for sexual excitement elicited feelings that were preponderantly or exclusively unpleasurable" (1905, 28). The symptoms that Dora produces after this event—anorexia and pain in the upper part of the body—lead Freud to an interpretation that says more about his hermeneutic wishes than about Dora's actual experiences. Filling in the gaps in her fragmentary representation, he adds his own phantasied "reconstruction of the scene. I believe that during the man's passionate embrace she felt not merely his kiss upon her lips but also the pressure of his erect member against her body. This perception was revolting to her; it was dismissed from her memory, repressed, and replaced by the innocent sensation of pressure upon her thorax, which in turn derived an excessive intensity from its repressed source. Once more, therefore, we find a displacement from the lower part of the body to the upper" (30). In this belated reconstruction, narrated by Freud not only after its occurrence but also after Dora had broken off her analysis, the erect member, of which she had said nothing, becomes crucial to him because as he converts the actual woman Ida Bauer into Dora, a tropic figure for petite hystérie, he needs to encode all experiences of vulnerability within phallic terms.

The second key scene occurred two years later, shortly after Dora had seen Freud for the first time, so that his implication in the events is directly addressed. During a vacation trip with Herr and Frau K., Dora suddenly decided to return to Vienna with her father. In contrast to the prior scene, however, she does speak about this event to her mother, though she waits two weeks to do so. The story she relates is that Herr K. had declared his love for her during a walk they took by a lake. Once she understood his intentions and without letting him finish his proposal, she had slapped his face—significantly, after he had declared, "You know I get nothing out of my wife" (98). In the course of the analysis Freud comes to connect this statement to a similar one Herr K. had apparently made to a governess he had employed and with whom he had had a sexual affair, thereby suggesting that Dora's slap must be interpreted as an act of revenge for the fact that Herr K. was treating her like a servant. At the same time, Freud, recognizing that his role in Dora's transference was obviously ambivalent, suggests to her in their last session that by waiting fourteen days before she told him that she had decided to break off the analysis with him, she was imitating the Viennese custom of giving servants two-week notices, thereby displacing her sense of denigration at the hands of her lover onto her analyst. Yet implicitly Freud, who throughout his rendition seems to identify himself first and foremost with Herr K., understood her termination of their analysis as an analogous act of revenge, with Dora interrupting him before he could finish his analytic proposal as she had her prospective lover.

Herr K., naturally, denied Dora's accusations and instead denounced her, explaining that (according to his wife) Dora had been reading Mantegazza's *Physiology of Love* while staying with them, and had shown interest only in sexual things. Her erotic phantasies having been aroused by her reading, she had merely imagined the entire scene. Her father, siding with Herr K. against his daughter, wrote Freud a letter, explaining, "I myself believe that Dora's tale of the man's immoral suggestions is a phantasy that has forced its way into her mind; and besides, I am bound to Frau K. by ties of honourable friendship and I do not wish to cause her pain. The poor woman is most unhappy with her husband, of whom, by the by, I have no very high opinion. She herself has suffered a great deal with her nerves, and I am her only support. With my state of health I need scarcely assure you that there is nothing wrong in our relations. We are just two poor wretches who give one another what comfort we can by an exchange of friendly sympathy. You know already that I get nothing out of my own wife. But Dora, who inherits my obstinacy, cannot be moved from her hatred of the K.'s. She had her last attack after a conversation in which she had again pressed me to break with them. Please try and bring her to reason" (26). Freud, questioning the truth of the father's explanation, instead sympathizes with Dora's sense of having been used. Indeed, he readily understands why Dora, who had initially supported her father's desire in relation to the K.'s, suddenly turned around to accuse him after having rejected Herr K. Yet his entire interpretive reconstruction of the case is based on the presupposition that there must have been a clandestine, either repressed or still unconscious love between Dora and Herr K., regardless of the fact that his patient persistently denies this. At the same time he admits that what puzzled him throughout, though he came to recognize this only after his patient had already walked out on him, is why she never accused Frau K., even though it appeared as though she had betrayed Dora. Belatedly he realizes that the question he should have addressed was not Dora's disgust at Herr K.'s errected member but rather her admiration for Frau K.'s " 'adorable white body,' " which, he notes, she spoke of "in accents more appropriate to a lover than to a defeated rival" (61).

Using his narrative to prove his theory that there is a sexually traumatic etiology for every case of hysteria, Freud believes that the key to her enigmatic behavior—her symptoms and her reticence—must lie in the solution to two riddles: First, "What is her desire and, concomitant with that, why does she reject the position of femininity ascribed to her by her father?" and second, "Where does her sexual knowledge come from?" What is manifestly clear in the analysis he puts down on paper is that, regardless of whether he is interpreting Dora's symptoms—her coughing, aphonia, melancholy—or the two dreams she offers him, in either case he assumes a rivalry between Dora and Frau K.: on the one hand in relation to her unacknowledged erotic fascination for Herr K., on the other hand in relation to her father, where Dora's jealousy stands in for the mother, who is so strikingly absent from the entire intrigue except as the addressee of her daughter's complaint. As Lacan suggests, one wonders why Freud insists on reading aphonia, brought on during the absences of Herr K., as a symptom for the fact that when the prospective lover is absent, the daughter need not speak, but fails to see this as "an expression of the violent appeal of the oral erotic drive when Dora was left face to face with Frau K., without there being any need for Freud to invoke her awareness of the fellatio undergone by the father when everyone knows that cunnilingus is the artifice most commonly adopted by 'men of means' whose powers begin to abandon them" (1951, 98). Indeed, one could just as easily speculate that Dora's aphonia was a response not to an absence but rather to an abundant presence that called forth a transgressive desire and thus recast the Oedipal configuration in a manner Freud was not willing to entertain for his *petite hystérique*. Only after the event did he come to recognize that Dora had actually harbored a desire for the woman who had taken her mother's place in the love life of her father, in the gesture of a psychic compromise, which had allowed her to abandon yet also adore the maternal body. Perhaps the fact that she withdrew from the masculine lover (whom the players in her family's intrigue had sought to offer her, even though her father openly admitted that he had no high opinion of this man) was less at issue than her hysteria's allowing her to articulate obliquely the masculinity forbidden to her. Aimed at rebuking her father's command, but uncannily also refuting Freud's dictum of the daughter's Oedipal trajectory, Dora's transgression seems to have revolved around the gender of those she chose to address: presenting her complaint about Herr K. to her mother, falling silent before her desire for the feminine body offered to her in the figure of her mother's surrogate and in the image of the Madonna she talks about in her second dream.

In the second and the third section of his *Fragments*, Freud relates the two dreams Dora recounts to these two sexually traumatic events. The first dream enacts a scenario in which Dora and her family flee from a burning house, with her father prohibiting her mother from returning to her room to look for the jewel box she has forgotten. In the second dream Dora enters an unfamiliar room where she finds a letter from her mother that tells her about the death of her father. As she heads for the train station, she suddenly finds herself in a deep woods and equally suddenly ends up in her own home, only to discover that her mother has already gone to the cemetery. In both interpretations Freud emphasizes Dora's ambivalent feelings for her father. However, completely ignoring any reading that might lead in the direction of paternal death and paternal infallibility or maternal knowledge and maternal resilience, he encodes this ambivalence within phallic terms. On the one hand, thus he argues, these dreams articulate Dora's infantile love for her father (her wish that he might protect her), while on the other hand they allow her to enact her fear that he might destroy her, or infect her with his illness. And in both cases the ambivalence inherent in her relation to the paternal figure is projected onto Herr K. In other words, her dreams broadcast the message she will not consciously accept, namely, that she desires this lover even though she also sees him as an agent of threat; like her father, he may be the carrier of sexual infection. In a more structural sense, she is fully aware that to enter into this phallic exchange is coterminous with abandoning her autoerotic desire and adoration of the maternal body. For Freud, her psychic anguish, converted into a myriad of somatic disturbances, can ultimately be reduced to her inability or unwillingness to submit herself to the love of a man, whom her father desires she accept and who stands in her father's place. In one and the same gesture Freud's interpretive solution supports his own screen phantasies, namely the family romance he has constructed between Dora and Herr K. and the theory romance of the Oedipus complex. Consequently, the final interpretation he offers of the second dream is that it is an unconscious reworking of the scene by the lake: "If it is true that you were delivered of a child nine months after the scene by the lake, and that you are going about to this very day carrying the consequences of your false step [*Fehltritt*] with you, then it follows that in your unconscious you must have regretted the upshot of the scene. . . . So you see that your love for Herr K. did not come to an end with the scene, but that (as I maintained) it has persisted down to the present day—though it is true that you are unconsious of it." Significantly, Freud adds, "And Dora disputed the fact no longer," (104) suggesting that her silence finally signals the consent he so desperately needs. Yet I would add that what the last words Freud addresses to Dora make perfectly clear is, above all, his own phantasmic implication in the solution. Knowing that she will not return for another session, so that he feels pressed to give closure to this fragmentary tale, he suggests, "Indeed, if your temptation at L. had had a different outcome [*Ausgang*], this would have been the only possible solution for all the parties concerned. . . . You will agree that nothing makes you so angry as having it thought that you merely fancied the scene by the lake. I know now—and this is what you do not want to be reminded of—that you *did* fancy that Herr K.'s proposals were serious and that he would not leave off until you had married him" (108).

At least in Freud's reconstruction of the case, Dora behaves like a classic petite hystérique to the very end. Seemingly offering him the consent and complicity he requires to validate his analytic theory, she nevertheless ultimately slaps him, as she had slapped her potential lover. Freud notes, "Dora had listened to me without any of her usual contradictions. She seemed to be moved; she said good-bye to me very warmly, with the heartiest wishes for the New Year, and—came no more." The reader, of course, is left as puzzled at this silence as Freud was, though perhaps more willing to speculate in directions he did not. For example, rather than simply accepting that her final silence signified her support, one might equally surmise that Dora had finally recognized that it was useless to interpolate her own voice into the theoretic model her interpellator insisted on so. Had she tired of continually saying no, so that her silence was an enactment of the words? Or was she perhaps tired of the game she had been playing with Freud? And if one entertains the thought that she had been playing a game of deception with him, then her silence, far from signifying consent, could be an expression of Dora's satisfaction at her addressee having so perfectly fallen prey to the false traces she had laid for him that no more need be said.

Freud, however, valiently screens out any self-doubt her sudden and atypical silence might provoke, filling in the gap in knowledge she enacts with a narrative about the repression of heterosexual desire. Dora, he concludes, had initially wanted her father but, having felt disappointed in him owing to his affair with Frau K., and also having felt anxious about his sexual disease, she had simulated hatred. Her rejection of Herr K., who in Freud's reconstruction serves as the privileged surrogate for paternal authority, thus becomes in part a hysterical refusal to acknowledge her own heterosexual desire and in part, however, also a rejection of the Oedipal law. Yet one point of difference cannot be effaced from Freud's case history, precisely because it is also the very condition of its narration: Dora refuses to make the confession he seeks to extort from her and instead falls silent, much as she had used her *tussis nervosa* to symptomize a disturbance in speech. As Lisa Appignanesi and John Forrester maintain, "The Freud who is so certain of the pathology of her response is the Freud whose psychoanalytic knowledge is a violation of her psychosexual privacy, the Freud whose interpretations are like erect, violating members requiring her assent, even if it comes in a form which he, at least, regards as satisfactory, that of her vigorous *dissent*. This Freud is reenacting in his conversations with Ida the sexual advances of Herr Zellenka. Out of self-defence, perhaps, Ida slipped away at this point, declining to follow up Freud's pursuit of Herr Zellenka's forgotten erect member, instead continually reproaching her father and dwelling, with much pain, on her father's love affair with Frau Zellenka" (1992, 150).

According to Peter Brooks, the impasse Freud found himself confronted with in relation to Dora is in fact endemic to any reading of the hysterical body, for this psychosomatic disorder "threatens a violation of basic antitheses and laws, including the law of castration and the conditions of meaning." Any attempt to read this body forces the analyst to "renounce mastery and law-enforcing discourse in a way that Freud, at the time of Dora, cannot do. The hysterical body challenges the interpreter not only to find its story, but to revise conventional stories, to recognize that bodies exceed and infringe the social constructions of gender and desire" (1993, 244). One must not lose sight, however, of the fact that this case history offers itself so readily to a critique of Freud's work on hysteria precisely because it so self-consciously admits its own failure.[4] Stavros Mentzos attributes the popularity of this particular case history among psychoanalytic critics to the double fascination this story exerts on the reader. Fascination, he suggests, is perhaps the crucial trait of the hysteric, who quite seriously addresses the question of her own truth and identity, but does so through a game of deception. Constantly shifting between "subtle intimation and simultaneous conceal-ment," he argues, the confusion and obfuscation thus performed defers all "final revelations, clear positions, definitive decisions ad infinitum" (1993, 133). Yet this fascination, evoked by virtue of an incessant oscillation that defies closure, not only characterizes the hysteric in the text but also the strategy of the narrative itself. As Freud attempts to piece together the frag-ments into a conclusive case history [*"lückenlose Beschreibung"*] he actually admits that this case study both illustrates a failure of interpellation and is itself fallible. For, justifying himself, he notes that it was "only committed to writing from memory after the treatment was at an end, but while my recol-lection of the case was still fresh," and although the record can "claim to possess a high degree of trustworthiness" without being absolutely exact (1905, 10), its rendition is nevertheless ridden with footnotes that contradict the very narrative he expounds, oscillating between revelation and conceal-ment and opening space for alternative readings. The hysteric's gaps in con-sciousness and memory, one could say, seem to have infected not only the analytic scenario between Freud and Dora but also his belated transcript, forcing him to produce an equally gap-riddled text. Still, Freud's profes-sional integrity becomes nowhere more evident than in the fact that even while he seeks to establish the validity of his solution, he admits that Dora usually responded to the interpretation he was offering her with a flat No. Subsuming her resistance into his theory, he takes recourse in the psychoan-alytic dictum that declares, "The 'No' uttered by a patient after a repressed thought has been presented to his conscious perception for the first time does no more than register the existence of a repression. . . . 'No' signifies the desired 'Yes'" (58). One of the exchanges between Freud and his resistant patient is particularly striking because it not only registers the way he seeks to turn interpretive fallibility into a strength, but unwittingly also discloses that Dora might perhaps have been playing cat and mouse with him, offer-ing Freud precisely the images she knew he desired and enjoying the fact that he duly fell prey to this bait. When he suggested that the mother's jewel box in the first dream should be read as a symbol for the female genitalia, Dora responds, "I knew *you* would say that," with Freud adroitly recasting her rebuke to fit the narrative he seeks to confirm, "That is to say, *you* knew it [was so]," and adding in a footnote, "A very common way of putting aside a piece of knowledge that emerges from the repressed" (69).

If then, in one sense, such a rhetoric sleight of hand can be seen as typical for Freud's phallic violence toward Ida Bauer, it nevertheless also illustrates his impotence, for all his efforts at proving to his readers that he had the knowledge she lacked resonate against his patient's adamant refusal to ac-cept his solution, her silence and abrupt departure once her contradictions and negations no longer seemed in place. Thus this text, which discloses the sexuality of the hysteric as one inscribed with gender slippage, is itself a slippery affair. In the same gesture that Dora rejects Freud's interpretive authority, the gaps and negations she uses to respond allow a very different story to emerge from the midst of his text than he purports to transcribe. The other story Dora may well have given such duplicitous articulation to would be that the failure in interpellation played through in their exchange resulted from the fact that she will not recognize herself in the Other's construction and more from Freud's misunderstanding the source of her self-image. Rather than the realm of the erect penis, so crucial to his theory-romance, her distress addressed the realm of adored femininity, recalling how during her visit to a famous picture gallery in Dresden she had "remained two hours in front of the Sistine Madonna, rapt in silent admiration" (96). Once again we find hysteria demarcating the limit of a representational system, interrogating the position of authority it also supports. Whereas Freud's investigation questions Dora's desire and the source of her sexual knowledge, Dora, by her negations and her sudden silence, turns the text back on the narrator, forcing it to also question Freud's desire and the source he is willing to ascribe to his knowledge of hysteria.

In his postscript Freud directly addresses the failure of his analysis, which, significantly, he does not attribute to any incorrect reading of her symptoms on his part, but rather to his being unable at the time to deal with the transference at work in their analytic scene. Lacan astutely attributes Freud's inability to face Dora's homosexual tendency to the fact that he had "put himself rather too much in the place of Herr K." to fully untangle his countertransference (1952, 101). Indeed, in contrast to the opinion of Dora's father, Freud had explained in a footnote, "I happen to know Herr K., for he was the same person who had visited me with the patient's father, and he was still quite young and of prepossessing appearance" (1905, 29). In other words, part of the failure in interpellation played through in Dora's case can be attributed to Freud's inappropriate presupposition that there could be a heterosexual solution to this case of hysteria by identifying with the position of the male lover. In Hitchcock's *Marnie*, which I will discuss as the toxic inversion of the classic Freudian case history, this countertransference is brought to the fore because the two positions nominally separated in Freud's *Fragments*—namely the scientist and the rejected lover—collapse into one. However, in these fragments, the issue of transference seems to be more complex, for part of Freud's blindness could equally be attributed to his inability or unwillingness to identify with Dora in their mutual enterprise whose nominal aim was to discover family secrets and disclose parental fallibilities, that is, acknowledging the identification between analyst and patient he had come to discover in his dream of Irma's injection. More crucially, Freud may also have been unable or unwilling to imagine that the transference at stake was not merely that Dora had recast him in her phantasy as the repetition of her father and her rejected suitor, but rather that the love relation she found herself repeating in the analytic scene was that he had come to represent Frau K. Again, Freud self-consciously addresses this blindness in a footnote, explaining that "The longer the interval of time that separates me from the end of this analysis, the more probable it seems to me that the fault in my technique lay in this omission:

I failed to discover in time and to inform the patient that her homosexual (gynecophilic) love for Frau K. was the strongest unconscious current in her mental life. I ought to have guessed that the main source of her knowledge of sexual matters could have been no one but Frau K., the very person who later on charged her with being interested in those same subjects. Her knowing all about such things and, at the same time, her always pretending not to know where her knowledge came from was really too remarkable. I ought to have attacked this riddle and looked for the motive of such an extraordinary piece of repression" (120).

Taking a different route than the one Freud privileges, one might speculate that Dora was fully aware that the object of her desire and the source of her sexual knowledge were one and the same person and that she was not repressing but quite willfully withholding this information. Adept at laying false traces, she could just as easily have been in control of their analytic scenario, all along fully possessing the knowledge Freud belatedly thought he might have helped her discover. Read in this way the deception performed in these fragments is that even while Freud sought to convince Dora that her hysteria was a symptom, broadcasting a message about her repressed desire for Herr K.—which she staunchly resisted to the end—she seems to have functioned as *his* symptom, broadcasting to him a message about his identification with the feminine position, which he in turn resisted by proclaiming that when she said no she meant yes.

Reading Freud's own negation against the grain, I would speculate that Dora's homosexuality causes him to falter [*steckengeblieben*] and leaves him completely confused [*in völlige Verwirrung geraten*] (as he notes in his footnote) precisely because it broadcasts to him a message about the hysteria in himself he seeks to disavow. For Dora seems to perform an analytic phantasy scenario in which she asks him to alternate between the paternal authority with which the hysteric daughter takes issue (her father and his surrogate, Herr K.) and the maternal position, which is both the source and the addressee of her sexual knowledge. In other words, even as Freud sought to replace a dialogue between a maternal surrogate and a daughter (the gynecophilic currents of love she felt for Frau K.) with the heterosexual couple he needs to privilege (the confession Dora refuses—her unconscious desire for Herr K.), he is belatedly forced to recognize that Dora had been using him all along as a figure in a very different scenario. While he thought he was masterminding an analytic scenario that replicated the heterosexual family romance, the marriage between Herr K. and Dora that he fancied would be the "only possible solution for all parties concerned" (108), the transference at work was that he was actually repeating the enigmatic and clandestine scenario of a duplicitous orality between two women, which as Appignanesi and Forrester suggest, was sensual and discursive in one and the same gesture. This other scenario, existing in tandem with the phallic reenactment Freud sought to privilege, shows him implicated in the very realm whose enigma he seeks to solve (so that it might be abandoned once and for all) namely, the magical fascination eminating from the maternal body. Although Freud can discover the origin of Dora's secret—the clandestinely shared orality with Frau K.—only in the belated and intermittent rhetoric of his own hystérikè, Appignanesi and Forrester insist that he could not or would not imagine that in the course of countertransference he was actually taking on the roles of the governess and Frau Zellenka (Frau K.): "He did not want to have his latinate language of psychoanalysis defiled by proximity with the oral exchanges between these women." However, as Appignanesi and Forrester add, Freud was perfectly willing to play another female part, "this a traditionally Jewish one that came naturally to his active analytic stance" (1992, 162). Phantasizing how the case could have found a happy ending if only the participants had accepted his proposal of a double wedding, Freud proves himself to be a thwarted matchmaker.

Unlike Augustine, who simply disappeared after she walked out of Charcot's clinic (but more like Maria Theresia Paradis, whose musical talent continued to charm Vienna's salon culture for many decades after her failed treatment by Mesmer), Dora does not vanish after she leaves Freud's office on 31 December 1900. Appignanesi and Forrester sight her again in the Vienna of the 1930s, when bridge playing had become a popular among female members of the Jewish bourgeoisie. Ida Bauer had turned into a highly successful teacher and player of this social game—with Frau Zellenka as her partner. Having resisted both her father's and her analyst's heterosexual family romance as the "only possible solution" to the hysteric daughter's discontent, she seems to have constructed for herself a more viable scenario of alliance. As they note "it was as if, across the years, they had finally dispensed with the superfluous men who had previously been their partners in their complex social games and contracts, yet they had retained their love of those games whose skill lies in the secret of mutual understanding of open yet coded communications within and across a foursome. Ida, adept at keeping her hand secret, also knew when and how to play it." And, as if to exonerate the analyst they had accused of rhetorical violence, they quickly add, "Freud might also have thought Ida's choice of occupation as a bridge master as an example of that rarest of all skills, successful sublimation" (167). At this point in her life at least, Dora seems to have been successful at juggling the contradictions in her hysteria—playing a game with her female partner that she had learned from identifying with her analyst.

II

As Hitchcock confided to François Truffaut in the famous set of interviews with the French director, *Marnie* (1964) much like the earlier film *Vertigo*, revolved around "the fetish idea. A man wants to go to bed with a thief because she is a thief" (Truffaut 1983, 301).[5] Yet in contrast to the novel by Winston Graham, whose heroine agrees to see a psychiatrist and where long

passages concern her self-analysis, Hitchcock admits he "was forced to sim-
plify the whole psychoanalysis aspect of it." "In the picture," he explains,
"we had to telescope all of that into a single scene, with the husband doing
the analysis himself" (304). Taking my cue from Hitchcock, I read *Marnie*,
the last of the Hitchcock trilogy that began with *Psycho* (indeed the last of
his classic Hollywood thrillers), as a cinematic narrative that refers explicitly
to the language of psychoanalysis as it plays through a case history of hysteria, but that is itself hysteric in Schindler's sense of a "misappropriation of
a master narrative." In my reading I will explore how this horrific inversion
of the case history, far from simply telescoping the "whole psychoanalysis
aspect" into one scene, in fact extensively interrogates the premises underlying Freud's cathartic method that by the early 1960s had become household
knowledge. Its performative magic consisted in Freud's and Breuer's claim
that "the moment at which the physician finds out the occasion when the
symptom first appeared and the reason for its appearance is also the moment
at which the symptom vanishes. . . . It can only be supposed that the psychical trauma does in fact continue to operate in the subject and maintains the
hysterical phenomenon, and that it comes to an end as soon as the patient
has spoken about it" (1893–95, 35). In Hitchcock's version, recreating a
primal scene of trauma so as to exorcise the mental demons, the foreign
bodies of nonabreacted memories that haunt the afflicted woman prove to
be anything but a wholesome solution.

I am returning here to issues already raised in my discussion of Freud's
writings on the etiology of hysteria as well as of his *Studies in Hysteria*.
These questions are whether one is ever able, given that memory traces reproduce traumatic scenes, to get beyond the register of representation or
whether one is not inevitably caught up within two cycles of repetition feeding on each other: hysteric conversion, producing ever new symptoms, and
analysis, producing ever new scenes. In other words, the disquieting question underlying Freud's and Breuer's cathartic method, I had suggested, addresses the uncertainty of whether one can fully approach and appropriate
an original scene of trauma or whether the attained scene is necessarily performative, or generated within the discursive formation at whose origin it is
supposedly located. My argument will be that, by telescoping "the whole
psychoanalytic thing," Hitchcock enacts in a cinematic scenario the recognition that when an analysis culminates in the recreation of an originary phantasy scene of trauma, this is not only a belated reconstruction but also a
reproduction within the register of representation, which by definition is
delimited from the originary trauma by a gap in the psyche. The theoretical
presupposition subtending my rereading of Freud's theory on the traumatic
etiology of hysteria has, in turn, been the claim that any analysis can solve
the after-pressures [*Nachdrängen*], the traumatic impact, inscribed into individual memory traces but can never resolve or efface the psychic material
connected with originary repression [*Urverdrängung*]. Following Slavoj
Žižek's claim that the problem with jouissance is not that we cannot get

enough of it, but rather that we cannot get rid of it, my point has been that while the cathartic method of psychoanalysis allows the patient to exchange the neurotic phantasies that incapacitate the afflicted subject with more viable life stories, this transformation does not get rid of traumatic affect. By interrogating the heterosexual couple that Freud postulates is the only possible solution to hysteria, Hitchcock presents a cinematic phantasy that cruelly enacts how the family romance of happy genital sexuality screens an enjoyment I have been calling traumatic, an enjoyment connected both with a misappropriation of the law and with self-expenditure, with a dissolution of the self. This enjoyment addresses the nothing around which symbolic conventions and personal phantasies of plenitude revolve, the nothing which we cannot get rid of, which makes us move from one thing to another, and about which one can only make much ado.

Like Elisabeth v. R. or Dora, Marnie is asked by her analyst-husband to confess the knowledge about herself she is either willfully withholding or unconsciously repressing so that the origin of her symptoms—her hallucinations, kleptomania, and heterosexual frigidity—might be found and made to vanish. Yet Hitchcock not only interrogates the premises of the very psychoanalytic language he uses to tell a story about a hysteric woman who performs different roles, constructing fictional identities for herself and a fetishistic man who has a pathological fixation on criminal women. Rather, as director of the tale he takes on the feminine position Freud so staunchly rejected in his encounter with Dora; indeed he mimes his hysteric heroine's language by laying false traces for his viewers, yet also quite self-consciously pointing to his game of deception. At the end of the film, when Marnie's husband, Mark, extorts a confession from her that in one magical swoop offers a primal phantasy scene for her sexual disinterest in him and her need to steal, conflating the two and apparently resolving the one deviancy through the other, Hitchcock explicitly points to the fallacy underlying Mark's hermeneutic project.[6] For, as I will show in greater detail, Marnie's confession might explain her repulsion of men but not her kleptomania, nor does it begin to address her adoration of the maternal body. Furthermore, given the artificiality with which this scene of revelation is enacted, Hitchcock articulates not only the fact that Mark falls prey to the solution he wants to hear, but also that any cure he believes can eradicate the traces of traumatic knowledge must fail. With Hitchcock's aesthetic strategy of pointing to the representational quality of the revelation of trauma he insists that any interpretation—whether the analyst-husband's or ours—works like a protective fiction shielding us from the recognition that in all cases the trauma that haunts the heroine is overdetermined and cannot be fixed. Furthermore, like Ida Bauer who was bright enough to mimic the vocabulary her analyst used to interpret her, Hitchcock has not only read his Freud but is fully adept in laying hermeneutic traps. This tale of analytic fallibility discloses how the analyst's desire deceives him into believing a phantasy scenario to be the entire truth about his wife. And it also plays a self-conscious game of deception with the viewer, with his heroine's phantasies so obviously equating money with the phallus that he seems to be imitating Dora's attitude toward Freud. When we as readers fall into the trap (of what by the 1960s had become a cliché of Freudian interpretation) of equating a bag containing stolen money with female genitalia, he implicitly counters, "I knew you'd say that," only to force us to confront our own hermeneutic gullibility.

The scenario Hitchcock unfolds, then, is a misappropriation of Freud's Oedipus story, showing how a woman, initially fully self-sufficient in her existence within her symbolic network, ends up infantilized and helpless, incapacitated not only by the traumatic knowledge inherited from her parents but also by her husband's violent insistence that she accept the position the Freudian Oedipal story designates as so-called healthy femininity. That position is relinquishing the maternal body and desiring the father's erect member in the surrogate version of a husband to whose authority she defers; relinquishing, in other words, her oscillation between masculinity and femininity, between the truth of her identity and deceptive self-fashionings. Contemporary with Hitchcock's *Marnie*, Anne Sexton's poetry reworks this Oedipal story, fashioning a persona of the poet-daughter who oscillates between an Oedipal inquiry into hidden family secrets and Jocasta's wish to conceal what she knows to be traumatic truths. The cinematic image repertoire he stages returns to haunt the *Film Stills* that the American photographer Cindy Sherman recreates some twenty years later, commemorating the films her mother would have seen at the time of her own conception.

At this point, so as to frame my analysis of Hitchcock's revisitation of the Freudian case history, I will offer two intertextual references the contemporary viewers of *Marnie* would have brought with them as they entered the darkened space of the movie theater. They would already have been familiar with "Tippi" Hedren from *The Birds* (1963), the actress whom Hitchcock was to call "his ultimate actress, the one he had waited decades to direct" (Spoto 1983, 501) and who, in *Marnie*, he claimed, was giving the finest performance of all his films. Viewers would also have been somewhat familiar with the fate of the female protagonist, for the plot development of *The Birds* runs along a similar trajectory as the film that was to follow. It also begins with a self-assured, though perhaps somewhat vain, heroine, Melanie Daniels, daughter of an influential newspaper publisher, who decides to seduce an equally self-content and self-confident lawyer, by bringing two lovebirds to his family home in Botega Bay, nominally to celebrate his sister Cathy's birthday. At their very first meeting in a pet shop Mitch Brenner, annoyed at her narcissistic self-sufficiency and threatened, yet also fascinated, by her carefree lifestyle, had explained to her that he wanted to tame her. In a scene staged to illustrate her resourcefulness, she takes a motorboat across the bay to arrrive clandestinely at the Brenner home and deposit the lovebirds at Mitch's hearth unnoticed. Having returned to her boat, she waits to see how Mitch will respond and to make sure that he sees her before she returns to the other side of the bay, forcing him to chase after her in his car. Just as she is about to land, glowing with pride at the success her seduction game seems to promise and already posing in the role of the blasé lover, a blackbird attacks her, pecking at her forehead. From one instant to the next, the clever, self-confident socialite is transformed into a vulnerable woman who cannot disembark from her boat or walk without being supported by Mitch.

Though Melanie regains her strength and her wit, wherever she goes, birds seem to follow, perching on the wires of the telephone poles outside the Brenner house, throwing themselves against Anne Hayward's door, where Melanie has decided to spend the night, and the next day launching their first attack during Cathy's birthday party, only to continue by assaulting all the inhabitants of the village. As a result, mass hysteria breaks out, beginning in the diner to which the women and children have fled after an attack on the school and where Melanie, having told her father over the telephone about the strange occurrence, defends herself by claiming, "No I'm not hysterical"; the customers become excited and histrionically exhibit their panic. After another onslaught one mother, maddened by anxiety, accuses Melanie, whom she considers the cause of the onslaught, of being evil. But hysteria also takes hold of Mitch's home, starting with his mother, whose traumatic sense of implenitude and vulnerability after the death of her husband is reawakened by the birds. Coming home from having witnessed the corpse of the first victim of the birds' mysterious assault, these wandering foreign bodies that seem to have come undone from their normal behavioral mode, she loses all composure and strength, and while Melanie brings her tea, she falls into a crying fit as she confesses her fear of again being abandoned. Then, after Cathy has witnessed the death of her teacher Annie Hayward, she, too, falls into a hysterical crying fit. Finally, waiting for the birds to attack the house after dinner, all three women exhibit hysterical incapacitation, alternatively screaming at Mitch, crying uncontrollably, throwing up, or waiting (as in Charcot's description of the aura) anticipating a new attack, huddling together trancelike, running aimlessly from one corner to the next to cower, curling up into sofa corners, and leaving Mitch on his own to fortify the house and protect them.

That Melanie is an incipient hysteric, however, is shown most clearly when, not unlike the gothic heroines of Radcliffe, she waits for everyone to fall asleep after the birds seem to have gone (their cries have ceased) and in a last moment of resourcefulness mounts the stairs to enter the parental bedroom on the second floor. In a strange scene, which could either be read as the phantasmic punishment of the heroine for her self-reliance or as her experiencing that perverse enjoyment of self-destruction against which Mitch's paternal authority is erected, a mass of birds attacks Melanie. As she waves her arms and hands above her head in an effort to protect her eyes, the sounds she emits are soft orgasmic moans, rather than loud cries for help. Indeed, in a gesture that can only be seen as articulating ambivalence, she sinks to the ground, softly and almost inaudibly whispering Mitch's name, in a posture that contradictorially blocks the door from inside.

The couple formation Hitchcock offers is indeed highly duplicitous. For the woman Mitch finally leads out of the house, the woman his jealous mother can finally accept, is someone fully incapacitated, physically wounded and psychically traumatized; instead of the self-secure mobility she exhibited at the beginning of the film, she must now be supported as she walks. Her clever wit has been exchanged for silence; her seductive glances, transformed into a catatonic staring into space. Infantilized in her trauma, she no longer seems to recognize her lover, responds anxiously to the call of the birds, and then gratefully surrenders to the protective touch of Mitch's mother's embrace. Yet perhaps even more perturbing is the fact that the moment she wakes up after her fainting attack, with Mitch leaning over her, her first response is to repeat the softly moaned gasps and wave with her hands before her face as she had done with the birds, continuing until Mitch can restrain her. One might read this as signifying that she now fears Mitch's touch as a threatening repetition of the traumatic assualt she experienced in the parental bedroom. Far more worrisome, however, is the thought that perhaps she can only imagine him as a satisfying object of erotic desire by reencoding him within this phantasy scenario of trauma.

One final point links *The Birds* to Hitchcock's revisitation of hysteria that he was to make the year the film was released. Having interviewed Tippi Hedren about the filming of the scene where she is assaulted by the birds, Donald Spoto offers the following description: "At the end of the attic sequence, when Melanie is on the floor being pecked by birds, elastic bands were tied around Miss Hedren's legs, arms, and torso. Attached to these bands were nylon threads, and one leg of each of several birds was tied to this string so the birds would not fly away. After several seconds of shooting, a tear was made in her clothing, "blood" was painted on—and shooting resumed. Eight hours daily, for an entire week, she was subjected to this nerve-racking experience. Birds flew at her, and birds were tied to her. 'Finally, one gull decided to perch on my eyelid, producing a deep gash and just missing my eyeball. I became hysterical.' She suffered a severe physical and emotional collapse and was put under a doctor's care while filming was suspended for over a week" (Spoto 1976, 393). One can only call uncanny the way the mental states of the heroine and the actress had strangely collapsed into one, offering a matrix of hysterical traumatization on which the next film, Hitchcock's greatest box office disaster, could be erected.

Within the literature about Hitchcock *Marnie* occupies a unique place in that critics are torn between embarrassment and admiration. As Donald Spoto notes, those who regard Marnie as a failure accuse it of being "contemptuous of an audience's technical naïvité with its laziness in the use of painted sets and ugly rear projection, and worst of all, with uninspired casting," (1976, 397); while those who admire it see the stylistic artificialities as a self-conscious homage to German Expressionism, such as *The Cabinet of Dr. Caligari* (1919), Robert Wiene's exploration of psychic disturbances, a cinematic language Hitchcock had been exposed to during his work in Germany in the 1920s. What seems indisputable is that this film continues to fascinate us with a strange, haunting quality.[7] It fascinates us in part because it is a composite of so many other Hitchcock films—visually, musically, as well as in relation to the mise-en-scène recalling *Spellbound*, *Notorious*, *Vertigo*, *The Man Who Knew Too Much*, *North by Northwest*, and *Psycho*. It also hystericizes us, by awakening cinematic reminiscences we have not got rid of. Indeed, *Marnie* was the last film in which Hitchcock worked with the cinematographer Robert Burks and the last time he used a muscial score by Bernard Herrmann. Undoubtedly it also fascinates us because of 'Tippi' Hedren, the last great Hitchcock blond; Donald Spoto rightly claims that her performance of the hysterical play between subtle intimation and simultaneous concealment was completely miscalculated by most critics at the time the film came out. Finally, however, it fascinates because it performs a phantasy scene, which, insofar as it revolves around larcenies—beginning with the narrative cut between a full purse and an empty safe and ending in a scene of recognition, where the hysteric finds herself simultaneously confronted with too much destructive knowledge and a gaping abyss that can neither be filled nor covered, a loss for which there is no clearly demarcated beginning but only a chain of reenactments—it defers ad infinitum all final revelations, clear positions, or definitive decisions, both for the characters in the scene and for the spectators.

Finally, Hitchcock quite self-consciously meant *Marnie* to fascinate precisely because it was conceived as a film which, in the language of hysteria, elicits the very nosological desire it also cleverly defies, this aim being demonstrated nowhere more clearly than in the trailer he made to promote this film. As it begins, we see (in the top left corner of the frame) the obese body of the director perched on top of a crane, with a camera standing next to his seat. The crane begins to swoop down, while he fixes us with his gaze until, having come to face us directly, he introduces himself: "How do you do. I'm Alfred Hitchcock, and I would like to tell you about my latest motion picture, *Marnie*." As the camera moves into a closeup, he quickly adds, "*Marnie* is a very difficult picture to classify," and proceeds to differentiate it from the two other films of the trilogy. He thereby, however, also explicitly points to the connection between them: "It is not *Psycho*. Nor do we have a horde of birds flapping about and pecking at people willy-nilly." Once he launches into his positive classification of the film, he calls his protagonists "two very interesting human specimens" and suggests that a possible label for the film might be a "sex mystery," only to immediately revise this by saying, "but it is more than that."

The next shot begins a series of filmed scenes; the first two, which introduce these "interesting human specimens," pretend to be from the film but were actually made only for this trailer. They show first Sean Connery and then Tippi Hedren, self-consciously aware of the presence of the camera, indeed looking directly into it in a manner forbidden by the cinematic language code of Hollywood's continuity cutting. Mark walks down the stairs of his family home and stops in front of the camera, as the director had in the previous shot, though in contrast cutting across the picture frame from right to left. Alfred Hitchcock characterizes him as a "thoughtful man, dark, and brooding. He is in a sense a hunter." Tippi Hedren walks down the stairs of her mother's home, now from left to right toward the camera, imitating the director's downward flight, and finally stops to look at us with a smile that hovers between seduction and mockery, as Hitchcock's voice-over adds, "and this is what he is hunting, Marnie." This is the first of several moments in the trailer when Hitchcock intimates an identification not with his hero but with his so enigmatically disturbed heroine.

Indeed, the next shot, again made only for the trailer, shows Marnie caught in the act of clearing out a safe. Though she intermittently glances about furtively to make sure that no one is watching her, she appears quite composed and calm as she places the money into her purse. Hitchcock's ironic comment on the scene—"Marnie was going about her own business like any normal girl. Happy, happy, happy"—is not only poignant because it contradicts what we see but also because it repeats the way Marnie will in fact describe her life before she met Mark, once he asks her to explain her criminal and pathological behavior. Starting with the next scenes, the trailer focuses on Mark, presented as one who faces a hermeneutic task. Because Marnie, Hitchcock adds, "does seem a rather excitable type," he at first "doesn't know what to make of Marnie." Letting on that the film is about how Mark must probe the problem that seems to haunt this enigmatic woman, Hitchcock nevertheless ridicules his hero's sexual solution to the mystery. When we see him kissing the heroine a second time, Hitchcock's mocking voice-over exclaims, "Oh dear, they're at it again, let me assure you, it is all in the spirit of investigation." Furthermore, after a short dialogue in which Mark explains to Marnie that she is a wild animal he has tracked and caught and insists on keeping, the director cuts to the scene where Mark rapes his wife. At first he comments, "As for which one is a wild animal, there are times at which I'm not sure," only to add, "I don't think that was necessary. Actually I should withhold comment, since I'm not sure I understand this scene," after we have seen Mark forcibly tear off Marnie's nightgown and then enfold her in his embrace. As he cuts to the next shot, showing Marnie riding a horse that has gone wild, he nevertheless offers an interpretation that leaves as much intimated as it conceals: "It would appear that Mark has a single solution to all problems. That is not so. . . . He is a troubled man. Troubled because he cannot seem to unravel the mystery of the girl called Marnie." Again, at least on the manifest level of the promotion trailer, Hitchcock is suggesting to us a sympathetic identification with the heroine, not the hero, warning us that the solution Mark will offer at the end of the film should be taken with a grain of salt, and that the promise of a solution is a false trace he is laying from the start. After a red blot of color has exploded onto a gray background, for one brief moment covering the entire frame, the trailer ends by moving from film scenes to writing. Once again we find ourselves confronted with the issue of nosology. In rapid succession we read the following sentences, written in yellow print against the gray background that has been purged of the red stain: "Is Alfred Hitchcock's Marnie: A Sex Story? . . . / Mystery? . . . / Detective Story . . . / Romance? . . . / A Story of a Thief . . . / A Love Story?" until we end with a signifier of hysterical overdetermination, "Yes / Yes, and more." But we are also left with the problem about Marnie's identity, which Mark is troubled by in such a disturbing manner because it is self-consciously constructed as an unplumbable navel of the film, which nevertheless shows real consequences. The hysterical heroine, the girl called Marnie, and Hitchcock's hysterical narrative, the film called *Marnie*, inevitably conflate.

III

Marnie begins with a close up of a round yellow purse held under the arm of a woman dressed in a gray-tweed jacket, whom we see only from behind. The only sound we hear is the clicking of her heels on the pavement. Once the camera stops tracking her and instead allows her to walk into the center of the picture frame, we notice that she is walking along the platform of a train station. In the thirty seconds it takes her to reach the spot where she has chosen to put down her suitcase, indicating to us that she is waiting for a train, the only other details we notice about this traveling stranger are her shoulder-length, black hair, the fact that the gray-tweed skirt matches her jacket, and that she is carrying a suitcase in her right hand. After the cut the next thing we hear is the word "robbed," uttered by the angry Mr. Strutt, who is talking to two policemen about the secretary Marian Holland who, as the next shot shows us, has "cleaned out" his safe. Asked to describe her, he offers a list of clichés of feminine beauty, including her size, weight, height, hair, and eye color, which make it perfectly obvious that he had been taken in by her deceptive game of seduction. This is echoed when Mark Rutland, one of Strutt's clients, appears on the scene and, on being asked whether he remembers her, we describe her as "the brunette with the legs." Strutt's anger, we soon discover, is less over the loss of the money but primarily at the fact that she deceived him. While she had charmed him, because she hysterically flattered his sense of empowerment—eager to work overtime, never making a mistake—her theft dismantles his mastery. Not only does Strutt now lack the money her services had helped him accumulate, but more importantly her theft also tells him that she had only been playing the nice, efficient, resourceful secretary. And if this act of subservience had helped satisfy his sense of masculine consistency, to be shown this was mere appearance conveys to him a message of his symbolic fallibility. "The little witch," he threateningly tells Mark, of whose sympathy he feels assured, "I'll have her put away for twenty years." Yet significantly the scene ends with a close-up of Mark's face: he is smiling to himself as though, triggered by Strutt's remarks, he has begun phantasizing about the beautiful criminal.[8]

The next shot repeats the beginning of the film. Once again, we have a close-up of the yellow purse; however, as the camera allows the woman, who we now know to be a thief (though we still have not seen her face), to move into the center of the image, we see she is walking along the corridor of a hotel, with a bellhop carrying packages and bags for her. Before she enters a room, Hitchcock exits from the left door closest to the camera, gazes after her and then looks for a brief moment directly into the camera at us. While Strutt had pointed to an empty safe and had been forced to paint a verbal image of the absent woman, and while Mark had suddenly fallen into daytime reverie about this absent woman he has seen only once, Hitchcock, crossing her path from behind, explicitly points to her, calling on us to note her presence, as though watching her might fill the many traces of lack she seems to leave behind her. The next shot still shows her from behind, unpacking the boxes and placing the newly bought clothes into an equally new suitcase, emptying the stolen money into it as well, but putting the yellow purse into her old suitcase with the worn cloths she is about to discard. From inside a hidden compartment of her pocket mirror she extracts three social security cards, displaying the other personas she has assumed. She chooses what we will discover is her real given name, Margaret Edgar. What we know, without yet having seen her face, is that she is an accomplished thief and a woman of many personas, wearing not only several names but also several faces. For even while she plays to the masculine gaze, she is performing a game of deception that is not only used to rob her admirers of their money and with it their phallic authority, but also to disclose that the image of femininity she so perfectly embodies, the persona that so obviously satisfies the figures of symbolic power, is merely an appearance, a crafty masquerade. At this point in the film her empowerment is twofold. She has appropriated the phallic symbol that sustains the power relation between the businessmen, namely their money, and she has punished their fetishistic appropriation of her as an object of exploitation and masculine heterosexual desire—the secretary working overtime, the brunette with the legs—by showing them that this was merely a decoy.

Only after the heroine has been visually characterized as a deceptive and clever actress, who dismantles the authority of the very masculine gaze she also constructs herself for, are we shown the end of her transformation. After she washes the black dye out of her hair into the bathroom washbasin, she raises her head, pushing the blond hair back, and we are finally confronted with the face of Tippi Hedren, smiling contently to herself as she looks above the camera axis: although her physiognomy is finally being revealed to us, she is not addressing us directly. We watch her as she is apparently looking into the mirror above the sink: we are obliquely in the position of her mirrored image. Significantly, in the course of the film we will never again see Marnie smile in such a serenely satisfied manner, perhaps because in all the scenes to come she is either focalized through one of her spectators or in a subjective shot, as she presents herself to one of these spectators; never again is she shown outside this economy of fetishizing gazes. As this sequence that has established the heroine finds closure, we see her one last time from behind, now carrying two suitcases. Once she has placed the old one into a locker, she turns around to face us, and, noticing a grid in the floor, drops the key into a shaft, as though signaling to us that we will never retrieve the key that will fully disclose her secret. A loudspeaker announcement indicates that this is a train station. So we know the heroine of a film called *Marnie* only in this newly donned self-representation, as we have also been made perfectly aware, not least of all by Hitchcock's personal pointing gaze, that this is perhaps nothing more than one of her many appearances. And thus before Mark Rutland ever crosses her path, we are already fully caught up in the questions that begins to haunt him, once Strutt has infected his phantasies with stories about the "witch" who betrayed him: What true identity hides behind this appearance? Is there a truth behind the deceptive game or is the woman only the composite of many assumed representations, put on to sustain her spectator's fascination?

The next sequences unfold certain detailed information about this enigmatic and fascinating woman. We are shown the two objects of her love that are clearly positioned in opposition to the men whose desire and authority she plays with—her horse, Forio, and her mother. Visually the connection between these two love objects that deviate from the heterosexual norm is emphasized by virtue of the artificiality with which Hitchcock frames the scenes that enact Marnie's hysterical desire beyond the phallus. We see her mount Forio, after having caressed his snout and declaring, "If you want to bite somebody, bite me." As she blissfully gallops through a landscape, Hitchcock, by his glaring use of a rear projection of trees in motion, emphasizes that the locale of her happiness is a protective fiction, covering up the image of the empty safe and her play with multiple identities and standing in contrast to the phantasies of desire and betrayal she elicits in her male interpellators. But this protective fiction also stands in for a lack that we have not yet seen by representation, which, however, is presented from the very start as that nothing around which the deceptive game of larceny, multiple identities, and fetishistic desire seems to revolve. This lack in mimetic realism is only enhanced as the next shot shows a taxi driving up to one of the doors in a row of houses close to a harbor, with the ugly backdrop so many critics took issue with, showing a huge ship, towering threateningly over these brickstone buildings and the children playing on the street. It is as though we were suddenly watching a play, not a film, so that the episode that follows in which Marnie demonstrates an almost infantile love for her mother who pushes her away, seems to openly declare itself as a theatrical scene, the tragic enactment of a misrecognition between a mother and a daughter.[9]

We are shown how Marnie, who generously sends her mother money and brings expensive gifts when she visits, is forced to recognize that the latter prefers a surrogate daughter, Jessie Cotton. While Mrs. Edgar will not allow Marnie to kneel before her and place her head in her mother's lap, she beckons Jessie to rest in the same position while brushing her hair. We are also shown that although her mother is an object of adoration, she is nevertheless also the addressee of Marnie's hysterical play with identities. Only for her does Marnie play the role of the successful secretary, whose excellent work allows her to be independent of men. In this she supports her mother's wish that women might do well for themselves and not depend on men, a phantasy Mrs. Edgar subsumes under the notion of staying "a decent woman" who "don't have no need for no man." Hitchcock clearly names this fetishism at play, showing that the paternal absence—which Jessie addresses when she asks, "Didn't you all have a Daddy either?"—is covered over by the money Marnie appropriates and the gifts she can then make to her mother. The other lack, made equally explicit by Hitchcock, is maternal love.

Once Jessie has left, Marnie, performing a different hysterical version of the self, the adoring little girl suddenly changes her voice and plaintively asks the question at the center of her constant oscillation between roles and genders, which continues until the end of the film: "Why don't you love me Momma? I've always wondered why you don't." As the mother remains silent, Marnie's plea for affection turns into an interrogation of her maternal interpellator. Wanting to know why she always moves away from her daughter's touch, Marnie asks "What's wrong with me?" Her mother's answer, "Nothing," uncannily hits the mark, but Marnie responds by insisting that there is a trace of "something wrong" her mother has seen in her from the start. Seeking to extort an explanation by imposing guilt, she finally confesses, "God, when I think of the things I've done to try to make you love me." The crisscross of misunderstandings reaches its high point when Marnie taunts the mother, who resiliently keeps silent, voicing her phantasy that her mother's coldness derives from her believing her daughter to be the boss's mistress, and thus not "decent." As her mother slaps her, she wakes up from her trancelike state, and in the adult voice, which she used earlier, Marnie apologizes for the scene, declaring, "I don't know what got into me talking like that. I know you never thought anything bad about me." As Marnie goes upstairs to rest, Mrs. Edgar, like Jocasta, remains silent, staring into space, withholding any insight into the traumatic knowledge her daughter unwittingly harbors but only articulates (so resiliently) in her hallucinations and nightmares. Consequently this scene between mother and daughter also introduces those hysterical symptoms involving incapacitation, rather than the sense of empowerment Marnie gains from her game of identities. For one, the sight of red induces panic attacks, visually rendered by using a red lens to tinge the object she is looking at (Hitchcock offers several more occurrences of this before the dramatic revelation at the film's conclusion). For another, once Marnie has fallen asleep in her mother's house, we are shown the beginning of her recurring nightmare connected with the duplicity of the maternal figure, who forces the daughter to get up from her warm bed and go to a place she experiences as being cold. This is a horrifying phantasy for which Marnie can find no explanation and to which her mother, who has just woken her, turns her back, going back down the stairs and signalling that she will not encourage any further inquiry into the matter.

Marnie, the foreign body wandering from one employment to the next and enriching herself in the process, is thus shown to be a stranger to herself, harboring in her psychic topology residues of traumatic knowledge that she cannot interpret. And this psychic uncanniness is both empowering and disempowering; oscillating between masculinity and femininity, she appropriates the masculine ideal of feminine beauty so as to steal money from the men in power and, with it, their authority. She stages a self-reliance, however, not only because she can give back to the men the fetishism they project onto her, answering their reducing her to a "brunette with legs" by turning them into duped, sexist fetishists. Rather she also experiences an enjoyment, not in relation to their phallic power but to her horse, Forio, which she can afford only by stealing from the men she also despises. Finally (and here, significantly, empowerment and incapacitation conflate), even while she plays the man to her mother, supporting her financially, it is in her maternal interpellator that she also comes to recognize her own vulnerability. Not only is she repeatedly forced to admit that the gifts she makes remain unrequited—her mother will not give her the love she seeks—but, more importantly, the sense of lack, from which she seeks to protect herself, clearly stems from other causes revolving around the maternal body that obliquely link sexuality, money, and violence. For the traumatic knowledge that inhabits her and urges her to move from one employment and role to the next intermittently encroaches upon her, at times rendering her utterly helpless; she loses control over her body, falling into a trance and becoming immobile, and she loses control over her thoughts and words, producing memory gaps or speaking in a voice she neither consciously knows nor controls. This second set of hysterical symptoms contradicts her self-assurance, so that even while her criminalistic parody of femininity helps her support the protective fiction that she is an invincible and infallible subject, her hysterical representation of traumatic impact tells a reverse message of vulnerability and implenitude.

As the narrative unfolds, these two moments of hysterical foreignness become enmeshed in a trajectory proposing the development toward normal femininity, which we saw in the case history of Dora. For Hitchcock's own misappropriation of Freud's master narrative on the manifest level seems to

be that Marnie must be removed forcibly from an economy of desire encircling the adored maternal body and instead forcibly inserted into an economy of marriage under the auspices of phallic paternal authority. In contrast
to Dora, however, Marnie is not able to leave once she finds she has been
trapped in an inadequate scenario of analysis. Unlike Freud (who, more like
Mr. Strutt, is at pains to explain why the hysteric deceived him only to leave
him with an empty couch), Hitchcock stages this development toward femininity and the family romance of heterosexual-couple formation as an overt
act of force and curtailment, thus deconstructing the violence inherent in the
exclusion, which, (as Judith Butler has convincingly argued) is so radically
at stake in our cultural constructions of gender.

This trajectory toward the solution of femininity and the enigma that
hysteria poses is played through in the following manner. Mark Rutland,
clandestinely watches her job interview, posing as an "interested spectator,"
and hires Marnie as payroll clerk, seeing her as the phantasmic embodiment
of the woman he had begun to daydream about in Strutt's office. Her hair
color at this point is between the black she wore while working for Strutt
and the light blond she wore when we first saw her face. While Marnie uses
her position in the Rutland office to watch how money is put into and taken
from the safe, Mark watches Marnie studying the safe, as he also watches
her panic attack after spilling red ink on a white blouse—an attack she cannot remember once it has subsided, calling it "a lot of excitement over nothing." Fully assured in his mastery, Mark, who had worked as a zoologist
before taking over the publishing firm of his father, decides to test and en-
trap her; he asks her to work overtime to type a manuscript on the "instincts
of predators, the criminal class of the animal world." However, as a storm
breaks out he finds himself presented with a different spectacle than what he
had anticipated. Rather than witnessing her embarrassement at typing his
text about criminality in female animals, he instead becomes privy to a different disorder. Terrified by the thunder and lightning, Marnie has a hysteric
attack, which induces a cataleptic seizure and hypnotic state during which
she hallucinates colors. It lasts until, like her mother's slap, Mark's kiss
wakes her from her trance and she has amnesia about everything that has
occurred, including his embrace. As Hitchcock had already foretold in the
trailor, it becomes increasingly unclear how perversity and normalcy can be
distinguished, since Mark's typing ploy and sexual advance not only suggest
that he is as much a predator as she, but also that what he sexually desires
is precisely *not* the self-assured Marnie in her normal state, the efficient secretary who plays to his desire but shows him that she is aware of their mutual game. Rather, he desires the woman grown rigid with fear, caught in a
cadaverous trance, as she will be during their honeymoon when he finally
rapes the wife who in her conscious state forbids his sexual advances.

The next Saturday they spend together only serves to heighten his fascination for her; once again, her game of deception seems to run along two
paths. At the race track she is approached by a man who claims to know her

as Peggy Nicholson, though she denies this, which Mark reads as a sure sign that she is hiding events from her past. Her fear of red overcomes her once more as she sees the jockey riding Telepathy wearing a white jacket with red dots. Having told Mark earlier to bet on this horse, she now warns against him and abruptly leaves the paddock, leaving Mark as puzzled about the contradiction between her usual composure, careful grammar, and quiet good manners and her sudden instinctual behaviour, as the strange man is puzzled about her denial of their past acquaintance. Hitchcock offers us, the implied spectators, the language of psychoanalysis as a bait to satisfy our hermeneutic desire: in the dialogue between Mark and Marnie, after she declares that she believes in "nothing," he asks her about her "tough child-hood," calling her bluff, and she responds by turning the question back on him. But he manifestly distances himself from the simplistic way Mark chooses to interpret the enigma Marnie embodies for him, engaging in the very discourse of psychoanalysis he also seeks to interrogate. Twice we see the strange man, who recognized Marnie as Peggy Nicolson, standing be-neath a sign saying "mutuel windows"; clearly we are meant to notice the words because it is the only sign we see other than one telling us that the location is the Atlantic City Race Course. Reading the scene literally, this mysterious man, who remains unidentified throughout the film, watches Marnie under the auspices of the window where one not only bets on a horse but does so by betting at odds with all the other players, to heighten both the risk and the gain. And indeed, his insistence that he knows her from her former existence as Peggy Nicolson is a wager pitted against her bet that she can cover up this past and against Mark's bet that he will be the winner in disclosing her true identity. Furthermore, mutuel windows as a pun also invokes the concept "mutual," which in turn indicates that something is possessed in common, that something is directed at and received in equal amounts, that two views have the same relation each to the other. Given that this sign is backdrop to a puzzled man who will not be deceived watching an enigmatic woman, Hitchcock may be inviting us to understand this as the best trope to explain how to frame the elusive disturbance Marnie performs for viewing. For, in the course of watching and interrogating her, Mark has opened two windows that give seeming entrance into the knowledge about herself she either withholds or is unconscious of. Put another way, she proves fascinating to him as he wants both to prove she is a criminal by extorting a confession from her and to solve the trauma underlying her panic attacks and amnesia. Mark takes on all the positions Freud could only phan-tasize about, acting as suitor, detective, and psychoanalytically informed zoologist. Marnie, for her part, emerges as a hybrid between the criminal, usurping the phallus in the symbolic (stolen money) and a sexual deviant, rejecting the penis in the imaginary (her heterosexual frigidity). The distur-bance of paternal authority provoked by Marnie's hysteria—both the empty safe and her deceptive feminine fascination—must be solved by the "inter-ested spectator," and the solution must be a double one. Marnie must confess her larceny and recognize her sexual pathology. Yet Hitchcock, by so markedly signaling that Mark's interrogation takes place under the auspices of mutuel windows, seems to be saying not only that these two interpretations, which share something in common, exist side by side but that, furthermore, they are framed views rather than the entire picture. Hitchcock's own hysterical narrative revolves around the question, Whose truth is being confessed, realized, acknowledged and perpetrated? The truth Mark requires for his sense of consistency and infallibility, as both a scientist and a heterosexual man? Or Marnie's truth? And since these, too, are mutual windows, one must add the question, How do these truths relate? Indeed, are these two narratives possessed by something in common or do they miss each other? For even while Mark seeks to translate the one psychic disturbance into the other, finding a core scene of trauma that would allow him to decode Marnie's criminality as a displacement for her sexual pathology, Hitchcock suggests there may be more windows at stake, offering views in which a sexual traumatization need not be privileged at the expense of all other traumatic impressions, in which the enigma of the hysteric's love need not be reduced exclusively to genital sexuality.

Torn between two protective fictions—the family romance Mark offers and her own romance of self-sufficiency—Marnie, suddenly finding herself cornered by Mark's advances, initially chooses the latter, stealing his money rather than accepting his proposal to spend yet another weekend with him; once more dying her hair light blond, she flees to the one creature she trusts, her horse. At this point she seems to be back in the position she was when the film began: in possession of the purloined money and enjoying Forio, or, to invoke the Lacanian triangle of objects of desire proposed by Slavoj Žižek (1991), simultaneously in possession of the S($Ⱥ$), whose inconsistency is made evident by the fact that she could purloin this money, and the (Φ) of perverse love. In contrast to Strutt, however, Mark is able to catch up with her and proposes a deal in which she will not only ultimately lose both her appropriation of paternal power and object of perverse desire but in the course of which she must accept the single object of desire (a) he will allow her, his penis.

During their drive back to Philadelphia he stages a prolonged proposal of marriage resembling rather the hearings staged during the Puritan witchhunts or a police investigation. Mark begins by forcing Marnie to confess both her crimes and family history. As she continues to hysterically spin new tales about her past to hide her real family bonds, he forces her to confront her own fallibility. After Mark has admitted that he had seen her at Strutts, Marnie, formerly so sure that she was the one in control of laying false traces, realizes that all this time he has wanted to "trip me up, trap me." Mark offers her a clue to his desire, explaining, "We have established that you're a thief and a liar," and asking whether she is a compulsive thief and a pathological liar, which would make a difference to him because he has fallen in love with her. She begins a new round of hysteric simulation, playing to the romance he is proposing. As she breaks into tears she tells him of Strutt's sexual advances and her need to fend them off, using the hysteric's rhetoric of negation: "I did it. I don't know why, I kind of went crazy I guess." While Mark is perhaps duped because she is now telling him the story of sexual fetishism he seeks to privilege, Hitchcock again distances himself from the "single solution" his hero seems to be fixated on. For one, he has just shown us the calmly calculated manner in which Marnie goes about stealing. For another, Mark is willing to accept Marnie's assurance that despite hating Strutt's advances, she does not also hate him—she answers, "Oh no, not you," because this supports his need to assure himself that his masculine heterosexuality is irresistible—but we as audience are only too conscious of the glaring parallel. And while Mark the scientist is still wary enough to notice that "the chronic use of an alias is not consistent with your story of sudden temptation and unpremeditated impulse," Mark the lover adds that he is trying not only to understand but also to believe her, which his love makes him want to do.

At this point Marnie finally offers the second confession he has been seeking to extort from her, namely, that his sympathy for her is mutual. Changing from a shrill voice of self-defense and attack to the soft coo of the beloved, she explains that her theft at Rutland was the result of an amorous confusion ("I thought it was time to get out before I got hurt"), and Mark now finds the daydream that began in Strutt's office has come true. Blissfully entering into his own delusional phantasy, indeed casting himself in the role of successful hunter and protector, he counters her plea to let her go by explaining, "I can't let you go Marnie. Somebody has to take care of you and help you, I can't just turn you loose." When he questions her about other potential amorous attachments, she returns the hysteric's denial, "No lovers, no beaus, no steadies, no gentlemen callers, nothing." He is pleased, as though this satsified his own romantic phantasy that marriage would be the cure for both the woman's criminality and her hysterical simulations. Although Mark still seems to entertain the possibility that she only pretends to like him, that she lies when she says he is different from the other men she is so explicitly not interested in, this does not marr the marriage plot he has been constructing throughout the interrogation. Marnie is forced to recognize in horror that she has been caught in her own game of deception, that what for her was a seductive ploy meant to disentangle herself from a tricky affair has become reality for her opponent. One last time she resorts to a verbal attack, accusing Mark of being mad, indeed incriminating herself by saying, "You know what I am. I'm a thief and a liar." She counters his declaration of love by responding, "You don't love me. I'm just something you've caught. You think I'm some kind of animal you've trapped." But in this battle between the hysteric, who wants to keep moving from one identity to the next, and the obsessional fetishist, who wants to hold onto an embodiment of the phantasy woman he has tracked and caught, the former ultimately finds herself in check.

The hysteric ploy on Hitchcock's part throughout the scene, however, is the indecision he induces in the spectators. For we cannot be sure whether Marnie is really fond of Mark or whether she is merely playing to his desire to be attractive, in part because she is not sure herself and in part because her desires might well be contradictory. Equally we cannot know whether her kleptomania actually relates to the issue of her sexual proclivities or whether she is simply using this as a rhetorical device to convince Mark to let her go, much as Hitchcock plants so many obvious references to sexual pathology that we invariably begin to sense they are there to dupe us into believing we are hermeneutically astute. And ultimately we cannot even be sure whether Mark has simply satisfied himself that he can now enact his daydream, regardless of the costs, or whether he does in fact enjoy the violent power he can now exert over Marnie. For the fetishism involved in his desire for a thief is that he enjoys the anxiety over the loss of symbolic power her kleptomania poses even as he enjoys the revenge that he undertakes in lieu of Strutt, who had threatened to have the little witch put away. In both cases, however, his pathological fix on a female criminal can readily be reencoded as supporting symbolic law. Pretending to rescue her, he says, "Someone must take responsibility for you," and in a gesture that legally incapacitates her he explains that her options narrow down to either him or the police.

Yet in the second half of the film Mark finds that taking legal possession of the wild animal he has found is less simple than he thought, because his hysteric wife continues to be resourceful, if limited, in her evasion tactics. Once they return from the catastrophic honeymoon during which, after the rape, Marnie tries to commit suicide, they keep up the façade of a happy couple for his father and sister-in-law, Lil. But Lil herself is in love with Mark and will not be deceived; she undertakes her own detective plot, whose outcome is inviting Strutt to the ball given by her father-in-law on the evening before his great annual hunt. Confronted with her past, Marnie finally confesses all her crimes to Mark, who decides to see whether those who have been victimized by her can be bought off. On the following day, while Mark is trying to finish off the first of these deals with Strutt, presenting his wife as a "sick girl" one must pity, Marnie rides with the hunt. Her anxiety about a possible arrest, as well as the realization that her husband's buying her off has given him an almost invincible power over her, however, causes her to experience the chase as a hallucinatory enactment of her own sense of being hunted. As the color red once again induces a hysterical panic attic, she loses control over Forio, the last insignia of her self-sufficiency. He fatally wounds himself by not jumping high enough over a brick wall (yet another narrative signal of her curtailed ability to flee and transform herself), and she shoots him at the acme of her hysterical attack of panic. Ironically this is more than simply the last time that Marnie successfully acts according to her own dictate. This act also begs reading as a form of symbolic suicide, for by virtue of killing the one symbolic support she trusted

in—her ownership of and love for her horse, Forio—she seems to be renouncing all symbolic ties and enacting a complete suspension of the network of paternal law. She now finds herself confronted with the nothing—
visually articulated through the red color that kept intruding during her
hysteric attacks—around which her hallucinations made so much ado yet
which her protean role playing sought to disguise. In that she is now prepared to acknowledge this gap, which is revealed to her when for the first
time she fully experiences herself bereft of her most precious desired object,
and thus beyond all hysterical protective fictions, she has traversed her
phantasy. The killing of Forio can be understood, then, as an ethical act
(*passage à l'acte*) in the manner discussed by Slavoj Žižek: "After we pass
through the 'zero point' of the symbolic suicide, what a minute ago appeared
as the whirlpool of rage sweeping away all determinate existence changes
miraculously into supreme bliss—as soon as we renounce all symboblic ties"
(1992a, 42). This act performs the renouncing of renunciation itself, a recognition that one has nothing to lose in a loss. Indeed, far from having recourse
to any romantic phantasy that Mark might save her, Marnie instead finds
herself flooded with the traumatic knowledge that haunts her. In the child's
voice she will repeat when making her final revelation to her husband, she
says, "There, there now" when she realizes that Florio has suddenly stopped
writhing in pain.

Leading up to this moment of utter self-wounding, in a sense preparing
this attack of traumatic infantilization, are the many debates between Mark
and her that force her to confront the fallibilities inherent in her hysterical
game of deception and seduction. Not unlike the Freud so certain of the
pathology of Dora's response, of whom Appignanesi and Forrester argue his
"interpretations are like erect, violating members requiring her assent, even
if it comes in a form which he, at least, regards as satisfactory, that of her
vigorous dissent" (1992, 150), Mark seeks to convince Marnie of her helplessness, irresponsibility, ignorance, psychic disturbance, and legal incapacitation. During the wedding proposal, for example, Marnie at one point explains, "You don't know me. I am not like other people. I know what I am,"
to which Mark responds, "I doubt that you do." When she finally admits to
him during their honeymoon that she cannot bear to be handled, specifying
that this disgust is limited to "you, men," Mark again invokes the issue of
pathology, asking whether she has ever consulted a doctor. As she defends
herself by saying that her lack of heterosexual desire has never incapacitated
her before—"I didn't want to get married, it's degrading, it's animal. Anyway, I was doing alright the way I was" (incidentally, repeating the way
Hitchcock introduces his heroine in the trailer), Mark conflates her unwillingness to have sex with him and her larceny. He counters by suggesting that
because she would have continued to steal, "I'd say you needed all the help
you can get." As she continues in this battle over the right interpretation of
her refusal to consummate their marriage, admitting that if she needs help,

it is not his, Mark again invokes her moral deficiencies, "I don't think you're capable of judging what you need, or from whom you need it." If Marnie has been caught, she has not yet been tamed. All her protean qualities—her role playing, her irritating oscillation between self-assurance and vulnerability, her interrogation of masculine power—must be arrested by framing these enigmatic and elusive symptoms into a coherent case history of psychic illness that privileges sexual deviancy as its diagnosis. And if Marnie is initially still able to see through Mark's urge to pathologize her, explaining to her requited husband, "Oh, men, you say no thanks to one of them and bingo, you're a candidate for the funny farm," she ultimately gives in to this desire. Still we can never be sure whether she succumbs to the case history he wishes to construct, whether she plays to his desire to "play doctor," or whether she simply accepts this as one of many possible arbitrary encodings for the traumatic impressions that haunt her. The point at stake, after all, is not whether she is traumatized. Rather, the issue is whether the traumatization can be reduced to a story about heterosexual desire, or whether it is simply one of many "mutuel" windows. After all, by the time Marnie tells her husband that she never wanted anyone to touch her, we have already seen her unabashed bliss at touching Forio, as we have also seen her give herself so unconditionally to her mother's touch.

In a scene that explicitly evokes the Freudian scene of analysis as its intertext, the successful hunter seeks to demonstrate his prowess as analyst of instinctual behavior as well. The scene sets in with Marnie's nightmare, and once again we see her asleep, calling out to her mother not to cry. As Mark approaches, trying to calm her, still in her dreamstate, she sees in him a figure of masculine aggression and, repeating the "no" she called out before the rape (also not unlike Briar Rose, in Sexton's transformation of the Grimm fairy tale, who mistakes the prince for her drunken, abusive Daddy and who, like her, requires sleeping pills to go to sleep), she calls out to him, "No, don't." While Mark hesitates, Lil also enters the room, and finally succeeds in waking her up. Mark seizes the opportunity to enact the books he has been reading at night, with titles like *Sexual Aberrations of the Criminal Female*, rather than taking "legal possession" of his wife. In imitation of Freud, he asks her about her dream, and she, like Dora, answers, "No, I don't know what it means, nothing." At his prodding, she begins to tell bits of the dream in the voice of the child she will don again in the final scene of revelation. This is only one of her personas, however, for as she changes back to the conscious woman, she reveals the presuppositions underlying the scene they have been enacting by mockingly asking, "You Freud, me Jane?" As in the proposal scene, she is initially able to counter his accusation, "I think you're sick," turning the issue of mental pathology back on him by explicitly naming what Hitchcock has been at pains to illustrate: that Mark is caught up in his own dreamworld, with "a pathological fix on a woman who is not only an admitted criminal but who screams if you come near her." Indeed, she demonstrates perfect mastery of the psychoanalytically informed criminological discourse she is meant to confirm, for as Mark continues to show himself unwilling to heed a voice that is independent of the text he seeks to confirm, she concedes to playing the game of doctor with him.

One last time we are privy to what was so disturbing at the beginning of the film—a scene in which a woman performs the role her male interpellator wants her to enact, namely, the neurotically frigid wife, though she is fully aware that this is an impersonation, not her truth, and makes sure that he knows this is a game. In this parody she can at first reflect back to him his own desires, in their game of free association, as she links the word air to "stare, and that's what you do." But because it also contains the traumatic knowledge that haunts her, the game ultimately causes Marnie to transform back into the figure of vulnerability in the nightmare scene, whom he had watched before Lil woke her up. The word death elicits the response "me," and as he says red, she desperately calls out the word "white," turning from him and falling into a hysterical crying fit. As he forces her into his embrace, she calls out to some unspecified person, "Oh, God, somebody help me." As in the previous scene, where an analytic battle is staged over the most viable interpretation of the enigma Marnie embodies and performs, the point is not that Mark is wrong in seeking to locate a traumatic etiology to her hysterical symptoms. Rather he misses the point when he believes this origin can be framed within a particular discursive window, as when he assigns more truth to what Marnie says in trance than to what she tells him in her conscious state.

Again, my point is not that the performances she offers in her hallucinatory mode should not be regarded as broadcasting a truth that her conscious self rejects. Rather, the mistake is in believing that while the conscious woman (clever, self-sufficient, and interrogative) is a deception, the unconscious woman (incapacitated, speaking her own foreignness) necessarily tells nothing but the truth. To return to the trope of mutual-mutuel windows, what Mark is not willing to entertain is that both states of consciousness exist side by side and are possessed by a traumatic truth they have in common, which, however, they not only articulate in different modes but can also only articulate obliquely. In other words, both the hallucinating and the rhetorically self-conscious Marnie are telling bits of truth. This is not only significant in so far as Mark's preference for the tranced woman reflects the fact that he is able to make love only to the incapacitated version of Marnie—the woman transfixed in terror or utterly exhausted after a panic attack. Rather, it also suggests that the voice of the child that breaks through in her hallucinations may be nothing other than one of her hysteric impersonations, articulating a bit of her truth but not all of it. For, as in the case of Dora's finally falling silent, one wonders whether at this point Marnie, giving in to Mark's desire to have her perform her privileged phantasy of trauma, is not simply exhausted by resisting her husband's analytic gaze, which prevents her from sleeping at night; or whether perhaps she is satisfied that she has finally found someone for whom she can enact her nightmare scenario, which her mother, after all, turns her back to. We are equally unsure whether the call for help with which this scene ends is actually directed at Mark, authorizing him to help her reenact the demons that torment her, or whether it is directed at someone outside this pathologically tinged bond, who might help her escape the marital trap that seems to require such a retraumatization.

IV

In her critical reading of Freud's writings on femininity Kofman is particularly interested in the way that the woman patient is translated into a figure of enigma, which the analyst must lay bare. Within this analytic scenario, she argues, the woman must remain silent about her truth while the man discovers the riddle hidden in the female body. Given that the hysteric performs femininity par excellence, Kofman uses the language developed in relation to this most elusive psychosomatic disorder to return to the construction of femininity within psychoanalytic discourse: "Because woman does not have the *right* to speak, she stops being *capable or desirous of speaking.*" "She 'keeps' everything to herself, and creates an excess of mystery and obscurity as if to avenge herself, as if striving for mastery. Woman *lacks sincerity*: she dissimulates" (1980, 43). Through this rhetorical sleight of hand, the riddle that woman seemingly embodies quickly turns into a form of deception. Because woman remains silent she creates a mystery, and this obscurity transforms into an undecipherable enigma. Her inability to decode herself is reencoded as her lack in honesty. Transposed onto Hitchcock's reiteration of the Freudian case history, one could say that Marnie, responding to the desire of her interpellator Mark, says of herself in the proposal scene, "I am a liar and a cheat." In his search for truth, the interested observer Mark tries to decode the enigma Marnie apparently embodies, so as to figure out which woman remains silent. At stake, however, is whether woman indeed has a riddle of which she is unaware, which she hides from herself, or whether she is perfectly cognizant of her secret and willfully keeps it hidden from her interpellator. Added to this is whether she is willing to collaborate with her interpellator in his effort to solve the riddle her symptoms broadcast or whether she refuses such collaboration.

Positioned within the psychoanalytic scenario as a silent body, riddled with an enigma and proclaiming that it has a story, woman, according to Kofman, can take on three positions, which I would argue are telescoped together in Hitchcock's film. Marnie traverses all three before her interested spectator, Mark, finally comes up with a solution. First, she belongs to the type Kofman calls the classic, hysterical woman if she admits that the reason for her illness is her silence about what makes up her enigmatic nature and if she is willing to collaborate with the speculating observer, so that in the course of interpretation the revelation of a hidden scene comes to be equivalent to a cure. In her case the observer requires the complicity of the woman to legitimate his solution, even as he is fully aware that this solution is externally injected, or an addition coming from outside the hysteric subject and imposed on her. By definition, then, this solution never fully fits, for the truth that is apparently discovered at the body of the hysteric, so resiliantly posing an enigma to her analyst, in some sense always proves to be not her truth but rather the truth the interpellator seeks. By accepting his solution, she supports his desire, but his success is also the sign of his fallibility, because it is predetermined by his interpretation and ricochets back to represent not the woman but the observer himself. As he falls prey to her staging of his desire for a coherent interpetation, the scene the classic hysteric offers, as I explored in my discussion of Charcot, ultimately reflects not her but rather his presuppositions about the truth of hysterical symptoms, the etiology and its cure. The failure of such a cure, one could say, is that his truth is confirmed through her complicity. "Because the 'patient's insincerity,' not only is unconscious but also involves willfully holding back things she is perfectly well aware of," Kofman notes, "the analytic treatment cannot be seen as a simple restitution of woman's right to speech; it is also an attempt to 'tear' from them their secret, to make them 'admit' or 'confess'—in short, an attempt not to give them speech but to extort speech from them. Woman is not only a patient, a hysteric; because she dissimulates, she is always also a criminal, and the psychoanalyst a policeman on the alert for the slightest clues that may betray her" (44). Within the course of this analytic scenario, the alterity of the hysteric remains undiscovered and unarticulated, although or maybe because she has been brought to speak. Thus dissimulation can be located not only in the behavior of the surveilled hysteric but also in the interpellator himself, performing a point I have repeatedly invoked: that the analyst, once drawn into the play of hysteria, is ultimately confronted with his desire to fall prey to the hysteric's dissimulations.

The second type of femininity, arising from the classic hysteric but performing a slightly different relation to her interpellator, is the narcissistic woman—usually extremely beautiful—an enigma owing to her self-sufficiency [*Selbstgenügsamkeit gegenüber anderen, Unzugänglichkeit*] (51), which Freud compares to cats and beast of prey, as well as to the child and the humorist. In *Marnie* this type entails both Mark's conception of his bride as being a "wild animal" and Hitchcock's self-conception as being an arch-ironist. This narcissistic woman, who seems not to care about those who court her, fascinates precisely because to her interpellator she embodies the preservation of an original narcissism that he has been forced to relinquish, a proximity to the maternal body. And if the analyst projects a lack of self-knowledge onto the classic hysteric so as to fulfill a phantasy that he could be the one to retrieve for her what she has no access to, a similar projection occurs in his relation to the narcissistic hysteric. In her the analyst can rediscover precisely the plenitude that he lacks—without, of course, the threat of psychosis that a real attachment to abundant maternal presence would entail. However, the refusal on the part of the self-satisfied and self-contained narcissist to reveal her secret also threatens the interpellator in the sense that it disempowers the very sense of infallibility and potency he seeks to confirm in his relation to her. For her insurmountable self-sufficiency, her resistance to discovery, her inevitable impenetrability deny all actual relations to the observing analyst, not only thwarting his desire to find himself confirmed in her but also undercutting the very desire for plenitude that caused him to turn to her in the first place. In the figure of Marnie, Hitchcock splices together the classic and the narcissistic hysteric, offering us a self-sufficient, beautiful criminal whose hysteria revolves around a double theft aimed at broadcasting a message of fallibility to those fascinated by her beauty—the theft of money and the denial of erotic desire.

As Kofman concludes, "The problem is to determine whether Freud . . . completely unaware of his own criminality, his own femininity, proceeds with his inquiry into the feminine enigma as if he were dealing with a criminal or rather a hysteric" (66). This, I want to argue, is precisely also the problem Mark encounters as he seeks the dual confession from his wife, which began with the proposal scene. As Kofman, speaking of Freud, adds, his dilemma is the following: "Does he admit that woman is the only one who knows her own secret, knows the solution to the riddle and is determined not to share it, since she is self-sufficient, or thinks she is, and has no need for complicity?" That is, is she the criminal type? Or does he proceed "as if woman were completely ignorant of her own secret, were disposed to help the investigator, to collaborate with him, persuaded that she must be, that she is 'ill,' that she cannot get along without man if she is to be 'cured'"? (66). This is the option Mark chooses, hoping to confirm in one and the same gesture his potency as lover and as scientist. If we read Hitchcock's film from the point of view of the interpellator Mark, namely as his wish-fulfillment phantasy, meant to confirm the consistency and infallibility of his masculine authority, Kofman's analysis of this argumentation is apt. For she continues, it is "as if Freud (and men in general) 'knew,' dream-fashion, that women were 'great criminals' but nevertheless strove, by bringing about such a reversal as occurs in dreams, to pass them off as hysterics, for it is very much in men's interest that women should share their own convictions, should make themselves accomplices to men's crimes, in exchange for a psycho-cure, a poison-remedy, a 'solution' that cannot help being pernicious since it restores speech to women only in order to model it on men's, only in order to condemn their 'demands' to silence" (67).

But as Dora so provocatively illustrates, the hysteric is precisely the one who wants a master even while she wants to question paternal authority, so that her hysteria emerges as a failure of interpellation. By questioning Freud as source of her own self-image, Dora demonstrates her refusal to recognize herself in the other's construction. This leads to the third constellation that Kofman calls the affirmative woman. Fundamentally undecidable, giving herself without abandoning herself, a fetishist of sorts, this affirmative hysteric oscillates between a denial and an acknowledgment of that lack in knowledge which she is meant to embody; safeguarding her provocative inaccessibility and self-sufficiency, and also showing herself indifferent to any one of her individual self-representations, nonchalantly moving from one performance of the self to the next, she oscillates between an embodiment of truth and dissimulation. She maintains a notion of the truth, even though she doubts the validity of any one individual manifestation of truth; she accepts femininity without accepting the notion of castration, and thus without taking on a clear, sexual determination; deferring all definitive decisions and clear positions.

Indeed, Lucien Israël's characterization of the language of hysteria illustrates how profoundly the three positions Kofman sketches actually conflate. Not only is the hysteric's language characterized by medical discourses as malice, performance, and deception because it performs an "exaggeration of the traits of femininity" (1976, 49), promising her masculine interpellator to show him what he seeks to discover, only to disappoint him by not fulfilling her promise (55). The hysteric also oscillates between hiding the lack she possesses and offering it to the master whom her broadcast addresses. Yet in this exchange, the Other, as Israël argues, does not simply reflect back to the hysteric her own image, but rather, in a sense, the hysteric attaches herself to him. She no longer "perceives merely herself represented by the other but also something more: she has moved to the other side of the mirror" (84), which is, incidentally, the position we take on in the scene when we first see Marnie's face. In Hitchcock's film, then, this oscillation plays itself out as Marnie, in her role as thief, first steals from the figures of paternal authority, whereas, in her exchange with Mark she accepts that she is possessed by a lack, encoding this nothing within the sexual language he privileges: "I won't be handled by men." Yet Israël also insists that one of the aims subtending hysterical performance is to refuse "that her sexuality be reduced to genitality, to the functions of reproduction. What she battles against is the confusion of a feminine desire with the maternal function," and this is an economic, political battle "because society, under the pretext of morality and happiness, turns the creativity of desire, which is always in the process of becoming, into a repetitive and gloomy satisfaction of need, often artificially created" (114). If the male Other, to whom the hysteric addresses her performance, does not realize that she is struggling for another type of love, another sexuality, her love remains purely narcissistic (195). In Mark, then, we find the deceived lover who, because he will not understand Marnie's desire in any but his single, sexual terms, finds himself first flattered, misrecognizing that this is a game, taking himself to be the master; then he becomes as angry as Strutt had at the deception he had initially encouraged.

Apodictically put, the hysteric both complies with her interpellator's desire to solve her riddle and completely recedes from his grasp, because her

desire is more; it is attached to his representation of her and differs from the
conflation of genitality and sexuality he proposes. In Hitchcock's appropriation of the Freudian construction of femininity, Marnie adeptly moves back
and forth between the clever, efficient criminal; the self-absorbed narcissist;
the traumatized hallucinator, the deprived daughter; and the woman enjoying a sexuality that is not reduced to genitality when she is with her horse,
Forio. Yet significantly, and indeed tragically, the most compelling image of
the hysteric's other desire, of the affirmative mode of hysteria, comes not at
the end of her scene of cathartic revelation but at the very beginning of the
film—in the shot of Marnie's face, looking at herself in the mirror, after she
has dyed her hair light blond and is about to don a new guise. In this omphallic representation of a woman's giving birth to herself, in the vortex of
a complex relay of gazes, the heroine's look is sustained but intentionally
aimed just above the camera axis, so that we as spectators just miss being in
the position of the reflection of herself in the mirror.

At this moment she is not yet disclosed as she will apparently be at the end
of the film when, imitating the voice and body language of an abandoned,
abused, and violent child, she comes to support Mark's phantasy that he has
solved her traumtic symptoms and rescued her from the law. Nor is she
completely impenetrable, as she was during their honeymoon, when Mark
insisted on consummating their marriage, and, not heeding her "no," ripped
off her nightgown and raped her while she fell into a catatonic trance.
Rather, at this point in the film, Hitchcock breaks open the opposition of
complete disclosure and complete self-effacment by rendering his heroine
fully visible to us, yet also obviously not directing her gaze at anyone. She is
addressing someone, and we can retrospectively reconstruct that it may be
Forio, whom she is about to visit. Or, as Bellour suggests, in staring with
intensity at her own image in the mirror, she seems to "admire the trium-
phant image of a split identity which answers, with theft and metamorphosis, the sexual aggression which her reality as an image has sealed in her
nature" (1977, 80). But we do not know and cannot ever definitively decide.
In contrast to all the following scenes, where she is staged either as the explicit object of someone's gaze or where the camera takes on the narrative
position of observer, it seems here to be an intruder. It joyfully, almost hysterically, affirms her inaccessibility by offering excessive visibility but by also
refusing to stage her as the bearer of an enigma. There is nothing deceptive
about this rendition of Marnie/Tippi Hedren; she holds no secret of which
an implied or explicitly staged spectator is unaware. She is not hiding anything, but she is also showing nothing. Rather, in this one moment she simply is—enjoying herself, dependent on nothing for this self-enjoyment,
performing for no one but herself. Furthermore, given that this shot is introduced by a prior sequence, which shows Alfred Hitchcock coming out of a
room, watching Tippi Hedren from behind and then gazing directly into the
camera (and thus at us), one can surmise that the director is also self-consciously framing this moment. Hitchcock seems to point to us as spectators

and with his gesture to the representational quality of what we are about to see. The hysterical indecision thus induced in the spectator is that even as we seem to be privy to the one moment of intimacy Hitchcock is willing to stage with his heroine, this moment is completely self-reflexive, fully indicating its own mise-en-scène.

Its horrific inversion, I will argue in the concluding part of this chapter, is the red stain with which Marnie's reenactment of her privileged phantasy of trauma ends. Both mark the moment where artificiality is evoked to point to the inevitable representationality of any performance of traumatic knowledge as well as any experience of real enjoyment—given that the navel of both is that kernel of traumatic enjoyment subtending but also inaccessible to its signification. In these moments, Hitchcock points to the blind spot, the traumatic impossibility of the cinematic frame, hysterically confirming the very representational system it also undermines. Thus the final sequence of *Marnie* knots together these hysterical disturbances of her interpellator's and her spectator's wish to achieve a final revelation, a clear position and a definite picture. For one, she enacts that the question of whether the hysteric woman is a criminal (the exploited working girl), sick (kleptomaniac), or a narcissist (frigid) is ultimately undecidable because the opposition is itself merely a screen phantasy. As the trailer promises, yes, she is all these things, but she is also more. Moreover, the self-consciously artificial rendition of Marnie's symptoms, her catalepsy, her hallucinations about red, and her nightmares, finds its acme in this scene, where the diegetic level of the film breaks its frame, thereby pointing to its own technique.

V

The scene imitating the psychoanalytic notion of cathartic revelation is introduced by Marnie's utter vulnerability. Having killed the only viable support she has in the symbolic, she tries one last time to flee her husband who will not willingly let her go. She returns to the Rutland office with the intention of clearing out the safe. But in contrast to her earlier, successful larceny, she is now as if in a trance state, indeed enacting the scene she had made up for Mark as he was interrogating her during their car drive, acting under the influence of sudden temptation and unpremeditated impulse. Given that she can not take the money in this state of psychic incapacitation, Hitchcock seems to suggest in retrospect that all her other (successful) larcenies were unconnected to her psychic distress, that they cannot be subsumed within a discourse of pathological kleptomania and indeed were never anything other than criminal offenses. In this sense Strutt is perfectly astute when he counters Mark's wish to treat Marnie as a "sick girl" by saying that this is a protective fiction ("the fashionable attitude") for what is simply a breach of the law.[10] To recall Kofman, it is easier to accept a hysteric than a criminal, precisely because the disturbance the former embodies can be located in the register of phantasms, while the latter implies actual transgressions within the symbolic network of codes, laws, and the exchange of paternal authority. The irritating ambivalence of Hitchcock's film is that Marnie is in fact both—a criminal appropriating money and with it power, which is what she has been deprived of, and a hysteric using her criminality to articulate the psychic larcenies at the navel of her phantasy life. Both labels are nothing but mutual windows into the enigma of a woman called Marnie, and can neither be conflated, so that resolving one is coterminous with resolving the other, nor be used to cover over and thus efface one another. If Marnie, within the logic of the narrative plot can no longer take the money in the Rutland safe, this is not because she has been cured of her kleptomania but because she is too traumatized to go about the business of stealing.[11]

Mark, who watches this spectacle of the castrated thief, waits until she has stepped back from the safe, exhausted at her own failure. He then over-powers her and explains that they will go to her home in Baltimore, where he hopes to extort from the mother a confession that is meant to cure the daughter. Fitting for the theatricality that had been connected with the ma-ternal home from the start, we are once again shown the ugly backdrop with the huge ship looming over the shabby street in which Mrs. Edgar lives, and because this is necessary to trigger Marnie's hysterical panic attack, the scene is also staged during a storm. As Mark forces her to enter the mother's house, Marnie flees to the staircase, cowering in terror from the thunder and lightning. Initially unable to talk, she watches the combat of Mark con-fronting Mrs. Edgar about her "accident," claiming that Marnie is sick and needs help in the form of a truthful account of the occurrences of the fatal night she cannot remember. The mother retorts, "You must be plumb crazy," and he begins a sequence of threats, declaring that he knows every-thing that happened and will tell her the whole story if she does not. Mrs. Edgar counters, "Oh, no, you won't Mister, because you don't know the whole story, and nobody does but me." One could say, a battle is being staged over who will be Marnie's privileged interpellator, or in the language of demonology invoked by Mr. Strutt, a battle over who will possess her soul. Mark, overtly voicing that his hurt narcissism is at the core of his want-ing to find a sexual etiology to her psychic disturbance, explains to Mrs. Edgar, "Do you know that your beautiful young daughter cannot stand to have a man touch her?" pointing angrily at himself as he adds, "Any man." As Freud said of Dora, Mark claims that Marnie does not know why the erect male member disgusts her, though we cannot be sure whether, like the analyst he is imitating, he is not merely blinded by his own desire, unable to entertain the possibility that she may be fully cognizant of what her sexual desire is actually aimed at. In other words, to cure Marnie's frigidity is coter-minous with his fetishistic desire to cover up the threatening knowledge of his own impotence, encoded as being sexually resistible. The mother, in turn seeking to protect her own fetishistic phantasy—that a life of decency might cover up her previous life as a prostitute—resists his challenge, saying that regardless of what made her the way she is, her sexual resistance to men is a sign of plain luck. And like Dora, Marnie remains silent about her desire, as she continues to watch Mark attacking her mother with the last of his many mistaken presuppositions, namely, that she was not only earning her living "from the touch of men" but that on the night of her accident she had murdered one of her clients.

At this point Marnie wakes up from her catalepsis, though from the way Hitchcock directs the scene it is not clear whether she has also belatedly understood that her mother was a prostitute or whether she is merely indicating the completion of her transformation into her former self that began as she entered her mother's house. Fearing she might not be successful in protecting Marnie from the terrible family secret, Mrs. Edgar attacks Mark, screaming to him to get out of her house and throwing herself against him, while Mark overpowers her as he had previously overpowered her daughter. Now, fully transformed by the scene she has witnessed into the little girl of the early "accident," Marnie begins to speak in the tiny child's voice we have already heard her use intermittently, as though she were a medium for the foreign body of encrypted knowledge that has been feeding on her: "You let my Momma go, you're hurting my Momma." Given that it is the physical assault that causes her to break her silence, not the verbal confessions made so far, it seems as though Hitchcock was once again pointing to the fact that the lack—about which Marnie, Mark, and the mother make so much ado—involves the issue of violence and protection in a structural sense, with frigidity and promiscuity or theft and prostitution only the semantic encodings, on the level of the after-pressure, not the traumatic impact itself.

While her mother, staunchly holding on to the position of Jocasta, pleads "Shut up, Marnie," Mark calls out in true Oedipal fashion, "No, remember, Marnie" and, knocking against the wall to trigger her reenactment of her nightmare, Marnie begins to relate her recollection of the accident. Significantly, Hitchcock visualizes this in the form of a flashback, so that we are again presented with mutual windows—a staged scene and a verbal narration existing side by side. In the course of Marnie's belated reenactment, Hitchcock oscillates between the scenic staging of this nightmare phantasy, where we hear the voices of the three actors, and the verbal narration by the grown-up Marnie, commenting on the scene she describes to her husband in the voice of her former self, but speaking the thoughts and feelings she did not speak then (and that we, therefore, cannot hear in the phantasy reenactment). What this shifting between two forms of narration accentuates, I would argue, is that the scene we are offered and Marnie's interpretive commentary on it are both representations of this horrific event that, not having been abreacted, has existed as a crypt in her psychic topology, functioning as her privileged phantasy scene of trauma, though not the origin of trauma. In other words, the point is not to say the accident never occurred, but rather

that Mark's belief that this one scene should explain everything there is to
know about Marnie's psychic distress, let alone that this would explain both
her larcenies and her frigidity, is his own analytic protective fiction.

What we see is the mother, waking Marnie and bringing her from her
bedroom into the living room, to allow the sailor who has just entered to
take her place in the mother's bed. Frightened by the lightning, the child
wakes up, and as the sailor touches her to calm her, she cries out for her
mother's, not his, embrace. The mother, misunderstanding her daughter's
cry, or perhaps accurately reading the sailor's actions as an articulation of
sexual abuse, attacks her client. While the narrating Marnie, prodded by
Mark to continue in her story, calls out, "Make him go, Momma," Hitchcock shows us the struggle between Mrs. Edgar and her client, in which,
using an iron poker to defend herself against his blows, she hits him on the
back but herself falls over backward, hurting her leg, once the mutilated
sailor has fallen on top of her. Recreating in her phantasy enactment her
mother's call for help, the narrating Marnie explains to Mark, "I got to help
my Momma," and Hitchcock once more cuts to the scenic rendition to show
us the child, jumping out of bed and, without blinking an eye, grabbing the
poker and hitting the threatening intruder, only to double this unexpected
exertion of violence by cutting to an image of the narrating Marnie who
explains, "I hit him. I hurt him." Hitchcock then cuts back to the scenic
representation, and we see the girl aim her final thrust at the sailor's head,
with a stream of blood trickling down his forehead. In the terrified but silent
gazes of both the mother and the daughter we recognize that she has murdered him. The narrating Marnie, however, can speak, whereas the actors in
her phantasy can only remain silent. As Hitchcock cuts back to the grown-
up woman, we see her calmly repeating the words she had spoken after the
death of Forio, "There, there now." Once more Hitchcock cuts back to the
scenic rendition, showing the dead sailor, a shot of the tearful, screaming
mother, another one of the screaming girl, and then a piece of white cloth,
almost completely covered by a blot of red, which the camera pans along in
an upward motion until, for a few seconds, it completely fills the frame.
This, as I have already suggested, is a complete break within the film's diege-
sis, because the shot belongs neither to the scene of narration (Marnie recounting the event to Mark and her mother) nor to the scene being narrated.
Furthermore, the trickle of blood we have been shown is obviously too slight
to account for such an enormous stain on the sailor's white T-shirt, as it is
also never made clear who the focalizer of the upward swing of the gaze
would be. Finally, the blot is filmed in such a way that we readily recognize
that it is obviously paint, not blood.[12] In other words, the heroine's and her
director's signifier for trauma pierces through the matrix of the film's representational language. Only after we have been confronted with this moment
of traumatic recognition, positioned like the footnote about the navel in
Freud's dream of Irma's injection, between two forms of representation—

the scenic rendition of the nightmare phantasy and Marnie's belated narration—do we see Marnie's face again. Though she is gasping, in contrast to the figures we have seen, she is not screaming as she wakes up from her hallucination. This blot functions like an omphalos; it marks Marnie's twofold rebirth. It indicates the parturition of the encrypted knowledge that has haunted her, as well as her cut from the maternal body she has invested with too much affection. Yet what this scar knots together is not only the past and the present scenes of narration. Rather it also knots these two scenes without belonging to either of them, indicating on the extradiegetic level of the film's aesthetic construction that the traumatic accident at the core of these larcenies, multiple identities, and parental abandonment is a nothing, which can be represented and narrated but not framed by any one interpretive window.

In a film that so overtly plays with Freud's language of psychoanalysis, we are coerced into reading this primal phantasy of trauma as a rearticulation of the Oedipal scene—the child wishing to sleep with the mother (stay in bed with her), then killing the paternal figure that disturbs this bond and threatens both her and the mother. Yet, it not only enacts the dream that Freud says is common to all of us. It encodes this mythopoetic story within a scene of sexual abuse against the child but also a scene of violence against the mother who protects her daughter. And in this narrative transformation it also enacts the duplicity of the daughter's violence—killing the figure of paternal authority who, in her phantasy, not only threatens to sever her from her mother but also threatens to hurt the adored mother. Furthermore, even as we are confronted with two narrators—the hysterical Marnie, responding to Mark's questions by explaining her feelings throughout the scene, and the seemingly omniscient narrator of the enacted phantasy scene, who offers us three subjective points of view—we are also confronted with more than one addressee. We watch the impact this story has on Marnie, who in the act of recounting the scene she has repressed discovers belatedly not only the forgotten event but also the affects attached to it, most crucially her own murderous impulses. We also see Mark, asking her to continue with her story and, once she has finished, assuring her that everything is all right, that everything is all over. But we also see her mother, listening to her daughter in quiet distress and helpless sympathy, as she not only hears a recreation of the horrific scene she has remembered only too well but also, for the first time, her daughter's experience of the event.

However, having offered us a double take on the the daughter's confession, Hitchcock opens up one last window. As the mother offers her confession, we become aware that there is not only more to the story than Mark's phallic solution allows but that the exclusion on which it is based opens up more discrepancies than it solves. For one, the maternal body in this Hitchcock film is not one whose abundant presence leads to psychosis, as in *Psycho*. Rather, as the object of her daughter's adoration the mother reciprocates this excessive love by an oblique manifestation of maternal protection. Seated in her armchair Bernice Edgar explains to her bewildered daughter and self-righteous son-in-law that she interpreted her daughter's amnesia as a sign of God's forgiveness. By telling the police she had killed the sailor in self-defense, she had not only covered for her daughter but also taken the punishment in her stead, keeping the truth secret even when they threatened to take her daughter away from her. Hearing of her mother's sacrifices, Marnie repeats the question around which her hysteria has revolved, a question which significantly has nothing to do with Mark's penis or the phallic money she usurps, declaring, "You must have loved me Momma? You must have loved me!" In what is perhaps the most painful moment of the entire film, the mother counters, "Why you're the only thing in this world I ever did love," so tragically moving not only because it marks the complete misrecognition on which their love is grounded but also because this impossibility of any direct declaration of love leads to the confession of another primal phantasy. This second scene of origins, furthermore, is precisely one Mark has never even known to ask about because it does not at all involve him.

Mrs. Edgar, having watched Marnie recount one phantasy of origins, the birth of her own leg impairment, her prison sentence, and the knot of her daughter's hysterical symptoms, finally recounts the story about her daughter's conception. She begins by explaining, "It was just that I was so young, Marnie. I never had anything of my own. You know how I got you Marnie? There was this boy, Billie. And I wanted Billie's basketball sweater. I was fifteen. And Billie said if I let him, I could have the sweater. So I let him. And then later on when you got started, he run away. I still got that old sweater." In the course of this monologue, Hitchcock cuts between Marnie, watching her mother with rising expectation and glowing with adoration, and the mother, smiling to herself as she recollects this moment of the past. When, in proud pleasure she turns her gaze to her daughter, adding almost as an afterthought, "And I got you, Marnie," her daughter can no longer contain herself and runs to kneel before her, so that she can look up at her demurely while Mrs. Edgar concludes her story: "And after the accident, when I was in the hospital, they tried to make me let you be adopted. But I wouldn't. I wanted you. And I promised God right then. If he let me keep you and you not remember, I'd bring you up different from me. Decent." In response to this oblique confession of her love, Marnie can only offer as oblique a response, declaring that her mother surely has realized her ambition: "Of course, I am a cheat and a liar and a thief, but I am decent." And while we hear Mark interpreting her larcenies as an expression of pathological kleptomania, explaining that when a child cannot get love, "it takes what it can get, any way it can get it," Marnie enacts how profoundly her husband's solution once again completely misses the point. Rather than turning to him, she gazes at her mother as though she were satisfied with the answer she has finally been given and places her head on her mother's knee. For a brief moment the latter barely brushes over the back of her daughter's head, and only then, because she realizes that the scar inscribed in their bond is not erasable, asks her to get up because she is hurting her leg.

If I have described the artificial red blot as an omphalos, marking the scar that knots together the daughter's scenic recollection, her two interpellators' responses to it, and our reception of these mutual windows, I can locate one last omphalic moment in *Marnie*. This becomes particularly poignant in light of the fact that the European video now distributed by Universal contains a cut of about thirty seconds in the mother's monologue, which eliminates everything she has to say about Billie's baseball sweater.[13] Though only a tiny cut, this deletion of Bernice's account of her daughter's conception has enormous consequences, for it suggests that her scene of origin does not revolve around a story of adolescent romance but rather about an accidental exchange. Insofar as a point of origin can be determined for the traumatic chain of psychic deprivations, abandonments, and abuses that Marnie's hysteria symptomizes, the encrypted maternal secret they address is the experience of being dispossessed, of having nothing of one's own. In other words, the trauma of fetishism at the navel of Hitchcock's film and his heroine's psychic reality involves not only a continual attempt to cover this fundamental lack in possession, whose necessary counterpart is the deferral of desire and definitive decisions, clear positions, and final revelations. More importantly, it involves the recognition that in the love life of one's mother the child not only takes the place of a supplement, meant to screen out the sense of implenitude, but that one's conception is contingent and arbitrary. The protective fiction that is maintained, if the story about Billie's baseball sweater is cut from Bernice's monologue, is the Oedipal romance that the daughter stands in for the lost father. What Hitchcock's original inclusion of this disturbing detail provokes is an interrogation of a narrative solution to this case history of fetishism and trauma, one that bases its interpretation on stories of blighted romance (the adolescent Bernice abandoned by Billy) or violent abuse and murder (the prostitute Bernice wounded by her client). Instead it insists, as Pierre Janet had proposed in his discussion of hysteria, that trauma is an accident. It articulates itself only as a sequence of contingent exchanges whose objects are arbitrary and interchangeable and that encircles the desire to possess, even as it also subtly intimates what one wants to conceal: the knowledge of one's fundamental and inevitable dispossession; that one has been robbed from the very start. At the end of Bernice's speech, Hitchcock leaves us to choose between three mutual windows: Mark's version of the sexually abused, frigid kleptomaniac whom he can rescue by teaching her to trust him; Marnie's performance of the protean and resilient language of hysteria, which hovers indeterminately between the intimation of truth and deception; and Bernice, who, by relating the prehistory of Marnie's psychic distress in all its bleak honesty, offers the only reliable narrative that does not appear as an interpretive phantasy scenario constructed to fill the gap in memory. She simply tells the story about a double possession—a sweater and a daughter—that came about in the course of a contingent exchange.

Pushed away from her mother, Marnie asks her husband in the voice of the child, "What am I going to do, what's going to happen?" now finally accepting him as her privileged interpellator. Deferring to his authority, she transforms the role of infantilized daughter she had been playing to Mrs. Edgar into that of submissive wife, willing to abandon her self-sufficiency and her self-enjoyment, and asks whether she might have to go to jail. He, believing he has won his battle against the mother and has rescued his wife from the demons that have haunted her, which is to say believing himself once more to be the master, assures her, "No, not after what I have to tell them." We are offered two more shots of Mrs. Edgar, the first of her face, now completely lifeless, staring into space, the other of her equally depleted body, nodding to them, as Marnie wishes her good-bye. Only once her daughter has closed the door behind her does Bernice's face become alive again, and addressing the place Marnie had occupied, the place that, now empty, marks the trace of her absence, she smiles adoringly and proudly, as she adds, "Good-bye, sugar pop." In other words, to the very end she insists that any admission of love can only exist side by side with an admission of lack. On the other side of the closed door, Marnie finally offers her husband the confession of trust he has sought to extort from her all along, "Oh Mark, I don't want to go to jail. I'd rather stay with you," but we begin to suspect that perhaps this is nothing but the beginning of a new game of seductive deception.

For while he smiles, leading his wife into the car and driving off, two details mar any assurance that they will now live the happy family romance with which a fairy tale about a prince and a pauper conventionally ends. For one, like the voice of Mrs. Fletcher, which, contradicting the reporter's story about her daughter's harmonious family, unpleasantly resonates in the final shots of Eudora's and Zelig's marriage ceremony, so too Bernice's smile remains with us even after the door has been shut, leaving her behind. For she continues to encrypt the knowledge Mark seeks to exclude from his marriage phantasy. On the one hand, she knows that the truth about Marnie is not that she is frigid or that she is a "thief, a liar, and a cheat," but that she is capable of single-mindedly killing to protect her mother, or rather to respond to her mother's desire to be her ally against men, be it a sailor-client, or Mark, the son-in-law. On the other hand, she also knows that her maternal love and Marnie's adoring fascination will persist because in the course of their gynecophilic talk, under the very eyes of the rivalrous husband, Bernice has taught her daughter that their bond is consumed precisely when it is severed, because there can be no solution to the larceny on which the psychic life of each individual is built. Like the navel's knotted scar, any confession of love inevitably comes after the cut, once the door separating them falls shut. Finally, we hear the children singing the nursery rhyme they had already sung at the beginning of the film when Marnie had hesitated briefly on the threshold to look at these representatives of her former self before entering her mother's house: "Mother, mother I am ill, send for the doctor over the hill. Call for the doctor, call for the nurse, call for the lady with the alligator purse."

Owing to this song, we recognize, as the film closes, that things inevitably return, and as at the end of *The Magic Flute*, one cannot help but wonder whether some residue of traumatic knowledge does not attach itself to Mark as he successfully severs his Pamina from her mother. If we have no guarantee that in relating the phantasy scene about the murdered sailor Marnie has actually reproduced the origin of her trauma and not merely its most significant representation, so, too, we have no guarantee that Marnie has really left all traumatic impression behind, locked up together with her mother in her former home. Furthermore, it is not only a question whether Mark is once again falling prey to Marnie's seductive staging of the penitent, infantilized wife he so desperately needs to assure himself of his own potency, his own plenitude. For the fetish he has finally secured—Marnie, the wild animal fixed in a frame, like the photograph of the jaguar Sophie on his desk, of whom he told her that he had trained her to trust him—commemorates his vulnerability as much as it does his prowess. Not only is she an uncanny figure, the adult woman masquerading as a helpless child. It was also as a vulnerable child, not as an empowered thief, that she killed the man who threatened her and her mother. How can he, and with him we, be sure that the murderous violence she has been able to convert into a hysterical play with identities, kleptomania, and a resistance to heterosexuality should suddenly have disappeared, not to resurface? After all, during their last car ride from Philadelphia to Baltimore Marnie had threatened to kill him if he told her mother about her. Indeed, owing to Mark's rescue mission, Marnie is now no longer the ignorant host of an encrypted traumatic family secret. Instead, she has turned this intimate, traumatic kernel into an extimate foreign body, now speaking with the hybrid voice of the murdering child and the submissive wife. If the film began with Mark beginning to phantasize about loving a thief because the sight of an empty safe arouses a complex knot of anxieties and desires involving the fear that he might be robbed, he now loves a murderess, whom he is neither conducting to a clinic nor a police station, but rather whom he is bringing home.

PART FOUR

▶ PERFORMING HYSTERIA

aesthetic debate revolving around the uncanny power of psychic reality, of hallucinations privileged over actual presences, draws its force from the spectral being made visceral. So that the strange, toxic side effect of a postmodern desire to evade the body's mutability is a hysteric language celebrating corporeality gone awry, with a disturbance in psychic topology not only finding a correspondence in the dysfunctioning of a body interior, but also in an externalization of both disturbances. Along the lines that I discussed with Marie-Ange Guilleminot's *Points Communs*, what Cronenberg stages is an inversion. What has remained unvisualized—because it belongs either to the psychic reality, whose only representation is through phantasy, or to the realm of a body interior not readily open to sight—is horrifically rendered external. This postmodern uncanny is a corporeal visualization, manifested on the skin or as a materialized hallucination, with scenarios emanating from an internal, private theater acted out on the scene of the external world. Though it harks back to a crisis in self-representation that emerged as the outcome of the enlightened project, what postmodern gothic hysterics veers toward is a complete conflation of a spectralized neutral space, with a body interior as scene for the peregrinations of unruly body parts and actions committed in external reality.

Indeed, David Cronenberg's self-portrait allows me to isolate three interrelated aspects of what I will be calling postmodern gothic hysterics, given that they address the interface between a pathogenic imagination heralding psychic estrangement and a hysterical strategy of psychosomatic articulation whose communication, always directed at an interpolating addressee, broadcasts a message about the frailty of symbolic codes, protective fictions, and mutable corporeality. First, we have highlighted the discrepancy between any outside, quasi-*objective* perspective on psychic processes and the subjective realization of these phantasies: that is, the discrepancy between the way someone presents him- or herself to others and how he or she *really* is, radically putting into question any essentialist notion of the subject, the mode of quasi-altered, self-presentation the psychoanalyst Stavros Mentzos designates as hysteric. Second, Cronenberg addresses the anxiety provoked when a given phenomenon (be this a person or an event) stages an uncanny boundary fluidity between what appears to be (or rather presents itself as being) of a friendly, helpful, kind, and articulate nature, and what appears to be dangerous, disgusting, horrible, and irrational. Again the notion of an essential, unified subject is radically questioned once a single subject shows him- or herself to be both *healthy*, and integrated, as well as *diseased*, and disintegrating. With the perfect and the monstrous configured in and over one and the same body, of course, we touch on one of the staples of gothic literature—namely, the duplicitous gothic person, be it the beautiful mutant, the femmes fatals, or the figure of social authority gone mad, the Monks and Dr. Frankensteins. Not only does this uncanny duplicity stage the mutual implication between perfection and monstrosity, as Roland Barthes suggests, given that "what is *beyond* no longer differs from what is *short* of a limit; the essence of the code (perfection) has in the end the same status as what is outside the code (the monstrous)" (1970, 71). It also illustrates that a neat boundary cannot be drawn between the realm of body surface, personal appearance and body interior, personal kernel, and the being beneath any surfaces. For if perfection and monstrosity both appear on the surface, on the skin, in the chosen manner of self-presentation, then perhaps, thus the disquieting message, the subject in its essence is a knotting of the pure with the impure, of the intact with the disintegrating; imaginary plenitude appears always inscribed by vulnerability and fragility.

Finally, and here I want to argue that we can locate the particular postmodern transformation of gothic's hysterics, David Cronenberg insists that both of these confusing discrepancies—the unresolvable noncoincidence between subjective experience, its translation into phantasies and self-fashionings, and its reception by an outside spectator and the uncanny blurring between what is nice and what is disgusting—must be dealt with in relation to the touch. These issues regarding the image one has of someone, or the way someone fashions him- or herself for others, can only be negotiated within the register of the body, as a tangible, palpable phenomenon. The postmodern film, of course, is particularly apt for such a project, because it crosses narrative and poetic tropes with the vibrancy of the visual and the implied three-dimensionality of the staged theatrical scene.

In order to explore how Cronenberg recasts a figuration of the uncanny within the context of postmodern cultural anxieties and desires, and to link this articulation of psychic estrangement with that of hysteria, it is useful to recall Tzvetan Todorov's argument that one of the narrative kernels of gothic texts is the "hesitation experienced by a person who knows only the laws of nature, confronting an apparently supernatural event" (1975, 25). The uncertainty evoked by such gothic oscillation between the real and the imaginary can either result in faith, entertaining new laws of nature to account for the phenomena (the genre of the marvelous), or in incredulity, leaving the laws of reality intact and seeking an explanation of the phenomena within the confines of this reality—he terms the genre the uncanny or, to avoid confusion with psychoanalytic terminology, the explained supernatural. The mark of fantastic texts, in turn, lies in a sustained hesitation both on the part of the characters toward the narrated events and on the part of the reader toward the characters and the text as a whole. What will prove seminal to my discussion of David Cronenberg's pathologies of the image, significantly, is an aspect that Todorov omits from of his classification system: namely, the shift from the fantastic into horror, when undecidability is retained even though the metaphors of fantasy have also become flesh.

In connection with doubt as the mark of the gothic, it is equally useful to also recall that when Sigmund Freud introduced the concept of the uncanny (*das Unheimliche*) into psychoanalytic discourse, he chose the term to designate those psychic moments when a subject is confronted with phenomena that force him to hesitate between whether something is agreeable and familiar or concealed and kept out of sight—for example, Cronenberg's description of himself as being both nice and disgusting. Yet what the subject confronting an uncanny scenario ultimately discovers is that "the unheimlich is what was once heimisch, familiar; the 'un' is the token of repression" (1919, 245). As an event of disjunction, when fixed boundaries become fluid, the *unheimlich* may refer to situations where whether something is animate or inanimate, real or imagined, unique or a repetition inspires a hermeneutic hesitation. Yet, significantly, the example Freud offers for the conflation of the familiar and the *unheimlich* is the site of the womb: "It often happens that neurotic men declare that they feel there is something uncanny about the female genital organs. This *unheimlich* place, however, is the entrance to the former *Heim* of all human beings. . . . There is a joking saying that 'Love is home-sickness'; and whenever a man dreams of a place or a country and says to himself, while he is still dreaming: 'this place is familiar to me, I've been here before,' we may interpret the place as being his mother's genitals or her body" (245).

It is, then, this sequence of terms, all mutually representing each other—gothic pathology of the image, moments of psychic hesitation or estrangement and the womb—that allows me to read Cronenberg's cinematic phantasy scenarios within the context of the language of hysteria, given that in this malady of the womb, this *mal de mère*, Freud's uncanny anatomic site, once it articulates itself as a wandering foreign body, makes strange the afflicted person's mental topography and its corresponding body organs, and in so doing it enacts an overdetermined performance of the uncanny. For as I have been arguing, the notion of the wandering womb of hysteria can continue to be a useful image, even if the medical discourse it emerged from is no longer tenable, once one treats it not as an empirical reality but rather as a cultural trope for dissatisfied desire in general. Concomitant with this, phantasy scenarios revolving around a womb gone awry offer a displaced representation of traumatic knowledge that links the subject's origin with its telos; that links its navel, marking parturition from the womb, with its internal counterpart, the foreign body of mutability introduced into the human body at conception, ensuring that a tomb of sorts will be the subject's ultimate destination. And if, by virtue of phantasy, these hysteric scenes (whether as hysteric fits, where the body plays through an organic disorder, or as hallucinations, where it plays through a disorder of the imagination) render the otherwise invisible traces of traumatic impact visible, the mise-en-scène of anxiety or desire they stage allow the afflicted subject to negotiate its relation to this uncanny anatomical site. What emerges, however, is not only a negotiation of one's desire in relation to two laws—the law of corporality in all its mutability and vulnerability, as this is dictated by the womb as the subject's actual site of origin, and the law of culture in all its fallibility and inconsistency, as this is dictated by a paternal decree to abandon the maternal body and accept the psychic protection that symbolic difference affords. These phantasy scenarios also articulate an uncanny psychic ambivalence about the anatomical site, configured as the conflict between a desire to have control over the womb and with it the fundamental fragility of the human subject it stands for, and a desire for disempowerment, for being taken into possession by the womb—which, once it begins to wander as a foreign body, comes to embody the traumatic truth of psychic alterity fundamental to the structure of subjectivity.

Mapping the discourse of hysteria onto Freud's claim that the womb is uncanny from the very start, familiar and unfamiliar, the forgotten and hidden site resonant of the maternal origin all subjects must abandon, one can speculate whether, once the womb begins to wander, the blurring between origin and telos, between invisibility and visibility does not go far that the resulting symptoms serve phantomatically to objectify the psychic gap in knowledge along which these distinctions had been constructed. As the unruly womb sets out on its trajectory, it infiltrates the entire body with its uncanniness, making internal the *Unheimlichkeit* external. In precisely this way, Cronenberg's cinematic phantasies repeatedly stage scenes where what was hidden breaks into the open, where what was inside the body appears on or indeed pierces the skin. But the contagion, the blurring, will even go farther and infect the spectator of this disruption until the inversion is complete. In Cronenberg's many phantasy scenarios the external living space of his protagonists is so fully flooded with the hallucinatory intoxication emerging from the uncanny wandering uterus, the hysterization is so complete, that interior and exterior conflate, and the space the protagonist is placed within fully transforms into its own uncanny point of origin. The lived space, enveloping the protagonist's body from outside, itself becomes a womb by representation, and it mirrors the internal womb that has begun to wander.

In connection with such a blurring of the boundary between internal and external body spaces, we should recall Jacques Lacan's term for the *Unheimlich*, "extimacy." As Jacques-Alain Miller has argued, he uses this concept to discuss psychic events that perform the gesture of inverting interiority into exteriority so as to illustrate that the most interior part of the psyche has a quality of exteriority, that the most intimate is radically Other, a foreign body, a wandering parasite (1988). This notion of extimacy is particularly useful for discussing Cronenberg's deployment of horror as metaphor-become-flesh, because it can so usefully designate the phantomatic, encrypted presence of kernels of real traumatic knowledge in the Symbolic, where repressed material returns not only as a hallucination but as an embodiment with both psychic and somatic reality.[1]

The issue that the infamous malady of the womb conflates with a process that dismantles the stability of images, however, allows me to address one final connection between late-eighteenth-century European Enlightenment, which produced the gothic imagination as one of its unacclaimed side effects, and postmodern horror imagination: reviving this sense of uncanny self-estrangement, this split between rationality and nightmare. For it allows me to reexplore the way hysteria performs a malady of and by representation, knotting together a disturbance of the body with one of the imagination in a psychosomatic scenario whose dysfunctioning body parts and pathogenic images come to stand in for inaccessible, resiliently present traumatic knowledge. Freud emphasized that hysteria should be seen as the psychosomatic language a subject uses to articulate how she is haunted by the memories and stories she has incorporated and cannot shed—texts occupying her body as though it were their host, using the body to speak their alterity, regardless whether these nonabreactable psychic traces are inherited phantasies or conversions of actually experienced events. The link between postmodern phantasies of horror at the contingencies of corporality and the invention of the uncanny in the late eighteenth century, though using Freudian psychoanalysis as its point of mediation, turns on another issue of the infamous malady of the matrix. For Freud's discussion of hysterical conversion, according to which psychical excitation becomes pathological by converting exclusively into the somatic register, concurs with the medical opinion of the eighteenth century, which claimed that the hysterical body was "given over to that disorder of the spirits which, outside of all organic laws and any functional necessity, could successively seize upon all the available spaces of the body" (Foucault 1961, 147). As a result, hysteria emerges as the neurosis par excellence that articulates an inundation of the psychic apparatus by the foreign body of spirits, by the pathological abundance of imaginations, of phantasies gone awry, precisely by hooking the message of a return of repressed desire or a repressed gap in knowledge into the body. At the same time, in the medical discourses of the Englightenment, hysteria figures as a key concept in a debate over the crisis in representation, namely in relation to the question of the diseased imagination as a source of body-dysfunctions.

As Foucault argues, hysteria, more than gout or dropsy, is the true eighteenth-century disease because it alone was explained within the transformed dualism that emerged from the Cartesian model, the operation of the imagination in relation to the body: "Hysteria thus appears as the most real and the most deceptive of diseases; real because it is based upon a movement of the animal spirits; illusory as well, because it generates symptoms that seem provoked by a disorder inherent in the organs, whereas they are only the formation, at the level of these organs, of a central or rather general disorder; it is the derangement of internal mobility that assumes the appearance, on the body's surface, of a local symptom" (1961, 148). Once Cartesian dualism had been transformed to such a degree that the powers of triggering physical illness could be relegated entirely to a diseased imagination, hysteria, known in the eighteenth century as the English Malady, uncannily spliced together a disorder of the imagination with that of the animal spirit. Indeed, in 1771 J. D. T. de Bienville published a book called *Nymphomania or a Treatise on Uterine Furor* in which he discusses the concept of *metromania* (womb fury), which, as G. S. Rousseau astutely points out, from the start was not only synonymous with *nymphomania* but also confused with *metermania* (a rage for reciting verses) (1991, 46). The compelling aspect of Bienville's confusion of the two concepts, however, is that for him, metromania "begins with a melancholy delirium, the cause of which is found in a defective matrix"; the deeper cause, however, proves to be not of a somatic but rather a psychic nature, a "mental derangement caused by the imagination" (quoted in Rousseau 1991, 46). It is against the backdrop of such medical discourses, well in place by the end of the eighteenth century, that the emergence of gothic literature could be mapped. Because I want to present Cronenberg's work as a postmodern transformation of this literary genre, I will return often to the way he transforms a medical discourse that splices the diseased imagination and defective womb together with an excessive production of verses (be these textual or visual meters).

II

In his article "A Gothic Revival" Wayne Drew explicitly discusses Cronenberg as a postmodern variant of the gothic. He argues that Cronenberg's films embody contemporary fascinations and paranoid obsessions, but interrogate them through the gothic genre, the dream vision, and automatic writing. His obsessive, scatalogical vision "rests in the equation between sexuality, horror and death. As such he is firmly within the Romantic tradition in that the fatal allure which resulted from the fusion of beauty and death in eighteenth-century European literature is fundamental to the literature of romanticism" (1984, 16). Repeatedly he touches on themes that are prevalent in the gothic genre: the relation of mind to body, involving anxieties about bodily and mental vulnerability and fallibility, as well as the question of sexual identity; of the position of the individual in relation to the family and social institutions (negotiating the oppressive and the nourishing aspects of these filial bonds); and the deployment of metaphysical and moral codes. In this Cronenberg is like a literary traveler of the late eighteenth century (Grünberg 1992, 32), exploring the thematic and formal terrain only to redefine it within the needs of postmodernism.

Indeed, in interviews Cronenberg has been particularly explicit about his relation to this cultural heritage. At the navel of his voyage through gothic terrain is his exploration of the connection between the physical and the spiritual. As he explains to Chris Rodley, "It's still a conundrum that drives me mad: the old Bertrand Russell riddle. What's mind? No matter. What's matter? Never mind" (1992, 129). In his work, this body-mind schism, acknowledging the inevitability of bodily demise as well as a human desire for immortality, evolves into two mutually implicated phantasy scenes of transformation, where metamorphosis means both reformation and mutation. Whatever particular versions the oscillations between mental and somatic register take—between phantasy and flesh, between interiority or exteriority—that is to say, regardless whether he confronts us with an embodiment of thought or the penetration of the body by mental processes, the basic premise is that while it is difficult to accept mortality, vulnerability, and the tragedy of human loss, these are also inevitable. "We've all got the disease— the disease of being finite," he explains in the same interview, "and con- sciousness is the original sin: consciousness of the inevitability of our death" (1992, 128).[2]

This ineluctable trace of mortality, voiced in the register of the body, can be understood in Lacan's term of extimacy, for the most intimate part of the psychic apparatus, the nodal point of mind and body, is also the foreign body that threatens to disband the subject whom it also holds together. Fit- tingly, at another point in the interview, Cronenberg offers his reading of the Latin quote, The fear of death disturbs me; "Death is the basis of all horror, and for me death is a very specific thing. It's very physical. That's where I become Cartesian. Descartes was obsessed with the schism between mind and body, and how one relates to the other. . . . The idea that you carry the seeds of your own destruction around with you, always, and that they can erupt at any time, is . . . scary. But there is no defence against it. . . . I don't think that the flesh is necessarily treacherous, evil, bad. It is cantankerous, and it is independent" (1992, 58, 80). The conjecture I especially wish to explore, however, involves medical discourses that describe hysteria as re- sulting from the wandering animal called uterus, reappearing at any mo- ment and disturbing the normal functioning of the body; they recode pre- cisely this sense of a palpable mortality.

Cronenberg's work shows the body to be fundamentally diseased because all living means dying; thus the body produces mental hallucinations. The mind is equally diseased because imagination is comparable to a virus, natu- ral and dangerous, and it produces body disturbances. At the navel of his postmodern transformation of gothic hysterics we find the impasse of the body-mind schism, a dilemma that becomes particularly compelling, as Cronenberg's cinematic phantasy scenarios repeatedly enact, when the so- matization of the imaginary veers into pathology. Repeatedly exploring the theme of the evanescence of human lives, the fragility of our mental states, and, therefore, the fallibility of reality, he recognizes that "one of our touch- stones for reality is our bodies. And yet they, too, are by definition ephem- eral. So to whatever degree we centre our reality—and our understanding of reality—in our bodies, we are surrendering that sense of reality to our bod- ies' ephemerality" (1992, 145).

Cronenberg's cinematic plottings of gothic hysterics all revolve around what Laplanche and Pontalis call the core of phantasy work: modalities of the primal scene, picturing the origin of the subject in relation to heritage, castration, or seduction. These phantasies (see chapter 3) depict the subject's desire to solve the riddle of her existence by exploring the issue of her ori- gins. Phantasy scenes engage this quest by enacting three core questions: Who am I in relation to my parents, my heritage? What is the origin of my body's anatomy, its castration? What is the cause of my drives, my desires? In contrast to the strict Freudian model, Cronenberg's cinematic phantasy scenes offer slight semantic transformations. Interrogating one's heritage becomes a question of the law of the body's mutability (its inevitable trans-formations), and the issue of castration emerges as the subject's subjection before the law of the Other, its possession by this alterity—its extimacy. Seduction in turn translates into ceding to the call of the diseased body and the diseased imagination.

If we accept Lucien Israël's formula with which I have been working, namely, that the hysteric is one whose psychic existence depends on setting up a mode of communication with a figure of alterity to whom she or he can repeatedly pose the question of identity, we can now reformulate the content of the questions raised by Cronenerg's phantasy scenarios. For his postmod-ern transformation of gothic hysterics moves beyond the question psycho-analysis traditionally ascribes to the hysteric—the hesitation between being masculine or feminine. It has grown to a resilient string of questions: Am I alive or dead? Am I mutating or transforming? Can I control the images that not only pervade my psychic apparatus but also take on somatic shape and wander through my body?' Within Cronenberg's oeuvre, such films as the *The Fly* or *Dead Ringers* stage scenarios involving representations of the womb as site for the subject's origins, as well as the corpse as figure for where the subject is headed. Films such as *Videodrome* or *Naked Lunch* play with the cultural archive of images as catalyst for and matrix within which to formulate the subject's desires and notions of gender. In all, however, he reenacts precisely the etymological splice of metromania and metermania so endemic to hysteria.

Therefore, I want to suggest two interrelated phantasy scenarios of hys-teric desire for Cronenberg's films. One includes phantasy scenes performing a *malady of the womb*. Here the womb, having become unhooked, pere-grinates through the body to signify a wandering desire with a transforma-tion and location at various body sites, the body speaking, as part of this transformation or mutation, above all its mutability. Ultimately this malady of the womb performs the interface between desire and anxiety: the mutual implication of womb envy and womb anxiety. The second scenario per-forms a *malady of representation*. Here the so-called diseased imagination (corrollary to the other staple of medical discourses on hysteria, the wander-ing *hystera*), but also the diseased body, expresses itself through a chain of substitutes standing in for or replacing the core trauma that is outside and beyond representation. In this respect, Cronenberg's insistence that the dis-junction between the intact body (the person who appears to be so nice) and the disgusting body (the person who presents monstrous phantasies) is pal-pable refers to another psychoanalytic maxim. Traumatic traces wander in the body. As a phantom, objectifying, in Nicolas Abraham's words, an in-herited or preserved gap in the psychic apparatus, this traumatic impact has a latent presence even if, or precisely because, it is not accessible. While the

body forgets nothing, acts out what we have no power over, and thwarts all
our phantasies of power, the peregrinations of the foreign body of trauma,
for which the wandering uterus of classical medical texts is a metaphor,
remains encrypted. By virtue of conversion, this foreign body is preserved as
an omphalic kernel, constructed into a space enveloping nothing. It is not
sublimated through translation into symbolic representation, so that precisely when language fails, the body acts, and we find ourselves momentarily
confronting of the *unheimlich*, extimacy, with the flooding of the symbolic
space with material from the real.

In Cronenberg's cinematic phantasy scenes both the malady of the womb
and the malady of representation have as their visualized point of knotting
some version of the navel. These scenes either enact a cut between breast and
genitals that allows the insertion and removal of videocassettes and other
objects (*Videodrome*), or highlight the cutting of the umbilical cord (*Dead
Ringers*), or stage the womb externalized to avoid natural denaveling
(*Brood, The Fly*). Given their hysteric blurring of reality and (the psychic
reality of) hallucinations, these cinematic narratives show protagonists living phantasies of the womb or responding to such phantasies with anxiety.
But even as the protagonists of these scenes oscillate between an appropriation of the matrix and its rejection, Cronenberg's enactment draws us into
the space of fantasy, touching on our own enjoyment as images of pathology
become palpable and not only as desires projected onto an external screen.
Rather, he uncannily diminishes the distance between the visual representation and our own somatic reenactment of this spectacle. Apodictically put,
his cinematic scenarios hystericize us. As Cronenberg explains, "The basic
appeal of art is to the unconscious and I try to communicate with my audience at that level. The dream quality of film is central in this experience. It is
in dreams that our inhibitions are down and things from the unconscious
emerge. I am not a staunch Freudian by any means but I think the mechanisms that he describes are quite accurate. It is this function that I have tried
to release and allow to work when I write a script. I think it is what is
released in audiences when they watch my films" (Drew 1984, 16).

III

I will turn my focus to what I call the navel scenes in several Cronenberg
films, beginning with the first hysterical modality of desire, the malady of the
matrix as womb envy or womb anxiety. In all his early films, David Cronenberg explored the notion of a wandering foreign body used to articulate not
only individual psychic discontent and distress, but also the way this personal hysteria responded to or imitated a cultural malaise. In *Shivers* (1975),
for example, hysteria is rendered in scenes where a body part—encoded as
foreign, as a parasite that has been created by a scientist to libidinize his
peers—goes awry and decides to have its own, independent existence, multi-
plying in the process. It transgresses the boundary between interior and exte-

rior, entering and exiting bodies through any orifice, and contaminating them in the process.[3] In a particularly gruesome case, the parasite, which had made its presence known to the character it was inhabiting through abdominal bulges seen through the skin, ultimately bursts wide open the skin around the navel in one long, bloody seam in its effort to leave the host body. The final scene of *Shivers* (which Martin Scorcese describes as "something I've never been able to shake. It's an ending that is genuinely shocking, subversive, surrealistic and probably something we all deserve" 1984, 54) stages mass hysteria taking over an entire housing complex. Celebrating a feast of destructive jouissance, the film ends by having the entire infectious cast embark into the Toronto night. In *Rabid* (1976), Cronenberg offers the phantasy scene of graft tissue gone awry to produce a female vampire, while in *Scanners* (1980) he develops a plot of women, medicated with a sedative during pregnancy, giving birth to monstrous, telepathic, mind exploders. This phantasy scenario, which I would call a splice between womb envy (the desire to create artificially) and womb anxiety (the fear of mortality) produces mutants. As symptoms of a communication with an Other site, with a point of other knowledge, these foreign bodies, turned into the hosts for pathological images (the scientists' notions of redesigning the body) offer precisely the coded message that we as the hystericized spectators seek—but they do so by representation. Entirely inverting the first, manifest intention (the scientists' desire to overcome the constraints and fallibilities of the human body), they somaticize the significant sentence, We are destructive, mutable, and disempowered, because possessed by alterity; in short, we are the carriers of the virus called mortality.

In the *Brood* (1979) Cronenberg quite explicitly visualizes the hybrid cerebral and visceral by inventing a plot about "creatures from the unconscious, making the mental physical" (Rodley 1992, 84). He presents us with the cinematic staging of extimacy—the embodiments of rage, anger, guilt, and disappointment—where, in a scene of horror, psychoanalytic metaphors become real. The overriding plot involves a deranged scientist, Dr. Raglan, who uses psychoplasmic surgery to palpably externalize his patients' psychic anger, with the body of the psyche revolting against the body of normalcy. These patients become paradigms of extimacy—the surface of their mutated body (lumps, scars, reshaped body tissue, signs on the skin) representing and substituting past traumatic impressions and their belated phantasy reenactment. Yet even as the privileged patient Nola is meant to embody the perfection of Dr. Raglan's project (hysterically giving shape to the core question of his therapy, Where does my anger come from?) she also is the symptom enacting for him how the perfection of hysteria is coterminous with the utter failure of his therapeutic project. Like her hysteric predecessors, she broadcasts the fallibility of his medical discourse, which seeks to find a cure for the body's mutability.

The gothic moment in this phantasy scenario (the literal, or real, embodiment of the metaphors of psychoanalysis) is that Raglan's therapy fatally goes awry. The stories of hatred and destruction Nola works through in therapy, when she shows Dr. Raglan her anger by reenacting it (in dialogue) through staged narratives, reappear as hallucinations in the real at another site—her mother's house, in the parental bed. Here her second set of children—the brood she gives birth to externally, children who have no navels because they were palpably but not naturally born—literally perform those deeds of violence she mentally conceives in her dialogue with Raglan, the primal scenes of child abuse at the center of her home. Owing to the fluid boundary between mind and womb, the omnipotence of thought Freud designated as one of the staples of the uncanny is visualized in its full, perturbing embodiment. The hysteric reenactment of trauma, once spliced with a gothic blur of fantasy and reality, produces scenes where the mentally recreated violence becomes palpably real.

The peripeteia of the narrative occurs when Nola finally enacts her mutation of the natural birth process for an audience other than her maker, the plastic surgeon Dr. Raglan. Responding to her husband's plea, "Let me be with you, I want to go with you wherever you go," she kneels before him and lifts up her long white gown, slit down the middle to expose her plastically refashioned body, the perfection of its white tissue emphasizing the monstrosity about to be revealed. What we see, as the camera moves back and forth between her proudly powerful gestures of self-exhibition and her husband's dismay turning into disgust, is the front of her body, between her breasts and genitals. Along with other disfigured bulges and tissue knots on her side and between her breasts, she reveals her second, external womb, filled with a fetus about to be born, attached by sack-shaped tissue to her body around the area of her navel. Once again, letting her white gown drop so that only the filled womb is exposed, she demonstrates to her husband the process of denaveling without a navel that produces her monstrous brood. Rather than pressing out a baby attached to her body by an umbilical cord that must be cut, Nola sensually and lovingly bites open with her teeth the womb-sack containing her psychosomatic progeny. She slowly rips apart the skin enveloping it, and, having gently extracted her newly born, licks its blood. This scenario of secondary, externalized birth quite compellingly enacts the uncanny turn by which Dr. Raglan's phantasies of transforming mutability through psychoplasmic surgery produce real, monstrous mutations. In this scene of horrible extimacy, Nola's hystericized body performs the scientific project of womb envy qua womb anxiety gone awry. In the film's resolution Nola senses her husband's disgust and her brood revolts in the shed next to the therapy room, killing Dr. Raglan who has entered it to save Nola's natural daughter, Candy. As the husband strangles the monstrous Nola, and by extension demolishes the brood that can exist only as somatic representatives of her psychic anger, Candy escapes. But the final close-up of the traumatized daughter, sitting silently in her father's car as he rescues her from the site of horror, shows bumps on her skin. The mother's hysteria has passed to the daughter.

In Cronenberg's remake of Kurt Neumann's *The Fly* (1986) we are again presented with a sequence of narrative events that involves the issue of body transformation as artificial birth or rather autoprocreation, leading to premature death. At an official function the solitary scientist Seth Brundel meets the attractive and ambitious journalist Veronica Quaife and explains to her that he is working on something that will change the world and human life as we know it. Intrigued, she follows him to his laboratory where she sees two teleportation pods connected by several thick rubbery wires to each other as well as to a computer that Seth can use to control them and learn whether teleportation has been successful. The first pod houses the body about to be transported whereas the second receives the reintegrated body; the computer decodes the organism placed in the first pod, indicates all the components that are being teleported on its screen, and during the teleportation sequence translates this reencoded information to the second pod.

Teleportation, we learn in the course of the film, is a process whereby the body is disintegrated at one site and reintegrated at a different location, as it moves from one pod through the connecting cords to the computer terminal and then again through cords to the second pod. These pods, iron beehive-shaped wombs large enough to encase the human body, with glass doors in the front for entrance and exit, are reminiscent of the Greek omphalos I discussed in my introduction, which as mound-shaped cult object came simultaneously to indicate religiously marked sites of birth and grave mounds. Playing on the same paradigm of associations, the cords connecting the three stations can be read as visualizations of artificial umbilical cords (Robbins; 1993). Indeed, this double meaning of the womb as a site where something is generated but also where mortality is perpetrated is at stake in Seth Brundel's scenario of teleportation. For the seminal anxiety that his scientific phantasy seeks to overcome explicitly relates to the disease of being finite. Seth has already formed a symptom to articulate this anxiety about the body's being transformed by age, by the agent of mutability wandering through the body, namely his motion sickness.

But in hysterically replacing this first symptom, motion sickness, with excessive mobility, teleportation, Seth enacts a self-generated triumph over all traces of transformation natural to human physiology, by virtue of his introducing an experience of artificial transportation that completely surpasses and transgresses all constraints imposed by nature on the human body. Entirely in the vein of gothic excess, Cronenberg displays that this second hysterical symptom formation is merely a transformation and not an effacement of the originary anxiety about body mutability. Now the representing phantasy of being unable to move becomes palpable, as a displaced articulation of the threatening other knowledge of the ineluctable body mobility toward dissolution, what Cronenberg calls "the disease of being finite." The internal "uterus" wandering through the body, which initially caused Seth's physical inertia, along the lines of hysterical exaggeration now exalts in its peregrinations so excessively that the result is an acceleration of body transformation.

As Seth moves from his first demonstration of teleportation, involving Veronica's silk stocking, to the unsuccessful and then successful teleportation of a baboon, only to complete the narrative sequence by teleporting his own body, Cronenberg once again stages the phantasy scenario of giving birth without the cutting of an umbilical cord (and thus without denavelment). This climactic scene of self-teleportation, however, is divided in two parts. The first is a reenactment of how Seth, drunk and jealous because Veronica seems to have left him for Stratis Borans, her former lover and the editor of the scientific journal *Particle*, carelessly goes through with the teleportation process despite a housefly's having accidently joined him in the pod. The second repeats this scene, replaying it on the computer screen and leading to Seth's tragically belated recognition of his ineluctable transformation into a mutant.

Significantly, Cronenberg uses three screens to visualize the fluidity between body interior and external refiguration. On the one hand, he highlights the two glass doors of the pods, one showing Seth's ecstatic face anticipating teleportation, the other revealing first the smoke and then his teleported body, emerging from its artificial womb. On the other hand, Cronenberg begins and ends the entire sequence with a shot of the computer monitor's dialogue with Seth, thus intertwining visual with verbal signs throughout this key scenario. After a shot of Seth claiming determinedly, "What are we waiting for? Let's just do it," we see the computer monitor responding to Seth's command "initiate sequence" with the assurance "sequence activated." Similarly, Cronenberg puts closure on the visualization of his protagonist's bodily dis- and reintegration by focusing on the computer monitor, which now blinks ironically "teleportation successful," although the spectators have been fully aware throughout the sequence of the fly's presence inside the first pod.

Controlling but also interfering with the information exchange between the twin pods, this computer monitor functions like Lacan's third element, troubling this narcissistically informed dyad because it puts to question any sense of plenitude, potency, or triumph over the mutable body that the pods sustain in the phantasy space of Seth Brundel. While the pods can only display integrated bodies, the computer monitor visualizes the interface between the external and the internal, giving in numbers, letters, and visual images a symbolic, not a somatic, representation of the teleportation sequence, a representation which is, furthermore, infinitely reiterable and replayable. The repetition of the teleportation sequence, the scene of Seth's distressing anagnorisis, is staged like the obscenely horrific inversion of the first scene, where lighting and music had endowed the initial teleportation with pathos and beauty. Now, responding to the onslaught of accelerated body transformation with the question "Is this how it starts when I die," Seth goes to his computer and, entirely in line with the gesture of the classic hysteric who interrogates her identity by addressing questions to an Other, whom she supposes to have the knowledge she seeks, he asks for the first teleportation of S. Brundel.

The camera begins to oscillate between the screen that splits in two parts, to indicate the primary and the secondary teleportation elements, and Seth's astonished face as he belatedly reconstructs the event in an effort to find out the identity of this secondary element and its relation to him. In other words Cronenberg now makes graphic, ironically on the level of symbolic and not somatic representation, the information of what happened on the most intimate—the molecular-genetic—level. Indeed, we have a visualisation of how hysteric metromania and metermania come to their orgiastic high point. While the first scene had offered us an external view of how Seth's so-called "diseased imagination," desiring to appropriate the womb as site for generating bodies, finds fulfillment in the hysteric enactment of self-teleportation, this second symbolic rendition of the sequence reiterates how, in the course of the first teleportation, the computer had gone awry. Seth, unable to learn the identity of the secondary element from straight verbal dialogue, asks the computer to run the sequence. With him we see a record of this teleportation sequence, where, misunderstanding the presence of the foreign body, of the other wandering *hysterus* that so fatefully was introduced into the act of teleportation, the computer had produced a fateful fusion. The malady of the womb quite visibly becomes a malady of meters, for the screen begins to throw up a plethora of images showing the breakdown of the human body, only to exchange these for images of the reconstitution of the fly body. The scene builds to the terrifying visualization of extimacy, as Seth discovers that the most intimate part of his identity is quite palpably Other, a fly, relentlessly facing him. It ends once more with an interpretive dialogue, in which Seth discovers that his fusion with this foreign body is ineluctable.

One can then say, as Seth turns himself into his own object of investigation, that the externalized phantasy becomes internalized and palpable. His hystericized body becomes the battleground for his conflictual desires about body transformation, where reintegration, though aimed at perfecting the body, runs the risk of mutation. What Cronenberg significantly leaves undecided is whether the repressed desire that comes to be articulated in the course of this hysterical enactment of phantasy images at the body is really a desire for a perfection of the impaired human body or for precisely the diseased transformation of the body. In either case, the navel of the scenario remains hooked to the hysterical uterus, understood as matrix and as wandering animal. If teleportation, on the one hand, was meant to overcome a natural vulnerability, Seth's motion sickness, it replaces this physiological imperfection by an excessive countergesture: the animal in Seth, the fly, wandering through his body like the unhooked uterus of classical medical texts—settling at various locations, infecting them, and completely transforming them.

On the other hand, we are shown scenes where the animal in him takes over the body, inducing the nymphomaniacal excess synonymous with metromania as well as eating disorders. But perhaps more significantly, the foreign organism wandering in his body also allows him to wander up ceiling and walls. It is as though the internal space of his body had been inverted and turned inside out, so that his unnatural peregrinations through his living space mirror the peregrinations of disease through his body interior. Furthermore, if the initial motion sickness was but a displaced psychosomatic representation of his anxieties about the body's vulnerability, so that the counterpart of this displacement, his scientific invention of teleportation, is to be seen as a displaced representation of his desire to avoid the dangerous register of the body entirely, its hysterical realization, the literal embodiment of the animal within him, is also an excessive disregard of all fear of the flesh. In one of his disputes with Veronica he accuses her of being afraid to dive into the plasma pool, of being destroyed and recreated. For Seth, in other words, the attempt to repress any knowledge of the disease of death, which all mortal subjects acquire in the maternal womb and for which the navel is the irradicable signature, forms two hysterical symptoms: first his motion sickness and then the invention of surrogate wombs, the teleportation pods, that briefly allow him the protective fiction of a body that has become fallible yet omnipotent because it has suspended all fear of the flesh, penetrated "beyond the veil of the flesh," embraced "the deep penetrating dive into the plasma pool."

Yet, as psychoanalytic discourse insists, repressed desires return as hallucinations in the real. In Cronenberg's *The Fly* this uncanny return takes on the gesture of postmodern gothic hysteria, where the womb at the heart of all of Seth's anxieties and desires becomes the only existent space. Controlling the site where organisms are generated, monitoring the act of dis- and reintegration of the human body, transforms into an exclusive embrace of the flesh with all its terrifying mobility, its vulnerability and mutability enhanced. Cronenberg ultimately presents us with a horrific enactment of the family romance, an inversion of the scenario Freud discussed (1909), where the child uses phantasy work to correct actual life and replace his ordinary parents with others of better birth. Seth's wish fullfilment ultimately revolves around a phantasy in which he imagines himself as the offspring of Brundle and housefly. The question Cronenberg thus inflicts on us is whether Seth's appropriation of the womb is merely an articulation of an anxiety about the death disease, as this translates into a fear of the flesh, symptomized by motion sickness on the one hand and a phantasmic appropriation of procreation, of generating bodies, on the other. Might these symptoms be screen phantasies, covering the far more disturbing repressed desire to be undone and redone precisely beyond the parameters of the natural body, to move outside the register of symbolic transformation into real mutation and destruction?

In support of the latter interpretation, Cronenberg offers a counterphantasy to Seth's malady of the womb: namely, Veronica's nightmare about giving birth to a mutant that occurs just after she realizes that she is pregnant with Seth's baby. She dreams that she is going into the hospital because she believes she will miscarry, only to find herself on the operating table with an oversized, blood-covered larva exiting from her womb and wiggling violently in the operating physician's hands. Within the context of *The Fly* this nightmare is especially significant because it uses the woman's focalization (Bal) of monstrous birth giving to critique the hysterical male's womb project. Entirely in the tradition of Mary Shelley's *Frankenstein*, it is the woman, fully responsible for her maternal function, who serves as the agent of conventional morality, deconstructing how (as Helen Robbins puts it) "jeopardized paternity breeds womb envy" (1993, 137). Indeed, only Veronica as the mother carrying Seth's natural child can put closure to his hysterical oscillations. She finally shoots the newly created hybrid Brundel-fly-telepod. Yet, even as she is the agent securing the recuperation of the symbolic order, the representative of the maternal reinstalling the fallible law of paternity against Seth's chaotically hysterical transgression of these two gendered functions, she is merely an instrument, fulfilling the act of death Seth designs for himself. As he pleads with her to shoot him, he is perhaps for the first time openly addressing the desire that has ridden him at his most intimate, Other site all along.

My final example of the modality of hysteria I have been calling a malady of the womb is *Dead Ringers* (1988), which also focuses on the sequences staging the protagonists' anxiety about and envy of the womb and its narrative resolution. Here Cronenberg addresses the issue of denaveling more directly than in any of his other films by enmeshing two plot sequences, scenes that represent a fascination for the feminine uterus, namely the gynecological work of the twin brothers Ely and Beverly Mantel, and a desire to avoid separation, namely the hysterical crossing of identity that these twins perform, especially for their female patients and lovers. These two strands come together in Beverly's nightmare phantasy that stages his separation anxiety as a repressed desire for psychic denavelment from his brother, only to find its narrative closure when the division he initially rejects is horrifically performed in the gesture of his real surgical cut into the body of his brother Ely.

As the dream begins, he wakes up to find himself lying in bed with Claire Niveau, the lover he initially shared with his brother, who broke up with them once she discovered their secret. Having met her again unexpectedly in an art gallery, he now wants to keep their love affair to himself. Articulating in dream language what has been perturbing his conscious mind—the fact that he wants to carve out a private space in his life that his brother will have no access to—he realizes that Ely is lying in bed with them, surveilling their intimacy. Terrified, he explains to Claire, "Look, honey, he's here. I don't want him to see this," and she responds, "Right, I'll just separate you." As she leans forward determinedly, we are shown blobs of body tissue over a meter long, connecting the two twins together around the area of their respective navels. Claire slowly bends her head forward and bites into what in the dark shadows of the blue lighting appears like the navel of the connecting tissue and extracts the cord of flesh that has tied them to one another, while both brothers lean backward, Ely flinching and Bev screaming in pain. Bev wakes up so violently that he falls out of the bed, and, still under the influence of the nightmare vision, will not let Claire take him into her arms. Only after she has given him some sleeping pills will he get back into bed with her. As she sits upright, he curls up, placing his head in her lap, seeking to mitigate the terrible nightmare representation of his lover who is forcing on him a second birth, an emotional life separate from his brother, by another representation, now not a traumatic but rather a protective fiction: the feminine lover's genitals as representative of the maternal womb.

As in *The Fly*, Cronenberg in this film also presents us with an uncanny blurring between womb anxiety and womb envy. The primal scene of the film, after all, shows the two boys in 1954 speculating on their origins, asking a little girl to have "sex" with them in their bathtub, and, because she rejects their proposal, turning instead to an anatomic doll for their investigation. This turn from body to model sets the pattern for two distinct but interrelated plots. On the one hand, Cronenberg sets up their medical specialization in gynecology as a metaphor for their desire to control and refashion the originary site of human life with all its vulnerability.[4] In this he self-consciously points to the well-known gothic motif of the scientist correcting fallible nature, taking over the role of creator by modifying the female reproductive organs. At one point Ely explains to one of his patients that he cannot help her, because her inability to get pregnant is not due to any defect in her organism but rather in her husband, placing her case beyond their jurisdiction: "We don't do husbands. We do female infertility, we do woman, that's our specialty."

On the other hand this hysterical obsession with the womb also articulates a defense against the possibility of symbolic castration, a belated anxiety about separation from the womb that Barbara Creed terms "phallic panic." In their effort to uncover, dissect, and control the mystery of the womb, the Mantel twins repeatedly stage their disavowal of sexual difference as well as psychic separation, their inability to accept a third position outside the narcissistic imaginary duality. In short, they demonstrate their unwillingness to acknowledge symbolic law because, as hysterics, they interrogate the infallibility of paternity, sensing only too acutely, as Creed puts it, "the impossibility of the individual male ever living up to the promise of the phallus" (1990, 131). As she concludes, "Unable to accept the possibility of symbolic castration, the male hysteric displaces his anxiety onto the body of woman, while simultaneously entering into a search for the impossible: abolition of sexual difference and reunification with the body of the Other" (145). For the twins, recognizing the impossible nature of the phallic ideal (and thus the sacrificial violence implied in accepting symbolic castration), means having recourse to the threatening but also desired womb, that uncannily familiar maternal site which offers protection from paternal law but inscribes a law of its own, the ineluctable "disease of being finite." For this reason I prefer to read the hysteria performed by the Mantel twins as more than symbolic castration. Instead, by focusing on the way their phantasy scenario revolves around a psychic cut that is repeatedly somatized—be it in

Bev's nightmare vision, the many dislocated operations on females, or finally their self-surgery—one can shift the critical discussion to the issue of denavelment, so as to emphasize that before and beyond the issues of sexual and symbolic difference what is at stake in this subjection is also the acknowledgment of the necessary fallibility of culture based on both paternal law and physical vulnerability.

Two symptom formations become enmeshed in the Mantel twins' performance of hysteria. For one, Cronenberg points to its misogynist streak, as for example in the scene where Bev, under the influence of a drug-induced hallucination, tries to use on a living woman the Mantel Retractor he and his brother developed for dissecting cadavers, and in so doing causes her extraordinary pain but justifies his actions to Ely by explaining, "There is nothing the matter with the instrument, it's the body that's wrong."[5] For another, Cronenberg stages the twins' pathological narcissism as a case history of borderline schizophrenia, playing with the fact that the identity boundary between them is entirely fluid. In both cases, however, what is at stake is the desire to have a womb of their own, bringing about an urge to penetrate the female body, to explore and reshape it.

But—and here one can locate the gothic turn of Cronenberg's rendition of this hysterical phantasy scenario—the intimate turns extimate in that the uterus they seek to discover inside women's bodies is also located outside, in the living spaces they inhabit. Both the apartment and the hospital, the two privileged places of their coexistence, architecturally come to represent the site of the womb, the space that harbors the intact bond between the twins and preserves them from denavelment. To stay with the metaphor of hysteria, once Claire has implanted in Bev a recognition of his repressed desire to separate from his twin, she causes the foreign body of strife, the figure of intimate and radical alterity at the basis of their fraternal bond (which they had successfully disavowed up to that point), to unhook and start wandering through the psychic space of the imaginary they share. The corollary to the disorder thus imposed on their shared psychic space is the growing disarray of precisely these two externally located womb sites. Ely's destructively performed inter-uterine operation, which one could call a cruel attack on a uterus during surgery that nearly kills the female patient, mirrors the manner in which the living and working space of the twins increasingly disintegrates, the latter the architectural victim of an equally cruel onslaught by the former—the twins' increased psychic instability.

We can then say, the womb—as object of scientific analysis and libidinal enjoyment—serves as the infiltrator and infector in this hysterical narrative about evasions and embraces of the disease of being finite. For the narrative of *Dead Ringers* moves along a circular trajectory that begins and ends at the navel. The turn from playmate to doll leads to a period of investigating the uterus, scientifically and amorously, whose acme is the nearly fatal operation performed by Beverly at the height of one of his delusions. At this point the twins turn away from the female body entirely, and, having withdrawn completely into their shared apartment, decide to cut into their own bodies instead. Yet if we look at the way the female protagonist, Claire Niveau, who comes to the Mantel twins to be treated and ends up as their lover, fits into the plot, we realize that Cronenberg pits two versions of hysteria against each other. For Claire is a hysteric in the classic sense. She quite literally suffers from a disease of the womb, a trifurcate cervix that makes it impossible for her to become pregnant. Owing to her unrequited desire, she is sexually promiscuous and emotionally unstable, having depressions and histrionic fits, so that the diseased body has as its counterfigure a diseased imagination, whose symptoms are masochistic, sexual phantasies, drug abuse, but also metermania. Not only is Claire an actress, but Ely, in an effort to get Bev to distance himself from her, argues that "she plays games all the time. You never know who she really is." As hysteric she infects the twins, injects her diseased imagination into their narcissistically informed phantasmic relationship, an incursion for which the drugs she gets Beverly to take are one of the most resonant tropic visualizations. In other words, she gets the uterus in their psychosocial apparatus to start its peregrinations, but in contrast to the male hysteria revolving around separation anxiety and a foreclosure of symbolic law, her hysterization of Beverly is coterminous with inducing in him the desire to separate from his twin.

She embodies the resilience of hysteria, constantly reshaping her symptoms. Yet the reason for this resilience is that she keeps the so-called castrative third term—the law of culture, gender difference, corporeal mutability, and mortality—floating. This preservation of the third term means positioning herself in relation to a figure of paternity, both accepting that the question of her existence can only be articulated in relation to this paternal figure and perpetually renegotiating her relation to this Other. To return to Lacan's formulation, the hysteric uses the interpellating Other to perform scenarios revolving around the question What am I, in relation to my dual castration by my sexual designation and by the contingency of my body? She splices together her indecision about whether to limit herself exclusively to either the masculine or feminine position with an oscillation between believing in the plenitude and infallibility of a perfect body, a wholly untroubled happiness, an eternal existence, and acknowledging the traumatic knowledge of human frailty, fallibility, and mortality. Articulating the enigma of her existence in a mise-en-scène of desire that knots together phantasies of procreation with those of mortality, the hysteric subject opens to question the consistency and infallibility of paternal law. Indeed, as Pam Cook argues, the disturbing impact of the film "derives from a laying bare of male fantasies in such a way that masculinity itself is revealed as fragile, unstable, even impossible" (1989, 4). The hystericized Mantel twins serve as representatives par excellence of masculinity in crisis. Yet while the female hysteric Claire negotiates her recognition that the symbolic is vulnerable, the male hysterics Ely and Bev are femininzed in the process. In contrast to Claire's histrionics that interrogate paternal law even though they remain firmly within the symbolic register, moreover the Mantel twins literally render the hysteric's peregrinations. But they then move into a state of foreclosing the symbolic, rejecting the third term of the law. Having traversed a complex sequence of phantasy scenarios oscillating between womb envy and womb anxiety, they ultimately find themselves fully engulfed by hallucinations that have become equivalent to the real, passing from the hysteric's abundant acting out of phantasies to the point where phantasy is transformed into an act.[6]

Claire, the resilient hysteric, emerges as the representative of this foreclosed third, this radical Otherness beyond narcissistic duality. Given her staunch refusal to support their dyadic relationship, it is significantly Beverly's inability to respond to her voice on the telephone after he has already performed the first part of his fatal enactment of denaveling that brings on the final image of mutual destruction. Cronenberg begins this final sequence by staging an uncanny birthday party. The twins, now disheveled and derelict, secluded in their apartment that has lost all semblance of order, decide to celebrate their total separation from the outside world. What emerges, however, is that Beverly is about to fulfill a separation of another kind. If up to this point he had been the more passive of the two, he has now decided to imitate the nightmare vision of Claire's giving him a second birth by biting through the cord connecting him to his brother. After he wishes Ely happy birthday and assures his astonished brother that this is quite literally the ritual they are about to celebrate, he declares that the tools meant to reshape mutant women are now to be used to enact the core scenario of the Mantle twins' diseased imagination—the phantasy that they are the original Siamese twins who need to come apart. While their malady of the womb began when they distanced themselves from the female body, by transforming the womb into a privileged object of investigation, their anxiety about and fascination for the palpability of the disease of being finite leads to their hysterization through the contact with Claire as their Other. This exchange finds its turning point when Claire, representative of the third element, insists on castrating their protective fiction of the invincible Mantel brothers by broadcasting to them the occluded difference on which this symbiotic duality is built. If the gynecological enterprise was a displaced phantasy of the repressed desire for death, its closure is not so much a return to the womb as a transformation into the womb. Finally united, they become the uncanny feminine body that had been the object of their destructive jouissance all along.[7]

As Ely lies anesthetized on the operating table, Beverly lovingly caresses his brother's skin, and crying over the terrifying separation that is about to occur, he begins to cut into his brother's body. Only in the next scene do we see that he has transformed Ely into an imitation of the representations of dissected figures, as these were used to illustrate the anatomical atlases of the sixteenth century (Sawday; 1995). As Beverly wakes up from what he believes to have been yet another terrible dream and, forlorn, wanders around the apartment, calling to his brother, we see the trace of this hallucination turned palpable: Ely's body, seated like the women patients in the earlier scenes in the gynecological chair with his legs apart, a huge whole cut around the navel, to expose the inside of the body's abdominal area. Though Beverly tries one last time to abandon the fatal family romance of the Mantel twins, dresses, packs his bag, and leaves their apartment to call Claire, he is forced to recognize that by cutting the umbilical cord between himself and his brother so as to release Ely into the womb, into the originary site of inanimate existence before birth, which they had been coveting in a displaced manner all along, he has ineluctably written his own end. As in *The Fly*, the work of the scientist, in this case the investigation into the fallibilities of the feminine womb, serves as a screen phantasy, veiling the desire to be undone beyond the parameters of natural existence. Leaving his bag behind in the phone booth, Bev returns to the overdetermined womb space—the shared apartment and Ely's body, cut open to expose its extimacy. In what is perhaps the saddest scene in all of Cronenberg's films, we follow the camera as it slowly pans down the shutters shielding the window and across the bloodied anatomical instruments, the burnt-down candle, and the needle containing a death drug, until it finally discloses Bev's corpse draped over Ely's abdominal cut. In the same gesture with which he had folded himself together over Claire's belly after waking up from his nightmare, Bev now lies over the opened womb of his brother, the knotted scar, the navel, covering and marking the wound of their second birth into death.

Cronenberg's gothic hysterics repeatedly stage the virus of mortality as it encompasses the mind-body schism, indeed exploring this interface. The wandering organ represents the disease of mortality in the register of the body, the wandering mind, its coterminous disease in the imagination. To reformulate Laplanche and Pontalis, one could speak of two primal scenes, revolving around questions of the subject's origin (castration, seduction, and heritage) and both sited in the womb. The matrix is represented either as the biological womb, the body's interior moving and turning outside, transgressing location and boundary designation—or as the image repertoire, externalizing and embodying phantasies and traumas one has introjected.

IV

In the interview with Chris Rodley, Cronenberg repeatedly critiques those who argue in favor of censoring images, by pointing out that like psychotics, censors confuse reality with illusion, that when someone watches images of violence they are seeing only a representation, not a real act. To focus on the pathology of the image rather than cleansing the image may be one of the ways to access the essence of subjectivity or to explore extimacy. "To make a metaphor in which you compare imagination to disease is to illuminate some aspect of human imagination that perhaps has not been seen or perceived that way before," he explains. "I think that imagination and creativity are completely natural and also, under certain circumstances, quite dangerous. The fact that they're dangerous doesn't mean they are not necessary and should be repressed" (1992, 168). As I conclude with my discussion of the second modality of hysteria performed in Cronenberg's films, namely the "malady by representation," I need to highlight the following difference. In the first set of films discussed, we as spectators remain outside the delusions, seeing only the consequences, as the inside of the body moves out and as phantasies are acted out over bodies. With this second modality, however, we move into the phantasy space of the protagonist's hallucinations. In other words, our hysterization now occurs because we are drawn into the space of his double consciousness, oscillating between reality and delusion, as the body of the protagonist is penetrated by images and turns the intimate into extimacy.

In his most radical performance of the image as virus, *Videodrome* (1982), Cronenberg offers another variation on the disturbance caused by an unhooked uterus, only now the analogy is between womb and video player; the peregrinating foreign body is at stake here through the viral images that float through the protagonist's body, flooding his imagination to such a degree that, whereas the classic hysteric loses control over her body functions, he loses control over his hallucinations. Significantly, too, here the peripeteia is staged as a navel scene that feminizes the masculine body and emphasizes its vulnerability. Max Renn, part owner of a private television station that shows pornography and a compulsive devourer of video images, becomes addicted to a television signal—Videodrome—that produces a diseased imagination. To be more precise, the S/M violence opens up the spine and makes the mind receptive to the videodrome signal, allowing it to seep in. Once it has infiltrated the organism, a tumor slowly develops in his brain. As this foreign body begins to move, hallucinations and double consciousness ensue. Part of Cronenberg's interest is to show how such addictive, viral hallucinations are a hysterical response to a hysterical culture, to a "highly excited state of overstimulation" and can serve a totalitarian deployment of mass hysteria. Thus the subplot of the film involves the two fascists Harlan and Barry Convex, seeking to take over Renn's TV station and use the videodrome signal to control the masses for their totalitarian purposes.

More seminal to my argument, however, is the way Cronenberg stages the fluidity between body and imagination once the infection has set in. In the course of his dissociations and reality overlaps, Max, in the style of the classic hysteric, believes he is experiencing scenes of violence that are, in fact, much ado about nothing. The first of these psychic absences occurs when Max's secretary brings him his wake-up call video; as she stands before him, he hallucinates hitting his lover Nicki Brand. Nicki runs an emotional rescue show, even though she is a practicing sadomasochist and as addicted as he to the videodrome program, where torture, mutilation, and murder are so fascinating because the scene appears to be utterly realistic. Indeed, given that she enacts his sadomasochistic phantasies of body mutilation for him, Nicki serves as the somatic counterpart to the videodrome images on his television screen. Both function as symptom for him, representing his repressed desire for body violence. Precisely this uncanny layering of lived reality, phantasy, and media images is at stake in the next sequence involving Nicki Brand.

Max uses a cyberhelmet to enter into the videodrome program, and as the camera moves from showing him from the outside into his mind screen, we see his next encounter with Nicki Brand, who hands him a whip only to change into an image on a television screen inviting him to "perform." As he whips the television, she writhes in ecstatic pain until utterly terrified at his own violence, he wakes up to find what he believes to be her corpse lying next to him in his bed. Having called Harlan to come over and help him, he is forced to recognize that the image of the mutilated Nicki was merely a phantasy of violence, staging himself and Nicki as its players—the representation of his repressed desires lacking all reference to physical reality. Indeed, the dialectic is such that Nicki transforms completely into a phantasmic image once she leaves him to audition for videodrome, returning uncannily on various television screens. At the same time, the television images appear to become ever more palpable, until, in the last scene, the relation between lived reality and television screen reality is completely reversed, and Max enters the torture room he has been watching so obsessively from the other side of the screen.

Cronenberg thus visualizes Max's hysterization by staging the fluidity between body and image-machine. After he has discovered that Brian O'Blivion is the creator of Videodrome, Max asks the scientist's daughter Bianca for an interview. Explaining that the monologue is her father's preferred mode of discourse, she sends him a cassette instead, which becomes animate in his hand. The television screen once more transforms into his hallucinatory mind screen, as Dr. O'Blivion broadcasts his general philosophy about the disease called artificial imagination. His broadcast consists in first explaining that because the screen is the retina of the mind's eye, whatever appears on the screen emerges as raw experience for those who watch it. He then transforms into Max's symptom, transmitting in inverted form the message Max desires. In this phantasy scenario played through first on the screen and then transgressing the boundary of the screen, O'Blivion appears as his alterego, explaining "I've been through it all myself, you see." Warning Max that his reality is already to a large degree video hallucination, he describes his addiction to the videodrome signal, visions causing a brain tumor by becoming uncontrollable flesh. In the scenario he describes, the tumor is not only coterminous with videodrome, but its creator also proves to be the first victim of this pathology of the image, given that he cannot survive its removal. What Cronenberg thus visualizes is the full complexity of extimacy. For part of the message O'Blivion transmits to Max is the fact that the virus of the image is so intimate a part of the subject that fades before it that removal will be fatal. At the same time, only through its externalization onto a video representation can the truth about this Other site be heard. In other words, we are presented with a semiotic short circuit, the fatal inversion of the hysteric's communication with alterity. To become cognizant of how the image's virus is seminal to the subject requires giving in to the temptation of the signal. But to enter into the exchange with videodrome is already the beginning of the demise of the subject.

This impasse is visually enacted. Max begins to hallucinate the death of Dr. O'Blivion, strangled by a masked figure who, responding to his questions, "Who's behind it? What do they want?" proves to be not only yet another representation but also the object of his erotic fantasies, Nicki herself. She is giving death to the inventor of the videodrome signal even as she keeps the system of hallucinatory visions floating. Replacing the voice of the father, she shifts the register from the public to the private, from conspiracy to eroticism, explaining, "I want you, Max." She beckons him to transgress the boundary between image and body, and in so doing collapse the distinction between externally induced and externalized, intimate fantasy spaces. As her lips take over the entire screen, the television set transforms into a pulsating, moaning body; the screen bulges outward to receive Max's head while he tries to enter into the televised mouth of his beloved. Significantly, the image fragment of the desirable feminine body he seeks to penetrate is a displacement of sexual genitalia, namely the mouth, as he also tries to do so not with his member but with his head, the locus of his metromania.

In this scene the image-machine transforms into an organic body in a moment of uncanny extimacy, when both the medium broadcasting the representation and the visual representation literally turn into the represented object; it enacts this hysterical uncontrollability of hallucinatory visions with recourse to the visual trope of a maternal orifice's engulfing the protagonist—the chiasmic inversion of this cinematic image is the navel scene of the *Videodrome*. Once he discovers not only that Dr. O'Blivion has no empirical body and exists only as a media representation, a talking head on the hundreds of tapes his daughter has collected of him, but also that he himself has ineluctably been damaged by the videodrome signal, Max interrogates the media image of this paternal Other, now understood entirely as a resilient representation, endlessly reiterable on videocassettes, but with no empirical reality except its own demise. Hoping to get some help with his videodrome problem by watching the tapes Bianca has given him, Max finds his body horrifically hystericized: it in turn has become an image-machine. In contrast to the first encounter with Dr. O'Blivion, the boundary blurring between image and body now moves from the masculine head being engulfed by a feminine image to the feminized male body penetrated first by the voice and image of Dr. O'Blivion and then by the phallic object par excellence that crosses eroticism with mortality: the revolver. Max watches the screen, demonstrating his potency by exhibiting to the feminized video screen his naked chest, banded by a gun strap; he then uses his gun to scratch his abdomen just above the navel. As O'Blivion drones on, his navel splits open, and, as though mirroring the exteriorization of his phantasies on the screen, he plunges the gun deep into the interiority of his body, and the body seam closes again.

This dialectic runs through to the film's final sequences. Videocassettes repeatedly become organic, while the various opponents fighting over who will control videodrome—Bianca, representative of the father sacrificed to the pathology of the image, or the obscene father Barry Convex, seeking to politically manipulate the pathology of the image—play the now fully suggestible Max like a video recorder. Each inserts preprogrammed videocassettes into his abdomen that instruct him about the acts of violence he is supposed to commit. On the one hand Barry Convext instructs him to kill the other owners of the television station, so he can take it over, on the other hand Bianca imposes on him the command to kill Barry and Harlan, the murderers of her father. Reminiscent of the hysterical patients at Charcot's Salpêtrière, performing the physician's invention of hysteria (Didi-Huberman 1982), his body has become the battleground for their competing ideologies of the pathology of the image—for Convex's political ambitions with videodrome and for Bianca's philosophy of the new flesh. Two points should be stressed. As his body is palpably penetrated by embodied images, the animate videocassettes, rather than imperceptibly by a nonrepresentable signal, Max Renn is feminized. Visually the body image that is emphasized is his own navel as a wound, metonymically referring to the disempowering vulnerability of the body, rather than the eroticized images of Nicki Brand's mutilated body, referring to an empowering fetishization of the body of the Other. Second, the phantasy scenarios Max plays through, once he has become aware of his ineluctable infection by the video signal, steadily shift away from the body as a pleasure-generating organism to the body as a generator of death.

If Max's hallucinations are representations revolving around nothing, the tumor that produces and controls these hallucinations is repeatedly described as a new organ, so that once more metromania and metermania converge. As Dr. O'Blivion explains, while the videodrome signal initially induces visions, symptoms without any organic lesion, it is these visions that produce the organic disorder, the tumor, that will eventually become a new outgrowth of the brain. Thus, the illness without any organic lesions ultimately produces its own organs, which proclaim that the only palpable reality lies in hallucinations. External and psychic reality conflate in the process of this hysterization, once the foreign body has become so autonomous that it both produces and controls hallucinations. At the same time, though externally introduced, videodrome nevertheless marks the extimate, for as Bianca explains to Max, although the tone of the hallucination is determined by the tape's imagery, the signal that does the damage is itself semantically uncoded, and can be delivered under anything. Max could have become infected through any image: it just happened to be through the S/M show because Harlan knew that this fed into his search for "something tough" in the area of pornography. Translated into the language of psychoanalysis, the representation does not cause addiction (in Max's case, the phantasies of violent sexuality). Rather the pathology of the image thrives on the non-representable pulse beneath representation, the traumatic *nothing* toward which, as Lacan suggests, all jouissance is directed, and for which sexuality is but the enticing protective fiction.

Indeed, as the film moves toward its implosive closure we recognize that the repressed desire Max encounters in his hallucinations is not sexual excess but the disease of being finite. The phantasy scenario he finally enacts at his own body, once mind space, body interior, and physical exterior have completely collapsed into each other, is not the scene of transgressive sexuality he initially was infected by, but rather one of vulnerability and destruction. Max, now completely dislocated between hallucination and reality, enters the room he has been watching on his television screen. Here his body, receptacle for and representative of violent images, after having committed preprogrammed acts of murder, ultimately has recourse to suicide. This Other law comes to him once again from the screen, showing a transformed Nicki, as though the paternal and the maternal were now spliced together—his final symptom, giving him the message of total transformation and enticing him to kill the old flesh so as to become the new flesh. Once more calling to him the very first message she had sent him—"Come to me"—she plays for him on-screen the scene of suicide he will then imitate as a hallucination but in the real, at his own body, in a final performance of extimacy, where media representation, the voice of the Other, and the embodiment of these images of mortality have become entirely indistinguishable.

V

I have been working with the assumption that gothic horror describes the uncanny moment when a metaphor takes over the full function and meaning of the object it symbolizes, effacing the distinction between figural and literal. But for Cronenberg, one might say, his postmodern transformation of gothic hysterics *represents* the embodiment of metaphor, the palpable materialization of phantasy. Not only do we find hallucinations narrated, they become mimetic reality within the diegetic space of the film. Breaking open, even troubling the categories set up by Todorov, Cronenberg floods our image repertoire with the reappearance of repressed desire as a traumatic hallucination in the real. My point, of course, is not that Cronenberg is hysteric, but rather that his cinematic phantasy scenarios perform hysterical anxieties in relation to the body's mutability and fragility. If I began by saying that hysteria is a malady by and of representation, that it performs symptoms without organic disturbances, the definition "by representation" transforms, in Cronenberg's postmodern version, into an abundance of organic problems. The nothing about which there is so much ado becomes tangible, palpable, and visible. As psychic metaphors come to be embodied, this radical negativity, against which phantasy scenes about body vulnerability are produced as a shield, and whose other message they perform by displaced representation, turns into organic disaster. Here the peregrinations of the unhooked uterus, a foreign body part wandering through an organism and functioning as the somatic signifier for a desire that has gone out of control, articulates the extimacy of the psychic apparatus. Being possessed by a foreign body part or externally introduced images translates into being possessed by the Other site of the unconscious. As thoughts are given somatic representations, the conventionally invisible interior of the body is turned inside out. In the dialectic of the hysterical strategy the imagination becomes diseased, owing to its anxiety about mutability and mortality, and tries to overcome this body problem by replacing reality with phantasy and hallucinations. But as the mind becomes disturbed because of these delusions, these idées fixes, the body in turn becomes diseased, somatizing the mental disorder by no longer functioning properly.

The point about hysteria, however, is not only that it incessantly dismantles fixed categories and boundaries but above all that it staunchly defies closure. As Freud so painfully realized, there is no solution to any case history of hysteria, nourished as it is by a resilience in symptom formations that encircles the pool of radical negativity, the extimacy of the subject, even as it interrogates the infallibility of symbolic law. In this resilient defiance hysteria radically questions all totalizing interpretations that feed off the promise of solution. Yet any aesthetic text must find closure. In the conventional genre of the gothic we have the options of explaining the uncanny, accepting it as the norm, or positing another reality. Cronenberg, in turn, offers two solutions: a psychotic shift into the register of the real, barring all doubt, as in *Videodrome*, *Dead Ringers*, or *The Fly* or, what is perhaps even more disturbing, a final cinematic shot, as in *Shivers* or *The Brood*, where the taint of trauma, the stain of the disease of being finite, resiliently remains.

Beyond Hysteria: Cindy Sherman's Private Theater of Horror

> The abject shatters the wall of repression and its judgments. It takes the ego
> back to its source on the abominable limits from which, in order to be, the
> ego has broken away—it assigns it a source in the non-ego, drive, and death.
> Abjection is a resurrection that has gone through death (of the ego). It is an
> alchemy that transforms death drive into a start of life, of new signifiance.
>
> —*Julia Kristeva*

I

As Laura Mulvey notes in her appreciation of the work of Mary Kelly, the women's movement inspired "debate and experiment around women's relation to language and images that drew feminist aesthetics into 'alliance' with avant-garde aesthetics during the seventies," and came to offer both "cultural identity and frame-work" (1986, 4) to visual artists, filmmakers, and theorists over the next two decades. At the same time, because feminist criticism came to address the influences a given culture's collective image repertoire has on the way women construct their identities, psychoanalytic theory proved to be one of this aesthetic project's most useful tools. With reference specifically to the representations of Augustine produced by Charcot in his photographic studio in the Salpêtrière, Mary Kelly decided to interrogate "the moment of middle age" in her series *Interim*.[1] After more than a hundred conversations with women that "focus on the recurring themes of body, money, history and power," she made thirty panels the size (three by four feet) of advertisement posters, dividing them into five sections. Each of these sections in turn comprised three pairs of double images that visually and verbally represented an article of woman's clothing: a leather jacket, leather purse, pair of short boots, black lace lingerie, and a white gown. The premise behind this installation, she explained, was that " 'Being a woman is but a brief moment in one's life!' Definitions of women's femininity are constructed primarily on the body: in its procreative capacity and as fetishized object—'to be looked at' " (cited in Pollock 1988, 188). On the left side of each panel, using the iconography of fashion advertisements, anatomic atlases, and popular medicine, as well as referring to the heroines of romantic fiction and Hollywood films, such as Alfred Hitchcock's blond actresses whose perfect poise quite self-consciously stages femininity as a masquerade, Kelly presented images of feminine clothing, which she drew over with a red highlighter. The articles of clothing, furthermore, were labeled with the same terms Charcot had used to impose an interpretive narrative on the hysteric's *attitudes passionelle* during her hallucinatory phase— *Menace* (leather jacket), *Appel* (purse), *Supplication* (shoes), *Erotisme* (lingerie) and *Extase* (nightgown). Furthermore, they were matched on the right-hand side with excerpts from the interviews with women who, owing to their middle age, felt themselves predominantly excluded from this image repertoire and had begun to question the representational discourses of fashion writing, medical literature, and family romances with happy endings that had come so pervasively to inform their sense of identity. The women nevertheless also admitted that their subjectivity was inextricably caught up in the very notion of feminine beauty that either reduced them to a commodity or excluded them once they no longer fit this function. Precisely because Mary Kelly's *Interim*, however, hovers (as Mulvey notes) between interrogating a cultural "appropriation of their image for masculine pleasure" and a "need to redefine women's relation to their image," this installation did more than offer the hysteric's misappropriation of a master narrative, namely Charcot's graph of the hysteric's passionate attitudes and our late-twentieth-century reiteration of her poses in advertisements and popular cinema. Rather, Kelly's work also performed the elusive and protean language of the psychosomatic disorder it invoked to critique Western culture's representation of feminine desire, sexuality, and identity. As Mulvey concludes, "One of the fascinating aspects of this work is this refusal to be pinned down or categorised. Although the written texts are not arranged as conventional stories, they contain many references to story-telling, swerving from anecdote and recounting 'personal experiences' to the fantastic world of fairy stories. The reader has to move from the register of real life and its unobtainable desires to that of the imagination where those desires can be 'lived out' in fantasy" (1986, 6).

The French artist Annette Messager admits a similar debt to Jean-Martin Charcot's work on hysteria. Though she does not directly appropriate the photographs and gravures he produced at the Salpêtrière, the manner in which she fashions herself as an artist as well as the techniques she develops invoke the medical discourse on hysteria I have been recounting. For one, she began early on to split herself into several artist personas: Anne Messager, collector; Anne Messager, artist; Anne Messager, practical woman.[2] As she explains in an interview with Barnard Marcadé, at the beginning of her career in 1970 when she considered herself to be a hybrid between collector and artist, she was living in a two-room apartment, a bedroom and a dining room. While her work as collector took place in the bedroom, where she kept her magazines, books, and camera, her work as artist took place in the rechristened dining-room, because there she kept the dirty tools she would use to craft objects. A friend, to whom she showed the double image of her working self was irritated, claiming that these two aspects had nothing to do with each other, and Messager concluded, "If he didn't understand, then perhaps it meant that it was interesting" (1990, 109).

From this moment on she came to cultivate an oscillation between various sites of working identity. Moreover, in the past two decades she has perfected the technique of deceptive artist-collector, which recalls the way Hitchcock's hysteric heroine Marnie describes herself as "a thief, a liar, and a cheat."[3] As Messager explains to her interviewer, "I am the hawker of chimera, the hawker of monkey-like dreams, of gossamer deliriums. . . . I am the cheat, the cheat of repainted photos, of deformed enlargements, of double exposures of clichés, of huge troubling blueprints, of a multiple crash of images, of deforming lenses. . . . I am the liar, the messenger [*messagère*] of false premonitions, of questionable loves, of suspicious memories, the tamer of paper spiders." (1990, 114). Reassembling photographs or sketches of dismembered body parts into new structures, documenting passionate attitudes and clichés about human behavior by gathering random photographs into a sequence, or recounting the life story of one of her personas by mounting a plethora of graphic images next to each other on a given wall space, she presents this play with our collective image repertoire under labels such as "Femmes en pleurs" (Women Crying, 1973), "Mes clichés témoins (Clichés I Witnessed, 1972), "Mes gestes quotidiens (My Everyday Gestures, 1974), "Mes Trophées" (My Trophies, 1987), "Comment mes amis feraient mon portrait" (How my Friends Portray me," 1973) or "Les effroyables aventures d'Annette Messager truqueuse (The terrifying adventures of Annette Messager, cheat, 1975). Yet this reappropriation of a given iconography of physiognomies and stereotypical gestures, of the artificialities that make up what we consider to be the human body, occurs explicitly in relation to the medical and forensic photography of the late nineteenth century. Photography, she explains, "is the one technique of reproduction which from its very beginnings entertained an extremely close relation to the body, the sick body, the social body, the 'exotic' body, the eroticized body. . . . When it comes to the relation between the body and its photographic mise-en-scène, what greatly influenced me was the approach of Charcot at the Salpêtrière, within the context of his work on hysteria" (110). And like the classic hysteric, who plays a game of seduction to reveal to her interpellator his false sense of mastery, Annette Messager steals from the master narratives that have informed her as a visual artist so as to confront her viewers both with their and her own contradictions. Mimicking the stereotypes about the female and the human body, she also admits that her deconstructive parody is infused with an admiration for these cultural clichés. Finally, drawing yet another parallel between her work and that of Charcot's, as well as Hitchcock's great actresses, she explains, "Photography, like hysteria, is located in the realm of immodesty, shamelessness and insolence." (128). Like Mary Kelly, who refuses to be pinned down or categorized, Anne Messager, reiterating Charcot's grand gesture of nosology, gives subtle intimations of the monstrous, explaining it is "all that which exists inside and which one does not know how to name, which one does not know how to see; all which is fluid, sticky, flaccid, all the disgusting colors, the blood, the humours" (121). Yet this traumatic material, which threatens the integrity of any notion of an intact human or social body as well as the cultural laws and collective phantasies relying on representations of body plenitude, is concealed through of the aesthetic reassemblage of the images; like the hysteric, Messager defers ad infinitum all final revelations and clear positions and instead leaves us fascinated, implicated, but undecided.

Finally, looking for contemporary performances of hysteria, one would invariably point to the work of the French multimedia artist Orlan, who says of herself, "Being a narcissist isn't easy when the question is not of loving your own image, but of re-creating the self through deliberate acts of alienation" (Barbara Rose 1993, 83). Using plastic surgery, this woman, whose real name we do not know and who, not unlike Pierre Janet's patient Madeleine, has preferred to conceal any information about her family and her background, has been staging carefully planned and highly stylized operations under local anesthesia, so that while her body is being remodeled she can direct the action. During these scenes of body transformation, selected texts are read and accompanied by music and dance within a highly contrived scenario involving elaborate costumes, stage props, and video projections. The sale of videos, films, photographs, and huge billboard posters documenting these performances finances further operations to occur until her transformation into an artifically reincarnated body will be complete. In a sense her "theater of operation," from which she emerges each time with a new appearance and elaborate documentation of the various stages of her body alterations, recalls Charcot's lecture theater, where he used the female body to document the transformation from normalcy to contortions, paralyses, and anesthetizations of the body as well as to the passionate attitudes of hallucinations. And if these performances of hypnotized patients came to invoke notions of simulation and deception, Orlan's performance in her intimate theater of operation also calls into question, as Barbara Rose notes, "whether our self-representations conform to an inner reality or whether they are actually carefully contrived falsehoods fabricated for marketing purposes—in the media or in society at large" (83). Furthermore, like Charcot's reproductions of the graph of hysterical gestures, compiled under the influence of already-existing representations of demonic possession, Orlan explicitly stages her "carnal art" under the auspices of famous Renaissance and post-Renaissance paintings of idealized feminine beauty: the mouth of Boucher's Europa, the forehead of Leonardo's Mona Lisa, the chin of Botticelli's Venus, the eyes of Gérôme's Psyche, and the nose of Diana, painted by an unknown member of the School of Fontainebleau. Orlan incarnates in all its visceral actuality the hysteric's seductive, self-destructive game with her interpellator's desire, dismantling the very representations she also uses her body to enact. As Barbara Rose suggests, admitting her own bafflement at Orlan's courtship with danger, marginality, and psychopathology, "If the parts of seven different ideal women are needed to fulfill Adam's desire for an Eve made in his image, Orlan consciously chooses to undergo the necessary mutilation to reveal that the objective is unattainable and the process horrifying. Orlan the artist and the woman will never play the victim: she is both subject and object, actress and director, passive patient and active organizer" (125). To conclude my own passage through medical case histories as well as visual, narrative, and musical reinscriptions of this most elusive, protean, and resilient articulation of somatic, psychic, and cultural discontent, however, I will now turn to an artist who, though not explicitly invoking the culturally transmitted iconography of hysteria, addresses what I have been calling the troubling message of the hysteric's complaint. For in her photographic phantasy scenarios Cindy Sherman stages the subject as a representational knot, linking our clichéd notions of the gendered human body with a knowledge of the monstrous, the traumatic dissolution underlying any self-fashioning.

II

"I don't do self-portraits," Cindy Sherman explained to Andreas Kallfelz in an interview for the journal *Wolkenkratzer*, "I always try to get as far away from myself as possible in the photographs. It could be, though, that it's precisely by doing so that I create a self-portrait, doing these totally crazy things with these characters" (1984, 49). Sherman thus poses a serious challenge to cultural critics, because if not the artist herself, then who is the woman depicted in her photos? If she does not want to create portraits of herself, then why does Sherman use her own body, distorted by costumes, makeup, and props, as her main model? If it is not a question of self-representation, then what is the relationship between the depiction and the feminine body being represented? We must consider further, at least in relation to the work she produced up to 1991, that Sherman always stages her portraits of women in a scenario that quite self-consciously employs multiple references to American film and TV culture since the 1950s; to costume gothics and romances, science fiction and horror thrillers, film noir, melodrama, advertising, and, in the *History Portraits*, to classical paintings she studied at college. In view of this, one could certainly bring into play the distinction between self-portrait and self-performance, but one would immediately have to ask who is staging herself here, and why.

Sherman has explained that she uses her photographs to reveal the latent psychological material that one does not normally see on the surface, in a subject's face or gestures, namely, material that contains the subject's imagination. At the same time, however, this other self of the imagination can only be articulated through surface appearances, through the knotting together of different self-representations. The way she tells the story of how she became a photographer characteristically involves this contradiction. Her point of departure was the image of the solitary daydreamer, which by the time Gustave Flaubert came to write *Madame Bovary* had already become a commonplace in western cultural image repertoire. To be more precise, she invokes the young woman who withdraws from the world, finds refuge in her own room, and behind closed doors occupies herself with her own phantasies. In interviews, Cindy Sherman describes how she first felt alienated within her own family, how she later felt totally threatened existentially by the urban violence of New York City, and how, to reduce this threat, she learned to transform herself into other people, initially in her own room and later in her studio. There she started to study her own face continually from different angles, until it began to look like a stranger's face. She began to disguise herself by dressing up in different costumes until she could no longer recognize the figure in the mirror. Her portraits were produced precisely in such moments of complete dissociation emerging from her discontent with the gender roles prescribed to her by her family and later by the conditions of her existence as a woman in a major urban center. So these portraits always also articulate her sense of dissatisfaction with the prevailing expectations culture has of women.

In a television interview with Mark Stokes she describes how, as a child, she borrowed her mother's clothes to disguise herself, but, significantly, she transformed herself into an ugly old woman. Imbued with exactly the same gesture, her photographs are at once brilliant and painful parodies of the dictate imposed by media images on every American girl: that she should perfect her clothes, makeup, and posture so as to imitate an apparently desirable but simultaneously unattainable model of immaculate feminine beauty. Sherman chose never to represent herself as an idealized figure. Perfection, Roland Barthes poignantly argues, exalts insofar as it wipes out the distance between code and performance, between origin and result, between model and copy. Since this distance, however, is part of the human condition, Barthes concludes, "Perfection, which annuls it, lies outside of anthropological limits, in supernature, where it joins the other, inferior, transgression: *more* and *less* can be generically placed in the same class, that of excess, what is *beyond* no longer differs from what is *short* of a limit; the essence of the code (perfection) has in the end the same status as what is outside the code (the monster)" (1970, 71). This is precisely the dialectic that Sherman performs in her photographs. The perfectly beautiful body and the monstrous body are shown to be mutually dependent on each other.

There is yet a further distinction that Cindy Sherman's self-portraits, which are not self-portraits, undermine: namely, the difference between performance in aesthetic practice and performance in linguistic speech-act theory I have been working with, where the latter refers to a verbal utterance that simultaneously performs the action it also describes. Sherman presents us with a dual gesture. She stages herself in scenarios by distorting her appearance, putting on costumes, and performing a masquerade. But as a woman who grew up in a specific cultural context, she has also been performatively constructed *by* the discourse specific to her environment. By presenting herself other than what she is, by refashioning the media images and narratives that have influenced her self-image, she insists that the act of self-representation as a means of expression always also performs the act it designates. Her explanation, "I don't do self-portraits," thus also refers to the notion that the portraits she makes of herself are aesthetic *performances* of the following utterance: The subject of the portrait has been created performatively, in fact, it can only be articulated as a performance. The represented subject can, therefore, be understood as a knot, binding together the various languages that have shaped it and through which it is able to express, in a displaced and dislocated manner, its traumatic impressions, memory traces, desires, anxieties, and phantasies. In addition, this represented subject performatively embodies the laws and dictates imposed on it by the family and by society, as well as any culturally acquired image repertoire. In the course of every self-representation, the depicted subject is always also a cipher for collective wish fulfillments and anxieties; in Sherman's case, it is above all manifestly a cipher for the way in which perfection and monstrosity are enmeshed. If one recalls that the Latin etymology of the word *monster* links this concept with the omen and the miracle, given that miraculous phenomena were seen as warnings of an inevitable and threatening future event, one can begin to grasp how Sherman's disturbances of the self-portrait incorporate the notion of mutability as one of their central themes. These self-representations are proleptic; they point toward something that has not yet become visible, even as they articulate the fact that although non-visible, the event of the subject's demise is, nevertheless, also inescapable.

Adept in postmodern theories, Sherman quite consciously uses her photographs to transform herself into a representation, thereby rendering problematic the relationship between the image, the depicted body, and any citation serving as cultural model for the representation. She stages her memories of media images and personal phantasy images, simultaneously seeking to trigger memories and phantasies in her viewers by performing her specific understanding of this culturally given image repertoire. To do so she draws on a rich archive of images from childhood reading, television, film, and high-gloss magazines, as well as from the entire archive of high art. Significantly she says that she is of the first generation of American artists to have grown up with television. If postmodernist theory works on the assumption that the socialized body is already inscribed by the image repertoire of its surroundings, then Sherman, in turn, inscribes these culturally transmitted images with the performances recorded in her photographs. In the process, she unsettles the relationship between authentic body and its pictorial representation, between original image and body masquerade. Composite images emerge from her *non*-self-portraits, assembled from body parts and prostheses; bodies dissolve gender boundaries and trouble the distinction between human and animal, between living body and corpse or prosthesis. At the same time she also produces hybrid bodies, given the enmeshing of model image and body performance, between memory and self-fashioning, between latent psychic material and manifest expression. "I see myself as a composite of all the things I've done," she explains (quoted in Kellein 1991, 9).

Sherman's self-representations are the serial fashionings of a plethora of potential identities. On the other hand, they also question whether this highly intricate role playing stages the represented subject as a false self or a mimicry, whether the illusion of authenticity is preserved even though such a gesture is intended to deceive, or whether beneath the surface, beneath the media composite, an autonomous self nevertheless does exist. Are we irrevocably caught up in the free play of simulacrums, or can an authentic articulation of the self emerge in the midst of postmodern simulations? Can we spectators discern an intact subject behind the performance and can we recognize in these non-self-portraits a woman who is radically other than ourselves, or are we (as Sherman at least suggests) primarily expecting to find our own self-image mirrored in the representation of this Other? As she explains, "People are going to look under the make-up and wigs for that common denominator, the recognizable. I'm trying to make other people recognize something of themselves rather than me" (quoted in Schulz-Hoffmann 1991, 30). Sherman thus not only addresses the hermeneutic problem that any spectator will first and foremost find—his or her memories and phantasies reflected in the image. Rather, she also points out that to become meaningful each image requires an interpretive story, regardless whether in the process the series of individual representations is supplemented by a narrative or whether it is reshaped into our own phantasy scene.

By calling on us to exercise our own memory and imagination—but by staging stereotypic figures from the image repertoire of femininity, fairy tales, or horror films—Sherman succinctly raises the question whether the fantasies thus aroused are authentic, or perhaps nothing more than clichés. Concomitantly she forces us to consider whether we spectators might not like the represented hybrid bodies, be the composites of a play of simulacrums, as she asks us to equally consider whether in the process of spectatorship we are able to reach that realm of the imagination that is unique to each of us. In addition, by turning herself into the image and at the same time constructing this image herself, Sherman not only knots together otherwise separated entities—the cited media image, the model, the representation, and the effect of viewing. She also stages herself as a hybrid, oscillating between empowered subject and disempowered object of the gaze. She critically refashions the relationship of the artist to the traditional image repertoire of femininity out of and against which she designs herself. She does this by installing and as it were parodying the traditional analogy between femininity and the image, even as she performs the extent to which the femininity being represented is a viewing effect, since each photographic image implicitly elicits an interpretive narrative to accompany it.

Craig Owens argues, "Sherman's photographs themselves function as mirror-masks that reflect back at the viewer his own desire (and the spectator posited by this work is invariably male)—specifically, the masculine desire to fix the woman in a stable and stabilizing identity. . . . But while Sherman may pose as a pin up, she still cannot be pinned down" (1992, 183). No matter how much, therefore, we are tempted to see Sherman's photographs as a way of processing the media image repertoire that she quite explicitly sees as her artistic material, it must not be forgotten that the reason these photographs are not self-portraits in the conventional sense may be that they articulate that other, unconscious self who can only emerge in the process of staging the imagination—by virtue of a displaced representation. For although Sherman insists in the interview with Kallfelz that she does not do self-portraits, she quickly concedes that her photographs do have a real, psychic point of reference: "and that's the other aspect. It could be that I really do let out some crazy person inside me in this way."

Ultimately, Sherman's hybrid and composite technique aims at making manifest the way in which vulnerability and masquerade, as well as perfection and monstrosity are enmeshed. The performance of her masked, disfigured, or displaced body is meant to serve both as an apotropaic gesture against but also as a reference to the body's vulnerability, to the fallibility of identity, and to anxieties about destruction and death, regardless of whether these fears originate in an actual experience of threatening events or merely in childhood nightmares. While Sherman seeks to evoke memory and phantasy images in her spectators, on the one hand, to demythologize traditional stereotypes (especially of femininity) and deconstruct the primacy of the idealized body, she seeks, on the other hand, to evoke those images of horror that are usually represssed: anxieties about fragmentation, dissolution, or the substitution of the human body with artificial body parts and prostheses. Staging a masquerade of the self serves a critical, even if displaced, project. If the postmodern subject is conventionally conceived as a "network of quotations, a complete blurring of image and identity" (Bryson 1991, 98), Sherman shows the logical conclusion of the idealized image of the intact body, as well as the reference-free simulacrum: the female body petrified into a mask, a prosthesis, a doll. On the other hand, she points to the realm that is foreclosed by both of these representational gestures while nevertheless remaining a part of the visualization: the formless body mass, the abject, the decay, and the process of decomposition.

Her multifaceted performance of the female body thus deconstructs various codes, namely traditional images of femininity and aesthetic idealization, and the concept of an intact body of plenitude. Against these codes she sets the multiplicity of female identity, a collapsing of the distinction between designing an image and becoming an image, as well as images of the transcience of the body. Her photographic performance exposes what lies beneath the cosmetic surface (*Disaster Pictures*, *Fairy Tales*) or reduces everything to a simulacrum (*Film Stills*, *Centerfolds*, *Fashion*) and to anatomical body parts and prostheses (*Specimens*, *Sex Pictures*). The question is staged, Where is the subject located, given its performative constitution through trauma, sexuality, and media images? This performance, in turn, points to what has been foreclosed, to the traumatic material that inhabits each of us, just as it also brings out our subjectivity as the result of the discursive field which has inscribed us. In lieu of self-portraits Sherman offers the knotting together of a given cultural image repertoire with memory traces, creations of phantasy, and figures of the traumatic.

III

Unlike in her earlier work, Cindy Sherman no longer appears as the model in her photographic transformation of the Grimm fairy tale *Fitcher's Bird*. Her body is replaced by dolls and artificial body parts. Nevertheless, this series is perhaps the most manifest self-portrait by the artist to date. Like Anne Sexton, she draws on a familiar archive of culture, the image repertoire of fairy tales, and picks from it the story of a clever and sly girl who, after initial passivity, begins to revolt against the dictate of female obedience. She uses her curiosity as a form of self-protection, so as to act in ways that transcend gender roles. Not only ignoring the magician's prohibition against entering the room with the smallest lock, she also disobeys his command that she always carry the magic egg with her. In this story of violence, dismemberment, and resuscitation, furthermore, she carries out the act of creating artificially, an activity normally relegated to the masculine realm. Without a trace of sentimentality, the sly girl, having shed a few tears, puts back together the body parts of her dead sisters that she finds in the forbidden room. And she claims the magician's deadly power for herself. He had exercised power over other people's lives by hewing intact bodies, above all those of beautiful women, into pieces and then demonstratively putting them in a cauldron, which, consciously placed in the center of the forbidden chamber, resembles an exhibition display. In her photographic transformation of the fairy tale, Sherman stages this cauldron as the focus of a horrific display, illuminating it with a golden ray of light and placing it in front of a curtain with a skull, an iron chain, and barely recognizable instruments of murder. What is then seminal to the required happy ending to the story is that the girl ultimately destroys the wicked magician, this artist of dismemberment, but apparently she can only do so by creating new body objects, a transformation that occurs precisely on the border between life and death.

First, the dead body parts of the demonic artist's victims, with which Sherman recalls her own use of dolls, artifical body parts, and prostheses as substitutes for her own body in her recent work, are reassembled by the sly girl to form new body units. The sisters are resuscitated. In the photos, how-ever, it is still only fragments—hands, hair, nose, mouths—that are visible; in contrast to the fairy tale, Sherman uses her photographic language to insist on an analogy between the fragmentation of female bodies by the wicked magician and the fragmentation of the represented body as an object in any aesthetic image. Second, the girl transforms herself into a phantasy figure, a feathered hybrid between animal and human. In this image, too, Sherman represents only a section of the body from waist to knee, illumi-nated from behind. The two hands are held in front of the stomach, the left one hovering slightly above the navel while the right one almost rests on the hip bone. Some fingernails are visible through the feathers. Owing to this mimicry, the sly sister is able not only to leave the magician's house with impunity, but also to entice the evil bridegroom to his death. Significantly, she does this through one last creation on the threshold between life and death. She decorates a skull with flowers and jewels, and, placed on a small pedestal, she exhibits this composite body, resembling an art display, from her window. The decorated skull becomes a dual representation. It stands in for the sly bride, but it also is an inverted rendition of the magician's concep-tual coupling of bride and corpse, in that it corresponds to the dismembered body parts of the other beautiful women he had courted.

In both acts of creation—the magician's murderous performance of dis-membering and displaying his brides, and the girl's self-protecting act of exchanging a substitute body, the decorated skull, for her own presence—the concept *bride* is linked to dead body parts and to aesthetic display. If in Sherman's photographs of these brides, the female body appears to be dean-imate (the artificial body parts of the two dismembered sisters decoratively arranged in a pattern, the feathered body of the third, in which a human form is barely recognizable), the substitute bride—the decorated skull—by contrast, gives the impression of being animate. Both bride substitutes, how-ever, the bird-woman and the skull bride, make fluid the boundary between what is animate and what is deanimate. On approaching his home, the wicked bridegroom asks the bird-woman where his bride is, and she tells him that she is sitting at the window, waiting for him to return. In the Grimm version of the tale we read, "The bridegroom looked up, saw the decorated skull, thought it was his bride, and nodded to her, greeting her kindly" (1819, 260). With this statement, the sly daughter, working with but also against death, introduces a death performance of her own. Her correlate site to the magician's forbidden chamber of death, where she found herself confronting the traumatic spectacle of her dismembered sisters, is the magician's entire house. Set on fire by her father and her kinsmen, it has become the site of death for the magician himself. By emphasizing the nipple of the death artist, Sherman offers one last blurring of gender boundaries; the magician, too, is a hybrid, bearded and female.

These fairy-tale photographs thus illustrate the revenge that art can take. Sherman presents images of violence meant as an apotropaic gesture against a fatal art project, but also as a statement about the cost of artistic creativity.

Art needs dead bodies, art creates dead bodies. In the images of the beautiful but dead feminine faces, in the sisters' chopped-off heads and in the decorated skull, the perfection of aesthetic idealization meets its opposite, monstrosity. The former represent the traumatic spectacle of what the sly girl found in the cauldron. The bodies stand for death as the prerequisite for the masculine artists' creative act. They function as the representation of a destructive fragmentation externally imposed by an artist on his medium. The skull image, in contrast, offers an estheticized rendition of what the sly sister sets up against this spectacle of horror, a representation of death that stands for herself and constitutes her self-representation. In the movement between these two images, abjection (in Julia Kristeva's definition of the term) emerges, namely as a performance of the alchemy by which a horrific enjoyment of traumatic destruction produces a new series of representations. For the subject of abjection, Kristeva explains, "is eminently productive of culture. Its symptom is the rejection and reconstruction of languages" (1980, 45).

For *Fitcher's Bird* one can, then, isolate three aspects of the performative in Sherman's artistic practice, each thematizing how the survival of the self is coterminous both with the destruction of the intact body and its transformation into a new body. First, the image of the sisters' dead body parts points to the concrete materials Sherman uses in her performed scenes, the deanimate dolls and props, but also the iconographic bits and pieces she borrows from a collective image repertoire. On two scores the production of her photographs can therefore be seen as an act that consciously employs the process of assembling body parts and image fragments. Second, the image representing Fitcher's bird is a radical reference to Sherman's multifarious masquerades, to her playing with disguise and mimicry as a screening of the self, as though she wanted to demonstrate how it is only with the help of such a strategy of displacement that she can offer herself to the view of the photographic lens. Finally, the image of the dead and deadly substitute bride is staged by Sherman as though it were a self-portrait. The face is reproduced frontally, looking, with almost impudent candor, directly at the spectator; her other self of the imagination is represented by the image of a decorated skull.

Precisely this decorated skull allows me to return to the nightmare Emmy von N. described to Freud, in which she had had to lay out and decorate a number of dead people and put them in coffins, but would not put the lids on (1893–1895). In the dream phantasy Freud's hysteric patient ascribes to herself the role of a woman who refashions dead bodies, dresses and adorns them—indeed one could say embellishes the dead—at the same time that she commemorates the presence of the dead among the living through her feeling compelled to leave the coffins open. Using this analogy as a point of departure, I want to discuss Sherman's self-representations, which she says are not self-portraits, as articulations of a hysteric language of the body. As I argue that these photographic representations perform the hysteric's production—seduction as well as disregard of the cultural codes that construct our notions of femininity and masculinity, of normal and pathological, of human and monstrous—I however, invoke the analogy to this clinical concept so as to speak of Sherman's aesthetic strategy.

It will help to recall one last time Stavros Mentzos description of this elusive and enigmatic psychosomatic disturbance. "Those affected by hysteria move internally (in accordance with their experience) and externally (in accordance with public appearance) into a state in which they *experience themselves as quasi-other*, and in the eyes of those around them *appear as other than they are*," he argues. "They place themself into a psychic state in which their own body functions and/or psychological functions and/or character traits are experienced and appear in such a way that an (apparently) other, *a quasi-altered self-representation results*" (1980, 75). Furthermore, the formula reappearing throughout my discussion has been that the hysteric's histrionic much ado about nothing corresponds to the desire for an impossible something, whose most resilient trope is the wandering uterus of Greek medical literature. Given that within Western medical literature the feminine soon came to be constructed as an enigmatic, untamed, uncontrollable nervous system, while its counterpart in our cultural image repertoire was the construction of the feminine character with a proclivity toward inauthenticity, imitation, deception, and mimicry, as well as toward unrestrained and unpredictable phantasizing, hysteria readily came to stand for femininity par excellence. The ironic impasse inherent in any discussion of hysteria, as I have been arguing throughout, is that its discursive construction demarcates the blind spot, the x marking that which lies outside any categorization, thus putting to question the very system of nosology it is also invoked to support. Similarly the hysteric emerges in medical and cultural texts as the one who, fully versed in the language of her master, seduces him with her perfect performance of the nosological phantasies he projects onto her, only to disillusion and dismantle his desire in the course of their exchange. Thus, even while the language of hysteria marks the construction of femininity, and the curtailment of the female subject's voice within its discursive formation, it has always also been considered the language of feminine discontent with culture; the code of dissatisfaction and boredom, melancholy, world-weariness, effusive daydreaming, and narcissistic self-preoccupation, as well as the code of self-destructive anger with which many talented, young women reacted to the constraining gender role offered them within the bourgeois family.

At the same time, given that a lack of satisfaction places the afflicted subject in close proximity to melancholia, another aspect of the language of hysteria I have been exploring is the hysteric subject's insistence on voicing cultural discontents that also refer to the constriction of gender in the sense of genus, generation, and origin. Whether the malaise the hysteric voices refers to family secrets that have been inherited or to the return of the truth the dead know, or whether it addresses fallibilities and inconsistencies within symbolic laws, this disturbance, thus my argument, can be understood as a language that allows the afflicted subject to articulate memory traces of a psychic trauma—the traumatic knowledge of somatic and symbolic vulnerability.

Now, the reason I invoke hysteria in my discussion of an American artist who does not present herself to her audience as a regular visitor of psychiatric clinics, as was the case with Anne Sexton, and who does not directly invoke the language or image repertoire of the psychoanalytic case history, as was the case with Alfred Hitchcock, is that hysteria performatively stages precisely the same problem that characterizes Cindy Sherman's displaced self-representations. Both the hysteric and this postmodern artist use the body to repeat by representation an earlier traumatic impression and, in the course of this mimetic self-representation, to oscillate between memory and figuration, between masculine and feminine self-definition, between resuscitating what is dead, deanimate, or artificial and killing off what is animate or material. With the help of a body performance—the theatrical display of intimate phantasy scenes, the simulation of various roles toward each of which she affects a belle indifférence—both decorate the past and draw new life from the dead. Hesitating between consciousness and trance, both use these performances to render the concealed visible. They allow the other self of the imagination to speak, staging the body in relation to a past trauma or retained memory traces, whose vanishing point is death. As Georges Didi-Huberman has shown, even while the hysteric articulates her discontent with the performance of gender that her culture expects of her, she does so by recourse to precisely the same representations of femininity that this culture dictates to her. She imitates, represents, and parodies in her body the feminine roles celebrated in Western art—the woman possessed by demons, the daydreamer, the seductress. Because she experiences herself and appears to others as being other than what she is, her self-representation stages the incongruity between any so-called genuine feminine being and any visualization or staging of femininity. Viewed as precisely such a strategy, the language of hysteria can, I suggest, be useful to any discussion of the way the self is constructed by representations. As something goes awry in the process of imitating given cultural codes of gender identity and perpetuating the simulacrum of inscribed media images, the self that emerges ultimately proves to result as a knot formed in the context of and the conflict between traumatic psychic material and its representations. In other words, it is at exactly this interface that both the hysterical and the postmodern subjects emerge.

IV

To read Cindy Sherman's photographic work as a postmodern performance of hysteria involves, on the one hand, an interpretation of the content of her images, given that the themes of her portraits of women are often the somatizations of a wandering desire, a bodily imitation of culture and an expression of discontent with it, a malady caused by phantasy, representation, and reminiscences. Repeatedly, her portraits represent the vagabonding, the boredom, the daydreaming of the female subject. On the other hand, the undecidable question posed by art criticism—Are Sherman's portraits of woman only meant as surface phenomena, a free play of signifiers without any specific nonsemiotic point of reference, or can a feminine essence, an authentic woman be discerned beneath the surface of the image?—mirrors the question posed by any hysterical self-representation. Owing to her somatic disorder that has no contingent organic disturbance, even as this disorder nevertheless reflects an authentic trauma, the hysteric oscillates between the critical exposure of her discontent with the identities that her culture either offers or prescribes to her, on the one hand, and the imitation of precisely this image repertoire, on the other. In hysteria, whose symptoms are so different for every epoch, what is performatively articulated, however, is not only a discontent with society's prescription of specific gender roles. Rather, a knowledge of all the traumatic impressions that subtend any representational gesture is also at stake. After all, the hysteric suffers as much from memory traces whose origins she cannot determine as she does from her need to commemorate the dead, whose graves she is compelled to leave open.

The series of photographs Sherman has been working on for almost twenty years now, all under the auspicious label "Untitled," offer us various modalities of the language of hysteria. My suggestion is that they do so by enmeshing, in the gesture of a negated self-representation, the performance of her body (and later of the artificial body parts that take its place) with performance as a discursive constitution of the self. Sherman stages herself primarily as an image, but perhaps above all as a knot of traumatic material that finds articulation owing to ideational representations in a substitute, namely in representations of the materiality of the body caught in the act of decomposition—of having become completely mechanical, nothing but matter, abject flesh, plastic, or wood. Possessed by memory traces, suffering from representations, her other self of the imagination oscillates between the play of simulacrums, the essence of the aesthetic code of perfection, and a traumatic mass, the monstrous. Apodictically, Sherman repeatedly stages traumatic disturbances connected to the body, as it is turned into a series of representations that themselves hysterically perform the disturbance in the image and of the image, notably a language of the body that veers ever more urgently toward the crisis of representation itself.

I would like to speak of Sherman's self-representations as a hysterical language of the body because she performs, albeit self-consciously, as Freud's early patients did not, the disjunction between feminine identities traditionally offered by Western culture and what feminine subjectivity "actually" is. As Laura Mulvey argues, "Because Sherman uses cosmetics literally as a mask she makes visible the feminine as masquerade" (1991, 142). In her first photographs, the *Untitled Film Stills*, she presents reconstructions of film scenes of the 1950s and 1960s (film noir, melo, nouvelle vague) in which she quite consciously poses as the stereotypical heroine of postwar-Hollywood films, indeed turns her body literally into a representation, the prototypical signifier Woman. If we also consider that she was born in 1954, then we realize that the media images she cites include those representations of femininity her mother would have identified with as she was conceiving and giving birth to her daughter. These photographs stand as the legacy of the maternal image repertoire. Reconstructing these imaginary film scenes allows Sherman to identify with her mother's attempt to try out the feminine roles American postwar culture offered her. But still, the scenes also represent phantasy scenarios about her own origins, and as such revolve around three central questions coupling phantasies of origin and the origin of phantasy (Laplanche and Pontalis 1973): Where do I come from? What is my gender? What do I desire? Significantly, Sherman performs these questions in relation to the way they find their source in the phantasmatic register of her own mother.

Because Sherman pays scrupulous attention to the details in her strategy of citation, the photographs appear entirely familiar to the spectator. They uncannily evoke memories of films, but of films that never existed, because her photographs are quite consciously designed as pure simulacrums, as authentic copies without an original. The represented subject and the representing image are identical. The disjunction between empirical woman and woman as representation is here endowed with a very special variation, given that the actual models of these photographs could potentially be other cinematic photographs, but that these are all purely invented film stills. If the classic hysteric suffers from nonabreacted reminiscences, finding herself subject to belated memory traces whose origins are unknown to her, Sherman provokes both in herself and her viewers the analogous effect confronting freely floating and overdetermined memory traces. She represents one moment from a film, capturing a whole film in a single image. With every image she suggests that something is about to happen, but leaves open what event it is that will occur. These women, self-preoccupied, pausing in midsentence, hesitating in midaction, recall the hysteric whose unsatisfied desire produces a permanent state of feverish expectations and fragile anxieties. But we, too, are drawn into the spell of momentary hesitation, of uncertainty. Arrested at the interface between memory and expectation, we, too, begin to dream or to anticipate hysterically.

Above all, however, Sherman presents the other self of the imagination and of representation as a knot of given cultural representations precisely because the constructed subject neither refers to any one earlier representation nor to herself as model; rather, the function of the act of self-representation, once we perceive the *Film Stills* as a series, stages her represented body as the nodal point of multiple identities. The subject appears to be wandering to return again to that resilient metaphor for hysteria, the uterus that has become unhooked—and gives body to roaming feminine desire, to inconstant feminine phantasy. This heroine does not appear to be a firmly established character but the integrational knot of curious nonintegrated details, "the sum of curious particularies" (Kellein 1991, 10). That is to say, Sherman deconstructs the tradition of Western iconography, which equates woman with the image. She discloses the performance of femininity as a fake in the gesture of the hysteric's so-called dissimulation: the hysteric woman who in her self-representations pretends to be another person, without ever fully identifying with this assumed other role.

Schulz-Hoffmann writes about the heroine of the *Untitled Film Stills* that we are presented with a woman pretending to be someone else but never quite getting fully into the role, so as never to fully expose either herself or the other (1991, 31), which applies equally to the strategy of hysteria. This pretense is not only owing to the analogy between the dissimulation of the hysteric's and Sherman's heroines and the reduction of self-expression to pure surface phenomena. Rather, the hysterical subject can only be represented as oscillating between various positions; hesitating between expression and imagination, between subtle intimation and simultaneous concealment; appearing even as she vanishes and at the very end withholding all final resolution from any self-expression, even as the trace of a residue constitutively influences the self-representation. By her hysterical gesture, Sherman self-consciously demonstrates to what extent the reality of femininity is produced by the representational medium and how the represented subject exists as a knotting of signifiers of femininity, as the integration of arbitrarily assembled details from our cultural image repertoire without any material nonsemiotic referent. As Rosalind Krauss argues, the portrayed feminine subject is imagined and embodied by virtue of the function of the signifiers, and so her identity is purely a function of the mise-en-scène, of lighting, distance, and camera angle (1993).

Thus, when Sherman repeatedly insists that it is futile to seek her true identity behind the woman performed in and by the image, that there is no depth to these photographs, that beneath the surface of the photographic image no intact, authentic self can be found, she is really emphasizing that her identity emerges only obliquely, as the conglomerate performance of her many masquerades and displacements of the self. Here, too, one can locate an analogy with the hysterical mode of self-reproduction. For like the hysteric, Sherman articulates herself by adopting other bodies and figures, by resorting to the histrionics of different self-fashionings and a belle indifférence toward any one of these. After all, her works all remain untitled. Indeed when she speaks about her mode of working, the scenario she offers resonates with the language of Freud's hysterics. "The level of energy brought to the otherwise faked emotions, as well as the staging of my photographs, leaves me drained," she explains. "The only way I can keep objective toward the characters I'm portraying is to physically distance myself from the activity. . . . I don't see that I'm ever completely myself except when I'm alone. I see my life as a training ground because I'm acting all the time;

acting certain ways to certain people, to get things done, what I want, to have people act toward me the way I want them to" (cited in Stockebrand 1985, 33).

While Laura Mulvey argues that in the *Untitled Films Stills* "Each of the women is Sherman herself, simultaneously artist and model, transformed chameleon-like into a glossary of pose, gesture, and facial expressions" (1991, 137), Judith Williamson opposes such an essentialist interpretation. She suggests that because Sherman offers a lexicon of represented feminine identities, each image calls on the viewer to construct the inextricability of femininity and the image; the enmeshment of femininity as a phantasy projection onto any single image, and the depiction of a woman concretely given figure to by any single image. Sherman's work is neither exclusively a witty parody of media images of femininity, a deconstruction of the supremacy of the simulacrum, nor merely a series of self-portraits in search of identity: "The two are completely mixed up, as are the imagery and experience of femininity for all of us. . . . Femininity is trapped in the image—but the viewer is snared too" (1983, 106).

Where the classic hysteric, rather more disempowerd by than in control of her strategy, performs femininity as a symptom without any clear lesion, Sherman self-consciously and with self-control elicits the false search for a real, coherent, homogeneous identity. She performs a maladie par représentation rather than becoming its victim, as is the case with the hysteric, even as she also takes recourse in the undecidable interchange between surface and essence. As Williamson puts it, Sherman's photographs are to be understood as a "surface which suggests nothing but itself, and yet in so far as it suggests there is something behind it, prevents us from considering it as a surface" (1983, 102). Because her photographs turn the viewer into an accomplice in an act that constructs the represented woman as an image, the ideology inherent in this aesthetic act is disclosed.

Clearly we should question the univocal, allegorical reading of Sherman's work, such as Arthur Danto offers reading the *Untitled Film Stills* as a representation of the essential woman, eternally the same in the midst of all her guises: "The Girl is an allegory for something deeper and darker, in the mythic unconscious of everyone, regardless of sex. For the Girl is the contemporary realization of the Fair Princess in the Far Tower, the red-clad child in the wolf-haunted woods, the witch-sought Innocent lost in trackless forest, Dorothy and Snow-White and The Littlest Revel in a universe of scary things. Each of the stills is about the Girl in Trouble, but in the aggregate they touch the myth we each carry out of childhood, of danger, love, and security that defines the human condition where the wild things are" (1990, 14). By interpreting the represented woman as a cipher for universal characteristics of the masculine psyche, Danto has been taken in by Sherman's hysterical performance; he thereby enacts precisely what she is trying to demythify. Above all, however, such an interpretation deflects the disturbance that emerges from Sherman's deconstructive staging of stereotypes of femininity, transforming this unsettling gesture into a stabilizing tropic reading. Such an allegorizing interpretation is blind to the critical moment in Sherman's work: when she performs the disjunction, between ideational notions of the self, self-representation, and identity.

I would argue instead that works from the series *Untitled Film Stills*, *Rear-Screen Projections*, *Centerfolds*, and *Fashion* produce an effect of uncanny and irritating recognition that elicits a gesture of counterdirection. They seem to call for an interpretative oscillation between the desire to integrate the free-floating signifiers into a narrative that would mitigate the sense of disturbance evoked by the images precisely through recourse to metaphors of danger, desire, or phantasizing. At the same time, however, they force on the viewer a recognition that the engendered composite is inhabited by an internal dissolution, by the traumatic psychic material as well as the real body subtending any representation and its interpretation. These photographs illustrate that to be subject to representation means neither an image-produced falsification of the represented self (signifier without signified) nor an identity between image and self (transparency between the signifier and the signified) but rather the production of a knotted subject that in one and the same gesture is conscious of being represented as well as of the dissolution inherent in any image representing it; a hysterical, postmodern subject that articulates itself precisely in the interface between monstrous, formless materiality beneath the suface of the image and an outward appearance of perfection, the coherence af any aesthetic object.

This counterdirectional gesture, this oscillation between integration and dissolution or sublimation and desublimation of aesthetic coherence, is no longer merely the privileged subject, but rather it transforms into the privileged strategy itself in such series as *Disasters*, *Fairy Tales*, and *Sex Pictures*. Although the protagonists in the *Untitled Film Stills*, *Rear-Screen Projections*, *Centerfolds*, and *Fashions* depict, in a variety of ways, the hysterical body performing a *maladie par représentation,* this hysterical body nevertheless remains intact within the frame of the representation. The displacement and dissolution of the subject here took place, as Rosalind Krauss argues, primarily through the photographic medium—the lighting, depth of field, grain, and framing. In the later works, by contrast, the subject fades almost completely from the field of vision, disfigured into monstrous body shapes or cut up into body fragments. It is reduced to a gaze without any reference point, or appears only by virtue of the objects that metonymically refer to the absent subject. In these representations, the hysterical body appears to be wounded, fractured, and dissolving. It is often absent, replaced by or supplemented with prosthetics. In Mulvey's words, we are shown "a monstrous otherness behind the cosmetic facade" (1991, 144).

At the same time, these photographs make manifest what had been implicit in Sherman's earlier demythification of cultural images of femininity; the conflation between the depiction of a disintegrating female body and a disintegration of the cohesive formal organization of the photographic image. These photographs self-reflexively stage phantasy scenarios of bodily fragmentation as an aesthetic principle; they form a horrific inversion of the earlier scenes, in which, analogous to the hysterical self-performance, an illness by representation was staged. What is now being performed is the malady aroused by a traumatic knowledge of one's own mutability, transformation, and decay. The represented monstrosity inundates the aesthetic coherence of the image and turns idealized perfection inside out. Both the represented body and the strategy of representation seem to be caught up in a movement of desublimation, dissolving, and disseminating. These photographs elicit a different kind of hysterization in the viewer, now no longer in relation to assimilated memory traces without origins but rather in relation to the viewer's own anxieties about fragmentation and dying.

Thus, two modalities of a language of hysteria emerge in Cindy Sherman's work. On the one hand, her photographs stage the hysteric's proclivity to extravagant phantasy, daydreaming, and self-preoccuption as the thematic subject of the *Untitled Film Stills* and *Centerfolds*. As viewers, we are outside the scene, permitted to watch the self-contained, seductive, dreaming, psychically and physically vagabonding heroine as she appears to be tormented by anxiety, engrossed in her desires, and consumed by her anticipations. We gaze at her from outside, but she is caught in the act of phantasizing something whose content, in the fashion of the true narcissist, she keeps to herself. The gesture of dreaming is staged here, while we are forced to interpret, to come up with the content of these phantasy scenarios. In the *Disasters*, *Fairy Tales*, and *Sex Pictures*, this relationship is reversed. Because the subject of the image has begun to fade, we ourselves partake of the phantasy scenario and are no longer excluded from its content. We do not see the dreamer; rather we have entered the realm of her phantasy space. We are now presented with the intimate drama we were only able to guess at in the earlier photographs. We are drawn directly into the intimate spectacle, the other self of the imagination. Now we are asked to look into the evil magician's cauldron, and, much like the sly sister in *Fitcher's Bird*, we are not spared its horrific sight—the dismemberment of the body, the monstrous dissolution of the self, the fantastic composites that create hybrid creatures.

On the other hand, Sherman repeatedly displays the hysteric's oscillation between positions of fixed identity. According to psychoanalytic theory, the hysteric defines herself in relation to a figure of paternal authority by constantly renegotiating her relationship to this Other. In dialogue with this interpellator she constantly reposes the question What am I? in relation to my gender and in relation to the contingency of my existence? Sherman's work performs a similar strategy of self-interrogation as a means of self-fashioning, though here it is quite specifically the spectator who serves as representative of the paternal code. For the photographs are constructed so as to draw the viewer into the exchange, indeed this implied viewer serves as the Other to whom the staged interrogation of identity is addressed. In such sequences as the *Centerfolds* and the *Color Tests*, we find the classic hysteric indecision Am I feminine or masculine? In the *Untitled Film Stills*, the *Rear-Screen Projections*, and *Fashions*, the question is Do I exist or am I the mere repetition of an image? In the *Disasters* and *Fairy Tales*, the questions are Am I human or animal, human or fantasy creature? Do I exist as an animate body, or do I negate my existence through deanimation? Am I human or model, doll or prosthesis?

Norman Bryson has poignantly described the transition within Cindy Sherman's work as going from the conventional postmodern notion that "all is representation" to a reformulation that privileges "the body as horror"; from a notion that the simulacrum is the only reality we have to the breakdown of the simulacrum into a body of disaster (in Krauss 1993, 217). It is in the counterdirectional gesture so typical of the language of hysteria, that is, the gesture of hesitating between two diametrically opposed registers of pure representation and of horror—that I would locate the common denominator of all of Cindy Sherman's work. In her early series, the heroine, composed of citations from invented film stills, advertisements, and pornographic images, functions as a serial display of stereotypes of femininity perpetrated by the image repertoire of western culture. Sherman not only stages a vulnerable, precarious, hesitant, vagabonding, and seductive female protagonist in them. Rather, the performance itself aims to highlight the exclusively semiotic quality of this photographic subject. In her later work, however, Sherman turns surface beauty inside out to reveal human mutability—the decomposed, vulnerable body and the monstrosity inherent in any aesthetically coherent image, meant to remain occluded by the perfection of sublimation. Now her performance aims to make manifest what is excluded from and foreclosed by the representation, the alterity that crosses cultural constructions of femininity with the real.

As I had argued about Freud's specimen dream of Irma's injunction, I would call this aesthetic strategy the language of hysteria because it doubles the dissolution of the represented subject by offering a threat to the coherence of representation itself. However, what Sherman privileges is neither the sublimation performed by representation (perfection as the essence of the code) nor a desublimating disturbance of the image (the monstrous situated outside the code). Rather, we see an oscillation between the two. She traces two modalities of feminine self-representation within the discursive formulations of Western cultural practices, thereby transforming representation into performance. On the one hand, there is the simulacrum heroine as a knot of traditional images of femininity: woman as a fetish, as a seemingly integrated body symptom, uncannily screening the truth of human vulnerability and contingency. On the other hand, there is the feminine body as representative for denaveling and mutability, for those moments of castration that are irrevocably inscribed into all human existence beyond gender. The disgusting fragments of the body and abject body fluids stand in for the real that can never be entirely captured within the frame of aesthetic coher-

ence. As the logical conclusion of her trajectory into the interiority of the
body and into scenes of the body's woundings, Sherman takes leave of the
human body completely in such sequences as *Specimens* and *Sex Pictures*,
only to replace it with dolls and anatomical figures. In so doing she seems to
deconstruct certain tacit presuppositions about gender and the body that
continue to be held so dear in our culture. For are not dolls the artificial
bodies given to girls, so that by playing with them they might learn the
power of feminine masquerade? And are not anatomical figures the plastic
reconstructions given to the medical students, so that, as David Cronenberg's *Dead Ringers* illustrated, by probing into them they might explore the
secrets of the human body that lie beneath the skin?

V

Cindy Sherman's photographs, all labeled "Untitled," urge us to endow
them with a title and bind them into narratives. But like the case histories of
the hysterics, so disconcerting and at the same time so heuristically stimulating to the analyst Freud, to whom they were addressed precisely because he
was incapable of finding any solution to them, this series, too, is interminable. Sherman says of the *Untitled Film Stills*, "What I was trying to do was
to make people make up stories about the character so they could imagine a
whole film, perhaps based around that character." In forcing us to invent
narratives for her images, however, she hystericizes us. Like her, we are
haunted by the images that remind us of familiar images, even as they always
miss their mark. Like her, we are possessed by memory traces that have no
clear origin. Her performances of femininity, of the monstrous, and ultimately of the mechancial body, compel us to see this staging as a performance. In one and the same gesture she urges us to focus both on the process
of figuration and on the traumatic material that is screened out by any aesthetic figuration, or, if it cannot be contained, that emerges from it in its
excessive, monstrous shape. If the starting point of her self-displacements
was her sense of dislocation and alienation in her home, its end point is the
fact that her photographs have the same effect on us. We, too, begin to feel
uncannily dislocated in our own image repertoire, in the phantasy scenarios
transmitted to us by the media, and in the protective fictions we construct to
give meaning to our contingent existence. If in her self-portraits, which are
no self-portraits, Sherman articulates her discontent with culture, her performance of this dissatisfaction consists precisely in making this discomfort
disturbingly our own.

In a television interview with Mark Stokes, Cindy Sherman describes how
she at first dismissed the suggestion, made to her by a doctoral student, that
her entire work was one long confrontation with death, but after reflection
recognized that her interest in horror films, artificial body parts, and fairy
tales, could indeed be understood in this way; these representations allow

her to prepare herself for the potential incursion of violence and death. "I don't know why I think of death perhaps every day, but maybe it's living in Manhattan, and reading the paper, and thinking how it can happen at any moment. . . . There are so many variables," she explains. "I think what's fascinating is that you are never prepared for it. And I'm not exactly afraid to die; once you're dead, what is there to be afraid of? It's just the unknown, and I think that is what's triggered in the films that I like, and somehow, I guess, I try to come to terms with it in my work, somehow." All of Sherman's work, one could say, revolves around staging this hesitation, this somehow. It performatively transforms her sense of being haunted by nightmares, memory traces, and inherited representations into renditions of a coherent photographic subject. Yet at every turn she makes sure that we never lose sight of the underlying traumatic knowledge of our inevitable vulnerability.

NOTES

INTRODUCTION
NAVEL INVERSIONS

1. Thomas Pynchon (1963) tells a version of this story in chapter 1 of *V*.

2. I thank Linda Gregerson for this anecdote; she offers a poetic rendition of this scene in "The Woman Who Died in Her Sleep," describing the navel as "The wound / she hadn't yet / learned to ignore—the mortal one—was where / the child had once been joined / to something else" (*Yale Review*, forthcoming).

3. Material circulated for the exhibition of her first set of navel plaster casts on June 20, 1992, and personal correspondence with the artist.

4. In their dictionary of folklore imagery, Bächtold-Stäubli and Hoffmann-Krayer (1937) have an entry for *Umbilicomantie* or *Omphalomantie*, a practice in antiquity whereby doctors read the skin folds around the navel to prophesy the character and fortune of a given person, or midwives read the knots and entwinements on the umbilical cord as a means of divination (p. 1307).

5. I purposely will not be consistent about gendering the term hysteria, sometimes referring to the hysteric in the feminine, when the conventional encoding of this psychosomatic disorder is discussed, then again either to him or her, depending on the gender of the protagonist in a literary narrative or a case history under consideration.

6. It seems significant that the editors, Joanne Morra and Marquard Smith, of a new journal *Parallax* included in the first issue a questionnaire on the state of cultural studies and philosophy, asking critics, among other items, to respond to the question, "What are the implications of the recent return to 'ethics' as a site of love, friendship, tolerance and the acceptance of difference within the discourses of cultural studies and philosophy?"

7. In a similar vein, Richard Sennett (1994, 25) argues that if people learned to accept their flawed nature, their exile from the Garden, they might find a home in the city. His plea is that we learn to negotiate between body images of completeness, wholeness, oneness, coherence, and those of the body as a source of suffering and unhappiness: "People who can acknowledge this dissonance and incoherence in themselves understand rather than dominate the world in which they live. This is the sacred promise made in our culture."

8. Though her interest is directed toward conceptualizing femininity in representation and subjectivity, and recognizing retroactively prenatal traces in later experiences, Bracha Lichtenberg-Ettinger (1992, 1994) undertakes a similar project; she introduces the concepts *matrix* and *metamorphosis* as supplementary symbolic perspectives. She, too, seeks to open the symbolic register dominated exclusively by the phallus in Freudian and post-Freudian theory.

9. In a similar manner, Françoise Dolto (1984) refers to the notion of castration by umbilical cutting ("castration ombilicale"), suggesting that birth should be seen as the first event of castration. In line with Lacanian theory, she defines castrations as those events in the developmental process of the subject when it learns from another that the fulfillment of its desire in the precise manner it seeks is forbidden

owing to symbolic law. I am concerned with the fault line between what is linguistically informed and what emerges from the real, and Dolto emphasizes here that birth is both a natural act and one fraught with symbolic significance: in both registers the cutting of the umbilical cord is the first gesture that fully defines the infant's body as distinct from the mother's. Dolto argues that the umbilical cut, functioning as a traumatic partition, is the pattern for all further castrations; that is, forbiddances of desire voiced through the contradicting desire of the other. The crux, of course, is that the umbilical castration is the one gesture of fragmentation whose symbolic differentiation accompanies an actual moment of separating two body parts from one another.

10. I would suggest that psychoanalytically speaking, the "invisible guide" leading him to rush so violently to her bedroom can be interpreted as his destructive drives.

11. Though their conclusions are different from those I propose here, both Luce Irigaray (1981) and Monique Schneider (1980) place matricide at the center of their discussions of subjectivity and culture.

12. I borrow the term from Roland Barthes (1957).

13. In a similar manner, Louise J. Kaplan (1991) argues that male and female perversions should be read as fetishistic or sadomasochistic scenes that are scripted retroactively to compensate for deprivations and traumas of childhood. For the person performing the act of perversion, the sexual encodings that structure these scenarios are actually transformations of nonsexual insults and injuries to their sense of bodily integrity experienced at an earlier date, but whose traumatic impact finds only belated articulation.

14. See Henry George Siddell and Robert Scott (1968, 1229). For a summary of artistic and religious representations of the omphalos, see Bruno Kauhsen (1990).

15. Harrison, (1927, 429) offers one version of this myth in which the guardian snake of Gaia is at first feminine and becomes a male serpent only when it has to be killed by Apollo—for only as a masculine being is it a "foeman worthy of Apollo's steel." A similar narrative forms the basis of Mozart's *Magic Flute*, as I will argue in chapter 2.

16. For a frame-by-frame analysis of this film, see William Rothman (1982).

17. William Rothman (1982), interpreting *Psycho* as an allegory about the making and viewing of films that self-reflexively comments on the camera's appetite as a murderous act, sees Marion in the position of the viewer, entranced by Norman Bates, who appears to her like a creature of her imagination, her mirror reflection.

18. I take this concept from Slavoj Žižek's (1992) interpretation of Hitchcock's films, including *Psycho*.

19. Donald Spoto (1983) points out that Hitchcock made two important additions to Bass's design of the shower sequence, one of which was the shot of the knife about to penetrate Marion's abdomen, filmed as a fast-motion, reverse shot, and the other, the shot of blood and water running down the drain: these suggest that it was particularly important for him to include a chain of navel imagery at the traumatizing core of his film. As Carol J. Clover points out, one of the reasons this sequence has evoked so much study may be that like the navel, at the core of its construction, it "suggests so much but shows so little." We see only the body being stabbed once, whereas all the other shots are of the knife; the shower; Marion's face, arm, and feet (1992, 41).

20. For a discussion of how Hitchcock forces us to see death's face directly, which

up to this point we had seen reflected only in the gaze of horror in Marion's and Arboghast's expression, see Hans Schmid (1993).

21. In "The Aetiology of the Neuroses" Freud writes about his work with Breuer: "Traumatic hysteria was well known; what we asserted beyond this was that *every* hysteria that is not hereditary is traumatic. In the same way I am now asserting that *every* neurasthenia is sexual," (1892–1899, 179). I will explore the implications of his shift to a sexual model for hysteria (see chapter 5), discussing what Freud gained by insisting that a phantasy of sexual seduction, rather than an actual scene of sexual experience, was to be found at the origin of all hysterical symptoms—as well as what he had to screen out for his theory to hold.

22. In my discussion I am shifting away from the debate about femininity staged in the 1920s when Freud claimed that libido has only one gender, namely, masculine. Meanwhile Ernest Jones, Karen Horney, and Melanie Klein argued for a polarization including a feminine libido as well. For a discussion of this dispute, see Juliet Mitchell (1984) and Jacques Lacan (1975) who also explores the possibility of a libido beyond the phallus.

23. Juliana Schiesari (1992) makes a similar claim for hysteria as an articulation of loss, without offering detailed examples, though she reads this in relation to the particular historical situation of women.

24. In a letter to Wilhelm Fliess, Freud argues, "There is a kind of conversion in anxiety neurosis just as there is in hysteria. . . . But in hysteria it is psychical excitation that takes a wrong path exclusively into the somatic field, whereas here it is a physical tension, which cannot enter the psychical field and therefore remains on the physical path. The two are combined extremely often" (1892–99, 195).

25. Concerned with the same representational difficulty, Jacques Lacan sees trauma as one of the "faces of the real," as Bruce Fink notes. Because trauma implies fixation or blockage, it "always involves something which is not symbolized" (Fink 1995, 26), thus pointing to the remainder that persists after symbolization. That is, it points to two moments of the real, "a real before the letter, that is, a presymbolic real, which, in the final analysis, is but our own hypothesis (R_1) and a real after the letter which is characterized by impasses and impossibilities due to the relations among the elements of the symbolic order itself (R_2), that is, which is generated by the symbolic" (27).

26. See Alaida Assmann (1995). On the issue of the belatedness of traumatic representation, at the core of Freud's work on the unconscious, see also Jean Laplanche (1989).

27. I illustrate in chapter 7 how Hitchcock's psychoanalytic films trouble this wholesome narrative about a successful cure of trauma.

28. As Ragland-Sullivan notes, Lacan chose to define the hysteric as being hors-sexe, because, plagued by "the chaos of identifying as neither/nor," her discourse is structured by a question that will allow no firm set of sexual identifications to serve as an identity basis for being, but rather performs an endless oscillation between masculinity and femininity (1995, 124).

29. For the hysteric, truth emerges from an encounter with the real; thus, her discourse mirrors that of psychoanalytic theory itself. The aim of analysis, after all, is to make visible the inconsistencies and impossibilities in the analysand's symbolic representations—her symptoms and phantasies—and translate these into encoded interpretive narratives.

30. André Green, distinguishing between hysteria and obsessional neurosis ar-

gues that the hysteric is "mad about her body"; she converts somatically, whereas the obsessional converts into thought, and the phobic is anxious (1986, 227). As I will discuss in chapter 4, Georges Didi-Huberman (1982) has convincingly argued, however, that even though the hysteric converts her phantasies into body language, the gestures she uses are deeply embedded within the cultural system of media images and texts available to her.

31. I am implicitly working with Jacques Derrida's (1977) discussion of the crypt as a place in the psychic apparatus containing knowledge that has been insufficiently repressed and kept present without adequate linguistic representation.

32. This is one seminal distinction between hysteria and paranoia; although hysterics will experience psychotic attacks and indeed are often classified in contemporary psychiatry as borderline schizophrenics, the hysteric *sustains* the symbolic system while the paranoid *forecloses* it. Thus, the paranoid builds walls and requires hermetically sealed off, consistent phantasy systems of order, whereas the hysteric aims to keep everything fluid and mobile.

33. In his interview with Stig Björkman (1994), Allen explains that he changed the script whenever he made new discoveries in the documentary material he looked at and that he used all the old film equipment from the 1920s, as well as flicker mattes for the lighting and scratches on the negatives to make the reshot scenes seem authentic. In addition, most of the actors, those interviewed and those speaking on the screen, were amateurs, who were able to create a realistic feeling, responding to the story that they heard from the film team as though it was a story they learned from the popular culture of the time. Although Allen made his own footage, it looked as though it were of another era, the cameleon technique mirroring the cameleon man it depicts.

34. It is interesting to note that in the course of the narrative, Zelig disappears twice more, only to reappear precisely because his transformations produce him as a foreign body, disturbing first Pope Pius's appearance before Saint Peter and then Hitler's speech at the Nazi Party rally in Munich.

35. I will return to this gesture of the subject dissolving into a prior image, when I discuss Jean-Martin Charcot's representations of the cycle of hysteria, where the women performing the stages of the cycle blend in with previous visual iconography about demonic possession, as well as in Cindy Sherman's *Film Stills*, where the heroine seems to dissolve into reconstructions of prior cinematic scenes caught in the frame of the film still.

36. In my own pun I am, of course, playing on the Elizabethan usage of the word 'nothing' with its feminine connotation, given that the nothing of gender difference in Shakespeare's *Much Ado About Nothing* refers to the issue of chastity, as this produces dramatic strife at the intersection between a real and an imaginary lack of the bride Hero's so-called bodily integrity.

CHAPTER 1
THE NAVEL OF SIGMUND FREUD'S INAUGURAL DREAM

1. Erik Erikson, contributing a somewhat different interpretation of the feminine in the dream, argues that Freud here aligns the resistance of Victorian women to being undressed and examined to the resistance of a dream to being totally disclosed: "The Dream, then, is just another haughty woman, wrapped in too many mystifying

covers and 'putting on airs' like a Victorian lady. . . . In the last analysis, then, the dream itself may be a mother image; she is the one, as the Bible would say, to be 'known' " (1954, 46).

2. For further material on Freud's life at the time he wrote his *Interpretations of Dreams*, see Lisa Appignanesi and John Forrester 1992 and Peter Gay 1988. The formula for trimethylamine can be reproduced graphically as follows:

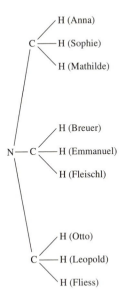

3. Monique Schneider (1980, 127–137), countering the more doctrinaire Oedipal reading of this dream, also connects the image of a toxin that will be eliminated with the dirty syringe. She argues that the desire for purgation, expressed in the dream, represents not so much Freud's debunking of his colleagues and figures of authority as his matricidal and infanticidal fury.

4. Though in this interpretation Lacan does not analyze the footnote, in his later seminar on the four fundamental concepts of the unconscious (1973, 23) he discusses the navel of the dream, saying that Freud invokes this term to designate, in the final analysis, the center of the unknown, which, like the anatomical navel that represents it, is nothing other than the gap, the abyss irrevocably inscribed into the subject of the unconscious.

5. Gilles Deleuze and Félix Guattari (1972) work with a similar topography when they propose the critical trope rhizome to explain the interface between psychic and social processes.

6. The counterimage to the thallus, of course, is the formula for trimethylamine that Freud sees at the end of the dream; it, too, emerges from nowhere, without roots and any point of origin.

7. I want to thank Judy Simons for pointing out to me that Freud, in a strange irony, suffered late in life from mouth cancer. This detail elicits a biographical story: the man who discovered psychoanalysis after a dream about the horrific vision inside

a hysteric woman's mouth (articulating his identification with her hysteric complaint about mortality by virtue of his feeling the same pain she feels—in his shoulder) ends up with the illness inside his mouth. The last photographs show this master narrator of the unconscious with a bandaged mouth.

8. I will discuss the point that hysteria is a language about keeping coffins open and adorning or discoursing with the dead, which I touched on superficially in the introduction, at greater length in the chapter on gothic hysteria and again in the chapter on Freud's case studies.

9. Barthes explicitly evokes Freud's discussion of the uncanny (1919), notably that although neurotic men often feel there is something uncanny about the female genital organs, this strange familiarity indicates how the womb evokes associations of repressed psychic material. By inversion, when a place is perceived as being familiar, Freud insists this can be decoded as a representation of the womb or the maternal body. I will return to this passage in my own effort to unpack what is contained in the metaphorical discussion of hysteria as a "wandering uterus," the familiar womb made strange by virtue of its peregrinations.

10. Jacques Derrida calls the Winter Garden photograph the overall punctum of the entire book (1981, 286) because in commemorating the death of Barthes's mother it also heralds the certainty of his own death. Martin Jay (1993, 450) notes the morbid irony that Barthes's own accidental death in February, 1980, shortly after *Camera Lucida* was published, only adds "to the poignancy of his argument for later readers."

11. Though Freud clearly presents his choice for a given formula at the end of his interpretation of the dream of Irma's injection, he nevertheless admits that there are other, less pacifying, interpretive choices available, an issue I will address in discussing Wagner's *Parsifal* in chapter 4.

12. I want to thank Benjamin Marius for this observation.

CHAPTER 2
MEDICINE'S HYSTERIA ROMANCE

1. I am referring to the transcripts of a seminar Slavoj Žižek held at Zurich University in the fall, 1994.

2. Ilza Veith (1965) notes that many symptoms attributed to hysteria at various historical periods would now no longer be designated as such, and the word itself no longer appears in the *Standard Nomenclature of Diseases* or in the *Mental Disorders Diagnostic Manual* of the American Psychiatric Association (as of 1952), having been replaced by the term *conversion symptom*.

3. See Stephen Greenblatt (1988) for a discussion of the cultural circulation of social energy, which I am implicitly invoking here.

4. In this brief overview I am primarily following the chronicle presented by Ilza Veith (1965) and Etienne Trillat (1986). The latter notes that for Plato, the uterus or matrix was like a living organism possessed by the desire to make children, but that this animal had no soul; that is, unlike all the other human body parts, it had no corresponding part in the immortal soul, the cosmos enveloping all human beings. Woman was distinct from man, thus Plato's conclusion, precisely because she harbored in her body this soulless, uncorrelated foreign body. Physicians after him would reformulate this image. Soranus suggested that the womb was no foreign body dominating the female genitals, but rather that woman herself was the cause of her

desire for progeny, Galen felt one should locate the origin of hysteria not only in the womb but also in the male semen and sperm so as to include the category of male hysteria. In an exploration of the resiliency of cultural formations of hysteria, the point is not the validity of any particular medical explanation but the rich proliferation of the metaphors and imagery employed as will be my focus in discussing David Cronenberg's films in a later chapter, where the notion of a uterus as voracious foreign body finds its postmodern transformation.

5. Veith records the writings of a Latin Hippocrates, Aretaeus, who asserts the existence of a hysteria unconnected with the uterus, which could also affect men, while Soranus sought to refute the idea of a uterus literally wandering about, suggesting instead that the disease emanated from the uterus but could affect the entire body. Galen, equally opposed to the notion that the uterus could wander about, saw hysteria as the result of a poisoning whose source, he believed, was the absence of semen in women and the retention of sperm in men.

6. In his interpretation of his dream of Irma's injection, Freud clearly refers back to this ancient image repertoire, using the representation of a woman who feels a hysterical lump in her throat to produce among other narratives his phantasy about curing the sexual dissatisfaction of spinsters and widows.

7. I will return to this intertextual issue in chapters 4 and 5, in discussion of both the iconography Charcot perpetrated at his clinic and Freud's translation of this theatrical and photographic spectacle into the narratives of case histories.

8. For G. S. Rousseau, Sydenham emerges as the unacknowledged hero of hysteria because he was the first to argue that the hysteric imitates other diseases and, by implication, also imitates culture. He explains, "Sydenham observed that the crucial hysteric symptom was always produced by tensions and stresses within the culture surrounding the patient or victim," and while the symptoms in part proved to be constant over time, the cultural tensions producing these symptoms varied. From this Rousseau speculates about a possible inference never explicitly stated by Sydenham, namely, that "the symptom leading to the condition of hysteria 'imitated' the culture in which it (the symptom) had been produced" (1993, 102).

9. For a feminist discussion of Foucault see Beret E. Strong (1989). It is interesting that Foucault, working with the French translations of British texts, mistakenly treats Sydenham as a contemporary rather than a precursor of such physicians as George Cheyne, whose treatise *The English Malady* appeared in London in 1735; Robert Whytt, whose observations on hypochondria and hysteria appeared in Edinburgh in 1764; William Cullen, whose work on hysteria also appeared in Edinburgh in 1796; or Joseph Raulin, whose treatise on hysteric vapours appeared in Paris in 1758. This is significant: while the mid-eighteenth–century medical literature does return to a sexualization and thus a gendering of hysteria, even as Whytt supports his theories by recourse to the "sagacious Sydenham" and his discovery "that the shapes of proteus, or the colours of the chameleon, are not more numerous and inconstant, than the varieties of the hypochondrian and hysteric disease" (1961, 95), the inclusion of hysteria within a discussion of sensibility is entirely foreign to Sydenham. Though the conflation of organic and moral discourse at the body of the hysteric results from Sydenham's construction of hysteria as the arch fallacy, to read only this result ignores the way Sydenham always also noted the message of vulnerability underlying the resilient simulations of his afflicted patients. As Foucault focuses on the construction of sexuality in the mid-eighteenth century, he falls prey to the same rhetorical gesture Freud undertakes at the start of modernism, when he too

turns from a traumatic to a sexual reading of hysteria. For both theorists, to have the sexual model hold requires other voices, such as those connecting hysteria with melancholia, be designated as leading far afield.

10. I am indebted to Julia Kristeva's work on the interplay of the semiotic and symbolic registers of the psychic apparatus, which not only incessantly negotiate affects, imaginings, and cultural codes, but require a thetic moment of violence for the symbolic order to take precedence. She has repeatedly argued (1987) that the subject needs to commit psychic matricide, in order not to remain melancholic or turn into a psychotic murderer. In chapter 5 I will return to the issue of nostalgia and crime in relation to a nonabreaction of maternity. As an aside to my reading of *The Magic Flute*, I would simply note that in this case matricide is significantly performed by the paternal figure of authority, while Pamina remains indecisive, vacillating in her alliances between Sarastro, the Queen of the Night, and Tamino. Her psychic ambivalence is such that she acknowledges her need for her mother even as she also recognizes that she must relinquish her unbearable, abundant presence.

11. Perhaps it is no longer necessary to point out that the opera works with race and gender as discussed by Gilman (1985), given that the one overtly evil character in Sarastro's world is a moor, whose dark skin ultimately proves to be the surface signal of an equally dark soul. Monostates is the only character to change sides in favor of the Queen of the Night, whereas the three boys whom she had initially asked to lead Tamino to Pamina, as well as the prince himself, shift alliances in favor of Sarastro. Madness in the queen, in German designated as a nocturnalization of the psyche, *Umnachtung*, and racial darkness in Monostatos mark both as being dangerous creatures of the night—murderous, irrational, indeed stereotypes of the Other, which the normative self sacrifices to reconfigure the parameters of its world.

12. If we recall that Erikson read Freud's dream of Irma's injection as a dream about male initiation, we see a similarity in narrative structure between the two parts of Freud's dream and the two acts of Mozart's opera. In the first act Tamino, like the dreamer Freud, finds himself in the realm of the imaginary, with several more or less hysteric women knotted together in a cluster—the Queen of the Night and her lady attendants—stirring in him the wish to identify with the female figure as an image. Significantly, Tamino falls in love with Pamina because he has seen her portrait. In the second act he, too, bonds with his colleagues against the knot of women and subjects himself to a symbolic formula that appears as mysteriously before his eyes as the one for trimethylamine does before Freud, namely, the insignia on the temple of wisdom calling the initiate to undergo the trial of fire and water.

13. This definition of an ethical act is taken from Lacan's discussion of Antigone in his seminar on ethics (1986), as well as from Žižek's application of Lacan's concepts in his discussion of Rossellini's films (1992a). I will return to the issue of an embrace of self-expenditure as an ethical act in my discussion of Richard Wagner's character Kundry.

14. Ivan Nagel isolates three experiences of death within Pamina's development. The first is her carefree defiance of death as she challenges Sarastro, saying she will accept punishment for her crime of wishing to flee but not a false existence—submitting herself to one she does not love. The second experience is her weariness when she yearns for suicide, while the third is her willingness to sacrifice herself for Tamino, of which Nagel says, "Death miraculously pledges not the destruction but the survival of the autonomous self." For him, Pamina, along with Leonore and Iphigenie, taught the authors of the German Enlightenment "to admit that autonomy is initiated and

sustained not by heroes, but by the weakest creatures—and that self-determination does not exclude or oppose rescue, but is its very model" (1988, 83).

15. I want to thank Michael Baumgartner for helping me with the analysis of the Mozart score.

16. For a rendition of Maria Theresa von Paradis's biography I have relied primarily on Mesmer's own account of the incident in his autobiography, fully aware of course that certain aspects of this case must remain speculative because we have no written evidence from Maria Theresa herself. Other critics, such as Eva Weissweiler (1981), simply assume that the gossip surrounding Mesmer can be taken at face value. She calls his treatment of Maria Theresa Paradis the work of a charlatan and accuses him of having not cured but rather sexually abused the blind girl in the same manner his peers had, though she had no concrete evidence to support her claim. Given that the case can no longer be decided, I find it significant for my own chronicle of the cultural language of hysteria that the stories engendered by the Paradis-Mesmer incident sexualize family alliances and appropriate the hysteric's body as the site where this "protective fiction" can take hold.

CHAPTER 3
GOTHIC HYSTERICS

1. Castle explicitly refers to Max Horkheimer and Theodor Adorno's *Dialectic of Enlightenment* as the first critique of the once-conventional view that the eighteenth century be seen as an era of progress, adding a psychoanalytic dimension, however, to their Marxist discussion of political and social alienation.

2. I will address the connection between late-eighteenth-century and late-twentieth-century sensibility in my discussion of David Cronenberg's films as a postmodern reversion of the body-mind problem raised by gothic literature.

3. I will return to the destructive enjoyment of traumatic knowledge that occurs once the subject has traversed a phantasy scene in my discussion of Jaspers' nostalgic, killer nannies in chapter 5.

CHAPTER 4
JEAN-MARTIN CHARCOT'S VAMPIRES

1. See Manfred Schneider (1988) for a discussion of how, in the representations Charcot produced of the hysteric symptoms and attacks, the seemingly pure hysterical automatism traverses a series of cultural signs and emerges as the effect of cultural codes, knotting together notions to the aesthetic rendition of passions and character, with notions of deviancy explored by pathology.

2. In his theoretical considerations *Studies in Hysteria* Josef Breuer takes issue with Pierre Janet's argument that hysteria is based on an innate psychological weakness, explaining that his educated patients are often of clear intellect, strong will, great character, and highest critical power, but in so doing he also invokes the figure of the martyred saint: "No amount of genuine, solid mental endowment is excluded by hysteria, though actual achievements are often made impossible by the illness. After all, the patron saint of hysteria, St. Theresa, was a woman of genius with great practical capacity" (1893–1895, 232). See also Jacques Lacan's discussion of St. Theresa's ecstatic enjoyment as an articulation of desire located outside the parameters of paternal law in his seminar *Encore* (1975).

442 — NOTES TO CHAPTER 4

3. For a description of the two categories of symptoms and the phases of the hysterical attack see Charcot (1887), Manfred Schneider (1988), and the exhibition catalogue edited by Alpha-Fnac (1982). The hysterical lump in the throat reappears in Freud's interpretation of Irma's injection.

4. It is significant that although Charcot in his published lectures transcribes the dialogues with both male and female patients, and although the gravures show both men and women, the photographic illustrations of hysteria that have influenced artistic representations of the possessed body in later decades exclusively show women hysterics.

5. As Sander Gilman argues, "The idea that the photograph supplied an objective source from which observations could be made, the underlying concept of scientific photography in the nineteenth century, had been unquestioningly transferred to psychiatric photography," offering among others the plates in Sir James Crichton Browne's *West Riding Lunatic Asylum Medical Reports* and *Doctor Diamonds Portraits of the Insane* as examples for this shift to visual verification (1982, 85). At the same time he understands Charcot's shift from photographic to graphic rendition as a skepticism toward the ability of the medium to transform the particular into the universal: "The complexity of even the relatively subjective depiction of the hysteric through the camera's eye was too great to present the desired schematic nature of the appearance of the hysteric."

6. Sander Gilman argues that Freud, more interested in the underlying causality of hysteria than in its external manifestations, became wary of illustration, and in his refusal to depict the insane in his own publications, in fact, he worked against what had become common practice in the closing decades of the nineteenth century, namely, illustrating neurological and psychiatric studies (1982, 204). Deborah Silverman explains the ubiquity of the visual in Charcot's work biographically in part, pointing out the direct involvement that members of his family had with decorative arts as well as his own artistic efforts as a painter, recalling that Freud called Charcot not a "thinker" but an "artist," and quoted him saying, "Je suis un visuel": "Charcot's definition of art as flat reportage was accompanied by his interest in arts as complex interior voyage; in secret, separate regions of his identity and in his own practice of the arts we can glimpse his uneasy movement from Realism to Symbolism and back again" (1989, 100). At the same time she argues that Charcot's new psychological discovery that the human psyche's design was heavily based on visual thinking, imagistic suggestibility, and subjective self-projection also came to alter the meaning of interior decoration at the end of the nineteenth century.

7. For a discussion of Luce Irigaray's notion of reiteration see Judith Butler (1993) and Mary Russo (1986).

8. The best collection of recent criticism on Bram Stoker's *Dracula* is Margaret Carter (1988). For a discussion of the blasphemous implications of Charcot's work, see Emily Apter (1991). Like Nina Auerbach (1982), who discusses the analogy between Stoker's vampirized women and Freud's hypnotized hysterics, Jennifer Wicke (1992) also notes the connection between the mesmeric and hypnotic world of Charcot and Stoker's rendition of Mina as medium, without, however, elaborating this intertextual connection. John L. Greenway (1986) in turn reads *Dracula* as a critique of the explanation of mental activity in physiological terms, which was the dominant scientific paradigm of Stoker's times.

9. For a discussion of hysteria seen as a version of spiritualism whenever medicine pathologized a belief in spiritualism, such as Frank Podmore's statement, "In the hysterical patient we see the same exaggerated self-consciousness which characterises

the magnetic somnambule and her successor, the spirit medium," see Alex Owen (1989, 150).

10. For a discussion of how the crisis and uncertainty about acts of symbolic investiture on the threshold of modernity found another transformation in Daniel Schreber's psychosis, see Eric Santner, 1996.

11. Even Van Helsing at one point admits, "You may think that I, Van Helsing, am mad—that the many horrors and the so long strain on nerves has at the last turned my brain" (469).

12. The iconography Stoker presents uncannily returns in Freud's speciman dream, in which he designs a nocturnal scenario where he and his three colleagues bend over the patient's, Irma's body, whose symptom of gasping for breath reveals a wound inside her throat, while Lucy dermographically shows her wound on the outside of her throat.

13. In his letter dated Vienna, 6 April 1897 Freud writes to Fliess, "The point that escaped me in the solution of hysteria lies in the discovery of a new source from which a new element of unconscious production rises. What I have in mind are hysterical phantasies, which regularly, as it seems to me, go back to things heard by children at an early age and only understood later" (1985, 235).

14. An observation Freud writes to Fliess on 6 December 1896 shows how astutely Stoker reworked the details about hysteria prevalent from medical literature in his description of vampirization, though I am arguing against the sexual encoding implied by Freud. He notes, "A hysterical attack is not a discharge but an *action*; and it retains the original characteristic of every action—of being a means to the reproduction of pleasure. . . . Thus patients who have had something sexual done to them in sleep have attacks of *sleep*. They go to sleep again in order to experience the same thing and often provoke a hysterical fainting-fit in that way. Attacks of giddiness and fits of weeping—all these are aimed at *another person*—but mostly at the prehistoric, unforgettable other person who is never equalled by any one later" (1985, 212).

15. In his letter to Fliess dated 17 January 1897 Freud picks up an analogy he had already commented on in his obituary of Charcot, asking his friend, "Do you remember how I always said that the mediaeval theory of possession, held by the ecclesiastical courts, was identical with our theory of a foreign body and a splitting of consciousness? . . . Why are their confessions under torture so like the communications made by my patients in psychical treatment?" (1985, 224)

16. Like Madame Bovary before her, Mina has them read the burial service for her, having convinced herself that she is dying and drawing her friends and stricken husband into this macabre scene (427).

17. Carolyn Abbate notes a parallel passage in Wagner's *Der Ring des Nibelungen*: "Legend tells us that Brünnhilde laughed in exultation upon witnessing (or, in some versions, upon hearing of) the death of Siegfried" (1991, 206). For a discussion of the manner in which Kundry exhibits the symptoms of hysteria most prevalent in the medical literature of Wagner's time—namely somnambulance, mutism, amnesia, paroxysms of laughter, and ecstatic convulsions, see Manfred Schneider (1994). He argues that her dying while imitating the figure of Maria Magdalena further supports the representation of Kundry as a hysteric, given that this biblical figure was considered to be both the prototype and the patron saint of hysterics.

18. The problem with Wagner, Žižek suggests, "is not his hysteria, but rather that he is not hysterical enough" (1997, 11). Arguing that *Parsifal* is structured around an opposition similar to the one between hysteria and possession proposed by Oughourlian, Žižek emphasizes the tension between a hysterically overexcited chro-

maticism, represented by Kundry, Amfortas, and Klingsor on the one hand, and a static diatonic tonality, a mythical timelessness represented by the Grail community and by the asexual purity as Parsifal's ultimate denial of passion. However, although the disappearance of the domain ascribed to the luxuriant (or putrefying) abundance of hysterical histrionics at the end of act 3 indicates that Wagner stages a "psychotic resolution of the deadlock of hysteria" (22), Žižek artfully points to a disturbing detail that remains, arguing, as I do, that Wagner's hystericism undermines the very aesthetic-political vision he seeks to realize (though he locates it at a different site than the one I propose). In Klingsor, the "maimed, obscene ludic father, author of fantasmagorias," writes Žižek, Wagner has inscribed himself into his work "in the very guise of what his work is striving to reject" (23), only to reemerge as Nietzsche's symptom, the figure whom the latter desperately needs to project onto him all he seeks to reject from his philosophical system—even as he finds himself infected by the hysterical hallucinations and the delusionary ramblings of the former. While I have discussed Van Helsing's relation to his dead, symbolic father, Charcot, as a commemorative transference, I will return to this dialectic of rejection and infection in my discussion of Hitchcock's rewritings of Freud.

19. For a discussion of Kundry within the context of a different contemporary medical debate, namely, syphilis, see Linda and Michael Hutcheon (1996). Marc Weiner, in turn, explores the way in which Kundry is representative of yet another contemporary medical debate, the one about race and degeneracy that sought to construct Jewishness as a pathology: "Doomed to wander the earth in multifarious guises (dishevelled hag, seductress, and penitent)," Weiner argues, her death at the end of act 3 recalls Wagner's ambiguous statement that "The only salvation for the Jews is *der Untergang*," which begs the question, whether this term meant "destruction" or "assimilation." It also recalls his more unequivocal statement, however, in "Das Judentum in der Musik," where he explicitly advocated the forcible ejection of corrupting foreign elements (1995, 240). Though this is not a line of argument Weiner follows, the fact that Kundry as representative of Jewishness is presented as a wandering foreign body who must be eliminated conflates a discussion about race with that about hysteria.

20. Luce Irigaray offers another alignment between medical discussions of hysteria and our mythopoetic image repertoire by invoking the figure of Pythia, who "apes induced desires and suggestions foreign to her still hazy consciousness." Like Kundry, Pythia is shown to perform the dual gesture of prostitution, broadcasting a message but contaminating her own radically other truth: for "by resubmitting herself to the established order, in this role of delirious double, she abandons, even denies, the prerogative historically granted her: unconscious. She prostitutes the unconscious itself to the ever present projects and projections of masculine consciousness" (1974, 141).

21. One could see this as analogous to the scene in Lucy's crypt, where Lucy begs her bridegroom to kiss her but is restrained by Van Helsing, who seeks to protect him from the contagion Lucy embodies.

CHAPTER 5
TURNINGS OF NOSTALGIA

1. I thank Birgit Erdle for reminding me that a reader open to speculative associations might recall the end of Hitchcock's *Psycho*, where the police use an iron umbilical cord to return another foreign body out of oblivion: the car contain-

ing Marion's corpse and the stolen money, which Norman had hoped would be forgotten.

2. Didier Anzieu argues that the specimen dream about Irma's injection should, in part, be read as Freud's psychic representation of the ambivalences connected with the Emma Eckstein episode: on the one hand, with the image of Irma's opened mouth, paying tribute to the ideas of Fliess in which he claimed that a pain in the abdominal or genital area should be treated as a distant [transferred] symptom [*Fernorganleiden*] whose organic lesion could be located in the ear, nose, and throat area; on the other hand, a feminization that occurs at the moment when he identifies with Irma's pain, expressing his wish to be treated by his friend whom he casts as an omnipotent healer, a magician, but whose corollary is the anxiety that this treatment might have fatal results. The fact that Freud defends himself in the dream against the accusation of professional error in judgment is read by Anzieu as a transference of guilt; namely, that he was to blame "because he had failed to make a sufficiently clear distinction between a hysterical and an organic symptom. The Irma dream was a posttraumatic act of repetition aimed at reparation. It harks back to the Emma incident so that the matter can be closed once and for all and any lurking doubts about Fliess' professional competence and moral honesty can be scotched" (1975, 144).

3. In a letter written on 14 August 1897 Freud explicitly names the analogy between patient and analyst: "I am now enjoying a period of bad humor. The chief patient I am preoccupied with is myself. My little hysteria, though greatly accentuated by my work, has resolved itself a bit further. . . . The analysis is more difficult than any other. It is, in fact, what paralyzes my psychic strength for describing and communicating what I have won so far" (Freud and Fliess 1985, 261).

4. Discussing the relation between representation and affect, Borch-Jacobsen offers a useful reformulation of Freud's insistence that everything psychical, everything available to the unconscious, is representable. "It is because Freud stubbornly continues to think that affect hides *representations*, because he thinks of it only as 'tied' or 'attached' to representations, that he wants to see it as an obstacle to the becoming conscious of the 'repressed,' that is, as a 'not-wanting-to-*know*' the unconscious." Claiming instead that "Affect does not resist anything, especially not itself," he suggests that, rather than claiming a patient "does not want to *know* anything about the representations that haunt him," one should reformulate this as the patient "*cannot* know anything, at least in the sense of representation" (1991, 144). Hysterical language, as I have been arguing, keeps affect encrypted, and as such it is effective precisely insofar as it is known by representation, yet each representation also misses the mark. Though the hysteric has a plethora of representations available to her, the traumatic affect around which she so incessantly revolves is precisely what moves the subject, what acts in the mental typology in excess of representation.

5. In his discussion of hysteria Alan Krohn points to the importance of the loss of significant love objects, usually by death, for the formation of hysterical symptoms, arguing, "The hysterical personality usually handles such loss by identification with the lost object or an unconscious, continuous, sometimes lifelong search for it" (1978, 153), though he places this within the Oedipal trajectory of the daughter. The death of the father, he suggests, evokes repressed fantasies concerning anger and guilt, while the ritual of mourning usually hinders a recognition of the ambivalence of these feelings.

6. At two points in his correspondence with Fliess, Freud relates the danger female servants might pose, though his point is that rather than violence, they introduce sexuality into the family. The first passage, sent to Fliess on 2 May 1897, is part

of his architecture of hysteria entitled "The Part Played by Servant-Girls." Here he describes the immense load of guilt, with self-reproaches, that hysterical women concoct in phantasy, owing to their identification "with these people of low morals who are so often remembered, in a sexual connection with father or brother, as worthless female material" (1985, 241). The second mention, in a letter from 3 October 1897, describes his own interaction with these intruders in the home. Seeking an etiology for his own sexual awakening, he claims, "I can only indicate that the old man plays no active part in my case ... that in my case the 'prime originator' was an ugly, elderly, but clever woman, who told me a great deal about God Almighty and hell and who instilled in me a high opinion of my own capacities" (1985, 268). He adds in the next letter, "She was my teacher in sexual matters and complained because I was clumsy and unable to do anything."

7. For a discussion of the function of violence in fairy tale narratives for disciplinary measures, see Maria Tatar (1992).

8. In an overview article on hysteria Janet discusses the case of a hysteric whose drunkard father died of delirium tremens, while her mother, a confirmed psychasthenic, died of pulmonary tuberculosis. The patient herself, he explains, "has been infected with typhoid fever, was worn out by poverty, overwork, and night watching. At the time of her mother's death, which was very dramatic and shocking, the patient suffered a terrrible shock. After this, for ten years, she had a succession of the most remarkable neuropathic disturbances." He then adds, however, "Though I followed her case attentively and knew all her thoughts in all the psychological states, I can affirm that she never had sexual disturbances, properly speaking, nor sexual experiences which had made a lasting impression. A working girl, born and raised in an easy-going environment, she had early become acquainted with all sexual matters without attaching special importance to them; she is capable of experiencing normal sexual sensations, but does not seek them nor repel them. It is difficult to imagine a more normal sexual life; nevertheless she is one of the greatest hysterics I know" (1914–15 165).

9. Ian Hacking, also commenting on the argument between Janet and Freud over the traumatic etiology of hysteria, offers a somewhat different account. In Janet's cases, he argues, "trauma itself is not a human action. It is not somebody doing something to you or to another. It is an event, or a state. Freud's traumas almost always involved somebody doing something, an intentional action. People and their deeds were central to Freud's traumas; the world at large was the stuff of Janet's" (1995, 192).

10. Reading Anne Sexton's poetry as a hysterical imitation of the psychiatric or psychoanalytic case history, I will return to the issue of divine identification and suicide to explore how the hysterical language of Madeleine, discontent with her bourgeois world, resonates uncannily in the work of the dissatisfied, suburban Boston housewife of post–World War II.

CHAPTER 6
ANNE SEXTON'S BUSINESS OF WRITING SUICIDE

1. In the first publication of Anne Sexton's correspondence, Linda Gray Sexton and Lois Ames decided to give pseudonyms to those recipients of letters who had asked to remain anonymous. Although Diane Middlebrook's biography (1991) offers some decipherings (such as Anne Wilden for Anne Clarke) I have decided to

follow Linda Gray Sexton's practice in the second edition of the Anne Sexton letters of preserving the pseudonyms since, as she argues, this was the way the collection originally appeared. For my purposes, furthermore, the actual historical persons whom Sexton addresses are not crucial, but rather the language she chooses to represent herself and her psychic condition is the more significant aspect.

CHAPTER 7
"YOU FREUD, ME JANE"

1. In a footnote to the first dream Dora offers him, Freud notes that her I do not know "was the regular formula with which she confessed to anything that had been repressed" (1905, 69). One is strangely reminded of Wagner's Parsifal in Act I, responding to Gurnemanz's questions about his origins and his knowledge of the Grail with a similar denial of knowledge.

2. Unpublished response read at a conference entitled "One Hundred Years of Hysteria" at the art academy in Zurich, 27 October 1995.

3. See Bernheimer and Kahane (1985), as well as the special volume of *Diacritics* (1983) edited by Neil Hertz, for a collection of some of the best articles on the case history of Dora. See also Hélène Cixous, who read the case of Dora as the story about "a very beautiful feminine homosexuality, a love for woman that is astounding" (Cixous and Clément 1975, 153–4), and who wrote a play (1976) commemorating this; see also Kim Morrissey's (1994) theatrical rewritings.

4. Janet Malcolm, arguing that Freud's case histories are rhetorically ineffectual, "a kind of doomed literary experiment in a genre whose center cannot hold," nevertheless insists that Freud also realized how much neurosis was ineluctably inscribed into the human condition, with therapy mitigating human suffering but never fully dismissing, dispatching, or destroying the phantasies that haunt us. Given that "the people with florid symptoms who came to him for treatment were only a little further along a continuum," he also came to understand "that every analysis is a failure" (1992, 30).

5. In discussing fetishism, Freud contests that "in every instance, the meaning and the purpose of the fetish" could be reduced to the following formula. The fetish is "the substitute for the woman's (the mother's) penis that the little boy once believed in and—for reasons familiar to us—does not want to give up" (1927, 152). Read in a more structural sense, however, one could say fetishism refers to a process whereby one denies the lack in the other that one is visually or actually confronted with. A substitute stands in for the lack, whether one agrees with Freud's sexual encoding and calls it the maternal penis or prefers to leave the lack uncoded and see it as a signifier of fundamental loss, lack in plenitude, fallibility, or vulnerability (the vocabulary I have been using). But this substitute, which allows denial of the lack one has also come to accept, has a radically ambivalent effect: as Freud notes, "The horror of castration has set up a memorial to itself in the creation of this substitute." In other words, even while it is a "triumph over the treat of castration and a protection against it," it always also points to the horrifying sense of lack, loss, and implenitude it seeks to mitigate.

6. Highlighting precisely the fallacy of Mark's solution, Michele Piso notes that Mark is "mistaken in presuming that Marnie is healed by the knowledge of her trauma. And if we follow him in thinking that we have found in the murder the secret truth of Marnie's sexuality, we too, like Marnie, are led astray." Because the trauma

buried within the film does not involve only the scene with the murdered sailor but rather a chain of woundings of the mother and the daughter, Piso adds that marriage "is not salvation but subjugation, less a recuperation and recovery than the deepening of a wound that won't close" (1986, 302). To discuss this unplumbable navel of the film, I will focus my discussion of *Marnie* on two representational cuts.

7. In his biography of Alfred Hitchcock's darker side, Donald Spoto, who had initially considered Marnie to be "one of Hitchcock's dozen great works" (1976, 397), revises his opinion by arguing that the film's sloppy technique can be adduced as the disastrous falling out between Hitchcock and Tippi Hedren, which had led the director to become disinterested in the final product. Nevertheless, he continues to admit to the film's fascination, allowing that it "has an intimate and curious appeal unique in Hitchcock's output. Its lack of structure and its dreamlike, almost hallucinatory texture draw the viewer into an empathy with its lacerated emotions" (1983, 507). Given that labels such as "great flawed film," which Truffault (1983, 327) attaches to the film, are ultimately a question of aesthetic taste, I will leave the case undecided and focus instead on the point of stylistic aberration and on what is so visually jarring, discussing its representational value, not its aesthetic merit.

8. I take this point from Raymond Bellour, who offers a shot-by-shot analysis of the first scenes of *Marnie*, beginning with the credits and ending with the heroine riding Forio, reading this as an enactment of the fetish inscribed in the gaze of masculine desire. Nevertheless, I disagree with his conclusion that Hitchcock "becomes a sort of double of Mark and of Strutt who have just contributed to the creation of his image but who, at the same time, are caught in it" (1977, 73). Instead I would argue that he hysterically undermines the very fetishism he is invoking by their relay of gazing, by so explicitly pointing out that this is fetishism, or rather by affirming the duplicity of the fetish: namely, that the phantasy image of the enigmatic woman both does and does not stand in adequately for what I as fetishist-spectator lack, because what he lacks is located in the matrix that subtends representations.

9. For a sympathetic marxist-feminist reading of the maternal figure see Michele Piso (1986); for a psychoanalytic discussion of Marnie's need to relinquish the desired mother see E. Ann Kaplan (1990).

10. Clinically, the term kleptomania describes an obsession to steal, without there being an economic necessity to do so. Given that Marnie, though not poor, does in fact need money to support her mother, the film seems to leave open the question of her pathology. For a discussion of the relation between phantasies about childhood deprivations and humiliations and kleptomania, see Louise J. Kaplan (1991); for a discussion of the typical delicts and crimes attributed to hysterics, see Regina Schaps (1982).

11. In the novel version of *Marnie* by Winston Graham (1961) the resolution is significantly different. After the death of her mother, Marnie discovers that she had gone out with other sailors while her father was away. He had divorced his wife, once he found out about her adultery, and she had been forced to kill her newly born baby. Because the heroine is thus not implicated in any murderous acts, the crimes she must atone for are also not pathologized. As she is about to confront Mr. Strutt, she briefly phantasizes that Mark might save her, but this is shown to be an impossible solution. The novel ends with her recognizing that she will have to take the responsibility for her breaches in legality on her own. In contrast to Hitchcock's heroine, Graham's does not regress into a phantasy enactment of trauma. Instead she

is about to fully assert herself within the symbolic network of the law, accepting its codes and its punishments.

12. This blot, I suggest, functions like the traumatic detail of a photograph, which Roland Barthes (1980) calls the punctum and Slavoj Žižek (1991) calls a traumatic stain of the real. One could speculate, though there is no evidence from Hitchcock to this point, that this is also a reference to the monochromatic style of painting introduced at the time by artists like Jackson Pollock.

13. This double cut, which is absent from the American video version on sale, and which could be either accidental or the result of censorship, has led to the fact that copies of *Marnie* dubbed into continental languages such as German also contain this cut. I have noted in brackets the passages cut from the version now distributed in Europe on video: "It was just that I was so young, Marnie. I never had anything of my own. You know how I got you Marnie? There was this boy, Billie. [And I wanted Billie's basketball sweater. I was fifteen. And Billie said if I let him, I could have the sweater. So I let him.] And then later on when you got started, he run away. [I still got that old sweater. And I got you, Marnie.] And after the accident, when I was in the hospital, they tried to make me let you be adopted. But I wouldn't. I wanted you. And I promised God right then. If he let me keep you and you not remember, I'd bring you up different from me. Decent."

CHAPTER 8
A WOMB OF ONE'S OWN,
OR THE STRANGE CASE OF DAVID CRONENBERG

1. See Mladen Dolar (1991) for a comparative discussion of Freud's "uncanny," Todorov's "fantastic" and Lacan's "extimité."

2. In her compelling discussion of representations of femininity in the horror film, Barbara Creed uses Julia Kristeva's notion of maternal authority and paternal law to suggest that images of horror, especially involving body disintegration, signify a split between these two registers: "On the one hand, these images of bodily waste threaten a subject that is already constituted, in relation to the symbolic, as 'whole and proper'. . . . On the other hand, they also point back to a time when a 'fusion between mother and nature' existed." Representations of bodily waste thus elicit both disgust from the audience, insofar as it views from its position within the symbolic, and also perverse pleasure, on a more archaic level. Such visualizations of disintegration, disease, and disgust deliberately point "to the fragility of the symbolic order in the domain of the body where the body never ceases to signal the repressed world of the mother" (1993, 13).

3. To Chris Rodley, Cronenberg describes his fascination with organs' developing a trajectory of their own in a way that resonates with the medical discourse on the vagabonding uterus of the hysteric: "It's like a tumour or a liver or a spleen that decides it will have its own independent existence. It still needs to share the common blood that flows through all the organs, but the spleen wants to go off and do a few things. . . . That's fascinating to me. I don't think of it as a threat. . . . At a certain point the chaos equals destruction. But at the same time the potential for adventure and creative difference is exciting" (1992, 29).

4. In the interview with Chris Rodley, Cronenberg explains, "Gynaecology is such a beautiful metaphor for the mind/body split. Here it is: the mind of men—or

women—trying to understand sexual organs. I make my twins as kids extremely cerebral and analytical. They want to understand femaleness in a clinical way by dissection and analysis, not by experience, emotion, or intuition. 'Can we dissect out the essence of femaleness?' 'We're afraid of the emotional immediacy of woman-ness, but we're drawn to it. How can we come to terms with it? Let's dissect it.'" (1992, 145).

5. Though Cronenberg explicitly uses images from Abroise Paré's *On Monsters and Marvels* (1840) in the title sequence, one might also see this Mantel detractor as a visual reference to the contraptions used by physicians well into the nineteenth century in their efforts to lure the uterus back to its proper place.

6. While in my discussion of Jasper's nostalgics this passage *à l'acte* entailed in-fanticide, in Cronenberg's *Dead Ringers* it entails the scene of double suicide.

7. Mary Russo suggests that this final surgery be read not merely as "a cutting out of the fraternal bond, but a reconfiguration of the twinned body as a mutant woman." As the twins and the mutant body conflate, what emerges is a "grotesque rewriting of the script of castration" (1994, 120).

CHAPTER 9
BEYOND HYSTERIA

1. For a discussion of Mary Kelly's work within the context of 1970s feminist aesthetics, see Pollock (1988). For another example of a visual artist explicitly appro-priating Charcot's photography in her work, see Nicole Jolicoeur's work *La Vérité Folle* (1989), which splices together psychoanalytic statements by Jean-Martin Char-cot, Sigmund Freud, and Melitta Schmideberg, with her own texts and with repro-ductions of photographs of hysterics she has traced over in silver ink.

2. See the catalogue of the first retrospective of her work, put together by the Musée de Grenoble (1990), as well as the catalogue edited by Sheryl Conkelton and Carol S. Eliel (1995).

3. In the same interview Messager admits her fascination with Hitchcock's som-ber stories, which though entirely idiotic are also excessively troubling. Indeed she confesses that she wants to be considered the Hitchcock of painting (1990, 117).

BIBLIOGRAPHY

Abbate, Carolyn (1991). *Unsung Voices. Opera and Musical Narrative in the Nineteenth Century*. Princeton, N.J.: Princeton University Press.

Abbate, Carolyn, and Roger Parker (1989). *Analyzing Opera. Verdi and Wagner*. Berkeley: University of California Press.

Abraham, Nicolas, and Maria Torok (1987). *The Shell and the Kernel*. Vol. 1. Chicago: University of Chicago Press, 1994.

Adams, Parveen, ed. (1991). *Rendering the Real. A Special Issue. October* 58 (Fall).

Adams, Parveen, and Elizabeth Cowie (1990). *The Woman in Question. M/F*. Cambridge, Mass.: MIT Press.

Allen, Woody (1987). *Three Films of Woody Allen*. New York: Vintage.

Alpha-Fnac (1982). *J. M. Charcot et l'hystérie au XIXe siècle*. Catalogue for the exhibition at the Chapelle de la Salpêtrière 2–18 June.

Anzieu, Didier (1975). *Freud's Self-Analysis*. Translated by Peter Graham. Madison, Wis.: International Universities Press, 1986.

Appignanesi, Lisa, and John Forrester (1992). *Freud's Women*. New York: Basic Books.

Apter, Emily (1991). *Feminizing the Fetish. Psychoanalysis and Narrative Obsession in Turn-of-the-Century France*. Ithaca, N.Y.: Cornell University Press.

Aragon, Louis, and André Breton (1928). "Le cinquantenaire de l'hystérie. 1878–1928." *La Revolution Surréaliste*, no. 11; 4th year (15 March); 20–22.

Assman, Alaida (1995). "Stabilisatoren der Erinnerung—Affekt, Symbol, Trauma." Manuscript.

Assoun, Paul-Laurent (1995). *Leçons psychoanalytiques sur le regard et la voix*. Vols. 1 and 2. Paris: Anthropos.

Auerbach, Nina (1982). *Woman and the Demon. The Life of a Victorian Myth*. Cambridge, Mass., Harvard University Press.

Bächtold-Stäubli, Hanns, and Eduard Hoffmann-Krayer (1937). *Handwörterbuch des deutschen Aberglaubens*. Reprint, Berlin: de Gruyter, 1987.

Bal, Mieke (1991). *Reading Rembrandt. Beyond the Word-Image Opposition*. Cambridge: Cambridge University Press.

Barthes, Roland (1957). *Mythologies*. Paris: Éditions de Seuil.

—— (1961). "The Photographic Message." *Image. Music. Text*. New York: Hill and Wang, 1977.

—— (1966). "Introduction to the Structural Analysis of Narratives." In *Image. Music. Text*. New York: Hill and Wang. 1977.

—— (1970). *S/Z*. New York: Hill and Wang, 1974.

—— (1973). *The Pleasure of the Text*. New York: Hill and Wang, 1975.

—— (1975). *Roland Barthes by Roland Barthes*. New York: Hill and Wang, 1977.

—— (1980). *Camera Lucida. Reflections on Photography*. New York: Farrar, Strauss and Giroux, 1981.

Baudrillard, Jean (1976). *L'échange symbolique et la mort*. Paris: Gallimard.

Beizer, Janet (1994). *Ventriloquized Bodies. Narratives of Hysteria in Nineteenth-Century France*. Ithaca, N.Y.: Cornell University Press.

Bellour, Raymond (1977). "Hitchcock, the Enunciator." *Camera Obscura* 2: 66–91.

Bernheimer, Charles, and Claire Kahane, eds. (1985). *In Dora's Case. Freud-Hysteria-Feminism*. New York: Columbia University Press.

Björkman, Stig (1994). *Woody Allen on Woody Allen*. London: Faber and Faber.

Boothby, Richard (1991). *Death and Desire. Psychoanalytic Theory in Lacan's Return to Freud*. New York: Routledge.

Borch-Jacobsen, Mikkel (1991). *The Emotional Tie. Psychoanalysis, Mimesis, and Affect*. Stanford, Calif.: Stanford University Press (1993).

Botting, Fred (1996). *Gothic*. London: Routledge.

Bourneville, Désiré M., and Paul Régnard (1876–77). *Iconographie photographique de la Salpêtrière* (Service de M. Charcot). Vol. 1. Paris: Aux Bureaux du Progrès Médical. Delahaye & Lecrosnies.

———— (1878). *Iconographie photographique de la Salpêtrière* (Service de M. Charcot). Vol. 2. Paris: Aux Bureaux du Progrès Médical. Delahaye & Lecrosnies.

———— (1879–80). *Iconographie photographique de la Salpêtrière* (Service de M. Charcot). Vol. 3. Paris: Aux Bureaux du Progrès Médical. Delahaye & Lecrosnies.

Bronfen, Elisabeth (1992). *Over Her Dead Body: Death, Femininity, and the Aesthetic*. Manchester University Press, Manchester.

Brooks, Peter (1993). *Body Work. Objects of Desire in Modern Narrative*. Cambridge, Mass.: Harvard University Press.

Brüder Grimm (1819). *Kinder- und Hausmärchen*. Reprint, Munich: Winkler (1973).

Bryson, Norman (1991). "The Ideal and the Abject: Cindy Sherman's Historical Portraits." *Parkett* 29.

Burton, Robert (1621). *The Anatomy of Melancholy. What it is, with all the kinds, causes, symptomes, prognostickes & severall cures of it*. Reprint, New York: Dutton, 1932.

Butler, Judith (1990). *Gender Trouble. Feminism and the Subversion of Identity*. New York: Routledge.

———— (1993). *Bodies That Matter. On the Discursive Limits of "Sex."* New York: Routledge.

Byatt, A. S. (1987). "Identity and the Writer," *Identity. The Real Me. Postmodernism and the Question of Identity. ICA Documents* 6.

Carroy-Thirard, Jacqueline (1979). "Figures de femmes hystèriques dans la psychiatrie française au 19e siècle." *Psychoanalyse à l'université* 4 (March): 313–24.

———— (1980). "Possession, extase, hystérie au 19e siècle." *Psychanalyse à l'université* 5 (June): 499–515.

———— (1982). "Hystérie, théâtre, littérature au dix-neuvième siècle." *Psychoanalyse à l'université* 7 (March): 299–317.

———— (1993). "L'hystérique, l'artiste, et le savant." In *L'âme au corps. Arts et sciences 1793–1993*, ed. Jean Clair. Paris: Gallimard.

Carter, Margaret l. (1988). *Dracula. The Vampire and the Critics*. Ann Arbor, Mich.: UMI Press.

Cartwright, Lisa (1995). *Screening the Body. Tracing Medicine's Visual Culture*. Minneapolis: University of Minnesota Press.

Caruth, Cathy, ed. (1995). *Trauma. Explorations in Memory*. Baltimore, Md.: Johns Hopkins University Press.

———— (1996). *Unclaimed Experience. Trauma, Narrative, and History*. Baltimore, Md.: Johns Hopkins University Press.

Castle, Terry (1995). *The Female Thermometer. 18th-Century Culture and the Invention of the Uncanny.* Oxford: Oxford University Press.

Cave, Terence (1988). *Recognitions. A Study in Poetics.* Oxford: Oxford University Press.

Charcot, Jean-Martin (1886). *Neue Vorlesungen über die Krankheiten des Nervensystems insbesondere über Hysteria.* Translated by Sigmund Freud. Leipzig: Toeplitz & Deuticke.

———— (1887). *Lectures on the Diseases of the Nervous System.* Translated by George Sigerson. London: New Sydenham Society.

Charcot, Jean-Martin, and Paul Richer (1887). *Les démoniaques dans l'art.* Paris: Macula (1984).

———— (1887–88). *Leçons du mardi à la Salpêtrière. Policlinique.* Paris: Progrès médical/Delahaye & Lecrosnier & Babé. German translation by Sigmund Freud. Leipzig: Franz Deuticke (1892).

———— (1888–89). *Leçons du mardi à la Salpêtrière. Policlinique.* Paris: Progrès médical/Delahaye & Lecrosnier & Babé; German translation by Max Kahane. Leipzig: Franz Deuticke (1895).

———— (1889). *Clinical Lectures on Diseases of the Nervous System.* Translated by Thomas Saville. Three vols. London: New Sydenham Society.

———— (1971). *L'hystérie.* Edited by Etienne Trillat. Toulouse: Edouard Privat.

Cheyne, George (1735). *The English Malady.* London: Strahan & Leake.

Cixous, Hélène (1976). *Portrait de Dora.* Paris: Éditions des femmes.

———— (1981). "Castration or Decapitation?" *Signs: Journal of Women in Culture and Society* 71 (Autumn): 41–55.

Cixous, Hélène, and Catherine Clément (1975). *The Newly Born Woman.* Translated by Betsy Wing. Minneapolis: University of Minnesota Press (1986).

Clément, Catherine (1979). *L'opéra ou la defaite de la femme.* Paris: Grasset.

———— (1990). *La syncope. Philosophie du ravissement.* Paris: Grasset.

Clover, Carol J. (1992). *Men, Women, and Chain Saws. Gender in the Modern Horror Film.* Princeton, N.J.: Princeton University Press.

Colburn, Steven E. (1985). *No Evil Star. Selected Essays, Interviews, and Prose. Anne Sexton.* Ann Arbor: University of Michigan Press.

Colvin, Howard (1994). "Letter." *Times Literary Supplement,* no. 4764 (July 22): 15.

Conkelton, Sheryl, and Carol S. Eliel, eds. (1995). *Annette Messager.* Exhibition Catalogue of Los Angeles County Museum of Art/ The Museum of Modern Art, New York. New York: Harry N. Abrams.

Cook, Pam (1989). "Dead Ringers," *Monthly Film Bulletin* (January): 3–4.

Cooke, Lynne, and Peter Wollen (1995). *Visual Display. Culture beyond Appearances.* Seattle, Wash.: Bay Press.

Copjec, Joan (1994). *Read My Desire. Lacan against the Historicists.* Cambridge, Mass.: MIT Press.

Cowie, Elizabeth (1990). "Fantasia." In *The Woman in Question,* edited by Parveen Adams and Elizabeth Cowie. Cambridge, Mass.: MIT Press.

———— (1996). *Representing the Woman: Cinema and Psychoanalysis.* London: MacMillan.

Creed, Barbara (1990). "Phallic Panic: Male Hysteria and Dead Ringers." *Screen* 31, 2 (Summer): 125–146.

———— (1993). *The Monstrous-Feminine. Film, Feminism, Psychoanalysis.* London: Routledge.

Cullen, William (1796). *First Lines of the Practice of Physic, with practical and explanatory notes by John Rotheram*. Edinburgh: Bell & Bradfute.

Cummings, Katherine (1991). *Telling Tales: The Hysteric's Seduction in Fiction and Theory*. Stanford, Calif.: Stanford University Press.

Dadoun, Roger (1989). "Fetishism in the Horror Film." In *Fantasy and the Cinema*, edited by James Donald. London: British Film Institute; 36–61.

Danto, Arthur C. (1990). "Photography and Performance. Cindy Sherman's Stills." *Cindy Sherman: Untitled Film Stills*. New York: Rizzoli.

David-Ménard, Monique (1983). *Hysteria from Freud to Lacan. Body and Language in Psychoanalysis*. Ithaca, N.Y.: Cornell University Press (1989).

de Lauretis, Teresa (1984). *Alice Doesn't. Feminism, Semiotics, Cinema*. Bloomington: University of Indiana Press.

de Man, Paul (1984). *The Rhetoric of Romanticism*. New York: Columbia University Press.

de Marneffe, Daphne (1991). "Looking and Listening: The Construction of Clinical Knowledge in Charcot and Freud," *Signs* (Autumn): 71–111.

Decker, Hanna S. (1991). *Freud, Dora, and Vienna 1900*. New York: The Free Press.

Deleuze, Gilles, and Félix Guattari (1972). *L'Anti-Oedipe*. Paris: Les Editions de Minuit.

Derrida, Jacques (1977). "Fors," *The Georgia Review* 31: 64–116.

——— (1981). "The Deaths of Roland Barthes." In *Philosophy and Non-Philosophy Since Mereleau-Ponty*, edited by Hugh J. Silverman. New York: Routledge (1988).

Didi-Huberman, Georges (1982). *Invention de l'hystérie. Charcot et l'iconographie de la Salpêtrière*. Paris: Macula

——— (1984). "Une notion du corps clichè au XIXe siècle," *Parachute* 35 (June): 8–14.

Dijkstra, Bram (1986). *Idols of Perversity. Fantasies of Feminine Evil in Fin-de-Siècle Culture*. Oxford: Oxford University Press.

Dolar, Mladen (1991). " 'I Shall Be with You on Your Wedding-Night': Lacan and the Uncanny." In *Rendering the Real. A Special Issue,* edited by Parveen Adams. *October* 58 (Fall): 5–23.

Dolto, Françoise (1984). *L'image inconsciente du corps*. Paris: Editions du Seuil.

Drew, Wayne. (1984). "A Gothic Revival: Obsession and Fascination in the Films of David Cronenberg." In *David Cronenberg*, edited by Wayne Drew. *BFI Dossier*. No. 21. London: British Film Institute.

Drinka, George Frederick (1984). *The Birth of Neurosis*. New York: Simon and Schuster.

Eisler, Kurt R. (1985). "A Farewell to Freud's *Interpretation of Dreams*." *American Imago* 42 (1985): 111–29.

Ellenberger, Henri F. (1970). *The Discovery of the Unconscious. The History and Evolution of Dynamic Psychiatry*. London: Fontana Books (1994).

——— (1973). "Freud in Perspective: A Conversation with Henri F. Ellenberger." *Psychology Today* (March).

Ender, Evelyne (1995). *Sexing the Mind. Nineteenth-Century Fictions of Hysteria*. Ithaca, N.Y.: Cornell University Press.

Erdle, Birgit (1995). "Fatal Answers." Manuscript.

——— (1996). "Traumatisierte Schrift. Nachträglichkeit bei Freud und Derrida." Manuscript.

Erdle, Birgit (1996a). "Plötzliche Entstellung eines 'guten Bildes': Grauen, Begehren, Spur in Roland Barthes' *Fragments d'un discours amoureux.*" In *Mimesis, Bild und Schrift. Ähnlichkeit und Entstellung im Verhältnis der Künste*, edited by Birgit. R. Erdle and Sigrid Weigel. Cologne: Böhlau.

Erikson, Erik Homburger (1954). "The Dream Specimen of Psychoanalysis." *Journal of the American Psychoanalytic Association* 2 (1954): 5–56.

Erikson, Kai (1995). "Notes on Trauma and Community." In *Trauma. Explorations in Memory*, edited by Cathy Caruth. Baltimore, Md.: Johns Hopkins University Press.

Evans, Martha Noel (1991). *Fits and Starts. A Genealogy of Hysteria in Modern France*. Ithaca, N.Y.: Cornell University Press.

Felman, Shoshana (1981). "Rereading Femininity." *Yale French Studies* 62 (1981): 19–44.

——— (1985). "Postal Survival, or the Question of the Navel." *Yale French Studies* 69: 49–72.

——— (1993). *What Does a Woman Want? Reading and Sexual Difference*. Baltimore, Md.: Johns Hopkins University Press.

Fink, Bruce (1995). *The Lacanian Subject. Between Language and Jouissance*. Princeton, N.J.: Princeton University Press.

Flaubert, Gustave, and George Sand (1981). *Correspondance*. Paris: Flammarion.

Flournoy, Théodore (1901). *From India to the Planet Mars. A Case of Multiple Personality with Imaginary Languages*. Princeton, N.J.: Princeton University Press (1994).

Flower MacCannell, Juliet (1991). *The Regime of the Brother: After the Patriarchy*. New York: Routledge.

Forrester, John (1980). *Language and the Origins of Psychoanalysis*. London: MacMillan.

——— (1990). *The Seductions of Psychoanalysis. Freud, Lacan and Derrida*. Cambridge: Cambridge University Press.

Foster, Hal (1993). *Compulsive Beauty*. Cambridge, Mass.: MIT Press.

Foucault, Michel (1961). *Madness and Civilization. A History of Insanity in the Age of Reason*. New York: Random House (1965).

——— (1969). *The Archaeology of Knowledge*. London: Routledge (1972).

——— (1976). *The History of Sexuality. Vol. 1: An Introduction*. Translated by Robert Hurley. New York: Vintage Books (1990).

Freeman, Lucy, and Dr. Herbert S. Strean (1987). *Freud & Women*. New York: Continuum.

Freud, Sigmund (1892–1899). "Extracts from the Fliess Papers." *Standard Edition*. Vol. 1. London: Hogarth Press (1950/1966).

——— (1893): "On the Psychical Mechanism of Hysterical Phenomena: A Lecture." *Standard Edition*. Vol. 3. London: Hogarth Press (1962).

——— (1893–95). *Studies on Hysteria. Standard Edition*. Vol. 2. London: Hogarth Press (1955).

——— (1896). "The Aetiology of Hysteria." *Standard Edition*. Vol. 3. Hogarth Press, London (1962).

——— (1900–1901). *The Interpretation of Dreams (1900). Standard Edition*. Vols. 4 and 5. London: Hogarth Press (1953).

——— (1905). "Fragments of an Analysis of a Case of Hysteria." *Standard Edition*. Vol. 7. London: Hogarth Press (1953).

Freud, Sigmund (1908). "Creative Writings and Day-Dreaming." *Standard Edition.* Vol. 9. London: Hogarth Press (1959).

———— (1908a). "Hysterical Phantasies and Their Relation to Bisexuality." *Standard Edition.* Vol. 9. London: Hogarth Press (1959).

———— (1909). "Five Lectures on Psycho-Analysis." *Standard Edition.* Vol. 11. London: Hogarth Press (1957).

———— (1909a). "The Family Romance." *Standard Edition.* Vol. 9. London: Hogarth Press (1959).

———— (1909b). "Some General Remarks on Hysterical Attacks." *Standard Edition.* Vol. 9. London: Hogarth Press (1959).

———— (1912). "A Note on the Unconscious in Psycho-Analysis." *Standard Edition.* Vol. 12. London: Hogarth Press (1958).

———— (1913). "The Theme of the Three Caskets." *Standard Edition.* Vol. 12. London: Hogarth Press (1958).

———— (1913a). "The Claims of Psycho-Analysis to Scientific Interest." *Standard Edition.* Vol. 13. London: Hogarth Press (1955).

———— (1914). "On the History of the Psycho-Analytic Movement." *Standard Edition.* Vol. 14. London: Hogarth Press (1957).

———— (1915). "Repression." *Standard Edition.* Vol. 14. London: Hogarth Press (1957).

———— (1917). *Introductory Lectures on Psycho-Analysis. Standard Edition.* Vol. 16. London: Hogarth Press (1963).

———— (1919). "The 'Uncanny.'" *Standard Edition.* Vol. 17. London: Hogarth Press (1955).

———— (1926). *Inhibitions, Symptoms, and Anxiety. Standard Edition.* Vol. 20. London: Hogarth Press (1959).

———— (1927). "Fetishism." *Standard Edition.* Vol. 21. London: Hogarth Press (1961).

———— (1932). *New Introductory Lectures on Psycho-Analysis. Standard Edition.* Vol. 22. London: Hogarth Press (1964).

Freud, Sigmund, and Karl Abraham (1965). *A Psycho-Analytic Dialogue: The Letters of Sigmund Freud and Karl Abraham, 1907–1926.* Edited by Hilda C. Abraham and Ernst L. Freud. London: The Hogarth Press and the Institute of Psychoanalysis.

Freud, Sigmund, and Joseph Breuer (1895). *Project for a Scientific Psychology. Standard Edition.* Vol. 1. London: Hogarth Press (1966).

Freud, Sigmund, and Wilhelm Fliess (1985). *The Complete Letters of Sigmund Freud to Wilhelm Fliess 1887–1904.* Edited by Jeffrey Moussaieff Masson. Cambridge, Mass.: Harvard University Press.

Gaultier, Jules de (1892). *Le Bovarysme. La psychologie dans l'oeuvre de Flaubert.* Paris: Léopold Cerf.

Gay, Peter (1988). *Freud. A Life for Our Time.* New York: Norton.

George, Diana Hume (1987). *Oedipus Anne. The Poetry of Anne Sexton.* Urbana: University of Illinois Press.

Gilman, Sander (1982). *Seeing the Insane.* New York: John Wiley & Sons.

———— (1985). *Difference and Pathology. Stereotypes of Sexuality, Race, and Madness.* Ithaca, N.Y.: Cornell University Press.

———— (1991). *The Jew's Body.* London: Routledge.

———— (1993). *The Case of Sigmund Freud. Medicine and Identity at the Fin de Siècle.* Baltimore: Johns Hopkins University Press.

Gilman, Sander (1993a) et al. *Hysteria beyond Freud*. Berkeley: University of California Press.

——— (1993b). *Freud, Race, and Gender*. Princeton, N.J.: Princeton University Press.

Goldstein, Jan (1982). "The Hysteria Diagnosis and the Politics of Anticlericalism in Late Nineteenth-Century France." *Journal of Modern History* 54 (June): 209–239.

——— (1987). *Console and Classify. The French Psychiatric Profession in the Nineteenth Century*. Cambridge: Cambridge University Press.

——— (1991). "The Uses of Male Hysteria: Medical and Literary Discourse in Nineteenth-Century France." *Representations* 34 (Spring): 134–65.

Graham, Winston (1961). *Marnie*. London: Chapmans (1992).

Green, André (1976). "Die Hysterie." In *Die Psychologie des 20. Jahrhunderts. Band II. Freud und die Folgen (1): Von der Klassischen Psychoanalyse . . .* , edited by Dieter Eicke. Munich: Kindler.

——— (1986). *On Private Madness*. London: The Hogarth Press.

Greenblatt, Stephen (1988). *Shakespearean Negotiations. The Circulation of Social Energy in Renaissance England*. Berkeley and Los Angeles: University of California Press.

Greenway, John L. (1986). "Seward's Folly: *Dracula* as a Critique of 'Normal Science.' " *Stanford Literature Review* 3: 213–30.

Grimm Brüder (1819). *Kinder- und Hausmärchen*. Reprint, Munich: Winkler (1949).

Grosz, Elizabeth (1994). *Volatile Bodies. Toward a Corporeal Feminism*. Bloomington: Indiana University Press.

Grünberg, Serge (1992). *David Cronenberg*. Paris: Cahiers du Cinéma.

Hacking, Ian (1995). *Rewriting the Soul. Multiple Personality and the Sciences of Memory*. Princeton, N.J.: Princeton University Press.

Hall, Caroline King Barnard (1989). *Anne Sexton*. Boston: Twayne Publishers.

Handling, Piers (1983). *The Shape of Rage. The Films of David Cronenberg*. A Publication of the Academy of Canadian Cinema. Toronto: General Publishing Co.

Harrison Jane Ellen. (1927) *Epilegomena to the Study of Greek Religion and Themis: A Study of the Social Origins of Greek Religion*. New York: University Books (1962).

Heath, Stephen (1978). "Difference." *Screen* 19 (Autumn): 51–112.

——— (1982). *The Sexual Fix*. London: MacMillan.

Hertz, Neil, ed. (1983). *A Fine Romance. Freud and Dora*. Special issue of *Diacritics* (Spring).

——— (1985). *The End of the Line. Essays on Psychoanalysis and the Sublime*. New York: Columbia University Press.

Homans, Peter (1989). *The Ability to Mourn. Disillusionment and the Social Origins of Psychoanalysis*. Chicago: University of Chicago Press.

Hunter, Dianne (1985). "Hysteria, Psychoanalysis, and Feminism: The Case of Anna O." In *The (M)other Tongue. Essays in Feminist Psychoanalytic Interpretation*, edited by Shirley Nelson Garner, Claire Kahane, and Madelon Sprengnether. Ithaca, N.Y.: Cornell University Press.

Hutcheon, Linda (1988). *A Poetics of Postmodernism. History, Theory, Fiction*. New York: Routledge.

——— (1989). *The Politics of Postmodernism*. New York: Routledge.

Hutcheon, Linda (1994). *Irony's Edge. The Theory and Politics of Irony*. New York: Routledge.

Hutcheon, Linda, and Michael Hutcheon (1996). *Opera. Desire, Disease, Death*. Lincoln: University of Nebraska Press.

Irigaray, Luce (1974). *Speculum of the Other Woman*. Ithaca, N.Y.: Cornell University Press (1985).

———— (1977). *This Sex Which Is Not One*. Ithaca, N.Y.: Cornell University Press (1985).

———— (1981). *Le corps-à-corps avec la mère*, Montréal: Les éditions de la pleine lune.

Israël, Lucien (1976). *L'hystérique, le sexe, et le médecin*. Paris: Masson.

Jacobus, Mary (1986). *Reading Woman. Essays in Feminist Criticism*. New York: Columbia University Press.

Jameson, Fredric (1981). *The Political Unconscious: Narrative as a Socially Symbolic Act*. Ithaca, N.Y.: Cornell Univesity Press.

Janet, Pierre (1893). "L'amnésie continue." *Revue Générale des Sciences Pures et Appliquées*. 4: 167–79.

———— (1894). *The Mental State of Hystericals*. Washington, D.C.: University Publications of America (1977).

———— (1914–15). "Psychoanalysis." *The Journal of Abnormal Psychology* IX: 1–35, 153–187.

———— 1926. *De l'angoisse à l'extase. Etudes sur les croyances et les sentiments*. Paris: Félix Alcan.

Jaspers, Karl (1909). "Heimweh und Verbrechen." In *Gesammelte Schriften*. Vol. 1. Berlin: De Gruyter.

Jay, Martin (1993). *Downcast Eyes. The Denigration of Vision in Twentieth-Century French Thought*. Berkeley: University of California Press.

Johnson, Barbara (1994). *The Wake of Deconstruction*. Oxford: Blackwell.

Jolicoeur, Nicole (1989). *La Vérité Folle*. North Vancouver: Presentation House Cultural Society.

Juranville, Anne (1987). "Hysterie und Melancholie bei der Frau." *Riss. Zeitschrift für Psychoanalyse* 4.11 (June 1989): 53–80.

Kahane, Claire (1989). "Hysteria, Feminism, and the Case of *The Bostonians*." In *Feminism and Psychoanalysis*, edited by Richard Feldstein and Judith Roof. Ithaca, N.Y.: Cornell University Press.

———— (1995). *Passions of the Voice. Hysteria, Narrative, and the Figure of the Speaking Woman, 1850–1915*. Baltimore, Md.: Johns Hopkins University Press.

Kallfelz, Andreas (1984). "Cindy Sherman. 'Ich mache keine Selbstportraits.'" *Wolkenkratzer Art Journal* 4.

Kaplan, E. Ann (1990). "Motherhood and Representation. From Postwar Freudian Figurations to Postmodernism." In *Psychoanalysis & Cinema*, edited by E. Ann Kaplan. New York: Routledge.

Kaplan, Louise J. (1991). *Female Perversions. The Temptations of Emma Bovary*. New York: Doubleday.

Kauhsen, Bruno (1990). *Omphalos. Zum Mittelpunktsgedanken in Architektur und Städtebau dargestellt an ausgewählten Beispielen*. Munich: Seaneg.

Kellein, Thomas (1991). "Wie schwierig sind Portraits? Wie schwierig sind die Menschen!" In *Cindy Sherman*. Basel: Edition Cantz.

Kilgour, Maggie (1995). *The Rise of the Gothic Novel*. New York: Routledge.

Kofman, Sarah (1980). *The Enigma of Woman. Woman in Freud's Writings*. Ithaca, N.Y.: Cornell University Press (1985).

—— (1995). *L'imposture de la beauté*. Paris: Galilée.

Krauss, Rosalind (1993). *Cindy Sherman. Arbeiten von 1975 bis 1993*. Munich: Schirmer/Mosel.

Kristeva, Julia (1974). *Revolution in Poetic Language*. New York: Columbia University Press (1984).

—— (1977). *Desire in Language. A Semiotic Approach to Literature and Art*. Oxford: Basil Blackwell (1980).

—— (1980). *Powers of Horror. An Essay on Abjection*. New York: Columbia University Press (1982).

—— (1987). *Black Sun. Depression and Melancholia*. New York: Columbia University Press (1989).

Krohn, Alan (1978). *Hysteria: The Elusive Neurosis*. New York: International Universities Press.

Kumin, Maxine (1981). "How It Was." In *Anne Sexton. The Complete Poems*. Boston: Houghton Mifflin.

Lacan, Jacques (1951). "Intervention on Transference." In *In Dora's Case. Freud, Hysteria, Feminism*, edited by Charles Bernheimer and Claire Kahane. New York: Columbia University Press (1985).

—— (1966) *Écrits: A Selection*. Translated by Alan Sheridan. New York: Norton (1977).

—— (1973). *Four Fundamental Concepts of Psycho-Analysis*. Translated by Alan Sheridan. New York: Norton (1981).

—— (1975). *Le séminaire XX. Encore, 1972–73*. Paris: Seuil.

—— (1978) *The Seminar of Jacques Lacan. Book II: The Ego in Freud's Theory and in the Technique of Psychoanalysis, 1954–1955*. Edited by Jacques-Alain Miller, translated by Sylvana Tomaselle. New York: Norton (1988).

—— (1986) *The Seminar of Jacques Lacan. Book VII: Ethics of Psychoanalysis 1959–1960*. Edited by Jacques-Alain Miller, translated by Dennis Porter. London: Tavistock/Routledge.

Langbauer, Laurie (1990). *Women and Romance. The Consolations of Gender in the English Novel*. Ithaca, N.Y.: Cornell University Press.

Laplanche, Jean (1974). "Panel on 'Hyteria Today.' " *International Journal for Psycho-Analysis* 55: 459–69.

—— (1989). *New Foundations for Psychoanalysis*. Oxford: Basil Blackwell.

Laplanche, Jean and J.-B. Pontalis (1964). "Fantasy and the Origins of Sexuality." In *Formations of Fantasy*, edited by Victor Burgin, James Conald, and Cora Kaplan. London: Methuen (1986).

—— (1973). *The Language of Psychoanalysis*. London: Karnac Books (1988).

Lichtenberg-Ettinger, Bracha (1992). "Matrix and Metramorphosis." *Differences* 4 (Fall); 176–210.

—— (1994). "The Becoming Threshold of Matrixial Borderlines." *Travellers' Tales. Narratives of Home and Displacement*. Edited by George Robertson et al. New York: Routledge.

Lowell, Robert (1978). "Anne Sexton." In *Anne Sexton. The Artist and Her Critics*. Edited by J. D. McClatchy. Bloomington: Indiana University Press.

Lubtchansky, Jacqueline (1973). "Le point de vue économique dans l'hystérie à partir de la notion de traumatisme dans l'oeuvre de Freud." *Revue Française de Psychoanalyse* XXXVII: 373–405.

Malcolm, Janet (1992). *The Purloined Clinic. Selected Writings*. New York: Alfred A. Knopf.

Massé, Michelle A. (1992). *In the Name of Love. Women, Masochism, and the Gothic*. Ithaca, N.Y.: Cornell University Press.

Masson, Jeffrey Moussaieff (1984). *The Assault on Truth. Freud's Suppression of the Seduction Theory*. New York: Harper Perennial.

Matlock, Jann (1994). *Scenes of Seduction. Prostitution, Hysteria, and Reading Difference in Nineteenth-Century France*. New York: Columbia University Press.

Matus, Jill L. (1995). *Unstable Bodes. Victorian Representations of Sexuality and Maternity*. Manchester: Manchester University Press.

MacCannell, Juliet Flower (1991). *The Regime of the Brother. After the Patriarchy*. New York: Routledge.

McCann, Graham (1990). *Woody Allen*. London: Polity Press.

McGrath, William J. (1986). *Freud's Discovery of Psychoanalysis. The Politics of Hysteria*. Ithaca, N.Y.: Cornell University Press.

Melman, Charles (1984). *Nouvelles études sur l'hystérie*. Paris: Denoël.

Mentzos, Stavros (1980). *Hysterie. Zur Psychodynamik unbewußter Inszenierungen*. Munich: Kindler.

——— (1993). "Nachwort." *Sigmund Freud. Bruchstäck einer Hysterie-Analyse*. Frankfurt am Main: S. Fischer.

Mesmer, Franz Anton (1779). *Mémoire sur la découverte du magnetisme animal*. Paris: Didot.

Messager, Annette (1990). *Comédie tragédie. 1971–1989*. Edited by Serge Lemoine; exhibition catalogue. Grenoble: Musée de Grenoble.

Micale, Mark S. (1990). "Charcot and the Idea of Hysteria in the Male: Gender, Mental Science, and Medical Diagnosis in Late Nineteenth-Century France." *Medical History* 34: 363–411.

——— (1995). *Approaching Hysteria. Disease and Its Interpreations*. Princeton, N.J.: Princeton University Press.

Middlebrook, Diane Wood (1984). "Becoming Anne Sexton." In *Anne Sexton. Telling the Tale*, edited by Steven E. Colburn. Ann Arbor, Mich.: University of Michigan Press.

——— (1985). "Poet of Weird Abundance." *Parnassus* 12–13 (Spring–Winter): 293–315.

——— (1991). *Anne Sexton. A Biography*. Boston: Houghton Mifflin.

——— (1992). "Coda." *Anne Sexton. A Biography*. New York: Vintage.

Middlebrook, Diane Wood, and Diane Hume George (1988). "Introduction." In *Selected Poems of Anne Sexton*. London: Virago.

Miles, Robert (1994). "Introduction." In *Female Gothic Writing*. Special issue of *Women's Writing: The Elizabethan to Victorian Period* 1(2): 131–42.

——— (1995). *Ann Radcliffe. The Great Enchantress*. Manchester: Manchester University Press.

Miller, Jacques-Alain (1988). "Extimité." *Prose Studies* 11 (December): 121–30.

Mitchell, Juliet (1984). *Women. The Longest Revolution: Essays in Feminism, Literature, and Psychoanalysis*. London: Penguin.

Mitchell, Juliet, and Jacqueline Rose (1985). *Feminine Sexuality. Jacques Lacan and the école freudienne*. New York: Norton.

Modleski, Tania (1982). *Loving with a Vengeance*. New York: Methuen.

———— (1988). *The Women Who Knew Too Much. Hitchcock and Feminist Theory*. New York: Methuen.

Moi, Toril, ed. (1986). *The Kristeva Reader*. Oxford: Basil Blackwell.

Montrelay, Michèle (1977). "Inquiry into Femininity." In *French Feminist Thought. A Reader*, edited by Toril Moi. Oxford: Basil Blackwell (1987).

Morra, Joanne, and Marquard Smith (1995). "Cultural Studies and Philosophy. Questionnaire." *Parallax* 1 (September): 93.

Morrissey, Kim (1994). *Dora. A Case of Hysteria*. London: Nick Hern Books.

Mullen, John (1984). "Hypochondria and Hysteria. Sensibility and the Physicians." *The Eighteenth Century*, 25, no. 2. (Summer): 141–74.

———— (1988). *Sentiment and Sociability. The Language of Feeling in the Eighteenth Century*. Oxford: Clarendon Press.

Muller, John P., and William J. Richardson, eds. (1988). *The Purloined Poe. Lacan, Derrida, and Psychoanalytic Reading*. Baltimore, Md.: Johns Hopkins Press.

Mulvey, Laura (1986). "Impending Time." *Mary Kelly. Interim*. Edinburgh: The Fruitmarket Gallery.

———— (1991). "A Phantasmagoria of the Female Body. The Work of Cindy Sherman." *New Left Review* 188.

Munthe, Axel (1930). *The Story of San Michele*. London: John Murray.

Nabokov, Vladimir (1969). *Speak, Memory. An Autobiography Revisited*. Harmondsworth: Penguin.

Nagel, Ivan (1988). *Autonomy & Mercy. Reflections on Mozart's Operas*. Cambridge, Mass.: Harvard University Press.

Nietzsche, Friedrich (1888). "Der Fall Wagner." In *Sämtliche Werke. Kritische Studienausgabe*. Vol. 6, edited by Giorgio Colli and Mazzino Montinari. Berlin: de Gruyter (1967–77).

Oppenheim, Janet (1991). *Shattered Nerves. Doctors, Patients, and Depression in Victorian England*. New York: Oxford University Press.

Ostriker, Alicia (1982). "That Story. The Changes of Anne Sexton." In *Anne Sexton. Telling the Tale*, edited by Steven E. Colburn. Ann Arbor, Mich.: University of Michigan Press.

———— (1986). *Stealing the Language. The Emergence of Women's Poetry in America*. Boston: Beacon Press.

Oughourlian, Jean-Michel (1982). *Un mime nommé desir. Hystèrie, transe, possession, adorcisme*. Paris: Bernard Grasset.

Owen, Alex (1989). *The Darkened Room. Women, Power, and Spiritualism in Late Victorian England*. London: Virago.

Owens, Craig (1992). *Beyond Recognition: Representation, Power, and Culture*. Berkeley: University of California Press.

Paré, Ambroise (1840). *On Monsters and Marvels*. Edited by Janis L. Pallister. Chicago: University of Chicago Press (1982).

Piso, Michele (1986). "Mark's Marnie." In *A Hitchcock Reader*, edited by Marshall Deutelbaum and Leland Poague. Ames: Iowa State University Press.

Plato (1961). *Symposium, The Collected Dialogues*. Edited by Edith Hamilton and Huntington Cairns. Princeton, N.J.: University Press, Princeton.

Poizat, Michel (1986). *The Angel's Cry. Beyond the Pleasure Principle in Opera*. Translated by Arthur Denner. Ithaca, N.Y.: Cornell University Press (1992).

Poizat, Michel (1991). *La voix du diable. La jouissance lyrique sacrée.* Paris: Éditions Métailié.

Pollitt, Katha (1991). "The Death is Not the Life." *The New York Times Book Review* (18 August).

Pollock, Griselda (1988). *Vision & Difference. Femininity, Feminism, and the Histories of Art.* New York: Routledge.

——— (1991). "Degas/Images/Women; Women/Degas/Images: What Difference Does Feminism Make to Art History?" In *Dealing with Degas. Representations of Women and the Politics of Vision*, edited by Richard Kendell & Griselda Pollock. London: Pandora Press.

Pontalis, J.-B. (1977). *Entre le rêve et la douleur.* Paris: Gallimard.

Porter, Roy (1993). "The Body and the Mind, the Doctor and the Patient. Negotiating Hysteria." In *Hysteria beyond Freud.* Sander Gilman et al. Berkeley: University of California Press.

Pynchon, Thomas (1963). *V.* London: Jonathan Cape.

Radcliffe, Ann (1791). *The Romance of the Forest.* Oxford: Oxford University Press (1986).

Ragland, Ellie (1995). *Essays on the Pleasures of Death. From Freud to Lacan.* New York: Routledge.

Raulin, Joseph (1758). *Traité des affections vaporeuses du sexe avec l'exposition de leurs symptômes, de leurs différentes cause et la méthode de les guérir.* Paris.

Rich, Adrienne (1974). *On Lies, Secrets, and Silence. Selected Prose 1966–1978.* New York: Norton (1979).

Richet, Charles (1880). "Les démoniaques d'aujourd'hui." *Revue des deux mondes* 37 (January): 340–72.

Ricoeur, Paul (1970). *Freud & Philosophy. An Essay on Interpretation.* New Haven, Conn.: Yale University Press.

Robbins, Helen (1993). " 'More Human Than I Am Alone.' Womb Envy in David Cronenberg's *The Fly* and *Dead Ringers*." In *Screening the Male. Exploring Masculinities in Hollywood Cinema*, edited by Steven Cohan and Ina Rae Hark. New York: Routledge.

Rodley, Chris, ed. (1992). *Cronenberg on Cronenberg.* London: Faber and Faber.

Rohde-Dachser, Christa (1991). *Expedition in den Dunklen Kontinent. Weiblichkeit im Diskurs der Psychoanalyse.* Berlin: Springer.

Romanyshyn, Robert D. (1989). *Technology as Symptom & Dream.* New York: Routledge.

Rose, Barbara (1993). "Is It Art? Orlan and the Transgressive Act." *Art in America* (February): 82–87, 125.

Rose, Jacqueline (1986). *Sexuality in the Field of Vision.* London: Verso.

Rothman, William. (1982) *Hitchcock. The Murderous Gaze.* Cambridge, Mass: Harvard University Press.

Rousseau, G. S. (1991). *Perilous Enlightenment. Pre- and Post-Modern Discourses. Sexual, Historical.* Manchester: Manchester University Press.

——— (1991a). *Enlightenment Crossings. Pre- and Post-Modern Discourses. Anthropological.* Manchester: Manchester University Press.

——— (1993). " 'A Strange Pathology.' Hysteria in the Early Modern World, 1500–1800." *Hysteria Beyond Freud.* Sander Gilman et al. Berkeley: University of California Press.

Russo, Mary (1986). "Female Grotesques. Carnival and Theory." In *Feminist Studies. Critical Studies*, edited by Teresa de Lauretis. Bloomington: Indiana University Press.

——— (1994). *The Female Grotesque. Risk, Excess, and Modernity*. New York: Routledge.

Salecl, Renata (1994). *The Spoils of Freedom. Psychoanalysis and Feminism After the Fall of Socialism*. New York: Routledge.

Santner, Eric L. (1996). *My Own Private Germany. Daniel Paul Schreber's Secret History of Modernity*. Princeton, N.J.: Princeton University Press.

Sawday, Jonathan (1995). *The Body Emblazoned. Dissection and the Image of the Body in Renaissance Culture*. New York: Routledge.

Schaps, Regina (1982). *Hysterie und Weiblichkeit. Wissenschaftsmythen über die Frau*. Frankfurt am Main: Campus.

Schiesari, Juliana (1992). *The Gendering of Melancholia. Feminism, Psychoanalysis, and the Symbolics of Loss in Renaissance Literature*. Ithaca, N.Y.: Cornell University Press.

Schindler, Regula (1994). "Hysterie." *RISS* 27 (August): 51–69.

Schlesier, Renate (1981). *Mythos und Weiblichkeit bei Sigmund Freud*. Frankfurt am Main: Anton Hain.

Schmid, Hans (1993). *Fenster zum Tod. Der Raum im Horrorfilm*. Munich: Belleville Verlag.

Schneider, Manfred (1988). "Nachwort." *Jean-Martin Charcot und Paul Richer. Die Besessenen in der Kunst*. Göttingen: Steidl Verlag.

——— (1994). "Die Allegorie der Hysterie und das Tête-à-tête der Wahrheit." In *Allegorien und Geschlechterdifferenz*, edited by Sigrid Schade et al. Cologne: Böhlau Verlag.

Schneider, Monique (1980). *La parole et l'inceste*. Paris: Aubier Montaigne.

Schulz-Hoffmann, Carla (1991). "Cindy Sherman—Kommentare zur hehren Kunst und zum banalen Leben." *Cindy Sherman*. Basel: Edition Cantz.

Schur, Max (1972). *Freud: Living and Dying*. New York: International Universities Press.

Scorcese, Martin (1984). "Internal Metaphors. External Horror." *David Cronenberg*, edited by Wayne Drew. *BFI Dossier*. No. 21. London: British Film Institute.

Sedgewick, Eve Kosofsky (1980). *The Coherence of Gothic Conventions*. New York: Methuen.

Sennett, Richard (1994). *Flesh and Stone. The Body and the City in Western Civilization*. New York: Norton.

Sexton, Anne (1966). "The Barfly Ought to Sing." *Triquarterly* 7 (Fall).

——— (1973). "The Freak Show." *No Evil Star. Selected Essays, Interview, and Prose*, edited by Steven E. Colburn. Ann Arbor, Mich.: The University of Michigan Press.

——— (1974). "Interview with Barbara Kevles." *No Evil Star. Selected Essays, Interview, and Prose*, edited by Steven E. Colburn. Ann Arbor: The University of Michigan Press.

——— (1981). *The Complete Poems*. Boston: Houghton Mifflin.

Sexton, Linda Gray (1991). "A Daughter's Story. I Knew Her Best." *New York Times Book Review* (18 August).

Sexton, Linda Gray, and Lois Ames, eds. (1979). *A Self-Portrait in Letters*. Boston: Houghton Mifflin.

Shamdasani, Sonu (1994). "Encountering Hélène. Théodore Flournoy and the Genesis of Subliminal Psychology." In Théordore Flournoy, *From India to the Planet Mars. A Case of Multiple Personality with Imaginary Languages*, edited by Shamdasani. Princeton, N.J.: Princeton University Press.

Shaviro, Stevan (1993). *The Cinematic Body*. Minneapolis: University of Minnesota Press.

Sheman, Cindy (1987). *Cindy Sherman*. Munich: Schirmer/Mosel.

Shorter, Edward (1992). *From Paralysis to Fatigue. A History of Psychosomatic Illness in the Modern Era*. New York: Free Press.

Showalter, Elaine (1985). *The Female Malady. Women, Madness, and English Culture, 1830–1980*. New York: Pantheon Books.

———— (1997). *Hysteries. Hysterical Epidemics and Modern Media*. New York: Columbia University Press.

Siddell, Henry George, and Robert Scott (1968). *A Greek-English Lexicon*. Oxford: Clarendon Press.

Silverman, Deborah L. (1989). *Art Nouveau in Fin-de-Siècle France: Politics, Psychology, and Style*. Berkeley: University of California Press.

Silverman, Kaja (1988). *The Acoustic Mirror. The Female Voice in Psychoanalysis and Cinema*. Bloomington: Indiana University Press.

Simons, David (1987). *Mesmer's Friends. The Therapeutic History of Altered States*. London: Delacourt Press.

Smith-Rosenberg, Carroll (1985). *Disorderly Conduct. Visions of Gender in Victorian America*. Oxford: Oxford University Press.

Sophocles (1954). *Oedipus the King, The Complete Tragedies*. Vol. 1. David Greene and Richmond Lattimore. Chicago: University of Chicago Press.

Spoto, Donald (1976). *The Art of Alfred Hitchcock. Fifty Years of His Motion Pictures*. New York: Doubleday.

———— (1983). *The Dark Side of Genius. The Life of Alfred Hitchcock*. New York: Ballantine.

Sprengnether, Madelon (1985). "Enforcing Oedipus. Freud and Dora." In *The (M)other Tonge. Esssays in Feminist Psychoanalytic Interpretation*, edited by Shirley Nelson Garner, Claire Kahane, and Madelon Sprengnether. Ithaca, N.Y.: Cornell University Press.

———— (1990). *The Spectral Mother. Freud, Feminism, and Psychoanalysis*. Ithaca, N.Y.: Cornell University Press.

Stafford, Barbara Maria (1991). *Body Criticism. Imaging the Unseen in Enlightenment Art and Medicine*. Cambridge, Mass.: MIT Press.

Stallybrass, Peter, and Allon White (1986). *The Politics & Poetics of Transgression*. Ithaca, N.Y.: Cornell University Press.

Stockebrand, Marianne (1985). *Cindy Sherman. Photographien*. Münster: Westfälischer Kunstverein.

Stoker, Bram (1897). *Dracula*. Harmondsworth: Penguin, 1993.

Strong, Beret E. (1989). "Foucault, Freud, and French Feminism. Theorizing Hysteria as Theorizing the Feminine." *Literature & Psychology* 35: 10–26.

Suleiman, Susan Rubin (1990). *Subversive Intent. Gender, Politics, and the Avant-Garde*. Cambridge, Mass.: Harvard University Press.

Sydenham, Thomas (1679). "Epistolary Dissertation to Dr. Cole." *The Works of Thomas Sydenham*. Vol 2. London: The Sydenham Society (1843).

Tatar, Maria (1978). *Spellbound. Studies on Mesmerism and Literature*. Princeton, N.J.: Princeton University Press.

——— (1992). *Off with Their Heads! Fairy Tales and the Culture of Childhood*. Princeton, N.J.: Princeton University Press.

——— (1995). *Lustmord. Sexual Murder in Weimar Germany*. Princeton, N.J.: Princeton University Press.

Till, Nicholas (1992). *Mozart and the Enlightenment. Truth, Virtue, and Beauty in Mozart's Operas*. New York: Norton.

Todorov, Tzvetan (1970). *The Fantastic. A Structural Approach to a Literary Genre*. Ithaca, N.Y.: Cornell University Press (1975).

——— (1989). *Nous et les Autres. La réflexion française sur la diversité humaine*. Paris: Seuil.

Trillat, Etienne (1986). *Histoire de l'hystérie*. Paris: Seghers.

Truffaut, François (1983). *Hitchcock*. New York: Simon and Schuster (1985).

Turner, Victor (1977). *The Ritual Process: Structure and Anti-Structure*. Ithaca, N.Y.: Cornell University Press.

Ussher, Jane (1991). *Women's Madness. Misogyny or Mental Illness?* Amherst: The University of Massachusetts Press.

van den Berg, Sara (1994). "Textual Bodies: Narratives of Denial and Desire in Studies on Hysteria." In *The Good Body*, edited by Mary G. Winkler and Letha B. Cole. New Haven, Conn.: Yale University Press.

van Gennep, Arnold (1960). *The Rites of Passage*. Chicago: University of Chicago Press.

Veith, Ilza (1965). *Hysteria. The History of a Disease*. Chicago: University of Chicago Press.

von Braun, Christina (1985). *Nicht Ich*. Frankfurt am Main: Verlag Neue Kritik.

——— (1995). "'Frauenkrankheiten' als Spiegelbild der Geschichte." In *Von der Auffälligkeit des Leibes*, edited by Farideh Akashe-Böhme. Frankfurt am Main: Suhrkamp.

Wajeman. Gérard (1982). *Le maître et l'hysterique*. Paris: Navarin/Seuil.

——— (1988). "The Hysteric's Discourse." *Hystoria*. Special issue, edited by Helena Schulz-Keil. *Lacan Study Notes* 6–9: 1–22.

Weber, Samuel (1982). *The Legend of Freud*. Minneapolis: University of Minnesota Press.

Weiner, Marc A. (1995). *Richard Wagner and the Anti-Semitic Imagination*. Lincoln: University of Nebraska Press.

Weininger, Otto (1903). *Geschlecht und Charakter*. Munich: Matthes und Seitz (1980).

Weissweiler, Eva (1981). *Komponistinnen aus 500 Jahren. Eine Kultur- und Wirkungsgeschichte in Biographien und Werkbeispielen*. Frankfurt am Main: S. Fischer Verlag.

Welsh, Alexander (1994). *Freud's Wishful Dream Book*. Princeton, N.J.: Princeton University Press.

White, Allon (1993). *Carnival, Hysteria, and Writing*. Oxford: Clarendon Press.

Whitford, Margaret (1994). *Luce Irigaray. Philosophy in the Feminine*. New York: Routledge.

Whytt, Robert (1764). *Observations on the Nature, Causes, and Cure of those Disorders which have been commonly called Nervous, Hypochondriac, or Hysteric:*

to which are prefixed some Remarks on the Sympathy of the Nerves. Edinburgh: J. Balfour.

Wicke, Jennifer (1992). "Vampiric Typewriting. *Dracula* and Its Media." *ELH* 59 (2); 467–93.

Williams, Linda Ruth (1995). *Critical Desire. Psychoanalysis and the Literary Subject*. London: Edward Arnold.

Williamson, Judith (1983). "Images of 'Woman': The Photographs of Cindy Sherman." *Screen* 23 (6).

Wright, Elizabeth (1984). *Psychoanalytic Criticism. Theory in Practice*. London: Methuen.

——— et al. (1992). *Feminism and Psychoanalysis. A Critical Dictionary*. Oxford: Blackwell.

Yalom, Irvin D. (1980) *Existential Psychotherapy*. New York: Basic Books.

Žižek, Slavoj (1991). *Looking Awry. An Introduction to Jacques Lacan through Popular Culture*. Cambridge, Mass.: MIT Press.

——— (1991a). *For They Know Not What They Do. Enjoyment as a Political Factor*. London: Verso.

——— (1992). *Everything You Always Wanted to Know about Lacan but Were Afraid to Ask Hitchcock*. London: Verso.

——— (1992a). *Enjoy Your Symptom. Jacques Lacan in Hollywood and Out*. London: Routledge.

——— (1992b). "Symptom." In *Feminism and Psychoanalysis. A Critical Dictionary*, edited by Elizabeth Wright et al. Oxford: Blackwell.

——— (1993). *Tarrying with the Negative. Kant, Hegel, and the Critique of Ideology*. Durham, N.C.: Duke University Press.

——— (1993a). "'The Wound Is Healed Only by the Spear That Smote You': The Operatic Subject and Its Vicissitudes." In *Opera Through Other Eyes*, edited by David J. Levin. Stanford, Calif.: Stanford University Press.

——— (1994). *The Metastases of Enjoyment. Six Essays on Woman and Causality*. London: Verso.

——— (1996). *The Indivisible Remainder. An Essay on Schelling and Related Matters*. London: Verso.

——— (1997). "'There Is No Sexual Relationship. Wagner as a Lacanian.'" *New German Critique* 69 (Fall): 7–36.

About the Author

Elisabeth Bronfen is Professor of English and American Studies at the University of Zurich. Her recent books include *Over Her Dead Body: Death, Femininity, and the Aesthetic* and a volume coedited with Sarah W. Goodwin, *Death and Representation*.